Pro Android Graphics

Wallace Jackson

Apress

Pro Android Graphics

ISBN-13 (pbk): 978-1-4302-5785-1

ISBN-13 (electronic): 978-1-4302-5786-8

Trademarked names, logos, and images may appear in this book. Rather than use a trademark symbol with every occurrence of a trademarked name, logo, or image we use the names, logos, and images only in an editorial fashion and to the benefit of the trademark owner, with no intention of infringement of the trademark.

The use in this publication of trade names, trademarks, service marks, and similar terms, even if they are not identified as such, is not to be taken as an expression of opinion as to whether or not they are subject to proprietary rights.

While the advice and information in this book are believed to be true and accurate at the date of publication, neither the authors nor the editors nor the publisher can accept any legal responsibility for any errors or omissions that may be made. The publisher makes no warranty, express or implied, with respect to the material contained herein.

President and Publisher: Paul Manning
Lead Editor: Tom Welsh
Technical Reviewer: Michael Thomas
Editorial Board: Steve Anglin, Mark Beckner, Ewan Buckingham, Gary Cornell, Louise Corrigan, Morgan Ertel, Jonathan Gennick, Jonathan Hassell, Robert Hutchinson, Michelle Lowman, James Markham, Matthew Moodie, Jeff Olson, Jeffrey Pepper, Douglas Pundick, Ben Renow-Clarke, Dominic Shakeshaft, Gwenan Spearing, Matt Wade, Tom Welsh
Coordinating Editor: Katie Sullivan
Copy Editor: Mary Behr
Compositor: SPi Global
Indexer: SPi Global
Artist: SPi Global
Cover Designer: Anna Ishchenko

Distributed to the book trade worldwide by Springer Science+Business Media New York, 233 Spring Street, 6th Floor, New York, NY 10013. Phone 1-800-SPRINGER, fax (201) 348-4505, e-mail orders-ny@springer-sbm.com, or visit www.springeronline.com. Apress Media, LLC is a California LLC and the sole member (owner) is Springer Science + Business Media Finance Inc (SSBM Finance Inc). SSBM Finance Inc is a Delaware corporation.

For information on translations, please e-mail rights@apress.com, or visit www.apress.com.

Apress and friends of ED books may be purchased in bulk for academic, corporate, or promotional use. eBook versions and licenses are also available for most titles. For more information, reference our Special Bulk Sales–eBook Licensing web page at www.apress.com/bulk-sales.

Any source code or other supplementary materials referenced by the author in this text is available to readers at www.apress.com. For detailed information about how to locate your book's source code, go to www.apress.com/source-code/.

This book is dedicated to everyone in the open source community who works so diligently at making professional new media software and application development tools available for anybody to use to achieve their dreams and goals. Last, but certainly not least, to my family, friends, clients, and neighbors for their help, assistance, and those great late night fiestas.

Contents at a Glance

Contents

About the Author

Wallace Jackson has been writing for vanguard multimedia publications about his work in new media content development since the advent of *Multimedia Producer Magazine* more than two decades ago, when he wrote about computer processor architectures for the magazine centerfold (a removable "mini-issue" insert) distributed at SIGGRAPH.

Since then, Wallace has written for numerous publications regarding his content production work in interactive 3D and new media advertising campaign design. He has written for industry trades such as *3D Artist, Desktop Publishers Journal, CrossMedia Magazine, Kiosk Magazine, Digital Signage Magazine, and AVvideo Magazine.*

Wallace Jackson was a COBOL and RPGII programmer in his early teens, and later he coded applications using Java, JavaScript, and HTML5. Wallace has written several popular application programming books on Java and Android development for Apress (Springer) over the past few years.

Wallace Jackson is currently the CEO of Mind Taffy Design, a multimedia content production and digital campaign design and development agency in Northern Santa Barbara County, located halfway between their clientele in Silicon Valley and Hollywood, Irvine, and San Diego. Over the past two decades, Mind Taffy Design has created i3D digital new media content deliverables using leading open source technologies such as PDF, HTML5, WebGL, Java, JavaFX, and Android for many of the top branded manufacturers in the world, including Sony, Samsung, IBM, Epson, Nokia, Tyco, Sun, KDS, Micron, CTX, EIZO, TEAC, SGI, and Mitsubishi.

Wallace Jackson received his undergraduate degree in Business Economics from the University of California at Los Angeles (UCLA), and his graduate degree in MIS Design and Implementation from the University of Southern California (USC). His post-graduate degree in Marketing Strategy is also from USC, where he completed the USC Graduate Entrepreneurship Program.

About the Technical Reviewer

Michael Thomas has worked in software development for over 20 years as an individual contributor, team lead, program manager, and Vice President of Engineering. Michael has over 10 years experience working with mobile devices. His current focus is in the medical sector using mobile devices to accelerate information transfer between patients and health care providers.

Acknowledgments

I would like to acknowledge all of the fantastic editors and their support staff at Apress who worked so very long and hard on this book, making it the ultimate all-around Pro Android Graphics book.

Tom Welsh, for his work as the Lead Editor on the book, and for his vast experience and invaluable guidance during the process of making the book leading-edge.

Katie Sullivan, for her work as the Coordinating Editor on the book, and for her unwavering diligence in making sure I either hit my writing deadlines, or even surpassed them.

Mary Behr, for her work as the Copy Editor on this graphics book, and for her attention to detail and to conforming the text to the current Apress writing standards.

Michael Thomas, for his work as the Technical Reviewer on this book, and for making sure I don't make any mistakes because code with mistakes does not run properly, if at all, unless they are very lucky mistakes, which is quite rare in computer programming, but when it happens, it's beautiful....

And finally Steve Anglin, Acquisitions Editor, for acquiring me as an author for Apress and Springer.

Android Digital Imaging: Formats, Concepts, and Optimization

In this first chapter, you will see how digital imaging is implemented inside of the Android operating system. We will take a look at the digital image formats that are supported in Android, the classes that allow imagery to be formatted on the screen, and the basic digital imaging concepts that you will need to understand to follow what we will be doing in Android graphics design.

We will also take a look at how to optimize your digital image assets for Android application development. We'll explore digital image optimization both from an individual image asset data footprint standpoint and from an Android device type market coverage standpoint.

As you know, Android devices are no longer just smartphones, but run the gamut from watches to phones to tablets to game consoles to 4K iTV sets. The significance of this to the graphic design aspect of Android application development is that you must now create your digital image assets in a far wider range of pixels, from as low a resolution as 240 pixels to as high a resolution as 4096 pixels, and you must do this for each of your digital imaging assets.

We will look at the facilities that Android has in place for doing this as a part of your application development workflow and your asset referencing **XML** (eXtensible Markup Language) markup. Markup is different from Java code in that it uses "tags" much as **HTML** (HyperText Markup Language) does. XML is very similar to HTML in that it uses these tag structures, but different in that it is customizable, which is why Google has selected it for use in Android OS.

Since this is a Pro level book I assume that you have a decent level of experience with developing for the Android platform, and have already been through the learning process in an Android educational title such as my *Learn Android App Development* (Apress, 2013).

Let's get started by taking a look at what image formats Android supports.

Android's Digital Image Formats: Lossless Versus Lossy

Android supports several popular digital imagery formats, some which have been around for decades, such as the Compuserve GIF (Graphic Information Format) and the Joint Photographic Experts Group (JPEG) format, and some are more recent, such as the PNG (Portable Network Graphics) and WebP (developed by ON2 and acquired and made open source by Google).

I will talk about these in their order of origin, from the oldest (and thus least desirable) GIF through the newest (and thus most advanced) WebP format. **Compuserve GIF** is fully supported by the Android OS, but is not recommended. GIF is a **lossless** digital image file format, as it does not throw away image data to achieve better compression results.

This is because the GIF compression algorithm is not as refined (read: powerful) as PNG, and it only supports **indexed** color, which you will be learning about in detail in this chapter. That said, if all your image assets are already created and in GIF format, you will be able to use them with no problem (other than the mediocre resulting quality) in your Android applications.

The next oldest digital image file format that Android supports is **JPEG**, which uses a **truecolor** color depth instead of an indexed color depth. We will be covering color theory and color depth soon.

JPEG is said to be a **lossy** digital image file format, as it throws away (loses) image data in order to achieve smaller file sizes. It is important to note that this original image data is **unrecoverable after compression** has taken place, so make sure to save an original uncompressed image file.

If you zoom into a JPEG image after compression, you will see a discolored area effect that clearly was not present in the original imagery. These degraded areas in the image data are termed **compression artifacts** in the digital imaging industry and will only occur in lossy image compression.

The most recommended image format in Android is called the **PNG** (Portable Network Graphic) file format. PNG has both an indexed color version, called **PNG8**, and a truecolor version, called **PNG24**. The PNG8 and PNG24 extensions represent the **bit depth** of color support, which we will be getting into in a little bit. PNG is pronounced "ping" in the digital image industry.

PNG is the recommended format to use for Android because it has decent compression, and because it is lossless, and thus has both high image quality and a reasonable level of compression efficiency.

The most recent image format was added to Android when Google acquired ON2 and is called the **WebP** image format. The format is supported under Android 2.3.7 for image read, or playback, support and in Android 4.0 or later for image write, or file saving, support. WebP is a static (image) version of the WebM video file format, also known in the industry as the **VP8** codec. You will be learning all about **codecs** and **compression** in a later section.

Android View and ViewGroup Classes: Image Containers

Everything in this section is just a review of Android Java class concepts and constructs, which you, as an intermediate level Android programmer, probably understand already. Android OS has a class that is dedicated to displaying digital imagery and digital video called the **View** class. The View class is subclassed directly from the **java.lang.Object** class; it is designed to hold imagery and video, and to format it for display within your user interface screen designs. If you wish to review what the View class can do, visit the following URL:

http://developer.android.com/reference/android/view/View.html

All user interface elements are based on (subclassed from) the View class, and are called **widgets** and have their own package called **android.widget**, as most developers know. If you are not that familiar with Views and Widgets, you might consider going through the *Learn Android App Development* book before embarking on this one. If you wish to review what Android Widgets can do, visit the following URL:

http://developer.android.com/reference/android/widget/package-summary.html

The **ViewGroup** class is also subclassed from the View class. It is used to provide developers with the user interface element container that they can use to design their screen layout and organize their user interface widget View objects. If you wish to review the various types of Android ViewGroup Screen Layout Container classes, visit the following URL:

http://developer.android.com/reference/android/view/ViewGroup.html

Views, ViewGroups and widgets in Android are usually defined using XML. This is set up this way so that designers can work right alongside the coders in the application development, as XML is far easier to code in than Java is.

In fact, XML isn't really programming code at all; it's markup, and, just like HTML5, it uses tags, nested tags, and tag parameters to build constructs that are later used in your Android application.

Not only is XML utilized in Android to create user interface screen design but also menu structures, string constants, and to define your application version, components, and permissions inside the AndroidManifest.xml file.

The process of turning your XML data structures into Java-code–compatible objects that can be used with your Android application Java components is called **inflating** XML markup, and Android has a number of inflater classes that perform this function, usually in component startup methods, such as the onCreate() method. You will see this in some detail throughout the Java coding examples in this book, as it bridges our XML markup and Java code.

The Foundation of Digital Images: Pixels and Aspect Ratio

Digital images are made up of two-dimensional arrays of pixels, which is short for picture (pix) elements (els). The number of pixels in an image is expressed by its **resolution**, which is the number of pixels in both the Height (H) and Width (W) dimensions.

To find the number of pixels in an image, simply multiply the Width pixels by the Height pixels. For instance, an HDTV 1920 x 1080 image will contain 2,073,600 pixels, or slightly more than 2 million pixels. Two million pixels could also be referred to as two megapixels.

The more pixels that are in an image, the higher its resolution; just like with digital cameras, the more megapixels are in the data bank, the higher the quality level that can be achieved. Android supports everything from low resolution 320 x 240 pixel display screens (Android Watches and smaller flip-phones) to medium resolution 854 x 480 pixel display screens (mini-tablets and smartphones), up to high resolution 1280 x 720 pixel display screens (HD smartphones and mid-level tablets), and extra high resolution 1920 x 1080 pixel display screens (large tablets and iTV sets). Android 4.3 adds support for 4K resolution iTVs, which feature 4096 by 2160 resolution.

A slightly more complicated aspect (no pun intended) of image resolution is the image **aspect ratio**, a concept that also applies to display screens. This is the ratio of width to height, or **W:H**, and will define how square or rectangular (popularly termed widescreen) an image or a display screen is.

A 1:1 aspect ratio display (or image) is perfectly square, as is a 2:2 or a 3:3 aspect ratio image. You see, it is the ratio between the two numbers that defines the shape of the image or screen, not the numbers themselves. An example of an Android device that has a 1:1 square aspect ratio would be an Android SmartWatch.

Most Android screens are **HDTV** aspect ratio, which is **16:9**, but some are a little less wide, as in 16:10 (or 8:5 if you prefer). Wider screens will also surely appear, so look for 16:8 (or 2:1, if you prefer) ultra-wide screens that have a 2160 by 1080 resolution LCD or LED display.

The aspect ratio is usually expressed as the smallest pair of numbers that can be achieved (reached) on either side of the aspect ratio colon. If you paid attention in high school when you were learning about lowest common denominators, then this aspect ratio should be fairly easy to calculate.

I usually do this by continuing to divide each side by two. So, taking the fairly odd-ball 1280 x 1024 SXGA resolution as an example, half of 1280 x 1024 is 640 x 512, and half of that is 320 x 256, half of that is 160 x 128, half of that is 80 x 64, half of that is 40 x 32, half of that is 20 x 16, half of that is 10 x 8, and half of that is 5 x 4, so an SXGA screen is a 5:4 aspect ratio.

Original PC screens primarily offered a 4:3 aspect ratio; early CRT tube TVs were nearly square, featuring a 3:2 aspect ratio. The current market trend is certainly towards wider screens and higher resolution displays; however, the new Android Watches may change that back towards square aspect ratios.

The Color of Digital Images: Color Theory and Color Depth

Now you know about digital image pixels and how they are arranged into 2D rectangular arrays at a specific aspect ratio defining the rectangular shape. So the next logical aspect (again, no pun intended) to look into is how each of those pixels gain their **color values**.

Color values for image pixels are defined by the amount of three different colors, **red**, **green** and **blue** (**RGB**), which are present in varying amounts in each pixel. Android display screens utilize **additive color**, which is where the wavelengths of light for each RGB color plane are summed together in order to create millions of different color values.

Additive color, which is utilized in LCD or LED displays, is the opposite of subtractive color, which is utilized in print. To show the difference, under a subtractive color model, mixing red with green (inks) will yield a purplish color, whereas in an additive color model, mixing red with green (light) creates a bright yellow color result.

There are **256 levels** of each RGB color for each pixel, or **8-bits** of color intensity variation, for each of these red, green, and blue values, from a minimum of zero (off, no color contributed) to a maximum of 255 (fully on, maximum color contributed). The number of bits used to represent color in a digital image is referred to as the **color depth** of that image.

There are several common color depths used in the digital imaging industry, and I will outline the most common ones here along with their formats. The lowest color depth exists in an **8-bit indexed color** image, which has **256** color values, and uses the GIF and PNG8 image formats to contain this indexed color type of digital image data.

A medium color depth image features a **16-bit** color depth and thus contains **65,536** colors (calculated as 256 x 256); it is supported in the TARGA (TGA) and Tagged Image File Format (TIFF) digital image formats.

Note that Android does not support any of the 16-bit color depth digital image file formats (TGA or TIFF), which I think is an omission, as 16-bit color depth support would greatly enhance a developer image data footprint optimization, a subject which we will be covering later on in the chapter.

A high color depth image features a **24-bit** color depth and thus contains over 16 million colors. This is calculated as 256 x 256 x 256 and equals **16,777,216** colors. File formats supporting 24-bit color include JPEG (or JPG), PNG, TGA, TIFF and WebP.

Using 24-bit color depth will give you the highest quality level, which is why Android prefers the use of a PNG24 or a JPEG image file format. Since PNG24 is lossless, it has the highest quality compression (lowest original data loss) along with the highest quality color depth, and so PNG24 is the preferred digital image format to use, as it produces the highest quality.

Representing Colors in Android: Hexadecimal Notation

So now that you know what color depth is, and that color is represented as a combination of three different red, green, and blue **color channels** within any given image, we need to look at how we are to represent these three RGB color channel values.

It is also important to note that in Android, color is not only used in 2D digital imagery, also called **bitmap** imagery, but also in 2D illustrations, commonly known as **vector** imagery, as well as in **color settings**, such as the background color for a user interface screen or text color.

In Android, different levels of RGB color intensity values are represented using **hexadecimal notation**, the **Base 16** computer notation invented decades ago to represent 16 bits of data value. Unlike Base 10, which counts from zero through 9, Base 16 counts from zero through F, where F represents a Base 10 value of 15 (or if you are a programmer you could count from 0–15, which also gives 16 decimal data values, either way you prefer to look at it). See Table 1-1 for some examples.

Table 1-1. Hexadecimal Values and Corresponding Decimal Values

Hexadecimal Values:	0	1	2	3	4	5	6	7	8	9	A	B	C	D	E	F
Decimal Values:	0	1	2	3	4	5	6	7	8	9	10	11	12	13	14	15

A hexadecimal value in Android always starts with a **pound sign**, like this: **#FFFFFF**. This hexadecimal data color value represents a color of white. As each slot in this 24-bit hexadecimal representation represents one Base 16 value, to get the 256 values you need for each RGB color will take 2 slots, as 16 x 16 equals 256. Thus for a 24-bit image you need six slots after the pound sign to hold each of the six hexadecimal data values.

The hexadecimal data slots represent the RGB values in a following format: **#RRGGBB**. So, for the color white, all red, green, and blue **channels** in this hexadecimal color data value representation are at the maximum **luminosity**.

If you additively sum all of these colors together you'll get white light. As mentioned, the color **yellow** is represented by the red and green channels being on and the blue channel being off, so the hexadecimal representation is **#FFFF00**, where both red and green channel slots are on (FF or 255), and blue channel slots are fully off (00 or a zero value).

It is important to note here that there is also a **32-bit** image color depth whose data values are represented using an **ARGB** color channel model, where the **A** stands for **alpha**, which is short for **alpha channel**. I will be going over the concept of alpha and alpha channels, as well as pixel blending, in great detail in the next section of this chapter.

The hexadecimal data slots for an **ARGB** value hold data in the following format: **#AARRGGBB**. So for the color white, all alpha, red, green, and blue channels in this hexadecimal color data value representation are at a maximum luminosity (or opacity), and the alpha channel is fully opaque, as represented by an FF value, so its hexadecimal value is **#FFFFFFFF**.

A 100% transparent alpha channel is represented by setting the alpha slots to zero; thus, a fully transparent image pixel is **#00FFFFFF**, or **#00000000**. If an alpha channel is transparent, color value doesn't matter!

Image Compositing: Alpha Channels and Blending Modes

In this section we will take a look at **compositing** digital images. This is the process of **blending** together more than one **layer** of a digital image in order to obtain a resulting image on the display that appears as though it is one final image, but which in fact is actually a collection of more than one seamlessly composited image **layers**.

To accomplish this, we need to have an **alpha channel** (transparency) value that we can utilize to precisely control the blending of that pixel with the pixel (in that same location) on the other layers above and below it.

Like the other RGB channels, the alpha channel also has 256 levels of transparency as represented by two slots in the hexadecimal representation for the ARGB data value, which has eight slots (32-bits) of data rather than the six slots used in a 24-bit image, which can be thought of as a 32-bit image with no alpha channel data.

Indeed, if there's no alpha channel data, why waste another 8 bits of data storage, even if it's filled with F's (or fully opaque pixel values, which essentially equate to unused alpha transparency values). So a 24-bit image has no alpha channel and is not going to be used for compositing, for instance the bottom plate in a compositing layer stack, whereas a 32-bit image is going to be used as a compositing layer on top of something else that will need the ability to show through (via transparency values) in some of the pixel locations in the image composite.

How does having an alpha channel and using image compositing factor into Android graphics design, you may be wondering. The primary advantage is the ability to split what looks like one single image into a number of component layers. The reason for doing this is to be able to apply Java programming logic to individual layer elements in order to control parts of your image that you could not otherwise control were it just one single 24-bit image.

There is another part of image compositing called **blending modes** that also factors heavily in professional image compositing capabilities. Any of you familiar with Photoshop or GIMP know that each layer can be set to use different blending modes that specify how the pixels for that layer are blended (mathematically) with the previous layers (underneath that layer). Add this mathematical pixel blending to the 256 level transparency control and you can achieve any compositing effect or result that you can imagine.

Blending modes are implemented in Android using the **PorterDuff** class, and give Android developers most of the same compositing modes that Photoshop or GIMP afford to digital imaging artisans. This makes Android a powerful image compositing engine just like Photoshop is, only controllable at a fine level using custom Java code. Some of Android's PorterDuff blending modes include ADD, SCREEN, OVERLAY, DARKEN, XOR, LIGHTEN, and MULTIPLY.

Digital Image Masking: A Popular Use for Alpha Channels

One of the primary applications for alpha channels is to **mask** out areas of an image for compositing. **Masking** is the process of cutting subject matter out of an image and placing it onto its own layer using an alpha channel.

This allows us to put image elements or subject material into use in other images, or even in animation, or to use it in special effects applications. Digital image software packages such as Photoshop and GIMP have many tools and features that are specifically there for use in masking and then image compositing. You can't really do effective image compositing without doing masking first, so it's an important area for graphics designers to master.

The art of masking has been around for a very long time. In fact, if you are familiar with the bluescreen and greenscreen backdrop that the weather forecasters use to seem like they are standing in front of the weather map (when they are really just in front of a green screen), then you recognize that masking techniques exist not only for digital imaging, but also for digital video and film production.

Masking can be done for you automatically using bluescreen or greenscreen backdrops and computer software that can automatically extract those exact color values in order to create a mask and an alpha channel (transparency), and this can also be done manually (by hand) in digital imaging by using the **selection** tools and **sharpening** and **blur** algorithms.

You'll learn a lot about this work process during this book, using popular open source software packages such as GIMP 2 and EditShare Lightworks 11. GIMP 2.8 is a digital image compositing software tool, and Lightworks 11 is a digital video editing software tool. You will also be using other types of tools, such as video compression software, during the book to get a feel for the wide range of software tools external to Android that need to be incorporated into the work process for Android graphics design.

Digital image compositing is a very complex and involved process, and thus it must span a number of chapters. The most important consideration in the masking process is getting smooth, sharp edges around your masked object, so that when you drop it onto a new background image it looks as though it was photographed there in the first place. The key to this is in the selection work process, and using digital image software **selection tools** (there are a half-dozen of these, at least) in the proper way (work process) and in the proper usage scenarios.

For instance, if there are areas of **uniform color** around the object that you wish to mask (maybe you shot it against a bluescreen or greenscreen), you can use the **magic wand tool** and a proper **threshold** setting to select everything except the object, and then **invert** that **selection set** in order to obtain a selection set containing the object. Sometimes the correct way to approach something is in reverse, as you will see later in the book.

Other selection tools contain complex algorithms that can look at color changes between pixels, which can be very useful in **edge detection**. You can use edge detection in other types of selection tools, such as the Scissor Tool in GIMP 2.8.6, which allow you to drag your cursor along the edge of an object that you wish to mask while the tool's algorithm lays down a precise pixel-perfect placement of a selection edge, which you can later edit using control points.

Smoothing Edges in a Mask: The Concept of Anti-Aliasing

Anti-aliasing is a technique where two adjacent colors in an image which are on an edge between two colors are blended right on the edge to make the edge look smoother when the image is zoomed out. What this does is to trick the eye into seeing a smoother edge and gets rid of what is commonly called "the jaggies." Anti-aliasing provides very impressive results by using averaged color values of a few pixels along any edge that needs to be made smoother (by averaged I mean some color or spectrum of colors that is part of the way between the two colors that are colliding at a jagged edge in an image).

I created a simple example of this technique to show you visually what I mean. In Figure 1-1, you will see that I created a seemingly smooth red circle on a bright yellow background. I then zoomed into the edge of that circle and took a screenshot and placed it alongside of the zoomed out circle to show the anti-aliasing (orange) values of a color between (or made from) the red and yellow colors that border each other at the edge of the circle.

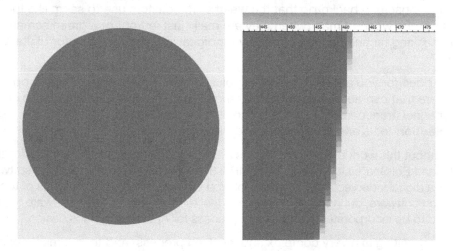

Figure 1-1. A red circle on a yellow background (left) and a zoomed-in view (right) showing the anti-aliasing

We will be looking at anti-aliasing in detail during the book. However, I wanted to cover all the key image concepts all in one place, and all in context, to provide a baseline knowledge foundation for you upfront. Hope you don't mind an initial chapter on theory before we start coding.

Optimizing Digital Images: Compression and Dithering

There are a number of factors that affect **image compression**, and some techniques that can be used to get a better quality result with a smaller **data footprint**. This is the objective in optimizing digital imagery: to get the smallest data footprint with the highest quality visual result.

We will start with the aspects that most affect the data footprint and examine how each of them contributes to data footprint optimization of any given digital image. Interestingly, these are similar to the order of the digital imaging concepts that we have covered so far in this chapter.

The single most critical contributor to the resulting file size, or data footprint, is the **number of pixels**, or the resolution, of a digital image. This is logical because each of these pixels need to be stored along with the color values for each of their channels. Thus, the smaller you can get your image resolution (while still having it look sharp), the smaller its resulting file size will be. This is what we call a "no brainer."

Raw (uncompressed) image size is calculated by **Width x Height x 3** for 24-bit RBG images, or possibly **Width x Height x 4** for a 32-bit ARGB image. Thus, an uncompressed truecolor 24-bit VGA image will have 640 x 480 x 3, equaling **921,600** bytes of original uncompressed data. If you divide 921,600 by 1024 (bytes in a kilobyte), you get the number of **Kilobytes** that is in a raw VGA image, and that number is an even **900KB**.

As you can see, image color depth is the next most critical contributor to the data footprint of an image, because the number of pixels in that image is multiplied by 1 (8-bit) or 2 (16-bit) or 3 (24-bit) or 4 (32-bit) color data channels. This is one of the reasons that indexed color (8-bit) images are still widely used, especially using the **PNG8** image format, which features a superior lossless compression algorithm than the GIF format utilizes.

Indexed color images can simulate truecolor images, if the colors that are used to make up the image do not vary too widely. Indexed color images use only 8 bits of data (256 colors) to define the image pixel colors, using a **palette** of 256 optimally selected colors rather than 3 RGB color channels.

Depending on how many colors are used in any given image, using only 256 colors to represent an image versus 16,777,216 can cause an effect called **banding**, where transfers between adjoining colors are not smooth. Indexed color images have an option to correct for this visually called **dithering**.

Dithering is a process of creating dot patterns along the edges of two adjoining colors in an image in order to trick the eye into thinking there is a third color used. This gives us a maximum perceptual amount of colors of 65,536 colors (256 x 256) but only if each of those 256 colors borders on each of the other 256 colors. Still, you can see the potential for creating additional colors, and you will be amazed at the results an indexed color image can achieve in some scenarios (with certain images).

Let's take a truecolor image, such as the one shown in Figure 1-2, and save it as a PNG8 indexed color image to show the dithering effect. We will take a look at the dithering effect on the driver's side rear fender on the Audi 3D image, as it contains a gradient of gray color.

Figure 1-2. A truecolor image source that uses 16.8 million colors, which we are going to optimize to PNG8 format

We will set the PNG8 image, shown in Figure 1-3, to use 5-bit color (32 colors) so that we can see the dithering effect clearly. As you can see, dot patterns are made between adjacent colors to create additional colors.

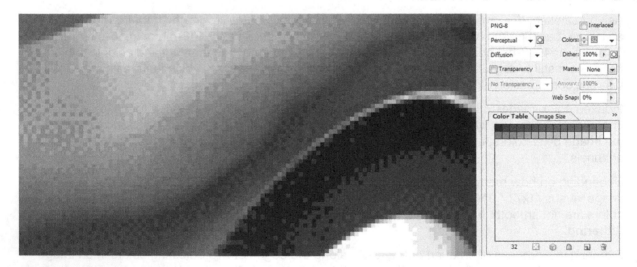

Figure 1-3. Showing the effect of dithering with an indexed color image compression setting of 32 colors (5-bit)

It is interesting to note that less than 256 colors can be used in an 8-bit indexed color image. This is done to reduce the data footprint; for instance, an image that can attain good results using only 32 colors is actually a 5-bit image and is technically a PNG5, even though the format is called PNG8.

Also notice that you can set the percentage of dithering used; I usually select either the 0% or 100% setting, but you can fine-tune the dithering effect anywhere between these two extreme values. You can also choose a dithering algorithm type; I use diffusion dithering, as it yields a smooth effect along irregularly shaped gradients such as those on the car fender.

Dithering, as you may imagine, adds data (patterns) that is more difficult to compress, and thus, it increases the data footprint by a few percentage points. Be sure to check the resulting filesize with and without dithering applied to see if it is worth the improved visual results that it affords.

The final concept (that you have learned about so far) that can increase the data footprint of the image is the alpha channel, as adding an alpha adds another 8-bit color channel (transparency) to the image being compressed.

However, if you need an alpha channel to define transparency in order to support future compositing needs with that image, there is not much choice but to include the alpha channel data. Just make sure not to use a 32-bit image format to contain a 24-bit image that has an empty (all zeroes, and completely transparent, and thus empty of alpha value data) alpha channel.

Finally, many alpha channels that are used to mask objects in an image will compress very well, as they are largely areas of white (opaque) and black (transparent) with some grey values along the edge between the two colors to **anti-alias** the mask. As a result, they provide a visually smooth edge transition between the object and the imagery used behind it.

Since in an alpha channel image mask the 8-bit transparency gradient from white to black defines transparency, the grey values on the edges of each object in the mask essentially average the colors of the object and its target background, which provides real-time anti-aliasing with any target background used.

Now it's time to get Android installed on your workstation, and then you can start developing graphics-oriented Android applications!

Download the Android Environment: Java and ADT Bundle

Let's get started by making sure you have the current Android development environment. This means having the latest version of Java, Eclipse, and the Android Developer Tools (ADT). You may already have the most recent ADT Bundle installed, but I am going to do this here simply to make sure you are set up and starting from the right place, before we undertake the complex development we are about to embark upon within this book. If you keep your ADT up to date on a daily basis, you can skip this section if you wish.

Since Java is used as the foundation for ADT, get that first. As of Android 4.3, the Android IDE still uses Java 6, and not Java 7, so make sure to get the correct version of the Java SDK. It is located here:

```
http://www.oracle.com/technetwork/java/javasebusiness/downloads/java-archive-downloads-
javase6-419409.html
```

Scroll down towards the bottom of the page, and look for the **Java SE Development Kit 6u45** download link. This section of the screen is shown in Figure 1-4.

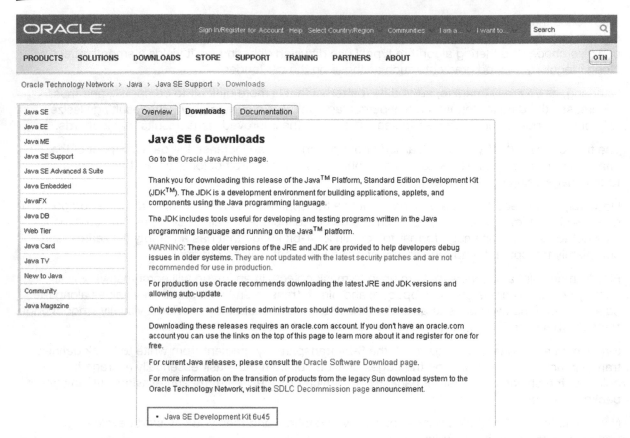

Figure 1-4. Java SE 6 Download Section of the Oracle TechNetwork web site Java SE archives page

Click the Java SE Development Kit 6u45 Download link on the bottom of the section and at the top of the download links screen. At the top of the downloads screen in the gray area shown in Figure 1-5, select the Accept License Agreement radio button option. Once you do this you will notice that the links at the right side will become bolder and can be clicked to invoke the download for your operating system.

If you are using a 64-bit OS such as Windows 7 64-bit or Windows 8 64-bit, which is what I am using, select the Windows x64 version of the EXE installer file to download.

If you are using a 32-bit OS such as Windows XP or Windows Vista 32-bit, select the Windows x86 version of the EXE installer file to download. Be sure to match the bit level of the software to the bit level capability of the OS that you are running. Figure 1-5 shows the download screen as it appears once the license agreement option radio button has been selected.

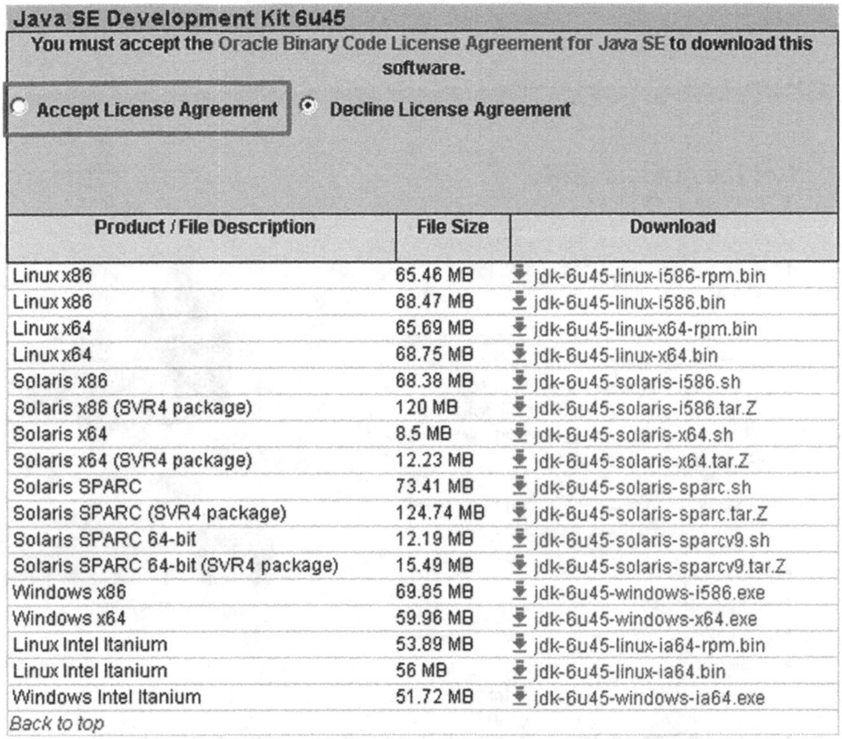

Java SE Development Kit 6u45

You must accept the Oracle Binary Code License Agreement for Java SE to download this software.

○ Accept License Agreement | ⦿ Decline License Agreement

Product / File Description	File Size	Download
Linux x86	65.46 MB	⬇ jdk-6u45-linux-i586-rpm.bin
Linux x86	68.47 MB	⬇ jdk-6u45-linux-i586.bin
Linux x64	65.69 MB	⬇ jdk-6u45-linux-x64-rpm.bin
Linux x64	68.75 MB	⬇ jdk-6u45-linux-x64.bin
Solaris x86	68.38 MB	⬇ jdk-6u45-solaris-i586.sh
Solaris x86 (SVR4 package)	120 MB	⬇ jdk-6u45-solaris-i586.tar.Z
Solaris x64	8.5 MB	⬇ jdk-6u45-solaris-x64.sh
Solaris x64 (SVR4 package)	12.23 MB	⬇ jdk-6u45-solaris-x64.tar.Z
Solaris SPARC	73.41 MB	⬇ jdk-6u45-solaris-sparc.sh
Solaris SPARC (SVR4 package)	124.74 MB	⬇ jdk-6u45-solaris-sparc.tar.Z
Solaris SPARC 64-bit	12.19 MB	⬇ jdk-6u45-solaris-sparcv9.sh
Solaris SPARC 64-bit (SVR4 package)	15.49 MB	⬇ jdk-6u45-solaris-sparcv9.tar.Z
Windows x86	69.85 MB	⬇ jdk-6u45-windows-i586.exe
Windows x64	59.96 MB	⬇ jdk-6u45-windows-x64.exe
Linux Intel Itanium	53.89 MB	⬇ jdk-6u45-linux-ia64-rpm.bin
Linux Intel Itanium	56 MB	⬇ jdk-6u45-linux-ia64.bin
Windows Intel Itanium	51.72 MB	⬇ jdk-6u45-windows-ia64.exe

Back to top

Figure 1-5. Java SE 6 download links for Linux, Solaris, and Windows (once software agreement is accepted)

Once the EXE file has finished downloading, make sure any previous version of Java 6 SDK is uninstalled by using the Windows Control Panel Add/Remove Programs dialog. Then find and launch an installer for the current version Java 6 SDK installer, and install the latest version of Java 6, so that you can install the Android Developer Tools ADT Bundle.

The Android Developer Tools (ADT) Bundle is comprised of the Eclipse Kepler 4.3 IDE (Integrated Development Environment) for Java and the Android Developer Tools Plug-ins already installed into the Eclipse IDE. This used to be done separately, and it took about a 50 step process to complete, so downloading and installing one pre-made bundle is significantly less work.

Next, you need to download the Android ADT Bundle from the Android Developer web site. In the past, developers had to assemble Eclipse and ADT plug-ins manually. Starting with Android 4.2, Jelly Bean + Google is now doing this for you, making installing an Android ADT IDE an order of magnitude easier that it was in the past. This is the URL to use to download an ADT Bundle:

```
http://developer.android.com/sdk/index.html
```

The screen shown in Figure 1-6 is what you should see on the Android SDK download page. Simply click the blue Download the SDK button to get started with the download process.

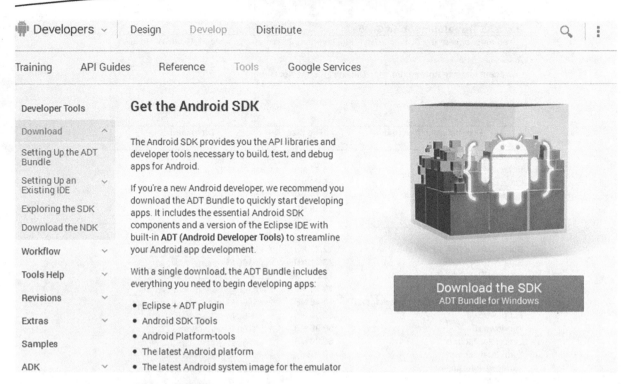

Figure 1-6. ADT Bundle Download the SDK Button on Get the Android SDK page of the Android Developer site

Once you click the Download the SDK button, you will be taken to the Licensing Terms and Conditions Agreement page, where you can read the terms and conditions of using the Android development environment and finally click the **I have read and agree with the above terms and conditions** checkbox.

Once you do this, the OS 32 or 64 bit-level selection radio buttons will be enabled so that you can select either the 32-bit or the 64-bit version of the Android ADT environment. Then the blue Download the SDK ADT Bundle for Windows (or your OS) will be enabled, and you can click it to start the installation file download process. This is the screen state that is shown in Figure 1-7.

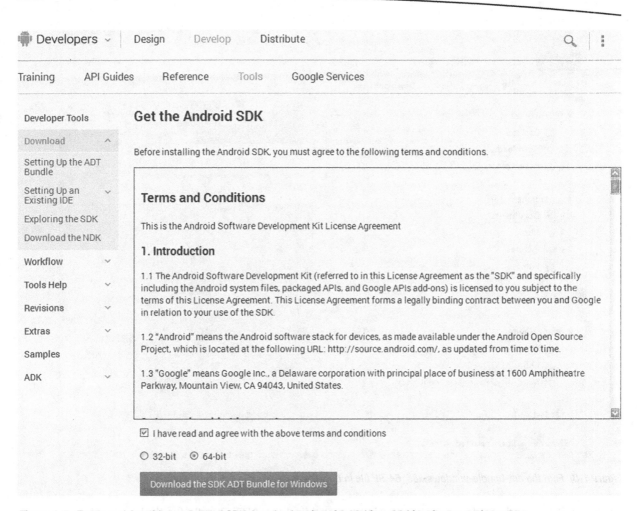

Figure 1-7. Terms and Conditions page and SDK download options for 32-bit or 64-bit software environments

Click the blue Download the SDK ADT Bundle button and save the ZIP file to your system downloads folder. Once the download is finished you can begin the installation process, which we will go through in detail in the next section of this chapter.

Now you are ready top unzip and install the ADT, and then update it to the latest version from inside of the Eclipse Java ADT IDE (after you install and launch it for the first time, of course). Are you getting excited yet?

Installing and Updating the Android Developer ADT Bundle

Open the Windows File Explorer utility, which should look like a folder icon with files in it (it is the second icon from the left in Figure 1-13). Next, find your **Downloads** folder, which should be showing at the top-left (underneath the Favorites section) of the file manager utility, as shown in Figure 1-8.

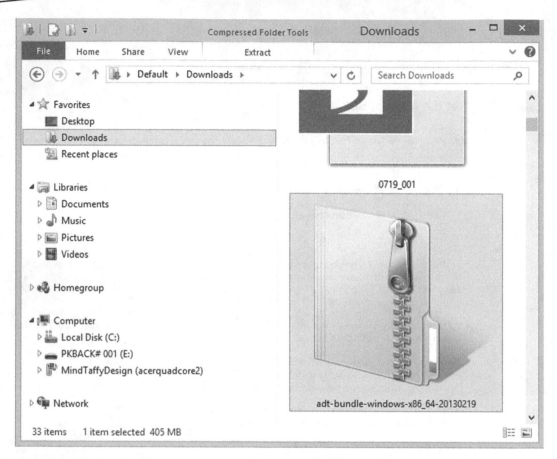

Figure 1-8. Find the adt-bundle-windows-x86_64 ZIP file in Downloads

Click the Downloads folder to highlight it in blue and find the ADT Bundle file that you just downloaded in the pane of files on the right side of the file management utility.

Right-click the `adt-bundle-windows-x86_64` file as shown in Figure 1-9 to bring up a context-sensitive menu and select the **Extract All** option.

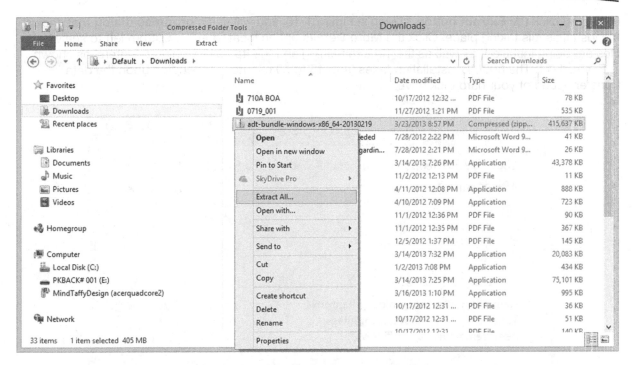

Figure 1-9. Right-click the adt-bundle ZIP file and select the Extract All option to begin the ADT installation

When the **Extract Compressed (Zipped) Folders** dialog appears, replace the default folder for installation with one of your own creation. I created an **Android** folder under my root **C:** hard drive (so, C:\Android) to keep my ADT IDE in, as that is a logical name for it. The before and after dialogs are shown in Figure 1-10, showing the difficult-to-remember path to my system Downloads folder and a new, easy-to-find **C:\Android** folder path.

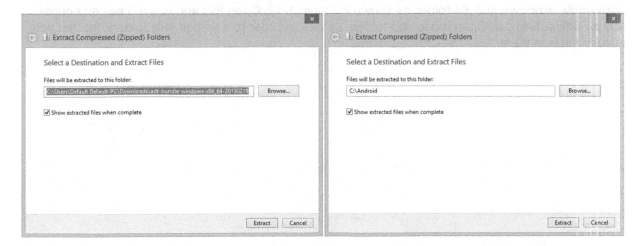

Figure 1-10. Change the target installation folder from your Downloads folder to an Android folder that you create

Once you click the **Extract** button, shown in Figure 1-10, you will see a **progress dialog** that shows the install as it is taking place. Click the **More Details** option located at the bottom left to see what files are being installed, as well as the Time remaining and the Items remaining counters, as shown in Figure 1-11. The 600MB installation takes from 15 to 60 minutes, depending upon the data transfer speed of your hard disk drive.

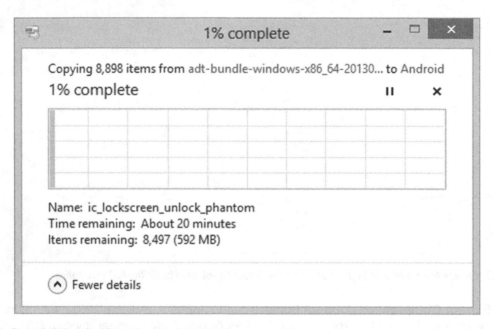

Figure 1-11. Expanded More Details option showing which files are installing

Once the installation is complete, go back into your Windows Explorer File Management Utility and look under the C:\Android folder (or whatever you decided to name it) and you will see the adt-bundle-windows-x86_64 folder, as shown in Figure 1-12. Open this and you will see an **eclipse** and an **sdk** sub-folder. Open those sub-folders as well, in order to see their sub-folders, so that you know what is in there.

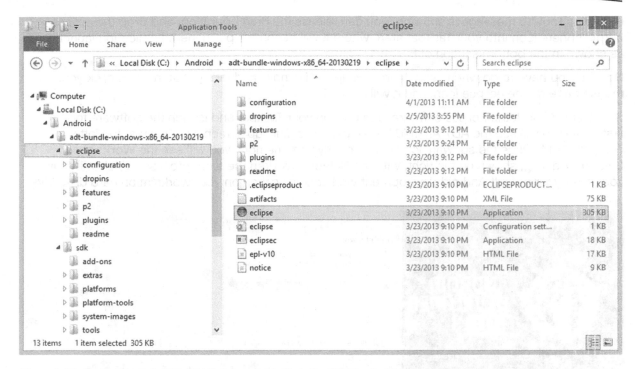

Figure 1-12. Finding the Eclipse Application executable file in the ADT Bundle folder hierarchy you just installed

Next, click the eclipse folder on the left side of your file management utility to show the file contents in the right side of the file manager. Find the eclipse Application executable file, which will be the one that has its own custom icon next to it, on the left. It is a purple sphere.

Click and drag the Eclipse icon to the bottom of your desktop (or wherever your Taskbar Launch area is mounted to your OS desktop), and hover it over your Installed Program Launch Icon Taskbar. Once you do this, you will see the **Pin to Taskbar** (Windows Vista, Windows 7) or **Pin to eclipse** (Windows 8) tool-tip message, as is shown in the top section of Figure 1-13.

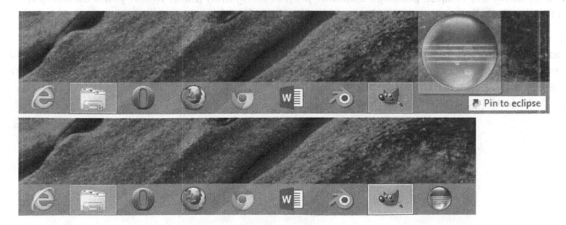

Figure 1-13. Dragging the Eclipse application onto the Windows Taskbar to invoke the pin operation

Once this tool-tip message is showing, you can release the drag operation, and drop the eclipse purple sphere icon into your Taskbar area, where it will become a permanent application launch icon, as shown in the bottom section of Figure 1-13.

Now, all you have to do when I say "launch Eclipse ADT now, and let's get started" is click your mouse once on the eclipse icon, and it will launch!

So let's try it. Click the Eclipse software icon once in your Taskbar and launch the software for the first time. You will see the ADT Android Developer Tools start-up screen, as shown at the left side of Figure 1-14. Once the software loads into your system memory, you will see the **Workspace Launcher** dialog, shown on the right, with the **Select a workspace** work process, which will allow you to set your default Android development workspace location on your workstation hard disk drive.

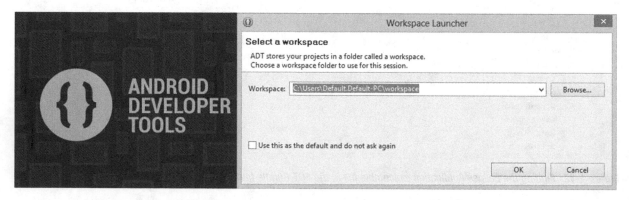

Figure 1-14. *Android Developer Tools start-up screen and Workspace Launcher dialog showing default workspace*

I accepted the default workspace location, which will be under your main hard disk drive letter (probably C:\) in your Users folder, under a sub-folder named using your PC's assigned name; your Android development workspace folder will be underneath that.

When you create projects in Android ADT, they will appear as sub-folders underneath this workspace folder hierarchy, so you'll be able to find all of your files using your File Management Utility software as well as using the Eclipse package Explorer project navigation pane, which you'll be using quite a bit in this book, to learn about how Android implements Graphics.

Once you set your workspace location and click the OK button, the Eclipse Java ADT start-up **Welcome!** screen will appear, as shown in Figure 1-15. The first thing that you want to do is make sure your software is completely up to date, so click the **Help** menu at the top right of the screen, and select the **Check for Updates** option about two-thirds of the way down, as shown in Figure 1-15 (and highlighted in blue).

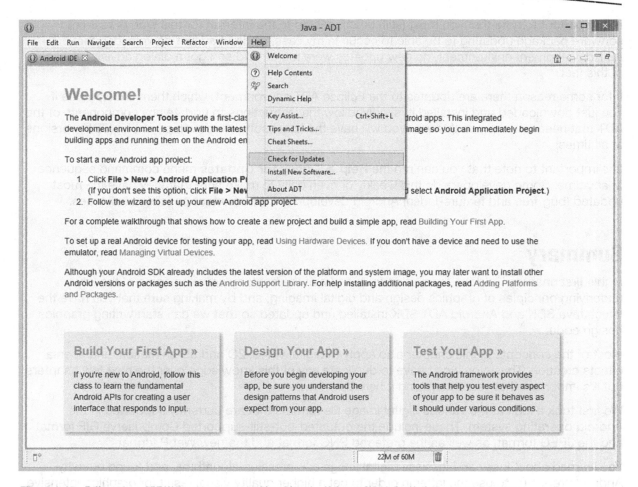

Figure 1-15. *Eclipse Java ADT Welcome screen and invoking the Help ➤ Check for Updates menu sequence*

Once you select this menu option, you will see the **Contacting Software Sites** dialog, shown in Figure 1-16 on the left-hand side. This shows the Checking for updates progress bar as it checks various Google Android software repository sites for any updated versions of the Eclipse ADT.

Figure 1-16. *The Contacting Software Sites dialog checking for updates to Eclipse ADT, with no updates found*

It is important to note that you must (still) be connected to the Internet for this type of real-time software package updating to be able to occur. In my case, since I had just downloaded the ADT development environment, no new updates were found, and so I got a dialog advising me of this fact.

If for some reason there are updates to the Eclipse ADT environment, which there shouldn't be if you just downloaded and installed it, simply follow the instructions to update any components of the ADT that need updating. In this way you will have the latest software development kit (SDK) versions at all times.

It is important to note that you can run the **Help ➤ Check for Updates** menu command sequence at any time. Some developers do this weekly or even daily to make sure that they have the most updated (bug-free and feature-laden) Android development environment possible at all times.

Summary

In this first chapter, I laid the foundation for the rest of the book by covering some of the key underlying principles of graphics design and digital imaging, and by making sure that you have the latest Java SDK and Android ADT SDK installed and updated so that we can start writing graphics design code.

Most of the concepts in this chapter also apply to digital video, 2D and 3D animation, and special effects creation. Thus, you won't have to duplicate any of this knowledge over the next few chapters, but it's important that you understand it here and now.

We first took a look at the various digital image file formats that are currently supported in the Android operating system. These include the outdated-but-still-supported Compuserve GIF format and the JPEG format, as well as the preferred PNG format and the new WebP format.

You learned about lossy and lossless digital image compression algorithms, and found out why Android prefers us to use the latter in order to get a higher quality visual result for graphics-intensive applications.

We then did a quick overview of the Android View and ViewGroup classes, which are used to hold and display digital images and digital video. We also reviewed the android.widget package, which holds many of the user interface classes that we will be utilizing frequently during this book.

Next, we looked at the building block of digital imaging and video, the pixel, and the fundamental concepts of resolution and aspect ratio. You learned how to calculate the number of pixels in an image in order to find its raw data footprint size. You learned all about aspect ratio and how it defines the shape of your image using a ratio of Width-to-Height multipliers.

Then we looked at how color is handled in digital images using some color theory and terminology. You also learned about color depth and additive color and how color is created using multiple color channels in an image.

Next, we looked at hexadecimal notation, and how colors are represented in the Android OS using two hexadecimal value slots per color channel. You learned that 24-bit RGB images use six slots and 32-bit ARGB images use eight slots. You learned that hexadecimal values are represented in Android by using a pound sign before the hexadecimal data values.

We then looked at digital image compositing and the concepts of alpha channels and pixel blending modes. We explored the power of holding different image elements on digital layers of transparency, using alpha channels, and algorithmically blending any pixel in an image with any of those layers via dozens of different blending modes in the Porter-Duff class in Android.

Next, we looked at the concept of using the alpha channel capabilities to create image masks, which allows us to extract subject material out of an image so we can later manipulate it individually using Java code or use it in compositing layers to create a more complicated images.

Then, we looked at the concept of anti-aliasing and how it allows us to achieve a smooth, professional compositing result by blending pixel color values at the edges between two different objects, or between an object and its background. We saw how using anti-aliasing in an alpha channel mask allows us to obtain a smooth composite between that object and a background image.

Next, we covered the main factors that are important in image compression, and you learned how to achieve a compact data footprint for these digital image assets. You learned about dithering and how it allows you to use 8-bit indexed color images with good results to reduce file size significantly.

Finally, you downloaded and installed the latest Java and Android ADT SDK software and then configured it for use on your workstation. You did this so that you are now completely ready to develop graphics-oriented Android application software within the rest of the chapters in this book.

In the next chapter, you will learn about digital video formats, concepts, and optimization. Thus, that chapter will be very similar to this one where you will get all the fundamental concepts regarding digital video under your belt, and you will also create the framework for your Android application, which you will be super-charging, from a graphics design perspective at least, during the duration of this Pro Android Graphics Design book.

Chapter **2**

Android Digital Video: Formats, Concepts, and Optimization

In this second chapter, we will take a closer look at how digital video is implemented inside the Android operating system. We will build upon the concepts you learned in the previous chapter, as all of a digital image's characteristics apply equally to digital video.

After all, digital video is really just a series of moving digital images. This motion aspect of digital video introduces a high level of complexity, as a fourth dimension (time) is added into the mathematical equation. This makes working with digital video an order of magnitude more complex than working with digital images, especially for the codec, which you will be learning about very soon.

This is especially true when it comes to video compression, and thus, this chapter will focus even more on video codecs and the proper way to get the smallest possible data footprint using a new media data file format that's traditionally been (and continues to be) a gigabyte-laden monstrosity.

We will take a look at the digital video file formats that are currently supported in Android, as well as the MediaPlayer class, which allows video to be played back on the screen. You will learn all about the VideoView user interface widget, which Android has created to implement a MediaPlayer for our ease of use in a pre-built UI container.

You'll learn basic digital video concepts that you will need to understand in order to follow what we will be doing with digital video during this chapter. We will take a look at digital video optimization from a digital video asset data footprint standpoint (app size) as well as from Android device types (a market coverage standpoint). You'll create a **pro.android.graphics** Java package and a **GraphicsDesign** Android application in this chapter.

Android Digital Video Formats: MPEG4 H.264 and WebM VP8

Android supports the same two **open source** digital video formats that **HTML5** supports natively, namely **MPEG-4** (Motion Picture Experts Group) **H.264** and the ON2 **VP8** format, which was acquired by Google from ON2 Technologies and renamed **WebM.** WebM was subsequently released as an open source digital video file format and is now in Android OS as well as all browsers.

This is very convenient from a **content production** standpoint, as the video content that developers produce and optimize can be used in HTML5 engines such as browsers and HTML5-based OSes, as well as in Android applications.

This open source digital video format cross-platform support scenario will afford content developers with a "produce it once, deliver it everywhere" content production situation. This will reduce content development costs and increase developer revenues, as long as these economies of scale are taken advantage of by the professional video graphics developer.

Like I did in Chapter 1, I will cover the MPEG and WebM video file formats from oldest to most recent. The oldest format supported by Android is MPEG H.263, which should only be used for lower resolution, as it has the worst **compression-to-quality** result because it uses the oldest technology.

Since most Android devices these days have screens that are using a medium (854x480) to high (1280x720) resolution, if you are going to use the MPEG file format, you should utilize the **MPEG-4 H.264** format, which is the most widely used digital video file format in the world currently.

MPEG-4 H.264 format is used by commercial broadcasters, HTML5 web browser software, Mobile HTML5 Apps, and Android OS. All of these summed together are rapidly approaching a majority market share position, to say the least.

The **MPEG-4 H.264 AVC** (**Advanced Video Coding**) digital video file format is supported across all Android OS versions for video playback, and under **Android 3.0** and later OS versions for **video recording**. Recording video is only supported if the Android device has video camera hardware capability.

There is also an **MPEG4 SP** (Simple Profile) video format, which is supported for **commercial video** file playback. This format is available across every Android OS version for broadcast-type content playback (films, television programs, mini-series, TV series, workout videos, and similar products).

If you are an individual Android content producer, however, you will find that the MPEG-4 H.264 AVC format has far better compression, especially if you are using one of the more advanced (better) encoding suites, like the **Sorenson Squeeze Pro 9** software (which you'll be using later in the chapter).

MPEG-4 H.264 AVC will be the format that you will use for Android video content production if you decide to use the MPEG-4 digital video format in your Android application rather than the WebM (VP8) video format from Google. The reason for the MPEG4 SP support is most likely because many commercial videos and films were originally compressed using this older video format, and playback of these commercial video titles on user's Android devices is a popular use for these devices these days, due to a dearth of interactive content. But you are going to do something about that, aren't you?! Great!

File extensions supported for MPEG-4 video files include **.3GP** (SP) and **.MP4 (AVC)**. I prefer to use the latter (.MP4 AVC), as that is what I use in HTML5 apps, and it is more common to use the superior AVC format, but either type of file (extension) should work just fine in the Android OS.

The more modern (advanced) digital video format that Android now supports is called the **WebM** or **VP8** digital video format, and this format provides a higher quality result with a **smaller data footprint**. This is probably the reason why Google acquired ON2, the company that developed the VP8 codec. You will learn all about codecs later in this chapter.

Playback of WebM video is "natively" supported in Android **2.3.3** and later, so most the Android devices out there, including an Amazon Kindle Fire HD as well as the original Kindle Fire, should be able to support this higher quality digital video file format. This is because it's **natively a part of the operating system** (OS) software installed on your smartphone or tablet.

WebM also supports **video streaming**, which you'll learn about in a later section of this chapter. WebM video format streaming playback capability is supported if users have Android OS version **4.0** (or later). For this reason I recommend using MPEG-4 H.264 AVC for captive (non-streaming) video assets and WebM if you are going to be streaming video. We will cover advanced video concepts such as streaming and the like in the last section of this book.

Android VideoView and MediaPlayer Class: Video Players

There are two major classes in Android, both subclassed directly from the **java.lang.Object** superclass, that deal directly with digital video format playback. They are the **VideoView** widget class, from the **android.widget** package, and the **MediaPlayer** media class, from the **android.media** package.

Most of your basic digital video playback usage should be accomplished by using the **<VideoView>** XML tag and its parameters, and designed right into your user interface designs, as you will be doing later on in the chapter.

Android's VideoView class is a direct subclass of the Android **SurfaceView** class, which is a display class that provides a dedicated **drawing surface** embedded inside a specialized Android View hierarchy used for implementing an advanced, direct-to-the-screen drawing graphics pipeline.

A SurfaceView is **z-ordered** so that it lives behind the View windows that are holding the SurfaceView, and thus a SurfaceView cuts this viewport through its View window to allow content to be displayed to a user.

Z-order is a concept that we will get into later on in the book when you start working extensively with layered composites, but in a nutshell, the z-order is the **order in the layer stack** of a given image or video source.

Layers are arranged, at least conceptually, from the top layer down to the bottom layer. This is the reason an image (or video) asset's order in this layer hierarchy is called the z-order, as layers containing the x and y 2D image data are stacked along the 3D **z axis**. Forget about learning about 3D z axes and z-order later on in this book; it looks like I just explained it!

As you now know, 2D images and video only use an x and y axis to "address" their data, so you will need to look at z-order and compositing from a 3D standpoint, as layers in a composite need to exist along a third z axis.

A SurfaceView class is a subclass of the **View** class, which, as you know, is a subclass of the Java **Object** master class. The **VideoView** subclass is thus a specialized incarnation of the SurfaceView subclass, adding more methods to the SurfaceView class methods, and thus is farther down within the View class hierarchy. There is more detailed information regarding this Android VideoView, and its methods and constructors, at the following web site URL:

```
http://developer.android.com/reference/android/widget/VideoView.html
```

Android's VideoView class implements a **Java interface** in an **android.widget** package called **MediaController.MediaPlayerControl**. This is so developers using the **VideoView** widget will have access to the Android **MediaController** class methods relating to **MediaPlayerControl** for digital video playback.

If you are going to code your own digital video playback engine, you should access the Android **MediaPlayer** class itself directly. In this scenario, you are essentially writing your own (custom) video playback engine (MediaPlayer subclass) to replace your use of the VideoView widget with your own (more advanced) digital video playback functionality.

There is more information about how this Android MediaPlayer class works, as well as a state engine diagram, at the following developer web site URL:

```
http://developer.android.com/reference/android/media/MediaPlayer.html
```

I could write an entire advanced programming book on how to code a video playback engine using this Android MediaPlayer class. However, since this intermediate book specifically covers Android graphic design and the inter-relationships between images, animation, digital video, compositing, blending, and the like, we'll utilize the VideoView class. Indeed, this is what Android prefers that we utilize, which is why it provided this class.

The Foundation of Digital Video: Motion, Frames and FPS

Digital video is an extension of digital imaging into the fourth dimension (time). Digital video is actually a collection of digital imagery that is displayed rapidly over time, much like the old flip-books where you could flip rapidly through the book's pages to animate a character or scene that was drawn on its pages to create **motion**. Each of the images in the digital **video sequence** is called a **frame**. This terminology probably comes from the olden days of film, where frames of film were run through a film projector at a rate of 24 frames per second, which served to create the illusion of **motion**.

Since each frame of digital video actually contains digital imagery, all the concepts you learned in Chapter 1 can also be applied to video. Related concepts include pixels, resolution, aspect ratios, color depth, alpha channels, pixel blending, image compositing, and even data footprint optimization. All of these can be just as readily applied to your work in digital video content development and implemented in your graphic designs.

Since digital video is made up of this collection of digital image frames, the concept of a digital video **frame rate**, expressed as **frames per second**, or more commonly referred to as **FPS**, is also very important when it comes to your digital video data footprint optimization work process.

The optimization concept with frames in a digital video is very similar to the one regarding pixels in an image (the resolution of the digital image) because video frames multiply the data footprint with each frame used. In digital video, not only does the frame's (image) resolution greatly impact the file size, but so does the number of frames per second, or frame rate.

In Chapter 1, you saw that if we multiply the number of pixels in an image by the number of color channels, it gives us the **raw data footprint** for that image. With digital video, we must now multiply that number again by the number of frames per second that the digital video is running at, as well as by the number of total seconds in the digital video.

To continue the VGA example from Chapter 1, we know one 24-bit VGA raw image is **900KB** exactly. That makes the math easy to take it to the next level in this example. Digital video traditionally runs at **30 FPS**, so one second of Standard Definition (SD) or VGA raw uncompressed digital video is 30 image frames, each of which is 900K, yielding a data footprint of **27000KB**.

To find out how many megabytes (MB) this would be, we need to divide 27000 by 1024, which gives us **26.3671875MB** of data for **one second** of raw digital video. Let's multiply this by 60 seconds, giving us **1582.0313** Megabytes of raw data **per minute** of 24-bit VGA digital video. Divide this again by 1024 and we have the amount of **gigabytes (GB) per minute**, which equals **1.54495**.

You think VGA resolution video has lots of raw data, at over 1.5GB/minute? **HD (High Definition)** video resolution is 1920x1080, times 3 RGB channels, times 30 frames, times 60 seconds, and that yields **10.43GB per minute**!

You can see why having a video file format that can compress this massive raw data footprint that digital video creates is extremely important! This is why Google acquired ON2, to obtain their VP8 video codec and the folks who created it! VP8 maintains a high level of video image quality while at the same time reducing file size by an order of magnitude or more. An order of magnitude, in case you might be wondering, equates to ten times (10X).

You will be amazed (later on in this chapter) at some of the digital video data compression ratios that you will achieve using MPEG video file format, once you know exactly how to best optimize a digital video compression work process by using the correct bit rate, frame rate, and frame resolution for your digital video content. We'll get into WebM video optimization more in Chapter 18 when I dedicate an entire chapter to advanced digital video data footprint optimization techniques and work processes.

Digital Video Conventions: Bit Rates, Streams, SD, and HD

Since we finished the last section talking about resolution, let's start out covering the primary resolutions used in commercial video. Before **HD** or **High Definition** came along, video was called **SD** or **Standard Definition** and used a standard pixel height (a vertical resolution) of **480 pixels**.

Commercial or **broadcast video** is usually in one of two aspect ratios: **4:3**, used in the older tube TVs, and **16:9**, used in the newer HDTVs. Let's use the math that you learned in Chapter 1 to figure out the pixel resolution for the 4:3 SD broadcast video.

480 divided by 3 is 160 x 4 is 640, so SD 4:3 video is VGA resolution, which is why I was using that particular resolution as an example in the previous chapter. There is also another 16:9 Wide SD resolution, which has become an entry-level screen resolution in Android touchscreen smartphones as well as in the smaller tablet form factor called mini-tablets.

Let's figure out what Wide SD resolution would be by again dividing 480 by 9 this time, giving us 53.4 times 16 is **854** so the new Wide SD smartphones and tablets feature an **854x480** "Wide SD" pixel screen dimension. This is largely so that the now-mainstream HD content can be downsampled directly from the **16:9 1920x1080** to **1280x720**, or to **854x480**.

HD Video comes in two resolutions, **1280x720**, which I call **Pseudo HD**, and **1920x1080**, which the industry calls **True HD**. Both are 16:9 aspect ratio and are now used not only in TVs and iTVs, but also in smartphones (Razor HD is 1280x720) and tablets (a Kindle Fire HD is 1920x1200, which is a less wide, or taller, **16:10** aspect ratio).

There's also **16:10 Pseudo HD** resolution that features **1280x800** pixels. In fact, this is a common laptop, netbook, and mid-size tablet resolution. Generally, most developers try to match their video content resolutions to the resolution of each Android device that the video will be viewed upon.

Regardless of the resolution you use for your digital video content, video can be accessed by your application in a couple of different ways. The way I do it, because I'm data optimization nuts, is **captive** to an application; that is, **inside** the Android application **APK** file itself, inside the **raw data** resource folder. We will be taking a look at this a little bit later.

The other way to access video within your Android app is by using a remote video data server; in this case, the video is **streamed** right from the remote server over the Internet and onto your user's Android device as the video is playing back in real time. Let's hope your server doesn't crash!

Video streaming is more complicated than playing captive video data files because the Android device is communicating in real time with remote data servers and receiving **video data packets** as the video plays. Video streaming is supported via WebM on Android 4.0 and later devices, using the WebM format. We will not be using streaming video in this book until chapter 19, as it requires a remote video server; you'll use captive video data so you can test your app!

The last concept that we need to cover in this overview is the concept of bit rate. **Bit rate** is a key setting used in the video compression process, as a bit rate represents the **target bandwidth** data pipe size that is able to accommodate a certain amount of bits streaming through it every second.

A slow data pipe in today's Internet 2.0 (mobile devices telecommunication network) IP infrastructure is **768 kbits/s** or **768 KBPS**, and the video file compressed to fit through this "narrower" data pipe will thus have a lower quality level and will probably also need to have lower resolution to further reduce its total data footprint. The older 3G networks feature these slower types of video data transfer speed.

It is important to note that an oversaturated (crowded) data pipe can turn fast data pipes into medium-fast or even slow data pipes, as more and more users try to access data through that data pipe during peak usage periods.

A medium data pipe in today's Internet 2.0 IP infrastructure is **1536** kbits/second (1.5 MBPS, or megabits per second). Notice that we are using bits here, and not bytes, so to calculate how many bytes per second this represents, divide by eight (eight bits in a byte). Thus, one megabit per second equals 128 kilobytes of data transferred per second, so one and a half megabits per second is 192 kilobytes per second.

Older **3G** networks deliver between 600 kbits/s and 1.5 mbits/s, so, on average, these will be 1.5 mbits/s and classified as a medium data pipe.

A faster data pipe is at least **2048** kbits/s, or 2 mbits/s or 2 MBPS, and video compressed at this higher bit rate exhibits a higher visual quality level. More modern 4G networks claim to be between 3 and 6 mbits/s, although I would optimize assets for 4G to 2 mbits/s just to make sure that your video assets will still play back (that is, stream) very smoothly if for some reason the network is yielding only 2MBPS.

Note that home networks often feature much faster MBPS performance, often in the 6MBPS-24MBPS range. Mobile networks are currently at 4G and have not yet achieved this bandwidth, so you will need to optimize for much more constricted data pipes in your Android graphics application development.

Bit rate must also take into consideration **CPU processing power** within any given Android phone, making video data optimization even more challenging. This is because once the "bits" travel through a data-pipe, they also need to be processed and then displayed to the device display screen. In fact, any **captive video asset** included in your Android application .APK file only needs optimization for processing power. The reason this is the case is because if you use captive digital video assets, there is no data pipe for your video assets to travel through, and no data is transferred! Your video assets are right there, inside your APK file, ready for playback.

This means that the bit rate for your digital video asset needs to be well optimized not only for bandwidth (or the APK file size, if you are using a captive digital video asset), but also in anticipation of variances in CPU processing power. Some single-core low-power embedded CPUs may not be able to decode the higher resolution, high bit rate digital video assets without dropping frames, so having a lower resolution, low bit rate digital video asset with ten times less data for a given CPU to process is a great idea.

Digital Video Files for Android: Resolution Density Targets

To prepare your digital video assets for use across the various Android OS devices currently on the market, you must hit several different resolution targets, which will then cover most of the screen densities on the market.

You will be learning more about the default screen densities in Android as they pertain to graphics in the next chapter on frame-based animation. In case you are wondering (as I was) why Android did not simply take one high-resolution asset and then scale it down using **bicubic interpolation** (or at least **bilinear interpolation**), the reason is that currently Android's Achilles' Heel happens to be scaling things, primarily imagery and video.

As you know, the screen sizes for Android devices span those smaller flip-phones and Android watches to the larger tablets and iTV sets. Within this spectrum are smartphones, eBook readers, mini-tablets, and medium tablets, so you will need at least four, if not five, different target DPI (dots per inch, or density pixel imagery) resolutions. For digital video, this also includes different target bit rates, so that you can try to fit all of the different device screen densities and the different processing power capabilities of single-core through quad-core CPU product offerings.

As far as digital video support is concerned, it is actually more about having three or four **bit rate targets** than it is about hitting display screens pixel for pixel, because the VideoView class can **scale** video up (or more preferably, down), as you'll see later on in the chapter and book.

Providing this evenly spaced range of bit rates is important because smaller Android devices tend to have less processing power to decode data-heavy (high) bit rate video smoothly, so you want a Android app to have a range of bit rates that can "curve-fit" to the processing power across all of the potential types of Android devices out there.

For instance, an Android watch or flip-phone will most likely have a single-core or maybe a dual-core CPU whereas an iTV will probably have at least a quad-core, if not an octa-core processor. The Galaxy S3 has a quad-core processor, and a Galaxy S4 has an octa-core (or dual quad-core) processor.

Thus, you should have bit rates that will decode smoothly on any processor, ranging from a low resolution 512 KBPS to a high resolution 2 MBPS target. The higher the resolution density, that is, the smaller the pixels, the better the video will look, regardless of the amount of compression.

This is because encoding artifacts will be more difficult to see (essentially they will be hidden from view) the smaller the **pixel pitch** (or the higher the **pixel density**) on any given Android device's screen. This fine pixel pitch, found on most Android device hardware, will allow you to get good quality video into a relatively small data footprint, once you know what you are doing with video editing or compression utilities such as the open source EditShare Lightworks 11 or Sorenson Squeeze Pro.

Optimizing Digital Video: Codecs and Compression

Digital video is compressed by using a piece of software called a **codec**, which stands for **code-decode**. There are two sides to a video codec, one that **encodes** the video data stream and the other that **decodes** the video data stream. The decoder will be part of the OS or browser that uses it.

The **decoder** is usually optimized for speed, as smoothness of playback is the primary issue, and the **encoder** is optimized to reduce data footprint for the digital video asset it is generating. For this reason, the encoding process could take a long time, depending on how many processor cores your workstation contains. A serious workstation these days offers eight cores.

Codecs (the encoder side) are like plug-ins in the sense that they can be installed into different digital video editing software packages in order to enable them to encode different types of digital video file formats.

Since Android supports H.263 and H.264 MPEG4 formats, and the ON2 VP8 WebM format for video, you need to make sure that you're using one of the video codecs that encodes video data into these digital video file formats. If you do this correctly, the Android OS will be able to decode the digital video data stream because the decoder side of these three codecs is built right into the Android OS, which is why you learned about these three formats.

More than one software manufacturer makes MPEG encoding software, so different MPEG codecs (encoder software) will yield different (better or worse) results as far as file size is concerned.

The professional solution, which I highly recommend that you secure if you want to produce video professionally, is called **Sorenson Squeeze**, which is currently at version 9. Squeeze has a professional version, which I will be using in this book, which costs less than a thousand dollars.

There is also an open source solution called **EditShare Lightworks 11** that does not currently natively support output to the WebM VP8 codec, so I am going to use **Squeeze Pro 9** for this book, until the codec support for Android is added to EditShare Lightworks, which they promise will be soon.

I still recommend that you go to the **editshare.com** or **lwks.com** web site and sign up for and download this software, as it's one of the most powerful open source software packages, along with Blender 3D, GIMP2, and Audacity.

When optimizing (setting compression settings) for digital video data file size, there are a large number of **variables** that directly affect the video data footprint. I will cover these in the order that they affect the video file size, from the most impact to the least impact, so that you know which parameters to **tweak** in order to obtain the result that you desire.

As in digital image compression, the **resolution**, or number of pixels, in each frame of video is the best place to start your optimization process. If your target users are using 854x480 or 1280x720 smartphones and tablets, then you don't need to use **True HD** 1920x1080 resolution video in order to get a good visual result for your digital video assets. With the super-fine density (dot pitch) displays out there, you can scale 1280 video up 33% [calculated via 1 minus (1280 divided by 1920)], and it will still look great. The exception to this would be if you are delivering an iTV app to GoogleTV users, in which case you might want to use 1920x1080.

The next level of optimization comes in the **number of frames** used for each second of video, assuming that the actual seconds of the video itself cannot be shortened. This is the **frame rate**, and instead of using the video standard 30 FPS, consider using a film standard frame rate of 24 FPS, or a multimedia standard frame rate of 20 FPS. You might even be able to get away with using a 10 FPS rate, depending upon your content.

Note that 15 FPS is half as much data as 30 FPS (or 100% reduction in data going into the codec), and some video content will play (look) the same as 30 FPS content! The only real way to find this out is to try these settings during your content optimization (encoding) work process.

The next most effective setting for obtaining a smaller data footprint is the **bit rate** that you set for a codec to achieve. Bit rate equates to the **amount of compression** applied, and thus to the **quality level** of the video data. It is important to note that you could simply use 30 FPS, 1920 resolution HD video, and specify a very low bit rate ceiling; however, your results would not be as good looking as if you first experimented with low frame rates and resolutions using the higher (quality) bit rate settings.

Since each video data stream is completely different, the only real way to find out what any given codec is going to do to your video data is to send it through the codec and view the end result. I would try to use 512 KBPS or 768 KBPS for your low end, 1.5 MBPS to 2.0 MBPS for your middle data, and 2.5 MBPS to 3.5 MBPS for your high end, if you can achieve a compact data footprint using these settings, which WebM or MPEG4 AVC will provide.

The next most effective setting in obtaining a smaller data footprint is the number of **keyframes** that the codec uses to **sample** your digital video. Video gains compression by looking at a frame, and then encoding only the changes, or **offsets**, over the next few frames, so that it does not have to encode every single frame in the video data stream. This is why a talking head video will encode better than video where every pixel moves on every frame (such as video using fast panning or rapid zooming).

A keyframe is a setting in a codec that forces that codec to take a fresh sampling of your video data asset every so often. There is usually an **auto** setting for keyframes that allows a codec to decide how many keyframes to sample, as well as a **manual** setting that allows you to specify a keyframe sampling every so often, usually a certain number of times per second or a certain number of times over the duration of the video (total frames). For the 480x800 digital video asset that you will be optimizing later in this chapter, I will set keyframes every 10 frames for a 400 frame 3D rendering planet fly-through total frames duration, or 40 times.

Most codecs usually have a **quality** or a **sharpness** setting, or slider, that controls the amount of blur applied to a video before compression. In case you don't know this trick, applying a very slight blur (0.2 setting) to an image or a video, which is usually not desirable, can allow for better compression as sharp transitions (edges) in an image are harder to encode (take more data to reproduce) than soft transitions. That said, I'd keep the quality or sharpness slider between an **80%** and **100%** quality, and try to get your data footprint reduction using the other variables that we have discussed here.

Ultimately there are a number of different variables that you will need to fine-tune in order to achieve the best data footprint optimization for any given video data asset, and each video will be different (mathematically) to the codec. Thus, there are no "standard" settings that can be developed to achieve a given result. That said, experience in tweaking various settings will eventually allow you to get a feel, over time, as to the settings you need to change to get your desired result.

Creating Your Pro Android Graphics App in Eclipse ADT

Let's pick up where we left off in Chapter 1 and create your new Pro Android Graphics application project in your virgin Eclipse ADT environment, which is currently open on your desktop. If you closed Eclipse, open it with your quick launch icon, and accept the default workspace (or the one you specified) and open up the blank Eclipse environment shown in Figure 1-16, way back in Chapter 1.

Click the **File** menu located at the top-left of Eclipse, and select the **New** sub-menu, and then select the **Android Application Project** menu option from the fly-out menu that will appear, as shown in Figure 2-1. I hope you are excited about finally getting down to creating the application for your professional Android graphics development experience during the book!

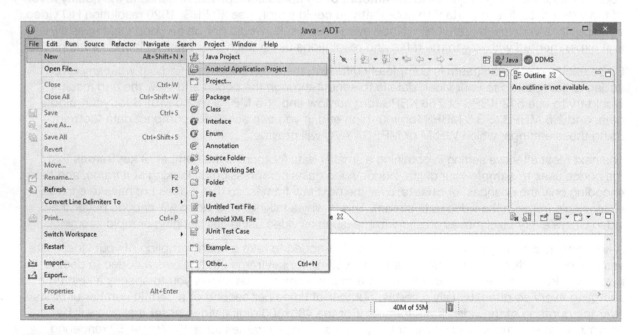

Figure 2-1. Using File ➤ New ➤ Android Application Project work process to create your Pro Android Graphics app

Once you select this, you'll see the first in a series of five **New Android Application** dialogs. These dialogs will guide you through the process of creating a new Android application "bootstrap," or framework, that will hold all of your assets and classes and methods and XML files and so on.

The dialogs will ask you a series of questions or, more accurately, allow you to select from a series of options, and specify information using data fields, so that Eclipse ADT (the Android OS, essentially) can create your application bootstrap code in the most optimal fashion using the standard conventions that Android wants to see implemented in the way that it wants to see them implemented. As you will see during this book, Android is very particular about how it wishes developers to structure or code their apps.

The first dialog, shown in Figure 2-2, allows you to name your **application** and the **project folder** in Eclipse, and finally to establish the **Java package** name for your project.

Figure 2-2. Naming your application, project, and package, and selecting a minimum and target SDK

These are the first three fields in the first dialog. Let's name this app and project **GraphicsDesign** and name your Java package pro.android.graphics after the name of this book. Throughout the book, you'll be developing this application project, implementing amazing graphics processing pipelines!

The next four drop-down menu selectors allow you to select **API levels** and **OS themes** that you will be developing for. I am accepting the default (or suggested) **minimum required SDK** of API Level 8 (Android 2.2 Froyo) with a **target SDK** of API Level 17 (Android 4.2 Jelly Bean). I'm going to **compile with** the latest API Level 17 and use the most modern **Holo Light** OS theme.

Once you have finished specifying all of these super important application specifications, click the **Next ➤** button to proceed to the next dialog in the New Android Application series of dialogs.

The second dialog in the series is the **New Android Application Configure Project** dialog, as you can see in Figure 2-3. This dialog will allow you to select options regarding how Android ADT will create the project file (directory structure) system, bootstrap Java code, and application icons for you inside Eclipse.

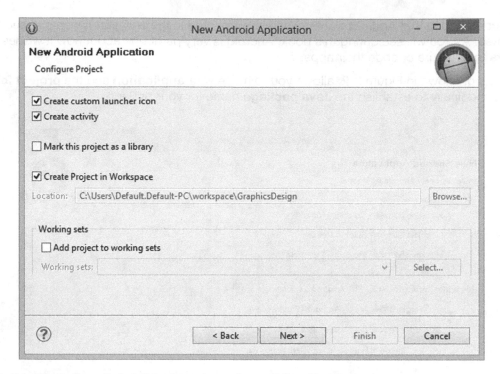

Figure 2-3. Using the Configure Project dialog to create your icon, activity, and project workspace

Although you will be designing your own custom application icon later in the book (after all, this is a book on graphics design), for now you will select the option for Android to create a placeholder application launcher icon for you, so place your checkmark in the first checkbox in this dialog.

The next checkbox in the dialog will instruct Android ADT to write some of your initial Java Activity subclass code for you, so let's be lazy and check this option as well, just to see precisely what Eclipse ADT will do for you.

Finally, accept the default **Create Project in Workspace** option by leaving this checkbox checked, as it will be checked already as the default.

This project is not so large that you need to **mark it as a library** within a larger application (with multiple libraries of code) or use **working sets**, so leave these options unselected. Once you are finished with this second dialog, click the **Next ➤** button, in order to proceed into the next dialog, which is the **Configure Launcher Icon** dialog.

This dialog, shown in Figure 2-4, will allow you to select from an Android-supplied asset, which you will use for now to define your application launch icon, which will be used temporarily for your Pro Graphics application.

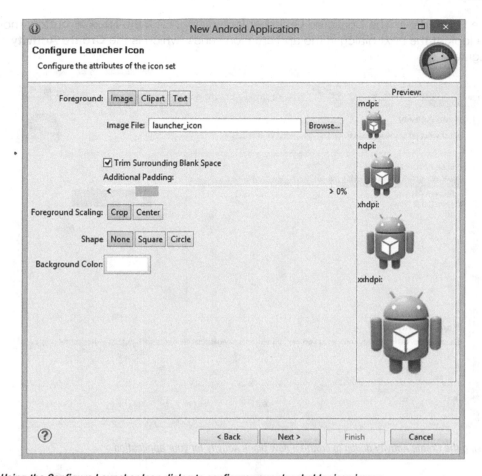

Figure 2-4. Using the Configure Launcher Icon dialog to configure your placeholder icon image

Since a professional application will always have a custom icon, and not a default Android icon, just select the defaults for this screen. Do this now because this icon will serve as a **placeholder icon** for your application until you get around to creating your own custom application icon, which you will be doing very soon so your application has an identity.

If you already have an image to use for your application icon, you could use this dialog to install it by selecting the **Image** button at the top, and then selecting the **image file** for the icon asset using the **Browse** button.

There are options to **trim surrounding blank space**, add **padding**, **crop** or **center** foreground scaling, pick an icon **shape,** and use a **background color**. You won't use them at this time (but feel free to play around with them).

Since this is a graphics design book, you will apply all of these image editing refinements to your application icon in your image editing software package where you have more control and options regarding the work process.

After you are finished with the Configure Launcher Icon dialog, click the **Next ➤** button, moving on to take a look at the next dialog in the app creation series, which is the **Create Activity** dialog, shown in Figure 2-5.

Figure 2-5. *Using the Create Activity dialog to create a new blank Activity for your application*

This dialog will allow you to select the type of Android Activity subclass Java code, which the Eclipse ADT environment will write for you. Let's look at the minimum bootstrap Activity code that ADT will write for you. To do this, select the **Blank Activity** option.

Since you're going to be creating your Pro Android Graphics application from scratch, so that you can learn how to customize your graphics assets inside Android, this is what you really want: a blank slate, if you will.

Once you have selected the first **Blank Activity** option, from the selection area underneath the **Create Activity** checkbox, click the **Next ➤** button and you will proceed to the final application configuration dialog within this New Android Application series of dialogs.

The **Blank Activity dialog**, shown in Figure 2-6, allows you to configure the blank Activity you selected in the previous dialog, by giving it a **name** and **navigation type**. Since you are coding your Pro Android Graphics application from scratch, select a **navigation type** of **none.** This is so that you can craft your own application navigation during the duration of this book.

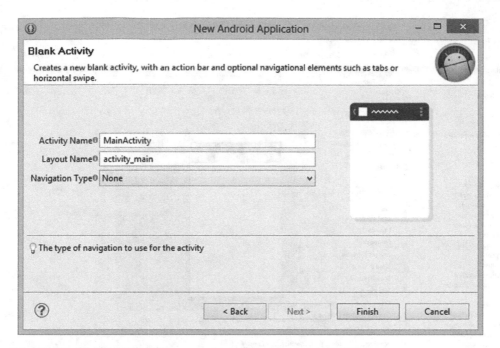

Figure 2-6. Using the Blank Activity dialog to name your Java Activity subclass and XML layout

For the **Activity Name** and **Layout Name** parameters, let's use an Android ADT suggested naming convention of **MainActivity.java** and **activity_main.xml** for your Java code and your XML markup files, respectively.

We will be following this naming convention throughout this first part of the book, as it makes it easy to see which Java Activity classes and their related Activity Layout User Interface Designs are paired with each other.

Once you have finished (doing absolutely nothing) on this dialog screen, click the **Finish** button. Now let's take a close look at the New Android Application Project bootstrap infrastructure that Android Eclipse ADT has so generously created for you using this series of five dialogs.

Once you select the **Finish** button, you will be returned to the Eclipse ADT IDE and you will see your new project displayed inside Eclipse's **Graphical Layout Editor** (or GLE) in a graphical format, as shown in Figure 2-7.

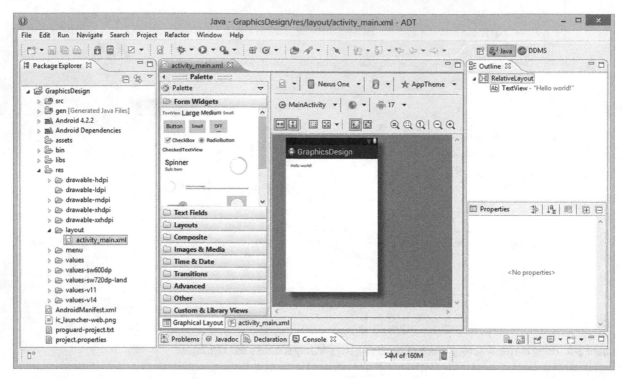

Figure 2-7. New activity_main.xml editing tab shown in central editing area of Eclipse after the new app is created

You will also see, on the left side of the IDE, the **Package Explorer** pane, which shows the **project hierarchy** and **folder structure** that was created by the New Android Application series of dialogs, which you just completed.

At the top is the **GraphicsDesign** folder, and under it are your **source code** (src), **resources** (res) or project assets, and the **AndroidManifest.xml** file at the bottom, which configures and launches your Android application.

Under the resources folder, you will find sub-folders for all your digital imaging DPI assets (folders named **drawable**), your **menu**, constants for your application (**values** folder), and user interface designs (**layout** folder).

Under your layout folder, notice that the **activity_main.xml** file name is highlighted; this is the XML markup that will be showing in the **central editing pane**, currently using the Graphical Layout Editor mode or view, in a view or "pane." On the far right you will see the **Outline** view or pane.

The Outline view shows you that the ADT selected a **RelativeLayout** UI layout container for your MainActivity UI design, and put a **TextView** UI element in it with a **Hello World** message. This means that Android ADT just wrote the **Hello World application** for you, and you didn't even have to write any code!

Next, let's take a look at your user interface XML markup in code format by clicking the **activity_main.xml** tab at the bottom right of your central editing pane in Eclipse. Once you do this, you can see the XML markup, which renders into the user interface screen view that was displayed in the GLE.

The default XML markup ADT wrote for your "Blank Activity" user interface screen layout definition is shown in Figure 2-8. This UI layout includes a RelativeLayout, which is Android's default or recommended layout type, and a simple TextView UI element or widget inside this layout container.

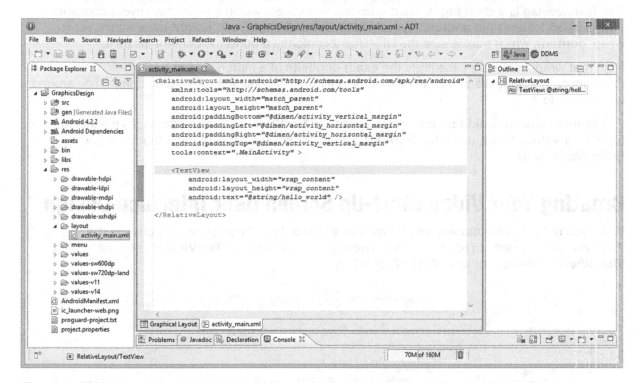

Figure 2-8. *Clicking the activity_main.xml tab at the bottom of the central editing pane to show the XML markup*

You are going to need to change this bootstrap XML markup to support a **VideoView** user interface element since you want your new MainActivity.java start up, or splash, screen to show something really cool after it launches.

Before you change this XML markup, let's take a quick look at what Eclipse ADT has crafted for you here, inside this RelativeLayout **parent tag** for your MainActivity class's UI layout container.

The first parameter in the parent (outer) tag is called the **xmlns:android** parameter, and this parameter sets a **URL** for the **eXtended Markup Language Naming Schema (XMLNS)**. This is done so that other tags and parameters used in this file can be validated as being correct, that is, conforming to the **XML schema** for RelativeLayout containers. If the URL is not present, Eclipse will put a wavy red underline under each tag parameters it can't validate.

There is also an **xmlns:tools** URL reference, which serves much of the same purpose as the xmlns:android parameter does for parameters starting with **android:**, only xmlns:tools does this for parameters starting with a tools: precursor, such as the **tools:context** parameter, which you will see at the very end of the <RelativeLayout> container parent tag.

There are also **android:layout_width** and **android:layout_height** parameters, which you set to **match_parent.** This makes sure the layout container scales to fit the display screen, which is the **parent** for this layout container.

There are also default **android:padding** parameters, which, as you can see, reference a **dimen.xml** file in the **values** folder as well as a **tools:context** parameter, which declares this context to be your **MainActivity.java** code.

The TextView tag is a **child tag**, since it is contained (nested) within the RelativeLayout container. This tag also features the **android:layout_width** and **android:layout_height** parameters, set to **wrap_content,** which makes sure the UI element conforms around the content inside it.

Note that wrap_content is essentially the **exact opposite** of a match_parent parameter, which does pretty much the opposite of this and expands to fill what is outside it rather than contracting around what is inside it.

Finally, there is an **android:text** parameter, inside the **TextView** tag, which references the **strings.xml** file in your **values** folder, using the **@string/** path to the **hello_world** <string> tag name and **Hello World** value.

Creating Your Video Start-Up Screen User Interface Design

While you're here in the **activity_main.xml** user interface layout container, let's change the RelativeLayout parent tag to be a **FrameLayout** parent tag and the **TextView** UI element to be a **VideoView** UI element or widget (see Figure 2-9).

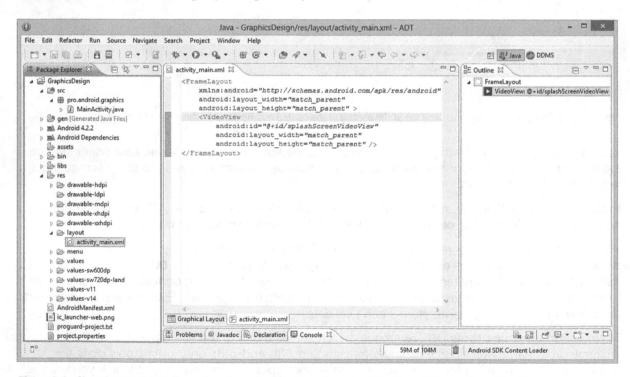

Figure 2-9. Changing the RelativeLayout container tag to a FrameLayout and TextView UI element to a VideoView

The reason that you want to use a **FrameLayout** user interface design container for your VideoView is because a VideoView inside a FrameLayout **maintains its aspect ratio** when it is scaled by Android. Later on in the book I will show you how to scale video to fit different aspect ratio screens, as long as the content you are **non-aspect-ratio scaling** is not prone to noticeable distortion (like a talking head video would clearly be).

Change the RelativeLayout opening and closing tags to FrameLayout and keep the **xmlns:android** and **android:layout** parameters, which as you now know are required. Then, change the TextView child tag to a VideoView and change its **android:id** to **@+id/splashScreenVideo**. Remove the **android:text** parameter and reference, as you will not be using it with your VideoView UI widget.

Now you're ready to take a look at how your Java code will implement your UI!

Taking a Look at Your MainActivity.java Activity subclass

Just to be thorough, since you are in the process of examining what the New Android Application series of dialogs created for you, let's take a look at your Java code as well. To do this, right-click a **MainActivity.java** file located under the **/src/pro.android.graphics** folder in the Package Explorer and select the **Open** option, or left-click and use an **F3** key if you prefer.

This file is highlighted in the left side of the IDE in the Package Explorer pane in Figure 2-10, and is shown already open for editing in the Eclipse central code editing pane. Notice that your application **package** name has been declared for you, and the necessary Android classes have been imported as well, using **import** statements along with package names.

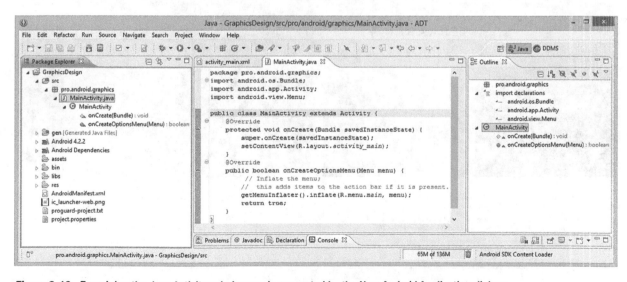

Figure 2-10. Examining the Java Activity subclass code generated by the New Android Application dialogs

Notice that MainActivity **extends** the Android **Activity** class, making it an Activity **subclass**, and that there is an **onCreate()** method written for you, which calls that Activity superclass's .onCreate() method using this code:

```
super.onCreate(savedInstanceState);
```

This code creates an Activity, passing a Bundle object containing system settings for your Activity, which is logically named **savedInstanceState**.

This Bundle object is used so that if this Activity needs to be terminated by the OS (to recover memory resources), it can later be restarted as needed, right where it left off, unbeknownst to the end user. The second line of code in the onCreate() method sets your application **ContentView** to your **activity_main.xml** definition. This is done using the **setContentView()** method call referencing an XML definition resource (**R** stands for resource) in the project **/res/layout** folder, with the file name **activity_main.xml**.

Creating Your Video Assets: Using Terragen 3 3D Software

Now I'm going to introduce you to one of the major secrets in professional software, used by all of the major studios to do 3D scene work. Terragen 3 just came out in the Summer of 2013. I got one of the first stable builds, since I am writing a 3D concepts book using the software, and, as you can see in Figure 2-11, the results you can get are truly photo-realistic.

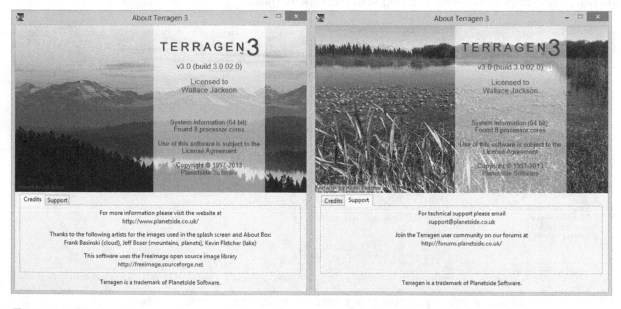

Figure 2-11. Terragen 3 start-up screen showing the credits panel as well as the technical support panel

Go to the **Planetside** Software web site and either download the free version or purchase the professional version. Then you will be able to render your own seamless fly-through using the 39KB source file, which I am including along with the other application data files used for this book.

If you're wondering how a file that's less than 40KB can contain an entire world definition (wait until you render 340MB of animation using it), that is what's so amazing about 3D. Like Java code, 3D is essentially all math, and as such, it is text and compresses very, very well.

Once you download and install Terragen 3, create a shortcut icon for it on your system launch Taskbar. After you do that, launch the software, and open the **loopingOrbit_v03.tgd** file, as shown in Figure 2-12. TGD stands for **TerraGen Data** file, in case you might be wondering.

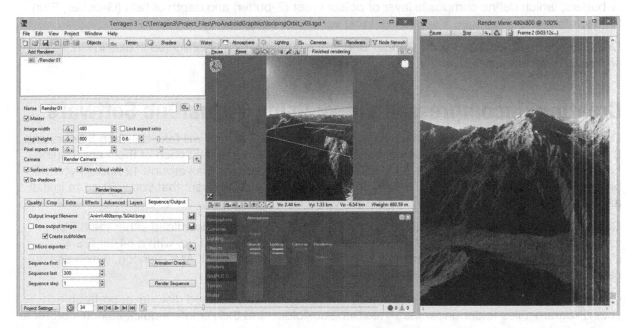

Figure 2-12. *Terragen 3 Rendering Panel and Render Settings area, as well as Render View window on the right*

Click the **Renderers** tab on the top right of the software, as shown in blue in Figure 2-12, and then click the Render01 object at the top left of the software to open up the render settings control area shown under it in Figure 2-12. Set an image width value of **480** and a height value of **800**.

Leave the other top panel settings as-is, and in the bottom of the panel, click the Sequence/Output tab on the right-hand side and set an Output Image file name. Mine goes to an Anim folder under my Terragen3 file folder hierarchy (Terragen3/Project_Files/ProAndroidGraphics/Anim folder).

I named my file **Anim\480temp.%04d.bmp**, which is a filename format that will generate numbered files using the format 480temp.0000.bmp and so on, as you will see in a future screenshot (Figure 2-16, if you are chomping at the bit). Terragen3 is a professional 3D program and has complex features.

Thus, the **%04d** part of this file name signifies that you wish to have four decimal places in your file name, or four zeroes for the first file name, in this case. Once this is set, you can set the **Sequence first** and **Sequence last** data fields to **1** and **400** respectively. Make sure all the other fields are blank, and that the **Sequence** step data field is set to a value of **1**.

If the **Extra output images** checkbox is not checked, then the **Create subfolders** checkbox can be either checked or unchecked as it will not be used unless the **Extra output images** checkbox is activated, so you can leave that one checked.

In case you are wondering, extra output images are useful for generating advanced ancillary imagery used in the advanced compositing of Terragen 3 output. This includes things like Z-buffers or G-buffers, which define composite layer or object order (Z-buffer) and depth of field (G-buffer; Blur) for each frame in a Terragen 3 sequence. I told you it was complex!

Once everything is set up, click the **Render Sequence** button, which I highlighted in blue in Figure 2-12, and watch your workstation render!

Creating Uncompressed Video: Using VirtualDub Software

Once your 400 frames of 3D animation have finished rendering, which will take between 8 hours and 8 days, depending on how many processor cores you have and how fast each of them are running (my system has 8 cores running at 3.4GHz each and my render time was around 12 hours), you will be ready to download and install the VirtualDub 1.9 open source software that you will use to install all 400 of these files into an uncompressed AVI video file format.

Google "VirtualDub Video" or go to the VirtualDub.com web site and download either the 32-bit version, or, if you have a 64-bit AMD processor based workstation (as I do) with a 64-bit OS (I'm using the 64-bit version of Windows 8.1), then download the 64-bit AMD version, which as you can see in Figure 2-14, is the version I am currently running.

Once it is downloaded, install the software by unzipping it onto your hard disk drive, preferable in your /Program_Files folder under the VirtualDub sub-folder, and then create a quick launch icon for it on your Taskbar.

Once you launch the software, you will see three key dialogs. The first is the **GNU** open source licensing, which you accept by clicking the **OK** button. The next dialog gives you the option of viewing your **Help File**, which is always a good idea before using any advanced graphics software package.

Figure 2-13 shows the three dialogs that you should familiarize yourself with, before you click the **Start VirtualDub** button to launch the software.

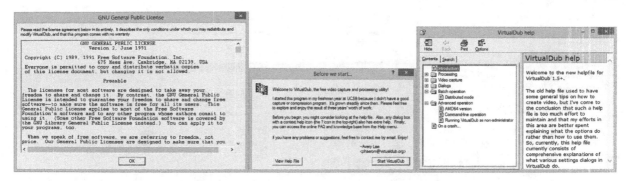

Figure 2-13. VirtualDub 1.9.11 GNU General Public License, Before we start, and the VirtualDub Help dialogs

Once you click the Start VirtualDub button and launch the software, you'll be greeted by an expansive, empty window with nine menus at the top. This is VirtualDub before any video files are loaded; let's configure your environment using the Video menu and several of its sub-menu options next.

We will configure your video **compression**, **framerate**, **color depth**, and **range**. As you can see in Figure 2-14, I included one of these menus in the screen shot so as not to waste any space on a huge empty screen. The **Video ➤ Compression** menu will open a **Select video compression** dialog; keep the default **Uncompressed RGB/YCbCr** setting, and click **OK**.

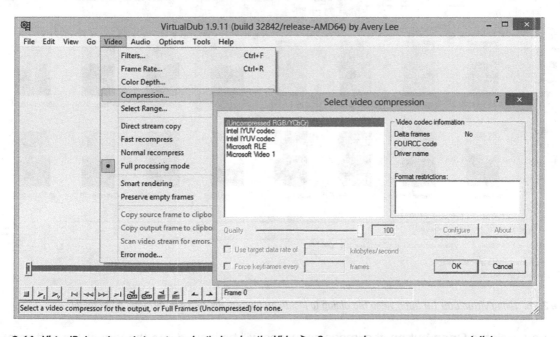

Figure 2-14. VirtualDub on launch (empty project) showing the Video ➤ Compression menu sequence and dialog

Next, set the **Frame Rate**, **Color Depth**, and **Select Range** menu options, which are also shown in Figure 2-14 and whose dialogs are shown in Figure 2-15. Accept the default 10FPS in the Frame Rate dialog, select a 24-bit RGB (888) setting for both sides of the Color Depth dialog, and leave the auto-detected zero to 400 frames range in the Select Range dialog. You can leave the audio options checked, but you're not using audio.

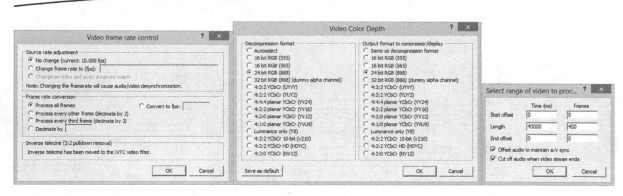

Figure 2-15. VirtualDub Video Frame Rate Control, Video Color Depth, Select Range of Video to Process dialogs

The next thing you want to do is to use a **File ➤ Open video file** menu sequence, which, if you need to visualize it, is shown in Figure 2-18, and find your numbered BMP Terragen 3 3D animation files in your Anim folder, as shown in Figure 2-16. Select the first name in the numbered file series of **480temp.0001** through **480temp.0400** BMP files, which you can see (along with my 360 pixel portrait resolution data files, which you'll be optimizing in Chapter 18, an advanced digital video optimization chapter).

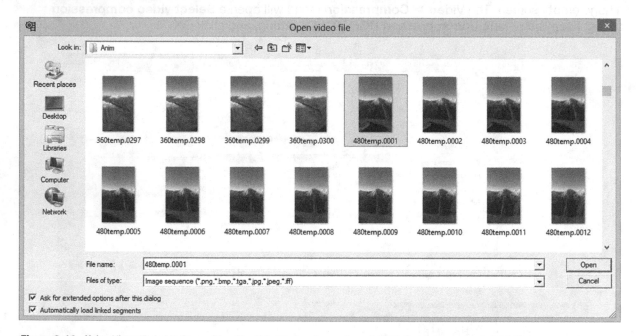

Figure 2-16. Using VirtualDub 1.9 Open video file dialog to locate numbered .BMP files in Terragen Anim folder

Once you click the **Open** button, the image sequence will be loaded into the VirtualDub software, and the first frames will be shown in the main window of the software, as shown in Figure 2-17.

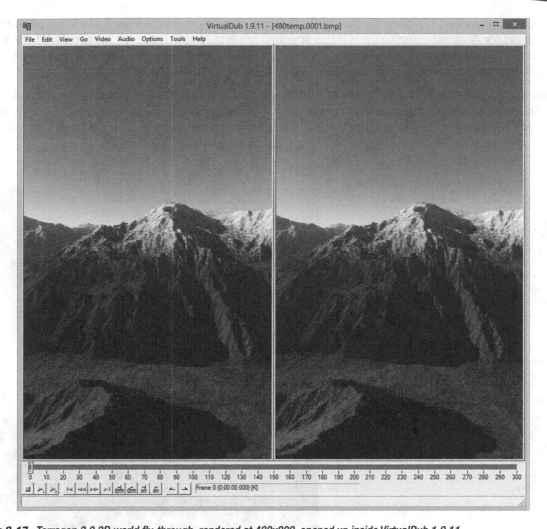

Figure 2-17. Terragen 3.0 3D world fly-through, rendered at 480x800, opened up inside VirtualDub 1.9.11

Once VirtualDub is loaded with the digital image frame sequence, it's time to use its ability to load these still image frames into an **AVI** container. This is one of the formats for digital video that supports an **FFU** version (**Full Frames Uncompressed**) of your digital video data.

AVI stand for **Audio-Video Interleaved**, and it is a video file format that was originally made popular by the Microsoft Windows OS and its popular Windows Media Player.

The reason you want to have full frames of uncompressed digital video going into your compression process is simply because you want to do all of your compression in one algorithm pass so that you're not compressing prior **compression artifacts**, which can add to the final data footprint tally.

The reason that you are using VirtualDub to perform this intermediate step is because Sorenson Squeeze Pro 9 does not support loading image sequence data, which I have strongly recommended to them that they add support for in a future version of their software, for obvious reasons.

EditShare Lightworks 11.1 does support this importing-numbered-image-files feature, so once they add support for Android-specific (or HTML5-specific) codecs, you could use Lightworks 11 for a digital video optimization work process that would go directly from Terragen 3.0 into Lightworks 11.1. Now that VirtualDub's loaded with Terragen data, you're ready to create an AVI.

To save as AVI, press the **F7** function key on the keyboard, or click the **File** menu at the top left of VirtualDub and select the **Save as AVI** option. As you can see on the menu in Figure 2-18, VirtualDub shows you the function key **shortcuts** that will make your work in the software package go faster.

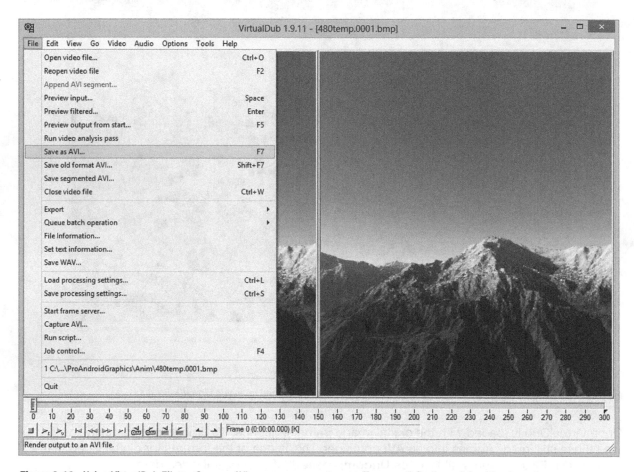

Figure 2-18. Using VirtualDub File ➤ Save as AVI menu sequence to save Terragen 3 fly-through in video format

Once you invoke the Save as AVI dialog, which is shown in Figure 2-19, you will need to create a folder called **AVIs** at the same level as your Anim folder, so that the AVI files will be kept separate from the numbered BMP files, primarily for organization purposes.

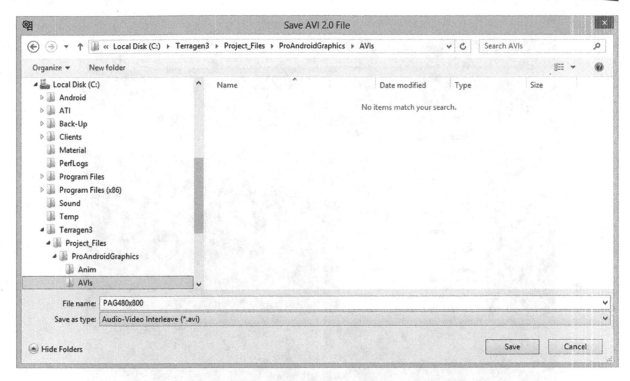

Figure 2-19. VirtualDub Save AVI 2.0 File dialog and Terragen3/Project_Files/ProAndroidGraphics/AVIs path

I used a **Terragen3/Project_Files/ProAndroidGraphics/AVIs** folder structure, as you can see on the left side of Figure 2-19. Select this folder or the one you created, and then type in the filename that you want to use for the AVI file (I used **PAG480x800)**, and the VirtualDub software will add the **.avi** file extension.

Once you have set everything up, click the **Save** button, and get ready to watch the video frames fly by your screen (if you have an eight core PC).

Once you have started the process of loading the static image frames into a full frames uncompressed AVI container so that it is compatible with the Sorenson Squeeze Pro 9 software, you will see the frames being loaded into the AVI on the main screen of the software.

There will also be a progress dialog with a number of statistics on it, which will tell you the current frame of digital video that is being processed is, as well as the amount of video data processed so far; in Figure 2-20, it is frame 136 and 149MB of data.

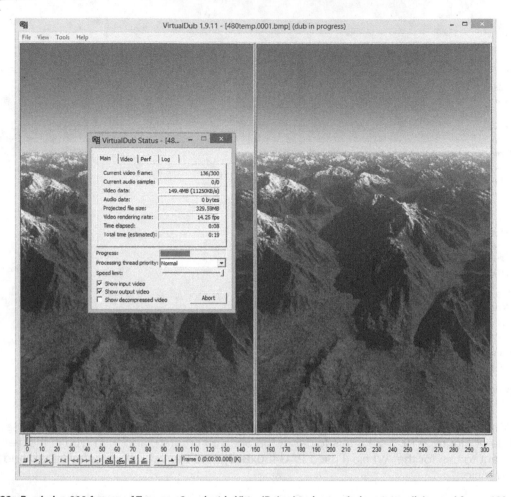

Figure 2-20. Rendering 300 frames of Terragen 3 project in VirtualDub, showing rendering status dialog and frame 136

This dialog will also project the final rendered AVI file size; in this case, it gets pretty close, estimated at **329.59** megabytes, the actual result, as you will see at the end of the next section when you optimize your video using Sorenson Squeeze, is actually 439.47070313, or 450,018,000 bytes, divided by 1024, which allows you to find the amount of megabytes.

The dialog also tells you the video rendering rate, which is essentially a barometer as to how fast your system processor is. My system got close to 15FPS, so it actually looked like the camera was flying through this 3D world that was created using Terragen 3.

Finally, there are time elapsed and estimated time values provided for those who have slower systems, and who are hungry and need to get a good meal in during this processing of video data.

Now that you have your data in an AVI digital video file format that Squeeze Pro can accommodate, you can get into the professional digital video data optimization software package and really get down to the business of data footprint optimization.

This is a critical step if you are using captive digital video assets in your Android applications because this will be the major factor in your .APK (Android package) data footprint (file size) for your entire app.

Compressing Your Video Assets: Using Sorenson Squeeze

When you start the Sorenson Squeeze 9 Pro package, you will see a copyright start-up screen, as shown in Figure 2-21, with progress text telling you what stage of loading the software you are in, like **initializing the UI**.

Figure 2-21. Squeeze Pro 9 start-up copyright screen

The next screen that you will see (Figure 2-22) is the **Welcome to Squeeze** dialog, which contains **video tutorials** and **squeeze resources**. As I did with VirtualDub, I recommend that you take advantage of assets such as this in order to familiarize yourself with the software package before you leverage it in your work.

Figure 2-22. Welcome to Squeeze screen offering seven video tutorials and five Squeeze resources

When you close the tutorial window using the **Close Tutorial** button on the bottom right, you will see the main Squeeze user interface window that is shown in Figure 2-23. This has areas for input options and video editing.

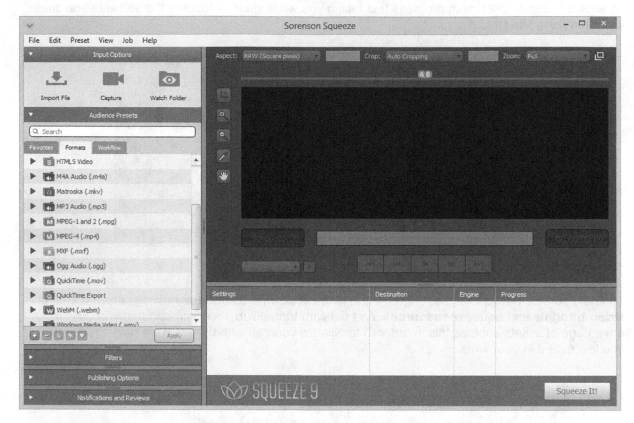

Figure 2-23.   Sorenson Squeeze application showing video codec formats on left and the Import File icon at top left

Click the **Import File** button at the top left to open the dialog shown in Figure 2-24, allowing you to navigate to the **AVIs** folder and **open** a file.

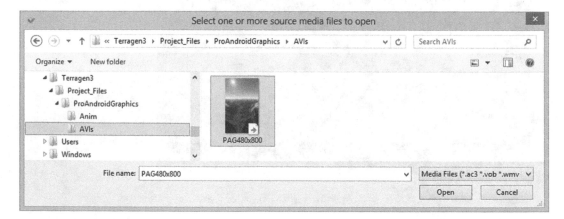

Figure 2-24.   Squeeze 9.0 Professional's Import File dialog, showing Terragen3 path and PAG480x800 file name

Once you find the PAG480x800.avi file and highlight it and click the Open button, or double-click the file itself once you find it, the AVI will be opened up in the video editing section of Squeeze 9 on the right side, as shown in Figure 2-25. Note that your **source** file is also designated in the bottom "processing" area of the software and that I have opened the MPEG-4 codec setting presets up in the **Formats** tab in the **Audience Presets** section of the software, which is shown on the left side of the software.

Figure 2-25. Squeeze showing imported PAG480x800.avi file at bottom (in blue) and the right-clicking of the Edit menu item

Right-click the current preset for 480p video, which is what you are going to compress, and select the **Edit** option. You will be editing these presets (compression parameters) for use in Android. This means taking a bit rate from 1200 to 1024, and a few other adjustments, which you will make next.

The first thing that you will want to do in the Presets dialog, which you can see in Figure 2-26, is to give your new **Android480x800p** preset a name, as well as a new description of **Android 480 by 800** in the Desc data field.

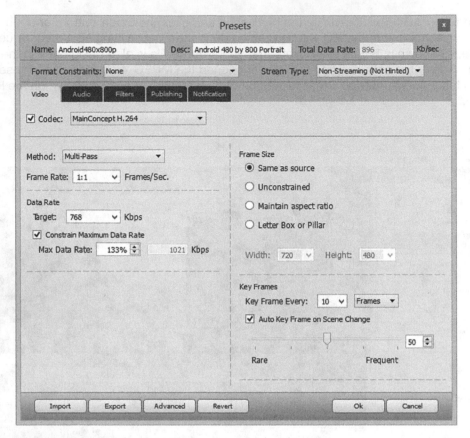

Figure 2-26. Squeeze 9 Video Compression Presets dialog and settings

Make sure the **Format Constraints** drop-down shows **None**, and the **Stream Type** drop-down shows **Non-Streaming not Hinted**, as you're creating captive video.

Make sure that the **Codec** is selected (checked) and set to **MainConcepts H.264,** as that codec has the best size-to-quality performance. The **Frame Rate** selection should be set to the default **1:1** setting, instructing the codec to compress every frame in your Terragen 3 animation sequence AVI.

The compression **method** should be set to a **multi-pass**, which takes the most data processing cycles (the longest time to compress), but also yields the best results, as you will be seeing at the end of this section.

Change your **data rate target** to **768 KBPS**, and select the **Constrain Maximum Data Rate** option and set a **max data rate** target overshoot allowance of 33% or one-third by setting a value of **133%** in this data field. This will give you the **1024 KBPS**, or **1 MBPS**, data amount that you want Android to process.

On the right side of the dialog, select the **Frame Size** option of **Same as source** so that your pixels are not scaled in any way, and set the **Key Frames** option to **Key Frame Every 10 Frames**, or once per second, as you are using **10 FPS** currently for your animation to give a slow but steady fly-through effect.

Finally, leave the **Auto Key Frame on Scene Change** box selected (checked), and the **Rare to Frequent slider** set to the median **50%** value, and click the **OK** button. This will save your settings into the new Android480x800p preset, which is shown on the left side of the Squeeze software in Figure 2-27.

Figure 2-27.   Squeeze showing newly created Android480x800p video codec settings applied to PAG480x800.avi

The next step in the work process is to apply this new preset to your .AVI file that you have imported. This is done using the Apply button located at the bottom right corner of the **Formats** (or the presets) pane.

Before you click the **Apply** button, be sure that the **Android480x800p** preset is selected (blue), so that it is the preset that's applied to your .AVI digital video asset's full frames uncompressed source data.

Once you click the Apply button, you will see the format preset applied to your Source AVI right underneath it, as shown in Figure 2-27. Make sure that you see this before you click the Squeeze It! button in the bottom right corner of the software (you can see this button in Figure 2-25).

Once you click the Squeeze It! button you will get a **blue progress bar**, which is shown on the right-hand side in Figure 2-27, and next to the **Job** status bar at the top of your **Project Settings** area at the bottom of the Squeeze software. Once the compression process has been completed, you will see an icon of your video asset with a **Play** button over it, as shown in Figure 2-28. You can click it to preview your compressed MP4 file.

Figure 2-28. Squeeze showing completed compressed MP4 file, Play icon, video codec used, and other settings

Use Explorer to compare original and compressed size, as shown in Figure 2-29.

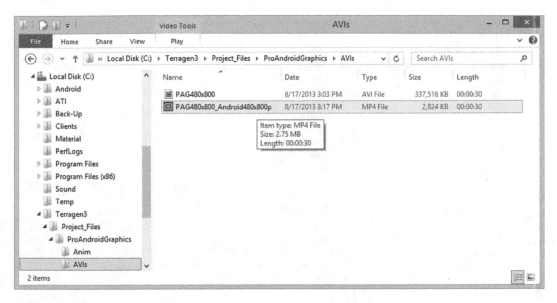

Figure 2-29. Using Windows Explorer to compare relative file size (compressed vs. raw)

Let's do the math to see what magnitude of compression you have obtained using these settings. If you divide these two numbers into each other, in either direction (swap numerator and denominator if you wish; it is the same as inverting the result) you get close to a 120:1 compression ratio, or, looking at it from the other (inverted) direction, the compressed file is 0.8367% of original raw data footprint, or 99.16% more compressed than the original file. I told you that you'd be amazed at what codecs can do!

Installing a Video Asset in Android: Using the Raw Folder

Next, to use this digital video asset in your GraphicsDesign application you must install this MP4 digital video asset file into the proper folder in your /res resources folder in your Android project folder hierarchy, which was shown in Figure 2-7. Digital video and other "developer compressed" assets that you do not want Android to "touch" or compress further are kept in a /res/raw folder. Since that folder doesn't exist, you'll need to create it, so right-click the **/res** folder and select a **New ➤ Folder** option. You can see the progression in Figure 2-30 (I left each selected in blue).

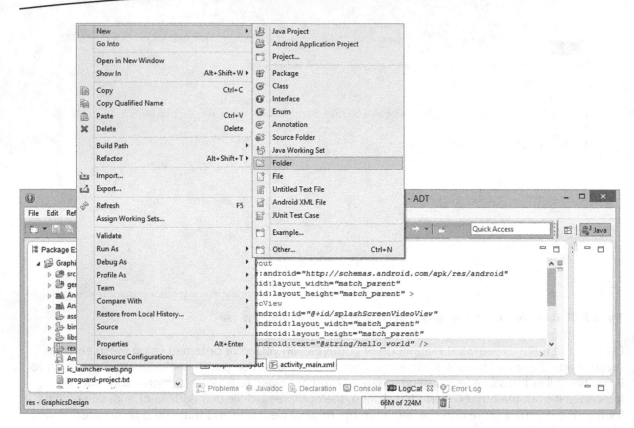

Figure 2-30. *Right-clicking the /res folder and selecting a New ➤ Folder menu sequence to create the /res/raw folder*

In a **New Folder** dialog, specify the **raw** folder name, shown in Figure 2-31.

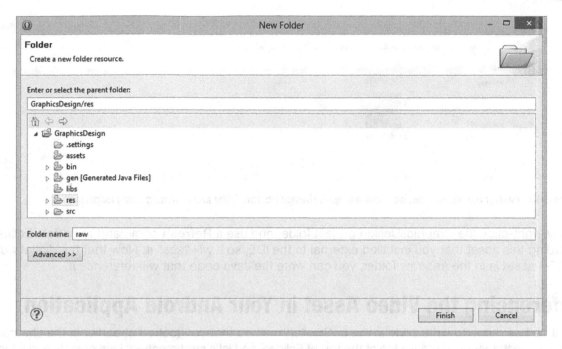

Figure 2-31. Using the New Folder dialog to specify a GraphicsDesign/res/raw path

Find the MP4 you created in Squeeze, and copy it, as shown in Figure 2-32.

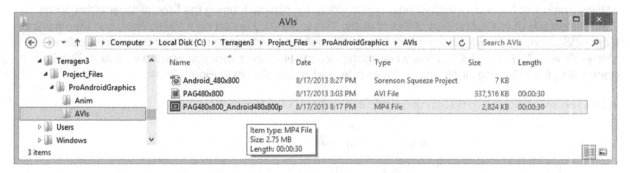

Figure 2-32. Finding the MP4 file generated with Squeeze and right-clicking to copy and paste it into the /res/raw folder

Put the MP4 in **/res/raw**, and name it **pag480portrait**, shown in Figure 2-33.

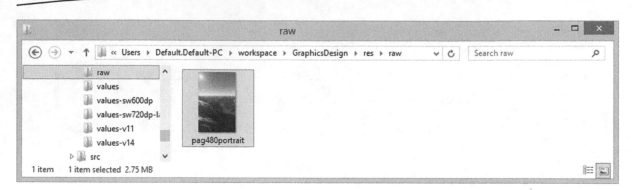

Figure 2-33. *Pasting the file into the /workspace/GraphicsDesign/res/raw folder and renaming it pag480portrait*

Finally, right-click the GraphicsDesign project folder and use a **Refresh** command to update Eclipse regarding this asset that you installed external to the IDE, so it will "see" it. Now that the digital video MPEG4 asset is in the /res/raw folder, you can write the Java code that will reference it.

Referencing the Video Asset in Your Android Application

The time has come to write code in the onCreate() method that you looked at earlier in the chapter! So, click the MainActivity.java tab at the top of Eclipse, and let's start creating Java objects and wiring them together so that they do something cool. If MainActivity.java is not open currently, find it in the /src folder, left-click it, and press the **F3** function key, or right-click it and select the **Open** menu option.

The first thing that you need to do is to instantiate your VideoView object, which you defined in your activity_main.xml file and which will hold digital video, for playback using the MediaPlayer class, which you learned about in the first part of this chapter. This is done by declaring a VideoView, and then naming it splashScreen, and finally, using a findViewById() method to reference the splashScreenVideoView <VideoView> XML (object ID) definition or configuration, whichever way you wish to look at it. This is done using the following single line of Java code, and is also shown in Figure 2-34:

```
VideoView splashScreen = (VideoView)findViewById(R.id.splashScreenVideoView);
```

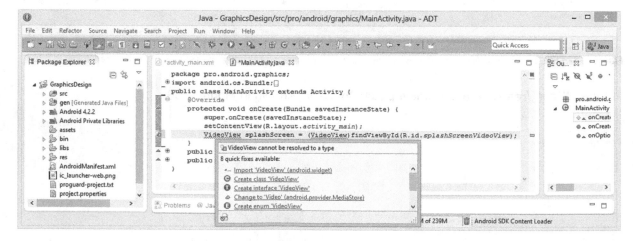

Figure 2-34. *Instantiating a VideoView object named splashScreen and mousing-over the Import VideoView option*

Next, create a URI object using the Android **Uri** class, and name it **splashScreenUri**, and load it with the **path** to a digital video asset in much the same way that you did with your VideoView. This is done using the following code, and is also shown in Figure 2-35:

```
Uri splashScreenUri = Uri.parse("android.resource://"+getPackageName()+"/"+R.raw.pag480portrait);
```

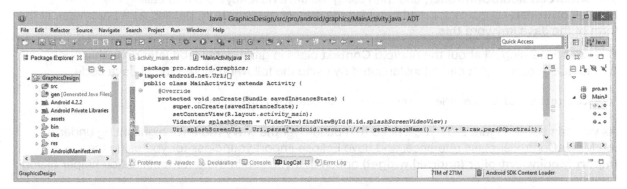

Figure 2-35. Instantiating a Uri object named splashScreenUri and using a Uri.parse() method call to specify a path

A **URI** is similar to the **URL** that you are familiar with using over the HTTP internet protocol, and is used in Android OS in a similar way to reference a data path to a resource. As you can see in Figure 2-35, both of the last two lines of code that you just wrote have wavy yellow warning highlighting under the object names, which is because you haven't utilized either object definition as of yet. The next line of code that "wires" these two objects together, using the **.setVideoURI()** method call, will rectify this problem.

As you can see in Figure 2-36, calling a **.setVideoURI()** method off of the **splashScreen** VideoView object and then passing it the **splashScreenUri** Uri object as the parameter for the method call indeed rectifies these warning highlights and eliminates them, so use the following line of Java code:

```
splashScreen.setVideoURI(splashScreenUri);
```

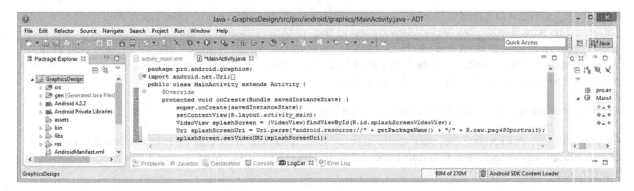

Figure 2-36. Using .setVideoURI( ) method to configure splashScreen VideoView to reference splashScreenUri Uri

Now you've created your VideoView and wired in (referenced) your video asset, but you still cannot play it because you have to utilize the MediaPlayer in order to accomplish that. So let's set up a **MediaController** object next.

You'll instantiate a MediaController by declaring a MediaController object, naming it **splashScreenMediaController**, and then using the Java **new** keyword and calling the **MediaController()** constructor method using the current app **context**, passed as a parameter, in the form of the Java keyword **this**.

You will be learning all about the Android **Context** class in great detail a bit later on in this book. A MediaController object can be instantiated by using the following single line of Java code:

```
MediaController splashScreenMediaController = new MediaController(this);
```

As you can see in Figure 2-37 you'll need to mouse-over the wavy red error highlighting under the MediaController class reference, and have Eclipse import your class for you using the **Import MediaController (android.widget)** option that you see in the error rectification helper dialog.

Figure 2-37. *Instantiating a MediaController object named splashScreenMediaController via the Java new keyword*

Now that you have created a MediaController object that you can use to play back your video asset, you need to wire it into your VideoView by using the .setAnchorView() method to establish what View object will "anchor" or host the MediaController UI controls, which you will see when you test your code later on in the chapter. Anchoring your MediaController object to your VideoView object is done by using the following single line of Java code:

```
splashScreenMediaController.setAnchorView(splashScreen);
```

As you can see in Figure 2-38, your code is error-free, and now that you've told the MediaController object about the VideoView, you can proceed to tell the VideoView object about the MediaController, thereby cross-wiring them.

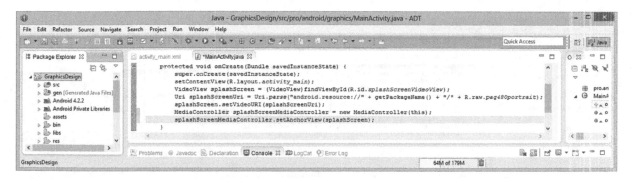

Figure 2-38. Wiring splashScreen VideoView to splashScreenMediaController using .setAnchorView()

You tell the VideoView about the MediaController that you want it to use by calling the **.setMediaController()** method off of the **splashScreen** VideoView object and passing it a **splashScreenMediaController** object as a parameter. This is done using the following line of Java code, shown in Figure 2-39:

```
splashScreen.setMediaController(splashScreenMediaController);
```

Figure 2-39. Wiring splashScreen VideoView to splashScreenMediaController using `.setMediaController()` method

The final thing that you'll need to do to start your digital video playback is to call the Android VideoView class's **.start()** method call off of your **splashScreen** VideoView object that you instantiated and configured earlier. This is done using the following Java statement, as shown in Figure 2-40:

```
splashScreen.start();
```

Figure 2-40. *Starting the splashScreen VideoView playback by calling a .start() method off the splashScreen object*

You've just implemented digital video playback in your MainActivity class's onCreate() method, using only seven well-placed lines of Java code. As you can see in Figure 2-40, your Java code is error-free and you're now ready to test your new Android application using the Nexus One emulator AVD.

Right-click your **GraphicsDesign** project folder and select the **Run As ➤ Android Application** menu command sequence to launch the Nexus One emulator, as shown in Figure 2-41. As you can see, the video playback is perfect.

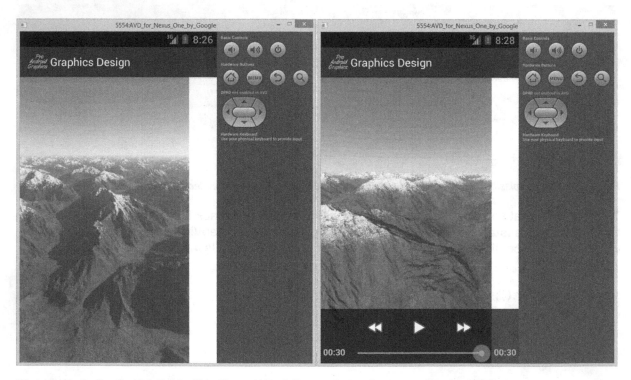

Figure 2-41. *Testing the MainActivity VideoView and MediaPlayer objects using the pag480portrait.MP4 video data*

Notice that if you click the digital video when it stops playing, you can bring up the MediaController UI and control your video using the usual video transport controls of **rewind**, **play**, **end**, or via a **jog-wheel**.

Also notice that, as I mentioned earlier when you were learning about <FrameLayout>, the video aspect ratio is being preserved, as indicated by the white background color that is showing through on the right side of the video. Later in the book you will learn how to scale a video asset to fit a screen size and shape by using a different type of layout container.

Summary

In this second chapter, you learned about digital video concepts, formats, terms, settings, and optimization. You also created the foundation (which is also known as the app bootstrap code) infrastructure that will contain your **pro.android.graphics** package and your **GraphicsDesign** application.

We started by looking at two primary video formats used in Android and HTML5, the **MPEG-4 H.264 AVC** and Google's **WebM VP8** format. You learned that MPEG-4 playback is supported in all versions of Android and that WebM is supported in 2.3.3 and later, with streaming support in Android 4.0 and later versions. You learned that **H.263** is mainly used for video conferencing.

We then took an overview of the Android **VideoView** and **MediaPlayer** classes. These classes are utilized to play digital video via XML markup and Java code within an application. You also implemented a VideoView user interface element in your Main Activity user interface design to hold your video data.

Next, we looked at the foundation of digital video, **frames** and **frame rates** expressed as **frames per second**, or **FPS**. We looked at how to calculate the **raw data footprint** "impact" of different resolutions and frame rates, so you know how to measure the data that is going into your compression work process. This allows you to calculate your actual data footprint reduction.

We took a look at industry standard **SD** and **HD** resolutions for traditional video, and at the concepts of **streaming** versus **captive** video and **bit rate**. You learned that bit rates are not only useful in fitting your data through a given network **bandwidth** capacity (**data pipe** size), but also to take into account the amount of **processing power** in a mobile (embedded) device. This is because it's important for the user to be able to decode this amount of data per second (bit rate) smoothly so they have a good user experience.

Next, we looked at **video scaling** in Android and the need to provide a few **resolution density targets** for your video so that Android does not have to scale it video to any great (drastic) amount. Currently, Android does not have a bicubic interpolation algorithm (it does have a bilinear filter).

Finally, we looked at what codecs do and the compression setting types used for digital video optimization. We looked at the digital video characteristics and codec settings that affect data footprint the most down to the least. You learned that there's no silver bullet for optimizing digital video, that each data stream is unique (at least as far as the codec sees it), and that optimizing your digital-video-data footprint-to-playback-quality ratio is an iterative process at best, and takes both time and experience.

To make sure that you made steady progress on your Pro Android Graphics app, you also took some time to create a shell for your application using the **New Android Application** series of dialogs. We took a look at what they gave you as a bootstrap, and configured an **XML user interface design** to play video on the splash screen in a MainActivity.java Activity subclass for your **GraphicsDesign** app in your new **pro.android.graphics** package.

You then created your video asset by installing and using the **Terragen 3** 3D animation software to generate **400 frames** of virtual world animation, and then installed and used the **VirtualDub 1.9** software to load those frames using an **AVI** digital video format container. You imported that AVI into the **Sorenson Squeeze Pro 9** software and compressed it to less than 1% of its original size so that you could include it inside your app's APK (**captive**).

Finally, you wrote the Java code to implement this video in your onCreate() method and learned about the **VideoView**, **URI**, and **MediaController** classes.

In the next chapter, you will learn about **frame animation** concepts, formats, terms, techniques, and optimization. You will implement a frame or **bitmap animation** in your GraphicsDesign app by using the **AnimationDrawable** class.

Chapter 3

Android Frame Animation: XML, Concepts, and Optimization

In this third chapter, we will take a close look at how digital images are utilized to create **frame-based animation** in the Android operating system. We will build upon the key concepts that you learned about in the previous two chapters, as all of the digital imaging characteristics you learned about in Chapter 1 apply equally well to frame-based animation.

Like digital video, frame-based animation is a series of numbered digital images. For this reason, many of the key concepts that you learned about in Chapter 2 also apply to frame-based animation. Thus, we are covering these initial graphics design topical chapters in the most logical order!

A combination of this knowledge from Chapters 1 and 2 is needed when we consider frame-based animation compression, and thus, this chapter will focus once again on digital image compression codecs and the proper way to get the smallest possible data footprint using the optimal new media data file format and framerate for the best end result.

We will take a look at exactly how your frame-based animation needs to be set up inside of the Android OS, using XML and an **<animation-list>** XML Tag Parent Container. An animation-list tag allows individual animation frames to be added into your XML-based 2D frame-based animation multimedia assets.

We will also take a look at how to wire these XML frame animation data definitions up to your Java programming logic in your application code. We will do this by actually creating the splash screen frame animation asset for your graphics design project using only nine image frames of a 3D logo!

Frame Animation Concepts: Cels, Framerate, and Resolution

Frame-based animation could also be called **cel-based animation** because of the original 2D animation created by Walt Disney. Disney animators drew on what at that time were called **cels** in order to represent each individual frame in their cartoon animation.

Later on, with the advent of film, the term **frames** replaced the term **cels** for the most part. This was because analog film projectors displayed **24 frames per second** of film. These frames of film were played via large reels of sequential film that was run through a film projector in the theater's projection room above the audience.

The technical term for digital frame-based animation is **raster animation**, as the frames or cels are made up of collections of pixels, also known as **raster images**. Raster images are also commonly called **bitmaps**, and in fact there is a **bitmap (.BMP)** file format in Microsoft Windows, although this digital image file format isn't currently supported within the Android OS.

For this reason, raster animation is also commonly called **bitmap animation** in the multimedia production industry. I will utilize these various terms interchangeably throughout this book, so that you will get used to using all of these different (but accurate) terms to refer to your frame-based 2D animation, which uses digital imagery to produce the 2D animation.

Android supports the same open source digital image data file formats that you use for 2D images in your application for usage within the frame-based animation asset. If you think about it, this is logical, as a 2D animation is defined by using those individual digital images as a foundation.

The significance of this is that we can use indexed color images in order to create an 8-bit frame animation, using the PNG8 or GIF formats. We can also use truecolor imagery to create 24-bit or 32-bit frame animation, by using the PNG24, PNG32, or JPEG digital image data file formats.

As with the digital image data file formats, Android prefers a PNG data format over a GIF or JPEG format for use in frame-based animation. This is due to its lossless image quality and reasonably good image compression results, which will yield a high quality user experience given a capable developer.

It is also important to note here that Android does not currently support Animated GIF, also known as animGIF, or aGIF, as a file format.

There are some work-arounds being discussed online until support for this format is added to Android, but given that a PNG8 gives better compression results, and defining frames via XML and controlling them via Java gives us far more control over the end results that we are trying to achieve, I am going to focus on currently supported Android solutions and methodologies in this edition of the book.

So, until Android adds this support, your best bet is to use digital video or frame-based animation, which is why we're covering these two topics in such fine detail very early on in this book, as we'll be using them often and in many different ways throughout this book.

This selection of several mainstream digital image file formats gives us a decent amount of latitude to be able to optimize our frame animation data footprint; due to the PNG32 support, it also allows us to implement robust image compositing work processes by utilizing alpha channel transparency.

Image compositing and data footprint optimization will become veritable cornerstones in your Pro Android 2D Graphics Design work process, as you will see throughout this book, as we leverage codecs, alphas, and blending.

Optimizing Frame Animation: Color Depth and Frame Rate

In frame animation, there are three primary ways to optimize for a smaller data footprint: reduce the resolution, reduce the color depth, and reduce the framerate. Since we have to provide four different resolution density targets as of Android 4.3, we'll focus on the other two, as we are kind of locked into having to provide resolutions spanning at least 100 pixels through 640 pixels or more, as you will see later on in this chapter.

Since there's a choice between lossless PNG32, or a truecolor PNG with a full 8-bit alpha channel, and an indexed color PNG8 with a 1-bit (on-off) alpha, you can use lossless PNG8 for animated elements that do not need to be composited (using an 8-bit alpha channel) later on in your application.

If you don't need to composite your animation over other graphics, you can also consider using the lossy JPEG format to get a far smaller per-frame data footprint by throwing away some of the image data and resulting quality. It is important to note, however, that this approach can increase image artifacts in each frame of the animation. If you happen to apply too much compression when you animate artifacts, it causes something called **pixel crawl**. With JPEG animation, not only do you have artifacts but because the medium is animated and the artifacts are on different pixels on each frame, it's like they are waving their hands and saying "Here I am! I'm an important artifact!" Not a good user experience.

Just as you can optimize your 2D animation by using an indexed (8-bit) color depth, you can also optimize your 2D animation using framerate (FPS), as the same concepts hold true with bitmap animation as with digital video: fewer frames to store means less data, which leads to a smaller application size.

Thus, the lower the framerate you can use to achieve realistic motion, the fewer frames will have to be defined in your XML markup. More importantly, fewer frames will take less processing power to play your frame-based animations, as well as fewer memory resources to hold those frames before they are displayed to the device's view screen. In fact, you'll get professional results in this chapter by using only nine frames of animation for your Pro Android Graphics animated 3D logo treatment.

Data footprint optimization becomes more important as more frame animation is included in your application. New media applications such as games and eBooks tend to have several frame animations running at any given time in the application Activity screen. Thus, you need to consider that your user's processor power and system memory are probably going to be scarce, so treat them like they are your most valuable resources! It will require careful optimization for your Android application not to use up your user's Android device hardware resources, once your app is fully operational.

Finally, the number of pixels within each frame, or the **frame resolution** of the frame-based animation, is of great importance to the optimization of your frame animation asset's data footprint. Review the raw image data mathematics that we covered back in Chapter 1 and apply them to each frame in your animation in order to calculate the exact raw data system memory space (footprint) necessary to hold your frame-based animation.

Just like you did with your static digital imagery, you will need to provide at least four density-matched raster animation image target resolutions to be able to span every popular Android device screen density. For this reason, if you can make your animation a few dozen pixels smaller in each dimension without affecting its visual quality, this will add up to memory savings in the end-game, no pun intended.

It's also important to trim any unutilized pixels within your animation so that the animated elements come as close (one pixel away) to touching the edges of your image container as possible. I have done this in all of the animation frame image assets used in this chapter, so you will be able to see exactly what I mean.

I trimmed an SVGA 800 x 600 pixel 3D rendered animation frame set down to 640 x 500; let's calculate the memory I saved by doing this. 800 x 600 is 480,000 pixels per frame, nearly half a million. 640 x 500 is 320,000 pixels per frame, so the difference (savings) is 160,000 pixels per frame, or 33% less data, right off the bat. Let's calculate the memory savings.

160,000 x 4 (ARGB) color channels yields 640,000 pixels of data per frame of system memory needed. Multiply that by 9, and I've saved 5,760,000 pixels of data (memory). Finally, divide that by 1,024, and I've saved **5.625 megabytes** of memory by trimming away unused pixels. The pixels I trimmed would only be used for representing alpha channel or transparency value, as they were simply space around the animated objects.

Similar to what you learned about static digital imagery in Chapter 1, Android will automatically handle the decision regarding which of your 2D frame animation pixel densities to implement for each device screen that the OS is running on. The largest 640 x 500 frame animation asset is for the **XHDPI** (iTV is 1920 x 1080, HD tablets are 1920 x 1200) resolution densities. Note that I also created three lower-resolution assets, all the way down to an 80 pixel version for watches and flip-phones.

As long as you support all of the major pixel density resolution levels within your frame animation cels, or frames, you will get superior visual results for your 2D bitmap animation assets every single time, on every type of Android device in the electronics market currently.

Creating Frame Animation in Android Using XML Markup

Your frame-based animation is defined in Android via an XML file containing XML markup. This XML file is stored in your /res/drawable folder, and you will create this XML markup using Eclipse later in the chapter in a hands-on example.

In case you are wondering why this XML file is kept in the /res/drawable folder, and not in the /res/anim folder, it is because there are **two types** of animation in Android. **Frame animation** uses the drawable resource folder, and **procedural animation** (covered in Chapter 4) uses the /res/anim folder.

The frame animation XML file will specify those individual frames in your frame-based animation definition (essentially, this is your 2D AnimationDrawable **object constructor**) by using special XML tags related to frame animation.

This XML construct specifies to your app Java code how the frames for the animation are to be loaded into an Android **AnimationDrawable** object. If you want to research more detailed information regarding the Android OS's AnimationDrawable class, you can find more details at the following URL:

developer.android.com/reference/android/graphics/drawable/AnimationDrawable.html

The AnimationDrawable class is the Android frame animation class that allows you to instantiate an AnimationDrawable object. This object will hold the frame animation data, which will later be loaded into the system memory at runtime, after you have instantiated your AnimationDrawable object inside your application Java code.

After this object has been instantiated, you can call it using a **.start()** method from within your application Java code, probably from the inside of an event handler if the animation is triggered interactively, or from the inside of an onCreate() method if the animation is intended to simply run on your Activity's start-up screen somewhere, as yours is going to.

Some types of frame animation in Android can also be **auto-started** simply by using XML markup, and do not have to be specifically started in your Java code by using the .start() method. We'll be looking at both of these ways to set up your frame-based animation during the course of this book.

The frame animation XML construct essentially creates an **array** of numbered digital image files, which represents the **frames** in the animation. There is also a parameter for each frame that specifies the **duration** that the frame is to be displayed on your screen. This duration value needs to be specified in **milliseconds**, using integer values representing increments of one-thousandth of a second. One second uses a **1000** integer value.

Android <animation-list> Tag: The Parent Frame Container

Most of your 2D frame-based animation assets will be created by using the **<animation-list>** XML parent tag and its parameters. The primary parameter you will be using is the **android:one-shot** parameter; it controls whether your animation will have a continuously looping or a "play once" animation playback setting.

Later on, you will reference the XML file containing this <animation-list> parent tag, and its children tags, by using its first name (the first part of the filename) without the extension. You will create a frame animation XML definition that uses an **anim_intro.xml** file name but references this file in Android XML markup and Java code as **anim_intro**. Once this <animation-list> is defined in XML, you will be able to reference the frame-based animation it defines in any of your UI or UX Designs.

Finally, there is an **android:id** parameter that you can utilize if you are going to reference your <animation-list> tag within your Java code—that is, if you're going to control your animation using a **.start()** method call. As you'll see later, there is also a way to auto-start your animation via XML so that you don't have to use an ID parameter, which is generally used to provide a way for your Java code to reference your XML tag constructs.

Android's <item> Tag: Specifying Your Animation Frames

The **<animation-list>** tag is always a **parent tag** because it is designed to contain **<item>** tags, which will always be **child tags**. The item tag is used to define the frames in your <animation-list> tag, with one <item> tag per each animation frame file name and frame display duration reference.

Each of the frames in your frame animation XML definition for your Android AnimationDrawable object will have its own corresponding <item> child tag, which references the drawable image file asset for that frame, as well as a frame display duration value specifying how long it stays on the screen.

These <item> tags will exist inside the parent <animation-list> container in the order in which they are to be displayed, just like you are loading your animation frames into a data array, which, essentially, you are.

It is important to note the distinction that the AnimationDrawable object or class uses drawable (bitmap image) assets, whereas an **Animation** object (or class, which you will learn all about in Chapter 4) does not.

An AnimationDrawable can be referenced by an Animation object, however, if you find that you need to apply procedural transformation or alpha blends to your frame animation to achieve a more complex effect. This is why we are going to cover the Animation class in the next chapter, regarding how to create procedural animation.

Creating a Frame Animation for our GraphicsDesign App

Let's get down to business and create a frame animation that will play over the top of your startup (splash) screen digital video asset. That way you can get into some advanced compositing of your digital video and your 2D animation assets right off the bat!

You will use PNG32 for your animation frames since you want a perfect result for your compositing. PNG32 has an 8-bit alpha channel, which will contain **edge anti-aliasing data** for your animated 3D text (Pro Android Graphics).

You will set it up this way so that even if you decide to change the digital video asset at a later time, or if you decide to allow your users to select from several digital video background options, the resulting composite 2D animated result will appear as if it is a part of the digital video data. Only us Android developers will know that it is in fact two separate content assets, and after the next chapter is over, it will be even more than two!

First, you will learn how to copy your nine animation frames into each of the proper project drawable resource folders. Next, you will create an XML file to hold your frame animation definition. Once that is accomplished, you will change the XML markup for your existing activity_main.xml user interface design to reference the new frame animation, using an ImageView widget.

Once you have put your assets in place and written all of your XML markup, you'll add in the Java code to load the XML data into an AnimationDrawable object and to start it on application startup. You'll do this by editing the **MainActivity.java** class in Eclipse, and by editing the **onCreate()** method where you will create your AnimationDrawable object, load it, and start it!

Copying Resolution Density Target Frames

The first thing that you need to do is to copy four sets of nine PNG animation frames into the appropriate folders. As of Android 4.3, this is the **/res/drawable-xhpdi** folder, the **/res/drawable-hdpi** folder, the **/res/drawable-mdpi** folder, and the **/res/drawable-ldpi** folder.

Let's do that now, so that your XML markup, which you will write in the next section, has something that it can reference. Open your operating system's file management software; for Windows 7 or 8 it's called Explorer, and since I'm using Windows 8, it looks like what is shown in Figure 3-1.

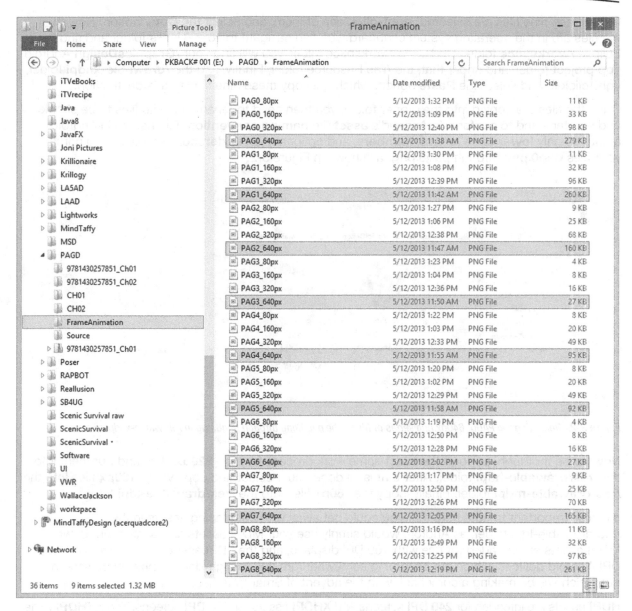

Figure 3-1. Control-selecting the eight animation files for copying to the XHDPI resolution density target folder

Hold down the **Control (CTRL) key** and select the nine PNG files that end in **_640px**, as shown in Figure 3-1. Holding a **Control** (modifier) key while you select the PNG files will let you select **random files,** instead of a range.

> **Tip** If you're wondering how you would select a **range of contiguous** files, the modifier key that you would use to accomplish that would be the **Shift** key.

Once these nine files are selected, **right-click** one of them, and select the **Copy** option. Now that the files are in the operating system clipboard, you can navigate to your **/Users** folder and find your Eclipse **/workspace** folder. Under the /workspace folder, you will find your **/GraphicsDesign** Android app project folder, and under that, the **/res** Resource folder. Finally, find the **/drawable-xhdpi** folder, right-click it, and select the **Paste** option, which will copy these nine files to this destination.

Once the files are copied into the proper folder, you then need to rename all nine files to be simpler and shorter—and to conform to Android's **asset file naming convention**. File names in Android must use only **lower case letters**, **numbers**, and optionally, an **underscore** character. So name your files **pag0.png** through **pag8.png**, as shown in Figure 3-2.

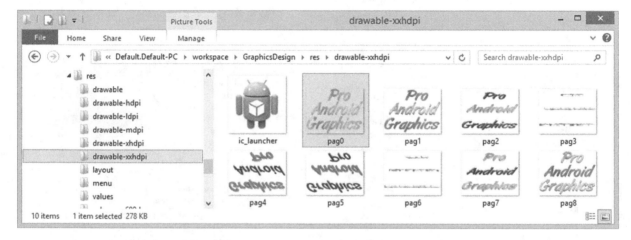

Figure 3-2. Renaming the PAG0_640px.png series of files to be pag0.png through pag8.png in /drawable-xhdpi

Now, to be thorough, perform the exact same work process for the **_320px** files, and put them into the **/res/drawable-hdpi** folder. After that is all done, multi-select and copy your **_160px** files into the **/res/drawable-mdpi** folder. Finally, copy the **_80px** files into the **/res/drawable-ldpi** folder.

It is also important to note here that you could get away with not placing assets in the /res/drawable-ldpi folder, as Android would simply use your MDPI assets and scale them down. MDPI assets are intended for use with 160 DPI displays, and the LDPI assets are for use with 120 DPI Android devices, which are becoming somewhat rare due to high-density pixel pitch screens, but which will be making a comeback with the advent of SmartWatches.

HDPI assets are intended for **240 DPI** screens and **XHDPI** assets for **320 DPI** screens. The **XXHDPI** folder and specification is new in Android 4.2 and is intended for **480 DPI** screens, and the **XXXHDPI** folder and specification is new in Android 4.3 and is intended for **640 DPI** screens. However, it is important to note that currently, as of Android Jelly Bean, XXHDPI is only used to hold the 144 x 144 pixel application launch icon assets, in case you're wondering why you are not using this drawable assets folder (yet).

Creating Frame Animation Definitions Using XML

Let's pick up where we left off in Chapter 2, and create a new XML file to hold the Frame Animation XML asset. Launch Eclipse ADT, if it is not open on your workstation already. Right-click your top-level GraphicsDesign folder, located in the Package Explorer pane on the left side of the IDE. Select the **New ➤ Android XML File** menu sequence, as shown in Figure 3-3.

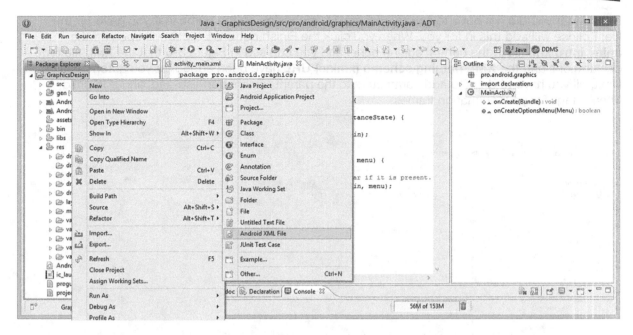

Figure 3-3. Right-clicking the GraphicDesign project folder to bring up the New ➤ Android XML File menu sequence

Once the **New Android XML File** dialog opens, select the **Drawable** resource type from the top drop-down menu selector, as shown in Figure 3-4. Next, name the file **anim_intro** and select the **animation-list** tag from the Root Element list near the bottom of the dialog. The **Project** name should be set automatically for you. Once everything's complete, click the **Finish** button.

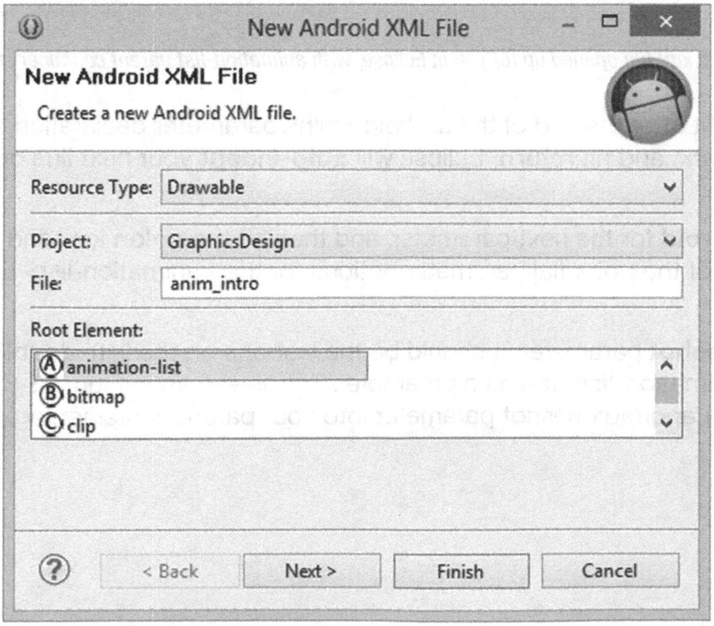

Figure 3-4. Setting parameters for the new XML file, anim_intro.xml

Notice that you did not have to specify the .xml file extension on the name that you gave for the file; Eclipse will add this in for you. When you click the Finish button, Eclipse will open up the **anim_intro.xml** file in the central editing pane, and you can see in Figure 3-5 that the XML file type declarations and the **XML naming schema (xmlns) URL** have been added for you automatically. Next, all you have to do is to add parameters to the parent <animation-list> tag, and add child <item> tags for your animation frames.

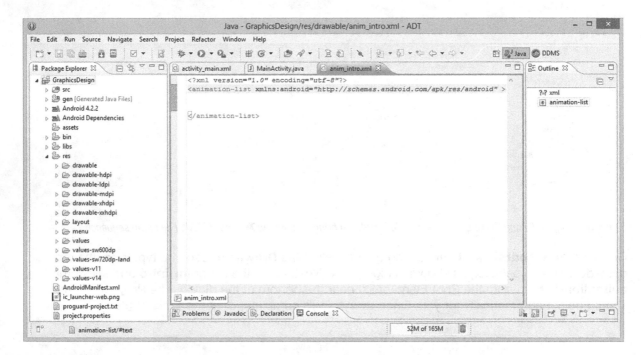

Figure 3-5. New anim_intro.xml file opened up for you in Eclipse, with animation-list parent container tag in place

Place your cursor right after the end of the android:xmlns parameter declaration, after the final (ending) quotation mark, and hit **return**. Eclipse will **auto-indent** your next line of code for you; pretty cool.

Type in the word **android** for the next parameter, and then hit the **colon** key, and up pops a **helper dialog** containing all of the potential parameter options for the <animation-list> tag, also a very cool and useful feature.

Find the **android:oneshot** parameter (it should be the last one on the list); **double-click** it to select and add it to the <animation-list> tag as a parameter. This is shown in Figure 3-6, right before the double-click adds the android:oneshot parameter into your parent container tag.

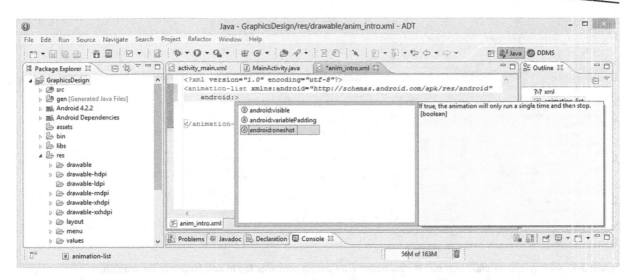

Figure 3-6. Typing android: will bring up an Eclipse helper dialog containing animation-list tag parameter options

You will notice that you still have to enter the **boolean value,** which is required for this parameter, as there will be quote marks provided, but nothing inside of them. You will then enter either **true** if you want your animation to **play only once**, or **false**, if you want your animation to **loop continuously**. Next, you need to specify frames using <item> child tags.

Place your cursor at the end of the <animation-list> tag, after the > character, and hit return to make Eclipse auto-indent your first <item> tag for you. Type in the following line of XML markup to specify your first frame of animation using the **android:drawable** source file reference parameter and **android:duration** frame duration value:

```
<item android:drawable="@drawable/pag0" android:duration="112" />
```

Notice that you omit the .png file name extension inside the file name reference, and preface it with an **@drawable/** path, which tells the Android OS to look in the **/res/drawable** folders in order to find an asset. Make sure **not** to reference a particular resolution density specific folder, as Android does that at runtime, depending on what device the user is using.

You may be wondering where I got the **112** milliseconds value from, which you are using for your **android:duration** value. Since I wanted this animation to play smoothly over a one-second duration, I divided the nine frames into 1000 milliseconds and got a value of **111**. Since 111 x 9 is 999, I made the first frame 112 and the rest 111 so that it adds up to an even 1000 **millis** (an industry term for milliseconds) or one second total animation duration.

Next, you need to copy and paste this first <item> tag underneath itself, using the same indentation, and change the value of android:duration to be 111, and change the android:drawable reference to @drawable/pag1, so that it will reference the file for the second frame of your animation sequence.

Once this is done, copy this second <item> tag seven more times underneath itself, making sure that the indentation lines up with the first two. Then change the @drawable/file names to **pag2** through **pag8**, as shown in Figure 3-7, where I show the final <animation-list> parent tag along with nine child <item> tags, which specify the animation frames and their durations.

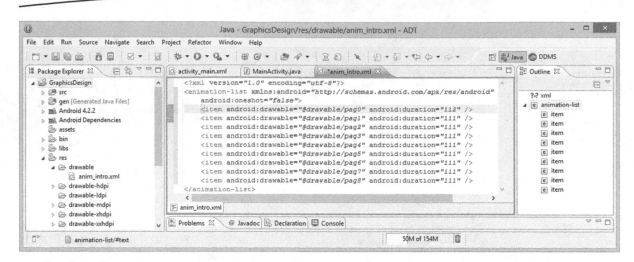

Figure 3-7. Adding <item> child tags inside <animation-list> parent container tag to add frames to the animation

Now that you have created your frame animation asset in the form of an XML file definition, it's time to reference that new asset from your existing activity_main.xml user interface XML definition. Let's do that next, using an Android ImageView widget so you can get some experience with ImageView.

Reference the Frame Animation Definition in an ImageView

Now let's add an ImageView widget to your activity_main.xml user interface definition. Click the activity_main.xml tab at the top of your Eclipse central editing pane, and temporarily remove the android:src parameter in the VideoView tag.

You're doing this at this time so that you can see what you are doing with your frame animation more clearly; you can replace the reference to the digital video source file later. This is one of the most convenient things about having things defined in an XML file; it allows you to "tweak" things about your UI during development to make development easier, as well as to experiment with different settings during the development process, instead of during the testing process, which can be more time-consuming.

Place your cursor after the end of the <VideoView> closing > character, and hit the return key, allowing Eclipse to indent your next tag for you.

Then you can type in the < character, which, as you know, will bring up the <FrameLayout> tag helper dialog, which will tell you exactly which tags are available for use inside this Framelayout UI container parent tag.

Scroll down inside this FrameLayout tag helper dialog until you see the **ImageView** tag, and then **double-click** it to select it. This will insert the ImageView widget tag inside your FrameLayout user interface container. This work process is shown in Figure 3-8 and Figure 3-9.

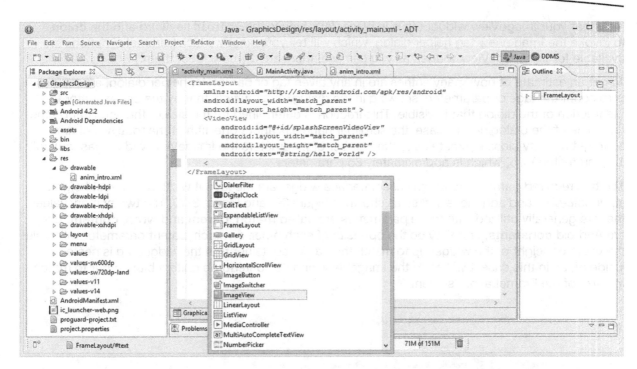

Figure 3-8. Typing a < character to bring up the helper dialog for the FrameLayout parent container tag in Eclipse

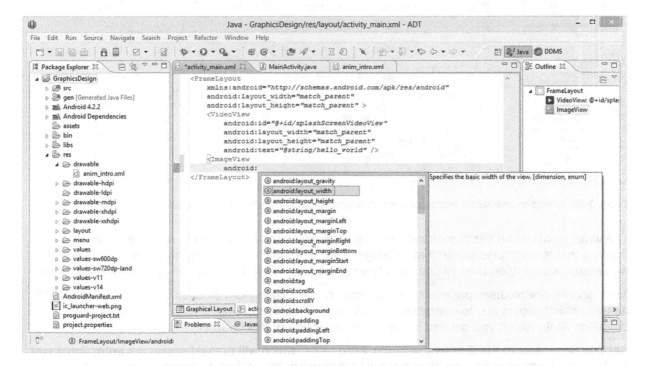

Figure 3-9. Typing android: inside an <ImageView> tag to bring up helper dialog of all ImageView tag parameters

Now that your ImageView widget tag is in place, let's type in the android keyword and the **colon** to invoke the ImageView tag helper dialog, which will tell you exactly which parameter options are available for the ImageView widget; as you can see, there are a whole lot of them!

To get an estimate of how many entries are in any given tag or parameter helper dialog, a cool trick is to count the tags or parameters showing in the dialog, and multiply that by the denominator for the fraction of the dialog that is visible. This fraction is determined by the size of the scrollbar on the right side of the dialog. In this case, the scrollbar handle is about one-fifth of the total scrollbar area, so to get a pretty close estimate as to the number of parameters the ImageView widget has, multiply 17 (parameters) x 5, which is approximately 85 parameters.

The two required parameters for any user interface widget are the layout width and layout height, so double-click and add those in first, as shown in Figure 3-9 and Figure 3-10. The two primary values that are generally utilized with these parameters are called **match_parent** and **wrap_content**. Both are Android **constants**, and they do the opposite of each other. A match_parent parameter will scale the width or height of the widget up to match the parent container that the widget tag is nested inside of, so in this case it will scale the ImageView (and its content) up quite a bit in order to match the size of the FrameLayout screen.

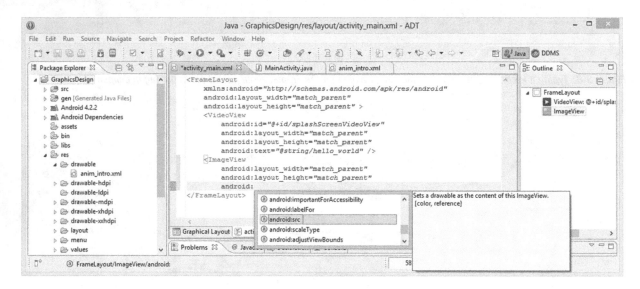

Figure 3-10. Adding an android:src source parameter to reference the anim_intro.xml file you created earlier

The wrap_content, on the other hand, will scale the user interface widget to match the size of the content that is contained within that UI widget. I will use match_parent first to show you what that parameter will do, then later I'll change it to wrap_content so you can see what that parameter does.

Next, add an **android:src** parameter; the android: helper dialog work process is shown in Figure 3-10 as well, which allows you to reference the XML source file that contains your frame animation definition XML, which you created in the previous section of this chapter.

Set this parameter to the **@drawable/anim_intro** value, which will then reference the **anim_intro.xml** file that you created earlier, which is in the **/res/drawable** folder. This parameter is shown in Figure 3-11.

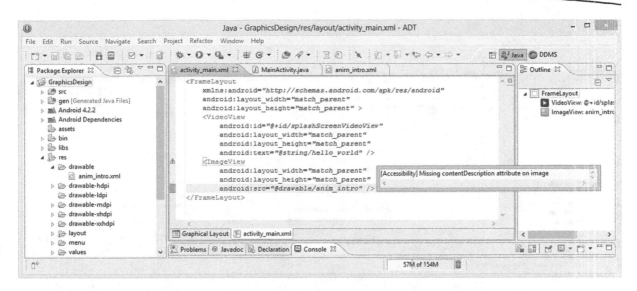

Figure 3-11. Mousing over a wavy yellow underline warning under ImageView tag in Eclipse to see the warning dialog

Also shown in Figure 3-11 is a **warning** in Eclipse that is denoted by a **wavy yellow underline** under the opening ImageView tag as well as a **triangular yellow warning icon** in the left margin of your code editing pane. To read the warning, mouse-over or click the wavy yellow underline or warning icon; an info dialog will appear to explain the problem.

In this case, it is an accessibility issue, as you can see in Figure 3-11. Android wants you to provide an **android:contentDescription** parameter that will tell the disabled (sight) what this ImageView user interface element contains, so add this parameter so that you will have warning-free XML markup. Add a return character at the end of the android:src parameter line of markup, but before the closing /> tag delimiter.

Then type in **android** and a **colon** to bring up the parameter selector dialog, and then find and double-click on the **contentDescription** parameter to insert it into the tag parameter list, as shown in Figure 3-12. Once you have done this, you can insert the reference to a string constant, which you will be creating next, inside the quotation marks, using the following markup:

```
android:contentDescription="@string/anim_intro_desc"
```

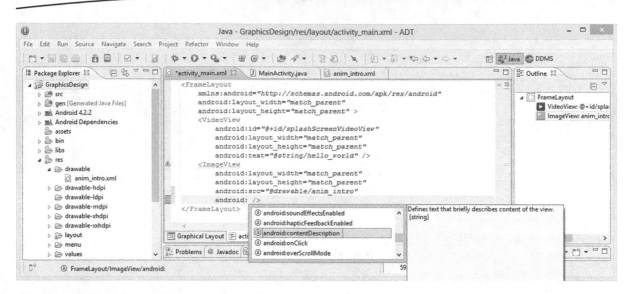

Figure 3-12. Adding an android:contentDescription parameter to the ImageView tag to remove warning in Eclipse

Next you will need to create the string constant for the contentDescription parameter inside of the **strings.xml** file in the **/res/values** folder using a <string> tag, as shown in Figure 3-13. Open the /values folder by clicking the arrow-head icon next to it and right-click the strings.xml file and select the **Open** option from the menu, or simply select it and press the **F3** key on the top of your keyboard. This will open up the strings.xml file for editing in the Eclipse central editing pane where you can add in the <string> tag for the anim_intro_desc string constant. Let's do that next.

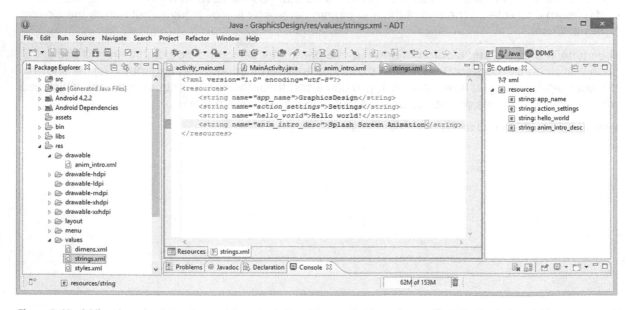

Figure 3-13. Adding the anim_intro_desc <string> tag to the strings.xml string resource file in the /res/values folder

The <string> tag requires only a name to reference it by and the string's text value inside of the tag. Thus your string constant would be defined as follows using this additional line of XML markup in the strings.xml file:

```
<string name="anim_intro_desc">Splash Screen Animation</string>
```

Once you have added this string constant and pressed **CTRL-S** or **File ➤ Save** menu sequence, you will have an error-free project. You can right-click the project folder and **Run As ➤ Android Application**, so that you can see how the match_parent layout parameters makes the first frame of your frame animation fill the display screen. This is shown in Figure 3-14 on the left hand side of the screen shot. Next, you'll use the wrap_content parameter to see how it provides a different result, so don't take a peek at the right hand side of Figure 3-14 or you'll spoil the surprise!

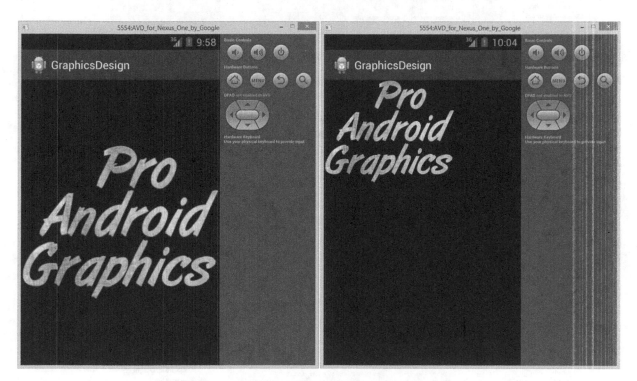

Figure 3-14. Running the XML markup in the Android Nexus One Emulator to see just how the parameters look

Next, let's change the android:layout_width and the android:layout_height parameters from match_parent to wrap_content so that you can see how these very important parameter values differ. You need to get a good handle on this early on in the game, as it affects how ImageView user interface elements scale their content; making sure you have control over your asset scaling is one of the cornerstones of professional graphics design.

As you can see in Figure 3-14, the ImageView content is now pixel-for-pixel and not scaled, and placed in the upper-left corner of the display at the pixel location of 0,0 (X,Y). You can see the XML markup in Figure 3-15.

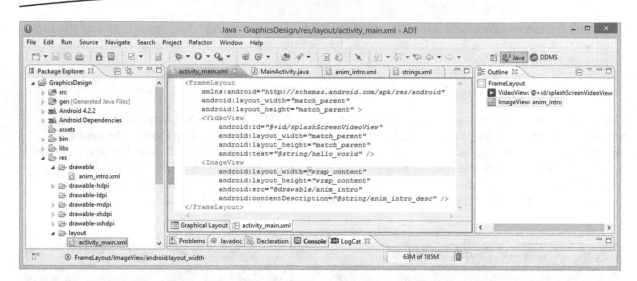

Figure 3-15.   Changing the android:layout_width and height constants from match_parent to wrap_content values

This animation is going to look kind of funny sitting in the upper left corner of the display screen, so let's use the android: work process, and add an **android:layout_gravity** parameter to the bottom of the ImageView tag, and set it to **center** the ImageView. This will center the ImageView user interface element; see Figure 3-16.

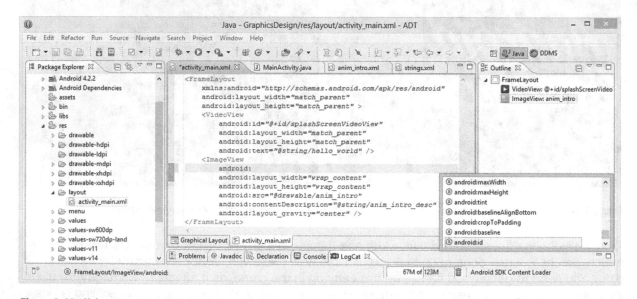

Figure 3-16.   Using the android: work process to find the android:id parameter for the ImageView tag

Layout gravity is useful for positioning user interface elements without having to specify any pixel or DPI (also DP) values. It is often used for centering UI elements; it is also used for aligning elements to the left or the right side, or to the top or bottom of a display or parent container.

Next, you need to add an **android:id** parameter, so that you can reference the ImageView user interface element widget inside your MainActivity Java code. Place your cursor after the word ImageView in the opening tag, and press the return key in order to add a new parameter line on to the beginning of the tag container, as shown in Figure 3-16.

Type in the word **android**, and press the **colon** key to bring up the parameter selector helper dialog; scroll to the bottom, find the **android:id** parameter, and double-click it to add it. You should be getting used to this work process by now—and enjoying how easy it makes writing your XML markup!

All you have to do now is to name your ImageView logically, so call it **pagImageView**. Now you're ready to animate through the frames using the AnimationDrawable class and object inside your MainActivity.java code.

Type the **@+id/pagImageView** reference name value inside of the quotation marks of the empty android:id parameter that you just generated, as shown in Figure 3-17. Android always uses the **@+id** prefix to reference XML tag android:id parameter values, so memorize this now, as you will utilize it often in your Android application development process from here on out!

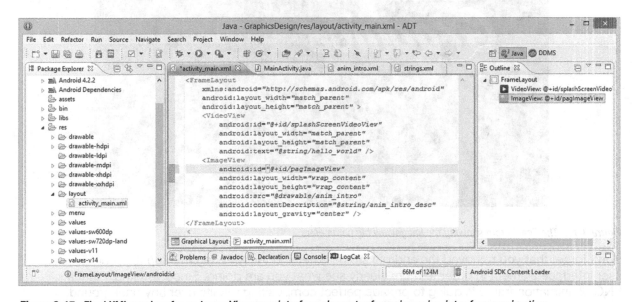

Figure 3-17. Final XML markup for an ImageView user interface element referencing anim_intro frame animation

Next, let's use the **Run As ➤ Android Application** work process to see the final result of the newly added ImageView user interface element XML markup. As you can see in Figure 3-18, you now have a professional end result.

Figure 3-18. The final output showing the ImageView tag parameters

Don't forget that you removed the android:src parameter in the XML tag markup for your VideoView user interface element in order to more clearly see what you are doing. Since you know that a PNG32 animation frame is going to provide perfect compositing results over any background, you can use a black background for now.

We could use a solid black or white background for the purpose of showing what we are doing in this chapter, but black will show this particular frame animation sequence the most clearly.

We will utilize this temporary background replacement (only while we are developing the animation assets) technique in this chapter, and in the next chapter on Procedural animation, to show you that XML allows you to be very flexible and innovative in how you go about developing graphics applications. So, if you need to turn on or off certain compositing layers or even application UI elements or features, it's quite easy to do in XML.

We do this so that we can isolate exactly what the XML code is doing to make it more clear to you, the reader. Once that is accomplished, you can add the android:src parameter back into the XML markup. This will serve to turn back on the background video so you can see a final visual result.

Now let's switch from writing XML markup to writing Java code, so that you can implement everything you've built using XML markup within the existing MainActivity.java file's Java program logic, using the onCreate() method.

Instantiating the Frame Animation Definition Using Java

If it is not open already, open Eclipse and click the **MainActivity.java** tab at the top of the central editing pane. Add a line of space (a return) after the Java code that sets your ContentView, and instantiate your ImageView user interface element, which will reference the XML definition you've been working on. This is done via the following single line of code:

```
ImageView pag = (ImageView)findViewById(R.id.pagImageView);
```

As you can see in Figure 3-19, there are some red wavy underline error flags that you need to address, as well as a red X error icon in the left margin.

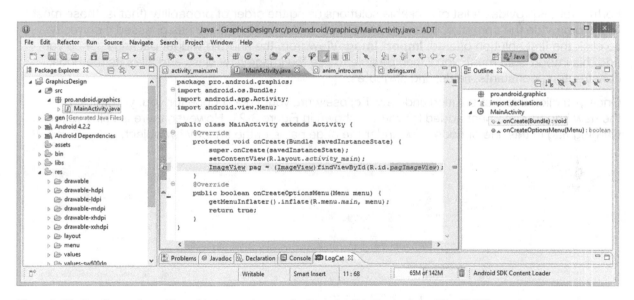

Figure 3-19. Creating an ImageView object named pag and referencing it to the pagImageView ID XML construct

By now you should be getting familiar with the work process in Eclipse for researching why errors and warnings are appearing, so mouse-over and (or) click the error flag icons, or highlighting, and let's see what Eclipse thinks is amiss inside your application logic at this point in time.

As you can see in Figure 3-20, Eclipse is now complaining that it cannot resolve (use) the ImageView object type because the class that is used to create (instantiate) that object type is not available to it (imported).

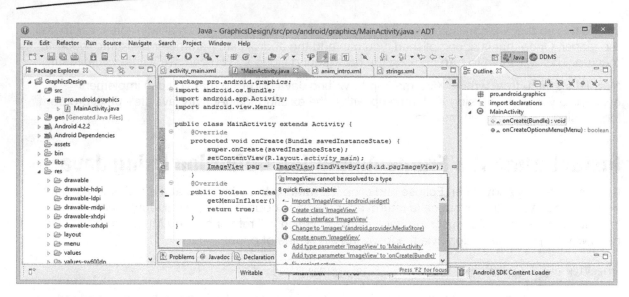

Figure 3-20. Mousing over the error highlighting in Eclipse to bring up the error message and quick fixes dialog

Fortunately, it provides a list of clickable solutions using the order of probability (that is, those most likely to provide the correct solution are listed first). In this case, Eclipse has guessed it correctly, so click the first solution offered, **Import ImageView** from the android.widget package. Once you add this import statement, you'll then be able to use the ImageView class and all of its methods, constructors, constants, fields, and attributes.

Once you click this first solution and have Eclipse write your import code for you, you will see the new import statement added for you, as shown in Figure 3-21. However, there is still a yellow warning flag in this line of code, now under the page name of the ImageView object.

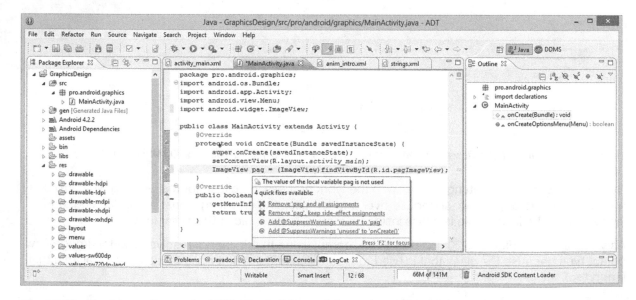

Figure 3-21. Mousing over the warning highlighting in Eclipse to bring up the warning message and quick fix dialog

Again mouse-over and (or) click to read the warning; in this case, it is simply that you have not yet implemented (utilized) this pag object that you have just created. Since you are about to use this object next, you can safely ignore this warning, and proceed to your next line of Java code.

Next, you need to instantiate your AnimationDrawable object, which will do all of the heavy lifting of generating your frame animation. Name this object **pagAnim**, and then use the **.getDrawable()** method, called off of your **pag** ImageView object, to load this new AnimationDrawable object with your frame animation's drawable assets. This is accomplished by using the following single line of Java code, as shown in Figure 3-22:

```
AnimationDrawable pagAnim = (AnimationDrawable) pag.getDrawable();
```

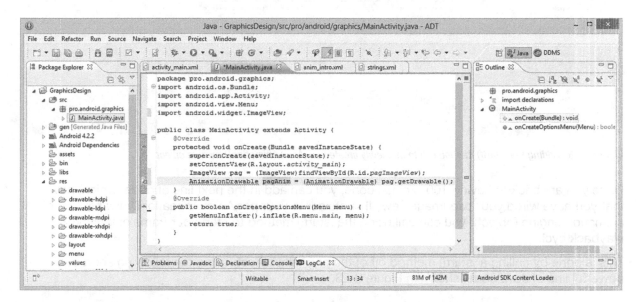

Figure 3-22. Creating a AnimationDrawable object named pagAnim and wiring it to pag object via .getDrawable()

As you can see in Figure 3-22, you again have error flags in this line of code, which we now suspect are related to adding an import statement that is necessary to utilize the AnimationDrawable class.

Mouse-over and click the error messages to generate the error message and fix-it solution dialog, and then click the link that will write the Java import statement for you. You've heard of agile development?! This is lazy development. It's far superior, in my opinion. You can see the import code that Eclipse has again written for you in Figure 3-23 if you're interested.

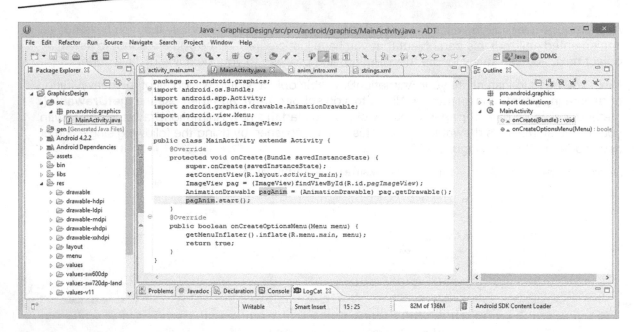

Figure 3-23. Adding the .start() method call to the newly created pagAnim AnimationDrawable object

Once you are back to having 100% clean code, you can add in the next line of code, which, now that you have wired your pag ImageView UI container to your pagAnim AnimationDrawable frame animation engine (object), you can call using the .start() method to start your frame animation playback cycle.

This is done by calling a .start() method off of the pagAnim object, using the following short but powerful line of Java code, shown in Figure 3-23:

```
pagAnim.start();
```

Now you are ready to use the **Run As ➤ Android Application** work process and test your frame animation to see if it works properly. Let's do that next!

Run the application in your Nexus One emulator, and you will see that the Pro Android Graphics logo is animating smoothly on your startup screen after your application launches. Congratulations, you have implemented a full-screen startup (splash screen) animation in Android, using only 2MB to cover all of the resolution density Android devices that are out there!

Summary

In this third chapter you learned all about frame-based animation concepts, formats, XML setup, and optimization, as well as creating four resolution-density–optimized animations for your **pro.android.graphics** package startup splash screen for your **GraphicsDesign** Android application.

We started out by looking at some of the basic concepts that relate to frame-based animation, such as the component **Cels** or **Frames**, how they are played over time using a **framerate** (expressed as **FPS** or frames per second) and **frame resolution** (or the size of each frame in pixels).

Next, we looked at how all of these attributes can work together to allow us to optimize our frame-based animation's new media assets so the Android app has a small data footprint. We talked about the different ways to optimize frame-based animation, such as adjusting the frame resolution, using a lower **indexed color** depth (8-bit color), and being really careful with the number of frames used to create the illusion of motion. We looked at **PNG32** for compositing animation and the concept of **pixel crawl**.

We then took a look at how frame animation is implemented in Android using XML markup. We looked at how the frame animation assets are held in their respective **/res/drawable-dpi** folders and how the XML file is held in the **/res/drawable** folder. We pointed out that frame animation uses the drawable folders and procedural animation, which we're covering in the next chapter, uses the **/res/anim** folder.

We took a look at the `AnimationDrawable` class, which contains the pre-built Java code that we use to implement frame-based animation. We looked at the **.start()** method and the **duration** variable and its **milliseconds** value.

Then we looked at the XML **<animation-list>** and **<item>** tags that are used to implement frame animation structures in XML markup. You learned about the oneshot parameter and how the parent animation-list container holds the child item tag objects inside it.

Next, you got down to business and actually created a frame-based animation for your Graphics Design project in Eclipse. You copied your nine frames into the resolution density folders and renamed them to be simpler and to conform to the Android **lower-case letters and numbers only** file naming rule.

You then created a new Drawable XML file, named it anim_info.xml, added an <animation-list> root element (and parent tag container), and then added the **android:oneshot** parameter. You then filled this with nested child <item> tags, configured for a one-ninth of a second duration and that also referenced your nine animation frames, now named pag0.png through pag8.png.

Once this was completed, you added an `ImageView` user interface element into your **FrameLayout** UI container inside your **activity_main.xml** UI screen layout XML definition file. You then referenced the anim_intro.xml file inside of this ImageView using the **android:src** parameter and added other parameters to make the screen layout of the ImageView look professional, as well as able to be referenced by your Java code.

Finally, you wrote Java code in the MainActivity.java file, instantiating the ImageView object, as well as the AnimationDrawable object, and then you "wired" them together using Java code. You then started looping the frame animation object construct by using the trusty **.start()** method.

In the next chapter, you will learn about Android **procedural animation** and its concepts, transforms, techniques, and optimization. You will learn how to combine transformational power, afforded to you via procedural animation in conjunction with your frame-based animation. This will allow you to boost the motion graphics effects that you are creating to a new level of power and complexity.

Chapter 4

Android Procedural Animation: XML, Concepts, and Optimization

In this fourth chapter, we will take a close look at how XML markup can be used to create **procedural animation** in the Android operating system.

Procedural animation is significantly more complex than raster animation, which simply displays a sequence of images on the display, so that we can create the illusion of motion. Frame animation only allows us to control the individual timing of each frame that is displayed, after we specify what frames will be utilized for the animation. Procedural animation takes this to the next level of complexity, as you will see during this chapter.

Procedural animation actually uses **code**, in most cases via XML markup, to define **transformations** in 2D space to actually change our Android assets. "Code" makes it sound a bit more complex than it actually is, as there are procedural animation **parameters** already defined in Android, and we supply these with various **values** that then cause all these procedural animation parameters to work together in order to achieve the resulting animation.

The Android assets that can be animated procedurally include user interface widgets (which we explore in detail later on in this book), images, digital video (via the VideoView widget), and even frame-based animations. So yes, frame animations can be procedurally transformed in Android, if you set it up correctly, which we will be doing in this chapter. It is important to note that although procedural animation can be set up using XML via a much easier work process, it can also be done using Java code. Procedural animation parameters can be changed via Java at runtime in order to make the animation more interactive or responsive to other inputs or triggers.

Procedural Animation Concepts: Tweens and Interpolators

The foundation of procedural animation is the concept of the **tween**, which is short for **in-between**. Back in the old days of cel animation, the senior animators drew the primary or key cels (or keyframes if you will), and the junior animators would then generate the **tween cels** to provide smooth motion between the cels that senior animators created.

This in-between cel creation process came to be termed **tweening**, and it is important to note that sometimes procedural animation is called **tween animation** because of this. Because frame animation uses raster technology, and procedural animation uses vector technology, you will also see **vector animation** as a term that is often used for procedural animation.

When tweening became a digital phenomenon, the process turned into what in Math class we learned about as **interpolation**. Since now everything is done numerically, we supply number values for our **key frames** and the Android OS does the rest for us by using the **Animation** class code to **interpolate** the **tweens** (the interim frames) automatically, using an **interpolator**.

The math for interpolation is fairly straightforward: determine the range, say from a starting value of 1 and an ending value of 8, divide it by the **resolution** of tween frames, and each frame becomes some fraction of that range. To generate 8 interpolated values between 1 and 8, you would have a new value calculated at each whole number; to have 16 frames between 1 and 8, you would have newly calculated values at 1, 1.5, 2, 2.5, 3, and so on.

The more interpolated values that are calculated, the higher the **resolution** and the smoother the animation movement provided by this interpolation. On the other hand, the more processing power that is used to do these calculations, the less processing power that is left over for other functions. Fortunately, Android determines (optimizes) this for you, and so all you have to do is to specify start (from) and end (to) values.

However, there is a more complex side to interpolation in Android. The **13 interpolator types** in Android further allow you to fine-tune the way that your values are interpolated over the numeric data range that you provide.

The interpolation types in Android are provided as predefined **interpolator constants** in the **Resources**, or **R**, area of the operating system. You can see exactly which types of interpolators are offered at the following URL:

```
http://developer.android.com/reference/android/R.interpolator.html
```

There are currently 13 different types of interpolators in Android; look for more to be added over time to allow more varied types of movement options for your procedural animation. These 13 interpolator constants are actually **mathematical equations**, in the form of Android Java classes that implement them. These interpolate, or tween, your values in different ways along your range, providing **different types of movement** during that range.

You can see the actual Android interpolator classes, which we are about to go over in great detail next, and which are based on the **android.animation** package's **TimeInterpolator** class, at the following URL:

```
http://developer.android.com/reference/android/animation/TimeInterpolator.html
```

The type of interpolation (or interpolator) that you learned about earlier is called the **linear interpolator** in Android, because it evenly spaces the values out across any specified data range in a linear (even) fashion. However, there are another dozen interpolators that change this even spacing between interpolated data values in order to create different types of movement, such as **bouncing**, **anticipation**, or **acceleration** effects.

The Android **AccelerateInterpolator** class is the basis of the first three interpolator constants, which are **accelerate_cubic**, **accelerate_quad**, and **accelerate_quint**, and which provide an **ease out** motion function that eases the motion out of the starting gate (thus accelerating the motion as time goes on, over your specified range of data values).

The Android **DecelerateInterpolator** class is essentially the counterpart of the AccelerateInterpolator class, and also features the three interpolator constants, only this time they are **decelerate_cubic**, **decelerate_quad**, and **decelerate_quint**. These provide an **ease in** motion function that eases the motion into the finish line, thus decelerating the motion as time goes on, towards the end of your specified range of values.

The **cubic**, **quadratic**, and **quintic** specifications define the mathematical **shapes** for these acceleration or deceleration **curves**. As with any of these interpolators, you will need to experiment with them in order to ascertain exactly what they will do in any given procedural animation scenario.

There is also an **AccelerateDecelerateInterpolator** class, which provides **both** an acceleration curve at the start of the motion range and a deceleration curve at the end of the motion range. Thus this motion type will accelerate slowly out of the gate, and slow down at a similar rate, before it reaches its final destination (the end of range "to" value).

The Android **AnticipateInterpolator** class provides a type of motion that will act like it is anticipating something, that is, it will start back a little bit at the start of the range of motion (imagine how you move, or adjust your body, when you think that you are about to get press), and then will fling forward (like a reaction) over the remainder of the data range.

Just as the AccelerateInterpolator has an AccelerateDecelerateInterpolator counterpart, AnticipateInterpolator has an **AnticipateOvershootInterpolator** class counterpart. This adds an **overshoot motion** at the end of the range, where the motion overshoots its target, and then **drifts back** to the final range value as a correction of that overshoot. If you wanted the overshoot motion feature without an anticipation part at the beginning of the range, there is an **OvershootInterpolator** that will accomplish this motion effect.

Remember that all of these different types of interpolators, which you can think of as **motion curves**, are simply trying to **mimic** the motion that you see in real-world scenarios every day by using basic mathematics to apply tween frame interpolation along a cubic or quadratic curve of data values.

Interpolators do an amazing job of controlling motion. You simply need to practice using them in order to see which particular interpolator constants you should use for any given procedural animation situation.

There is also a **BounceInterpolator** class that simulates a bouncing object, such as a beachball, and this interpolator should be used specifically when you need something to bounce off of something else. Finally, there is a **CycleInterpolator** class, which mimics cyclical motion by using the **sinusoidal** mathematical pattern with a developer-specified cycling value.

Next, we will take a closer look at how ranges of values are specified, as well as how they can be controlled (skewed) even further using **pivot point** specifications. Once you have all of these advanced procedural animation parameters (controls) in your quiver, you will find that you can do just about anything that you can imagine using procedural animation in Android.

Procedural Animation Data Values: Ranges and Pivot Point

In order to be able to interpolate, we need to specify more than a single numeric value because interpolation, or tweening, involves creating new interim values between a starting and ending value. So, information from the previous section (interpolation) will be applied to information found in this section (ranges), and then in the next section, we will cover the transformation types that all these fine-tuned controls can be applied to.

To have any procedural animation, we will always need to specify a **range**, from a **starting value**, called a **From** value, to an **ending value**, called a **To** value. This seems logical, as we need something to animate over time!

Besides a range, many procedural animation transformations involve a **pivot point**. A pivot point tells the Android OS how to **skew** the transform into a given direction, as you will see in the next section when we get into the three primary different types of transforms and how they function.

Like the value range, a pivot point also requires two values to establish. However, unlike a value range, which utilizes a From and To value, a pivot point uses a **2D (two dimensional) location** on our 2D image, using **X and Y coordinates**.

Pivot points are also used extensively in 3D animation, where setting the pivot point requires three (X, Y, and Z) data coordinates, in order to be specified accurately. Currently, Android uses 2D procedural animation in its Animation class, with 3D animation being accomplished via a different **android.opengl** package, a discussion of which is best suited for an Android 3D book. In this book, we're covering Graphics Design, which is primarily 2D.

When we look at the various types of transforms, which we will do in the next section, you will see how this pivot point allows a more fine-tuned result to be obtained. This gives the developer additional power over the procedural animation transform effect that they are trying to achieve.

Procedural Animation Transforms: Rotate, Scale, Translate

There are three primary or core types of transformations that are used in both 2D and 3D animation. One of them involves **movement**, and the technical animation term for this is **translation**. One of them involves **size**, and the technical animation term for this is **scale**. The last one involves **orientation** (which direction that something is facing), and the technical animation term for this is **rotation**.

We will cover each of these transformation types individually within this section so that you have a clear understanding of what each of them does before you implement each of these transforms, both individually as well as collectively, later on in the chapter in your GraphicsDesign application.

Let's start with the most common form of transformation, which is a movement or translation from one location on the screen to another locale. To create a movement between two points along a straight line or **vector**, we need to have a starting point, using an X, Y coordinate, as well as an ending point, also using an X, Y coordinate pair. Since we move along a vector, also sometimes called a **ray**, which is a **directional vector**, you can see why procedural animation is sometimes called vector animation.

The next most common form of transformation is to scale an object up or down by a **scaling factor**. Scaling can take place along the X-axis as well as the Y-axis, so to scale an object uniformly, make sure to keep your X and Y scaling value ranges exactly the same.

To scale an object along its X-axis (left to right) requires a starting (**fromXScale**) value for the X-axis scaling, say, for instance 1.0 or 100%, as well as an ending (**toXScale**) value, say 0.5 or 50%. Similarly, to scale an object along its Y-axis (up and down) requires a starting (**fromYScale**) value for the Y-axis scaling, say, for instance 1.0 or 100%, as well as an ending (**toYScale**) value, say 0.5 or 50%.

So, in order to uniformly scale an object to half of its original size, we would use those X-axis and Y-axis Scale From and Scale To setting values.

The next most common form of transformation is to rotate an object by a specified number of **degrees**, ranging from zero to 360 (or a full circle). This is done by specifying a fromDegrees value, say 0, and a toDegrees value, say 360, which would generate a full rotation of the object.

If you wanted to rotate your object around its center-point, you would specify the **pivotX** and **pivotY** values to both be set at 50%, which would place the pivot point in the center of the object you are rotating.

Procedural Animation Compositing: Alpha Blending

There is one other attribute that can be animated procedurally in Android, but it is not a transformation, and is more akin to a compositing feature. Transforming an object changes it physically in some way, moving it to a different location, changing its size, or how it is oriented (rotated).

Alpha blending an object with its background using a change in the object **alpha value**, commonly known as a fade-in or a fade-out, is a compositing function. However, in Android it is included with the procedural animation toolset, as the alpha value is a logical attribute to animate, especially if you are creating a ghost story, or a transporter beam special effect.

The **alpha** attribute of an object that you are animating procedurally can be controlled, allowing **alpha (transparency) blending** to be combined with the translation, scaling, and rotation transformations already available for your use in creating animation procedurally, that is, by using XML or Java code to specify data values to the **Animation** class.

Like most of the other procedural animation attributes, with the exception of pivots, which are denoted using a percentage such as 50%, and degrees, which are denoted using integers between 0 and 360, alpha blending amounts are set using **real numbers** between **0.0** (transparent) and **1.0** (visible).

It is important to note that using more than one decimal place is allowed, so if you wanted your object to be one-third visible, you could use 0.333 or, for three-quarters visible, you could specify 0.75 as the starting or ending value for your object's alpha value.

Alpha starting and ending values are set by using the **fromAlpha** and the **toAlpha** parameters, so to fade-out an object, you would set fromAlpha to 1.0 and toAlpha to 0.0.

To combine multiple different types of procedural animation parameters together, you would create a **set** of animation transformation parameters. Using a procedural animation set will allow you to **group** transforms and compositing together in a logical and organized fashion. This will allow far more complex procedural animation to be created. I will cover how to create procedural animation sets in detail a bit later on in this chapter.

Procedural Animation Timing: Using Duration and Offsets

You might be wondering how to set the **timing** that is used between all of these different range data values. Setting a timing value for a range will also to some extent define how many interpolated data values are created over that range. It is important to note that the Android OS decides this value based on the device processing power and what it thinks will provide the most optimal visual-result-to-processing-power-use ratio or trade-off.

The duration of any given procedural animation range value setting is set using a **duration** parameter, which takes an integer value in milliseconds. A millisecond is one-thousandth of a second, not one-millionth of a second as it sounds like it would be. Most programming languages, Java included, use millisecond values for all of their timing functions and operations.

Thus, if you wanted the fade-out discussed in the previous section to take four seconds, the XML parameter would be **android:duration="4000"**, as four thousand milliseconds equals four seconds. If you wanted the fade-out to take 4.352 seconds, you would use a millisecond value of 4352, and thus you would have a one-thousandth of a second granularity available for accuracy.

Each transformation (or alpha blend) range that you define has its own separate duration setting, allowing for a great deal of precision in the XML markup definition of the effect that you are trying to achieve.

There is one other important timing-related parameter that allows you to **delay** when the specified range will start play. This is called an **offset**, and it is controlled by the **startOffset** parameter data value.

Say you wanted to delay your four second fade-out by four seconds as well. All you would have to do is to add an **android:startOffset="4000"** to your <alpha> parent tag (which you will be using for real a bit later on in this chapter), and this timing delay control would then be implemented.

This startOffset parameter is especially useful when it is utilized in conjunction with looping animation behaviors, which we are going to be covering next. The reason for this is that when used in an animation loop scenario, the startOffset parameter will allow us to define a **pause** during each of the animated element's loop cycles. Let's take a look at loops and the parameters available to us to control looping animated elements next.

Procedural Animation Loops: RepeatCount and RepeatMode

Like a frame animation, a procedural animation can be played once and then stop, or it can be played continuously in a loop. There are two parameters that control looping: one that controls whether the animation will loop or not, and another that controls the way in which the animation will loop.

The procedural animation parameter that controls the number of times that an animation, or a component (part) of that animation set, will loop is called the **repeatCount** parameter. The parameter requires an **integer** value.

If you leave this repeatCount parameter out of (that is, unspecified in) your procedural animation definition, your animation will **play once**, and then stop, meaning that the default setting is **android:repeatCount="1"** for this parameter. The exception to the integer value for this parameter is the **infinite** constant. Therefore, if you want to have your animation loop forever, you should use the **android:repeatCount="infinite"** setting. In case you are wondering, the numeric value that the predefined constant "infinite" defines is -1, so **android:repeatCount="-1"** should work as well.

The parameter that defines what type of looping is used is the **repeatMode** parameter. This parameter can be set to one of two predefined constants; the most common of these is **restart**, which will cause procedural animation to loop seamlessly (unless you have defined the startOffset parameter). In case you are wondering, the numeric value that the predefined constant "restart" defines is 1, so **android:repeatMode="1"** should work as well.

The other type or mode of animation looping is the **reverse** mode, which is also called **pong animation,** as it causes the animation to reverse at the end of its range, and run backwards until it reaches the beginning again, at which time it runs forwards again. Like the game Pong. Back and forth. In case you are wondering, the numeric value that the predefined constant "reverse" defines is 2, so **android:repeatMode="2"** should work as well.

All these parameters may seem fairly simple on their own, but combined in complicated structures using the animation set, which we are going to talk about next, they can quickly become very complicated and produce some very complex and detailed animation results. So, don't underestimate the power of these parameters when they are put together by a savvy developer in the right way. Soon, you will be that savvy developer, so let's look at sets!

The <set> Tag: Using XML to Group Procedural Animation

An **animation set** defines a **group** of procedural animations that need to be played together as a set or group. Sets are defined using the procedural animation XML file; in fact, they provide the grouping structures for our core transformation tags. This is done using a **<set> parent tag** to contain (or to group) any transformations we want to structure together logically in your procedural animation's overall design.

Sets can be **nested** to create even more precise and complicated structures. All we have to do is to make sure that the <set> tags and their transform tags that they contain are properly nested. If you use proper code indents when you write your code, nesting should be fairly easy to visualize and to track. You will see this later on in the chapter when you start writing XML markup in order to create some cool procedural animation objectives in your GraphicsDesign app.

Android OS has a specialized Animation class just for creating Animation Sets. As you might imagine, this class is called the **AnimationSet** class!

The AnimationSet class is in the same package that holds the Animation class. This package is known as the **android.view.animation** package, as animations are played back in a **View**. We will be delving much deeper into the View class in a later chapter on user interface design, so stay tuned.

Procedural animation transformations contained within each AnimationSet are executed together as a **unified transform** by the AnimationSet class.

If the AnimationSet class observes any parameters that are set for the containing AnimationSet that are also set for its children's transforms, that is, those transform tags contained within the containing <set> tag, the parameters that are set for the parent AnimationSet <set> tag will override the child transform values.

For this reason you'll learn how **not to be redundant** and not place the same parameters in more than one place by following some simple rules that will minimize your chance of error, and thus maximize your chance of getting the animation results you are looking for on your first code (markup) go-round.

The way AnimationSet inherits parameters from an Animation transform, and vice-versa, is important to understand. Some parameters or attributes set in the AnimationSet, by inclusion in the <set> tag, will affect the entire AnimationSet itself. However, some of these will be "pushed down" and thus applied to the children's transforms, and some are even ignored! For this reason, let's learn **where to apply certain parameters** when using animation sets, so that you know exactly what Android wants upfront before you start.

The **duration, repeatMode, fillBefore**, and **fillAfter** parameters, also called **properties**, will be **pushed down** to all child transforms when they are set on an AnimationSet object; that is, specified inside of the parent <set> tag. A solution to this is to always set these parameters **locally,** within your transform tags, and to **never** set these in the parent <set> tag. If you do this, then Android has nothing to push down, and there is no confusion as to where the parameter is going to be applied in the processing cycle.

The **repeatCount** and **fillEnabled** parameters, or properties, are **ignored** for an AnimationSet altogether, and thus you will always apply these parameters locally to each animation transform that you wish to access properly.

On the other hand, the **startOffset** and **shareInterpolator** parameters can be applied to the AnimationSet itself. Note that the startOffset can also be applied locally to transforms to fine-tune the timing of the animation by introducing a delay into the looping cycle or when it starts animating.

So a good **rule of thumb** is to apply your transformational parameters locally, rather than at the group or AnimationSet <set> level unless it is a **shareInterpolator** parameter, which is obviously intended for usage in a group level operation, as that is the only way to "share" things in a procedural animation. So, **always set transform parameters locally**!

Another reason for following this rule of thumb is that prior to Android 4.0, all parameters placed inside of the <set> XML tag were ignored, but could be applied at runtime using Java code. Thus, if you are delivering to OSes prior to V4, you have to call the **.setStartOffset(80)** method on an AnimationSet object to obtain the same effect as declaring, in your XML markup, the **android:startOffset="80"** parameter inside your <set> tag for your procedural animation XML resource for your Animation Set object.

Procedural Animation vs. Frame Animation: The Trade-Off

Before we get into the XML markup and Java coding necessary to implement procedural animation in your GraphicsDesign application, I want to discuss some of the high-level theory, principles, concepts, and trade-offs that serve to differentiate frame animation from procedural animation.

Frame animation tends to be **memory intensive**, more than it is processing intensive, as the frames that are to be placed on the screen are loaded into memory so that they can later be used in an application. Displaying the image from memory onto the View is fairly straightforward and does not require any complex calculations, so all processing involves moving each frame's image asset from memory over to display screen.

Frame animation gives us more control **outside** of Android, as we can use production software (3D, digital imaging, digital video, special effects, particle systems, fluid dynamics, etc.) to manipulate all our pixels into exactly the animation effect that we're looking to achieve. Since Android does not have all of these advanced tools and pre-production capabilities as of yet, using frame animation will allow us to use powerful production tools outside of Android, and then bring the result into our Android app.

Procedural animation tends to be more **processing intensive**, as there is value interpolation and the application of interpolator motion curves to the resulting interim data values. Additionally, if sets and sub-sets are utilized to create a complex animation, there can be even more processing involved, as well as the memory space required to hold the plethora of data necessary to perform the processing.

Procedural animation gives us more control **inside** of Android because, since we are doing everything with code and data, it can be **interactive**. This is because other code and data (and even UI elements) can be crafted to interface with the procedural animation in real time, allowing it to be made interactive, whereas frame animation, at least by itself, is not as interactive. Frame animation by itself is a more linear medium, like video.

Since procedural animation can be applied to just about any View object in Android, including text, UI widgets, images, video and frame animation, if you set things up correctly, such as using image compositing techniques to their best results, you can achieve some impressive interactivity by using frame animation in conjunction with procedural animation.

If you are combining frame and procedural animation, as you will be doing, you will have a load on **both processor and memory resources**, so you must try to optimize what you are doing so that you don't use up too much of the system resources needed to run the rest of your application code and UI. This is why we covered data footprint optimization in Chapter 3 and why you're learning about the same type of optimization here.

Creating Procedural Animation in your GraphicsDesign App

Now it's time to implement procedural animation within your GraphicsDesign application, to enhance the frame animation on your splash screen by making it look as though the frame animation spins in from out of the distance. To do this using only frames would take about one hundred frames, instead of just nine for the seamless spin movement. You will utilize the <scale> transform tag to create this illusion.

Later on in the chapter you will implement an animation <set> tag in order to group this <scale> transformation tag with another transformation tag, the <alpha> (transparency or alpha blending) tag, which will fade the incoming spinning (frame) scaling (procedural) animation in, over time, in order to create an even more realistic out-of-the-distance special effect.

Finally, you'll use a <rotate> procedural tag to give this animation even more transformations by rotating your logo around the Z axis as it gets closer to its final resting place. This will allow you to create a <set> of three different transform types to demonstrate a complex animation set.

The first thing that you will need to do is to create a new XML file using Eclipse to define your procedural animation. So, let's get started!

Creating a Procedural Animation Definition Using XML

Let's use the work process of right-clicking the GraphicsDesign project folder and menu selecting the **New ➤ Android XML File**, a work process that we utilized in Chapter 3 (refer to Figure 3-3 to see this visually).

In the New Android XML File dialog, select the **Tween Animation** option by using the **Resource Type** drop-down menu, and then name this file **pag_anim** so that you can reference the file name in your Java code, which you will be writing a little bit later to set up the Animation object and wire it into your existing ImageView object.

Note that since this XML file will be placed in the **/res/anim** folder for you, rather than in the /res/drawable folder, that you could have named it anim_intro.xml, since the two files would actually be considered different assets since they are referenced inside of different folders in Android. However, I don't want to confuse any of the readers so I'll use a different name for the procedural animation XML than I did for the frame animation.

Next, you want to select your **Root Element**, which in this case is the type of procedural animation transform that you want to start out with. Since the most visual impact for bringing the logo in from the distance is going to be the <scale> transform, you need to select a scale tag option as your root element. Completed settings for the dialog are shown in Figure 4-1.

Figure 4-1. Creating a Tween Animation XML file for the <scale> transform

Once you are finished setting all of these dialog options, click the **Finish** button to create the **pag_anim.xml** file and open it up in Eclipse.

Once the pag_anim.xml tab opens up in Eclipse, you will see the **<scale>** and **</scale>** opening and closing tags for a scale transform parent container.

Since your scale transform is going to have lots of parameters but no child tags, let's change the way that this <scale> tag is written to better suit your purposes. You will do this by deleting the **</scale>** closing tag, and by changing your <scale> opening tag to be both an opening and a closing tag.

The simplest way to do this is by putting your cursor between the **e** at the end of the word scale and the **>** character, and pressing the **return** key. After you separate the opening tag onto two different lines, insert a **/** character before the **>** so that it becomes a **/> or short-hand closing tag**.

This will change <scale> to **<scale and />** and allow you to enter parameters for your scale transformation's **attributes** or **properties**. The way that this should look when you are finished can be seen in Figure 4-2, along with the next steps you are about to perform.

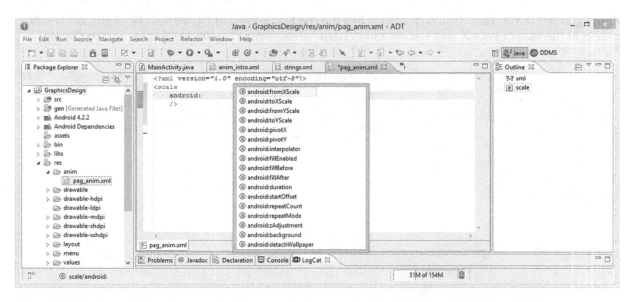

Figure 4-2. Use the android: work process to bring up options for a <scale> transform tag and select fromXScale

Next, place your cursor after the open **<scale** tag and press return to type in another line, and have Eclipse auto-indent for you. Type the word "android" and the colon key to bring up the scale tag parameter helper dialog, as shown in Figure 4-2, so you can see all 17 parameters that define what the scale transformation is going to do.

Double-click the first **android:fromXScale** parameter to add it to the <scale> tag. Notice in Figure 4-3 that Eclipse also added another needed parameter automatically, the **xmlns:android** XML Naming Scheme declaration and its URL, which is needed in every (XML file) opening tag that is used in Android. Let's set the value for the **fromXScale** parameter to **0.0,** and also cut and paste the xmlns:android parameter to the top of the scale tag next to the opening <scale tag (make sure and include at least one space).

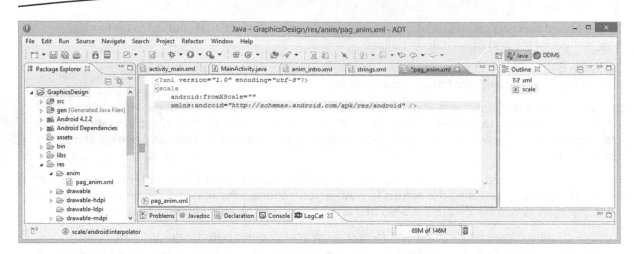

Figure 4-3. *Adding the android:fromXScale parameter, and auto-generating the xmlns:android URL reference*

When you are done, your XML should look like the markup shown in Figure 4-4. Now you are ready to add in the rest of your X and Y scale range parameters: **fromYScale**, **toXScale**, and **toYScale**.

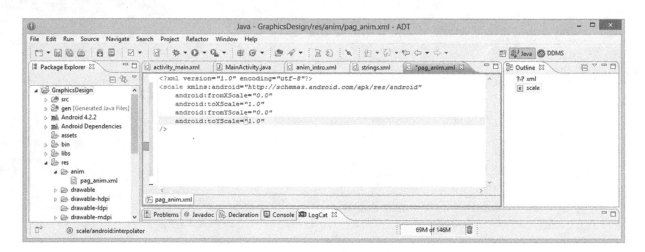

Figure 4-4. *Adding the X and Y To and From Scaling parameters to scale your PAG logo from zero to full scale*

Utilize that same android: work process to add in scale range definition parameters, and set both X and Y **From** parameters to **0.0** (invisible in the distance), and both X and Y **To** parameters to **1.0** (fully visible upfront).

Next, add your Pivot and Interpolator parameters to determine where the scale will emanate from and how it will move in from the distance. Use your android: work process and add **pivotX** and **pivotY** parameters and an **android:interpolator** parameter as well (see Figure 4-5). Since you want the spinning logo to scale in evenly from the center of the screen, you will use a value of **50%** for both X and Y pivot parameters. If you used the 0% setting, the spinning logo would appear to come out of the upper-left corner of the display, and that would not look nearly as natural as the more centered appearance for the scaling in of your Pro Android Graphics logo.

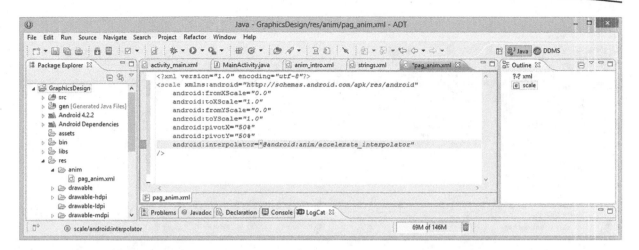

Figure 4-5. Adding pivotX and pivotY parameters as well as an accelerate_interpolation interpolator constant

Setting the value for the android:interpolator parameter can be a little bit more tricky, as it requires the correct **constant reference path** within the OS to be specified accurately. This is done by using the **@android:** to specify the Android OS resources area, as well as an **anim/** to path specify the animation resources, in this case interpolator constants, and then an interpolator constant name, in this case **accelerate_interpolator**.

You are using an acceleration interpolator now because you want your spinning Pro Android Graphics logo to zoom into the center of the screen, smoothly and naturally, and this accelerate_interpolator constant will reference a motion control curve algorithm that will provide this motion for you.

Next, you are going to specify your timing values for the animation using the **android:duration** and **android:startOffset** parameters, which you learned about earlier in the chapter. The duration parameter you are going to set at 9 seconds; this is because you want your spinning animation to appear slowly and smoothly out of the distance.

Remember that the duration and interpolator parameters work hand-in-hand, in this case to provide a smooth, realistic flight path for your spinning logo as it flies in from the distant horizon.

The reason you need to specify a startOffset parameter of 3000, which is 3 seconds, in this case is because this is a **splash screen** animation, and you do not want the animation to start the exact same moment that this screen loads. For this reason, you are going to give your end user a few seconds to realize that the app has launched and to look at the display screen before you start up-scaling your spinning Pro Android Graphics animation into view.

Since you have scaled this animation down to zero for its starting scale range value, the fact that your frame animation starts the logo spinning immediately does not matter, as the user cannot see it anyway, so it will not need an offset specified. You can see all of the nine parameters that you have specified for your scale transformation so far in Figure 4-6.

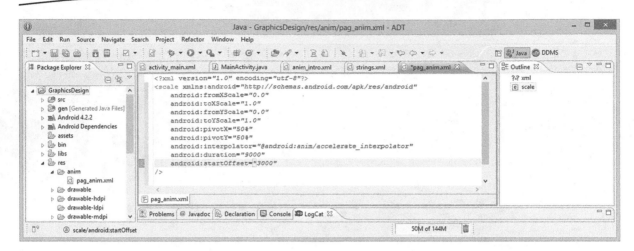

Figure 4-6. Adding an android:duration parameter set to 9 seconds and a 3 second animation start offset value

Next, you are going to specify your procedural animation looping parameters, the **android:repeatCount** and the **android:repeatMode**, which you learned about earlier in the chapter. These parameters will allow you to control how many times the procedural animation transforms are executed, which, in the case of this intro animation, happen to be critical to achieving a processional result. The final markup for your <scale> tag can be seen in Figure 4-7.

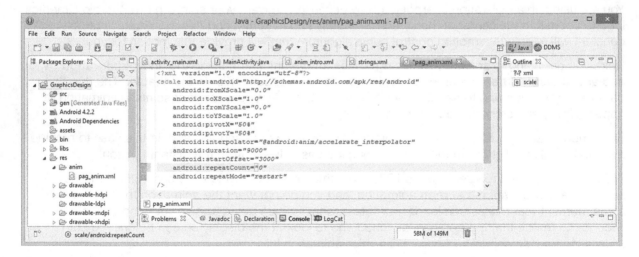

Figure 4-7. Adding an android:repeatCount value of zero specifying one playback cycle and a restart repeatMode

Since you want your logo to appear to fly in from the distance, and stop and spin in the center of the screen once it is full scale, you need to set the repeatCount to repeat this scaling operation only one single time, or your spinning logo frame animation will disappear again, virtually as soon as it arrives on the screen—actually, three seconds after it arrives, since you have specified the startOffset value to be 3000, or three seconds.

Since computers start counting at zero, the correct setting for this will be **android:repeatCount="0"**, so make sure not to use a 1 value. Next, you will set the repeatMode parameter to specify a seamless looping animation by using a restart value constant. Remember that a reverse value constant would give you a pong animation result, which might be cool to use if you wanted the spinning logo to be sucked back into the horizon (in which case you would specify repeatCount as 1, and repeatMode as reverse).

Since the animation is only playing once, you don't really even need to set the repeatMode parameter at all! I am doing so here so that you will have exposure to this important parameter, as most of the transform animations that you will set up will need to specify both the repeatCount value and a repeatMode parameter, as well as one of its two constant values.

Now that you have set up your procedural animation, all you have to do is to go into your project MainActivity.java Activity's Java code, instantiate your Animation object, wire it up to your **pag** ImageView object, and you're ready to enhance your frame animation with some cool procedural animation!

Instantiating the Animation Object in MainActivity.java

Click the MainActivity.java tab in the central editing area of Eclipse, as shown in Figure 4-8, showing all of your XML tabs as well, and add in a line of code that instantiates an Android **Animation** object named **pagAni** and loads it with the XML <scale> animation that you just defined in the **pag_anim.xml** file. This is done using the following line of Java code:

```
Animation pagAni = AnimationUtils.loadAnimation(this, R.anim.pag_anim);
```

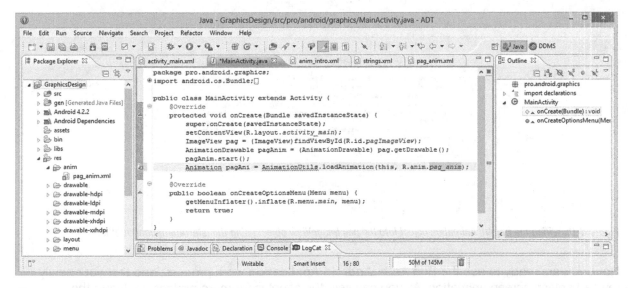

Figure 4-8. Instantiating an Animation object named pagAni, and referencing the pag_anim.xml XML definition

What this line of code does is to construct the **Animation** object and name it **pagAni** on the left side of the equals sign, and then, using the equals sign, load this pagAni Animation object with the result of the method call to the **.loadAnimation(context, reference)** method, which is called off of the **AnimationUtils** class using dot notation, since it is contained within that class. The current context is set using the **this** constant, and the reference to your <scale> procedural animation XML definition is set using the **R** (Resources), **anim** folder, and **pag_anim.xml**, which are concatenated together by using the period character, like this: **R.anim.pag_anim**.

As you can see in Figure 4-8, Eclipse ADT (Android) has a problem with the Animation and the AnimationUtil classes being utilized without first being imported, so let's mouse-over both of the class references and select the **import** option in order to have Eclipse write some Java code for you.

Once the two classes have been imported, your code will be clean, and you can enter the second line of code. This shorter line of code wires your newly created pagAni Animation object into your existing pag ImageView object.

This is done using the following single line of Java code, which calls the **.startAnimation()** method off of the pag ImageView object and passes it the pagAni Animation object, thus essentially wiring the constructs together:

```
pag.startAnimation(pagAni);
```

The completed implementation of your Animation object using only two lines of code can be seen in Figure 4-9.

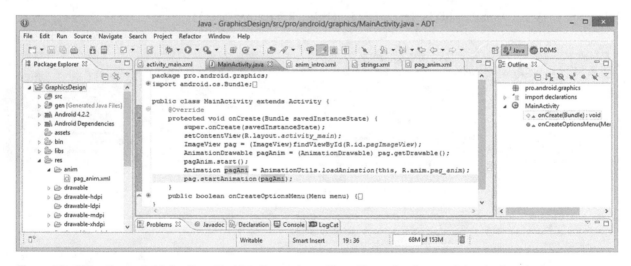

Figure 4-9. Wiring the pagAni Animation object into the pag ImageView object using the .startAnimation() method

Now, you are ready to use the **Run As ➤ Android Application** work process, and test your newly revised splash screen animation. As you can see, the effect is far more professional, and the animation now appears out of nowhere and lands spinning in the middle of the screen. I will forgo the screen shot here as there is currently no way to provide an animated screenshot, and you have already seen the static one in Chapter 3 (refer to Figure 3-14).

Next, you're going to add even more refinement to this Pro Android Graphics logo animation special effect in order to make it even more believable and professional. You are going to add alpha blending to your animation to make the animation more realistic. You will do this so that the spinning logo is more and more visible as it comes in from the distance, so that it appears more and more solid the closer it gets to the camera (your display screen).

You will accomplish this by putting a <set> parent tag construct outside of your current <scale> tag, and then adding an <alpha> child tag into your new <set> group. In this way, both of these procedural transformations will be performed as a single, unified procedural animation processing operation.

Let's get going on that now. Since you already have a procedural animation XML definition file, click the **pag_anim.xml** tab under the Eclipse central editing pane, and go back in and modify that markup from being a <scale> transform animation definition to becoming a group animation <set> definition that contains a <scale> transform definition and much more.

Using Set to Create a More Complex Procedural Animation

Click the **pag_anim.xml** tab to put yourself back into XML editing mode, and put your cursor at the very end of the first tag that you have in this file, **<?xml version="1.0" encoding="utf-8"/>**, and then press the **return** key to add a new line of markup before the opening **<scale** tag.

Type in the <set> tag, and then cut and paste the **xmlns:android** parameter from the first line of the <scale> tag into the patent <set> tag instead, as shown in Figure 4-10. You do not need to have this parameter in an XML file more than one time, and it should go into the first (usually parent) tag container.

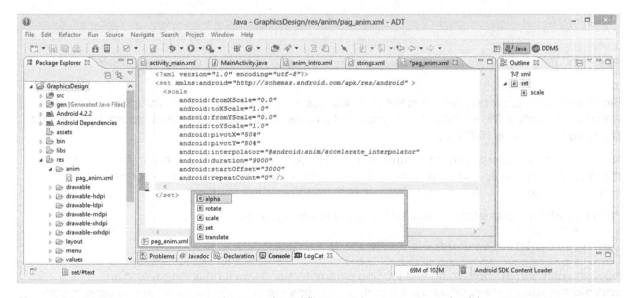

Figure 4-10. Adding a <set> parent tag to the pag_anim.xml file to contain your <scale> and <alpha> parameters

Once this is done, place your cursor at the end of the <scale> tag XML, and press the return key to add a line of space for your <alpha> tag, and then type a **<** character, as shown in Figure 4-10, to bring up the <set> tag parameter helper dialog. Double-click the <alpha> tag option to add it.

Next, make sure the tag is represented on the screen as **<alpha** and an **/>** closing tag delimiter, and then place your cursor after the word <alpha and press the return key to add an indented line of code. Type the word android and a colon to bring up the <alpha> tag parameter helper dialog, and take a look at the 13 parameters that are available for use with this tag.

Double-click the first parameter listed, **android:fromAlpha**, in order to add it to your <alpha> tag. Your screen should look something like Figure 4-11 right before you double-click the **fromAlpha** parameter to add it to the list of alpha blending parameters you are going to be adding.

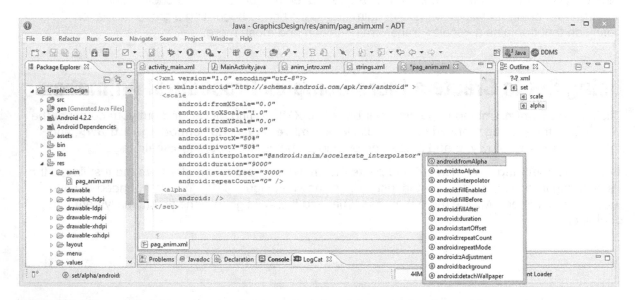

Figure 4-11. Using your android: work process to bring up tag helper dialog containing all the <alpha> parameters

Since the logo should be invisible in the distance, you're going to set your **fromAlpha** value to **0.0**, which will specify a **0%** visibility. Since you need a range, let's add the **toAlpha** parameter next and set its value to **1.0** or **100%** visibility.

Next, let's add an interpolator to control your motion or, in this case, the timing of the fade. To have the fade-in start evenly and slow down at the end, you'll try using the **deceleration** interpolator constant this time.

The interpolator parameter is specified using the following markup:

```
android:interpolator="@android:anim/decelerate_interpolator"
```

Now you can add in your timing and looping parameters and you'll be finished. Add an **android:duration** parameter, and set it to match up or **sync** with the same value you used in your <scale> tag of 9000, or 9 seconds. You want your transforms to run in parallel in this case so everything looks natural.

Do the same thing for the **android:startOffset** parameter and its 3000 or 3 second value, so again everything remains in sync.

Since you are not currently using the android:repeatMode parameter, due to a repeatCount value of zero, I have removed it from the <scale> transform tag, as you may have noticed in Figure 4-10 and Figure 4-11.

Add an android:repeatCount parameter to the <alpha> tag container and set its value to zero as well, so that the Pro Android Graphics logo does not fade in and out once it reaches the front of the screen.

The six <alpha> tag parameters can be seen in Figure 4-12 and, as you can see, their values are either synchronized with the <scale> tag, or moving exactly opposite of it, as in the case of the interpolator constant value.

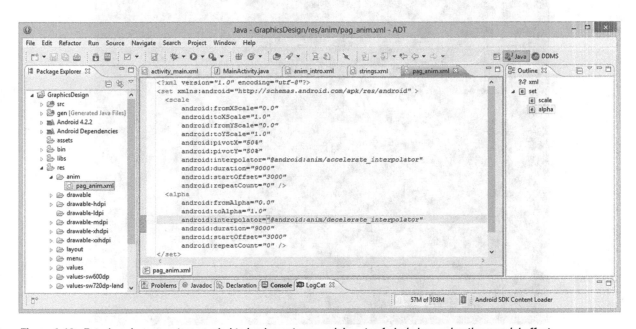

Figure 4-12. Entering six parameters needed to implement your <alpha> tag fade-in logo animation special effect

Let's take a look at the results in the Nexus One emulator by using your **Run As ➤ Android Application** work process, and see how this additional alpha blending gives you an even more realistic visual result for your animation.

Right-click the GraphicsDesign project folder in the Eclipse Package Explorer and use the **Run As ➤ Android Application** to launch the emulator. Watch as the Android OS emulation loads and the application automatically launches and runs the splash screen on start-up.

As you can see in Figure 4-13, now the animated logo both scales and fades into view, just as it would appear to do in real life. You've accomplished this using only 16 parameters, two transform containers, and a single group (set) container so far.

Figure 4-13. Testing your Animation <set> in the Nexus One Emulator

Let's add yet another transform type into your <set> parent tag container in order to demonstrate that you can build up as complicated a procedural animation structure as you like using this same work process and basic XML markup.

The rotate transform allows us to rotate in two dimensions (2D) around a pivot point in the X and Y image space. It's primary data range inputs are the X and Y location of the pivot points and the to and from range for the rotational degrees.

If you were animating a cream pitcher pouring, you would place the pivot point on the right-side of the pitcher halfway down from the spout, where the pitcher would normally tip/rotate, and then set the fromDegrees to 0 (upright pitcher) and the toDegrees to 90 (pitcher at full pour).

Next, let's add your <rotate> transformation, and rotate your logo around two different axes at the same time. You are rotating in 3D space around the X axis in your frame animation so let's rotate your logo (while it rotates in the frame animation) around the Z axis by using procedural animation!

Admittedly this is probably taking this particular effect way too far, but I wanted to show you several of the primary transforms in the chapter and to create a relatively complex animation set at the same time.

Rotation Transformation: Going a Bit Too Far with FX

Let's add the <rotate> transform tag by placing your cursor at the end of the <alpha> tag XML markup and pressing the return key. This will add the line of space you need for your <rotate> tag. Next, type the **<** character, as shown in Figure 4-14, in order to bring up the <set> child tag parameter helper dialog. Finally, double-click the <rotate> tag option to add it.

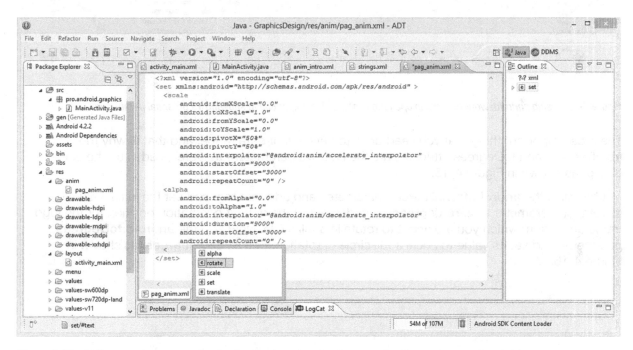

Figure 4-14. Adding a <rotate> procedural animation transform tag to your animation <set> parent container group

Next, type in android and a colon, and bring up the <rotate> tag parameter helper dialog, and take a look at its 15 parameters, shown in Figure 4-15.

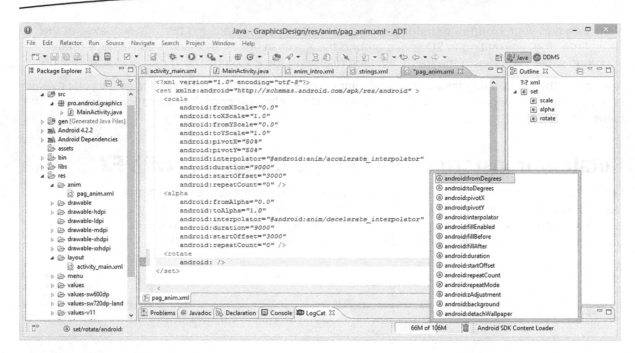

Figure 4-15. Using android: work process to open the <rotate> tag helper dialog showing 15 potential parameters

The most important thing that you need do is to define your data range, and that is why the fromDegrees and toDegrees attributes are the first two parameters that are listed in the helper dialog, as shown in Figure 4-15.

Double-click the **android:fromDegrees** parameter, and add that tag, and set the initial value for its rotation parameter to **zero degrees**. Zero degrees is the default orientation position for the logo frame animation, which you are about to rotate in a full circle. Now add the **android:toDegrees** parameter, and set its value to equal a full circle of rotation, that is, **360 degrees,** as shown in Figure 4-16.

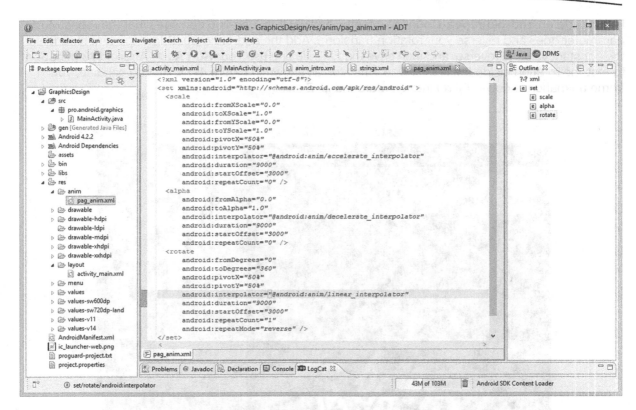

Figure 4-16. Adding nine parameters to your <rotate> transform tag in your procedural animation <set> parent tag

Next, set your pivot point X and Y, which is the next most important attribute in a rotational transform, as it defines where the center of the rotation transform will be located in your 2D image or frame animation. Add in the **android:pivotX** and **android:pivotY** parameters, and set them both to be 50% of the way into the image (frame animation) for both axes. This will set your pivot point to be in the **exact center** of the image, or frame animation (or widget, or shape, or text, or whatever you are rotating).

If you wanted to rotate from the upper-left hand corner, you would use **0%** for both values, and if you wanted to rotate around the lower-right hand corner, you would use **100%** for both values.

The next most important parameter is the motion interpolator, which for this case you will use a linear interpolation constant to rotate your logo smoothly and evenly. The markup specifying this tag is written as follows:

```
android:interpolator="@android:anim/linear_interpolator"
```

Now all you have to do is set your timing and looping parameters, and you will be ready to test your double-axis-rotating logo animation in the Nexus One emulator.

Add an android:duration parameter and set it to 9000 or 9 seconds to match up with your other two transform parameters. Now add an android:startOffset parameter set to 3000 (3 seconds) so your timing's synchronized completely.

Finally, add an **android:repeatCount** parameter, and set it to 1 so you can see what the repeatMode parameter does and reverse your rotation transform. Add the android:repeatMode parameter and set the constant value to reverse, and then save the XML file and use your **Run As ➤ Android Application** to test the rotation inside the Nexus One emulator, as shown in Figure 4-17. As you can see, your frame animation is now rotating into view around its Z axis.

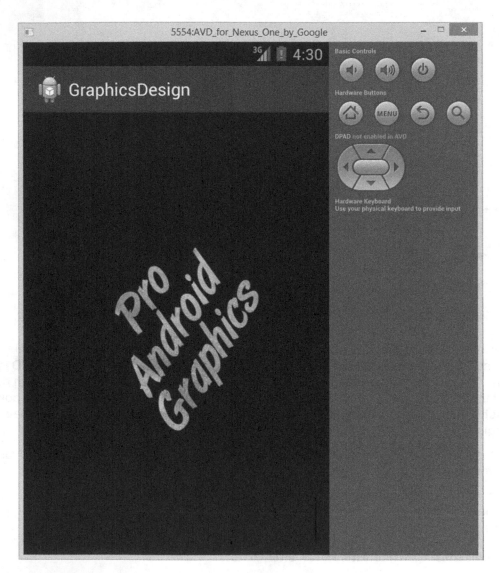

Figure 4-17. Viewing the rotate transform in the Nexus One Emulator

Next, you'll change your <rotate> transform parameters so that the rotation in both directions happens on the way in from the distance, just to show how easy it is to refine (called tweaking) animation values once they are initially put into place using your XML markup.

Tweaking Transform Values: The Ease of Adjusting XML

Go back into your <set> and change the **android:duration** value to **4400** and the **android:startOffset** value to **200**. Notice that 4400 + 4400 + 200 = 9000, so you are **syncing** your two rotation timings and the pause in between them to match up with your other two transform's 9 second durations.

Run the application again in the Nexus One emulator using a **Run As ➤ Android Application** work process, and notice that now both rotational directions happen coming into the final resting place of the frame animation. If you have trouble seeing both of them, you can also tweak the startOffset value of 3000 for the <scale> and <alpha> transforms to be O, so there is no delay in starting these animations, and there is 100% sync with all of the data values at this point (see Figure 4-18). Try more value tweaking until you are satisfied with the results and comfortable with the work process of tweaking values!

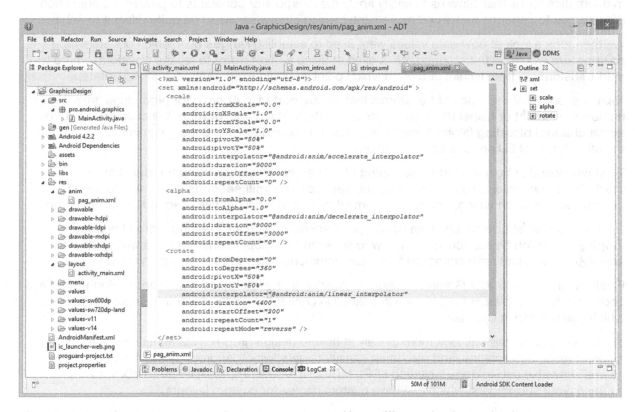

Figure 4-18. Tweaking your <rotate> transform tag parameters to achieve a different animation special effect

Summary

In this fourth chapter, you learned about procedural animation concepts, the Android application assets that can be animated procedurally, XML tags, how to set up complex procedural animation using XML parameters, and other related procedural animation design and optimization techniques.

You also put this information to actual use, creating procedural animations for your pro.android. graphics package start-up screen in your GraphicsDesign Android application, which utilizes several of Android's transform types.

We started by out looking at some of the basic concepts that relate to procedural animation, such as **tweening** and **interpolation**, and how these divide up the data ranges that your animation parameters specify so that they can be played back smoothly and attractively over time.

You learned about **motion curves** and their **Interpolator classes** in Android, which implement the mathematics for us that allow us to easily apply the interpolator constants to procedural animation data ranges to generate real-world movements, which otherwise would be quite difficult to achieve.

We then took a look at how data values were used to establish **ranges** over which our animation **parameters** would be transformed. We looked at using a **pivot point** to tell the transform where to start transforming from (scale) or around which point it should execute the transform (rotate).

Next, we looked at the types of transforms that are supported in Android for procedural animation, namely movement or **translation**, size or **scale**, and orientation or **rotation**. We also looked at how **alpha channel blending** (alpha transparency) can be controlled via procedural animation along with the other types of 2D **spacial** transformations.

Then we looked at how to control the **timing** of procedural animation using the **duration** and **startOffset** parameters. You learned that you need to use a **milliseconds** data value to specify procedural animation timing, and how to convert back and forth between seconds and milliseconds.

Next, we looked at how to delineate what type of animation you are creating, from **play once** to **looping** animation types. You learned how to set seamless looping animation, as well as how to specify the back and forth animation type, also commonly referred to as **pong** animation.

Finally, you went into your GraphicsDesign application and wrote some XML markup along with Java code to actually implement procedural animation in conjunction with your frame animation assets, which you created in Chapter 3.

In the next chapter, we will look more closely at how to design graphics elements across all of the different resolution screens, and resolution density targets, which Android defines and enforces via its /res/drawable sub-folders, including LDPI, MDPI, HDPI, XHDPI, XXHDPI and TVDPI, as well as /res/layout sub-folders, which can have custom names for custom layouts.

Chapter 5

Android DIP: Device-Independent Pixel Graphics Design

In this chapter, we'll take a closer look at how to design graphics assets to be able to span the wide range of Android device screen sizes currently on the market. With Android devices as small as watches up to as large as iTV sets, providing a range of pixel-based assets that will fit all of the screens on the market well and look great is certainly one of the major challenges in creating professional Android graphics.

There is no way around this challenge, short of using only vector (shape) graphics, which scale to fit any size screen, and user interface widgets with XML parameters such as **android:gravity** that do the screen layout math for you automatically. If you're going to use pixel-based assets of any kind in your app, this chapter, and all the information within it, should be of significant interest to you as a budding Pro Android Graphics designer.

You will find when you finish with this chapter that designing for all of the thousands of different Android device (product) screens out there is a game of trade-offs and "guestimation." The information in this chapter will allow you to make the decisions regarding which pixel density imaging resolutions to support, and if doing the extra asset creation work is worth the end result as a percentage of estimated market share (total end users) relative to visual quality on the screen due to scaling (or lack thereof).

We will take a look at the seven currently defined pixel density levels that are a part of the Android OS and API. We will also look at various density and scaling concepts and techniques as they relate to resizing and scaling pixels, and common display resolutions and how to target them effectively.

How Android Supports Device Displays: UI Design and UX

As we all know, the Android OS supports a wide variety of popular consumer electronics devices. Most all of them offer different screen sizes, screen shapes, screen aspect ratios, and screen pixel densities. We'll be looking at each of these areas of screen differences in this chapter.

For application development, Android's operating system attempts to provide a consistent user experience development environment across each supported hardware device. The OS will attempt to handle the task of adjusting your application's user interface to each screen type on which it is displayed.

Additionally, the operating system provides custom APIs that allow you to customize your application UI for a specific screen size and density. This is done to allow developers to optimize the UI design for different screen configurations. For instance, developers may want to specifically develop for a tablet UI, which may be different from a smartphone UI, smartwatch UI, or an iTV UI.

Even though Android will take care of scaling and resizing your UI design, in order to make your applications fit each disparate screen like a glove, you need to make an effort to optimize an application for different screen sizes and pixel densities. In this way, Android OS does not have to scale or resize any given imaging asset too drastically, and thus the user probably won't even notice such slight pixel adjustments, if any are made at all. Indeed, minimizing the scaling and adjustments is the name of the game, and what you're going to learn about in this chapter includes even more optimization techniques! Android development is a lot about optimization.

By providing the Android OS with a reasonable range of highly optimized pixel-based imaging assets inside your .APK file, you can allow the Android OS to go the rest of the way in maximizing the user experience across all Android hardware devices.

If the pixel-based asset optimization process is performed correctly, all your end users will be summarily convinced that the app that they are using was specifically designed for their device, rather than scaled, stretched, and rotated to fit their device screen's physical resolution, aspect ratio, and orientation (portrait or landscape). There is quite a bit involved in this process, and we will be covering all the various factors in this chapter.

Device Display Concepts: Size, Density, Orientation, DIP

An Android device **screen size** is simply the actual physical size, measured in inches, of any device display screen diagonal size measurement. The screen size is commonly given in product specifications, and is often included in the product name itself. For instance, the Nexus 7 or Nexus 10 tablets are 7 and 10 inches in their display screen diagonal measurement, respectively.

The Android OS classifies common screen sizes into four generalized **size constants**, including **small**, **normal**, **large**, and **extra large**. As of Android 4.2.2 there is also an XXHDPI drawable resource folder, so look out for an **extra extra large** size constant to be added in the future as well! Android 4.3 added an XXXHDPI constant as well recently, to support the new 4K iTVs currently appearing on the market.

Android device **screen density** is defined as the number of physical pixels contained in a one inch area of a given device's display screen. Physical pixels are actual hardware screen elements that generate one single pixel; so on LCD screens this would be one **cell**, and on OLED screens this would be one **organic LED**. A **low density** screen would have **120 pixels per inch**, and a **high density** screen would have twice than many pixels, or **240 pixels** per inch.

Screen density in the graphics industry has long been referred to as **DPI,** which stands for **dots per inch**. You are probably familiar with this term as it relates to printer specifications, and now that display screens are approaching similar resolutions as printers, the term now applies here as well. We will be discussing screen density in detail within this chapter.

The Android OS classifies common screen densities into six basic **density constants**, including **low** or **LDPI**, **medium** or **MDPI**, **tv** or **TVDPI**, **high** or **HDPI**, **extra high** or **XHDPI** and **XXHDPI**. As of Android 4.2.2 there is also an XXHDPI drawable resource folder, so look for an **extra extra high** screen density constant to be added as well at some time in the future, as well as an extra extra extra high (XXXHDPI) constant for 4K iTVs.

Android device **screen orientation** is defined as the way that the Android device is being held by the user, that is, the orientation of the screen from the user's current Android device usage point of view. Orientation can change at any time simply by a user rotating the screen by 90 degrees. The industry terms that have been defined over time for either orientation are called **landscape** (widescreen view) or **portrait** (tall, or up and down).

In terms of the **aspect ratio**, this means that a screen aspect ratio can be either wide or tall, depending on how the user is holding the device. This makes user interface and content development significantly more difficult.

It is important to note that different Android devices will operate using different orientations by default when they are powered up by the user. Also, the screen orientation can be changed at runtime by the user simply rotating the device. There are APIs in the Android OS to detect when this happens, so that you can change your content and user interfaces based on the device screen orientation if you so desire. As you can see, developing graphics for Android can get complicated, which is why this book exists.

Android device **screen resolution** is defined using **physical pixels**, and is usually specified using the total number of pixels along the X axis and Y axis, respectively. If a user's screen orientation changes, X axis becomes Y axis and Y axis becomes X axis, so the resolution specifications change.

Screen resolution is generally specified using the landscape or widescreen orientation parameters, so a WVGA **800x480** screen is held in **landscape** and a **480x800** WVGA screen is being used (viewed) in a **portrait** declination.

It is important to note for those developers who wish to include multiple device screen support in their apps that Android applications do not work directly via the screen resolution. The current development approach is to make your Android application concerned only with **screen size and density**, as specified by the **size** and **density** constants provided in and by the OS.

The way for Android developers to accomplish this is to use **DIP (density-independent pixel)** units, which can also be denoted in code and markup as DIP or dip. A DIP can be thought of as a "virtual" pixel representation of sorts, which you should get used to utilizing when you define the UI (user interface) layouts. As you will see later on in this book, we will use DIP units to express layout dimensions and user interface element positioning, providing a **density-independent** way of creating UI layouts across devices.

According to the Android Developer web site, a density-independent pixel is the equivalent to a physical pixel on a **medium** size, **MDPI** constant **160 DPI** screen. This is used by Android OS as a baseline screen density assumed by the operating system to be a "medium" density, or "normal," device screen. How this works is that at runtime the Android operating system transparently handles all scaling of units defined in DIPs after it looks at the current density of the device screen that is being used to run the application.

The way in which DIP units are translated into physical screen pixels can be calculated by developers in the following way:

Physical Pixels = DIP * (DPI/160)

For example, using an **XHDPI (320 DPI)** extra high density pixel screen, 1 DIP would equal 2 physical pixels. On an **XXHDPI (480 DPI)** extra extra high density pixel image screen, 1 DIP would equal 3 physical pixels. There's a chart (a table) in the next section of this chapter that collects all of this density-related information together into one place, so stay tuned.

In summary, Android developers need to use **DIP** (or **DP**) units when they define their application UI if they wish to ensure proper display of their user interface design across Android hardware device display screens that feature different pixel densities (different dot pitch, or pixel pitch).

To optimize your application user interface and content for many different screen sizes and pixel densities, you will provide **alternate resources** for each of the popular sizes and densities. Additionally, you will also create **alternative user interface layouts** to fit some of the different screen aspect ratios, as well as **alternative digital imagery** for different screen densities. So, this is where considering the trade-offs comes into play.

The trick is selecting what levels your app needs to support, based on the devices you are targeting. Developers don't have to provide an alternative asset for every single combination of screen size and density; to do this would yield a huge data footprint. Android provides compatibility features that can handle the work of rendering an application on any screen, if you have created your UI using a technique that will allow it to be resized.

Density Independence: Creating Similar User Experiencesl

An Android application is said to achieve **density independence** when it is able to preserve the physical appearance (from an end-user perspective) of the user interface elements when they are displayed across display screens that feature differing pixel densities or different **DPI**s (dots per inch) or **PPI**s (pixels per inch).

In case you are wondering why device independence is deemed so important, it is because without it, all of your UI elements will appear to be larger on a lower-density display and much smaller on a higher-density display. You will soon see that density-related user interface element size changes can cause visual (user experience or UX) problems within the application's layout, and this could significantly affect your application's usability.

The Android operating system will help your application achieve density independence in a couple different ways. First of all, Android will scale DIP units up or down as it deems appropriate for a current screen density.

Secondly, Android will scale your drawable resources to the appropriate size, based on the current screen density, **if it is necessary**. Optimally, it will not be necessary, which is why, in this chapter, I am going to go into great detail on how to attempt to create three or four different versions of your pixel-based assets, so that Android has several equally-spaced-apart resolution density targets to choose from. This is so that if Android is forced to scale, it can get close to the perfect visual result.

You may be wondering: Why not just provide one high-resolution asset, and have Android scale that down to fit? The short answer is that Android does not perform scaling all that well, has no bicubic interpolation algorithm like Photoshop and GIMP have, and so we must currently create scaled asset targets ourselves for Android to use, by using Photoshop CS6 or GIMP 2.8.

This is why I cover utilizing those external open source new media content production tools in my Android books; because to really nail that pristine result in Android, currently one has to leverage other software outside of the Android development environment in order to perform media optimization of one type or another. Android development spans many software packages!

In many cases, developers can obtain density independence in an application simply by specifying all UI layout dimension values in DIP or DP units. As you have seen in previous chapters already, the use of **match_parent** and **wrap_content** constants can match or scale UI areas for us as well. If you have pixel (image) assets, it's not quite as easy!

Android will scale PNG, GIF, or JPEG bitmap drawables, as well as any video assets, in an attempt to display them at an optimal pixel resolution based on an optimal scaling factor relative to the current screen density. It is important to note that pixel scaling can often result in **blur** or **pixelated** results, again, due to a currently-less-than-advanced scaling algorithm.

To avoid **scaling artifacts**, developers are encouraged to provide several alternative bitmap resource levels for three or four different densities. How many of these you provide is entirely your call, and deciding this is what this chapter is in the book for, so you can calculate this trade-off.

For example, you should at least provide a high resolution level of bitmap assets for large (iTV) and high-density (HD smartphone) screens. Android will intelligently use those high resolution assets, instead of up-scaling raster (pixel-based) assets designed for medium-density "normal" screens.

You should also at least have one other set of assets that targets **normal** size mainstream device screens, which feature **MDPI** (medium pixel density). With the advent of SmartWatches, you might also consider having well-optimized LDPI (low density pixel image) assets as well, especially if your application is targeting SmartWatches. SmartWatches are currently exploding onto the Android market, with a dozen major manufacturers releasing models this year.

A **160 DPI MDPI** screen density asset is exactly a **2X downsample** of the **320 DPI XHDPI** screen density asset, and is exactly a **3X downsample** of the **480 DPI XXHDPI** screen density asset, as you will see a bit later in the chapter when you create launcher icon assets for your GraphicsDesign application.

Table 5-1 summarizes Android **density qualifiers**, **screen size constants**, **pixel density** DPI, **pixel multiplier** (relative to the default normal MDPI), as well as Android-defined **minimum screen** sizes for each level specified in DIP, and finally app **system icon** types, specified with **physical pixels**.

Table 5-1. Android Device DPI Chart Showing Six Levels of Pixel Density Screens Specifically Supported in Android

Android Device DPI Chart	Screen Size	Pixel Density	Pixel Multiplier	Minimum DP Screen Size	Launcher Icon Pixel Size	Action Bar Icon Size	Notify Icon Size
LDPI (Low Density Pixels)	small	120	0.75	426x320	36x36	24x24	18x18
MDPI (Medium) (Default)	normal	160	1.0	470x320	48x48	32x32	24x24
TVDPI (HDTV 1280x720)	HDTV	213	1.33	640x360	64x64	48x48	32x32
HDPI (High Density Pixels)	large	240	1.5	640x480	72x72	48x48	36x36
XHDPI (Extra High Density)	xlarge	320	2.0	960x720	96x96	64x64	48x48
XXHDPI (Extra Extra High)	xxlarge	480	3.0	1280x960	144x144	96x96	72x72
XXXHDPI (Extra Extra Extra High)	xxxlarge	640	4.0	1920x1440	192x192	128x128	96x96

When deciding which of these seven target digital image asset density levels to develop assets for, I also factor the delivery of new media assets onto platforms other than Android, such as HTML5 apps and even digital signage.

It is important to remember the fact that currently doing your image asset down-sampling in Photoshop or GIMP, optimally by an even 2X or 4X, is sure to yield a far superior result to the resampling that the Android OS will provide. Thus, the ultimate consideration is total app data footprint, and how many different image, frame animation, icon or UI element image assets that your application requires. At a minimum I would suggest providing the assets for MDPI, HDPI, and XHDPI, or at least MDPI (160) and XHDPI (320).

Android Multi-Screen Support Via <supports-screens> Tag

As you have seen so far in this chapter, Android will handle the majority of the work of rendering the application's user experience properly on device screen configurations by scaling layouts to fit a screen size and density. Android will also scale image, video, and frame animation drawables for any given screen density, if it becomes necessary.

There are some additional ways developers can optimize their XML markup, and Java code, that will allow the Android OS to further optimize visual results across many different screen configuration types. So, let's cover those here, over the next several sections of this chapter.

Android developers are allowed to **explicitly declare** in their application **AndroidManifest** XML file the different screen sizes that the application supports. You may have noticed the **AndroidManifest.xml** file in Eclipse in the project folder at the bottom in the root of the project folder itself. This "manifest" file essentially configures and launches, or "bootstraps," the Android application, much like an **index.html** file does for a web site.

Declaring the exact screen sizes that your application supports ensures that only device owners with screens that your app can support will be able to purchase and download your application. An obvious downside to doing this is that implementing this can severely restrict the potential market size, that is, your application's purchasing audience.

The other thing that specifically declaring screen size support across the different screen sizes will affect is how the Android operating system can render your application on larger screens. Specifically declaring a screen size will determine whether or not an application runs in Android's **screen compatibility mode**. Screen compatibility mode is a "band-aid" solution for Android applications that are not efficiently designed to scale for large display screens, such as those found in tablets and iTV sets.

Starting with OS Version 1.6, Android has added support for a wide variety of screen sizes and performs most the work of resizing application layouts so that they correctly fit on any screen. However, if the application does not follow the guidelines for supporting multiple display screens, Android could stumble across some rendering issues on some larger display screens.

For application designs that encounter this particular problem, the screen compatibility mode may make the application a little more usable on larger screens, but then again, it might not, so make sure to test your app well.

To declare the display screen sizes that your application supports, you'll need to include the **<supports-screens>** XML element in your **AndroidManifest** XML file. This tag is a **child tag** of the **<manifest> parent tag**, and allows you to specify all of the screen sizes your application supports and to enable screen compatibility mode for screens that are larger than what your application currently has the assets in place to support.

It is important that you leverage this element in your Android application manifest XML file, to specify every screen size your application supports. An application can be said to "support" a given screen size constant if it has all the assets it needs to resize your content and UI properly to fill an entire screen area, meaning at least **MDPI**, **HDPI**, and **XHDPI** image assets.

Thus, if you intend to include these three "suggested" (required) **normal**, **largeScreen**, and **xlargeScreen** resolution density assets, be sure to also include the following <supports-screens> tag (and parameter) configuration in your AndroidManifest.xml file, after the **<manifest>** tag as a child tag:

```
<supports-screens android:largeScreens="true" android:xlargeScreens="true" />
```

Note that you do not have to specify android:normalScreens="true" as this is the default <supports-screens> size specification, and thus is inherently specified, so just add largeScreen and xlargeScreen support via this tag. You will add this tag a little later on in the chapter, when you are editing your AndroidManifest.xml file, since you need to include this in your app.

Resampling applied by Android will usually work well for most applications, and you should not have to do any extra work to make your application work across screens that are larger than an HD smartphone or a tablet.

However, it's important that you optimize your application's UI design for different screen sizes by providing **alternative layout resources**. To offer an example, you may wish to modify the layout of an Activity when it is on a tablet, compared to when it's running on smartphones. We will be looking more closely at alternate layouts in the next section of this chapter.

If your application does not work well when it is resized to fit different screen sizes, you can use the **parameters** of the <supports-screens> tag to control whether your application should be distributed to smaller screens or have its UI scaled up or **zoomed** to fit larger Android screens using the system's **screen compatibility mode**. You can take a look at all of the tag parameters if you like by visiting the Android Developer site at this URL:

http://developer.android.com/guide/topics/manifest/supports-screens-element.html

If you haven't designed your application assets, layout, and user interface design to support larger screen sizes, and the normal Android scaling does not achieve an acceptable result, an Android screen compatibility mode can be invoked in order to scale your app up to fit on the larger screen size. Android does this by emulating a **normal** size screen (medium density **MDPI**). This emulation is implemented by **zooming** the MDPI density (normal sized) assets and UI designs, so that they fill the entire HDPI or XHDPI screen.

It's important to note that this **upscaling** causes **pixelation** and **blurring** of your content and user interface designs, as up-scaling invariably will. This is why Android strongly suggests (as do I) that you provide optimized content and user interface layouts for your application, across **MDPI**, **HDPI**, and **XHDPI** at the very least, so that you have image assets in place that can be optimized (scaled) by Android OS for use on larger display screens.

Providing Device-Optimized User Interface Layout Designs

Android will resize your application's user interface layout to fit any of your user's device screens. In many cases, this should work just fine. In other cases, however, your UI design might not look as professional as you might like it to, and in these cases it might need some further adjustment in order to fit different screen orientations, or aspect ratios, properly.

For example, on a larger device screen, or a screen with a vastly different aspect ratio (wide vs. square), you may wish to adjust the position and size of some user interface elements in order to take advantage of the new screen shape or additional screen space. Conversely, given smaller screens you would probably need to adjust user interface element and font sizes in such a way that everything fits attractively on a smaller display screen.

The configuration **qualifier** constants you can use to provide size-specific layout resources include **small**, **normal**, **large**, **xlarge**, **xxlarge**, and **xxxlarge**. For example, a user interface screen layout XML definition for those extra large device screens could go into the **/res/layout-xlarge** project folder. Starting in Android Version 3.2 (Honeycomb or API 13), the above-mentioned size groupings have been **deprecated** and you should instead utilize a newer **ScreenWidth-Number-DP** naming schema, which we will discuss further here.

Deprecated means **discontinued but still supported**, in case that you're not familiar with the terminology. It is recommended that when features become deprecated in Android, that you recode your application to use the new way of doing things, in this case naming layout resource folders using the new folder name standard, as described by ScreenWidth-Number-DIP (**sw-#-dp**).

This folder name configuration **qualifier method** defines the **smallest width** required by the layout resources using **density-independent pixels**. To give an example, if a given tablet layout will require a minimum of 480DP worth of screen width, you would place it inside the **/res/layout-sw480dp** folder.

The new DIP-size-specific qualifiers offer Android developers more control over the specific screen sizes their application can support, compared to the deprecated screen size groups (small, normal, large, and xlarge) supported prior to Android 3.2 Honeycomb API Level 13.

It is important to note that the DIP sizes that you can specify, by using these new qualifiers, are not the physical screen size specifications. The qualifiers are instead for use regarding your Activity, that is, the width or height specified in DIP units that are available to your Java Activity window, that is, its area (portion) of the physical display screen.

The reason for this is that the Android operating system might be using a portion of a physical display screen's pixel area for its own UI elements, such as the system utility bar, located at the bottom of a display screen, or the status bar, located at the top of the display screen.

What this means is that some portion of the physical display screen might not be available for your application user interface layout. The sizes you declare should therefore be specifically targeting the size of the area of the physical display screen that is needed by your app's Java Activity.

Android's operating system will take care of accounting for any of the other display screen space that is used by the operating system UI when the developer declares how much space is needed for their Activity layout.

It is important to note that the Android Action Bar will be considered a part of the application window space, even if your layout does not declare it specifically. This means the Android Action Bar will reduce the screen real estate (area) that would otherwise be available for your layout, and you must remember to account for it within the overall user experience design.

While using the new DIP qualifiers might seem more complicated than using the deprecated screen size constants, it might in reality be simpler once you determine the density pixel requirements for your UI layout design.

When you design user interface layouts, your primary consideration will be the actual size at which your application switches from a smartphone UI to a tablet UI to an iTV UI. Using the qualifiers we are going to go over in detail in the next few sections, you will be in complete control over the exact density pixel sizes at which the layout changes between XML designs.

Let's go over the three available screen configuration modifiers that look at minimum (smallest) width, total screen width, and screen height, and see how they differ. Between the three different methods you should be able to accurately specify any screen layout change trigger ranges that you need.

Using Android's SmallestWidth Screen Configuration Modifier

The Android **smallestWidth** screen configuration qualifier, which takes the format **sw#dp** (such as **sw480dp**), is meant to define the target size of a screen by indicating the **shortest width dimension** of the available screen. An Android device smallestWidth component is the shortest dimension of the display available height or available width, depending on the orientation. One might also conceptualize this as the smallest possible display width for the screen, which is obviously where the constant name came from.

You can use the smallestWidth qualifier to ensure that regardless of the display's current orientation, your application will have at least this number of DIPs of display width available for your Activity's UI layout. So, if your user interface layout requires a smallest width dimension of the display area be at least 720 DIP, then you would use this qualifier to create the layout resource folder named **/res/layout-sw720dp** to hold your user interface layout definition XML files for your app's Activities.

The Android OS will use the XML resources in this folder only when a smallest dimension of the available display is at least 720 DIP. It is important to note that this determination is done regardless of whether the 720 DIP side is the user-perceived height or width. The smallestWidth is a **fixed screen size characteristic** of the Android device display. A device's smallestWidth modifier does not change when the user display screen orientation changes.

A smallestWidth calculation made by the Android OS for a given device will take into account the Android OS UI elements. For example, if a device has some Android UI elements that are part of the display that account for some of the space that infringe upon the smallestWidth measurement, the system will calculate the smallestWidth to be smaller than the device's screen size, because those are display pixels not available to your UI.

Since the screen width is many times a determining factor in a UI layout design, using the smallestWidth configuration modifier to determine the appropriate screen size fit can often be helpful to the Android developer.

An available display width parameter can also be a factor in ascertaining whether or not to use a single pane UI layout, for example for smartphone, or a multiple pane layout for a tablet or iTV. For this reason, developers need this modifier to ascertain a smallestWidth device DIP parameter.

Using the Available Screen Width Screen Configuration Modifier

There is another configuration parameter that will allow the developer to specify a **minimum available display width** in DIP units, which does take the screen orientation into account. Unlike the smallestWidth configuration modifier, the **w#dp** (example: **w480dp**) width configuration modifier will in fact change when the display orientation changes between a landscape and a portrait orientation, thus reflecting the current visual width that is available for your UI layout from the end user's visual perspective.

This configuration parameter can be useful in determining which multiple pane UI layout design that your application will use in landscape mode or in portrait mode, depending on how an end user is holding their device.

This is due to the fact that even on the larger tablet devices, you often don't want to use the same multiple pane UI layout design for the portrait orientation as you do for the landscape orientation. With the width screen configuration modifier, you can use something like w640dp to specify a 640 DIP minimum available screen area width for your layout, instead of having to implement both the screen size qualifier and orientation qualifier.

Using the Available Screen Height Screen Configuration Modifier

There's a third configuration parameter that allows developers to specify **minimum available display height** in DIP units, which also takes the screen orientation into account. This **h#dp** (example: **h600dp**) height configuration modifier will also change when the display orientation changes between the landscape and the portrait orientation, thus reflecting the current visual height that is available for the developer's UI layout from an end user's visual perspective. Using the h#dp configuration modifier to define the height required by a layout is useful in the same way as the w#dp is for defining the width.

Providing Device-Optimized Image Drawable Assets

As you know, Android will scale your PNG, GIF, and JPEG bitmap drawable assets so they will render at an optimal physical size for each device. If an application provides bitmap drawables only for the baseline, medium screen density (MDPI), then Android scales them up when on a high-density screen, and will scale them down when on a low-density screen. This will cause artifacts in your bitmaps, especially regarding the upscaling side of things, as data that isn't there needs to be created to do upsampling.

To ensure that your raster image assets look pristine, you will essentially be forced to include alternative image versions, at different resolutions, to be used for different screen densities. I'll be showing you the optimal way to approach this work process throughout this book.

Current Android system **configuration qualifiers** that you can utilize for density-specific resources include LDPI (low), MDPI (medium), TVDPI (TV), HDPI (high), XHDPI (extra high), XXHDPI (extra extra high), and XXXHDPI (extra extra extra high). Based on size and density of the current user's device screen, the Android OS will leverage all size-specific and density-specific drawable assets that you provide in your application's **/res/drawable** folder(s) hierarchy.

For example, if your user's device has a high-density display screen, and your app implements drawable resources, Android will look for the drawable resource folder that matches to that device display density configuration.

Android also factors in the alternative resources available, so a resource directory with the **-hdpi** configuration qualifier, for instance a **/res/drawable-hdpi** folder, would provide assets matching that particular density level, so Android will use your drawable assets from that folder.

If, however, no density-matching assets can be located in your /res/drawable folders, Android will use your default assets, which are kept in the **/res/drawable** folder; if none are found there, Android will use the MDPI density resources in the **/res/drawable-mdpi** folder, and will then scale these up or down as needed to match the current screen size and density.

Since scaling down is preferable to scaling up, if you are going to leave out assets, I suggest that you leave out LDPI assets, unless you are developing for SmartWatch, and at least include MDPI, HDPI, and XHDPI assets, as we will be doing throughout this book. If you can, set it up so that Android, if it scales at all, is scaling pixels down, and not up, and then you should always obtain decent visual results.

It is important to note that any digital image resources kept in the **/res/drawable** folder are considered by the Android OS to be **"default"** drawable resources. I guess if you wanted to try using only HDPI or XHDPI assets and have Android downsample these, you could simply put them in the /res/drawable folder to accomplish this, leaving the other folders empty.

In my development practices, I keep only **XML definitions** for things like animations and transitions in this /res/drawable folder, and then keep all of my pixel-based digital imaging assets in those various density-specific /res/drawable-dpi folders. This is a more "surgical" way of doing things.

In this case, the MPDI assets would be considered the default. How do I know this? By looking at the **density constants** inside the **DisplayMetrics** class, which we will be covering in detail very soon. The **DENSITY_NORMAL** and **DENSITY_MDPI** constants have the exact same data value of **160 DPI**.

Fortunately, when Android is looking for a density-specific image asset and it does not find a suitable one in the default density-specific directory (either /res/drawable or /res/drawable-mdpi), it won't necessarily utilize the default (MDPI) resources. Android might instead use one of your other density-specific resources, if it ascertains that it will provide superior resampling results. Thank Heavens for small miracles.

For example, when looking for a low-density LDPI image asset, if one isn't available, Android will (correctly) scale down the high-density version of that image asset, because Android knows that scaling higher-density assets down to lower-density targets provides superior visual results.

Let's take a look at this from a math perspective. If we downsample by 2X from 240 DPI to 120 DPI, we are going to obtain a superior result than if we had downsampled by 1.5X from 160 DPI to 120 DPI. In image resampling, downsampling, or upsampling, you always want to use a factor of 2 or 4 if you can to provide the best quality result from the resampling algorithm.

You might be wondering: What if I don't want my image assets to be scaled, to compensate for different pixel density displays? If you want your image to be big on low-density displays, and tiny on high-density displays, for whatever your reason, there is indeed a way to accomplish this in Android.

The way to instruct Android to **never pre-scale** when appropriate resolution density assets are not available for use is to put image assets that are never to be scaled into a resource directory with the **-nodpi** configuration qualifier. This would, of course, equate to the **/res/drawable-nodpi** folder naming convention. When Android uses an image asset from this configuration qualifier folder, it will not scale it for any reason, even if it deems that it should based on the current device density and its internal when-to-scale algorithms.

Besides **density configuration modifiers** (LDPI, MDPI, HDPI, XHDPI, etc.), there are **orientation configuration modifiers** (**PORT** and **LAND**) in Android, as well as **aspect ratio configuration modifiers** (**LONG** and **NOTLONG**).

These can be used to create folder structures that contain custom designs that fit orientation (portrait or landscape) and aspect ratio (widescreen) display screen scenarios. These configuration modifiers can also be used in conjunction with the other modifiers, for instance, they can be chained together, so **/res/drawable-land-hdpi** would contain **landscape HDPI assets**.

The DisplayMetrics Class: Size, Density, and Font Scaling

You might be wondering if the Android OS has an API or class that allows developers to **poll the device** their application is running on and obtain information about its display characteristics. In fact, there is, and it is called the **DisplayMetrics** class.

The DisplayMetrics class is a member of the **android.util** operating system utilities package, which is no surprise, and it provides an object structure that, when polled (accessed) by the developer, gives the **display metrics information** regarding the current (end user) device's display screen. Information provided includes the **display physical size** in both the X and Y dimensions, the **pixel density** in both the X and Y dimensions, and the **font scaling factor** that is currently being used by the Android OS.

To access the DisplayMetrics class members, initialize the DisplayMetrics object using the DisplayMetrics() constructor, using the following code:

```
DisplayMetrics currentDeviceDisplayMetrics = new DisplayMetrics();
getWindowManager().getDefaultDisplay().getMetrics(currentDeviceDisplayMetrics);
```

There are eight constants in this class: **DENSITY_DEFAULT**, **DENSITY_HIGH**, **DENSITY_LOW**, **DENSITY_MEDIUM**, **DENSITY_TV**, **DENSITY_XHIGH**, **DENSITY_XXHIGH**, and **DENSITY_XXXHIGH**.

If you wanted to research this DisplayMetrics class further on the Android Developer web site, it can be accessed by using the following URL (this is also the source of the information in Table 5-1):

`http://developer.android.com/reference/android/util/DisplayMetrics.html`

The DisplayMetrics object also has seven data fields that can be accessed once the object has been instantiated. These are shown in Table 5-2.

Table 5-2. Android DisplayMetrics Class and Object Data Fields Plus Access Modifiers and Functions

Access/Type Modifier	Object Field Proper Name	Object Data Field Information Provided on Polling
public float	Density	The logical density of the display
public int	densityDpi	The screen density expressed as dots per inch
public int	heightPixels	The absolute height of the display, in pixels
public int	widthPixels	The absolute width of the display, in pixels
public float	xdpi	Physical pixels per inch in the X dimension
public float	ydpi	Physical pixels per inch in the Y dimension
public float	scaledDensity	A scaling factor for fonts on the display

As you can see, once you create a DisplayMetrics object, your applications can see precisely what the current Android device has in the way of screen size and pixel density, and how the OS is currently scaling fonts as well.

Optimizing Android Application Icons for LDPI to XXXHDPI

Although I cannot optimize all of the graphics assets that we'll be using throughout this book in this chapter, I will go through the down-sampling work process using the open source digital imaging software package **GIMP2** here for the **launcher icons**, since they are one of the few assets that you will want to have all five drawable target levels created under. The reason you are creating five levels for the application launcher icons is because on Android tablets, Android looks for launcher icons **one folder higher** than it uses for the rest of the application's drawable assets.

This means that to support XHDPI, which is one of the drawable levels that you will always want to support, you have to include a **144x144 pixel** launch icon PNG32 file in the **XXHDPI** folder. You do this in order to make sure your application icon (your app branding, if you will) looks crystal clear on the larger Android tablets, such as the Google Nexus 10.

If you don't have GIMP2 on your system yet, go to `www.gimp.org` and download the latest version (currently 2.8.6) for your operating system.

After you install and launch GIMP2, use the **File ➤ Open** menu sequence to open the **PAG_logo_288.png** PNG32 file of the Pro Android Graphics logo we used in Chapter 3 and Chapter 4.

In case you are wondering why I am using a **288 pixel** version of this logo, it is because when downsampling to the five different icon sizes required by Android, this particular pixel dimension will **resample evenly**, that is, it will leave no remainder (partial pixels) for the resampling algorithm.

> Note   If you want to use the XXXHDPI for 4K iTVs add a downsample to 192x192 pixels to the work process which follows.

Let's do the math. XXHDPI requires 144 pixels, which is half of 288, giving us a 2X downsample. XHDPI requires 96 pixels, which is a third of 288, giving us a 3X downsample. HDPI requires 72 pixels, which is half of 144 pixels and a fourth of 288 pixels, giving us a 4X downsample. MDPI requires 48 pixels, which is a sixth of 288, giving us a 6X downsample, and LDPI requires 36 pixels, which is an eighth of 288, giving us an 8X downsample.

If you had wanted to develop your icon artwork at **576**, which is twice the 288 resolution, that would also work, or even at **1152**, which is four times the 288 resolution, if you need to have print resolution icon assets.

Note that 2 x 1152 is **2304**, which happens to also be a common digital camera native pixel resolution. Remember, image and video (pixel) scaling works much better along **Power-of-Two** sampling multiples (1-2-4-8-16-32, etc.).

Once your launch icon logo at 288 pixels is open in GIMP2, it should look like the screen shot shown in Figure 5-1. The **checkerboard pattern** behind the logo denotes a **transparency** in GIMP, so you can see that we have just the pixels for our Pro Android Graphics logo for our application icon.

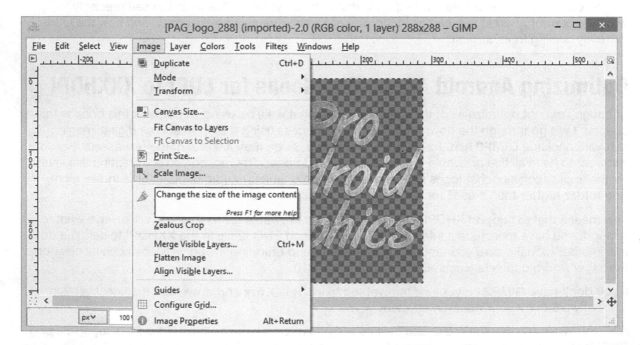

Figure 5-1. Using an Image ➤ Scale Image function to resize the 288 pixel asset to fit XXHDPI 144 pixel icon size

Android suggests using an alpha channel to provide transparency for your launch icons, in case users have wallpaper, or other background imagery, set up on their Android devices.

Now you are ready to resize the 288 pixel launcher icon image down to half of its original size, using the **Image** menu and the **Scale Image** option, as shown in Figure 5-1.

Selecting this menu sequence will bring up the **Scale Image** dialog, shown in Figure 5-2, which you will use to set your downsample resolution of **144** width and **144** height, as well as to set an **interpolation algorithm** to the value **Cubic** for your interpolation method or setting.

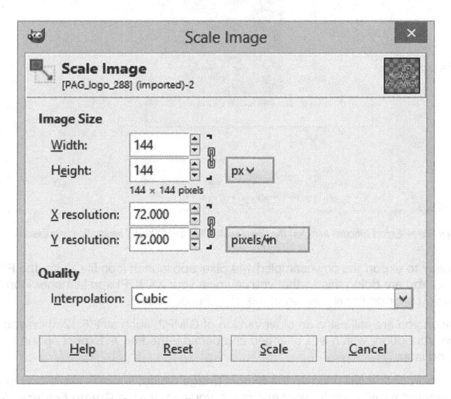

Figure 5-2. Setting the parameters in the Scale Image dialog

Cubic interpolation uses a high-quality downsampling algorithm that will take the edges in your image into account, and will **anti-alias** them during the downsampling process to provide smooth transitions to sharp edges or drastic changes between pixel areas in your image. A great example of this would be the edges of your Pro Android Graphics logo, for instance.

Cubic interpolation in GIMP2 is similar to the **bicubic interpolation** in Photoshop. If you are using Photoshop instead of GIMP2, then also select the **Bicubic Sharper** (for downsampling) option from the drop-down menu at the bottom of Photoshop's Image Resizing dialog.

The image should now be four times smaller than it was originally, or two times smaller along each of the X and Y axis, as shown in Figure 5-3.

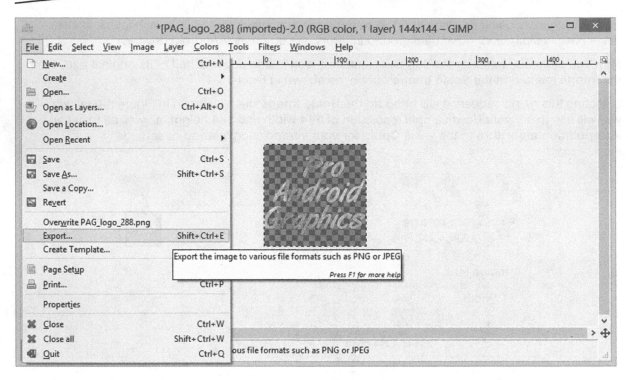

Figure 5-3. Using a File ➤ Export function to export the newly scaled 144 pixel XXHDPI application icon asset

You are now ready to export the downsampled 144 pixel app launch icon file, using the **File ➤ Export** menu sequence. You are doing this so that you can give your XXHDPI app launcher icon file a file name that tells you later on the resolution of this digital image asset.

If for some reason you are still using an older version of GIMP2, such as 2.6.12, then you would use the **File ➤ Save As** option, which was changed and became the **File ➤ Export** option as of GIMP2 version 2.8.0 and later.

Selecting the Export option will bring up the **Export Image** dialog, which is shown in Figure 5-4. If you haven't created a folder yet for your app icons, you can use the **Create Folder** button on the top-right of the dialog to do this now. I used it to create the **/Icons** folder under my Pro Android Graphics Design (PAGD) folder and its /CH05 sub-folder.

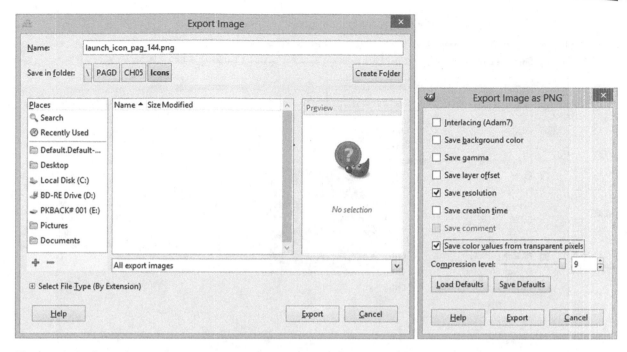

Figure 5-4. Setting the launch_icon_pag_144.png file name and selecting export options in Export Image dialog

Once you have a folder for your app icons, enter the descriptive file name **launch_icon_pag_144.png** in the **Name:** field at the top of the dialog. GIMP2 uses your file extension to determine which type of file format (codec) to use to save the file. You can also use the **Select File Type (By Extension)** widget at the bottom-left of the dialog to do this the long way. Once you have set everything, click the **Export** button at the bottom-right of the dialog, which will bring up the **Export Image as PNG** settings dialog, shown on the right side of the Figure 5-4 screen shot. Make sure that the **Save resolution** and the **Save color values from transparent pixels** are checked, and then set the **Compression level** slider to the maximum compression (9).

You might be wondering why a lossless file format such as PNG32 has this compression level setting in GIMP2 at all, as one would expect this with JPEG but not with PNG; one would assume max compression would be a given. It turns out that it controls the speed of the lossless compression, much like when you use the ZIP compression algorithm, which is also lossless. With a ZIP utility, you define a trade-off between how long the compression process is going to take and how much better (slightly smaller files) job the compression algorithm is going to do in compressing it. Since 9 is the default value for this slider in GIMP2, I simply left it alone. Feel free to play around with this, and observe the results, later on, if you wish.

Once you have exported the new 144 pixel XXHDPI launcher icon asset, you can return to your 288 pixel source file for further resampling of the other four launcher icon assets. This is most easily accomplished by using the **Edit** menu and the **Undo Scale Image** option, as shown in Figure 5-5.

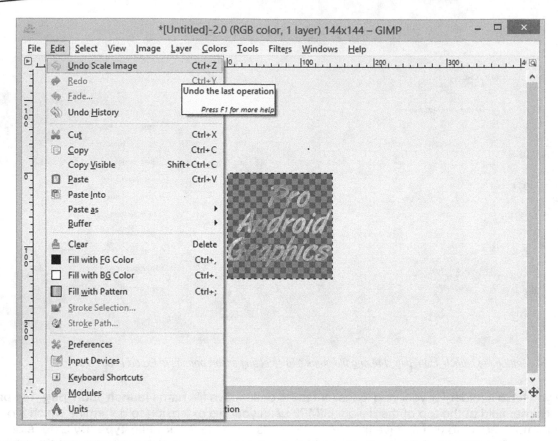

Figure 5-5. Using the Edit ➤ Undo Scale Image menu sequence to revert logo icon image data back to 288 pixels

In case you are wondering why you did not simply continue resizing the 144 pixel image data right on down the line, the reason you need to return to your original source file for subsequent resampling is because you want to give the resampling algorithm the most data to work with possible, which allows it to achieve the best visual result each time you resample.

This is why earlier I discussed using a 576 pixel, a 1152 pixel, or a 2304 pixel source artwork image, as the higher resolution you have going into an image resampling algorithm, the better chance you have for an acceptable result coming out of that algorithm, given you have bicubic interpolation algorithm mathematics (called cubic in GIMP) with which to downsample.

Generally you want to stay away from upsampling if you can help it, which you saw earlier in this chapter when we talked about an HDPI or XHDPI screen emulating (upsampling) an MDPI "normal" user experience (and user interface design). Upsampling forces the algorithm to create image data (pixels) that do not currently exist in the image, and this guesswork as to what these pixels should be, and where they should be, translates into either artifacts, or blurring, or both, in the resulting digital imagery.

Next, let's copy the newly downsampled application launcher icon assets into their proper folders, and write the XML markup that will be needed to implement them inside your Android GraphicsDesign application.

Installing the New App Icon in the Correct Density Folders

Open the file management utility for your operating system (for Windows 8, it is the Windows Explorer tool) and find the **/Icons** asset folder that you created for your icon assets and saved your launch icons in, (for me, this folder was called the **/PAGD/CH05/Icons** folder, and is shown in Figure 5-6).

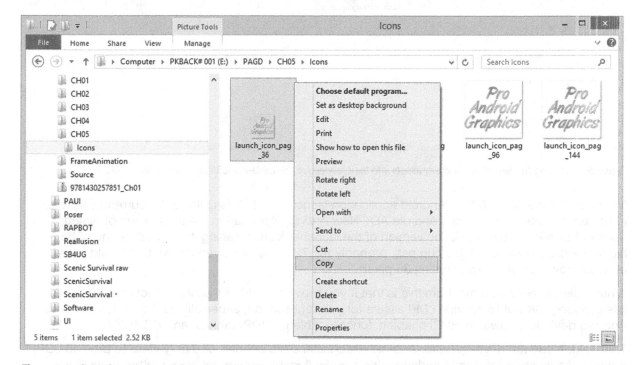

Figure 5-6. Selecting app launch icon density level assets from the /icon folder for copying to /drawable folders

It is important to create and maintain a logical asset folder hierarchy when developing a complex Android application that involves lots of new media elements and assets. Besides your /workspace/ project folder for your Android app, you should have a separate /project folder, with sub-folders for images, video, audio, animation, 3D, icons, and so on. These new media type sub-folders could then have their own sub-sub-folders such as /project/audio/music, or /project/audio/voiceovers; for your digital imagery you might have /project/images/mpdi, /project/images/hdpi, and /project/images/ xhdpi; and for digital video /project/video/mpeg4 and /project/video/webm, for instance.

Let's start copying the launcher icon image assets from the new media icon assets folder over to the appropriate Eclipse ADT workspace project folder, which is **/workspace/GraphicsDesign/res/ drawable-ldpi** now.

Select the **LDPI 36 pixel** resolution density asset, right-click it, and select the **Copy** option to put the file location reference into your operating system's clipboard, as shown in Figure 5-6.

Next, find your **/workspace/GraphicsDesign/res/drawable-ldpi** folder, right-click it, and select the **Paste** option to copy and paste this file into the folder, as shown in Figure 5-7. Repeat this work process for all five of the launcher icons, so that the pixel number in each of their name matches the density level for that resolution. If you forgot which density requires which icon resolution, refer back to Table 5-1 (the sixth column).

Figure 5-7. Pasting the launch icon density assets into their respective drawable-dpi folders in the resource folder

Notice that there is no default Android application launch icon in this LDPI folder currently, so it is important to note that even the Android ADT New Android Application creation series of dialogs does not provide a low-resolution version of the launcher icon, meaning it must scale one of the higher resolution icons for this purpose, probably the 72 pixel, HDPI version, as this would be an even 2X downsample, to a resulting 36 pixels.

What I take (infer or assume) from this is that if you provide a 240 DPI asset collection (HDPI), it is probably OK not to provide LDPI assets for your application, especially as the trend in today's Android devices is towards HDPI phablets (phone+tablet), XHDPI tablets, and HDPI iTVs.

That said, if you are developing for Android watches and flip phones, you may want to provide LDPI optimized assets, at least until Android adds a cubic (bicubic) interpolation algorithm to its OS. As you can see from Figure 5-8, Android does provide an MDPI icon asset, which we have pasted our custom launcher icon beside and will be renaming to something simpler.

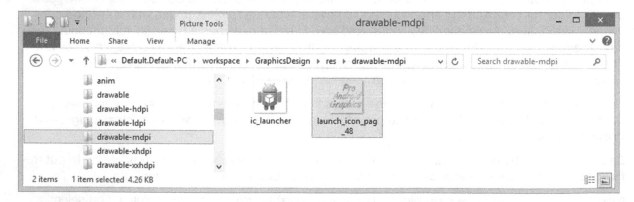

Figure 5-8. Android created ic_launcher.png icon and developer created launch_icon_pag_48 in /drawable-mdpi

Make sure that after you copy all of your files into the proper resolution density folders that you rename them with generic names (no pixel numbers) so they **all have the same name** in each folder, as shown in Figure 5-9.

Figure 5-9. *Renaming the launch_icon_pag_48.png file to generic (and simpler) file name of pag_icon.png*

As you can see in Figure 5-9, I chose the simple name **pag_icon.png**, and I closely followed the Android asset name convention of only using **lowercase letters**, **numbers**, and the **underscore character**.

Once you rename all five files to **pag_icon.png**, you will be ready to edit the XML parameters in your AndroidManifest.xml file to implement the new custom Pro Android Graphics launcher icon for your GraphicsDesign app.

Configuring the AndroidManifest.xml for Custom App Icon

Now that all of your assets are in place where they need to go, fire up Eclipse and right-click the **AndroidManifest.xml** file, which you will find located at the very bottom of your GraphicsDesign project folder on the left side of Eclipse in the Package Explorer navigation pane.

It is interesting to note the AndroidManifest.xml is the one exception in Eclipse as to how the top editing tab is labeled. Notice that the Android Manifest XML tab reads **GraphicsDesign** (Project Folder Name) **Manifest**.

The XML markup should look like what you see in Figure 5-10, and I have highlighted the **android:icon** parameter in the **<application>** tag, where you will reference your own custom launcher icon filename, which you'll do next.

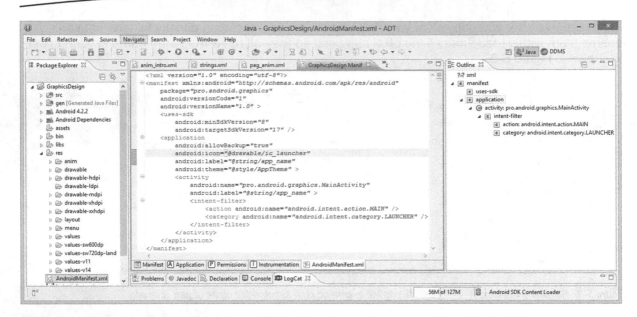

Figure 5-10. *Right-clicking the AndroidManifest.xml file in the Package Explorer to open it for editing in Eclipse*

You'll leave the other default AndroidManifest entries as they are, but you will change the **ic_launcher** reference to **pag_icon** so that you know how to add your own custom launcher icon reference if you want to. Take a look at the other tags in your application's Manifest that Eclipse set up for you.

It is important to note that you could have also left the ic_launcher file reference as-is and named your launcher icon assets **ic_launcher.png** in each of the resolution density folders as well, as an alternative work process.

While you're here, add that **<supports-screens>** tag which you learned about earlier, and fix an additional tag that could make your Android application more professional. Take a look one parameter down (underneath) the android:icon parameter, and you will see the **android:label** parameter.

This parameter controls the text value that is written at the top of your application's splash screen, as well as the text label that is utilized under your application launch icon. The application launch icon is always located at the "front" (i.e. the launch icons area) of the user's Android device; both the icon graphic and label underneath it need to be perfect. The changes to the initial AndroidManifest.xml, which was generated for you via the New Android Application dialog series, are shown in Figure 5-11.

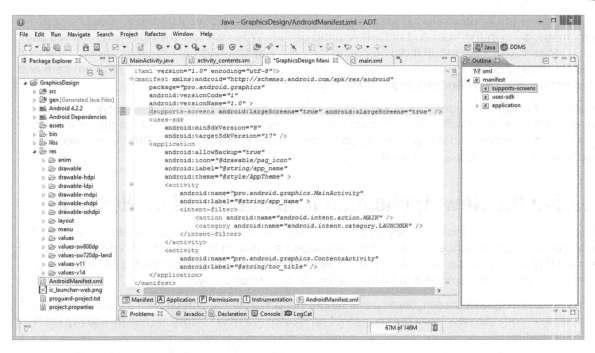

Figure 5-11. *Adding a custom android:icon parameter and a <supports-screens> tag to your AndroidManifest*

As you can see, the **android:label** parameter references a string constant in the **strings.xml** file that is named **app_name**. You need to edit the value of this string constant to add a space between the words Graphics and Design. Click the strings.xml tab, at the top of the central editing pane in Eclipse, and add a space into the app_name <string> tag, so that it reads **Graphics Design** instead of GraphicsDesign, as shown in Figure 5-12.

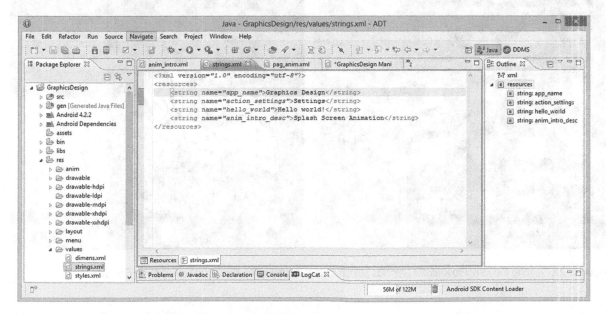

Figure 5-12. *Changing the app_name <string> tag constant to Graphics Design (two words) to fix icon wrap*

This will allow the Android OS to "wrap" the icon label more attractively on the end user's icon launch collection in the front end of their Android device. When we test the app next, you will see that it looks 100% better than it did before. In fact, the way the Android OS was wrapping the icon label has been bothering me for a couple of chapters now. So we're solving that problem here and now. Refinement of an Android app is done in stages.

Making this slight text modification will allow your application icon label to wrap more naturally underneath your new Pro Graphics Design icon, and it will also make your screen title at the top of your app far more readable as well, as you will soon see when you use a **Run As ➤ Android Application** work process in the next section.

Testing the New Application Icon and Label on Nexus One

Now it's time to take a look at how good your density-matched launcher icon looks, as well as the improved label appearance now that you have added a space in between the words Graphics and Design! Right-click the project folder, use the **Run As ➤ Android Application** menu sequence, launch the Nexus One emulator in Eclipse, and look at your app now.

At the top of the splash screen, shown on the right-hand side of the screen shot shown in Figure 5-13, you can see both the new launcher icon asset as well as the new Graphics Design Activity label for your application.

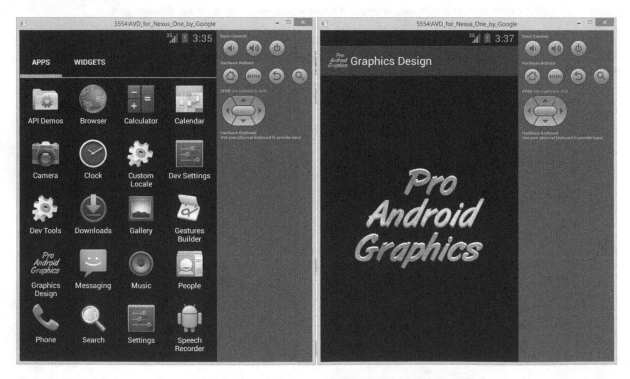

Figure 5-13. *Testing the new Pro Android Graphics launch icon and label in the Nexus One emulator in Eclipse*

To see the icon in the Android OS application icon area, hit the **Go Back** circular button on the top-right of the emulator. This button is the third button from the left in the second row of circular buttons in the upper-right corner of the emulator, and has an arrow on a curved line swooping back, indicating the Return or Go Back function.

Once you click this button, you will be returned to the Android OS Home Screen, where you can click the icons button at the bottom-middle of the screen to open the app icon launch area of the OS, where you will see your new application icon.

Figure 5-13 shows the launch icons area of the emulator on the left side, and the application's splash screen animation and your new title bar label treatment on the right side of the screen shot.

As you can see, subtle changes in code, scaling, and spacing can make all the visual difference regarding the professional appearance of your app! This is why I put this chapter in the book after the new media chapters, as I needed to give you some graphics foundation for the different types of imaging, video, and animation assets and their creation and optimization.

Summary

In this fifth chapter, we took a close look at why the Android OS requires us to provide so many different density versions of our pixel-based assets as well as different versions of our user interface design layouts. This is one of the most tedious areas in Android graphics design, and it is necessitated by the plethora of Android hardware device types, models, and consumer electronics manufacturers located around the world. The same thing that makes Android attractive for developers—the thousands of different Android devices that can run their apps—is also what makes the graphics design part of Android an order of magnitude more difficult that what most people would assume that it would be.

We first took a look at some Android device display characteristics, such as physical resolution, pixel density, DPI, DIP, orientation, aspect ratio, and so on. We looked at the common **screen size qualifier constants** used in Android, which include **small**, **normal**, **large**, and **extra large**.

Next we looked at the **screen density qualifier constants** used in Android, including **low** or **LDPI**, **medium** or **MDPI**, **high** or **HDPI**, **extra high** or **XHDPI**, **extra extra high** or **XXHDPI**, and the newest as of Android 4.3, **extra extra extra high**, or **XXXHDPI**.

You learned that you need to provide pixel-based raster image assets across as many of these **/res/drawable-dpi** folders as possible to give Android the most image assets possible to use in case Android needs to **scale** your digital image assets.

Then we looked at the Android **<supports-screens>** tag, and how it allows us to specify in our AndroidManifest.xml file exactly which screen density devices our applications are going to support. You learned that any screen density display not included will be excluded from being able to download and use your app, so you learned to be very careful about using this tag!

Next, we looked at providing custom layouts, and the various screen layout **configuration qualifiers** that are now available in Android, such as the **smallestWidth,** or **sw#dp** qualifier, and the **width** (**w#dp**) and **height** (**h#dp**) configuration qualifiers. You learned just how these qualifiers work in allowing you to define density ranges across different Android devices that might be using different layout designs, allowing developers to control exactly how an application UI design is going to span across different Android device screens.

We looked more closely at device-optimized density levels, and orientation and aspect ratio configuration qualifiers, so that we can control how our UI designs and content assets can span different display screen sizes, pixel densities, aspect ratios, and screen orientations.

Then we looked at the Android **DisplayMetrics** class and how to use it to be able to **poll** our user's current device display in order to find out which device display characteristics are actually being used with any particular Android hardware device.

Next, you put some of this new knowledge to use, and optimized the launcher icon for your GraphicsDesign application. You did this across all five of the density constant folders currently supported in Android, or at least the density constants that ADT sets up folders for when you use the New Android Application creation process in Eclipse.

In the next chapter, you will learn how to design layouts in Android using the Android **ViewGroup** subclasses. You will learn about the different layout containers that are derived from the Android ViewGroup class, and how to use them in order to design user interface layout containers that span across different types of Android devices. After you do that, you'll be ready to learn about the **View** subclasses and user interface widgets!

Android UI Layouts: Graphics Design Using the ViewGroup Class

In this sixth chapter, we will take a closer look at the different types of screen layout containers that Android offers, and how they can be used to hold our application new media content and user interface designs. This is a logical follow-on to Chapter 5, where I discussed providing UI layouts for different screen sizes, shapes, orientations, and densities.

User interface layouts are implemented in application Activity subclasses by leveraging a number of layout subclasses created using the Android **ViewGroup** superclass. ViewGroup is designed to be subclassed, and that has been done for us dozens of times already, providing custom Android layout container classes. We will be taking a look at several of these in detail in this chapter, as each has a logical use and implementation.

Screen layouts in Android can be bit tricky, not only because we need to design different layouts for different screen sizes, shapes, densities, and orientations, but also because there are several layout container classes in Android's API that are either deprecated, or not yet fully implemented.

This makes decisions regarding which user interface layout containers to use, and how to implement them across Android hardware devices in the market, the most important up-front decisions that you will make as a developer. At the same time, this is one of the most difficult foundational decisions for your Android application that you are likely to encounter in your Android Graphics Design work process currently.

A good analogy can be found in Database design. If you design your database structure incorrectly upfront, and then load data into it, but you forget something, you will have to go back and start over from scratch. At the very least, you will have to write code to read the incorrectly-designed database structure, add in the missing data structure (and data), and then write out the new database structure.

Just as your Activity subclass provides a Java foundation for controlling your application's activities on the screen, your application's XML layout container (ViewGroup subclass) is the XML foundation for the Activity UI.

Android ViewGroup Superclass: A Foundation for Layouts

Android provides the top-level layout class, **ViewGroup**, for use in creating layout container classes. FrameLayout, LinearLayout, and RelativeLayout are the three most widely used layout classes, and we will be covering these as well as more specialized ViewGroup sub-classes throughout this chapter.

The ViewGroup class is part of the **android.view** package, since a ViewGroup class is itself a sub-class of another superclass called the **View** class.

The View class is another class that is not directly used (constructed or instantiated) in your application but is used as a superclass (as a master class template) to not only define screen layout containers, such as ViewGroup and its subclasses, but also to define the many Android user interface widgets that are contained inside these layout containers.

We will be covering View and its widget-related subclasses over the next few chapters as well, as it is important to Android development. However, before we can cover View (widgets) you must master the layout container that holds these UI widgets in place (layouts), and that's exactly why I am spending the next couple of chapters delving deeply into ViewGroups and specialized layouts.

ViewGroup is not used directly in applications, but its many subclasses certainly are, so we are going to cover the major ones in detail next.

We are not going to focus on the ViewGroup class as a master class a whole lot here, but it's important to realize that you could create your own custom subclasses if you wanted to; however, that has essentially already been done for you, as you will see in this chapter.

Since what I am trying to do with this book is sling-shot you way ahead in your knowledge of Pro Android Graphics, we're going to focus on covering how to implement the existing layout classes (existing ViewGroup subclasses), which are the most commonly used and are implemented by other developers.

After we cover those primary ViewGroup subclasses, which are already coded for you and are available for your development use, chances are good that you will probably decide to simply utilize one of those for the UI layout.

In the next couple of sections, we will cover the primary ViewGroup layout parameters and constants as well as which of the many ViewGroup sub-classes are deprecated (discontinued and will be removed at some point in time) and experimental (not fully implemented and may be removed at some point in time). If you want to research ViewGroup even further, you will find a summary page on the Android Developer web site at the following URL:

```
http://developer.android.com/reference/android/view/ViewGroup.html
```

In deference to the reader, we will focus on those layout container classes that are here to stay and widely used, and that currently provide layout functionality which, when used optimally, provides a good user experience.

The ViewGroup LayoutParams Class: Layout Parameters

There are two different types of layout parameters for the ViewGroup class that span across all of its many subclasses. These are termed **base** layout parameters, and there are **constants** in Android to use for each of these.

The first one **expands the UI layout container** so that it fills the screen (the parent) above it in that dimension (width or height). We have already utilized the parameter constant **MATCH_PARENT** before in our GraphicsDesign application development. You may also use this as lower-case **match_parent**.

It is important to note that prior to Android 2.2 API Level 8 (Froyo) this was called **FILL_PARENT;** however, I suggest using MATCH_PARENT, since most current devices are Android 2.3.3 (Gingerbread) or later anyway. In fact, only 5% of the market currently is comprised of pre-Android 2.2 devices!

If you want to see the current market share percentages for the different API Levels, you can find them at the Android Dashboards web page:

http://developer.android.com/about/dashboards/index.html

The other layout parameter constant does the exact opposite of the match_parent parameter constant, and **contracts to fit around the content**, which is inside the layout container in that width or height dimension. This constant is called the **wrap_content** and it is aptly named as it can wrap itself around your content. It is important to note that since Android provides these constants for both the X (width) and Y (height) dimensions, they can be used together, as you'll be seeing later on in this book.

For example, if you wanted your Button UI element to span across a parent layout container, you would code the **android:layout_width="match_parent"** parameter, and then use **android:layout_height="wrap_content"** so the height of the button would then conform to the Button's (text label) content, and the width would then be defined by the entire UI layout container's width.

Since, as you know from the last chapter, you want your UI to **scale to fit** different display screens, these parameters are a good place to start to achieve this objective. Mastering these parameters makes the UI development easier, more accurate, more flexible, more elegant, and ultimately more powerful.

You can also provide an exact number for the layout_width or layout_height parameters, but in light of what you read in Chapter 5 and the deprecation of AbsoluteLayout containers, I suggest you do not use these "hard-coded" values unless you're delivering your application to one specific "captive" hardware device.

It is important to note there are subclasses of **LayoutParams** for different subclasses of ViewGroup. For example, the deprecated AbsoluteLayout class has its own subclass of LayoutParams, which adds in an X and Y value.

If you wish to review the Android LayoutParams class further, you can find it located at the following Android Developer web site URL:

http://developer.android.com/reference/android/view/ViewGroup.LayoutParams.html

Next, we'll take a quick look at the layout classes that we are not going to cover (in detail) or code with in this book. This is because they have either been discontinued for use (deprecated) or are not fully implemented (i.e. they are experimental) in the API as yet.

Deprecated Layouts: AbsoluteLayout and SlidingDrawer

There are two layout container classes that are still in the Android API but have been deprecated. The **AbsoluteLayout** layout container class was deprecated long ago in **API Level 3,** or Android Version **1.5**, known as **Cupcake**. The **SlidingDrawer** layout container class was deprecated quite recently in **API Level 17**, or Android Version **4.2**, known as **Jelly Bean**.

An AbsoluteLayout would be used for absolute positioning, that is, layouts that allow you specify the exact physical pixel locations (X and Y pixel coordinates) of the layout children tags. AbsoluteLayout is less flexible and more difficult to span across devices than other types of layouts that use a more relative positioning.

In fact, after learning all about across-device layout and asset support, as you did in Chapter 5, it is clear that this class was deprecated when it became obvious to Android OS API developers that there were going to be a plethora (currently hundreds) of widely differing Android manufacturers, and their products, to support.

Although there is no official statement from Google as to why the SlidingDrawer layout container was deprecated, there are a lot of developers asking in forums why it was deprecated. After all, it was a pretty cool UI container that could animate your UI into view from all sides of the screen.

In my opinion, it was eliminated for one of the following reasons. First, it animates an entire screen area over another screen area, which has to be hard on the device's processor. Secondly, it allows UI designers to do whatever they like, as far as UI location and functionality, and Android is moving towards more standardized UI approach across both OS and apps.

Finally, it may well be stepping on someone else's patent; there are other deprecated classes that seem to fall into this category, and there are a lot of lawsuits between major mobile OS players right now that pertain to UI design and UI layout methods and how they allow the UI to function.

Lucky for us developers, there is the **DrawerLayout** layout container class, which appears to have replaced the SlidingDrawer layout container class. For this reason, we will have a section on the DrawerLayout container in this chapter, and we will leave in-depth coverage of AbsoluteLayout and SlidingDrawers classes out of this book, as they are no longer supported.

Android's Experimental Layout: SlidingPaneLayout

Not only are there deprecated layout containers in Android, but there are experimental ones in the API as well. "Experimental" means that the layout container could be removed at any time. Use experimental classes at your own risk! One of these experimental classes is Android's **SlidingPaneLayout** class and layout container.

Since the SlidingPaneLayout is pretty cool, I'll give it a page or two in this chapter, but until it becomes a permanent part of the API I won't use it in any code, or go into further detail regarding it in future chapters, as I will do with most of the other layout containers we cover in this chapter.

The Android SlidingPaneLayout class is a sub-class of ViewGroup, and it is found in the **android. support.v4.widget** package in the Android OS. So if you want to import this class, the import statement reference would read

```
import android.support.v4.widget.SlidingPaneLayout;
```

This is one of the longer import statement references in the Android OS.

The SlidingPaneLayout container allows developers to create horizontal multiple pane layouts for use at the top level of their user interface.

The left and primary pane is usually treated as the content list or the content browser, and is subordinate to the primary detail viewport used for displaying the actual displayed content.

SlidingPaneLayout child tags (View) may overlap the pane if their combined width is greater than the available width within the SlidingPaneLayout.

When this occurs, the user will be able to slide the upper view out of the way by dragging it or by navigating toward the direction of the overlapped view using a navigation key on their keyboard, if they have one installed.

If the child view's content can be scrolled horizontally, a user can grab the layout container by its edge and also drag that content horizontally.

Because of its sliding attributes, SlidingPaneLayout could be deemed appropriate for creating layouts that will smoothly adapt across many different screen sizes. This would mean that the UI could expand completely when on larger display screens and "accordion" as necessary on smaller display screens.

A SlidingPaneLayout layout container should be considered as distinct from a navigation drawer, which we will be looking at in a future section of this chapter. A SlidingPanel and DrawerLayout should not be used in the same design scenarios, as you will soon see.

A SlidingPaneLayout container should be conceived as a way for your UI design to allow a two-pane layout normally used on a larger screen to be able to adapt to a smaller screen in a logical way.

The user interface interaction offered by this SlidingPaneLayout container should allow the end user to see an app's informational hierarchy between the UI panes. This inter-pane content relationship may not always exist with a DrawerLayout container design approach where the navigation UI elements take the user to different places or functions within the app and do not as directly relate to the content in the app screen at hand.

The Android Developer web site makes it clear that the logical UI design usage of the SlidingPaneLayout container should include pairings of panes with logical use bindings. An example of this would be a phone number list with related dial or tagging features, a city or street list with related map features, a contact list and UI allowing interaction with the contact, or a recent e-mail list with a content pane displaying the message in the selected e-mail.

UI design usage of a SlidingPaneLayout container that might be better suited to the DrawerLayout container would include high-level (Activity) function screen switching between more global functions within your app. Examples of this might include jumping from a Table Of Contents (TOC) view screen in an e-book app to a view screen of your bookmark setting utility.

UI designs for navigating amongst the functional areas of your application should use the navigation drawer pattern. As you will see later on in this chapter, as well as later on in the book, this DrawerLayout container can be used to provide access to top-level app navigation icons in a cool way.

Similar to the LinearLayout container, which we will be covering a little bit later in the chapter, the SlidingPaneLayout container will support the use of weight layout parameter **android:layout_weight** for any of its child views. It uses this parameter setting to determine how to divide remaining space after the screen width measurement is complete. The parameter value for android:layout_weight only applies to width in this layout container.

When views do not overlap, the android:layout_weight parameter will behave as it would with a LinearLayout. When the panes do overlap, weight on a slideable pane indicates that the pane needs to be sized to fill available space in its closed state.

Weight on a pane that is covered indicates that the pane should be resized to fit all of the available container width, except for a thin strip that the user should use to grab the slideable view and pull it back over into its closed state.

Until the Android Developer web site lists this layout as fully implemented (not experimental), you may want to consider using another layout container or be ready to recode your user interface design in the event that Android decides to pull this layout container back out of the API.

Next, we'll take a look at one of the most used layout containers of them all, the Relative Layout container, which allows complex UI designs to be assembled using a single parent layout container tag <RelativeLayout> containing the child tag UI widgets and parameters that position them relatively to each other.

Android RelativeLayout Class: Designing Relative Layouts

The Android **RelativeLayout** class is the type of layout container that is utilized if you specify the blank application template in the New Android App series of dialogs, as we saw in the first part of this book when we created an empty Android application bootstrap set of files to work from.

Android RelativeLayout is a **ViewGroup** class that renders its children View objects (widgets) in screen positions that are relative to one another. Earlier in the book you learned that the Android ADT IDE will look at the parent layout container that your UI widget is contained in, and then bring up a parameter list (which you learned is invoked by typing **android:** inside any given UI or layout container tag). Do you remember how long the parameter list was when you were inside the RelativeLayout container type? This portends the power that is afforded by RelativeLayout parameters and constants, of which there are literally dozens.

The position of a given View object contained in a RelativeLayout container can be specified as **relative to sibling elements**. There are two dozen constants that can be utilized for specifying relative positioning, including **ABOVE, BELOW, ALIGN_LEFT, ALIGH_RIGHT, ALIGN_BASELINE, START_OF, END_OF, ALIGN_PARENT_TOP, ALIGN_PARENT_BOTTOM, ALIGN_END, CENTER_VERTICAL, CENTER_HORIZONTAL**, and ten others. If you want to see the complete list of RelativeLayout constants, visit the Android Developer web site via this URL:

`http://developer.android.com/reference/android/widget/RelativeLayout.html`

The RelativeLayout container allows complex user interface designs in a **single layout container** by providing lots of layout parameters for the widget tags that are contained within the <RelativeLayout> parent tag.

For this reason, this user interface layout container has become popular with developers for designing complex user interface designs, because it can eliminate nested ViewGroups (layout containers), which keeps a layout container hierarchy flat. Less nested structures of any kind, especially other layout container structures, can save system memory, which improves application performance and reduces processor overhead.

If you find yourself being forced to utilize multiple nested LinearLayout containers in order to achieve your UI design objective, then you may wish to replace the many LinearLayout containers with one single RelativeLayout container. You would then utilize RelativeLayout compatible parameters and constants within the RelativeLayout container in order to achieve the same layout end result that would otherwise require using multiple (nested hierarchies) user interface layout containers.

Since we'll be leveraging RelativeLayout containers throughout this book, I will leave all other learning content relative to this XML tag (no pun intended) to the hands-on XML markup and Java coding that we will be doing in the rest of this book.

Android LinearLayout Class: Designing Linear Layouts

The Android LinearLayout class supports an instantiation in Java of layout containers styled using the <LinearLayout> XML tag. This layout container is meant to be used to define simple horizontal or vertical user interface layouts, such as a row of buttons along the top of the Activity screen, or a column of UI image icons at the left side of the screen, for instance.

A LinearLayout container always arranges its children in a single column or in a single row. The **orientation** of the row (the **horizontal** orientation constant) or the column (the **vertical** orientation constant) can be set by calling the **.setOrientation()** method in your Java code, or it can be set in your XML markup that sets up and configures your LinearLayout container.

The default orientation parameter, if you do not set it up specifically, will be horizontal, as most linear layouts span across the top or bottom of the screen. If you want a vertical UI layout, use an **android:orientation** parameter and set it to the **vertical** constant.

All children of the LinearLayout tag will be **stacked** on top of each other (in vertical orientation) or one after the other (horizontal orientation).

A vertical LinearLayout will have one UI element (child tag) per row, no matter how wide the UI element may be, although it looks more professional if the UI elements are all of uniform width. Horizontal LinearLayouts will always be one row high, and the height will be determined using the height of the tallest UI element (child tag) and will include any padding.

A LinearLayout will take into account any margins between its UI elements (the child tags) and the gravity (center, right, or left) alignment of any of the child tags.

You can also specify your LinearLayout's gravity using the **.setGravity()** method. As you know, specifying the layout gravity will set the alignment (center, left, right, etc.) of all of the child elements in that layout.

You can also specify that certain children grow to fill up any remaining space in the layout by setting a **weight** parameter. The LinearLayout weight indicates how much of the extra space (if there is any) in a LinearLayout should be allocated to the layout container if it does not fill its parent container. This is usually the screen if the LinearLayout is an Activity's primary layout container.

To set a weight, use a **zero** if the layout container is not to be stretched or use a decimal number between 0.0 and 1.0 to prorate any of those extra pixels amongst all of the UI elements (child tags) within the container.

If you need something more complex than a single row or column of user interface elements, consider using a RelativeLayout container, as it will be more memory efficient than nesting multiple LinearLayout containers.

Android FrameLayout Class: Designing Frame Layouts

We have already used the Android FrameLayout container to hold our Digital Video asset in Chapter 2. FrameLayouts are holders or "frames" intended to hold one other structure inside them, such as an image or video asset.

The FrameLayout was designed to allocate an area of the screen to display one single item. Although you can use it for your own UI designs, realize that is also often used as a superclass for many other useful UI layout container subclasses in Android, such as **AppWidgetHostView**, **CalendarView**, **MediaController**, **GestureOverlayView**, **HorizontalScrollView**, **ViewAnimator**, **ScrollView**, **TabHost**, **DatePicker**, and **TimePicker**.

Generally, a FrameLayout should be utilized to hold one single child View, because it can be difficult to organize your child views in a way that is scalable between differing display sizes without the children overlapping each other.

You can, however, add multiple UI elements (child tags) to the FrameLayout and control their position within the FrameLayout by assigning the gravity parameter to each child tag. This would make your FrameLayout scalable by Android at runtime, using one of the 27 **android:layout_gravity** constants, which are described in detail at the following Android Developer web site URL:

```
http://developer.android.com/reference/android/view/Gravity.html
```

The FrameLayout children tags (View widgets) are drawn as a stack with the most recently added child on the top. The size of a FrameLayout expands to fit the size of its largest child plus its padding, visible or not, if the FrameLayout parent tag supports a visibility parameter.

It is important to note that child tags (View widgets) that are currently invisible because they've been specified via an Android **View.GONE** constant instead of using **View.INVISIBLE** will be utilized for FrameLayout container sizing purposes only if the **.setConsiderGoneChildrenWhenMeasuring()** method is called using a **true** parameter.

As you can see, the FrameLayout container is deceptively complex, and is actually intended more for usage as a superclass for creating other more specialized layout containers than it is for use as a mainstream developer UI design container (like LinearLayout or RelativeLayout).

It can be useful for holding single UI element layouts such as full-screen digital video using a VideoView UI element widget, especially if the video needs to maintain its aspect ratio when it is scaled by the Android OS to fit different screen sizes or aspect ratios. This is a somewhat specialized use-case scenario, however, so don't try to use a FrameLayout if there is another layout container class that will fit your UI design usage better.

Next, let's take a look at the GridLayout container for use in grid UI layouts.

Android GridLayout Class: Designing UI Layout Grids

The Android **GridLayout** container class does just what its name suggests: it places its UI element child tags into a rectangular grid. This layout class is quite similar to the LinearLayout container; in fact, it has many parameters that are the same as or similar to LinearLayout's. If you change a <LinearLayout> container parent tag to a **<GridLayout>** container parent container tag in the XML definition, the chances are good that your child tags in both container types will work just as they are coded!

This GridLayout's virtual grid user interface container is comprised of a set of **infinitely thin** (that is, zero pixels used) lines that separate a viewing area into discrete user interface layout cells.

Within the Android GridLayout API, the grid lines are referred to by using **grid indices**. A grid with a certain number (N) of columns will have N + 1 grid indices, which will run from 0 through N inclusive.

Regardless of how your GridLayout container might be configured, a grid index of 0 will be fixed to the leading edge of the container and a grid index of N will be fixed to its trailing edge, after padding is taken into account, as we have seen in the other layout container types.

Your UI elements (child tags) will occupy one or more of these GridLayout cells, the number of which will be determined by the Android **rowSpec** (row specifier) and **columnSpec** (column specifier) grid layout parameters.

Each of these specifier parameters defines the set of rows or columns that are to be occupied, and how children should be aligned within the resulting group of cells.

The cells in a GridLayout container do not overlap; however, a GridLayout container also does not prevent child tag elements from being defined to occupy the same cell, or to span across a group of cells. So cells do not have to be square (1:1 aspect ratio); they can be portrait or landscape.

In the scenarios of same-cell occupation or spanning, there's no guarantee that child tags will not overlap each other after a grid layout operation completes, so make sure you test your creative GridLayout containers well!

If a GridLayout container child tag does not set any row or column indices for a given cell that it wishes to occupy, the GridLayout class will then assign a cell location automatically. This is done in a logical fill order specified within the class following the GridLayout orientation, rowCount, and columnCount parameter settings.

You can also set custom spacing between child tag elements by specifying a **leftMargin**, **topMargin**, **bottomMargin**, **rightMargin**, or **Margin** (which adds the value to all four margins) layout parameter. You can alternatively use the Android **Space** class to create empty space within certain GridLayout cells.

The Android Space class is a lightweight View subclass that can be used to create empty space between user interface elements in layout containers like GridLayout. There is more information on the Space class at this URL:

http://developer.android.com/reference/android/widget/Space.html

When the GridLayout parent tag's **useDefaultMargins** parameter has been set, a predefined margin is applied around each child tag. This margin space is calculated automatically by the Android OS based on an Android UI style guide.

Each of the global automatic margins defined by Android can be overridden at the local UI element level by an assignment of the aforementioned margin parameters.

It is important to note that these default values will generally produce an acceptable spacing result between your child user interface elements, but the automatic (style guide) values could also change between different releases of the Android platform, so it may be better to add a little more XML markup (parameters), and take control over your UI spacing yourself.

A GridLayout container's distribution of extra space is based on priority, rather than weight, since this container, unlike the LinearLayout, has no weight parameter options. In fact, this is one of the primary differences between the LinearLayout and the GridLayout user interface containers.

The child tag (UI element in grid cell) capability to span cells will be ascertained by the GridLayout class using the android:gravity parameter for the child UI element that sets the alignment property of its row and column groups. If alignment is defined along a certain X or Y axis, then the UI element in that cell is marked as flexible in that direction. If no alignment is set using the android:gravity parameter, then the UI element is instead assumed to be fixed in the grid and thus inflexible.

To assure that a row or column will resize, make sure that each of the UI elements defined inside it (via child tags) define the android:gravity parameter. To prevent your row or column from resizing, you need to make sure that at least one of the user interface elements inside that row or column does not define (set) the android:gravity parameter.

If you have multiple UI elements inside the same row or column (group), they will be considered to act in parallel. This type of grouping will be considered to be flexible if all of the components within it are flexible and defined using the android:gravity parameter.

You may be thinking at this point: Don't you mean android:layout_gravity? There are actually two layout gravity parameters, android:layout_gravity and android:gravity! How's that for confusion! You'll use android:gravity as your parameter selection when you are setting the layout gravity that is inside your UI element (View object) and android:layout_gravity for specifying gravity outside your layout container object or ViewGroup object.

To think about this in a slightly different way, just to make absolutely sure that you have it straight, an **android:gravity** parameter specifies the direction in which the UI element (View) content should align **inside of a child tag UI element** (View object).

Conversely, an **android:layout_gravity** should be used to specify an **outside gravity** for that View. This means specifying the direction for which that View should touch its parent tag's (ViewGroup object's) container border.

Row and column groups that exist on either side of a GridLayout boundary or internal border will be considered to act serially and not in parallel.

In keeping with the "flexibility principle" for GridLayouts, a group made up of these two elements will be flexible if one of its component elements is flexible. When this flexibility principle does not provide your UI with complete disambiguity, the GridLayout class algorithms will favor rows and columns that are located close to the layout container's right and bottom edges. This is logical because, as we know, graphics and layouts in Android begin at X,Y screen coordinates of 0,0 which is the upper-left corner.

As I mentioned earlier, unlike LinearLayout, the GridLayout container does not currently provide support for the parameter called **weight**. In general, it is therefore not currently possible to configure a GridLayout container to distribute the excess space between multiple components. If you need this functionality, use a LinearLayout container.

You can accommodate many of your auto-resizing needs for the GridLayout by simply using the android:gravity parameter with the CENTER value constant. This will add in equal amounts of spacing around your child UI element in your cell or cell group.

If you want to get really tricky, you can command complete control over the excess space distribution in your row or column by using the LinearLayout container as a child UI element to contain your UI components within those associated cells or cell groups. This will most likely take more memory to achieve, so make sure that it is really necessary before you implement it.

It is also interesting to note that you should not need to use either of the Android size value constants WRAP_CONTENT or MATCH_PARENT when you are configuring the child tags (UI elements) within your GridLayout container. The GridLayout parent tag, however, will normally utilize the MATCH_PARENT constant for the width and height layout parameters, so that it fills the Activity screen.

You can even use a GridLayout without specifying which cells your UI elements will be placed in and let the GridLayout class algorithm do this for you. The safe way to declare a GridLayout has each UI element (widget) layout parameters specifying **row and column indices**, which together define precisely where the UI element needs to be placed. When either or both of these values are not specified, the GridLayout class will calculate grid cell location values for you (rather than throwing an error or exception).

If you don't specify row or column indices (values, or integer numbers), the child UI elements will be added to a GridLayout. To do this, GridLayout keeps track of a **cursor position**, much like reading a SQLite database, which it will utilize to place widgets into cells that don't have anything in them. It will calculate this based on a GridLayout orientation parameter setting, since like a LinearLayout, a GridLayout can be either horizontal (landscape) or vertical (portrait).

In fact, to fit different device orientations, something we looked at in Chapter 5, you may want to design one of each of these specific GridLayout orientations to fit iTVs and tablets (horizontal landscape orientation) and one to fit smartphones and e-Readers (vertical portrait orientation).

When your GridLayout orientation property is set to **horizontal,** and you've specified the **android:columnCount** parameter that defines how many columns your layout will have, a cursor position will be maintained for automatic layouts with a separate height index stored for each column. If you supply your own indices, this never gets used, which is what I recommend.

Otherwise, when auto-generated UI element indices need to be created for you, the GridLayout class will first determines the size of a cell group by looking for any **android:layout_rowSpan** and **android:layout_columnSpan** parameters for the UI element, and then, starting at the cursor position, it will step through all of the available cell locations from left to right and then top to bottom, in order to find the row and column indices of the first location that is free for use.

When your GridLayout orientation parameter is set to vertical, all of the same principles apply, except that the horizontal and vertical axes are switched, so the population goes top to bottom and left to right and the cursor stores a width position (from left towards the right) rather than a height position from top to bottom.

So, a horizontal orientation is populated just like Westerners read a book, and a vertical orientation is populated like you would read ancient scrolls with hieroglyphics on them.

If you want multiple user interface elements to be placed into the exact same cell, then you would have to define their indices explicitly. This is because the automatic child element allocation procedure described above is designed to place the user interface element widgets in separate cells.

You may be wondering: Wouldn't it be more efficient to use a TableLayout than a GridLayout? In fact, the GridLayout is more memory efficient than the TableLayout and does not require the TableRows feature, so I would suggest getting comfortable with GridLayout, as it is one of the most flexible and efficient user interface layout containers in Android. Strangely, it is often overlooked by most developers. But not by you; you are going to master it in this chapter! RelativeLayouts can also be coded as GridLayouts with a little bit of creativity in defining the relative relationships into rows and columns.

As I mentioned earlier, basic FrameLayout configurations can be nested and accommodated inside the cells of a GridLayout because a single cell can contain multiple View or ViewGroup objects.

To switch between two View or ViewGroup objects, you would place both of them into the same cell, and then leverage each via a **visibility parameter** by using the constant **GONE** in order to switch between one ViewGroup to the other ViewGroup (or View) from inside your Java code.

As you can see, with a little creativity, something that seems as basic as a GridLayout container can become much more powerful due to nesting and the number of parameters and constants that it supports within Android OS.

Next, we'll take a look at another powerful layout container that was recently added to Android in Version 4, the DrawerLayout. In fact, a DrawerLayout could contain a GridLayout for a complex UI drawer treatment that would still be memory efficient, given that you set it up correctly.

The DrawerLayout Class: Designing UI Drawer Layouts

The **DrawerLayout** class is also a subclass of ViewGroup, and it is stored in the **android.support. v4.widget** package, which indicates that this is an all-new layout container as of Android 4.0 and later. A full import statement reference to this class is **android.support.v4.widget.DrawerLayout.**

A DrawerLayout container is designed to function as the top-level layout container for the user interface content that you wish to be contained inside an interactive "sliding drawer" user interface layout container.

These UI containers can be "pulled out" of the left or right sides of the screen by your users, using handles located at either side of the display screen. The UI Drawer position, as well as its layout, is controlled by using the **android:layout_gravity** attribute in your child views. These should correspond to the side of the screen from which you want your UI Drawer to dragged out from, so use either android:layout_gravity="LEFT" or android:layout_gravity="RIGHT." Be sure to not specify the CENTER constant, or any of the other gravity constants.

To use a DrawerLayout, position your primary content layout container View (ViewGroup) as the first child of the DrawerLayout tag, using layout_width and layout_height parameters set to **match_parent**.

Next, add your UI drawers as child tags (Views or ViewGroups) right after this primary content layout container, and set a layout_gravity parameter to be either the LEFT or the RIGHT layout_gravity constant.

Make absolutely sure not to use the TOP or BOTTOM (or any other constants) layout_gravity settings, as this class is not intended to provide vertical drawers, only horizontal ones, and will likely throw an exception.

To create one single UI drawer that spans the entire side of your screen, your UI Drawer content tag should make use of the **match_parent** constant for the **android:layout_height** parameter to set the full height of the screen.

For the **android:layout_width** parameter, you would next use the fixed width that you want to use for the UI Drawer width, specified using a **DIP value**.

The **DrawerLayout.DrawerListener** Java interface can be utilized to monitor the state and the motion of your UI drawer implementation so that your Java code can do things when the drawer is open, closed, or being dragged.

The Android DrawerListener has four methods that you can place custom Java code in to control what your Drawer UI does during these states. The methods are all declared as **abstract** and **void** and include **onDrawerClosed()** and **onDrawerOpened()** as well as **onDrawerSlide()**, which is called when your user is dragging the handle, and **onDrawerStateChanged()** to signal when the drawer goes from closed to open or vice versa.

It would be smart to avoid using expensive processing functions in your DrawerListener methods, such as using animation inside a drawer, as this may cause stilted performance as the UI Drawer is being dragged out.

If for some reason you must implement processor-expensive operations in a UI Drawer, be sure to invoke this code during the DrawerLayout **STATE_IDLE** state. The other state constants for DrawerLayout include **STATE_DRAGGING**, **STATE-SETTLING**, and for locking, **LOCK_MODE_UNLOCKED**, **LOCK_MODE_LOCKED_OPEN**, and **LOCK_MODE_LOCKED_CLOSED**.

There is also **DrawerLayout.SimpleDrawerListener**, which offers the default (no special options) implementation of each of the DrawerListener callback methods. Use this if you are just accessing the core functionality of the UI DrawerLayout class as it provides simpler, more memory efficient code.

To remain consistent with the Android OS design principles, any UI drawers located on the left side of the screen should contain UI elements that are intended for (global) navigation of your application. Conversely, UI Drawers that contain UI elements that invoke operations or functionality local to the current screen content should be positioned on the right side of the screen.

Staying true to these Android navigation rules will keep user confusion to a minimum by utilizing the exact same "navigation on the left, actions on the right" UI structure that is currently in use in the Android Action Bar and elsewhere within the Android OS UI design.

Navigation drawer user interface design is such an in-depth topic that there is a chapter on it later in the book, once you get a few more foundational user interface layout principles under your belt.

However, if you wish to take a closer look now, you can find some more in-depth information on it at the following Android Developer web site URL:

```
http://developer.android.com/reference/android/support/v4/widget/DrawerLayout.html
```

Adding Menu Items to Access the UI Layout Container

To really be able to develop a new user interface layout, you need to code a new Activity that has a functional screen, rather than using the Splash Screen for your application. Before you can code a new Android Activity, you will need to be able to access it from your MainActivity.java Splash Screen Activity. This will be done using an **Options Menu**, which was added to your app when you created a New Android App (blank Activity option), so all you have to do is modify the existing Menu XML markup and Java code.

All you have to do to add a couple new functions to your app is to add some Menu items in the XML file in your /res/menu folder, and the MenuInflater class code that is already in your MainActivity will inflate those values for you and configure your Options Menu object using those parameter values.

If you want to research the Android MenuInflater class further, there is a page that covers it on the Android Developer web site at the following URL:

```
http://developer.android.com/reference/android/view/MenuInflater.html
```

Let's open the Menu XML definition that was created for you in the New Android Application series of dialogs by opening the /res/menu folder, as shown in Figure 6-1, and right-clicking the main.xml file inside the folder, and selecting the Open command or pressing the F3 function key.

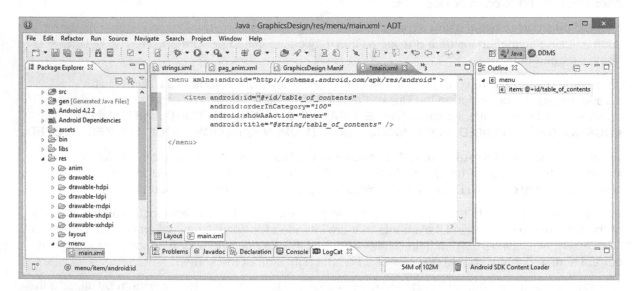

Figure 6-1. *Editing your first <menu> tag <item> tag to make it a Table of Contents options menu selection item*

Edit the android:id parameter to rename it with what its new function is, table_of_contents, and also edit the android:title parameter to match that as well using the @string/ reference prefix, which tells Android to look in the **/res/values/strings.xml** file to find the <string> constant definition.

Once you have this first <menu> parent tag <item> child tag created, you can then create a second menu item simply by copying this entire <item> tag structure and pasting it underneath itself, as shown in Figure 6-2.

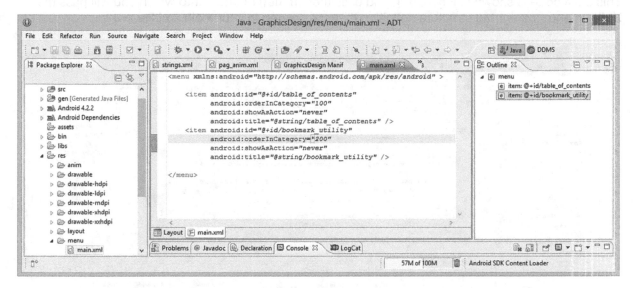

Figure 6-2. Copying and editing the first <menu> parent container <item> tag to create a second Bookmark menu item

Let's do that now, and change the second <item> tag's table_of_contents ID and menu title (label) references to **bookmark_utility**, so that you have bookmarking set up as well for your Pro Android Graphics e-book app. There's one other change you need to make to the **android:orderInCategory** parameter so that the Bookmark Utility menu option comes after the Table of Contents menu option. Set a value for this parameter to **200**, as shown in Figure 6-2.

Now all you have to do is edit the strings.xml file in your /res/values folder to change the existing menu option string constant to read **Table of Contents**, and then copy and paste it underneath itself to change its values to support your **Bookmark Utility** menu option, as shown in Figure 6-3.

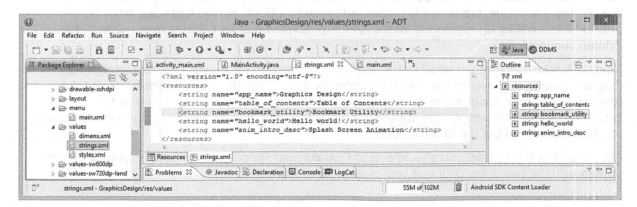

Figure 6-3. Adding <string> constants for Table of Contents and Bookmark Utility menu items to strings.xml file

Now let's click the **MainActivity.java** editing tab in Eclipse and take a quick look at the code that will **inflate** your new options menu items XML in your **main.xml** file and load it into a Java **Menu object** named **menu**.

This Java code is shown in Figure 6-4, and uses the **.inflate()** method, into which you will pass the XML <menu> parent tag structure definition that you created in your main.xml file.

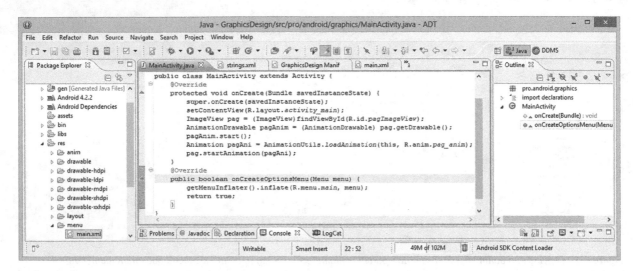

Figure 6-4. Looking at the onCreateOptionsMenu() method and getMenuInflater().inflate() method in MainActivity

You will pass your menu XML definition into the .inflate() method by using a reference path of **R.menu.main,** which breaks down into **R** (resource folder), **.menu** (menu sub-folder), **.main** (main.xml file).

This is called off of the **getMenuInflater()** method, using dot notation to **chain** the two methods together, as shown in the following line of code:

```
getMenuInflater().inflate(R.menu.main, menu);
```

After the MenuInflater class has populated the Menu object with the definition you created in XML, the return true; statement is processed to return a Boolean true flag value from the onCreateOptionsMenu() method to let the Android OS know that an Options menu object was inflated successfully.

Next, let's take a look at the results of your menu alterations in the Nexus One emulator in Eclipse to make sure everything is working correctly. Right-click the project folder, and use the **Run As ➤ Android Application** menu sequence to launch the emulator, and use the MENU button in the Nexus One emulator on the upper-right of the emulator. It is the second button in the second row of buttons from the top of the emulator.

After you click this button, you should see an Options menu pop up at the bottom of your Splash Screen with the two items on it that you created (see Figure 6-5).

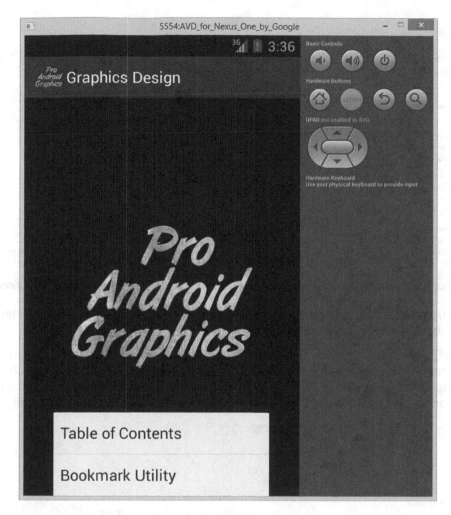

Figure 6-5. Testing your new Options menu in the Nexus One emulator

Now that you have your Options menu inflated with the existing Java and XML code that was in your app already, you will need to create a new method in your MainActivity.java Java code that will call new Activity screens once these Options menu items are selected by your users.

First, however, you will need a second Activity to call in that code, so let's create your app's second Activity class to hold a Table of Contents screen design for your Pro Android Graphics e-book app.

Creating a Table of Contents Activity for Your UI Design

Let's create a new Java Class in Eclipse. You do this by right-clicking your GraphicsDesign project folder at the top of the Package Explorer pane, as shown in Figure 6-6, and selecting the **New ➤ Class** menu command sequence.

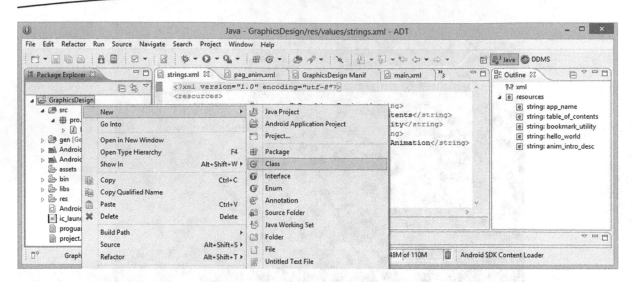

Figure 6-6. Right-clicking the GraphicDesign project folder and selecting New ➤ Class menu items to create a new Activity

This will open up the New Java Class dialog, which will allow you to specify the characteristics of the new Activity subclass that you want to create.

Make sure the Source folder is set to **GraphicsDesign/src** and the Package is set to your **pro.android.graphics** package name. Set the Name field to be **ContentsActivity**, which will create the name ContentsActivity.java for your file, and then click the **Browse** button next to the **Superclass** field and type an "a" character in the **Choose a type** field to narrow your search (see Figure 6-7).

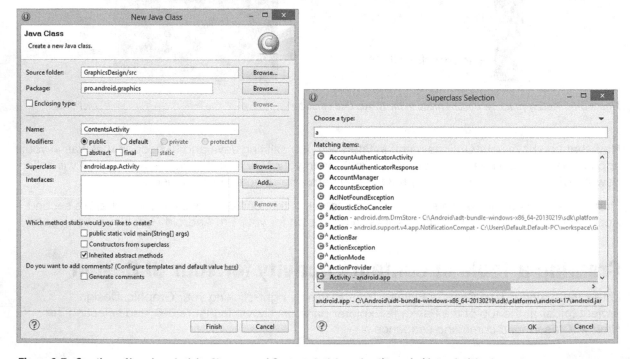

Figure 6-7. Creating a New Java Activity Class named ContentsActivity using the android.app.Activity Superclass

Scroll down until you see the Activity class and click it to select it for use as your Superclass value, and then click the OK button in the Superclass Selection sub-dialog to return to the New Java Class main dialog. Then click the Finish button to create the new Java Activity in Eclipse. Once this is done, you will see your new **ContentsActivity.java** class open in a tab in the central editing pane of Eclipse, as shown in Figure 6-8. Notice that your **package** declaration, **import statement**, and **public class ContentsActivity extends Activity** declaration are all in place and ready to add Java code into, which you are going to do next.

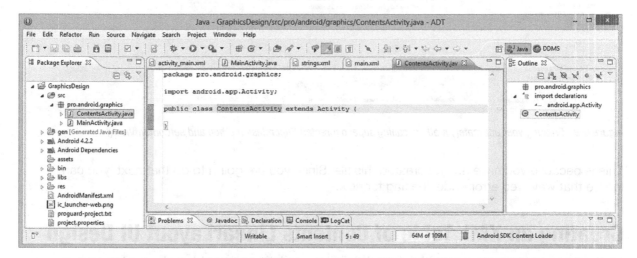

Figure 6-8. Your new public class ContentsActivity extends Activity Superclass in a pro.android.graphics package

To create your Activity, you will first need to call your Superclass Activity onCreate() method by using the **super.onCreate(saveInstanceState);** line of code inside your **protected void onCreate(Bundle saveInstanceState)** method.

You did the same thing in your MainActivity.java class. In fact, if you want to copy similar code from the MainActivity.java editing tab in Eclipse, it will save you some time typing it in!

The next line of code in your onCreate() method will give the Activity that you created in the first line of code a screen layout (user interface) by using the setContentView() method with a reference path to the layout XML file that you are going to create next.

Since you know that this is going to be in the /res/layout folder and that you are going to name it activity_contents.xml, you can insert the reference path now using the R.layout.activity_contents, so your method call looks like the following line of code:

```
setContentView(R.layout.activity_contents);
```

This is all you need to do in order to set up a new Activity; create it, and then set its ContentView to your XML screen layout definition. You may notice in Figure 6-9 that Eclipse has error flagged an XML file reference!

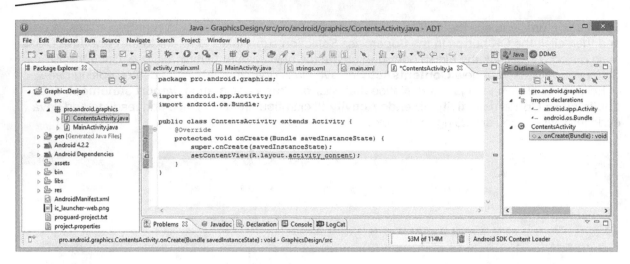

Figure 6-9. *Creating your onCreate() method, calling super.onCreate() Superclass method and setContentView()*

This is because you have not yet created this file. Since you are going to do that next, you can ignore that wavy red error underline flag for now.

Creating an XML Table of Contents LinearLayout UI Design

Next, you need to create a new XML layout definition, so let's again right-click your top-level project folder, and this time you will select the **New ➤ Android XML File** menu sequence, as shown in Figure 6-10.

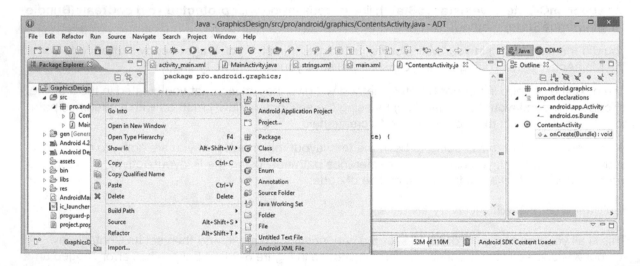

Figure 6-10. *Right-clicking the GraphicDesign project folder and creating a New ➤ Android XML File via menu sequence*

This will bring up the **New Android XML File** dialog, shown in Figure 6-11, where you can specify what type of XML file you want Eclipse to create.

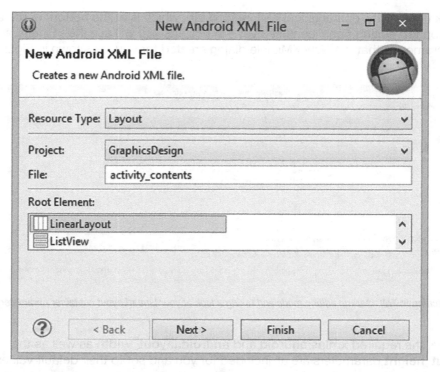

Figure 6-11. Creating a new Layout XML file named activity_contents

Select the **Layout Resource Type** and the **GraphicsDesign Project**, and then name the file
activity_contents, and select a **Root Element** of **LinearLayout**, and click on the **Finish** button to
create the **activity_contents.xml** file that is shown in Figure 6-12 in the **Graphical Layout Editor**
(I call it the GLE) pane inside Eclipse. The GLE can be accessed using the left bottom tab in Eclipse.
Since you want to review the XML tags and parameters that we have been talking about in this
chapter, click the other bottom tab and switch the editing view into XML editing mode so that you can
work directly with your XML markup, rather than using the GLE's drag-and-drop visual editing mode.

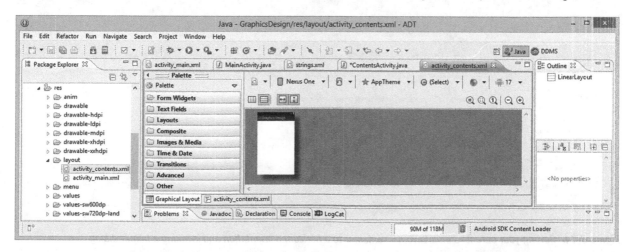

Figure 6-12. Newly created activity_contents.xml file shown in Eclipse central editing pane in Graphical Layout

Once you click the activity_contents.xml XML editing tab, which is at the bottom of the activity_ contents.xml top tab editing pane (confused yet?) in Eclipse, you will see the <LinearLayout> parent tag and the parameters that the New XML File dialog created for you, as shown in Figure 6-13.

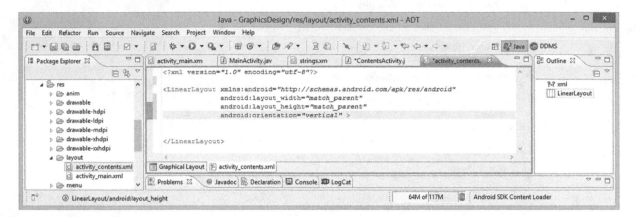

Figure 6-13. Switching to XML markup editing mode and taking a look at your LinearLayout container parameters

As you can see, the required **xmlns:android** and **android:layout_width** as well as the **android:layout_height** parameters are all included for you and set to their default values, which are correct, so let's leave them as-is.

The only LinearLayout parent tag parameter that you are going to change is the **android:orientation** parameter, which you are going to set to **horizontal** for the parent tag. You are using the horizontal orientation for the parent tag container because you are going to nest two vertical LinearLayouts next to each other, so the top-level orientation is going to be horizontal, as the two vertical sub-layouts are next to each other. Next, place the cursor after the **> (closing chevron)** on the opening LinearLayout tag and then press the return key to auto-indent your next line of code. Finally, press an **< (opening chevron)** to open the **child tag helper dialog**, as shown in Figure 6-14.

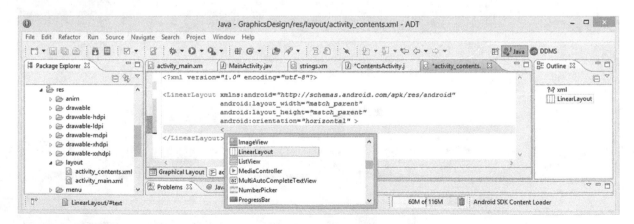

Figure 6-14. Setting your parent <LinearLayout> container to a horizontal orientation and invoking a helper dialog

Find the LinearLayout tag on the helper dialog, and double-click it to add a nested LinearLayout container underneath the current one. The nested LinearLayout tag is shown in Figure 6-15, with the parameters that you will need to add next in order to make it lay out vertically and fit the screen across many different types of Android devices, screen sizes, and shapes.

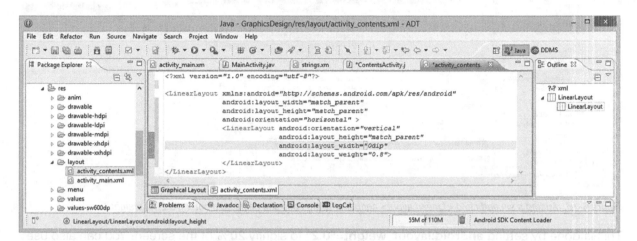

Figure 6-15. *Adding a child <LinearLayout> container and setting it to a vertical orientation, 0 dip, and 80% weight*

Copy the android:orientation parameter from the parent tag, and then paste it into the child tag, and change it to use the **vertical** constant value.

Next, copy the **android:layout_height="match_parent"** from the parent tag, and then use it inside the child tag as well, as you want the height of the nested child LinearLayout to conform to the full height of the screen.

Since you want to use an **android:layout_weight="0.8"** parameter to set this nested vertical layout to use **80%** of the screen width, you need to add an **android:layout_width="0dip"** parameter. Using the **0dip** setting is a little-known trick, and it will tell Android to **turn off device independent pixel sizing** for the layout, almost as if **0dip** means "no dip" to Android. This will serve to tell the Android OS to calculate the screen sizing based on the current device screen size, along with the **android:layout_weight** setting.

Next, you need to add another nested LinearLayout for the right side of the screen. The fastest way to do this is to simply to copy the <LinearLayout> tag that you just created, and paste it again underneath itself, as shown in Figure 6-16. Change the android:layout_weight parameter in the second nested layout to utilize the remainder of the display screen.

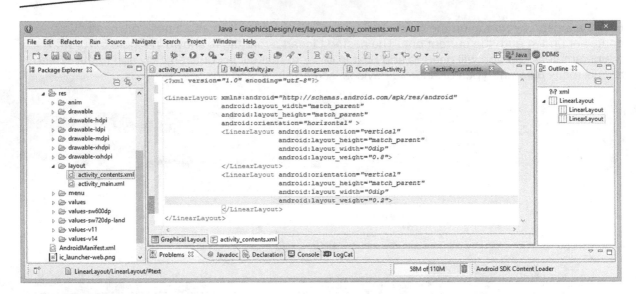

Figure 6-16. *Adding a second child <LinearLayout> container using copy and paste, and setting a 20% weight*

This is done by setting **android:layout_weight="0.2"** to signify **20%** of the screen. You can also use integers in the weight parameter, and Android will add them together to get a total and then obtain the fraction of the screen weight to use via division, so if you wanted to use 8 and 2, or 80 and 20, instead of 0.8 and 0.2 to specify these fractions, that would work as well. In fact, so would 4 and 1, as 4/5 is 0.8 and 1/5 is 0.2.

Now you have your empty, nested layout container structure of one horizontal LinearLayout that holds two vertical LinearLayouts together. Android does not like empty layout containers, so at some point Eclipse will place wavy yellow warning highlighting under your LinearLayout tags to let you know that you need to place child tags (widgets) inside these containers or you're just wasting valuable system memory.

Let's add a few TextView user interface widgets to these layout containers next, so we can show you how a simple Table of Contents is created by using the two nested LinearLayout structures that you have created.

Adding Text UI Widgets to the TOC UI Layout Container

Now you need to add your **TextView** UI elements, known as TextView widgets in Android, to the inside of your nested layout container structures. As you might have seen by now (if these are not showing up as yet, use the **CTRL-S** keystroke combination to **Save** your activity_contents XML file), your empty layout container is throwing warnings in Eclipse (unused layout container warnings). To alleviate this problem, let's add some basic Text UI elements to create a Table of Contents screen, with chapter titles on the left side and page numbers on the right side. The layout_weight parameter will allow you to easily fine-tune the precise spacing between these two data columns.

The first thing that you need to do is to create the **<string>** tag XML text constants that you are going to use to label your TextView UI objects, so click the **strings.xml** tab in Eclipse, and add eight <string> tags to the bottom of the file. The easiest way to do this is to copy the last <string> tag eight times, and edit the name parameters and data values.

Once you have added these eight <string> tags and changed their name parameters to chap_one through chap_four and page_one through page_four, you can add data values to them that represent the first four chapters of a Pro Android Graphics book, as shown in Figure 6-17. Add in some mock-up page ranges as well, so that there is data in the UI element to preview the UI design with, and then you will be ready to add in <TextView> tags.

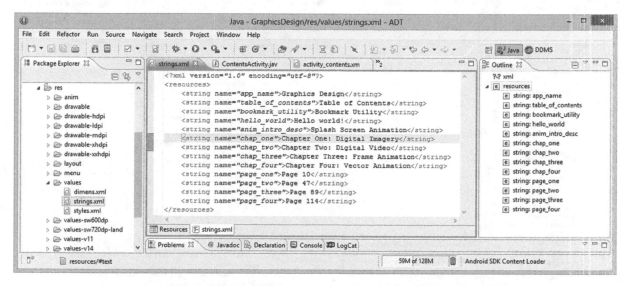

Figure 6-17. Adding <string> tags (constants) for four chapter titles and four page number TextView UI elements

Let's add in your first <TextView> user interface element tag, which will be a child tag inside your first nested <LinearLayout> tag. Once this tag has been coded, you can copy it three more time and simply edit the parameters for the copied child tags to save app development time.

You know that you need the android:layout_width and android:layout_height parameters as a requirement, so let's add these first with the constant value of **wrap_content,** since you want this UI element container to conform to the text data content that is held inside of it.

Next, you have to add an android:text parameter to reference the <string> tag constants that you have added in your strings.xml file earlier. This is done using the @string/ path preface to the <string> tag name parameter that you assigned to each of the string constants. So your first <TextView> tag UI container XML markup looks like this (also shown in Figure 6-18):

```
<TextView android:layout:width="wrap_content"
          android:layout_height="wrap_content"
          android:text="@string/chap_one" />
```

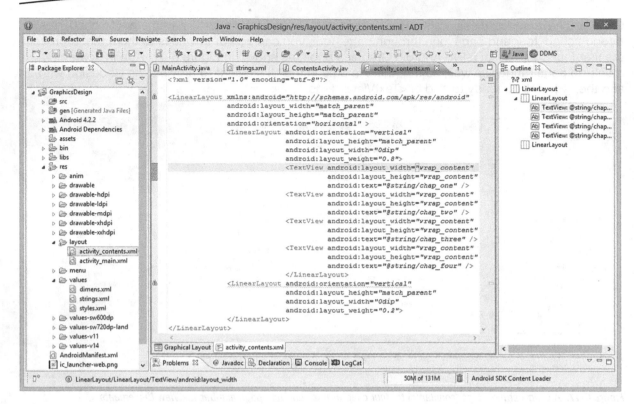

Figure 6-18. Adding TextView tags to the first nested LinearLayout container along with Eclipse warning icons and wavy yellow warning underline highlighting

Now you can copy and paste this UI container tag structure three more times underneath itself and change the android:text parameter values to reference the chap_two, chap_three, and chap_four <string> tag names. Once this is done, you will notice one of your error warnings has disappeared!

Now you only have two warning flags in Eclipse left to deal with, as you can see in Figure 6-18. Mouse-over the first, and you will get an Eclipse ADT recommendation that you utilize the **android:baselineAligned="false"** parameter in your parent tag layout container. Let's add that now, in the top-level parent LinearLayout container tag, as shown in Figure 6-19.

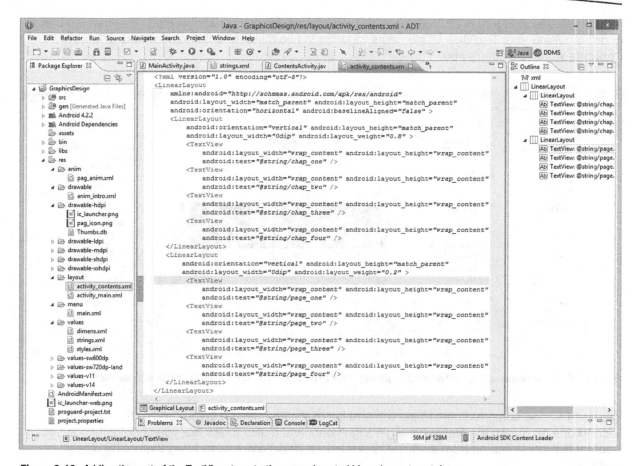

Figure 6-19. Adding the rest of the TextView tags to the second nested LinearLayout container

This particular warning will appear if you use the **android:layout_weight** parameter inside a nested UI container. This is because a LinearLayout is set to internally calculate child container baseline alignment when weights are involved. Since your child containers layout_height constants are set to match_parent, their baselines will be aligned anyway, so the warning suggests that you turn off this feature so that the Android OS does not take the processing time to do this needlessly or redundantly.

Now you can add four more TextView UI containers to your second nested LinearLayout container, which will eliminate the final warning highlight and allow you to test the basic UI layout and see if you need to add any other parameters, such as layout_margin parameters, to fine-tune it.

The easiest way to do this is to copy the four TextView tags from the first nested LinearLayout and paste them into the second nested UI container, changing the android:text parameter reference values from **chap** to **page**.

Now you can use the GLE tab at the bottom-left of the XML editing pane to preview your UI design. This is a shortcut that allows you to not have to take the time consuming Run As Android Application work process and invoke the Nexus One emulator, which unless you are developing on an 8-core workstation with 16GB of memory and a hyper-fast SSD, can take a very long time to load!

As you can see in Figure 6-20, your nested UI containers are doing exactly what you intended them to do: grouping your TextView UI elements together in two discrete columns, just like a Table of Contents would be configured.

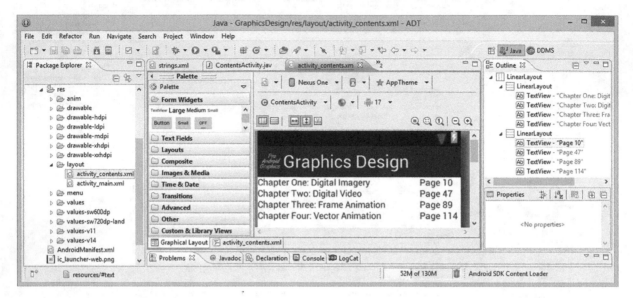

Figure 6-20. *Using Graphical Layout Editor tab to preview your UI design so you don't have to invoke the emulator*

You need to add some margins to the top and left of the first nested layout and to the top of the second one (to match the first top margin alignment), and it also looks like you should change your layout weight distribution from an 80%/20% mix to a 75%/25% mix to bring them a bit closer together.

Let's add in **layout_marginTop** and **layout_marginLeft** parameters to refine your nested LinearLayouts a bit more in order to perfect your UI design.

Since you want to add space on the left of the screen so that the TextView elements to not touch the left side of the screen, as they are now, you need to add an **android:layout_marginLeft="10dip"** parameter to the first (left) LinearLayout container, as shown in Figure 6-21.

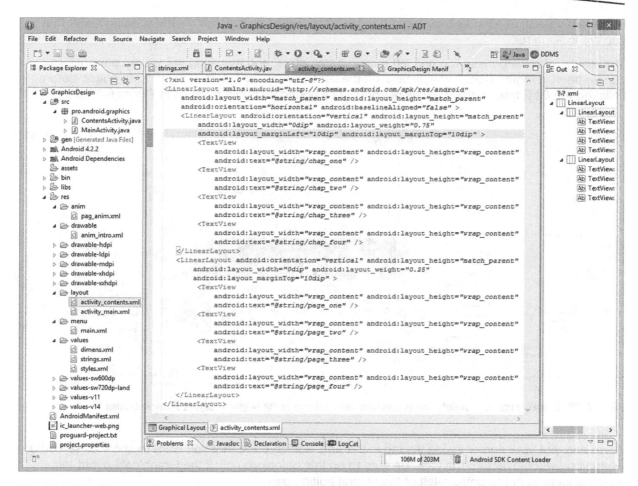

Figure 6-21. *Adding marginTop and marginLeft parameters and changing android:weight value to fine-tune spacing*

The reason that you're adding this to the LinearLayout container parent tag and not to every single TextView user interface element (which should also work) is because the TextViews are **children** of the LinearLayout, so you can just move the parent, and all of its children will move along with it.

Next, you want to do the same thing, only adding space to the top of the UI screen, so that the TextView elements don't touch the top of the screen. Add a similar **android:layout_marginTop="10dip"** margin parameter to the same LinearLayout container in order to bring the container's contents (the chapter titles) down a little bit on the display screen.

Finally, you need to bring the top of the right LinearLayout container down to match what you have done to the left LinearLayout container, so cut and paste the android:layout_marginTop="10dip" parameter from the first Linear Layout tag into the second one to duplicate the same DIP alignment.

Now that you have pushed the borders of the nested UI containers away from the side of the screen, all you have to do is adjust the spacing between the left and right nested containers by tweaking the **android:layout_weight** parameters to be a 75%/25% mix rather than the 80%/20% mix you tried first. This will serve to bring the right side of the screen closer to the left (and middle). You can tweak these two values, as long as they sum up to be 100%, until you get exactly the spacing result that you are looking for.

The results of adding these top and left margin parameters, and tweaking the weight parameters, can be seen in Figure 6-22. I specifically left the left UI container selected in the XML editor, before I clicked the GLE tab, so that the layout container's boundary could be seen in Figure 6-22.

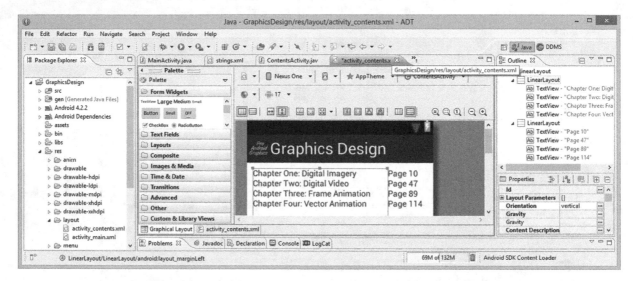

Figure 6-22. Checking your new weight and margin parameter settings in the Graphical Layout Editor in Eclipse

To do this, put your cursor inside the tag in the XML editing pane that you want to show as selected when you switch over into the GLE. Be sure to do this before you click the Graphical Layout tab, which is located at the bottom-left of the central editing pane.

Once you switch between the two editing vides, what you were last working on in XML editing mode will be shown as highlighted or selected in the other Graphical Layout Editing mode.

This valuable little trick shows that you can not only select and examine the bounds of your UI elements in the GLE, but also the layout containers in which they live. Pay close attention to the Eclipse IDE features!

Now, all you need to do is add in a dozen or so lines of Java code that will take your user's menu selections and then launch new Activities. In this case, it's the **ContentsActivity.java** class that you created earlier.

Once you implement the **onOptionsItemSelected()** method, which will be needed to accomplish your menu navigation implementation, you will then be able to test your new LinearLayout UI design inside the Nexus One emulator.

Using onOptionsItemSelected() to Add Menu Functionality

Add a new line after the onCreateOptionsMenu() method and add a **public boolean onOptionsItemSelected()** method and pass it a **MenuItem** parameter named **item** by using the following line of Java code:

```
public boolean onOptionsItemSelected(MenuItem item) {your method code goes in here}
```

The onCreateOptionsMenu() method is part of the Activity class, for which you already have an import statement, but you will see when you finish typing in this line of code that the MenuItem class in the android.view package will need an import statement. If you mouse-over the wavy red underline error highlighting, you will see an option to have that import statement written for you.

This MenuItem object, named **item** in the method declaration, is passed from the Android OS to this method whenever a user clicks one of the Menu object items that were inflated by the onCreateOptionsMenu() method. We then call the .getItemId() method off of this MenuItem object and pass that value into a Java switch statement using the following code:

```
switch(item.getItemId()) { individual case statements go inside of this structure }
```

Once you have set this method and switch structure up, you can add your **case statements** for each menu item. Within each of these case statements, you will add the lines of Java code that are needed to process whatever needs to be done when each menu item is selected by your user.

Inside of these case statements that you are going to write here, the Java actions you are going to take will involve using an Android **Intent** object to launch the Activity subclass that contains your application's functions, which will take the form of UI screen layouts.

Each of these Java case statements will use the following code format:

```
case R.id.table_of_contents:
    Intent intent_toc = new Intent(this, ContentsActivity.class);
    this.startActivity(intent_toc);
    break;
```

Let's analyze these case blocks of Java code, shown in Figure 6-23.

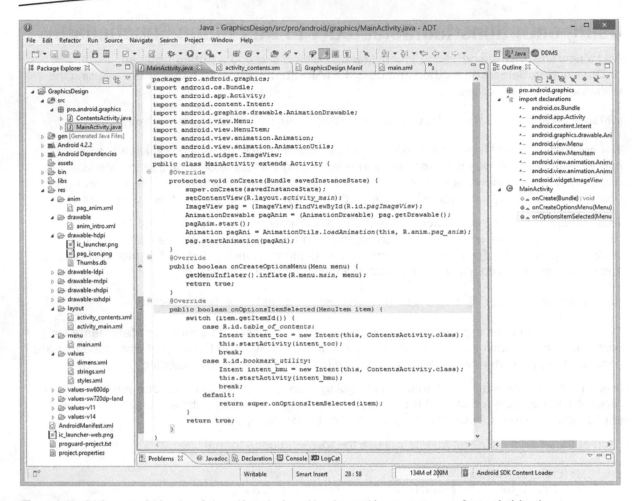

Figure 6-23. Adding an onOptionsItemSelected() method to add an Intent object to start a new ContentActivity class

The case statement itself is assigned to the resource ID for the menu item defined in your XML file (main.xml) and inflated into the Menu object named menu in your onOptionsMenuCreate() method. This ID for the Menu object is like its name, which tells you which menu item the user has selected, and you then execute the code inside this case statement. Code inside of a case statement comes after the colon and before a **break** statement, which will exit you from any particular case statement.

Next, you create an Intent object that carries your intent to start a new Activity subclass to the Android OS. This is done via the following code:

```
Intent intent_toc = new Intent (this, ContentsActivity.class);
```

This line of code instantiates an **Intent object**, names it **intent_toc**, and loads it with a new intent configured with the **current context** (this) and the target Activity class that you want to launch, the ContentsActivity.java class that you coded earlier, as specified in its compiled format via the name **ContentsActivity.class**. An intent in Android is used to communicate between different areas of the OS.

If you are not as familiar as you should be with intents, you can read up on them on this page of the Android Developer web site located at the following URL:

```
http://developer.android.com/reference/android/content/Intent.html
```

The next line of code starts the Activity using the .startActivity() method and the new intent object that you just created in the previous line of code. This launches the new Activity subclass onto the display screen. The method is called off the current context reference of this, like so:

```
this.startActivity(intent_toc);
```

This is all you need to launch the ContentsActivity.class onto the user's device display, so all you need now is a break statement, which breaks you out of the switch statement case matching loop, and you're ready to test!

Notice that I also put the Options menu item in for your Bookmark Utility (BMU), which we will be designing later on in the book. I did this to show more than one menu item on the menu, and also to show how you need to use different intent object names to differentiate your intent objects between menu items and the different Activity subclasses they will launch.

So the intent object for your BMU is named **intent_bmu**, and this intent will be loaded with a reference to a BookmarkActivity.class once you create the XML layout and Java code for that class.

For now, I just pointed it to the ContentsActivity.class, since that exists so that you have working code; thus both menu options will launch the layout container we have been working on.

Testing the Table of Contents Activity on the Nexus One

Now you can right-click your GraphicsDesign project folder and use the **Run As ➤ Android Application** work process to see if your new menu and layout container are working properly together. As you see in Figure 6-24, when you select the menu using the emulator menu button, and click the Table of Contents menu item, shown in blue on the left side of the screen shot, it launches the ContentsActivity Java Activity subclass and your LinearLayout user interface design, shown on the right side.

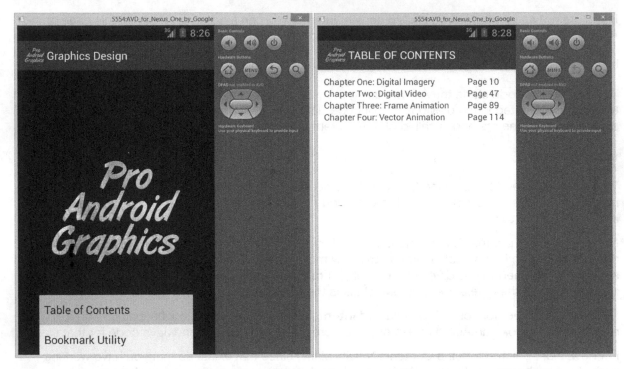

Figure 6-24. *Testing your new menu, Activity subclass, and Table of Contents layout design on the Nexus One*

Also shown on the right side of the screen shot is the Back button icon, highlighted in blue, which you can use to return to the splash screen and test the other menu item, which for now will also call the same Activity. Once you convert this UI to a RelativeLayout, you will add a Button widget, which you will be learning about in the next chapter. This UI Button widget will perform the return-to-home (splash screen) user interface function.

Later on in the book we'll transmute this into a RelativeLayout and more; since layout containers are fundamental to graphics and UI design, we will be working with them throughout the book. I wanted to use this chapter to give you an overview and show how one is implemented in the overall process of Activities, Manifest, XML, Java, and so on.

Summary

In this sixth chapter, you learned about Android **layout containers**, which hold user interface elements and content that is used on the device display screen by Android users.

We started by looking at the foundation class for layouts in Android, the **ViewGroup** class. You learned that the dozens of different types of layout containers found in Android are derived from this superclass, used to "group" View objects, which you will learn about in the next chapter.

We then took an overview of the Android **LayoutParams** class and its layout parameters, which are used by developers to configure and fine-tune how their user interface layout works and how it groups its child element View objects together. You learned about **match_parent** and **wrap_content** layout constants and how they are used in Android to allow layouts to auto-size.

Next, we looked at the Android layout container classes that have been **deprecated**, as well as the ones that were experimental and not yet fully implemented (permanent) in the Android OS. With many layout containers to cover, we'll be focusing on fully implemented layout classes in this book.

We looked at the Android **RelativeLayout** class, one of the most used layout containers, and the one that is used in the New Android Application series of dialogs when a baseline (blank) application is created.

Next, we looked at LinearLayouts, another often used layout container and one that is used for simple linear layouts of buttons or text.

Next, we looked at FrameLayouts, a high-level layout container usually used for holding more complicated layout containers or a single element UI like locked-aspect-ratio, full-screen digital video playback, usually via the VideoView widget.

Next, we looked at one of the newer Android layout containers, GridLayouts, which is quickly becoming popular for use in designing complex UI designs using a flat (non-nested) layout container design. We will be covering this UI layout container in detail in a future chapter on advanced layout design.

Finally, we looked at DrawerLayout, another new layout container for the design of advanced sliding drawer UI layouts that the user can pull out from the left or right side of the display screen and that contain the widget elements for global app UI (left side drawer) or local content UI function (right side drawer).

To get some hands-on experience you created your own layout container in XML, and then added a menu and coded an Activity class so that you could access a new Table of Contents screen for your application.

In the next chapter, you will learn about the View class and how it is used to create widgets that can populate the inside of your layout containers.

Chapter 7

Android UI Widgets: Graphics Design Using the View Class

In this seventh chapter, we will take a closer look at the Android **View** class and its many subclasses. We already looked at the Android ViewGroup, which is a View subclass, and some of its more mainstream layout container subclasses, and now we are going to take a look at some of Android's View subclasses that we can implement in order to create our user interface widgets and graphic designs within those ViewGroup layout containers.

Since layout containers (ViewGroup classes) are used to contain user interface elements, called **widgets** in Android, we logically had to cover those first in the previous chapter. Thanks to that foundation, we can now cover some of Android's most often used user interface widgets. These can be placed inside the parent layout containers as child UI elements.

Just like Android has dozens of ViewGroup layout container classes, so too does Android have hundreds of View (widget) subclasses. Thus, we will not be able to cover each of these widget classes in detail in this book, as this is not a book solely focused on UI design elements and how they work.

We will take a look at the most popular Android UI design widgets from a graphics standpoint, that is, which of those UI element widgets should be used to implement your app's graphics elements. We will also cover the UI widgets that allow developers to create customized graphical UI elements.

Customized GUI (Graphical User Interface) elements are those elements that can be enhanced (or styled) by utilizing additional graphics design content assets along with graphics design attributes such as alpha channel (transparency) for seamlessly compositing graphics with UI elements.

First, you'll learn about the Android View superclass, and then we'll cover its most often used UI design subclasses. The View widget classes that we will cover in detail during the course of this book include ImageView, TextView, EditText, Button, ImageButton, VideoView, Space, AnalogClock, CalendarView, DigitalClock, and ProgressBar.

Now that you can add new Activity subclasses to your Pro Android GraphicsDesign application thanks to the Menu system you added in the last chapter, you can create UI layouts using all of these widgets by using new Activity classes. Each functional screen for your Android application will have its own menu option, activity, layout container, and collection of View widgets, which you will learn about in this chapter.

The Android View Class: The Foundation for UI Widgets

The Android **View** class is a direct subclass of the **java.lang.Object** class, and it defines an area on the display screen called a View, whose core properties are defined by the View superclass. The View superclass is part of the **android.view** package and is imported into your application by using an **import android.view.View** Java code statement.

A View object in Android occupies a **rectangular area** on the user's display screen; it is responsible for drawing to that area of the screen and for **event handling** the interactions that happen in that area of the screen.

This View superclass is not used directly, but can be used to create other subclasses, which can then be used in your Android applications. There are so many View subclasses already, so chances are good that you won't have to do any of this programming work yourself! You can just find and utilize the View subclass that provides the functionality you require, and import and utilize that View subclass for your application development needs.

The View class is especially valuable to graphics designers as it provides the basic building block for user interface components in the Android OS. UI components (or elements, as I like to call them as a graphics designer) are termed "**widgets**" in the Android ecosystem. There are many specialized widget subclasses of View that act as UI controls and are capable of containing and displaying text, images, video, animation, or other content.

Since the View class is a base class for building widgets, which are used to create all of your interactive UI elements (button, text fields, etc.), you will be seeing the class name View quite a bit in your graphics design Android application development experience, so get familiar with View.

As you've learned already, a ViewGroup (View subclass) is a base class used for creating layout containers, which are those invisible containers that hold all of the Views (or nested ViewGroups) and define their layout properties. A ViewGroup object is exactly what it says it is: a group of View objects! In that sense, everything on your screen in Android boils down to being a View child object inside a parent ViewGroup container.

So many UI widgets have been developed for Android over the years that they are bundled together in their own Java package in Android called the **android.widget** package. If you want to see all the widgets that are currently in the package, you can visit the widget **package summary** page on the Android Developer web site at the following URL:

http://developer.android.com/reference/android/widget/package-summary.html

You can add Android View objects either using Java code or by specifying a collection of View objects using one or more XML files containing layout container parent tags. The latter way (by using XML UI description) is the more common (and easier) way to define your user interface design for your Android apps, and it is the way that you will be doing UI design in this book.

View Basic Properties: ID, Layout Positioning, and Size

Once you have defined the layout container (ViewGroup) that will contain your child UI elements (View objects), as you did in the previous chapter, the first thing that you will generally do is to define the properties of your child UI widget View objects by using Android parameters. Parameters in Android are always prefaced by **android:**, as you already have seen.

The reason for this, in case you were wondering, is due to that XML Naming Schema **xmlns:android** parameter, found in the parent container in every XML file definition that is coded for Android. This specifies your path to the current XML definition, kept in a central repository, which is located at

```
http://schemas.android.com/apk/res/android
```

Thus, the xmlns:android parameter is really saying, "Everywhere that you see android:, expand this to the path **http://schemas.android.com/apk/res/android** in order to provide the direct reference to the most current and centrally located XML parameter definition for any given parameter in this XML file."

So, your android:layout_weight parameter is really seen by Android OS as

```
http://schemas.android.com/apk/res/android:layout_weight
```

Now you know exactly what is going on in your XML files, and why that XMLNS parameter is needed in every parent tag that you add, and why Eclipse will throw errors if it is not there (a "this parameter does not exist" error).

If you are going to reference any View from your Java code for any reason, and this includes ViewGroup parent tags as well as View widget child tags, you need to utilize the **android:id** parameter to assign an **ID** to the widget (View object). This is done so that you can use the **findViewById()** method, which is used to connect the XML user interface element definition that you are writing with the Java object you are instantiating in your Java code to "inflate" your XML definition, which will populate the fields in Java objects. The **findViewById()** (View) and **inflate()** (Menu) methods in Android serve to "bridge" your XML markup with your Java program logic.

Populating a Java object with an XML definition of the object's attributes is generally termed **inflating the object** within the Android OS lingo.

An ID parameter is not required, so if you are not going to reference your View object in the Java code, you don't have to bother using an android:id tag to define it. A good example of this is using a **TextView** element (View) that is being included in your UI design simply for the purpose of placing a text label somewhere on your screen and is defined in the XML UI layout definition but is not used interactively within the Android application. You observed this in the previous chapter's XML UI definition.

Other parameters, like **layout_width** and **layout_height**, on the other hand, are always required to be defined for each of your View object's XML tags.

After you give your View (child tag) its ID parameter, you generally will want to give it layout positioning parameters for **height** and **width**. These are usually assigned one of two constants, **match_parent** or **wrap_content**.

This is so that Android can do the positioning for you. You can also use pixel or DIP values, but remembering our discussion in Chapter 5, try to use the Android system layout constants whenever you possibly can. These two parameters are always required to be supplied for each UI widget (View object) that will be contained within your ViewGroup layout container.

The size of a View object is expressed using a width and height; however, rarely does the developer have to specify these parameters if they have set their layout positioning parameters, because Android will do this for you.

In fact, Android OS internally tracks **two pairs** of width and height values for each View object. The first pair of values is known as **measured width** and **measured height**. Your measured width and height dimensions will define how big your View object wants to be inside its parent container. These **measured dimensions** can be obtained by calling the **.getMeasuredWidth()** and **.getMeasuredHeight()** methods on any given View object that has an ID that allows it to be referenced (to call methods on it) from within Java logic.

The second pair is known as width and height, or to be more exact, **drawing width** and **drawing height**. These **drawing dimensions** will define the actual size of a View on screen, at drawing time, and after layout calculations.

The drawing width and drawing height values may be, but do not have to be, different from the measured width and measured height values. The drawing width and drawing height can be obtained at runtime in your Java code by calling the **.getWidth()** and **.getHeight()** methods on any given View object.

To measure a View dimension, a View will always take into account padding. We'll be covering padding and margins in the next section of this chapter.

Padding is expressed in DIP for the left, top, right, and bottom portions of a View. Padding is used to space the content of a View by a certain amount of pixels. Even though a View subclass can define padding, it does not have support for a margin. However, Android ViewGroup subclasses can provide a margin parameter, and so margins and padding can be defined in ViewGroups.

View Positioning Characteristics: Margins and Padding

To position your UI layout elements relative to each other, there are two key classifications of layout parameters, **margin** and **padding**, that allow you to fine-tune how your UI looks on the display screen.

The **global positioning** is done by the Android OS via the layout_width and layout_height constants. This is so that Android OS is able to accommodate different device screen sizes, densities, aspect ratios, and orientations.

The developer is then allowed **local UI element positioning** control via use of the **android:padding** parameters for each child View tag UI element. Note that this parameter is called android:padding, not android:layout_padding, so you really don't have to remember "use margins for layouts, and padding for UI elements," as the designation of what they can be used for is built right into the parameter name itself! Since android:padding is not named android:view_padding, you know that padding parameters can be used for both the View (widget) and ViewGroup (layout container) subclass types.

Since there are less places that you can use margins, and since you have already experienced using them in previous chapters, let's start with those first. Margins push what they are assigned to away from themselves on the outside of the container, whereas padding does the opposite and pushes the boundaries of the container away from what is contained inside it. You will see this in detail during this book as you used both types of spacing parameters to achieve various types of graphic design end results.

There are four different margin setting parameters: **layout_marginBottom**, **layout_marginTop**, **layout_marginLeft**, and **layout_marginRight**. There is also a fifth option simply called layout_margin, which will set all four sides of margin with one single DIP value, providing evenly spaced margins all the way around your layout container.

Starting in Android 4.2 API Level 17 (Jelly Bean), there are two additional margin parameters, **layout_marginStart** and **layout_marginEnd** parameters. These "start" and "end" margin parameters were added as part of Android's support for right-to-left (RTL) design layouts for cultures that scan the screen from the right to the left, rather than from the left to the right.

For RTL screen design flows, layout_marginStart is equal to layout_marginRight, and layout_marginEnd is equal to layout_marginLeft.

For left-to-right (LTR) screen design flows, layout_marginStart is equal to layout_marginLeft, and layout_marginEnd is equal to layout_marginRight.

For detailed information on margin layout parameters, read the Android Developer web site **ViewGroup.MarginLayoutParams** page at the following URL:

```
developer.android.com/reference/android/view/ViewGroup.MarginLayoutParams.html
```

Just like with margin, Android has four different types of **padding** setting parameters: **android:paddingBottom**, **android:paddingTop**, **android:paddingLeft**, and **android:paddingRight**. There is also a fifth short-cut option, simply called **android:padding**, that will set all four sides of padding with one single DIP value, providing evenly spaced padding all the way around your View object's content.

Starting in Android 4.2 API Level 17 (Jelly Bean), there are two additional padding parameters, **android:paddingStart** and the **android:paddingEnd** parameter. These "start" and "end" padding parameters were added as part of Android's support for RTL design layouts for cultures that scan the screen from the right to the left, rather than from the left to the right.

For RTL screen design flows, the android:paddingStart is equal to the android:paddingRight, and the android:paddingEnd is equal to the android:paddingLeft.

For left-to-right (LTR) screen design flows, the android:paddingStart is equal to the android:paddingLeft, and the android:paddingEnd is equal to the android:paddingRight.

For detailed information regarding the view padding parameters, read the Android Developer web site **View** superclass page at the following URL:

```
http://developer.android.com/reference/android/view/View.html
```

Next, you'll take a look at the parameters that allow you to control how your View widgets utilize your graphics design assets, as well as composite with your graphics design (drawable) assets (imagery and animation) and digital video assets.

View Graphic Properties: Background, Alpha, and Visibility

Your widget's graphics property definition is done via XML parameters, just like everything else: naming, layout, spacing, orientation, and so on. The graphics properties, or parameters, that we are going to be most concerned with in this book are the ones that will allow us to seamlessly integrate our user interface design into our overall app graphics design process. These include background image capabilities, alpha blending value settings, and for some widgets and your app's icons, image source file references.

As you learned in Chapter 3, any slot or placeholder in the widget that can hold an image asset can also accommodate an animation asset. This ability to add motion to graphics and UI elements gives developers a lot of power to create amazing user experiences using their user interface design.

The most often used View property utilized for integrating graphics is the **android:background** parameter. This parameter allows us to set a background image source file, or a background color value, including an alpha value.

In some cases, to allow the image, animation, or video that is behind your UI widget View object to show through, you'll set your UI widget background property to be **transparent**. This is accomplished by using the hexadecimal color value with **eight** integer locations, including an alpha channel, via the **android:background="#00000000"** tag parameter, which sets the **ARGB** value of 100% transparent (essentially defining zero background imagery/pixels).

The next often used View property utilized for integrating graphics is the **android:alpha** parameter. This parameter allows you to set the transparency value for the UI widget as a whole, including its background image. So you would use android:alpha to make the entire UI widget translucent or opaque using a **real number** setting, such as **android:alpha="0.55"** for 55% opacity.

Since this is a book on advanced graphics and compositing techniques, we will be using alpha parameters extensively as the book gets more and more advanced as you learn the foundations of Android development that pertain to graphics design.

The next most often used View property is the **android:src** parameter, which is used to define a **source image** asset. In case you are wondering why this is not used more often than background imagery and alpha blending values, it is because all widget tags have the android:background parameter, but relatively few tags, such as the <ImageView> and the <ImageButton> as well as the <Bitmap> tag, support the use of the **android:src** image source referencing parameter.

This is because the source imagery would cover up the UI widget itself, so to have the UI element in front of your image assets (or animation assets) you would instead use the android:background parameter. There are a few other places that you would use the android:src parameter as well, such as in your AndroidManifest.xml file to assign icon assets to the application.

Finally, there is the **android:visibility** parameter, which is more memory and processor efficient than the **android:alpha** parameter. This is because the algorithms necessary for alpha blending, which is usually utilized to create semi-translucent effects where the background images or elements can show through for graphics design effects, are more complex than the simple code to display or not display an element on the screen. Alpha can also be animated in your Java code to smoothly fade in or fade out a given design element. So use alpha for graphics compositing and use visibility for layout or user interface usability implementations, as it is less "expensive."

If you just want to **show** and **hide** View objects, that is, instantly turn on or off the visibility on the screen, all View elements such as TextView, ImageButton, ImageView, Button, CheckBox, ViewGroup, and the like have a **visibility** property. The visibility of a View can be set to one of three predefined Android value constants: **VISIBLE** (currently visible onscreen), **INVISIBLE** (hidden with its screen layout space still enforced, even though it isn't visible), and **GONE** (hidden completely, including from the parent layout container's child layout placement calculation algorithm).

A View's Functional Characteristics: Listeners and Focus

Once you have designed the collection of View UI widgets using your layout container in an XML file containing XML tag markup, they will still need to be inflated and "wired up" to the operating system and device hardware.

This is accomplished inside your Java code by **"trapping"** your end user interaction with your user interface elements via Android OS **input events**.

Android input events are triggered by your end users as they interface with your application by using their Android device hardware navigation features, such as keypads, navigation keys, trackballs, and touchscreens.

Trapping these input events will allow your UI design to become functional and respond to user interaction. Trapping operating system input events can be accomplished by using Android **event listeners** in your Java code.

The Android **EventListener** superclass is a part of the **android.util** package; if you want to research the core superclass, you can find more information on the Android Developer web site at the following URL:

```
http://developer.android.com/reference/java/util/EventListener.html
```

Event listeners are methods that you can attach to your View objects after you import, instantiate, and inflate them from the XML definition using the **findViewById()** method.

Once the Java code setting up the View object is in place, you can attach an event listener method to that object, which will perform **event handling** for the View object, which in most cases is one of the UI design elements.

There are a half-dozen event handling methods that are used the most often in Android, including **.onClick()**, **.onLongClick()**, **.onTouch()**, **.onKeyUp()**, **.onKeyDown()**, **.onCreateContextMenu()**, and **.onFocusChange()**. If you want to research Android OS input events in more detail, visit the following URL:

```
http://developer.android.com/guide/topics/ui/ui-events.html
```

The last event handler I mentioned was the **.onFocusChange()** method, which tracks a change in **user focus**. This brings up another concept called **focus**, which is used to ascertain which of the UI widgets in the layout container your user is using or focusing on (interfacing with or using) currently.

The Android OS will handle determining which of the parent ViewGroup child View objects currently has the focus of your application end user. This is accomplished by tracking input events that can tell Android which UI widget the user is touching (using) currently, as well as how the user may be progressing from one UI element to the next.

You can also force your application to set its focus to any UI View object (user interface element) at any time. To do this, you would call the View's **.requestFocus()** method, which would then highlight the UI element for use.

Additionally, all View objects will let you set the .onFocusChange() event listener so that your application logic, if it needs to, can be notified and take appropriate action when the View object that it is attached to gains or loses the user's focus.

We will be looking at input events, event listeners, event handling, and focus in detail throughout this book as they are all fundamental to your application development, user interface, and user experience optimization.

Next, let's implement the Bookmarking Utility Activity subclass and also create your new RelativeLayout container so you can get some practice with that layout container type. You'll get this new Activity working with your Options menu, add it to your AndroidManifest.xml configuration file, and add a **TextView** widget as well. Later, you'll add other types of UI widgets (View subclasses) to this new Bookmarking Utility Activity as well.

Bookmark Utility UI: Using a RelativeLayout and TextView

Next, you are going to create your Bookmarking Utility and in the process learn about **RelativeLayout** container parameters and the **TextView** UI widget because these are the most commonly used classes in all of Android.

After you accomplish that, you can then move on to more advanced widgets and layout containers, but first I need to make sure all of my readers have this proper basic graphics design foundation and that I have covered the more basic ViewGroup and View subclasses.

Some of you might be wondering: What does text have to do with graphics design? If you take a close look at Photoshop or GIMP, you will find extensive text creation and alignment tools in these packages. The TextView class in Android provides nearly a hundred parameters that allow developers to simulate this type of design power and flexibility in their Android application development work process, which is fantastic.

You need to finish implementing your second MainActivity class options menu item, the **Bookmark Utility**, by creating a new **BookmarkActivity.java** class and an **activity_bookmark.xml** layout definition to hold your RelativeLayout container. You'll do that quickly over the next page or two so that you have the foundation to not only learn about the important TextView widget but also about the even more important ImageView widget that will hold your graphic imagery.

So fire up Eclipse if it's not open already, and enter your GraphicsDesign project, and right-click the GraphicsDesign folder, and use the familiar **New ➤ Java Class** menu sequence to bring up the **New Java Class** dialog shown in Figure 7-1. Specify your **pro.android.graphics** package and the **BookmarkActivity** name for the new Activity subclass, and then select the **android.app.Activity** for your superclass, and then click the **Finish** button when you are done configuring to show the empty class, which should look Figure 6-8 from the previous chapter.

Figure 7-1. Creating your new BookmarkActivity Java Class

Next, you need to add an onCreate() method to your BookmarkActivity that will call the **super.onCreate(savedInstanceState)** superclass's onCreate() method and use the **setContentView(R.layout.activity_bookmark)** method to reference the **activity_bookmark.xml** file that you are about to create. A quick way to accomplish this is to copy this block of code from your **MainActivity.java** file and then change the R.layout reference, as shown in Figure 7-2.

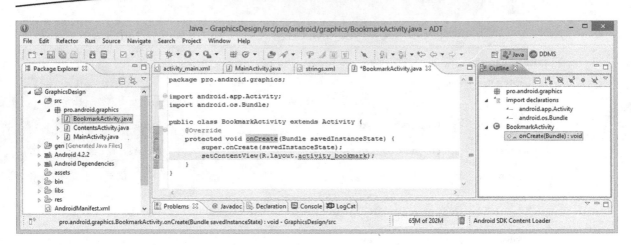

Figure 7-2. Entering your onCreate() method Java code and setting the ContentView to your activity_bookmark.xml

Since you have the red wavy line error highlighting in your BookmarkActivity class, let's create your **activity_bookmark.xml** file next to get rid of it and to create the RelativeLayout container for the markup you will be creating in the rest of this chapter.

Right-click your GraphicsDesign project folder, and this time use the **New ➤ Android XML File** menu sequence to bring up the **New Android XML File** dialog, shown in Figure 7-3. Select the Layout resource type and name the file **activity_bookmark** to mirror the BookmarkActivity class name, and then select a Root Element parent tag of type RelativeLayout in the center selection area of the dialog. Click the Finish button when you have set all the file creation parameters.

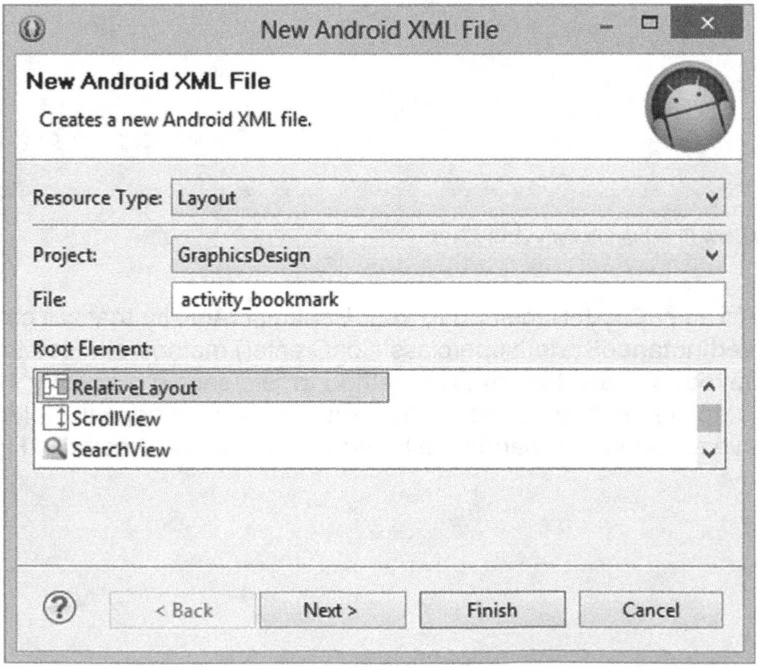

Figure 7-3. Creating a New RelativeLayout XML File

For now, you are going to leave this new RelativeLayout container empty, and you'll finish implementing the new BookmarkActivity class and MainActivity options menu so that everything will work in the Nexus One emulator.

You'll get all of this work out of the way now so that you can test your new Activity UI screen as you progress through the rest of this chapter.

The next logical thing to do, since you have the BokmarkActivity.java class created and error-free now, is to add that Activity subclass to your AndroidManifest.xml file using the <activity> child tag that will make it visible to the Android OS for use.

Right-click the **AndroidManifest.xml** file, and **Open** it, and then add the <activity> tag as you did for the Table of Contents Activity subclass in the previous chapter. When you are finished, it will look very similar to your ContentsActivity tag located right above it, but it will reference a different class name and label <string> tag constant, as shown in Figure 7-4. You are going to create the <string> constants in your strings.xml file and then you will be ready to get to work crafting your RelativeLayout container design.

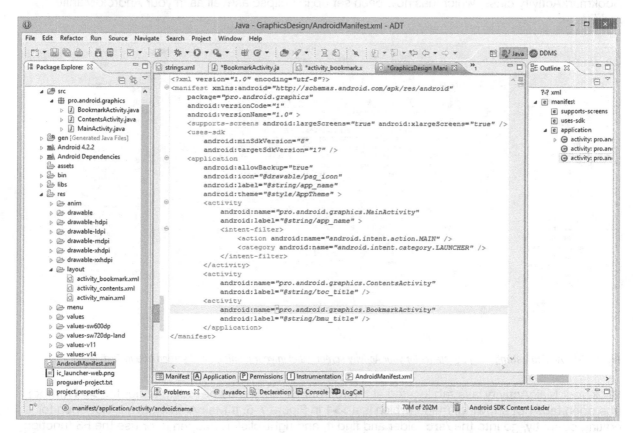

Figure 7-4. Adding a BookmarkActivity label and referencing your AndroidManifest.xml file using an <activity> tag

Next, click your strings.xml tab in the central editing area of Eclipse, or, if it is not open, go into your **/res/values** folder, right-click the strings.xml file name, and **Open** it, or use the **F3** key to open the file.

Copy and paste the last <string> tag constant entry, and then paste it two times underneath itself. You'll do this so you can add the bmu_title (label) string constant referenced in your AndroidManifest, as well as the TextView string constant that you will use next when you start crafting your widgets inside your RelativeLayout container XML definition.

Set the text value for the <string> tag named **bmu_title** to be "BOOKMARKING UTILITY" and the text value for the <string> tag named bookmark_text to be "Current Bookmark Page" using the following two lines of XML markup:

```
<string name="bmu_title">BOOKMARKING UTILITY</string>
<string name="bookmark_text">Current Bookmark Page</string>
```

Once your <string> tag XML constants are in place, as shown in Figure 7-5, you can then proceed to your MainActivity.java class, and make your second menu item operable by referencing your new BookmarkActivity class, which has now been set up in Eclipse as well as in your AndroidManifest. xml file.

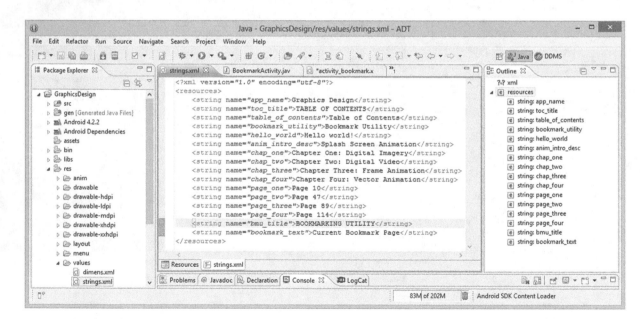

Figure 7-5. Adding <string> tag constants for your Activity screen label in your manifest and screen title in TextView

Click your MainActivity.java tab located at the top of Eclipse; it may be hiding under the **>> Number** (the open tabs not showing) menu, which is a **>>1** in Figure 7-5. If MainActivity.java is not open for editing currently, go into the **/src** folder and find it, and right-click it to open it, or use the F3 function key once you have selected (highlighted) it.

In the **onOptionsItemSelected()** method in the second switch statement case code block, change the reference from your ContentsActivity.class to your new **BookmarkActivity.class** so that your options menu will now launch the Bookmarking Utility Activity screen you have just wired into place.

You have now done everything necessary to be able to access the RelativeLayout container that you are about to begin filling with the basic UI widgets that we will cover in this chapter.

You needed to be able to access the BookmarkActivity.java class that calls the activity_bookmark. xml RelativeLayout container definition from the second options menu item, as shown in Figure 7-6, and so you had to not only call that Activity subclass from your MainActivity class Java code, but you also had to set it up in your AndroidManifest XML file.

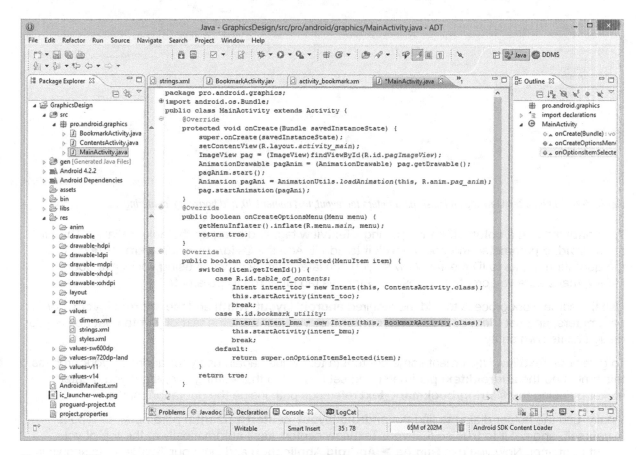

Figure 7-6. Adding a reference to your newly created BookmarkActivity.class to the Options menu in MainActivity

Finally, to get clean code, you had to add two new <string> tag constants to your /res/values/ strings.xml file and create the (currently empty) XML definition container by creating the new activity_bookmark.xml file.

Next, you'll add a TextView UI widget to the RelativeLayout container, and then you will test everything in the Nexus One emulator to make sure that everything is wired up correctly and that you are getting the results that you want to see from the TextView UI widget child tag's parameters.

Now you're ready to add a TextView UI element to the RelativeLayout in your activity_bookmark.xml screen layout definition file to add a bookmarked page label to the top of your Bookmarking Utility user interface design.

Click the activity_bookmark.xml tab at the top of Eclipse, and add an indented line of space after the opening RelativeLayout tab, and type in a < character to bring up the helper dialog, and double-click the **TextView** child tag in order to add it inside your RelativeLayout container, as shown in Figure 7-7. Now you'll add parameters to configure your TextView for use.

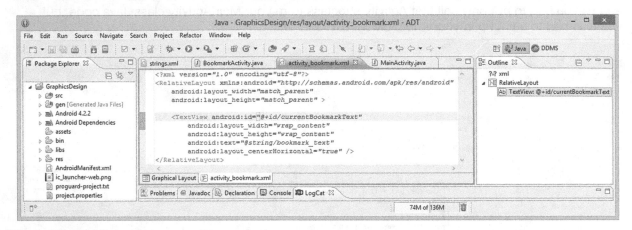

Figure 7-7. *Adding a TextView tag and basic parameters for layout, text content, ID, and horizontal centering*

Type **android** and a **colon** after the opening <TextView tag, and bring up the helper dialog. Then find an **android:id** parameter and double-click it to add it. Add the **@+id/currentBookmarkText** inside the quotation marks to ID the TextView so you can later change its value using your Java code. Finally, make sure you create the closing **/>** for this tag (after the ID parameter).

Use the same work process to add the required **android:layout_width** and the **android:layout_height** parameters, and set them both to **wrap_content**, as you just want the text object to float above your design as its own entity.

To give your TextView UI element some content (a text value), again use your android: work process; this time, find the **android:text** parameter and set it equal to that <string> constant you created earlier by using the **@string/bookmark_text** reference path inside the quotation marks.

Finally, use the helper dialog to find the **android:layout_centerHorizontal** parameter, or type it in yourself, and set it to **true** so that your TextView centers itself automatically at the top of your layout container. Now you can **Run As ➤ Android Application** and see your TextView, as shown in Figure 7-8.

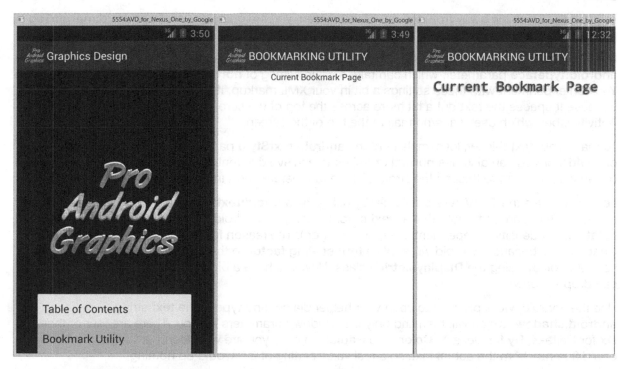

Figure 7-8. Testing your RelativeLayout and TextView in activity_bookmark.xml in the Nexus One emulator

Next, let's add some more advanced parameters to bring your text down a bit from the top of the screen, make it larger, change it to a monospace font, and give it some drop shadow special effects, just like you'd do if you were designing your UI in Photoshop CS6 or GIMP 2.8.6. To save some space, I'm going to use two parameters per line, as shown in Figure 7-9, since you are going to be adding more tags to this RelativeLayout container very soon.

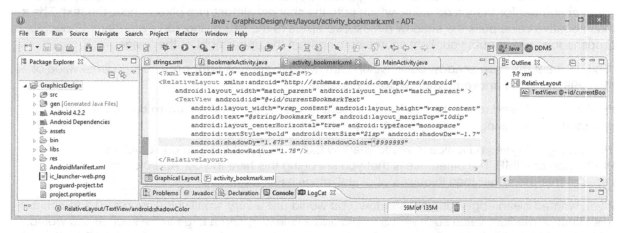

Figure 7-9. Adding advanced TextView tag parameters for typeface, style, size, and drop shadow special effects

To push the TextView away from the top of the screen, you are going to use an **android:marginTop** parameter and set it to a value of **10dip** (or 10dp).

Next, you can change to a monospace font (or serif if you like Roman fonts) using the **android:typeface** parameter, which can take a value setting of **normal**, **sans**, **serif**, or **monospace**. You can experiment with these settings a bit in your XML markup, if you like; I used **monospace** because it spaces the text out a bit more across the top of the screen and looks different from the Activity label (which uses sans/normal) at the top of the screen.

To make your text thicker, let's implement the **android:textStyle** parameter and set it to the value of "**bold**", or you can also use **normal** or **italics** to achieve different text styling effects. I used bold because I am trying to thicken the strokes of the font before I add in a drop shadow effect.

Let's also make the TextView's size larger by using the **android:textSize** parameter with a setting of **21sp**. It's important to note that all text or font settings in Android OS use **standard pixel** or **sp** notation, not density-independent pixel, or dip (or dp). The reason for this, which you learned in Chapter 5, is because Android will apply a **font scaling factor** to the fonts it uses in the OS, which you can poll by using the **DisplayMetrics** class. Now you have a big, wide, fat TextView object you can drop shadow!

Use the android: work process to open your helper dialog, and type in the text string **android:shadow**, which will then find only the shadow parameters for you. There are four of them: **Dx** for Delta-X, **Dy** for Delta-Y, **Color**, and **Radius**. In case you are wondering, a "delta" is an offset, or a difference from the actual text, so a real value setting of 0.0 would do nothing.

It is important to note that drop shadow FX do not render in the Graphical Layout Editor (GLE) tab, so you can't see these parameters in Eclipse! You must use a **Run As ➤ Android Application** work process, and view them in the Nexus One emulator. This is why I included the pane in Figure 7-8 showing the results on the far right side of the screen shot.

First, let's specify the drop shadow offsets from the text itself, using the **android:shadowDx** parameter set to a real data value of **-1.7**, and then the **android:shadowDy** parameter set to a real data value of **1.675**. Notice that I am taking advantage of this real number and providing a precise decimal number for the **y axis** value, which puts the shadow almost two pixels under the text. The **x axis** negative value pulls the shadow almost two pixels to the left, giving you a standard 45 degree dropshadow, which puts your light source coming from the upper right of the image.

Next, let's set the drop shadow color, which I am going to set to a **light grey** hexadecimal value of **#999999** using the **android:shadowColor** parameter.

Finally, you will need to set the shadow blur (soften) radius by using the **android:shadowRadius** parameter, again using a real value of 1.75 pixels.

This setting will give you a nice, realistic shadow blur radius, just like you could achieve in Photoshop or GIMP. The difference is that you are doing this here in your Android app using a few bytes of markup rather than kilobytes of digital image asset data.

If you wanted clean edges on your shadow, you would use a very small value such as 0.1 to achieve this effect. A medium value such as 0.5 would add a little blur, and a large value such as 2.0 would add a lot of blur of softening to the shadow. I recommend a value between 1.25 and 1.75 for the most realistic shadow, but lots of cool effects can be achieved using these four android:shadow parameters.

Another very important UI widget to us graphics designers is the ImageView widget. You'll take a closer look at that widget, and some of its important parameters in the next section when you add a picture of your bookmark page to the Bookmarking Utility Activity.

Using an ImageView Widget: The Cornerstone of Graphics

Before you add your ImageView UI widget to your RelativeLayout container, you need to put the digital image assets into their respective density pixel folders. Copy **bookmark0_240px.png**, **bookmark0_320px.png**, **bookmark0_480px.png** and **bookmark0_640px.png** into your **/res/drawable-ldpi**, **drawable-mdpi**, **drawable-hdpi**, and **drawable-xhdpi** folders, respectively.

Notice I am using resolutions that are twice the DPI targets for each of the pixel densities: 240 is twice 120 DPI (or two inches in size), 320 is twice 160 DPI, 480 is twice 240 DPI, and 640 is twice 320 DPI. Except for icons, you are not providing app image assets for the XXHDPI 480 DPI level.

If you did provide an XXHDPI image asset, it would need to be 960 pixels. Figure 7-10 shows your project's resource drawable-ldpi folder, and the app icon, and first bookmark page image placeholder (the splash screen), after the bookmark0_240px.png file has been copied and renamed to bookmark0.png.

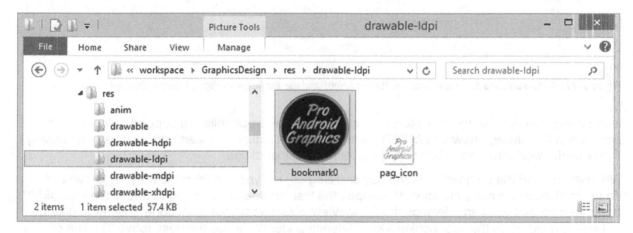

Figure 7-10. *Copy the bookmark0_240px.png file into the /res/drawable-ldpi folder and rename it bookmark0.png*

After you copy and rename all four image files into the four target pixel density folders that Android wants you to provide for pixel-based assets, you can add your <ImageView> child tag to your <RelativeView> parent layout container tag, as shown in Figure 7-11.

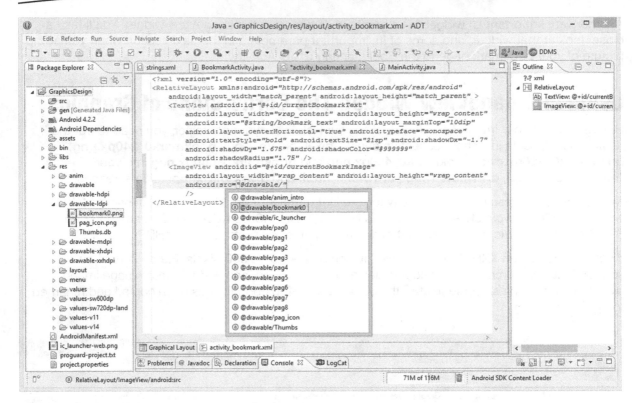

Figure 7-11. *Add parameters for ID and layout width and height, and use the helper dialog to locate @drawable files*

If you want, you can use the **<** key to bring up the RelativeLayout child tag support helper dialog, or just type in the **<ImageView** and **/>** begin and end tag delimiters and start adding parameters using the **android:** work process to bring up the parameter helper dialog.

Whether you find the parameter via the helper dialog or just type it in from memory, which you will do as you become a more proficient developer, the first parameter you need to add is the **android:id** parameter so that you can reference this ImageView object from your Java code in order to change the image used when the user bookmarks a different page. You'll use the descriptive ID value of **currentBookmarkImage**, so this ID reflects the ImageView functionality.

Next, add in the required **android:layout_width** and **android:layout_height** parameters, set to **wrap_content**, and then set the source file reference for the image using the **android:src** parameter set to **@drawable/bookmark0**, which will reference your **bookmark0.png** files in your **LDPI**, **MDPI**, **HDPI**, and **XHDPI** drawable folders, based on the user's Android device specifications.

Also note in Figure 7-11 that when you type in the **android:src="@drawable/** portion of the source file referencing parameter, that after you type in the **/** character, Eclipse will bring up a helper dialog listing all of the drawable assets that you currently have installed inside your project.

If the image assets that you copied earlier are not listed, you may need to right-click your project folder and select the **Refresh** command. This needs to be done every time you add assets when Eclipse is running (already launched) on your system, and is done to show Eclipse ADT that you have added in new assets that are external (not yet visible) to the Eclipse development environment.

Since you have used Windows Explorer, or another file management utility, to add these to the Eclipse project folder hierarchy (structure), the Refresh command will tell Eclipse to rebuild its internal file referencing to this new folder and/or asset file structure so that it knows what is in there.

Next, you need to either use the **Graphical Layout Editor** tab or your **Run As ➤ Android Application** work process and see how your initial ImageView object and parameters are working with your current TextView object and parameters.

As you can see in Figure 7-12, the ImageView object overlaps the TextView object at the top of the screen. If you had been using the simpler Linear Layout container with a vertical orientation, this would not have happened.

Figure 7-12. Nexus One preview showing TextView and ImageView overlap

Since you're using a RelativeLayout container, you need to provide parameters that tell your ImageView object how you want it to position itself relative to the neighboring TextView object. So, let's add in some more parameters!

After you use a **Run As ➤ Android Application** work process to run your Nexus One emulator, you will notice that because of a forced **Save** function used during this process you now have a **warning message** on your ImageView tag. Mouse-over it now, and you will see that Eclipse wants you to add in a **contentDescription** parameter (for accessibility reasons) for the sight impaired. As you can see in Figure 7-13, I added in this parameter.

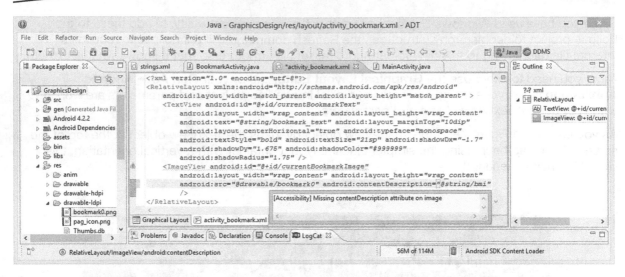

Figure 7-13. *Eclipse contentDescription warning message and android:contentDescription reference @string/bmi*

Make sure that you add in a <string> tag constant in your strings.xml file in your /res/values folder that adds in this text constant using the following markup:

```
<string name="bmi">Image of Currently Bookmarked Page</string>
```

Now you can deal with the relative layout positioning of your ImageView and TextView objects. Let's add in the **android:layout_below** parameter, which tells your ImageView object to lay itself out below the object that is referenced in the parameter; in this case, it is **@+id/currentBookmarkText**.

Here's yet another reason that you needed to give your TextView object an ID parameter: so that you can use relative layout alignment parameters to align other objects in the layout with the TextView using its ID.

Let's also downsize the image content inside your ImageView object UI widget container so that it does not touch the edges of the portrait layout, as you saw that it was doing in the Nexus One emulator. The best way to achieve this is to add an android:layout_margin parameter that will not only push the ImageView away from the sides of the screen but also down from the TextView UI element at the top of the screen, giving you a much nicer spacing result for the screen UI design. Use the value of 9dp this time, as shown in Figure 7-14, to demonstrate that you can use either 9dip or 9dp, and either one will work just as well in your XML markup.

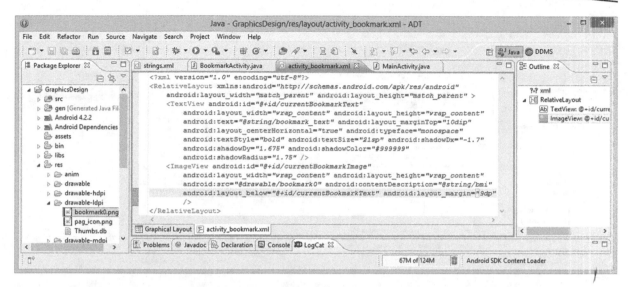

Figure 7-14. Adding parameters to correct TextView and ImageView overlap and add spacing around ImageView

Next, you will add an android:layout_centerHorizontal parameter and set it to a value of true. As you can see in Figure 7-12, your ImageView is already centering in a portrait layout, but when the user turns the device on its side, the ImageView will be on the left side of the screen. Thus, for your current portrait design, this parameter would be redundant, but to support both portrait and landscape orientations, it turns out to be a lifesaver!

This type of design is what I was talking about in Chapter 5; you need to think across all of the different devices, densities, and orientations.

Finally, you'll add an advanced parameter called android:clickable and set it to a value of true because later on you will want to allow your user to click the image of the bookmarked page and go to that page immediately. So you'll use some foresight, adding a tag parameter now, while you are here learning about some of these ImageView parameters. The new parameters you have just added can be seen in Figure 7-15.

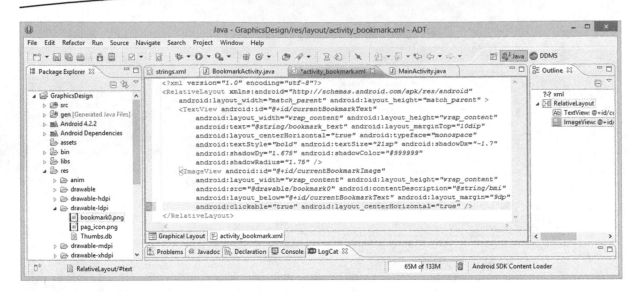

Figure 7-15. Adding parameters to make ImageView clickable and to center horizontally in landscape layouts

Now you're ready to again use your **Run As ➤ Android Application** work process and see how your user interface design looks with the dropshadowed TextView and centered ImageView underneath it.

As you can see in Figure 7-16, it looks very clean. All you have to do now is to test your UI design in the landscape orientation by turning your Nexus One emulator 90 degrees sideways and see if your new user interface design stays just as professional!

Figure 7-16. Testing your layout so far in the Nexus One emulator

Before you do that, there is one other detail that I want to add to the ImageView. Since you drop shadowed the TextView, you should also have the same effect on your ImageView, at 45 degrees under the left bottom side of the 3D hoop. Let's type in **android:** to take a look at the parameter list, and see if you can find the android:shadow parameters so that you can add the drop shadow to the ImageView object as well.

Although the ImageView has about 100 parameters, it does not seem to support the android:shadow parameters that the TextView supports yet. I am sure at some point in the future this will be added, but this is not an easy feature to support, given that Android can't just simply drop shadow the ImageView container, which is square, and would be much easier.

To correctly drop shadow this ImageView object, Android would have to look at the source image reference in the ImageView object and then incorporate (generate) the drop shadow effect based on the alpha channel (that image's transparency).

This is where Android's flexibility in allowing developers to use external software such as GIMP 2.8.6 or Lightworks 11.1 becomes very valuable. What you are going to have to do to achieve this matching drop shadow effect for your ImageView is to go into GIMP and create it using that program's tools.

I'll do that later on in this chapter; after all, this is a Pro Graphics book so you'll go through the work process in GIMP of how to create a drop shadow effect for your image asset instead of creating it using an Android ImageView parameter. You'll learn how to create semi-translucent alpha data while you're at it, just to make sure you learn the most advanced techniques!

Next, you're going to take a look at how to turn your Nexus One emulator 90 degrees to achieve a landscape orientation. You will do this so you can test your UI to see how it looks in a landscape orientation.

Testing Your UI Design in the Nexus One Landscape Mode

Next, you are going to learn the keyboard shortcuts that will turn your Nexus One emulator from portrait orientation to landscape orientation, so I hope you still have it running on your screen! If not, fire it up again!

The keyboard shortcut on Windows to toggle an emulator between landscape and portrait uses the (left side) **Control** or **CRTL** key modifier along with the **F11** function key. So hold down the CRTL key on the left side of your keyboard and then (while it is still being held down) tap the F11 key and voila, your emulator will rotate right there in front of your eyes.

Use **CTRL-F12** to rotate the display back to portrait orientation. As you can see in Figure 7-17, your android:layout_centerHorizontal works very well in landscape orientation and you have just as attractive a layout in that orientation as you do in portrait orientation.

Figure 7-17. Switching the Nexus One emulator into Landscape mode to test the centerHorizontal parameter

If you are using an Apple Macintosh, the Command key plus the 7 on the numeric keypad mimics the CRTL-F11 on Windows and the Command plus the 9 on the numeric keypad mimics the CRTL-F12 on Windows. Some users online claim that other keystrokes also work on Macintosh, such as CTRL+FN+F11 or CTRL+Command+F11 and CTRL+FN+F12 or CTRL+Command+F12, so just experiment.

If you are using the Linux OS, use CRTL-F11, just like you do in Windows. It is important to note that CRTL-F11 means "switch forward" and CRTL-F12 means "switch back," so both keystroke combinations may work as a toggle between the portrait and landscape orientations.

Adding a Drop Shadow Effect to an ImageView Image Asset

Now let's add a drop shadow effect to the bookmark0.png image asset using the GIMP 2.8.6 open source digital image editing and composition software.

Launch GIMP 2.8 and open the **bookmark0_640px.png** file that you copied into your **/res/drawable-xhdpi** folder. You always want to work with the highest number of pixels that you can, since you will have to downsample the image to provide assets in the other three resolution density folders. Figure 7-18 shows, from left to right, the first few things you need to do to set up your digital imaging composite for this project. First, widen your image by 40 pixels in each of the x and y dimensions to accommodate your shadow. In the **Set Image Canvas Size** dialog, click the **chain icon** next to the Width and Height fields to lock them together, and then enter **720** into the **Width** field, and click the **Center** button to center the original 640 pixel resolution image inside the new 720 pixel resolution image. Click the **Resize** button to apply these new parameters to your digital canvas and in your **Layers-Brushes** window right-click under the current layer and find the **Duplicate Layer** menu option to copy that layer data into a new layer.

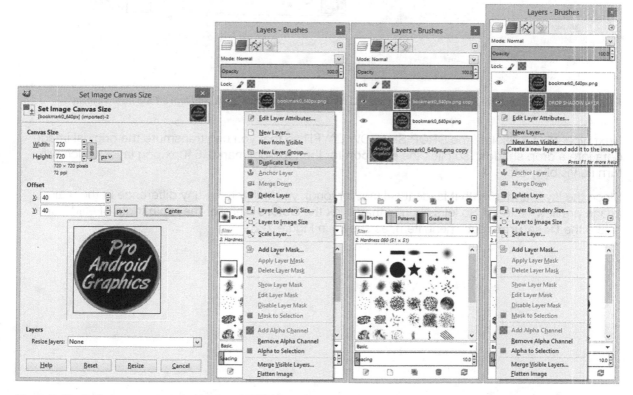

Figure 7-18. Setting up your 640 pixel bookmark PNG image for creating a drop shadow effect inside GIMP 2.8

Once you have your duplicate layer, drag it underneath your original image layer, as shown in the third pane of Figure 7-18. Double-click the copy (duplicated) layer, and name it **DROP SHADOW LAYER**, as shown in the fourth pane of Figure 7-18. Next, right-click underneath the layer and select the **New Layer** command to bring up a **Create a New Layer** dialog, which is shown in Figure 7-19. Enter a layer name of **White Background Layer**, and select a **White Layer Fill Type** (radio button option), and click the **OK** button.

This will create a new layer filled with the color white on top of the DROP SHADOW LAYER, but since you want the White Background Layer to be the background, you need to drag it down to the bottom of the layer stack, as shown in the center pane of Figure 7-19.

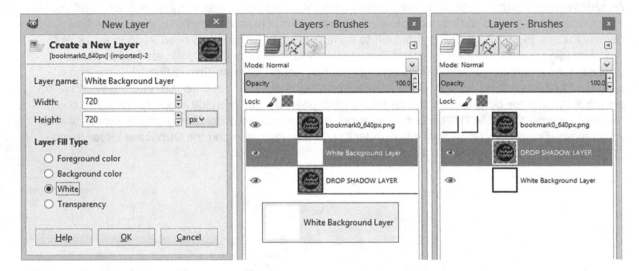

Figure 7-19. Create the White Background Layer, drag it to the bottom of the layer stack, and turn off top layer visibility

Next, you want to isolate the DROP SHADOW LAYER so that you can transmute the original image data into a drop shadow, so click the **eye icon** for the top bookmark0_640px.png layer, which will turn its visibility off.

Since the layer underneath it is identical (not for long), you will not see any difference in the main image preview window. So let's change that: click the **Colors** menu at the top middle of GIMP and select the **Desaturate** sub-menu item, as shown in Figure 7-20.

Figure 7-20. Using a Colors ➤ Desaturate tool to turn the DROP SHADOW LAYER from color to black and white

Notice in GIMP that if you hover your mouse over anything in the GIMP software package, including icons, menus, layers and so on, a tool-tip will pop up and tell you what that software function is used for.

The **Desaturate tool** or algorithm is used to remove color, or saturation, from an image while leaving its lightness, or luminosity, values intact. This essentially turns your image from a color to a black and white image, which in your case is the first step in achieving a medium gray shadow for your 3D hoop encased image.

The Desaturate (Remove Colors) dialog has three options that allow you to choose a shade of gray based on lightness, luminosity, or an average of the two. I chose the luminosity (radio button selector) as it provided me with the lightest gray coloration.

If you want visual feedback on what any given tool in GIMP will do, look for the Preview checkbox and make sure there is a check mark in it. Once you do this, you will be able to see the results of your settings in the main GIMP preview window, as shown in Figure 7-21.

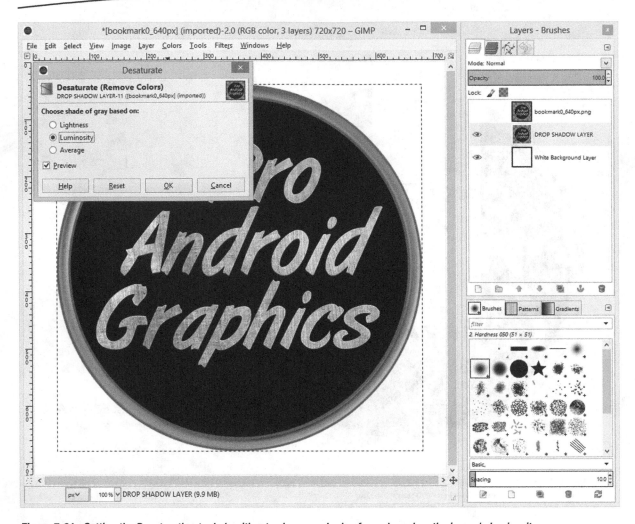

Figure 7-21. Setting the Desaturation tool algorithm to choose a shade of gray based on the image's luminosity

In case you haven't figured out your next "move" to create your drop shadow effect, you are going to **blur** these grayscale pixels to create the shadow effect. However, if you do that now, your blur will get **cut off** due to the edges of the current layer, which are denoted in GIMP using **dotted lines**.

As you can see in Figure 7-21 and Figure 7-22, although you have resized your canvas, which is the container that is holding your layers, the layers themselves are still at the original 640 pixel source data sizing.

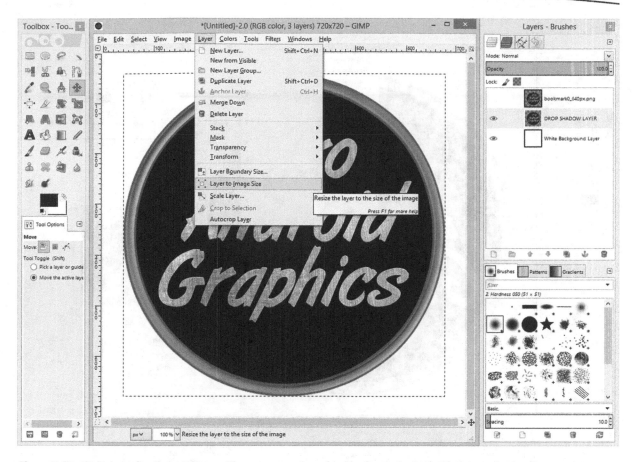

Figure 7-22. Use a Layer ➤ Layer to Image Size menu sequence to resize layer size to match the new image size

This is shown via the dotted lines, and although not a problem now, if you were to apply a blur operation with the edges set like this, you would get straight line areas on the resulting blur (shadow). This is because GIMP's blur algorithm cannot "see" space outside the current layer boundaries.

Somehow you need to find a way to push these boundaries out for just this layer, so that they match the edges of the new image (canvas) size that you specified earlier as 720 pixels. Fortunately, GIMP 2 has a command designed just for this purpose. It is located under the GIMP **Layer** menu, and it is called **Layer to Image Size**, and it is shown in action in Figure 7-22.

This is important to do before the blur operation, as a fuzzy blur looks unprofessional if it has razor sharp edges that show where its containing graphic's edges are. So don't forget this step!

As you can see in Figure 7-23, your blur algorithm now has more space to spread (blur) your monochrome image's pixels in order to turn it from a hard-edged metal hoop into a nice fuzzy shadow underneath your original image.

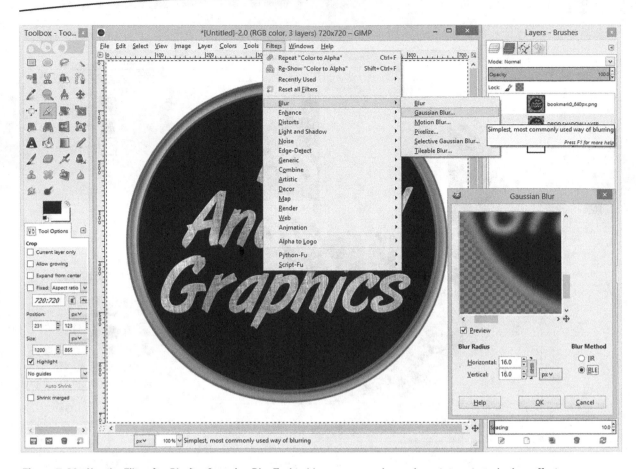

Figure 7-23. Use the Filters ➤ Blur ➤ Gaussian Blur Tool to blur your monochrome layer to create a shadow effect

To invoke the Blur algorithm in GIMP, go into the **Filters** menu, and find the **Blur** sub-menu, which will open up a fly-out sub-menu with the different types of Blur algorithms that GIMP supports. Blur's an important effect in digital imaging for both fine-tuning photography and for creating special effects, as you are doing here.

For your application, you are going to use the most popular Blur algorithm, which is called **Gaussian Blur,** named after the man who created the central mathematics algorithms that are utilized inside the Blur algorithm. It will give you the smooth, evenly-distributed blur effect that you are looking for without a complicated user interface, as you can see in Figure 7-23.

I combined the menu drop-down screen shot with the Gaussian Blur dialog on the right side to save space. As you can see, I **locked** the **Horizontal** and **Vertical** values using the **chain icon** to get an even blur, and selected the default **RLE** (Run Length Encoded) Blur Method (algorithm), and selected the **Preview** checkbox to show me the blur amount within the dialog preview.

In the next major version of GIMP (2.10), there won't be an IIR or RLE Blur Method selection option, as current machines are so fast that it will not be needed any more. It used to be that IIR was faster (optimized) for photographs and RLE for blurring edges and vector (shape based) artwork.

I am using a **Blur Radius** (in pixels) of **16.0** (the default is 5.0) to get a fair amount of blur on the hoop part of this image, which is the only part that's going to be visible underneath (and slightly to the left-bottom) of the original image. Remember that the original image is above this in the layer stack, but currently not visible, as the eye icon is turned off, so you can see exactly what you are doing on this layer for now. Click the **OK** button, and you can see a dropshadow effect in Figure 7-24 even before you move it!

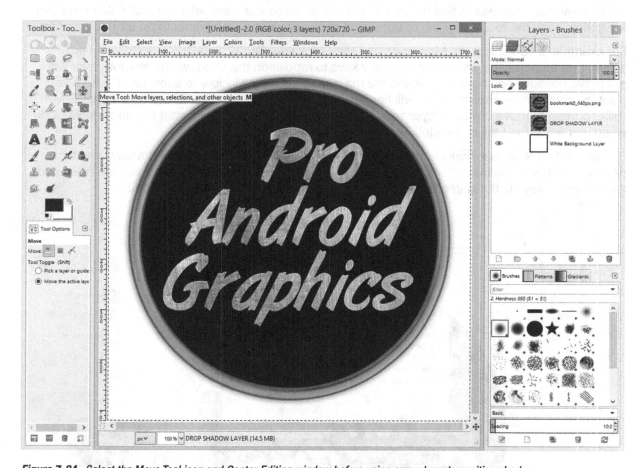

Figure 7-24. Select the Move Tool icon and Center Editing window before using arrow keys to position shadow

Next, you will use the Move tool to position the drop shadow layer down and to the left by a few pixels (I used 6 in each direction, as you will see).

First, you need to turn back on the original image layer visibility using the eye icon in the Layer palette, which you can see has been done in Figure 7-24. You can also see the highlighted Move tool icon as I left the tool-top fly-out active for the screen shot.

It is also important to notice that after I turn on the visibility of the top layer and make sure that the shadow layer is still selected, or **blue** when the Layer Palette is active and **gray** (as in screen shot) when another window is active, that I click on the titlebar of the image preview window itself (now gold in the screen shot) to make that window active before I use the arrow keys on my keyboard to move the layer pixel by pixel.

The reason that this work process is important is because digital image editing software such as GIMP is **modal**. This means that the software looks at which tools are selected and which windows are active (have the focus) in order to determine precisely what a user wants to do for that function.

For example, if you select the Move tool, and then click your DROP SHADOW LAYER to make it active, and then use the left and down arrow keys to reposition the shadow, the shadow layer will not move because you have not clicked the main image editing window to show GIMP where you want the move to be applied. What will happen instead when you use the arrow keys is that GIMP will use them to move between layer selections, which is what you would want the arrow keys to do when you are in the Layers palette!

So, select the Move tool, make sure the DROP SHADOW LAYER is selected and active, and then click the titlebar of the central editing window in GIMP, and press the down arrow key six times and the left arrow key six times in order to position the shadow as shown in Figure 7-25.

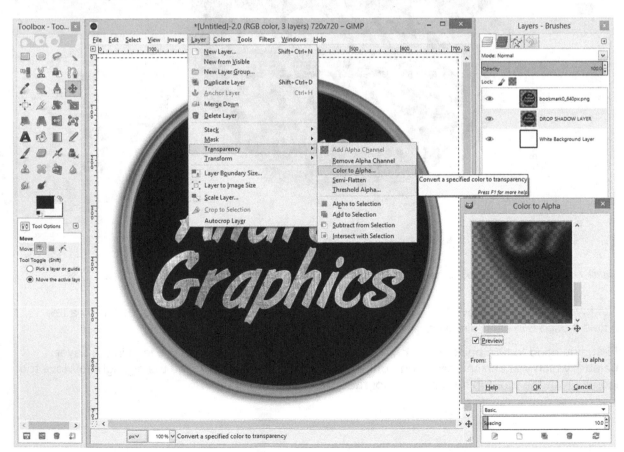

Figure 7-25. *Use a Layer ➤ Transparency ➤ Color to Alpha tool to create translucent alpha values from shadow*

Next, you are going to take the drop shadow greyscale values and transfer them to the alpha channel so that they will let some of the background color (or imagery) through into the shadow area of your image for a much more realistic compositing effect (result) once you are back in Android. This is done in GIMP by using the **Layer** menu and the **Transparency** sub-menu and the **Color to Alpha** algorithm on the fly-out, as shown in Figure 7-25.

As you can see in the **Color to Alpha dialog**, which is shown on the right side of Figure 7-25 (I have again combined the menu selection screen shot and the dialog that it brings up to save some space), you now have a **partial transparency** in your alpha channel where your shadow is. This will serve to mix pixel colors behind that area (the shadow) more realistically, whether those are solid color values or image color values (differing pixel color values). We will be going back into Android Developer mode soon and will be showing how to implement this in Eclipse and the visual results in the Nexus One emulator as well.

Now that you have created your drop shadow effect, you can get rid of some of that extra space around your image and its effect so that you don't go from a 640 pixel to a 720 pixel image just to add a drop shadow. To do this, you will again use the **Set Image Canvas Size** dialog, this time to cut the size back down from 720 pixels to 672 pixels, as shown in Figure 7-26.

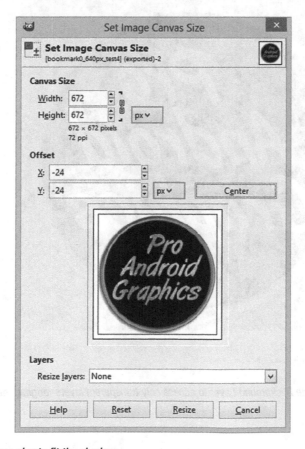

Figure 7-26. Shrinking the canvas size to fit the shadow

You'll use 32 more pixels than your 640 pixel image size was to start with. Notice you are using power-of-2 pixel increments (1-2-4-8-16-32-64 etc.) here, so that when you resize to the other density levels you get even pixel boundary numbers. In the dialog, click the **chain icon** to lock the dimension of the canvas size and enter **672** and then click the **Center** button. This will auto-enter **-24 Offset** values for you in the X and Y fields. Why -24 and not -48? This is because this is giving you the offset around all four sides of the image, as shown visually in the dialog, and half of 48 is 24.

Now you can turn off your white background layer visibility, using the eye icon, and take a look at the resulting effect and alpha channel values.

Select the primary image layer, as shown in Figure 7-27, and make sure the visibility is off for the White Background Layer, so you can see your alpha channel and transparency values, as denoted in GIMP using the checkerboard pattern. As you can see by the dotted-line, you haven't added too much image data (pixel space) to your original image to add this drop shadow effect.

Figure 7-27. *Turning off the White Background Layer to access only transparent layers (original image and shadow)*

Next to the **Layers tab** (stacked white or clear vellum icon), you will see the **Color Channels tab** (stacked Red, Green, and Blue icon). Click this tab now so that you can examine the red, green, blue, and alpha channel for your image next. You are going to make sure that your alpha channel defines as transparent around your image, as opaque (black) for most of the image, and as translucent (gray) where the shadow effect is positioned.

Once you are in the Channels tab you will notice that the channels work in much the same way that the layers do, and so let's turn off the visibility of the red, green, and blue channels, leaving only the alpha channel on, so you can see the data your alpha channel contains. The result of this can be seen in Figure 7-28, and your alpha channel does contain your shadow data.

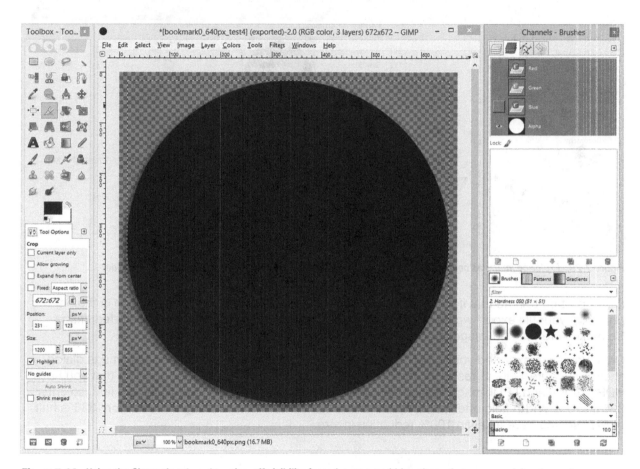

Figure 7-28. Using the Channels tab and turning off visibility for red, green, and blue channels to see an alpha channel

This translucent area of the alpha channel will let some of the color data from any pixel colors that may exist underneath your image mix (when you are compositing it, at least) into the gray shadow areas of the image itself.

This will result in a photo-realistic shadowing effect, regardless of what you place underneath this image and its new shadow effect. You will want to test this next in Eclipse once you finish up here by creating your different density target images, and saving the master file, and similar busy work.

Let's export this file to your /workspace/GraphicsDesign/res/drawable-xhdpi folder using the GIMP File Export dialog shown in Figure 7-29. You'll name the file **bookmarks0.png** (for bookmark shadow) so that you have both image versions intact. You will use the **Save color values from transparent pixels** option in the sub-dialog, shown on the right hand side of the screen shot.

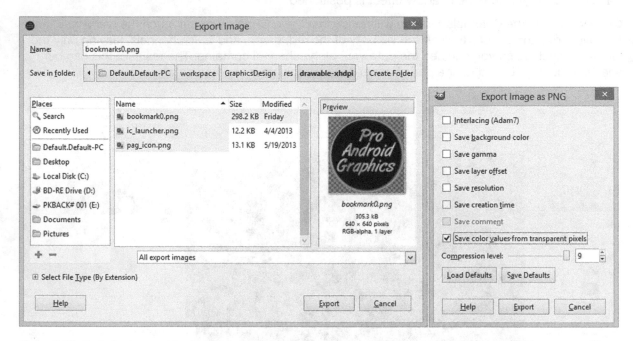

Figure 7-29. Exploring image as bookmarks0.png to your /workspace/GraphicsDesign/res/drawable-xhdpi folder

It is important to note that if you had left the White Background Layer visible (eye icon in the on position), your file export would have a white background visible in the resulting exported image. So make sure that the image looks as it does in Figure 7-27 before you do the export!

Once you have exported your XHDPI PNG32 asset, it is time to use the GIMP Scale Image dialog, shown in Figure 7-30, to resize your image data into the other resolution densities, so that you have HDPI, MDPI, and LPDI image assets for this new image. Let's do the 2X downsample first, so enter **336** into the **Width** field after you **lock** the image size x and y values using a **chain icon**. 336 is half of 672, so you have an even 100% reduction in size.

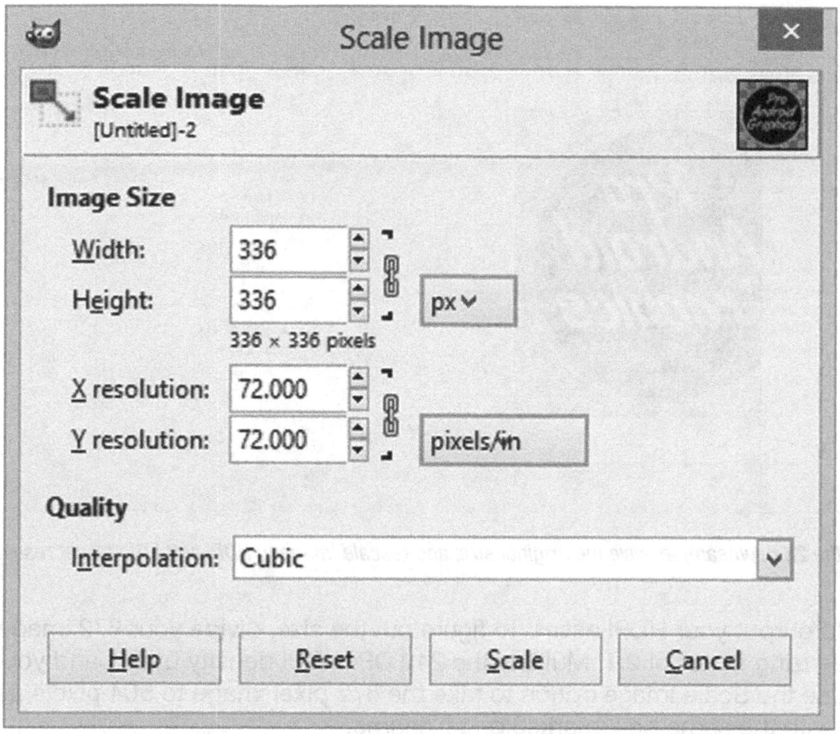

Figure 7-30. Scaling image down to create 336 pixel MDPI asset

You will use the high quality **cubic** interpolator to do these image rescale operations. Once you **export** the files to your **/res/drawable-mdpi/** folder, using the filename **bookmarks0.png**, use the **Edit** menu and **Undo** function to take you back to your original (highest) resolution XHDPI image asset, as shown in Figure 7-31. Also, this is a good time (after the Undo Scale Image option is invoked) to use the GIMP **File ➤ Save As** operation to save a GIMP native **.XCF** file of your layers, channels, and so on in your working directory for images. As you can see, for this book, mine is /PAGD/CH07.

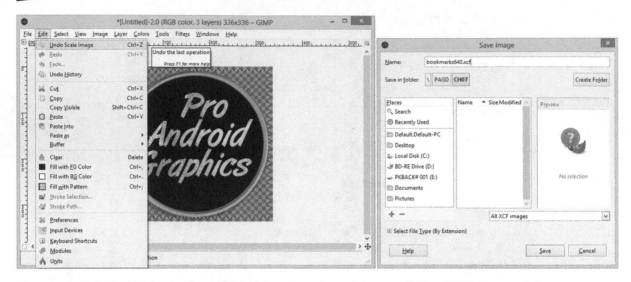

Figure 7-31. Undo the 2X downsample, save the original size, and rescale image to HDPI and LDPI target resolution

Now you need to output your HDPI asset. To figure out the size, divide your 672 image size by its 320 DPI to get a sizing factor of **2.1**. Multiply the 240 DPI HDPI density by 2.1 and you get **504** pixels, so next use the Scale Image option to take the 672 pixel image to 504 pixels and export it to the HDPI folder with the same bookmarks0.png filename.

Again, you will **undo** the Scale Image operation, and multiply the LDPI 120DPI density by 2.1 to get **252** pixels or take half of the 240 DPI 504 pixels to reach this same number. Perform the same Scale Image and Export operations on this 252 pixel digital image asset, and you will have all four of your resolution density targets provided for.

If you have already saved the file as a native XCF (eXperimental Computing Facility) on your hard disk, make sure to answer No to the Save dialog you get when you exit GIMP, or you will save a lower resolution version of the image to that file name (container) and lose your original hi-rez format.

Now you can go back into Eclipse and make the necessary changes to your XML file to implement the new drop shadow effect image version and learn how to put a background color or image in your RelativeLayout container so that you can have Android perform some image compositing for you. You can start to leverage the foundational knowledge you've learned in the initial chapters.

Changing Your ImageView XML to Incorporate a New Asset

Fire up your Eclipse ADT package if it's not still running and go into the **activity_bookmark.xml** editing tab, and edit your **android:src** parameter, as shown in Figure 7-32, so that it references your new **bookmarks0.png** image, which you have just created.

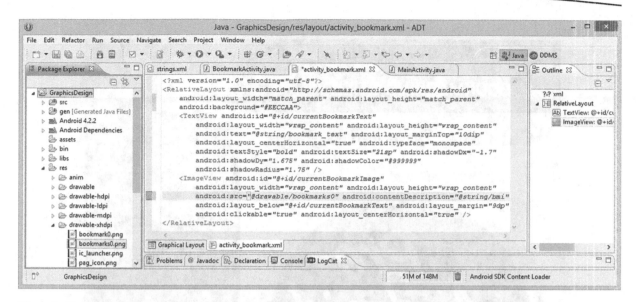

Figure 7-32. Changing the android:src image reference name and adding an android:background parameter in the parent tag

To see the resulting shadow against a white background (default) color for your RelativeLayout, you can use the **Graphical Layout tab** at the bottom of the editing screen, or use a **Run As ➤ Android Application** work process and take a look at it in the Nexus One emulator.

To show the partial alpha channel bleed-through in this new image, you will need to add an **android:background** parameter into your parent RelativeLayout container tag. First, you will use a pastel orange color value of **#EECCAA** to make sure that your color shadow is tinted grayish-orange, and then later you will add an image to make sure that image data is blending with your shadow alpha as well. The new parent tag parameter can be seen in Figure 7-32.

Next, use the **Run As ➤ Android Application** work process to preview the new UI design in the Nexus One emulator. Now that you know how, you can take a look at it in both portrait and landscape modes, and see how ultra cool it looks. It looks really great (see Figure 7-33).

Figure 7-33. Testing shadow alpha channel using background color

If you want to match the TextView drop shadow to the ImageView drop shadow, you can tweak the android:shadow parameters and their values so that the shadows are more similar (increase the offset and Dx and Dy values a bit). You can do this after you add a background image, to further test your alpha.

Now that you know your alpha channel is working with a solid color, in the next section you'll copy a JPEG image of a beautiful sunset into your XHDPI folder and see if your drop shadow effect works with photographic imagery.

Compositing a Background Image in Your RelativeLayout

Finally, you are going to install a background image called **cloudsky.jpg** in your UI's RelativeLayout container. Find this file in the book's Chapter 7 assets folder, and copy it to your project's **/res/drawable-xhdpi/** folder, and then utilize your Refresh function in Eclipse ADT so the development environment can "see" it when you reference it and not throw an error.

To reference the new JPEG image, simply change the hexadecimal color value that you had in the **android:background** parameter for its data value from a **#EECCAA** value to an asset reference value of **@drawable/cloudsky** and you're done! The XML markup for the new image reference and the refreshed /res/drawable-xhdpi folder image assets contents are shown in Figure 7-34.

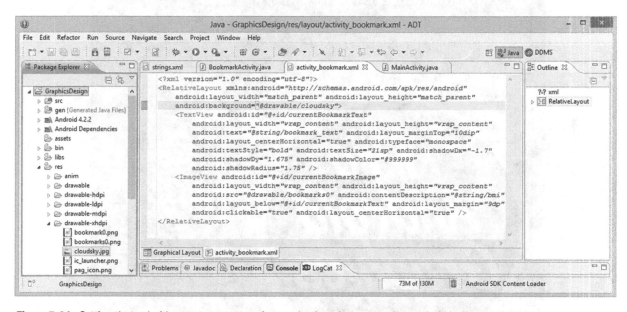

Figure 7-34. Setting the android:src parameter to reference bookmarks0.png and an android:background parameter

Notice that your Eclipse ADT utilizes a different icon for JPEG imagery in the IDE than it does for PNG imagery. The JPEG is 384 Kilobytes for a 1000 pixel square image, so I'm just going to use one XHDPI density resolution and let the Android OS downsample it since it's just a stock sunset image.

The other thing I did here that was kind of tricky was I used a 1:1 square aspect ratio image that could be **scaled asymmetrically** by Android into a portrait or landscape orientation. This can be done without a user knowing that what they are looking at is not original (undistorted) image content, since they can't see the 1000x1000 pixel image that is stored in the Android .APK file resource area. I'm going to show you a lot of cool tricks in this book; we have hundreds of pages to work with!

The image has 1000 pixels in each x and y dimension, thus there are plenty of pixels for the Android OS to work with when scaling, and no sharp edges in the picture. This photograph features just puffy clouds with gradients of sunset color, which is the perfect scaling scenario, as you will see when you test this new background image out in the Nexus One emulator using both portrait and landscape viewing orientations.

Let's get back on point, however. What you are really testing here are your drop shadow effects and the alpha channel compositing efficacy of the gray values (8-bit or 256 of them) in your alpha channel, which are allowing the underlying pixel color values to show through, or combine, with your shadow effect to various extents. As you can see in Figure 7-35, your GIMP-created drop shadow is compositing beautifully with the background sunset image.

Figure 7-35. Testing drop shadow alpha channel in the Nexus One emulator

This is more than I can say for Android's TextView parameter's algorithmic shadow compositing; however, this may be due to the current value settings!

The current TextView shadowColor parameter is optimized for a white color background, using a light grey #999999 hexidecimal color value setting.

You will need to change this value to a much darker grey setting to match the shadow greyscale value used on your ImageView. You should probably use a **#333333** hexidecimal color value, which is all the way on the other end of the greyscale spectrum.

To figure out the exact percentage gray value, from 0 to 16 (Hexidecimal), 3 is 25% (remember, 3 is really four, when counting from zero) of the way, so this gray would use **75%** black and **25%** white, so it's a 3/4 dark gray.

The #999999, on the other hand, is 10 of 16 which is 5 of 8, and 8 goes into 100 12.5 times, and 5 times 12.5 is **62.5%** white and **37.5%** black, so it's a 3/8 light gray, and as you can see in Figure 7-35, light gray doesn't work with the sunset image. Additionally, you need to add the alpha values into the RGB value to make it an ARGB value. Let's make it 75% (12/16) opaque, via a **BB** alpha value, yielding a resulting hexidecimal value of **#BB333333** for the new **android:shadowColor** parameter value, as shown in Figure 7-36.

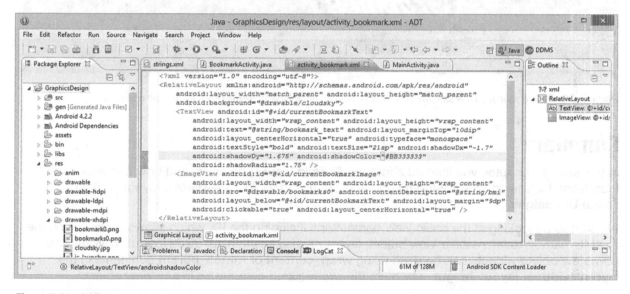

Figure 7-36. Adding the new alpha channel ARGB color value to your TextView android:shadowColor parameter

Now you're ready to test your alpha-channel-capable shadowColor parameter on your TextView to see if you can get closer to the result you are achieving on your ImageView. Use your **Run As ➤ Android Application** work process and run the Nexus One emulator and test the user interface design in both portrait and landscape modes. Figure 7-37 shows the UI design in landscape mode in the Nexus One emulator; the shadow darkness and transparency match up!

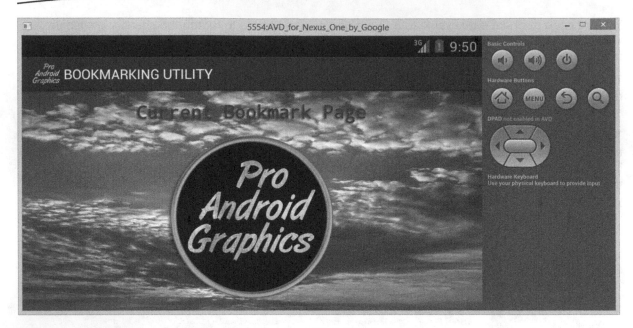

Figure 7-37. Testing your TextView shadowColor with alpha and ImageView in Nexus One's landscape orientation

Summary

In this seventh chapter, you learned about the Android **View** superclass, and how it provides the foundation for user interface **widgets** that you can use to fill your ViewGroup layout containers to create **UI designs**.

We started by looking at the basic View parameters, including the **ID,** which allows other Java code or XML markup to reference a View object; layout (global) positioning, using **layout_weight**; and how View object widgets can be sized using **wrap_content** or **match_parent** constants in the **layout_width** or **layout_height**, which are the two required parameters in any View object.

We then looked at View (local) positioning properties or parameters, which can use **margins** (space outside the View bounds) and **padding** (space inside the View bounds). These parameters allow localized View object (UI widget) positioning inside the layout container and relative to other UI elements.

Next, you looked at the **graphics properties** for any View object, which are controlled by **background** (image) and source (image) as well as **alpha** and **visibility** parameters. Most of the graphics design and special effects you will be learning about in this book will ultimately be implemented using these parameters, so we covered them in detail to leave no pixel unturned.

Finally, we looked at how one makes a View object **interactive** by setting the **focus** and by implementing **event listeners** and **event handling** routines.

The time had come to start writing Java code and XML markup, so you created a new Activity subclass to create a **Bookmarking Utility**, so that you could learn about the **RelativeLayout** container and the **TextView** and **ImageView** UI widgets, both View subclasses themselves and important in Android design.

You learned how to apply drop shadow effects to the TextView UI element and discovered that the ImageView UI element does not yet support this feature, so you learned how to go outside Android and accomplish this effect via another open source digital imaging software package called GIMP 2.8.6.

You learned the work process for creating a drop shadow using some advanced features in GIMP and your highest resolution digital image asset, and how to create new drop shadow versions of this asset for each of the other DPI density resolutions that are required for optimal graphics in Android.

Finally, you learned how to switch the Nexus One Emulator from portrait mode into landscape mode by using the **Control-F11** and **Control-F12** function key sequences in Windows and Linux and the **Command-7** and **Command-9** keys in the Macintosh OS. You also learned that some Mac OSes also support the Windows/Linux CTRL-F11 keystroke sequence, or something very similar.

In the next chapter, you will learn more about the other advanced ImageView concepts, parameters, techniques, methods, and optimization. You will learn how to utilize all the different properties and options that the ImageView UI element affords you, as it is the cornerstone of graphics in Android OS.

Advanced ImageView: More Graphics Design Using ImageView

In this eighth chapter, we will continue to look even more closely at the **ImageView** widget and its advanced property settings (parameters), as it is the most important user interface element for implementing graphics design inside the Android OS, along with its ImageButton subclass.

You got a head start learning about the ImageView user interface widget in the previous chapter, where you used it to hold an image for the currently bookmarked chapter in the bookmarking utility UI that you are designing.

You used the **android:src** parameter to define a **source image**, some UI layout parameters to position it, and a margins parameter to give it some breathing room in your design. However, you didn't really get into any of the advanced parameters or tricks, such as using both the source (foreground) image plate and the background image plate at the same time.

We did cover some fairly advanced digital imaging concepts using GIMP 2.8, which is always good to do in a Pro Android Graphics book, and I will try to do even more of that as the book goes on, in both GIMP and VirtualDub.

We will take a look in this chapter at some of the other unique properties and parameters of the ImageView user interface widget class, as well as how to implement them via XML markup and Java code. You already learned about one parameter that is primarily utilized in an ImageView, the android:src parameter or attribute. This is because the ImageView is a container for a digital image asset, and that image asset is referenced via a source (src) attribute or property (or parameter). Since **ImageButton** is subclassed from ImageView, it will also feature this same android:src parameter.

Graphics in Android: The Origins of the ImageView Class

The Android **ImageView** class is a subclass of the **View** Superclass, which is itself a subclass of the **java.lang.Object** master class. The View class has its own package, the **android.view** package, but ImageView is kept in a separate Android package for UI widgets called the **android.widget** package.

The **android.widget** package contains the ImageView class, as well as all of the other UI element classes that are subclassed from this View class. If you want to see exactly which widgets are included in the package, you can find this information at the following Android Developer web site URL:

```
http://developer.android.com/reference/android/widget/package-summary.html
```

The ImageView class displays any supported digital image format for areas of our application that require custom imagery that we as developers wish to supply. This would include things like the application icon, background imagery for a layout container, UI custom buttons, and so forth.

The ImageView class can access imagery from a variety of sources, such as internal application resources (the **/res/drawable** folders) or from content providers, such as **HTTP**. The ImageView class will compute its UI container measurement from the source image asset so it can be used with any layout container. Since this is a graphics book, we will be using digital imagery with every layout container that we utilize, for the most part.

ImageView provides various display options such as custom scaling and RGB value re-tinting, both of which we will look at in detail in this chapter.

It is interesting to note that the ImageView class has very few subclasses, which is the opposite of what one would assume for a pixel-centric OS such as Android. The ImageView subclass that we will be looking at the most is the **ImageButton** class, but there is also a **QuickContactBadge** subclass that is more niche-oriented, if your application is working with QuickContacts.

ImageView has only one known indirect subclass as well, called ZoomButton, which is a subclass of ImageButton. ZoomButton is used to zoom in and out of digital image based button assets using a zoom factor and zoom speed.

If you wish to examine the ImageView class in greater detail, please visit its page on the Android Developer web site, located at the following URL:

```
http://developer.android.com/reference/android/widget/ImageView.html
```

The ImageView class does, however, have one single **nested class**, which is called **ScaleType**. This **ImageView.ScaleType** nested class allows us to define how our digital image asset will be scaled to fit its View.

This makes ScaleType important enough to merit its own section within this chapter, so let's take a look at how this ImageView.ScaleType class works, and learn about all the powerful image scaling constants it offers us.

The ImageView.ScaleType Nested Class: Scaling Control

The Android ImageView has a nested class called **ScaleType,** which contains scaling constants, and related algorithms, for determining how to scale an ImageView object. This **ImageView.ScaleType** class is a subclass of the Java **Enum** class, which is a subclass of the java.lang.Object master class. The precise superclass ➤ subclass relationship between these is as follows:

```
java.lang.Object
  > java.lang.Enum<E extends java.lang.Enum<E>>
   > android.widget.ImageView.ScaleType
```

The ImageView.ScaleType class is a part of the **android.widget** package, as you would expect, and its import statement would thus reference a path of **android.widget.ImageView.ScaleType** if it is used in your Java code.

The reason the ScaleType class is a subclass of java.lang.Enum is because it uses this Java **Emuneration Types** class to create **numeric constants** for the different scaling algorithm types or **scaling options** that the scaling algorithm uses to ascertain which type of scaling needs to be implemented.

These numeric constants have also been assigned string (text) constants to make them easier to remember and to reference within your code. We will be covering each of these in detail in this section of the chapter.

There are 71 direct subclasses of java.lang.Enum in Android, as it is used to provide these numeric constants, which can be a common practice in Java programming. If you want to learn more about this Enum class, you can find its page on the Android Developer web site, located at the following URL:

```
http://developer.android.com/reference/java/lang/Enum.html
```

If you've used the **wrap_content** constant for the android:layout_width and android:layout_height parameters for your ImageView UI element, then using one of the ScaleType scaling type constants would equate to scaling the digital image asset itself. This is because your ImageView references, and thus contains, your source image, and the wrap_contant tells Android to conform the ImageView UI "container" around the image asset, pixel for pixel, which means that the ImageView container takes on the physical specifications of the image asset. If one of the ScaleType constants is specified via this nested class, the image asset (via the ImageView) would then be scaled to that given display screen size, density, and aspect ratio in a way which is based on the scaling type (ScaleType) constant which has been specified.

ScaleType is most useful for determining how to scale an image relative to different screen aspect ratio, that is, keeping the aspect ratio locked so as not to distort the image at all, or, on the other end of the spectrum, allowing the image scaling operation to rescale our image without regards to aspect ratio, as we did with our 1000 pixel square image in Chapter 7.

The ScaleType class also has a scaling type (constant) that allows us to match up each pixel of our digital image asset with each pixel of a user's Android device's physical hardware display. This is the **CENTER** constant.

If there are not enough pixels in an image asset, or rather in the closest resolution density image asset that matches up with the screen resolution, our image will perfectly center within the display. In this way the image is using one physical display pixel for each pixel in the image asset. Now this is my kind of digital imaging class!

Let's go over each one of these eight different types of Scaling Algorithm Constants individually, in detail. I'll outline them in Table 8-1, so that they are all together in one place, and then we can discuss each of them. The number in parenthesis after each scaling constant in the table represents the actual integer value that is represented by the scaling constant.

Table 8-1. ImageView.ScaleType Image Scaling Constants and Summary of How They Scale Digital Image Assets

Scaling Constant	Scaling Algorithm Result on the Digital Image Asset
CENTER (5)	Aspect Ratio Locked Scaling, which matches the image's pixels to the physical hardware's pixels while also centering the image.
CENTER_CROP (6)	Aspect Ratio Locked Scaling Algorithm, which fits an image inside the View for both of that image's X and Y dimensions.
CENTER_INSIDE (7)	Aspect Ratio Locked Scaling Algorithm, which fits an image inside the View for at least one of the X or Y image dimensions.
FIT_CENTER (3)	Scales an image to fit inside a View while maintaining image's aspect ratio. At least one (X or Y) axis will exactly match the View. The image will also be centered inside the View.
FIT_START (2)	Scales an image to fit inside a View while maintaining image's aspect ratio. At least one (X or Y) axis will exactly match the View. The image will originate from the View upper-left corner.
FIT_END (4)	Scales an image to fit inside a View while maintaining image's aspect ratio. At least one (X or Y) axis will exactly match the View. The image will originate from the View lower-right corner.
FIT_XY (1)	Scales an image's X and Y dimensions to match the View dimension, which will not maintain the image's aspect ratio
MATRIX (0)	Scales an image using a supplied Matrix class. The matrix can be supplied using the setImageMatrix method. A Matrix class can be used to apply transformations such as rotations to an image.

The **CENTER_CROP** algorithm centers the image in the display with the **aspect ratio locked** for the scaling operation, and **fits the shorter side** (X or Y) and **crops** the longer side of the image.

Cropping in digital imaging is an operation that truncates each side of an image by a certain number of pixels (centering the cropping operation, in this case) as long as your image resolution is divisible by two.

The **CENTER_INSIDE** algorithm **centers the image inside** the display, with the **aspect ratio locked** for the scaling operation. This scaling algorithm **fits the longer side** (whichever, X or Y) and **pads** the shorter side of the image dimension with an equal amount of background colored pixels on either side or on the top/bottom. If the pixels in the image are smaller than (fewer than or lesser than) the physical hardware pixels, this algorithm does the same thing as the CENTER scaling constant.

The **FIT_CENTER** algorithm also **centers the image inside** the display, with the **aspect ratio locked** for the scaling operation. This scaling algorithm is similar to CENTER_INSIDE, except that if the image has fewer pixels than the display, this algorithm will **upsample to fit the longer side** (whichever X or Y) and **pad** the short side of the image dimension with an equal amount of background colored pixels on either side or on the top/bottom.

The **FIT_START** is the same algorithm as the FIT_CENTER, except that instead of centering the result, it locates it at the **0,0 origin** of the View, which is the upper-left corner, commonly known as the origin of a View container in digital imaging jargon. So it Fits to the Start (origin) of the Image's Array, hence its name.

The **FIT_END** is the inverse of the algorithm used for FIT_START, so instead of locating the result at the top left (0,0), it will locate it starting with the last (END) pixel and work backwards. The coordinates of the View END (last or final) pixel would essentially always be the image's **X,Y resolution specification** for the View, and so the FIT_END constant will display starting at that END location, which is the bottom-right corner of the View container, and work backwards towards the center of the View. Thus a FIT_END constant will Fit to the End of the Image's Array; hence its name.

The **FIT_XY** algorithm is the one that unlocks aspect ratio and will fit the image to the size of the View, which may cause some distortion, so be careful with this one. That said, there are images, such as the one we used in Chapter 7, that are not nearly as prone to distortion, so this scaling constant can be used cleverly, especially in image compositing scenarios and with certain textures and photographic image backgrounds.

Finally, the **MATRIX** algorithm allows you to assign the output of a Matrix class transformation (Rotate, Scale, Skew, etc.) using a **.setImageMatrix()** method call. The Matrix class can be used to apply transformations such as rotations, scaled and skewed to an image, to achieve special effects within the View object. Essentially this option will allow you to substitute your own custom scaling and transformational algorithms in place of these other seven, which have generously been provided for you by the Android OS.

These scaling constants can also be set using tag parameters in your XML markup for any tag that supports the **android:scaleType** parameter. So, for instance, if you wanted to use the FIT_START constant, you would use the **android:scaleType="fitStart"** parameter in order to achieve this effect.

It is important to note that the ScaleType constants in XML use **CamelCase**, so CENTER_CROP would be **centerCrop**, CENTER_INSIDE would be **centerInside**, FIT_XY would be **fitXY**, FIT_CENTER would be **fitCenter**, and so on.

Using AdjustViewBounds and How it Relates to ScaleType

There is a parameter or attribute that can be used with ImageView objects called **AdjustViewBounds**, which accepts a **Boolean** value (true or false). In XML, this is the **android:adjustViewBounds** parameter, and in Java, it is the **.setAdjustViewBounds()** method call.

If you want the ImageView object to adjust its container boundary in order to preserve the aspect ratio of your referenced digital image asset, then set this Boolean flag value to be **true**.

If you want your ImageView object to adjust its boundaries in order to fit the aspect ratio of its parent layout container, which if you have set the layout_width and layout_height parameter value of **match_parent** is probably the physical display screen of the Android device, then you would set that Boolean flag value to **false**, which is the default value, so you really do not ever need to have an android:adjustViewBounds="false" parameter in the XML markup for an ImageView.

The more obvious reason to use a false value would be to **toggle** the on/off switch (or, more accurately, the true/false switch) using the **.setAdjustViewBounds()** method inside your application's Java code.

So, if you had used the android:adjustViewBounds="true" for your ImageView XML parameter definition, and you wanted to later tell Android to go ahead and unlock aspect ratio, and **scale to fit** your container dimensions (given you're using match_parent), you would call ImageView setAdjustViewBounds() method off of your ImageView object's name using the following Java code:

```
myImageViewObjectName.setAdjustViewBounds(false);
```

Next, I want to outline some caveats regarding using the **android:scaleType** that we discussed in the previous section with an **android:adjustViewBounds** parameter, which we are covering here. When your ImageView object(s) call their constructor methods from the ImageView class, this constructor looks at your XML and sets the android:adjustViewBounds parameter setting **before** it looks at (and sets) your android:scaleType parameter's constant value.

What the constructor method does when you set AdjustViewBounds to true is it also sets your ImageView object's ScaleType to the value of **FIT_CENTER**.

For this reason, if you set your android:scaleType parameter to some other constant value, even if the parameter comes after android:adjustViewBounds in your parameter list within your ImageView tags, your ScaleType constant (if other than FIT_CENTER) will override an android:adjustViewBounds="true" parameter altogether. Keep this in mind to avoid unexpected scale results.

This is because it's not as much about the order of the parameters in your ImageView tag XML definition, but more about the order which the ImageView class fetches and implements these parameters from the XML definition, and this is determined by Java code inside the ImageView.java class itself.

MaxWidth and MaxHeight: Controlling AdjustViewBounds

Just as there is a relationship between the ScaleType and AdjustViewBounds parameters (or properties, or attributes), there is also a similar type of relationship between the **android:maxWidth** and **android:maxHeight** parameters and the AdjustViewBounds parameter setting for the ImageView object type.

The android:maxWidth is an optional parameter that can be used if you want to stipulate a **maximum width** for the ImageView object. An android:maxWidth parameter setting data value needs to implement dimension value delimiters such as **DIP**, **DP**, **SP**, **IN**, **PX,** or **MM**.

Thus, your maxWidth parameter would specify a **floating point** number, which would be appended with a **unit indicator constant** such as **120.0dip**.

Available unit indicators for an ImageView include PX or px, representing **pixels**; DP, dp, DIP, or dip, representing **density-independent pixels**; SP or sp, representing **scaled pixels** that are scaled based upon a preferred font size and normally used for specifying font sizes in TextView parameters; IN or in, representing **inches**; and MM or mm, representing **millimeters**.

The exact same rules, constants, and unit indicators would also apply for your **android:maxHeight** parameter, only they would be applied to the other dimension of the ImageView object.

So, the caveat with maxWidth and maxHeight is that in order for these two parameters to function properly, your ImageView AdjustViewBounds attribute must be set to true. Note that this in turn means that your ImageView ScaleType must be set to FIT_CENTER.

You learned in a previous section of the chapter that if you set a ScaleType constant other than "FIT_CENTER" in your XML ImageView definition, the AdjustViewBounds will not work. The caveat applies to the maxWidth and the maxHeight as well, so if you try to use maxWidth and maxHeight parameters with ScaleType, and it isn't working properly, now you know why.

Setting a Baseline in ImageView and Controlling Alignment

The concept of a **baseline** is far more applicable to a TextView, as baseline alignment is often used to align things based on the bottom edge of a text font. However, the concept is also supported in ImageView via two different parameters, the **android:baseline** and the **android:baselineAlignBottom**.

The term "baseline" refers to an imaginary line at base of any View subclass objects, such as ImageButton, ImageView, TextView, and similar UI elements or widgets. When you set a baseline parameter, you are giving Android OS a location for the baseline you want to utilize to refer to that object when its parent (layout container) tag uses an alignBaseline parameter.

The android:baseline parameter allows a developer to set an **offset** of the baseline within the View object. This parameter probably should have been called baselineOffset to be more clear about that, especially since there is an android:baselineAlignBottom parameter as well, which we will take a look at next.

What the BaselineAlignBottom attribute does is to set the flag that tells the Android OS to use the **bottom edge of the image** asset in your ImageView as its baseline alignment setting. As far as digital images are concerned, this is usually what you're trying to do, so, if you are not getting the image alignment that you are looking for when using other layout_alignBaseline types of parameters inside your UI layout containers that contain ImageView UI elements, try setting this android:baselineAlignBottom parameter equal to true.

Using the CropToPadding Method to Crop Your ImageView

Another useful ImageView parameter is the **android:cropToPadding** attribute, which allows you to invoke a digital image crop operation to your digital image asset by using XML markup or Java code.

If you remember, in Chapter 7 you used digital image cropping as an integral part of your work process for achieving your drop shadow special effect. You did this by using the GIMP 2.8.6 Canvas Size (Crop) command.

If being able to crop the image asset in your ImageView seems like it is a trivial capability in and of itself, then consider its value within a more complex work process, one that is made possible by using XML and Java code within your graphics design application.

The way that you utilize this attribute is clearly evident within its name, CropToPadding. You use your android:padding parameters to set up your crop operation, and then you set your **android:cropToPadding="true"** parameter to invoke the crop operation.

So, to crop evenly around an image, use the android:padding parameter with a DIP value, or to crop a different amount on different sides of the image, use android:paddingTop or android:paddingLeft or android:paddingBottom or android:paddingRight.

If you have the background image set up in your layout container, what this will do is to let that image show through where the cropped portion of the ImageView is (was), so this can be used for **compositing** or **special effects** purposes as well. This is especially relevant when you animate the padding values using Java code by attaching them to interactive elements of your application, or even animate them using predefined programming logic.

Next, we'll take a closer look at changing the colors (**tint**) in your image asset, and using the **PorterDuff** class to invoke Android's blending modes.

Tinting an ImageView and Color Blending Using PorterDuff

The last of the parameters for the ImageView class that are not inherited from the View Superclass is the **android:tint** parameter, which allows us to augment the color of our image asset using an **ARGB** hexadecimal color value via an XML parameter.

It is also possible to change the **PorterDuff** class **blending mode** that is used to apply the ARGB color value to the underlying image; however, this is possible only if we use a .setColorFilter() method, via Java code.

The .setColorFilter() Java method takes two parameters, one defining the color value to use and the other specifying the PorterDuff.Mode constant and the method is called using the following Java code format:

```
.setColorFilter(int color, PorterDuff.Mode mode)
```

If you use the XML parameter **android:tint**, then the **PorterDuff.Mode** that is defined as the default is the **SRC_ATOP** pixel-blending mode constant. This, as you may have guessed, composites the color value specified onto the TOP of the SRC (source) image, which as the parameter specifies will tint it.

You can lighten or darken your image by tinting using **white (#FFFFFF)** or **black (#000000)** color data values, respectively. You will use this technique in a little bit to improve the **contrast** of your drop shadow effect, which you created for your bookmarking utility TextView and ImageView user interface elements in the previous chapter.

The PorterDuff.Mode **nested class** is yet another collection of number value constants, similar to ScaleType, only with far more constants defined. In this case, the constants represent **algorithmic pixel compositing blending modes**, which are algorithms that define how the two different pixel color values should be added (or subtracted, or multiplied) together.

Both GIMP and Photoshop have similar compositing modes that you set using the layer palettes within each of those respective digital image software packages. It is impressive that this same digital imaging power that is in Photoshop and GIMP is also available to Android developers via PorterDuff.

PorterDuff.Mode is one of the 71 Enum subclasses we talked about earlier; this nested class is kept in the **android.graphics** package and is specified via an **import** statement as **android.graphics.PorterDuff.Mode**.

If you want to peruse all of the **blending modes** currently available via the Android PorterDuff class, and see what the actual algorithms are for each of them, you can visit the following Android Developer web site URL:

```
http://developer.android.com/reference/android/graphics/PorterDuff.Mode.html
```

Next, you will get into implementing some of these ImageView attributes in the XML user interface definition that you started working on in Chapter 7. You'll lighten your background image using tint and play with aspect ratios!

Apply Tint to SkyCloud Image to Improve Shadow Contrast

Launch Eclipse ADT and open up your GraphicsDesign application if it's not open on your desktop already. You are going to perform some digital imaging procedures, just like you'd do in GIMP 2.8 or Photoshop, only you will do it using Android XML markup.

The first thing that you really need to do to put the final touches on the drop shadow effects that you created in the previous chapter is to lighten up the CloudSky digital image that you are using as a background plate for your BookmarkActivity.java Activity subclass.

Currently you are holding your background image inside the RelativeLayout parent tag using the android:background parameter, which is performing an automatic ScaleType of FIT_XY for you and filling the screen with your image asset with zero regard for aspect ratio, which is what you want, actually.

However, as powerful as Android's RelativeLayout container is, and as many powerful parameters as it does have, the **android:tint** that you need to use is not one of them, because RelativeLayout is for **UI Layouts** and ImageView is for **Digital Imaging**.

So let's remove that android:background parameter from your parent tag, and add a ImageView child tag at the top of the container, which will place it behind the other UI elements as far as Z-order is concerned. Next, you will start adding parameters, as shown in Figure 8-1, to configure it for use.

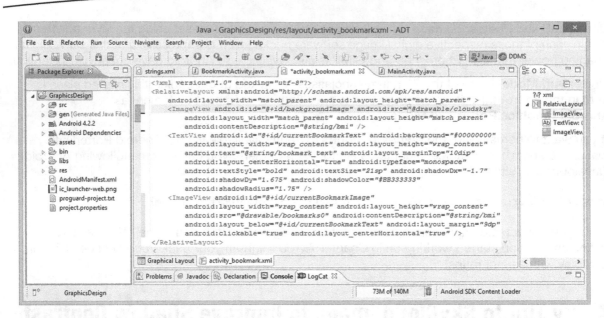

Figure 8-1. Adding an ImageView to hold the digital image backplate for the Activity, so you can apply tint and effects

Let's add an ID parameter set to backgroundImage and add in those required layout_width and layout_height parameters and set them to the match_parent constant so the ImageView container fills the RelativeLayout container.

You will notice (if you press **CRTL-S** or **File ➤ Save**) that Eclipse will flag your code with a wavy yellow underline because it wants contentDescription parameters for all ImageView classes and subclasses (such as ImageButton), so copy and paste the android:contentDescription parameter from the other ImageView into this one to solve that particular problem.

Finally, you'll need to add the reference to the digital image asset itself, so add an ImageView **android:src="@drawable/cloudsky"** parameter in order to reference your digital image. These parameters set up the basic plate for your background image and are shown in Figure 8-1.

Now, let's use a **Run As ➤ Android Application** work process, and take a look at the revised UI design, and make sure it is the same as it was before you started. As you can see on the left side of Figure 8-2, Android is scaling your source image asset using the **FIT_CENTER** ScaleType constant, so you are seeing the default white background color of the RelativeLayout container.

Figure 8-2. Testing your new ImageView settings in the Nexus One emulator before and after tint and scaleType

You are seeing here that the android:src parameter uses a **FIT_CENTER** and an android:background parameter uses a **FIT_XY** ScaleType algorithm constant, which is what you really want in this particular application (or UI Design scenario). So you need to fix this before you start your color corrections.

You can either use the android:background parameter to hold your image asset, which would involve changing your android:src to an android:background, or you can add an **android:scaleType="fitXY"** to override the **fitCenter** that is being used currently. Since you are learning about these ImageView specific parameters, and not about parameters that are inherited (like background) from the View Superclass, you'll go ahead and add in a ScaleType parameter, and set it to the **fitXY** scaling constant, as shown in Figure 8-3.

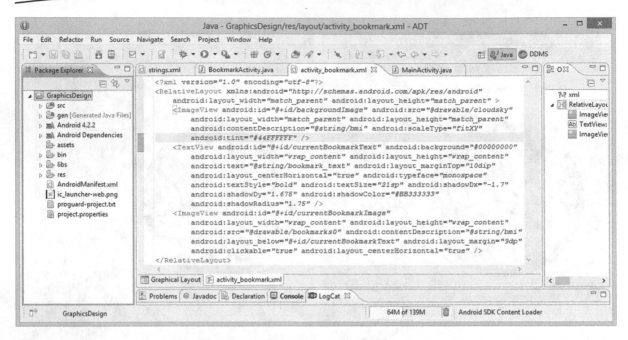

Figure 8-3. Adding parameters to lighten the image by 31.25% and scale to fit the parent container to match Chapter 7

Now that you've resolved the scale issue, it's time to use the **android:tint** parameter to do some **color correction** on the source image using the ImageView container's properties (attributes).

The way to control the amount of tinting that overlays your source image is by using an **alpha channel** to adjust the level (or the transparency) of the tint color, which in this case is **white**, or in hexadecimal value, **#FFFFFF**. Adding a white color value will invoke a **uniform lightening effect** across all of the pixels in your source image, just like the lightening algorithm in GIMP 2.8.6 or Photoshop CS6 would perform for you.

You'll specify a **31.25%** lightening of the image by using a level 4 (or 44) value in Hexadecimal, as 4 is 5, and 5/16ths is 31.25% of 16/16ths (100%). So your ARGB value, which you would need to specify inside this android:tint parameter, is **#44FFFFFF** or a 31.25% application of white to the image.

As you can see on the right side of Figure 8-2, the completed application of your android:scaleType and android:tint parameters has your image scaling properly, is looking 100% more realistic, and the shadows are now visible.

One last thing I wanted to cover before moving on is that a number of the digital imaging special effects that we are going to be using in this book do not **render** accurately, or at all, in the **Graphical Layout Editor** tab in Eclipse ADT, as you can see in Figure 8-4 in the pale yellow warning area.

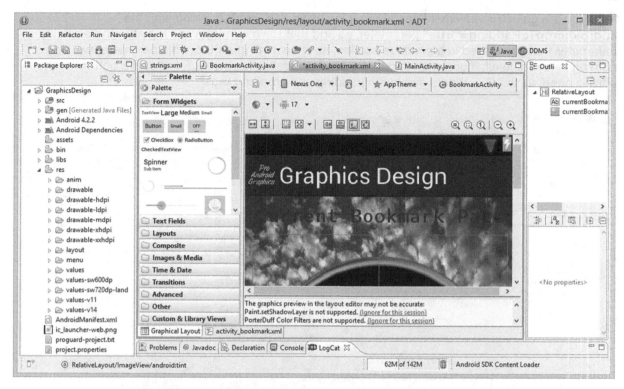

Figure 8-4. *Errors in Graphical Layout tab (see yellow area) advise that shadows and PorterDuff require an emulator*

The reason for this is that the code needed to render shadows and blending modes would have to be added into Eclipse ADT for the GLE module, and that is a significant amount of work and code, so for now, you will need to use the **Run As ➤ Android Application** work process to test or review your code.

Cropping Your SkyCloud Image Asset Using CropByPadding

Now that you have seen how to apply basic image lightening color correction in Android using XML markup and the ImageView widget, let's also learn to **crop** your image using the **android:cropByPadding** parameter, and at the same time get some practice in using the five **android:padding** parameters.

Cropping seems like something really simple, in and of itself, and it is; however, it can also become an integral part of more complicated "moves," as I like to call them, that can be made towards obtaining complex digital imaging special effects, like drop shadows, embossing, faux 3D, and so on.

Indeed, you have already seen what I am talking about in Chapter 7, when we took our source image and duplicated, grayscaled, blurred, moved and alpha channeled it into a semi-translucent, alpha-channel-integrated, drop-shadow, special-effect digital image using the very affordable GIMP 2.8.6 package.

Now you are going to implement image cropping using XML markup along with the **android:cropToPadding="true"** parameter, so add that to your ImageView tag after the android:tint parameter that you added in a previous section, as shown in Figure 8-5. This parameter will do nothing in and of itself; if you wish to prove that to yourself, click the GLE tab at the bottom of the editing pane, as the GLE works great with padding and cropping tags!

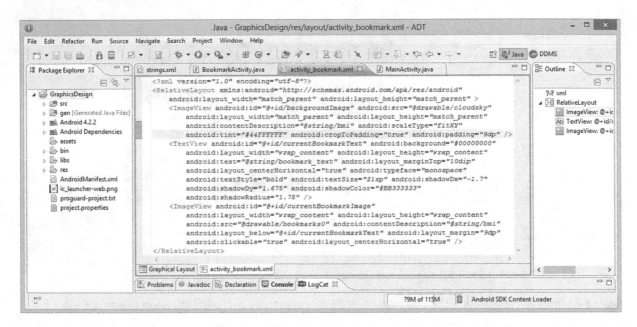

Figure 8-5. Adding android:padding and android:cropToPadding parameter to crop 9dip of perimeter border area

So, let's add in an **android:padding="9dp"** parameter next to give a 9 DIP of border around your UI design. Since there is no android:border or layout border parameter, this is a way that you can add borders into your design.

Notice that the default white color of the RelativeLayout container, which is behind the ImageView, is now showing through that area of the ImageView that has been **cropped out of the way** and is allowing those pixels to show through. If your RelativeLayout had a background image installed, it would composite with the ImageView source image, just like layers do in GIMP.

Use the **Graphical Layout Editor** tab or your **Run As ➤ Android Application** work process to see that the android:cropToPadding parameter is now doing its thing, as shown on the left side of the screen shot in Figure 8-6.

Figure 8-6. Testing your CropToPadding parameter and RelativeLayout background color value in the Nexus One emulator

Let's color this border with some of the color that is in the setting sun. You do this by adding an **android:background** into your RelativeLayout.

Add an **android:background="#FFEEAA"** parameter in the RelativeLayout parent tag, much like you had it set there before, except using a different color value. As you can see on the right-hand side of Figure 8-6, this new color value approximates (matches) colors in the clouds around the setting Sun.

Next, you are going to use the android:paddingTop parameter to push (crop) down the image so that the drop-shadowed TextView is in the yellow area of color at the top of the UI design, so that you get some practice with some of the more directional padding parameters.

As you can see in Figure 8-7, I have changed the android:padding="9dp" to an **android:paddingTop="50dp"** parameter, which changes the design to match what is shown on the left side of Figure 8-8.

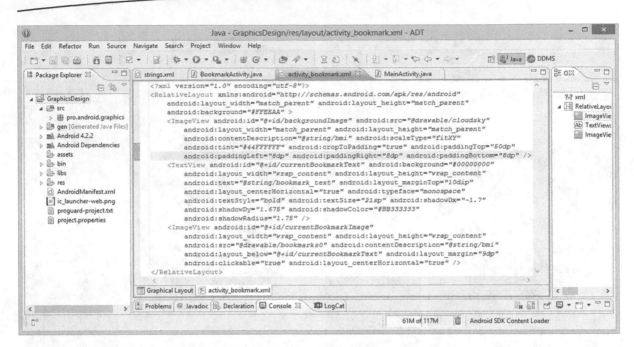

Figure 8-7. Add paddingTop, paddingLeft, paddingRight, and paddingBottom parameters to create a custom crop

Figure 8-8. Testing your custom android:padding and android:cropToPadding parameters in the Nexus One emulator

Since you lose your border effect, let's add in another **android:padding="8dp"** parameter, and again use either the **Graphical Layout Editor** tab or the **Run As ➤ Android Application** work process to see the result. What you will see when you do this is that your **android:paddingTop** parameter is not rendered correctly, and your UI screen reverts to looking like what is shown on the right-hand side of Figure 8-6. Back to the drawing (cropping) board!

What this means is that the **android:padding** parameter is applied **after** the other more specific android:paddingTop (and the others) parameters, so if you want to specify different padding values, you must specify each side individually, or the android:padding parameter will override the others.

So change android:padding="8dp" to **android:paddingLeft="8dp"** and then copy it **two more times** beside itself, as shown in Figure 8-7, and change the Left to be **Right** and **Bottom,** respectively.

Now your backplate (background image) ImageView has more parameters set for it than your currentBookmarkImage (subject matter) ImageView does! The XML markup for the first ImageView, which is on the bottom (in back) of the UI element compositing stock, should now include the following parameters:

```
<ImageView android:id="@+id/backgroundImage"
           android:src="@drawable/cloudsky"
           android:layout_width="match_parent"
           android:layout_height="match_parent"
           android:contentDescription="@string/bmi"
           android:scaleType="fitXY"
           android:tint="#44FFFFFF"
           android:cropToPadding="true"
           android:paddingTop="50dp"
           android:paddingLeft="8dp"
           android:paddingRight="8dp"
           android:paddingBottom="8dp" />
```

To see the new custom image crop (using padding values and cropToPadding), take a look at the right side of Figure 8-8. You now have the desired image effect of the TextView drop shadowed over a sunset yellow hue and the 8dip border the rest of the way around the image to add a little decoration. You were able to achieve your cropping, color correction, layout, ID, reference to the source digital image asset, and scaling by using a dozen parameters.

Next let's take a look at how to customize where the baseline alignment is set for your ImageView using the android:baseline ImageView parameter.

Changing the Baseline Alignment Index for Your ImageView

Instead of aligning your TextView relative to the layout container by using a **layout_marginTop="10dip"** parameter, let's instead align this TextView to the **backgroundImage** ImageView compositing backplate by using the baseline capabilities you have been learning about in this chapter.

Let's set the TextView's **layout_marginTop** parameter to **0DIP** and add an **android:layout_alignBaseline** parameter that references the **backgroundImage** ID so that your TextView aligns to your first ImageView baseline definition, which you are going to set next. This is done using the following XML markup, which you can see I added at the end of the tag in Figure 8-9:

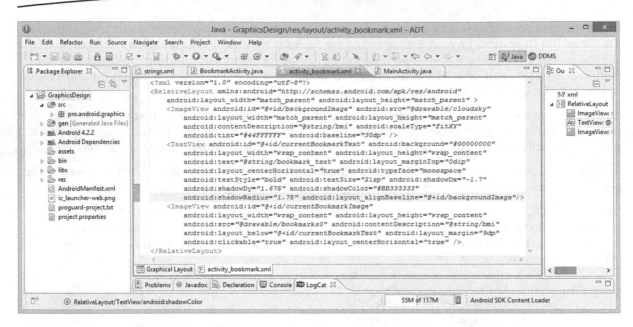

Figure 8-9. Adding an android:baseline definition to your ImageView and referencing it from your TextView object

```
android:layout_alignBaseline="@+id/backgroundImage"
```

To specify a custom baseline position for your backgroundImage ImageView, add an **android:baseline** parameter to the end of the ImageView tag parameter list, using the following XML markup, as shown in Figure 8-9:

```
android:baseline="30dp"
```

Now use your **Run As ➤ Android Application** work process to launch the Nexus One emulator, and you can see that the results are very similar to what you got when you were using your android:layout_marginTop="10dp" parameter.

As you can clearly see in Figure 8-10 (portrait) as well as in Figure 8-11 (landscape), the TextView object is now aligning its baseline, which is at the bottom of its text content, to an imaginary (invisible) baseline, which is 30dp from the top of the image.

Figure 8-10. Testing your portrait UI layout in the Nexus One emulator

Figure 8-11. Testing the android:baseline parameter in the Nexus One emulator using the landscape mode

It is a bit counterintuitive that a baseline would be set from the top of an image rather than the bottom, since a baseline represents the bottom of a font (where it sits) to most of us. The reason for this is because as we know, an image is indexed (numbered) starting in the upper-left corner at pixel 0,0 and so zero pixels in your baseline alignment setting would thus align with the top of the image.

That is probably why there's a shortcut **android:baselineAlignBottom="true"** parameter; all this does is simply get the Y (height) resolution of the image, and then set this value as the android:baseline parameter setting.

It is also interesting to note that if you forgot to set your marginTop to zero, it has no effect on the positioning, that is, the margin is not added to the baseline alignment setting, but rather is replaced by it.

To confirm this, set an **android:layout_marginTop="50dip"** and render the UI design, and you will see that it has no effect, which means that Android OS is prioritizing your android:baseline alignment parameter setting over the android:layout_marginTop alignment parameter setting.

It's important that you get used to noticing the different effects of your parameter settings in Android, as this is ultimately how you will get more familiar with how the OS is going to render your user interface designs in any given scenario.

Let's take a look at how this new user interface design will look when our user turns their Android device orientation 90 degrees on its side, so press the **CRTL-F11** keystroke combination to rotate the Nexus One emulator.

As you can see in Figure 8-11, the new user interface design using the baseline alignment for the TextView object works just as well as the top margin parameter. This demonstrates that there are often a number of different ways of achieving the same user interface layout in Android.

This makes Android user interface design both more flexible and more complicated, as there's often ultimately an optimal way to get a user interface to layout amongst all of the different device screen sizes and orientations. If possible, we as developers want to get a user interface design working across devices using only XML layout tags and parameters.

Next you'll take a look at how you can use the android:layout_margin and the android:padding parameter to perform image scaling for you via XML markup.

Performing Image Scaling: Margins and Padding Attributes

Besides using a ScaleType parameter for scaling ImageView objects globally within their layout containers, there is another way to scale digital image source assets referenced inside the ImageView container. Both margin as well as padding values will allow you to scale an ImageView source image asset within its container, as you're about to experiment with in this section.

First, let's change the android:layout_margin="9dp" parameter in your second ImageView tag (your foreground currentBookmarkImage asset) to zero DPI, as shown in Figure 8-12. You will do this so that you can first observe the image asset in its unscaled state (size).

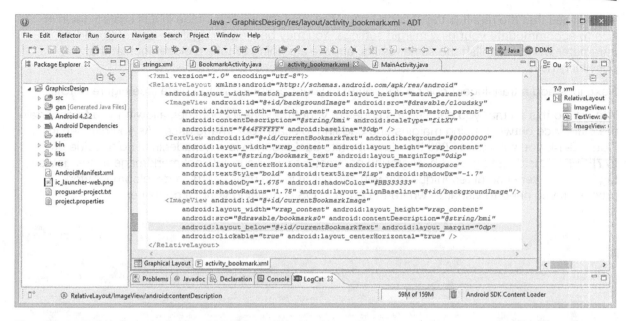

Figure 8-12. Setting the currentBookmarkImage ImageView layout_margin value to zero DIP to see unscaled asset

Use the **Run As ➤ Android Application** work process and take a close look at the image, as shown on the left side of the screen shot in Figure 8-13. Then change the 0DIP to 50 DIP, and run the emulator again.

Figure 8-13. Showing an unscaled ImageView asset on the left and an ImageView scaled using a 50dp margin

You will see that the result is the second ImageView with the source image in it is scaled down in size to accommodate your new margin settings. You may be wondering if the android:padding parameter will accomplish the same results, and we are going to take a closer look at that possibility next.

Next, let's add a translucent color background to your bookmark image plate (see Figure 8-13).

You will do this so that you can see the edges of your ImageView container, allowing you to ascertain the difference between using margins and padding to scale your image asset. As you can see in Figure 8-14, you will add a **50%** translucent white background via a hexadecimal color value of **#77FFFFFF** inside an android:background parameter to your currentBookmarkImage ID ImageView tag. This is a very useful technique that you can utilize in the user interface development work process if you need to visualize where the Android OS is drawing your UI container.

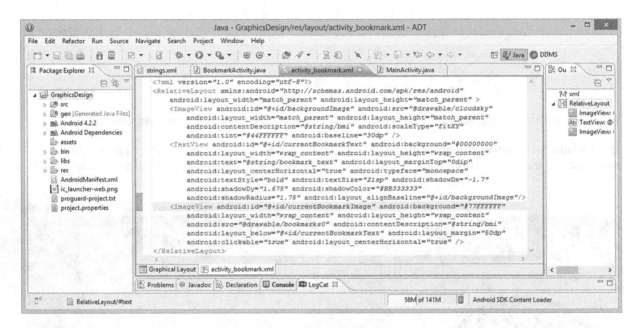

Figure 8-14. *Adding a 50% transparent white background to visually show 50dip margin and padding operations*

This technique will work even if your digital image assets use transparent alpha channels, as yours does in this instance with your drop-shadowed hoop. You will leave your android:layout_margin parameter set to 50DIP, as this is a perfect setting to show the difference between using margins and padding to scale an ImageView source image asset within its container.

As you can see in Figure 8-15, this hoop image produces its shadow effects correctly through both your translucent ImageView background color and the ImageView background plate held in the RelativeLayout container.

Figure 8-15. Showing your 50DIP image scale operation using padding on the left and using margin on the right

In the emulator view on the left, you are using an **android:padding="50dp"** parameter to scale your source image asset, and as expected, since padding adds space on the inside the container, the container stays the size of the match_parent layout specifications and still scales your image asset down close to 50%.

In the view on the right, you are scaling your source image asset using the **android:layout_margin="50dp"** parameter. Margins add spacing on the outside of the container, so your container scales down along with your image asset.

The reason that the second ImageView container doesn't completely fill the screen, as you can see in Figure 8-15 on the left, is because the TextView is baseline aligned 30dp into (below the top of) the first ImageView image backplate for your UI composite.

The second ImageView has the RelativeLayout parameter **android:layout_below,** which is referencing the TextView UI element. This pushes that entire View container down, as can now be seen due to your translucent background color value setting.

Now let's use a **Control-F11** keystroke combination to turn the Android Nexus One emulator 90 degrees, and take a look at padding versus margins scaling in landscape mode. As you can see in Figure 8-16, the results are similar, and the padding parameter scales the image asset inside the View object container, while the android:layout_margin parameter scales the ImageView object container as well as the source image asset it contains.

Figure 8-16. Showing 50dip image scale in landscape mode for padding on the top and for margin on the bottom

The only difference that I can detect in the landscape mode is that the android:layout_centerHorizontal parameter seems to be centering the ImageView container away from the sides of its parent RelativeLayout container. Sometimes differences such as this cannot be anticipated, and this points out why it is always important to test all user interface layout designs in as many different Android device emulators and orientations possible!

As you have seen in this chapter, with a little bit of creativity and good knowledge regarding what digital imaging operations consist of at heart, a significant portion of the digital image manipulation "moves" that you can implement in GIMP or Photoshop can also be accomplished in Android using XML markup and Java code.

Summary

In this eighth chapter, you learned more about Android's digital image user interface element container ImageView, which you had initially implemented in your application XML markup and Java code during the previous chapter.

We started by looking at the **ImageView** class and its various subclasses, nested classes, methods, attributes, and parameters. You learned that the ImageView class is used to create Android's **ImageButton** UI widget subclass (which you'll be learning about in the next chapter) and **QuickContactBadge**.

Next, we looked at the **ImageView.ScaleType** nested class, which is a very important class in Android, as scaling is an important concept in digital imaging. This is because scaling images correctly is the foundation for obtaining clean-looking visuals under any new media development platform.

You learned about the **java.lang.Enum** class and enumeration types, and then you looked at the **Scaling Constants**, which use this class to specify to the Android OS what type of scaling to use for your ImageView UI widget assets.

Then we looked at several of the **attributes** that are specifically part of the ImageView class. We started with the **AdjustViewBounds** flag and the **maxWidth** and **maxHeight,** which, if this flag is set to true (on), will let you specify your own custom width and height values; note that one generally doesn't want to do this in Android, but we covered it here just to be thorough.

Next, we looked at the concept of ImageView baselines, and the **android:baseline** and **android:baselineAlignBottom** attributes, which allow you to set your own custom baselines within the ImageView or set the baseline to be at the absolute very bottom of the image, rather than at the top of the image.

Then we looked at the **cropToPadding** attribute and how to utilize it with Android padding parameters in order to implement a digital image cropping operation using only XML markup.

Finally, we looked at the **android:tint** parameter and the **PorterDuff** blend modes, which allow us to use XML markup to perform basic color adjustment and correction to our digital image source asset.

To get some practice applying many of these ImageView class properties and attributes, you implemented some of them in the Bookmarking Utility and its RelativeLayout user interface design that we began creating in Chapter 7.

In the next chapter, you will learn about the ImageView subclass ImageButton and how to create complex, interactive, image-based buttons using XML markup and Java code.

Chapter 9

Advanced ImageButton: Creating a Custom Multi-State ImageButton

In this ninth chapter, we will continue to look at the **ImageView** class by delving into one of its most important subclasses: the **ImageButton** class.

The ImageButton is one of Android's most important user interface elements for implementing your leading-edge graphics design inside of a Button user interface element itself. Whereas Android has a standard Button class, it does not allow as much flexibility in implementing graphics design assets as the ImageButton class does.

Since this is a book focused on graphics, we are going to single out this ImageButton class. We'll take an entire chapter to learn how to define its many states and how to attach graphics elements to each state in order to achieve impressive visual results that the standard Android Button class cannot match.

We used the **android:src** parameter to define a **source image**, and used some UI layout parameters to position it and the margins parameter to give it some breathing room in the design. However, we didn't really get into any of the advanced parameters or tricks, such as using both the source (foreground) image plate and the background image plate at the same time.

We did cover some fairly advanced digital imaging concepts using GIMP 2.8, which is always good to do in a Pro Android Graphics book, and I will try to do even more of that as the book goes on, in both GIMP and VirtualDub.

Button Graphics in Android: ImageButton Class Overview

The Android **ImageButton** class is a subclass of the **ImageView** class, which is itself a subclass of the View Superclass, which, as you learned in the previous chapter, is a subclass of the **java.lang. Object** master class. The class hierarchy for the ImageButton class is structured as follows:

```
java.lang.Object
  > android.view.View
    > android.widget.ImageView
      > android.widget.ImageButton
```

The ImageButton, like its parent class ImageView, is kept in that separate Android package for UI widgets called the **android.widget** package because it is a UI widget used for custom Button UI elements crafted using images.

An ImageButton UI widget would be used when a developer wishes to create a custom UI Button element that displays that Button as an image instead of as a text label on a square background, such as a standard UI Button would appear, as you have seen in previous chapters.

Just like the Android Button class UI widget, an ImageButton UI widget can also be pressed (using a click or touch event) by the user, and has focus and hover characteristics as well.

However, the Button UI widget is subclassed from the TextView class, so it primarily targets text, as it is essentially a TextView UI element with a background that makes it look like a Button UI element. Your ImageButton UI widget, on the other hand, is subclassed from the ImageView class, so this gives it graphics features, which we are looking to harness in this book.

If you don't utilize any of its custom parameters, an ImageButton UI widget will have the visual appearance of the standard UI Button, but that gray button background will change color to blue when the button is pressed. Thus, don't use an ImageButton unless you are going to implement the various image assets and the multi-state features that we are going to cover within this chapter.

The **default image** for your ImageButton UI widget, which defines its **normal state**, can be defined staticly by using the **android:src** XML parameter in an **<ImageButton>** child tag inside of your XML layout container UI definition. It can also be defined dynamically at runtime in your Java code, and this is done by using the **.setImageResource()** method.

We'll be using XML to define UI designs, as Android prefers that we do, in this book. If you use the android:src parameter to reference image assets, this will replace your standard ImageButton background image. You can also define your own **background image** if you wanted to do some **compositing**, and you can also set the background color value to be **transparent** (#00000000).

ImageButton States: Normal, Pressed, Focused, and Hovered

The ImageButton class allows you to define custom image assets for each of the states of use: **normal** (default or not in use), **pressed** (user is touching or pressing down on click selection hardware), **focused** (recent touch released or click released), and **hovered** (user is over an ImageButton with a mouse or navigation key, but has not touched or clicked it). The hovered state was added recently in Android 4.0 API Level 14, possibly in anticipation of using the Android OS for the Google Chromebooks. The four primary ImageButton states, along with their mouse event equivalents, are shown in Table 9-1.

Table 9-1. *Android ImageButton Class Primary Image Asset State Constants and their Mouse Usage Equivalents*

ImageButton State	Description of the ImageButton State	Mouse Event Equivalent
NORMAL	Default ImageButton State when it is not in use	Mouse Out
PRESSED	ImageButton State when it is touched or clicked	Mouse Down
FOCUSED	ImageButton State when it is touched and released	Mouse Up
HOVERED (API 14)	ImageButton State if it is focused (not touched)	Mouse Over

ImageButton UI elements are not easy to implement because you will need to create a unique digital image asset for each of these ImageButton states. You must do this to visually indicate to a user your different ImageButton states, and as you will see in this chapter, this involves some digital imaging work!

You will be using GIMP 2.8 a bit later on in the chapter to create the many digital image states for each of the ImageButtons that you are going to implement in each of the resolution densities required by Android to span across different device types and screen sizes and resolutions. You will soon see that the number of digital image assets that must be created is calculated by the number of image buttons times four states times four density targets, or sixteen image assets per ImageButton implemented.

The standard work process to define ImageButton states is by using the XML drawable definition file that lives in your **/res/drawable** folder and that uses a parent **<selector>** tag and child **<item>** tags to define each of the ImageButton states with a custom digital image asset reference. You'll look at an example of exactly how to set this up a bit later on in the chapter.

Once you set up this XML definition, Android will automatically change the image asset for you based on the **state** of an ImageButton. The order of the state definitions is important, as they're evaluated in order. This is why the normal image asset comes last, because it will only be displayed after **android:state_pressed** and **android:state_focused** have both evaluated false.

ImageButton Drawable Assets: Compositing Button States

Let's get down to business, and jump into the work process for creating a multi-state ImageButton. This starts with creating the different digital image assets for each of these button states. To do this, you will use the GIMP open source image editing and compositing software package, so start GIMP now by using the quick launch icon on your Taskbar.

Use the **File ➤ Open** menu sequence to access the Open Image dialog shown in Figure 9-1, and find the ImageButton_Bookmark.png image, which will be your bottom (lowest) foundational image compositing layer for this ImageButton digital image asset. Once you locate the asset, select it so it turns blue, and click the Open button to load it into GIMP as an original image layer.

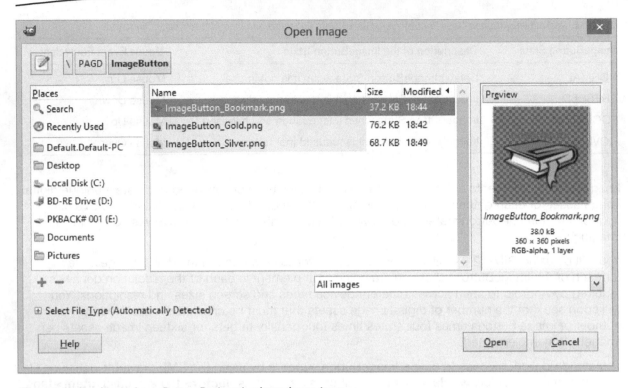

Figure 9-1. Opening the ImageButton_Bookmark primary image layer

The next thing that you want to do is to add an outer button element, say a metal ring around the perimeter of the button so that it actually looks like a button.

If you click on the other two original assets that are shown in Figure 9-1, the dialog will show a preview of them at the right-hand side, and you can see that they are a gold and silver ring UI design element that you will be compositing over the basic bookmark icon during the next few steps of this work process.

GIMP has a very useful tool or command for bringing in an external imaging asset and placing it into a compositing layer for use all in one very easy step. This tool or command is located under the **File** menu and is called an **Open as Layer** function.

Let's use this menu sequence, as shown in Figure 9-2, to go back into your ImageButton assets folder, and bring in your next image compositing layer.

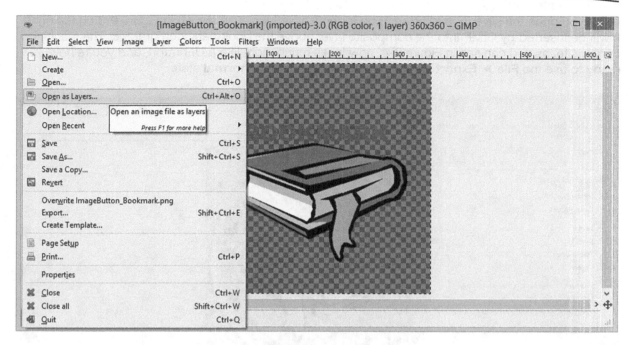

Figure 9-2. Using the File ➤ Open as Layers menu sequence to add a composite layer

As you can see in Figure 9-2, your foundation bookmark layer is already in place at 360 pixels in size for your **XHDPI** extra-high density pixel image asset size, so now you are going to select the next layer up in your image composite, which will be the ImageButton_Silver.png file shown in the **Open Image** dialog in Figure 9-3, which is accessed by using the **File ➤ Open as Layers** menu sequence shown in Figure 9-2.

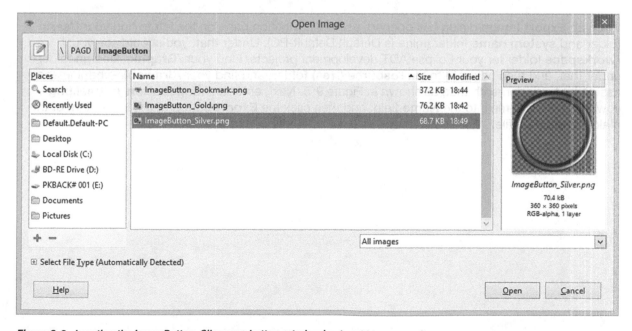

Figure 9-3. Locating the ImageButton_Silver.png button exterior ring to add to composite

Once you open the silver outer button hoop (or ring) asset, which is shown in Figure 9-3 on the right, it will be inserted by GIMP into the composite layer above the bookmark icon graphic. The resulting composite, as you can see in Figure 9-4, now looks much more like a UI button, and you're now ready to use the **File ➤ Export** menu sequence to create your **normal** state.

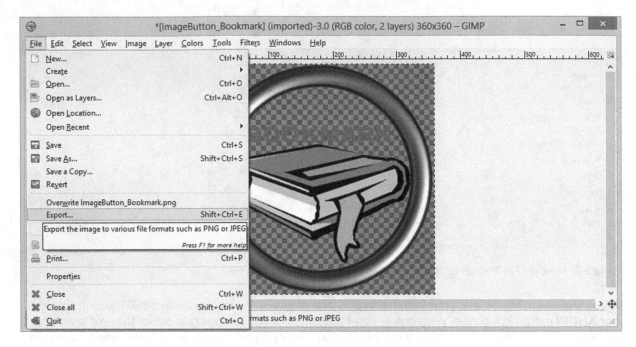

Figure 9-4. Using the File ➤ Export menu sequence to export the newly composited button

Once an **Export Image** dialog has opened, use the navigation pane on the left to find your **Users** folder and **system name** folder (mine is Default.Default-PC). Under that, you should see your **/workspace** folder for your Eclipse ADT development projects. Find your **/GraphicsDesign** folder under that, and then navigate to the **resource (/res) folder**, and find your **/drawable-xhdpi** image assets folder underneath that, as shown in Figure 9-5. Next, enter an **imagebutton_normal.png** (lower case) file name into the **Name** field, and then click the **Export** button at the lower-right of the dialog to create a file.

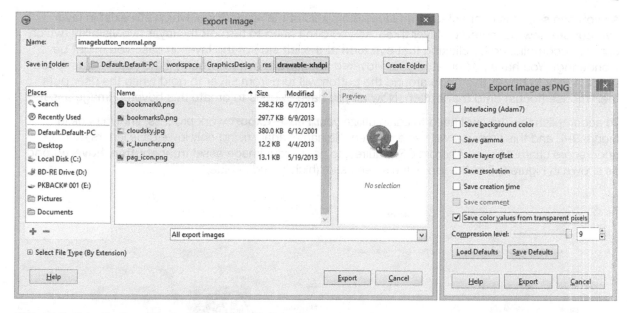

Figure 9-5. *Using the Export Image dialog to save the imagebutton_normal.png ImageButton normal state asset*

Once you click the Export button, you'll get an **Export Image as PNG** dialog with export options, shown on the right of Figure 9-5. I just use the **Save color values from transparent pixels** option to make sure all of the nuances of the alpha channels are saved along with the ARGB image data correctly.

Now you are ready to create your next ImageButton **hovered** state image asset, so again use the **File ➤ Import as Layers** work process shown in Figure 9-2, and this time open the **ImageButton_Gold.png** compositing asset, which will place this asset into a compositing layer above the ImageButton_Silver.png asset, as shown in the **Layers** palette on the right side of Figure 9-6.

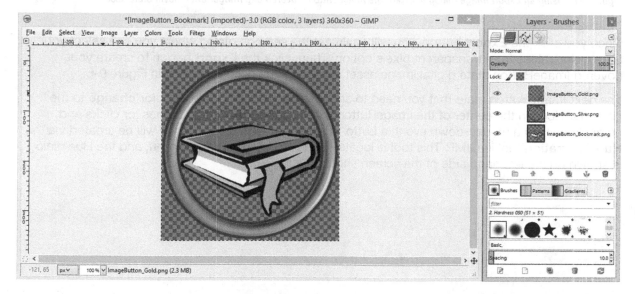

Figure 9-6. *Using the File ➤ Open as Layer to add the ImageButton_Gold.png image asset to a compositing layer*

As you can see, this overwrites or replaces the pixels of the silver hoop, which still exist in layer two but are now obscured by layer three, so you don't need to turn off the layer two visibility (which can be accomplished by clicking that **eye icon** at the left side of the layer, in case you might be wondering). You have just created your Hovered ImageButton state where, if the user has a mouse or the ability to hover, this hoop around the button will turn from silver to gold when the user puts their mouse (focus) onto that button. Now all you have to do is to create this hovered image asset!

To accomplish this, you will need to again utilize your **File ➤ Export** work process, shown back in Figure 9-4, and this time you will use a different file name, again using only lowercase letters and underscore characters, as Android OS requires, to name your image asset **imagebutton_hovered.png**, as shown in Figure 9-7 at the top of the screen shot (highlighted in blue).

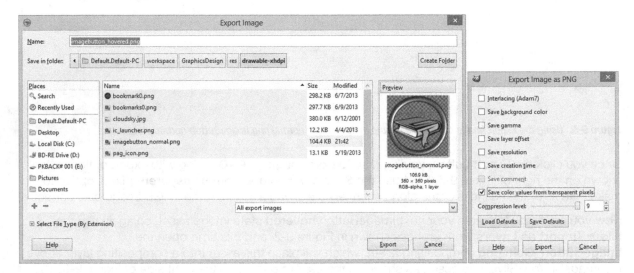

Figure 9-7. Using an Export Image dialog to export the imagebutton_hovered.png ImageButton hover state asset

Once you click the **Export** button, you will again get the settings dialog where you can select your Save color values from transparent pixels option. Then, click the **Export** button to create your hovered ImageButton state digital image asset, shown in 360 pixel resolution in Figure 9-6.

The next ImageButton state that you need to create is the **pressed** state. A **color change** to the bookmark icon in the center of the ImageButton happens when the user touches (or clicks and holds, known as a mouse-down event) a button UI element. The color change will be created via the **Hue-Saturation** tool in GIMP. This tool is located under the GIMP **Colors** menu, and the Hue dialog is shown on the left-hand side of the screen shot in Figure 9-8.

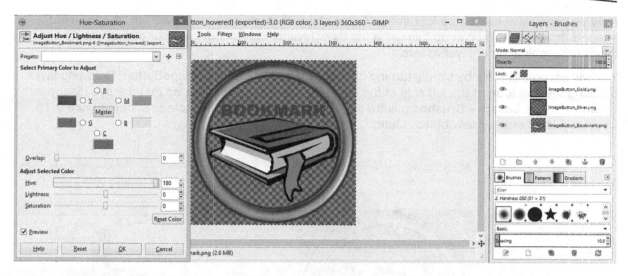

Figure 9-8. Using the Colors ➤ Hue-Saturation dialog to shift the ImageButton_Bookmark layer Hue 180 degrees

Make sure that your **bottom layer** is selected, as shown in gray in Figure 9-8, before you invoke and apply this Hue-Saturation tool, or you will end up color shifting one of your "UI hoop" compositing elements instead of your bookmark icon. If this happens, you can always use the **Edit ➤ Undo** feature.

I chose to shift the Hue 180 degrees, but you can use any color shift that you like, as long as it looks good with the golden outer ring UI element.

Once you click the OK button, which will apply this new Hue color shift to your bookmark icon's layer, use your **File ➤ Export** work process to access the **Export Image** dialog shown in Figure 9-9, and export the asset using the name **imagebutton_pressed.png** in a folder used for high-resolution density image assets in Android (/workspace/GraphicsDesign/res/drawable-xhdpi).

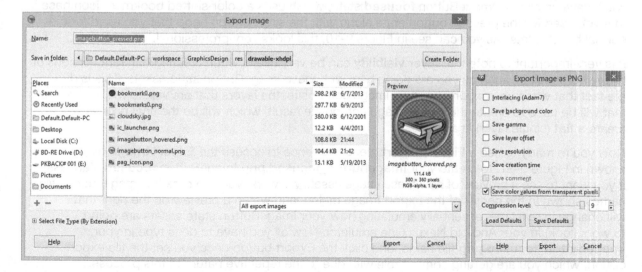

Figure 9-9. Using an Export Image dialog to export an imagebutton_pressed.png ImageButton pressed state asset

Now you only have one of the four ImageButton states that you need to create left, the **focused** ImageButton state. You can do this using the three layers that you have in your composite, in a different combination of layer assets.

You will accomplish this by simply turning off the layer visibility for the ImageButton_Gold.png layer, by using the **eye icon** at the left side of the layer. Click this eye icon now, so that the eye disappears, as shown in the **Layers - Brushes** palette on the right-hand side of the screen shot in Figure 9-10. The result is an entirely new button state.

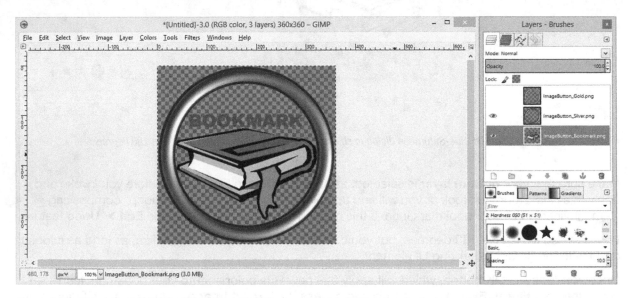

Figure 9-10. Using the visibility (eye) icon to turn off the ImageButton_Gold composite layer to create focused state

What will happen when you do this is that the **ImageButton_Silver.png** layer will now be visible, and you'll have an all new ImageButton **focused** state, which uses a color-shifted bookmark icon base that you used for the pressed button state along with the silver button hoop that you used for the normal button state. As you can see in Figure 9-10, this looks very professional.

It is very important to note that **layer visibility** can be very useful when creating different versions of image composites, such as you are doing here with these ImageButton state assets. This is due to the fact that when you export your final image composite, the layers that are visible will be the ones that will be used to create the digital image composite result, which will be the final pixels used to create a **flat** (single layer) image asset.

Now you're ready to use a **File ➤ Export** menu sequence to access the **Export Image** dialog, shown in Figure 9-11, to create your **imagebutton_focused.png** ImageButton **focused** state asset. If you want to see a preview of how these image assets will work, you can click the imagebutton_ file names shown in the center of the Export Image dialog, and watch a preview on the right that will change in real time, essentially emulating how your ImageButton state assets are going to work (look) in your Android Nexus One emulator. Now all you have to do is type in your **imagebutton_focused.png** file name, and click the Export button once you set the file export option, which you are getting comfortable with due to the repetitive nature of this process.

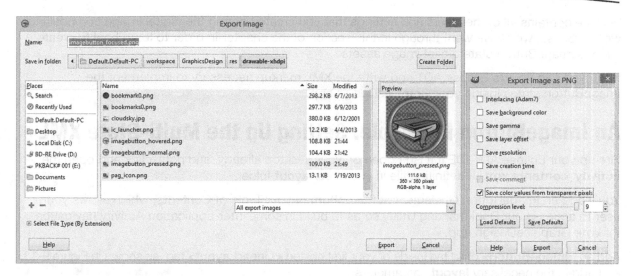

Figure 9-11. *Using an Export Image dialog to export a imagebutton_focused.png ImageButton focused state asset*

Now that you have output the extra-high resolution density assets for your multi-state ImageButton, you should probably save a GIMP native file format version of this image composite in case you need it in the future for any reason. This is done in GIMP by using either the **Save** or the **Save As** menu options under the **File** menu.

Doing this will access the **Save Image** dialog, shown in Figure 9-12, which will allow you to save your current GIMP project as a native .XCF file in the folder where your original image composite assets came from.

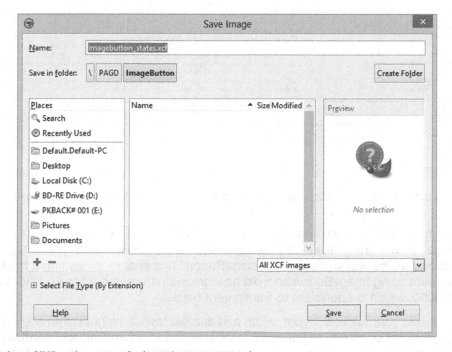

Figure 9-12. *Saving a GIMP native composite imagebutton_states.xcf,*

This file contains all of the layers and settings that you created during the digital image compositing work process, which we went through in this section of the chapter in order to learn how to create various ImageButton state digital image assets.

Next, you can go into Eclipse ADT and write the XML markup necessary to implement the ImageButton states inside your GraphicsDesign app.

An ImageButton Drawable: Setting Up the Multi-State XML

Fire up your Eclipse ADT IDE if it isn't open on your desktop already, and right-click and open the **activity_contents.xml** UI definition file in your **/res/layout** folder.

You'll add an ImageButton UI element at the bottom of your Table of Contents, which allows your user to access your Bookmarking Utility so as to build in some inter-application Activity navigation for your GraphicsDesign app.

Add an **<ImageButton>** child tag inside of your first nested **<LinearLayout>** tag, as shown in Figure 9-13, and add in the necessary **layout_** parameters.

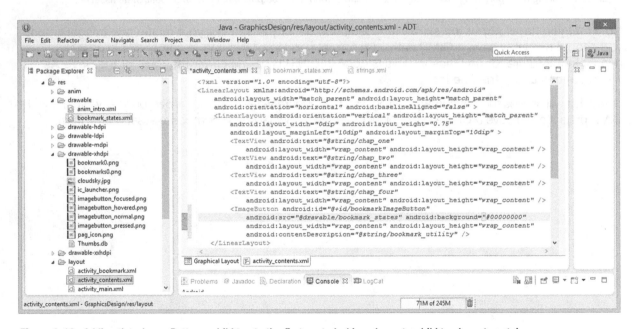

Figure 9-13. Adding the <ImageButton> child tag to the first nested <LinearLayout> child tag layout container

Let's use the android:id parameter, and name your <ImageButton> UI element **bookmarkImageButton**, and make sure your alpha channel, which is part of your ImageButton state assets, shows all the way through your ImageButton. This is done by setting a background that is 100% transparent using ImageButton android:background parameter set to an ARGB hexidecimal value of #00000000, which is equivalent to transparent black.

Since you already set your android:layout_width and android:layout_height parameters to the standard **wrap_content** constant, all you have to do now is add an **android:contentDescription** parameter that is required for every ImageView class (and subclass, such as ImageButton).

Since you already have a <string> constant that references your Bookmarking Utility, let's use that for the string value for the parameter as follows:

```
android:contentDescription="@string/bookmark_utility"
```

Finally, let's add in an **android:src** parameter that will reference the XML file that contains the markup defining the bookmark ImageButton states. Call this file **bookmark_states.xml** and put it in the /res/drawable folder. The XML markup for this parameter will read as follows:

```
android:src="@drawable/bookmark_states"
```

Now you'll need to create this bookmark_states.xml drawable XML definition, so you will use your **New Android XML File** work process by right-clicking on the **/res/drawable** folder and then selecting a **New ➤ Android XML File** menu sequence. This will open the dialog shown in Figure 9-14, and will auto-set the **Resource Type** drop-down to **Drawable** and **Project** drop-down to **GraphicDesign**.

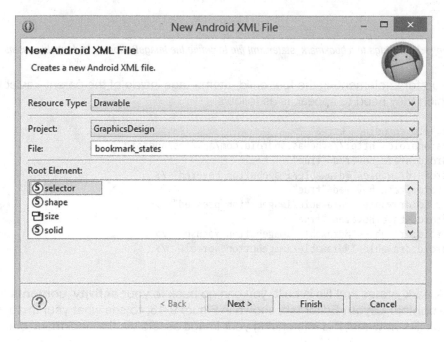

Figure 9-14. Creating a New Android XML File of Resource Type Drawable with <selector> Root Element

Name the File **bookmark_states** and select a **Root Element** of type **<selector>** and click the **Finish** button to create the bootstrap bookmark_states.xml file for your project in the **/res/drawable** folder.

Now you are ready to add in the **<item>** child tags for each of the states of your ImageButton drawable assets, as shown in Figure 9-15. As you can see, the order goes from **hovered** to **pressed** to **focused** to **normal**, just as it would if you put your mouse over an object, then clicked down, then released, and then removed your mouse from the object sphere of influence.

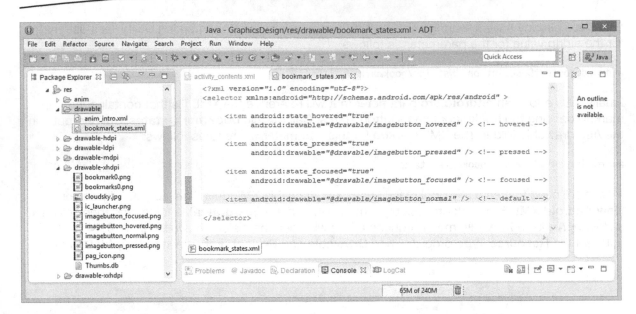

Figure 9-15. Adding <item> tags to a bookmark_states.xml file to define the ImageButton state drawable assets

The XML markup for implementing the four child <item> tags inside of the parent <selector> tag, in the order in which they need to appear, is as follows:

```
<? xml version="1.0 encoding="utf-8" ?>
<selector xmlns:android="http://schemas.android.com/apk/res/android"
    <item android:state_hovered="true"
        android:drawable="@drawable/imagebutton_hovered" />
    <item android:state_hovered="true"
        android:drawable="@drawable/imagebutton_pressed" />
    <item android:state_hovered="true"
        android:drawable="@drawable/imagebutton_focused" />
    <item android:drawable="@drawable/imagebutton_normal"  />
</selector>
```

Once this bookmark_states.xml file is built, you can go back to your **activity_contents.xml** file and use the **Graphical Layout** Editor tab, shown in Figure 9-16, to see what your ImageButton UI element will look like now that it is referencing your image assets via the bookmark_states.xml file.

Figure 9-16. *Using the Graphical Layout Editor tab to preview the <ImageButton> child tag and its parameters*

You will notice when you are in the Graphical Layout Editor tab that when you click the ImageButton, it selects it for editing rather than giving you the pressed state visual feedback that you are looking for!

What this means is that you will need to use a **Run As ➤ Android Application** work process so you can test your application in the Nexus One emulator in order to make sure that your XML markup is all working together correctly.

As you can see in Figure 9-17, your ImageButton color-shifts and turns gold when you click on it, but it looks a little bit too big to appear to users as a button UI element, so you need to shrink it down to a more button-like dimension. My first thought here was that Android only had the extra-high resolution image asset to work with, and was not downscaling it enough.

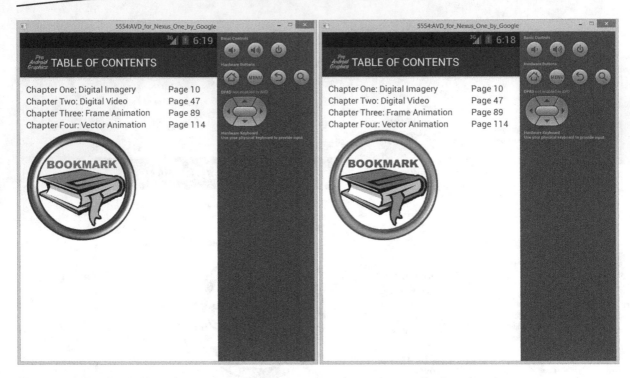

Figure 9-17. Running the Nexus One emulator to text the ImageButton states in an application run environment

So to make sure that this is not the problem, the first thing that you need to do is go back into GIMP and finish the work process that you started in the previous section of this chapter. As you know, you created the highest resolution version of these four image asset ImageButton states; however, you did not finish creating the other three resolution density versions of these assets for the **LDPI**, **MDPI**, and **HDPI** drawable folders. So the first thing that you need to do, since you have to do this anyway and are just putting a tedious work process off, is to create all your assets!

Create All ImageButton State Assets: Density Resolutions

Since you're using 32-bit PNG high quality digital image file format across all of your assets, you can simply open up the 360 pixel XHDPI image assets and downsample them to even multiples. These would include **120** pixels (3X downsample) for LDPI, **180** pixels (2X downsample) for MDPI, and **240** pixels (a 1.5X downsample) for HDPI.

Let's launch GIMP and use the **File ➤ Open** menu sequence to access the **Open Image** dialog, as shown in Figure 9-18. Next, use the left-side **Places** pane to navigate into your **/workspace/GraphicsDesign/res/drawable-xhdpi** folder, and select the **imagebutton_normal.png** file and click the **Open** button to open this digital image asset up inside of GIMP.

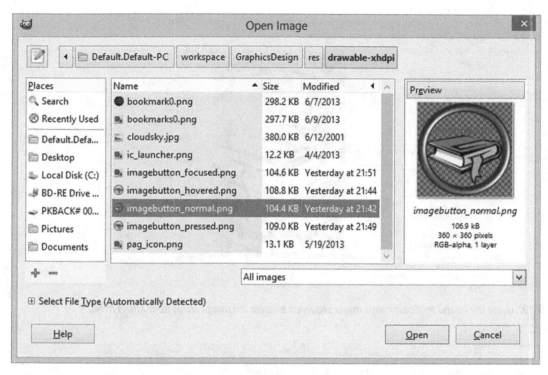

Figure 9-18. *Opening the XHDPI imagebutton_normal.png state*

The next step in this work process is to use the Image menu and the Scale Image tool dialog to downsample your image size from 360 pixels to half that size on each of the X and Y image axis to 180 x 180 pixels, which is a 2X or 100% downsampling of the image.

It is important to note that even (2X, 4X, 8X) downsample operations will yield the best results, so you will create the **MDPI** image assets first. You can make sure the lock on the X and Y resolution imput fields is set, and then enter the **180** in the first field; when you press return, or click in the sccond field, the second 180 will be entered for you.

Next, make sure that the **cubic** interpolation algorithm option is selected in the drop-down menu near the bottom of this dialog. Cubic interpolation in GIMP is the same as bicubic interpolation in Photoshop, so this is the highest quality sampling that you are going to get using GIMP. Once you're done setting the dialog parameters, click the **Scale** button, as shown in Figure 9-19, and the image will downsample to a size shown in Figure 9-20.

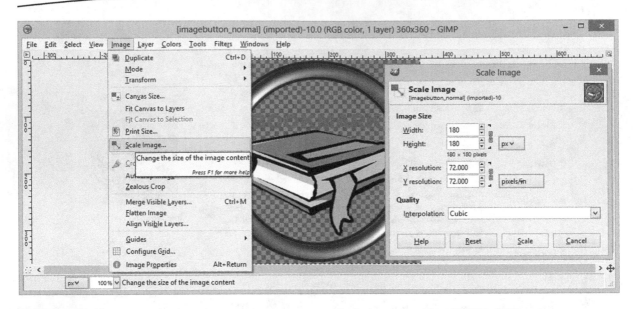

Figure 9-19. *Using the Image ➤ Scale Image menu sequence to scale the image asset from XHDPI to MDPI*

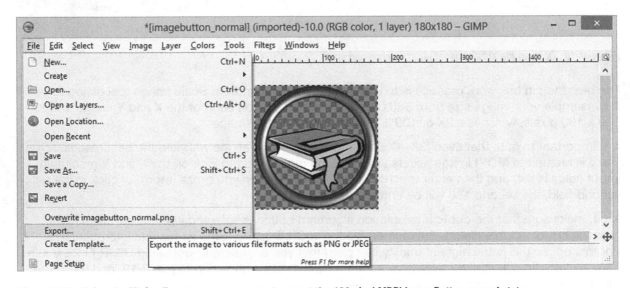

Figure 9-20. *Using the File ➤ Export menu sequence to export the 180 pixel MDPI ImageButton normal state*

Note the high quality downsample result for the new image in Figure 9-20. Now you are ready to use the **File ➤ Export** work process to export your new MDPI digital image asset. I dropped-down the menu and showed the selection in Figure 9-20 as well to get twice the mileage out of the screen shot.

You are going to use the **Export Image** dialog, shown in Figure 9-12, to save this MDPI image asset using the same exact file name, but into a different (res/drawable-mdpi) folder, making it a different file, at least as far as Android is concerned. Android uses the same file name in multiple folders!

If you export the file to the XHDPI folder, it will replace your 360 pixel asset, so do be very careful regarding what you are doing during this work process. Figure 9-21 shown the same file name highlighted in blue, and the different folder path in the **Save in folder:** line right underneath it.

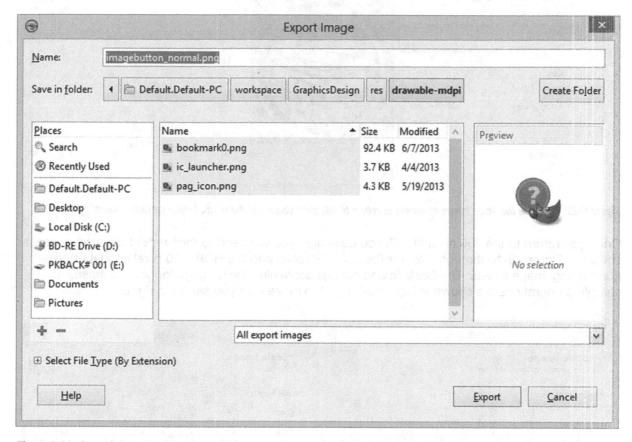

Figure 9-21. Exporting the 180 pixel imagebutton_normal.png asset to the drawable-mdpi folder

Once you have everything set correctly, click the **Export** button and the file will be created in your MDPI folder at a proper 180 pixel resolution.

The next step in your work process is to utilize an **Edit ➤ Undo Scale Image** menu sequence shown in Figure 9-22 to **undo** the 2X downsample and return to your XHDPI resolution image. You always want to downsample using a high resolution image source, so you get a good result from the cubic algorithm.

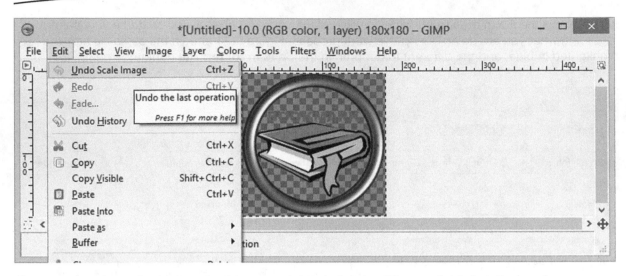

Figure 9-22. *Undoing the Scale Image operation to return to 360 pixel version of the normal state for better sampling*

Once you return to the 360 pixel XHDPI source image, you will need to then repeat the work process shown in Figures 9-18 through 9-22 for the LDPI 120 pixel and the HDPI 240 pixel imagebutton_normal.png image assets. The Scale Image dialogs containing the settings for both of these sampling operations are shown in Figure 9-23, just to make sure you set them right!

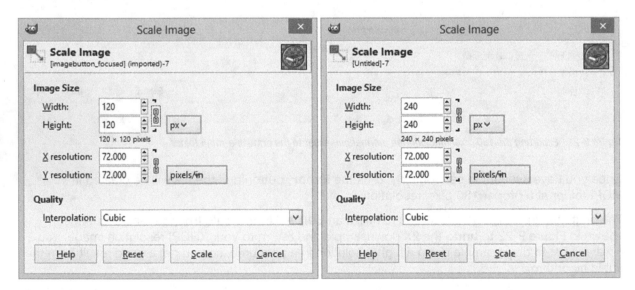

Figure 9-23. *Scaling normal state asset to 120 pixels (LDPI) and 240 pixels (HDPI) to create normal state assets*

The next steps involve repeating this work process using your other three image state assets. These will include the **imagebutton_pressed.png, imagebutton_focused.png**, and **imagebutton_hovered.png** image assets. These three ImageButton state assets need to be downsampled into an **LDPI**, **MDPI** and **HDPI** asset resolution. This can be done in any sequence that you wish, as long as it all gets done in the end.

The first step in doing this remaining downsampling (in addition to those steps shown in Figures 9-18 through 9-22) is to completely close out the imagebutton_normal.png 360 pixel asset, **without saving** it into any other (lower) resolution by accident. There are two ways to do this; I am going to show you how to be redundant and do both of them, so that you'll always be 100% assured that you do not "blow away" any of your high-resolution source assets by accident.

The first way is to always use your **Edit ➤ Undo Scale Image** work process, which is shown in Figure 9-22. The second is to use the **File ➤ Close** work process, which is shown in Figure 9-24, and to use the **Close without Saving** option in the dialog, which is shown on the right, even if you do use the Undo Scale Image work process. This will assure that the high-resolution asset that you opened at the beginning of the work process always remains intact on your hard disk drive, because you **Never Save Over It**!

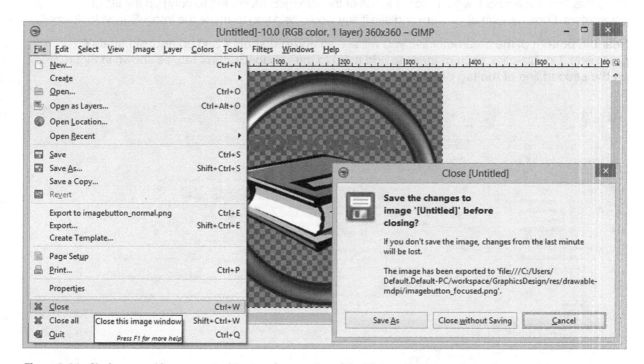

Figure 9-24. Closing normal image asset without saving over the original data so that you can open the next state

Next let's use this work process to close the **imagebutton_normal.png** asset and open one of the other assets and create the other three DPI resolution assets for that ImageButton state by using the work process outlined in Figures 9-18 through 9-24.

Once you do this for all four ImageButton states, you should have a pretty good handle on the digital image compositing and downsampling work process involved in creating a multi-state ImageButton for use in Android application development.

Once you have created all 16 multi-state ImageButton assets, you can go back into Eclipse ADT and see if having all of these smaller ImageButton state image assets will give you a smaller ImageButton UI element, or if you have to construct a solution to that problem through the use of additional XML parameters.

Scaling the ImageButton Down to a UI Element-Like Scale

Next, you need to go back and restart Eclipse ADT, or if Eclipse is already open on your desktop, be sure to right-click the project folder and use the **Refresh** option to allow Eclipse to "see" the new image assets that you have added into your various **/res/drawable-dpi** sub-folders.

Next, use the **Run As ➤ Android Application** work process to see if Android OS is using any of these smaller image assets that you have just created.

When you run the app again in the Nexus One emulator, you will see that it still looks like it did in Figure 9-17, so you need to see if there are any parameters that you can use to achieve your desired end result.

To do this, use the android: work process inside of the <ImageButton> tag to bring up the list of parameters. Look through all of them and see if any would help you to make the ImageButton look smaller.

Near the bottom of the parameter list, you will see an **android:scaleX** and an **android:scaleY** parameter. Double-click each of these to add them to the <ImageButton> tag, as shown in Figure 9-25, on the second line of the tag parameters.

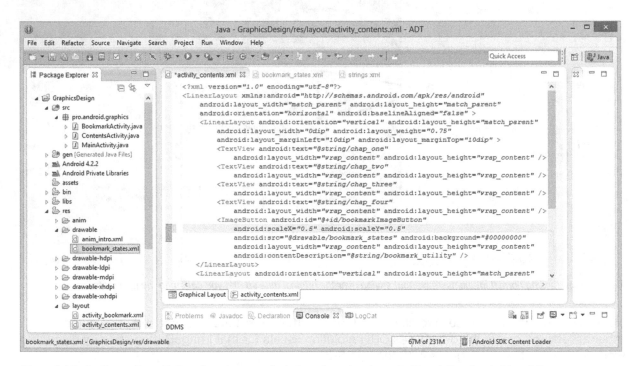

Figure 9-25. Scaling an ImageButton down to more of a button size using the android:scaleX and android:scaleY

Since you know that **even scaling** works the best, you'll use a real or float scaling value of 0.5, which is the equivalent of doing a 2X downsample.

To see the visual result of adding these android:scale tags without having to use the **Run As ➤ Android Application** work process, you can click the **Graphical Layout** Editor tab at the bottom of the XML editing pane. This will switch you over into Visual Editing Mode to see the results of the 50% scale operation (parameter).

As you can see in Figure 9-26, these android:scaleX and android:scaleY parameters give you exactly the end results that you were looking for, and the ImageButton now looks like a UI element under your Table of Contents.

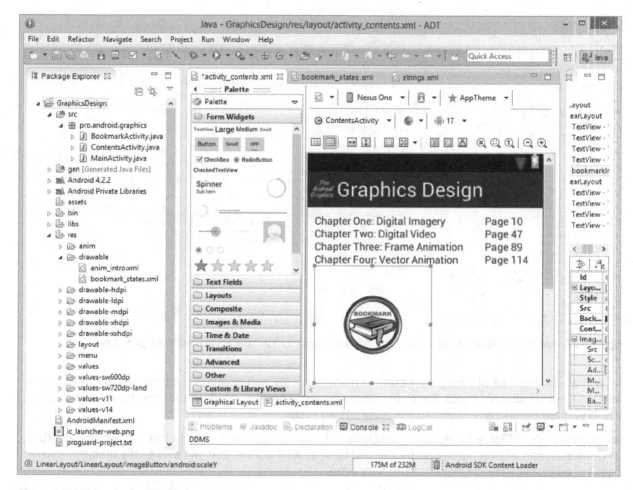

Figure 9-26. *Using the Graphical Layout Editor tab to preview the result of the ImageButton scaling parameters*

However, the android:scale parameters left your ImageButton container the original size, as you can see by the selection set (sizing handles) area shown in Figure 9-26. So you need to add some additional parameters into the mix to pull this ImageButton container up and to the left, which will involve using some negative margin parameters, which you will add in next.

First, let's add in an **android:layout_marginTop** parameter, with a negative value of 35 DIP to pull the newly resized ImageButton back up closer to the Table of Contents. You can use the Graphical Layout Editor tab to preview this setting to make sure that it is working well for you.

Next, let's add in the **android:layout_marginLeft** parameter with a negative value of 35 DIP to pull the newly resized ImageButton closer toward the left side of the screen. You can also use the Graphical Layout Editor tab to preview this setting to make sure that it's working well for you.

Figure 9-27 shows the android:layout_margin parameters in place inside of the <ImageButton> tag at the top of the tag next to the two android:scale parameters. Your ImageButton UI element now has ten custom parameters.

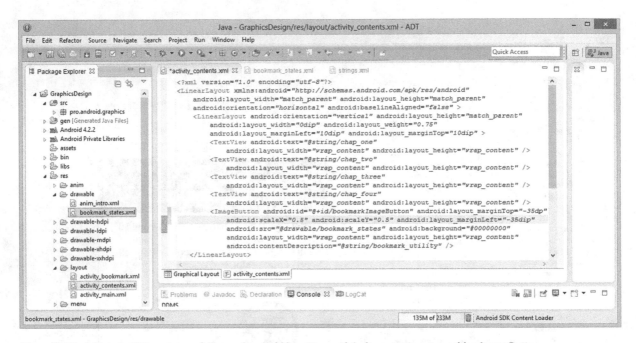

Figure 9-27. Add android:layout_marginTop and android:layout_marginLeft parameters to position ImageButton

Now that you have all of your parameters in place, to scale and position the ImageButton, let's again leverage the Graphical Layout Editor to quickly preview the XML markup that you have written, and see if you are getting any closer to the desired end result.

As you can see in Figure 9-28, the ImageButton UI element is now closer to the bottom of the Table of Contents, and will be perceived by the end user as a UI button that will eventually take the end user to the Bookmarking Utility Activity subclass.

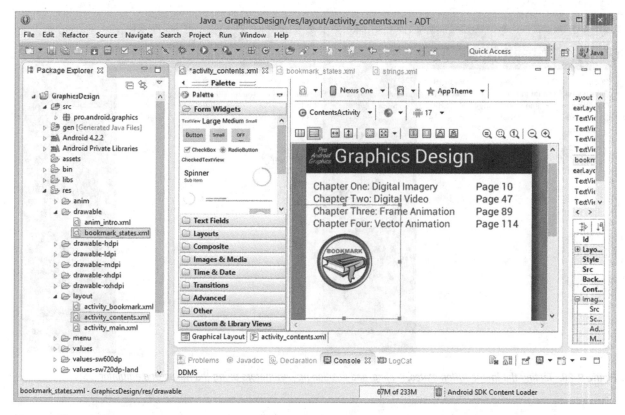

Figure 9-28. Using the Graphical Layout Editor to preview negative margin settings positioning your ImageButton

Since I have the <ImageButton> tag selected in the XML Editing pane, the UI element is also showing as selected in the Graphical Layout Editor pane, which shows how the negative margin parameter values have moved the unused portion of the UI widget container out of the way so that the scaled UI element can be positioned where it should be on the screen.

The other option is, of course, to downsize your image assets themselves to be half their original pixel sizes, or 180, 120, 90 and 60 pixels.

The way that you have the XML markup designed you can easily add more Table of Contents entries, as long as you keep the <ImageButton> child tag as the last tag inside of the first nested <LinearLayout> child tag container.

Finally, let's test the ImageButton in Nexus One, as shown in Figure 9-29.

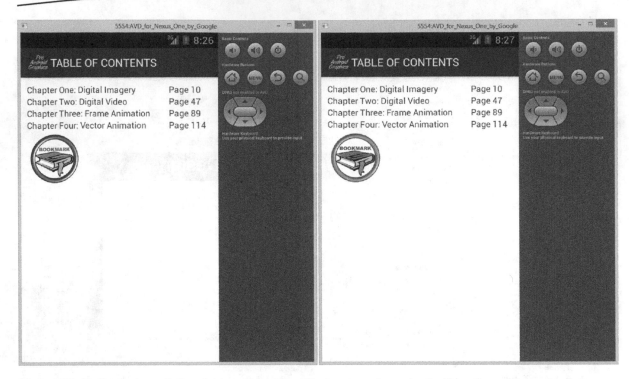

Figure 9-29. Testing the ImageButton states, scaling, and positioning parameters using the Nexus One emulator

Summary

In this ninth chapter, you learned about the Android ImageButton UI widget and how to use it to implement multi-state graphical buttons using XML.

We started by looking at the **ImageButton** class and how it differs from its Button UI widget counterpart. You learned that the **ImageView** class is used to create the Android **ImageButton** UI widget subclass, and that the **android:src** parameter references its source images and **android:background** controls the transparency used for compositing it over elements behind it.

Next, we looked at the **ImageButton States** that are used to provide users with visual feedback as to which use-state the ImageButton is currently in, using different images provided by the developer for each of these states.

You learned about the **hovered** state, and how it only applies to Android devices that feature a mouse, and how that state was introduced in API Level 14 probably to provide support for the use of Android on Chromebook.

You learned about the **pressed** state, which shows that the ImageButton is being clicked (the down part of the click) or touched if on a touchscreen. You learned that the pressed state is the equivalent of a mouse-down state on a "normal" PC programming environment.

You learned about the **focused** state, which shows that your ImageButton has been released (the up part of the click), and that the ImageButton is in use (has focus) until another UI element is accessed by the user.

You also learned about the **normal** state, or the unused ImageButton state, which is the default. All ImageButtons will use this state unless they are being used in some way (hovered, pressed, or have focus).

Next, we went through how to create the four ImageButton states using the GIMP digital imaging software package to create a digital image composite document that you could use to export four unique but pixel-synchronized image assets that would create a seamless multi-state ImageButton user experience.

Then we looked at how to implement an ImageButton into one of your existing layout containers, adding this new <ImageButton> child tag into one of your existing nested <LinearLayout> child tags.

Next, we created your bookmark_states.xml XML definition file, which created the multi-state drawable image asset definition that referenced the image assets created earlier in the chapter using GIMP 2.8.6.

In the next chapter, you will learn about the 9-Patch technology, and how to create 9-Patch image assets that can scale accurately without regards to aspect ratio. 9-Patch technology is also available for HTML5 apps.

Chapter 10

Using 9-Patch Imaging Techniques to Create Scalable Imaging Elements

In this tenth chapter, we will take a closer look at the Android **NinePatch** class, as well as the **NinePatchDrawable** class, and the **Draw 9-patch tool**.

Since this is a book focused on graphics, and we have now covered Android ImageView and ImageButton classes, which are used to hold and implement an image or animation graphics asset, we will start to focus more on graphics-related classes within Android OS. The first of these is NinePatch.

A NinePatch is one of Android's most important graphics design tools when it comes to developing image assets that can scale without distortion due to Android device display screen aspect ratio or orientation changes.

A NinePatch is a resizable bitmap whose scaling during resizing operations can be controlled via nine areas that we can define in our bitmap image (imagine a tic-tac-toe grid that has nine discreet areas).

The NinePatch type of image asset can be used for anything from a scalable button background to a UI layout container background that will scale to fit different screen resolution densities, aspect ratios, and orientations.

The advantage of a NinePatch Drawable object is that developers can define a single graphic element (in an example later in the chapter, this will be a 20KB .PNG file) that can be utilized across many different UI elements, including buttons, ImageButtons, sliders, backgrounds, and similar items.

Android NinePatchDrawable: A Foundation for NinePatch

The Android **NinePatchDrawable** class is a subclass of the Android **Drawable** class, and is therefore a part of the **android.graphics.drawable** package.

An import statement references **android.graphics.drawable.NinePatchDrawable** as the Android package "path" to an Android NinePatchDrawable class, which exhibits the following Android Java Class hierarchy:

```
java.lang.Object
   > android.graphics.drawable.Drawable
     > android.graphics.drawable.NinePatchDrawable
```

This NinePatchDrawable class has four Java constructors (methods) for the creation of a NinePatchDrawable object in Android. Two of the constructors are **deprecated**, as of Android Version 1.6 API Level 4, so do not use the following two constructors to create your NinePatchDrawable objects:

```
NinePatchDrawable(Bitmap bitmap, byte[] chunk, Rect padding, String srcName) - OR -
NinePatchDrawable(NinePatch patch)
```

Notice that they both access a NinePatch image asset directly, without using the Android R or Resource (/res/drawable) area of the OS. This end-run around the Android "Resource Bin" is what has been deprecated, not the NinePatch technology itself. The correct way to access the NinePatch asset is by using either of the following (non-deprecated) constructor methods:

```
NinePatchDrawable(Resources res, Bitmap bmp, byte[] chunk, Rect padding, String s)
```

This constructor method creates NinePatchDrawable objects using **raw Bitmap object** data for the NinePatch, setting the initial target density based on the display metrics of the resources. This constructor should be primarily utilized for advanced NinePatch usage via Java code. Since we're using XML to implement graphics design resources up-front, via a **static** declaration, we will be using the **NinePatch** class, which I'll be covering in the next section. It uses the following much simpler constructor method:

```
NinePatchDrawable(Resources res, NinePatch patch)
```

This constructor will create the NinePatchDrawable asset using an existing NinePatch asset, which can be found in the **/res/drawable** folder, using the correct file naming protocols for NinePatch assets. This NinePatchDrawable Java constructor will automatically analyze and then set an initial target image resolution density based on display metrics for the resource itself.

I'll focus on the second way as it is more standardized, straightforward, and much faster way to get to the end result that we are looking for here. In the next section I'll go over the NinePatch image asset concepts in detail, and then I'll cover the NinePatch class itself, and then I will finally get into how to create NinePatchDrawable image assets. This is done using the **Draw 9-patch** imaging tool that is hidden deep inside the Android SDK folder hierarchy, in the /sdk/tools folder.

NinePatch Graphics Assets: A 9-Patch Concepts Overview

The NinePatchDrawable object, also commonly referred to by using a number, that is, "9-patch," allows Android developers to develop a special type of morphable PNG8, PNG24, or PNG32 graphics asset. A 9-patch is able to apply different scaling factors to different areas within a given digital image.

So a 9-patch image asset is essentially an axis-independent, scalable .PNG bitmap image that uses nine distinct quadrants within the image asset to support scaling, or more accurately, pixel tiling, of any size and shape a View object or layout container might be.

Due to its built-in **NinePatchDrawable** class (and **NinePatch** class) support, the Android OS can automatically resize a developer's 9-patch image assets to accommodate the contents of any View object inside of which a developer has placed a 9-patch image asset as its background image asset reference. This is accomplished via algorithms that exist inside the Android NinePatch class and Android NinePatchDrawable class, as well as inside the Draw 9-patch software utility found in the /sdk/tools folder in the Android SDK.

A good example of a use for a NinePatch image asset would be on the inside of the background image placeholder (the android:background XML parameter) that is commonly used with the standard Android Button object UI widget. Button UI widgets almost always need to stretch in at least one dimension, and often in both X and Y dimensions, in order to accommodate text strings of various lengths, or different font types, or different font sizes.

This NinePatchDrawable object references Android's recommended **PNG** digital image format, and it also includes an **extra one-pixel-wide border**. There are three different "flavors" of PNG images that are supported in the Android OS: **indexed color** (8-bit) **PNG8**, **truecolor** (24-bit or RGB) **PNG24**, and a **truecolor with alpha channel** (32-bit or ARGB) **PNG32 image file format**.

To be recognized by Android as a 9-patch image asset, a NinePatchDrawable asset needs to be saved with the file name extension of **.9.png** and saved into the **/res/drawable/** directory of the appropriate Android project.

The **one-pixel border** I mentioned earlier will not be visible to our end users, and instead will be utilized by Android NinePatch class algorithms to define which areas of our image asset will be **scalable** and which areas of our image asset will be **static** (fixed and not scaled, just moved).

We will be able to indicate the **scalable sections** of our 9-patch imaging asset by drawing one (or more) single-pixel-wide **black** line segments within the left and the top portions of this one pixel border.

All of the other border pixels not utilized to define a scalable section of our 9-patch image will need to use the completely transparent color value (#00000000) or a white (#FFFFFF) color value.

We could even define both by using the **#00FFFFFF** hexadecimal color value (transparent white), if we want to be really tricky. Fortunately the Draw 9-patch tool that we will be looking at later will do all of this for us!

Interestingly, we may define any number of these scalable sections as we wish using these single-pixel black line segments. It is important to note that this **relative sizing** of each of these scalable sections to each other will always remain "ratio consistent." What this means is that the largest scalable section will always remain our largest scalable section, at each scale, no matter how large or how small this scale might become.

After we define our scalable (exterior) sections for the 9-patch asset, we then define (optional) **drawable areas** (interior) for the 9-patch image that are called "padding areas." Padding drawable areas tell Android where it can place the elements that are defined inside the View object or the ViewGroup (View subclass) layout container object.

This padding feature is included so that our NinePatchDrawable asset does not get overwritten by other application assets, or obscured visually. The padding definitions are created in the same way that scalable sections are defined, by using one-pixel black "padding lines" that are drawn onto the **right** and **bottom** one-pixel border areas of the 9-patch asset definition.

If a View object sets a NinePatch as its background, and it then specifies a View object text attribute, for instance, it will stretch this attribute so that all of the text attributes fit inside this area, which we have designated using our right and bottom one-pixel black border definitions.

It is important to note that if the 9-patch padding area definition lines are not specifically defined, the Android NinePatch algorithm will instead use our **left** and **top** scaling definition line segments to define the image asset padding (drawable) areas.

To summarize the differences between the use of the one-pixel black border lines, the left and top lines define which pixels in our image assets are allowed to be replicated in order to stretch or scale the 9-patch imagery. The bottom and the right one-pixel black border lines define our drawable areas on the inside (interior) of our 9-patch image asset where the View object contents (attributes or asset references) are allowed to overwrite.

The Android NinePatch Class: Creating a NinePatch Asset

A **NinePatch** class is a direct subclass of the Java java.lang.Object master class, which means that it is used to define the NinePatch Java Object and was coded uniquely to be its own Android asset. It is not based on another class hierarchy within the Android OS. As you might have guessed, it lives inside the **android.graphics** package. Its class hierarchy is as follows:

```
java.lang.Object
  > android.graphics.NinePatch
```

An object constructed by the Android NinePatch class allows the Android OS to scale and render this 9-patch image asset using nine discreet sections.

Another great analogy is that of a compass. The four corners of a 9-patch image, at NE, NW, SE, and SW are unscaled, whereas the four edges, N, E, S or W, are scaled along one axis. The middle of the compass (9-patch image) is scaled along both of its axes, just like a normal image would be scaled in Android.

Optimally, the middle of our 9-patch source PNG image assets will be 100% transparent, as yours will be later in this chapter when you get into using the Draw 9-patch software tool. This is so that our 9-patch can provide a scalable image framework around an open, rectangular content area for our View object to use for the content that it styles and references.

This design approach will allow developers to create custom graphics that will scale seamlessly in the way that they define them.

When content is added to our View object inside a 9-patch image asset, and this content exceeds the internal padding limitations of the 9-patch graphic asset, it can be easily adjusted with zero asset distortion.

The Draw 9-Patch tool, provided with the Android SDK in the **/tools** folder, gives developers a simple, useful tool for creating NinePatch image assets using a WYSIWYG (What You See Is What You Get) graphics editor.

I'm going to cover the use of the Draw 9-patch software in detail in the next section of this chapter, so let's get started!

The Draw 9-Patch Tool: Create NinePatchDrawable Assets

This section will cover how to create a 9-patch graphic using the Android **Draw 9-patch** tool. You will need the source PNG image with which you would like to create your NinePatchDrawable object; I have provided a sample PNG image asset named **NinePatchFrame.png**. This truecolor-with-alpha-channel PNG32 digital image asset can be located in a NinePatch sub-folder in the project assets repository for this book.

The reason I'm using an alpha channel to define transparency in the center area of the 9-patch that you're about to create is so that any image layers (intended composites) that are behind the image asset inside Android will composite perfectly with the 9-patch image asset in the compositing stack.

Let's get started by locating your **Draw 9-patch** tool in your Android SDK folder hierarchy, in the **tools** sub-folder. Open your OS's File Navigation utility; for Windows 8 this is the Explorer and is shown in Figure 10-1.

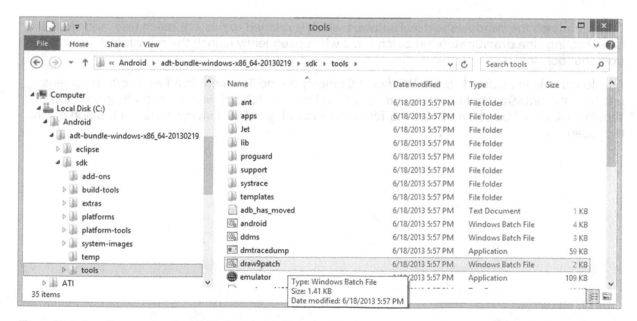

Figure 10-1. Locating your draw9patch Windows batch file in the Android folder SDK sub-folder, tools sub-folder

As you can see, I named my Android SDK folder **Android**, and it contains an **adt-bundle-windows-x86** folder that I unzipped to install the SDK. Under this folder is the **sdk** folder and underneath that is the **tools** sub-folder.

Once you click the tools sub-folder, as shown in Figure 10-1, you will see a **draw9patch.bat** Windows batch file; that is what you'll need to launch to run the Draw9patch software utility. Right-click the draw9patch file and select the **Run as administrator** menu option, as shown in Figure 10-2.

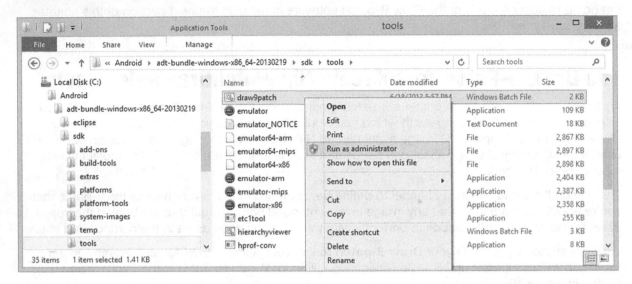

Figure 10-2. Right-clicking the draw9patch Windows batch file and selecting the Run as administrator option to run

This will launch the Windows terminal software which is needed to run .bat batch files, and since it is "executing" the **draw9patch.bat** batch file, it will subsequently launch the draw9patch application from the tools folder.

As you can see in Figure 10-3, the **Windows Command Line Terminal** (cmd.exe) software opens and runs the draw9patch.bat, which then opens a Draw 9-patch software editing window on top of a Terminal window. You can minimize the Terminal window if you like, leaving the Draw 9-patch editing tool open.

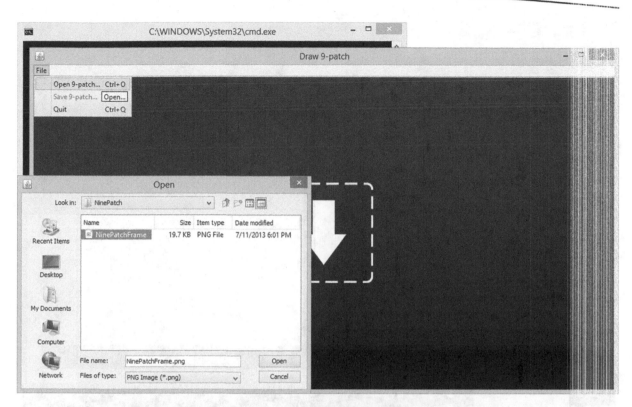

Figure 10-3. Launching the Draw 9-patch software and using the File menu to access the Open 9-patch dialog

There are two ways to open your source .PNG files for 9-patch development; either **drag** your PNG image onto the Draw 9-patch window, where the **drop it arrow** is, in the center, or use the **File ➤ Open 9-patch** work process to locate the file in your NinePatch sub-folder. Both of these ways are shown in Figure 10-3; however, I am going to use the conservative route with the **Open** dialog, shown in the bottom-left corner of the screen shot.

Once you find the NinePatchFrame.png 32-bit PNG source image asset, select it, and click the **Open** button. You will see your Draw 9-patch software, with your PNG file in the editing and preview areas. The left pane is your editing area, where you can create your one-pixel black lines that define patches or scaling areas, as well as your center (padding) content areas.

The right pane is your resulting 9-patch preview area, shown in Figure 10-4, where you can see what your 9-patch image asset will look like when it is scaled according to the one-pixel black border line definitions that you are defining in the left editing pane of the software.

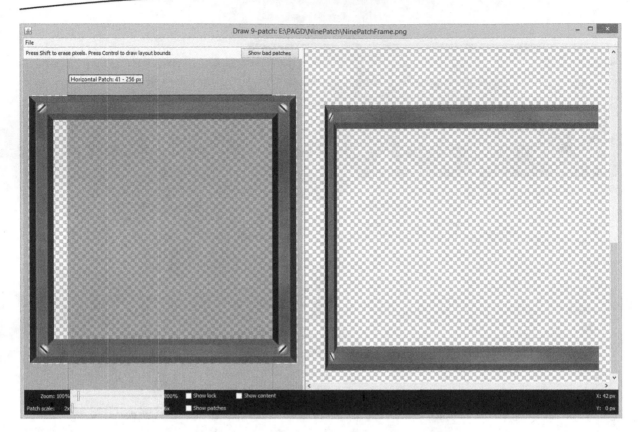

Figure 10-4. Drawing out the Horizontal Patch at the top one pixel black line segment to define active X axis area

Let's click in the top one-pixel transparent perimeter on the right side, near the corner, as shown in Figure 10-4, and then drag towards the left to draw the black line that defines the X dimension scalable patch. Once you draw in the rough approximation of what you want, you can fine-tune the line using the fine lines at each end of the one-pixel line segment. Put your mouse over these until your cursor changes into a double-arrow; then click and drag the grayed-out area until it fits pixel-perfectly with the transparency area in the center of your NinePatchFrame source image asset.

You can also right-click, or hold the Shift key and click on a Macintosh, to erase the previously drawn line. As you can see in the preview area on the right, you're still not getting the visual result that you're going for, so let's continue on and define the left one-pixel black border next.

First, let's use one of the more colorful options, located at the bottom of the Draw 9-patch software, so you can visualize your settings even better.

Look for the empty checkbox next to the **Show patches** option, and **check it** to turn this feature on. As shown in Figure 10-5, this will provide colors for your selected areas by using a combination of purple and green colors. This will make it clear which areas in your image asset are being affected.

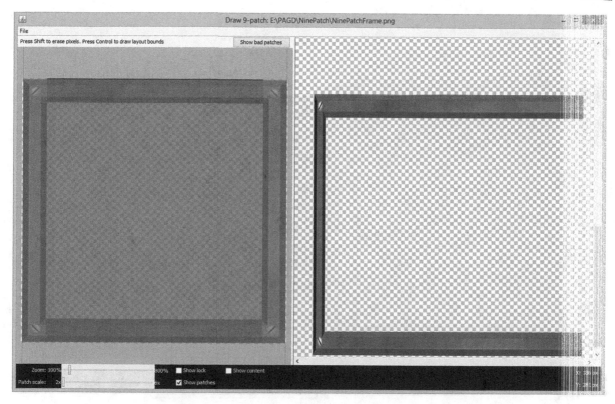

Figure 10-5. Turning on the Show Patches checkbox option, and finishing the top one-pixel black line segment

You can see in Figure 10-5 that several other useful controls exist at the bottom of your editing pane. One is a **Zoom slider**, which will allow you to adjust the zoom level of your source graphic in the editing area. The other slider is the **Patch scale slider**, which allows you to adjust the scale of the preview imagery shown in the preview area on the right. The **Show lock option checkbox** will allow you to visualize the non-drawable area of the graphic when you mouse-over it.

The **Show patches** option checkbox, which you have just enabled, allows you to preview your scalable patch definitions in real time in a left pane editing area. The pink color represents an area of the patch that is scalable.

The **Show content** option checkbox highlights your content area in a preview image, where purple shows the area in which View content will be allowed.

Finally, at the top of the editing area there is a **Show bad patches** button that will add a red border around patch areas that may produce artifacts in the graphic when it is scaled. Visual excellence for your scaled images will be achieved if you strive to eliminate all bad patches in the design.

Now it is time to draw in your **left one-pixel border**, shown in Figure 10-6.

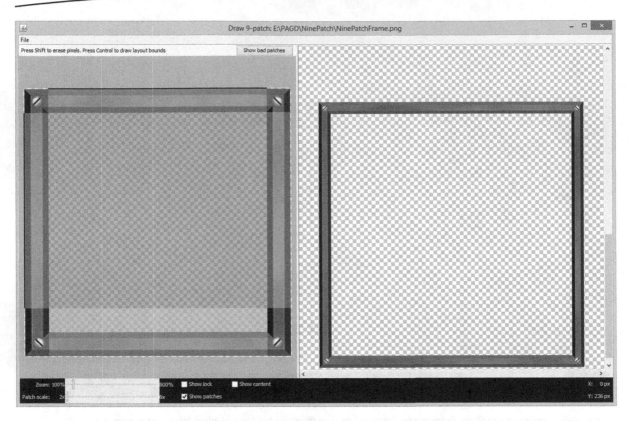

Figure 10-6. *Drawing out the vertical patch at the left one-pixel black line segment to define active Y axis area*

As you can see in Figure 10-6, I didn't draw a one-pixel black border line all the way down the left side. I did this so that you could visualize how well the **Show patches** option works. The option will allow you to visualize exactly what you are doing right down to the pixel level; this precision is absolutely necessary if you want to define the perfect 9-patch image asset.

Figure 10-7 shows the 9-patch image asset with both the top and left one-pixel border black line definitions in place; as you can see, due to the Show patches option, you have now defined your static areas and your scalable areas with surgical precision.

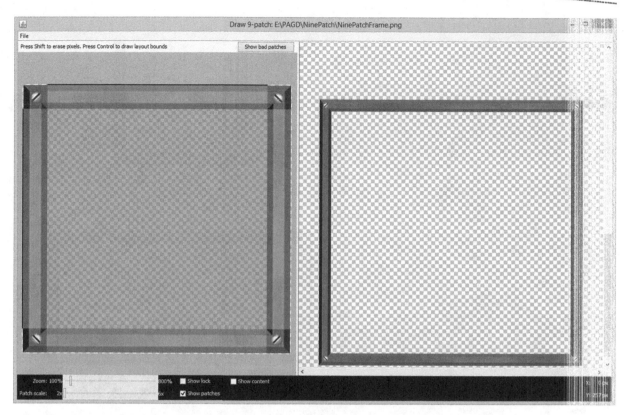

Figure 10-7. Both the horizontal and vertical patch one-pixel black line segments now define active axis areas

Also notice in Figure 10-7 on the right-hand preview side of the software tool that the result of your 9-patch image asset definition is giving you a very professional scaling result.

If you grab the scrollbar on the right side of the screen, and pull it up or down, you will see that the 9-patch scales into a portrait as well as a landscape container shape with perfect visual results.

Now that you have defined the scalable areas of the 9-patch image asset, it is time to define the **padding** areas of your 9-patch image asset, using the one-pixel black border lines on the **right** and **bottom** of the editing pane.

As you can see in Figure 10-8, I have drawn in, on the right-hand side, the one-pixel black border line segment that is needed to define the Y image dimension for the center (padding) area for the 9-patch image asset. Also notice in Figure 10-8 that I am in the process of drawing in the second bottom side one-pixel black border line segment in order to define the X dimension for the center (padding) area for the 9-patch image asset.

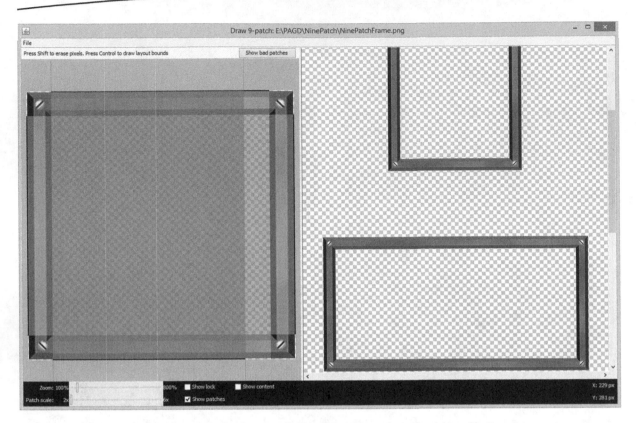

Figure 10-8. Defining the padding areas using the one-pixel black line segments on the right and bottom areas

Notice the muted colors that are used to show the different layers of the scalable versus padding area definitions. Your padding definitions utilize a grayish overlay on the green or purple (or pink, if you prefer) scalable area definition, which is more brightly colored, probably due to the fact that the scalable area is more important to define than the padding area.

Also, notice on the right-hand side in the 9-patch results previewing area that the 9-patch scaling result is giving you exceptionally professional results, regardless of the image's orientation or the dimensions that the 9-patch image asset is being scaled into.

Finally, notice in Figure 10-9 that I am pulling the right side one-pixel black border line segment up to show the patch adjustment guides and how the border allows you to adjust your 9-patch padding parameters precisely.

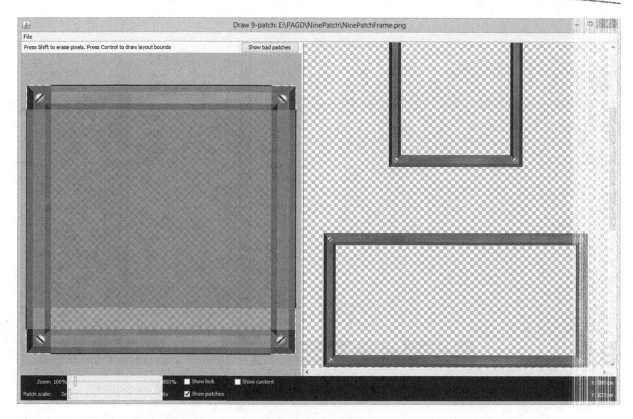

Figure 10-9. *Adjusting the padding areas via the right side one-pixel black line segment to show patch adjust guides*

Figure 10-10 shows the finished 9-patch image asset definition with both a scaling set of border line segments and the padding set of border line segments.

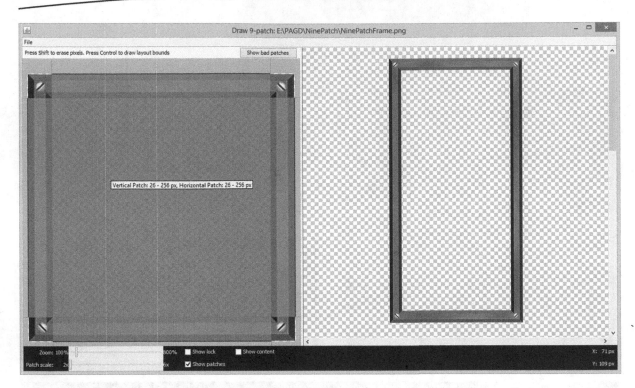

Figure 10-10. Final patch and padding areas defined and using mouse-over center area to get patch coordinates

It is important to note that if you place your mouse in the left editable pane, over the center section of your 9-patch definition, and then hold it there, the tool-tip pop-up will appear, giving you the precise pixel patch coordinates for your final 9-patch definition.

In my case, this shows that I have used 256 pixels minus 26 pixels, or 230 pixels of my total 280 pixel image dimension, for my center scalable area. This means that I have used 25 pixels, or half of the 50 remaining pixels, for the actual image assets (bars and screws) that will be scaled. This also means that the fixed areas of this 9-patch (in this case it is a corner of the frame with a standard screw in it to hold it down firmly, or so it appears at least) would thus each be 25 pixels square in size.

This is enough pixels, two dozen or more, to be able to scale up if necessary and to be able to have detail to appear photo-real if scaled down, or used at higher pixel densities, where it will look smaller.

As you can see in Figure 10-10 and Figure 10-11, on the right-hand side of the Draw 9-patch application preview pane, the scaling graphic looks crisp and realistic. If you scroll the preview pane, this holds across previews.

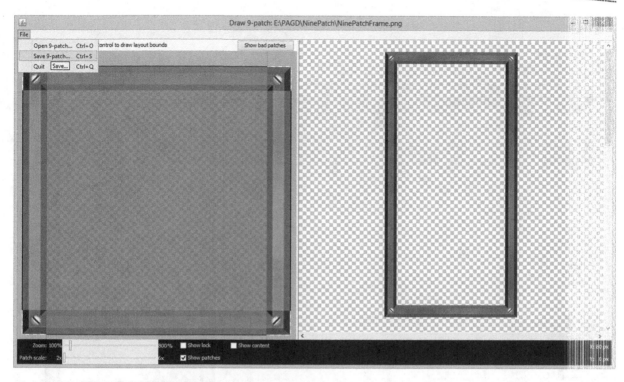

Figure 10-11. *Final patch definition, and using the File menu and Save 9-patch menu options to save a 9-patch*

Now it is time to save the 9-patch image asset using the File menu and the **File ➤ Save 9-patch** menuing sequence, which is shown in Figure 10-11.

Your Draw 9-patch software tool File **Save** dialog, which is shown in Figure 10-12, will automatically save your 9-patch image assets with the required **.9.png** file name extension required by the Android OS.

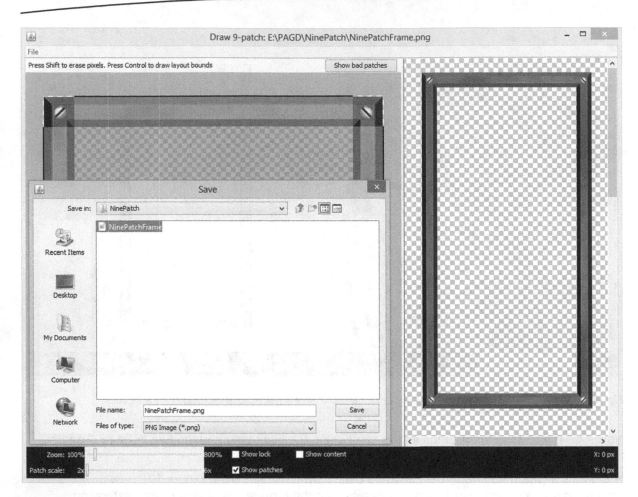

Figure 10-12. Exporting the NinePatchFrame.9.png file using the Save dialog

When Android sees this type of PNG file name in your **/res/drawable** folder, it automatically sets it up using the **NinePatch** class to load it, and also makes it into a NinePatchDrawable image asset once it's referenced in XML.

It is important to note here, since there is also the **Open 9-patch** menu option in the screen shot, that opening a normal (non-9-patched) PNG file (*.png) will load your PNG asset and add an empty one-pixel border around the image, into which you can draw your scalable patches and content area.

If you use this menu command to open up previously saved 9-patch PNG files (*.9.png), your 9-patch PNG asset will be loaded in as previously modified, with no one-pixel border drawing areas added, because that one-pixel patch definition area already exists within your file due to a previous editing session.

One final caveat for the **Save** dialog is that it will **not** show this **.9.png** extension in the dialog itself, but will insert it on your hard disk drive when it saves your file out as a new 9-patch image asset. This can be somewhat confusing the first time that you use this software utility, as the file it says in the Save dialog that it's going to save a **NinePatchFrame.png** but what it actually saves out is **NinePatchFrame.9.png**.

Make sure to keep this caveat in mind when you go to save out your file, so that you don't get a NinePatchFrame.9.9.png file. Even if you do, the next step in the work process will be to go into your OS file management utility to see your original file and the new 9-patch version, and see how much data footprint "weight" the 9-patch definition added to the file.

Launch your OS file management utility from your Taskbar; for Windows 8 it happens to be the Windows Explorer file utility, as shown in Figure 10-13. As you can see, in my /PAGD/NinePatch folder there's an original Photoshop file with the 280 pixel image asset source composite; a NinePatchFrame.png PNG32 image asset with alpha channel, ready for import into Draw 9-patch; and a **NinePatchFrame.9** PNG32 file generated by the Draw 9-patch tool.

Figure 10-13. Checking the NinePatch folder to see the original NinePatchFrame and the new NinePatchFrame.9.png

Let's find out how much data was added to the .9.png file, because, as the screen shot says, the 9-patch definition process added one full KB to my PNG file size, but this assessment is not accurate enough for me.

To find out your exact file size **delta**, or difference, between these two files, right-click each of these two PNG file assets, and use the **properties** option. This will allow you to see the actual file size data footprint for each file.

The original PNG is 19.7KB and the new PNG is 20.2KB. This means that the 9-patch definition added .5KB to this 280 pixel square image asset, or about 2.5% more data. Not bad for adding such a flexible image asset scaling capability right into the PNG digital image asset itself.

Now that you have created a usable 9-patch image asset, let's go into your XML assets and implement it in a couple of places to see how well it works within the context of your GraphicsDesign Android application.

Implementing Your NinePatch Asset Using XML Markup

The first thing that you will need to do for your XML markup to be able to reference this 9-patch PNG imaging asset is to install it into the proper project folder hierarchy location, where you know the Android OS is going to look for 9-patch image assets.

Go into your NinePatch **assets** folder, the one that you were just in, which is shown in Figure 10-13, and right-click the **NinePatchFrame.9.png** file, which is highlighted in the screenshot, and select the **Copy** option to copy the file into your system clipboard.

Next, use your left side navigation pane and navigate into your **/workspace** folder and **/GraphicsDesign** project sub-folder, and finally into your **/res** (resource) sub-folder and **/drawable** sub-folder, as shown in Figure 10-14. Then simply right-click the **/res/drawable** folder and select the Paste option. This will put a copy of the NinePatchFrame.9.png file there.

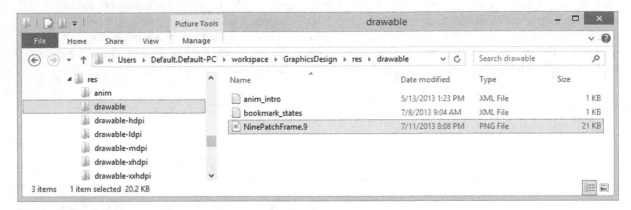

Figure 10-14. Using Copy + Paste to put a copy of the NinePatchFrame.9.png file into your drawable assets folder

Since Android OS requires asset file names to use only lowercase letters, numbers, and the underscore character, the next thing that you will need to do is to rename the 9-patch image asset file to use all lowercase letters and numbers, as ninepatchframe.9.png, as shown in Figure 10-15.

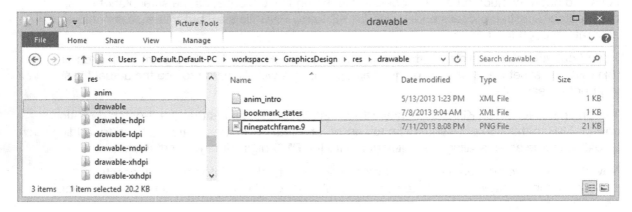

Figure 10-15. Right-clicking and using the Rename command to rename the file using only lowercase characters

Now you can add the 9-patch image asset into your Table of Contents Activity UI design **LinearLayout** container using the **android:background** parameter in the parent tag, as shown in Figure 10-16, using the following XML markup:

```
android:background="@drawable/ninepatchframe"
```

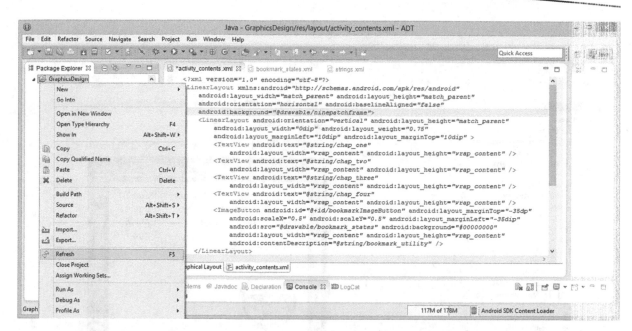

Figure 10-16. Adding an android:background parameter to reference the ninepatchframe 9-patch asset and Refresh

Also shown in Figure 10-16 is the **Refresh** operation, which you must invoke so that Eclipse ADT can "see" the new 9-patch asset that you have added in the /res/drawable folder. So let's do that as well, and right-click the GraphicsDesign project folder and select the Refresh option from the menu.

Once you do this, the 9-patch image asset will be visible in your project folder hierarchy, as you will see a bit later on in the chapter, in Figure 10-17, when you take a look at your 9-patch asset in use as a decorative UI layout container 3D frame graphics design element.

Figure 10-17. Using the Graphical Layout tab to preview your 9-patch asset in your parent LinearLayout container

Let's click the Graphical Layout Editor tab at the bottom of your XML editing pane, and see if the GLE can "render" 9-patch assets, since there are some graphics design elements, such as the **PorterDuff** blending modes, that the GLE is unable to preview.

As you can see in Figure 10-17, the Graphical Layout Editor pane renders a 9-patch asset perfectly, and thus the GLE can indeed show you how a 9-patch image asset will look in your application. That's great; so you can use the GLE in your 9-patch work process without having to launch the emulator every time you want to see how a 9-patch image asset works as a graphics design element!

As you can see in Figure 10-17, the 9-patch image asset you created works well as the decorative framing element for your Table of Contents UI design, and it looks quite nice. The only problem is that the center (padding) area that your 9-patch asset defines is making a couple of the longer text UI elements wrap, so you will need to add some XML parameters to adjust the font size for this text down slightly in size so that this wrapping to the next line does not occur.

To do this, you'll need to add in an **android:textSize** parameter and a value of 13 standard pixels (13sp) to decrease your TextView UI element font size slightly, by using the following parameter in each of your TextView tags:

```
android:textSize="13sp"
```

Once you add this parameter into each of the TextView tags, all of your Text elements will be the same size and fit inside your 9-patch frame perfectly.

Figure 10-18 shows the modified TextView child tags inside each of the two nested (child tag) LinearLayout containers. Remember to keep your textSize parameter values the same so that the text in your Table of Contents looks uniform. Users will be able to detect slight font size differences in your UI design, and will perceive this as a design flaw, and thus will deem your app as less than professional, so use the same SP value in all eight TextViews. I used 13sp to get the text as large as possible.

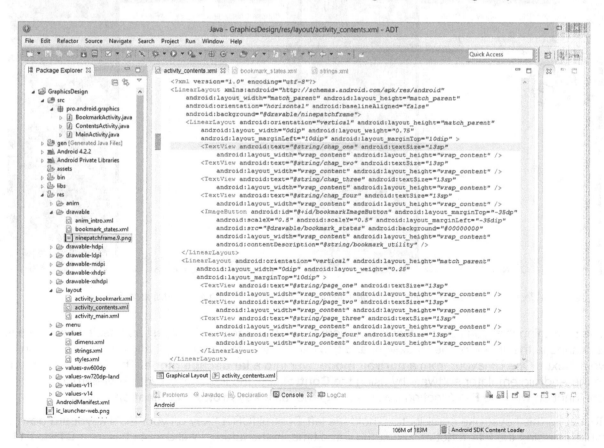

Figure 10-18. Adding an android:textSize parameter into eight TextView tags in the nested LinearLayout containers

Now you are ready to preview the new font size in the Graphical Layout Editor tab, so click the tab at the bottom of the editing pane and make sure that the font size allows all of the TextView objects to fit within the decorative 9-patch UI layout frame that you added in this chapter.

Next, let's take a look at what the 9-patch asset looks like in the Nexus One emulator, to see what it would look like on an actual Android phone. Use the **Run As ➤ Android Application** work process to launch your AVD Nexus One emulator, and make sure your TextView font sizes, 9-patch image asset background, and multi-state ImageButton all work together seamlessly.

As you can see in Figure 10-19, the 9-patch image asset frame around your UI layout container looks great, the TextView UI elements are the perfect size for a table of Contents, and your multi-state ImageButton composites perfectly and is still positioned attractively, relative to the balance of your UI layout design. As you can see on the right side of the screen shot, the ImageButton is still functioning correctly within the UI design.

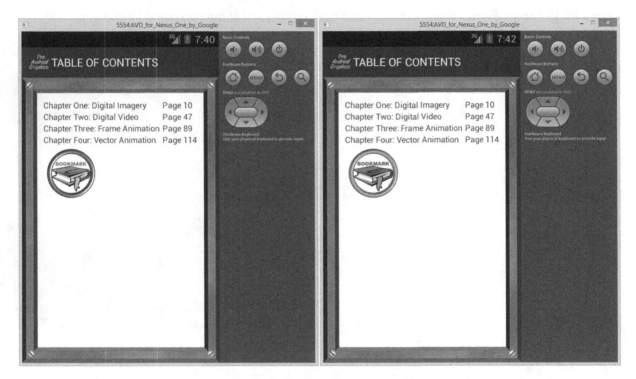

Figure 10-19. Testing the Table of Contents UI design in the Nexus One emulator with the 9-patch asset in place

The next thing that you need to test is how your 9-patch image asset will reshape itself when there is a change in the shape of the UI design, and this can be accomplished by changing the orientation of your Nexus One UI layout from a **portrait mode** over into a **landscape mode**. This is accomplished in the Android emulator software by using the **Control** key (the left one) on your keyboard in conjunction with the **F11** function key, used together as a **keystroke combination**.

To invoke this keystroke combination, hold the left Control (CRTL) key on your PC's keyboard down, while pressing the F11 function key at the same time. In the future, I will denote this as a **CTRL-F11** keystroke combination.

To rotate your Nexus One emulator back in the other direction, utilize the **CTRL-F12** keystroke combination. This will return the Nexus One emulator to its original portrait orientation mode.

Invoking CTRL-F11 this will cause your Nexus One emulator window to rotate 90 degrees, and will put the Nexus One emulator into landscape orientation mode, just as if you had turned your Smartphone on its side.

The results are shown in Figure 10-20; as you can clearly see, your 9-patch image asset conforms itself to the new shape of the UI screen as if it had been created for that exact screen aspect ratio in the first place.

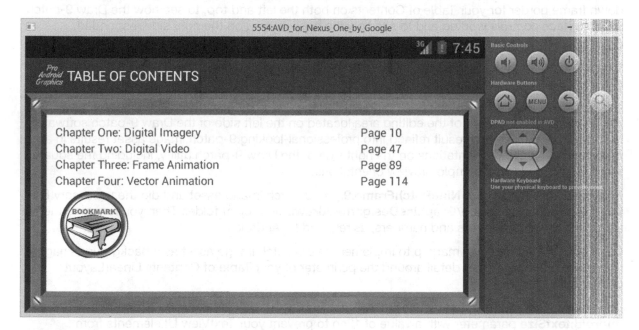

Figure 10-20. Testing the 9-patch asset in a different screen aspect ratio by using an emulator landscape orientation

Now that you know how to create and use 9-patch image assets, you'll be able to use them in future chapters for other types of graphic designs, or for UI element design, so make sure to practice using your Draw 9-patch tool.

Summary

In this tenth chapter, you learned about the Android **NinePatchDrawable** and **NinePatch** classes, as well as how to use the **Draw 9-patch** software tool.

We started by looking at the **NinePatchDrawable** class and how it allows developers to instantiate drawable objects (image assets) that utilize the NinePatch objects, which use 9-patch uneven image asset scaling technology.

Next, we took a closer look at the **NinePatch** technology and concepts, which you will need to fully understand to be able to implement the 9-patch image assets in your Android application. You learned how to use a one-pixel black border line segment to define both X and Y scalable areas within your 9-patch image asset, and how this also defines the areas of your image that will remain fixed and will not scale at all.

Then you learned how to utilize the right and bottom one-pixel border areas to define the center padding areas where the View content will live inside your 9-patch image asset. We looked at the NinePatch class, which allows us to create NinePatch objects that implement NinePatch technology.

Next, we took a look at the Draw 9-patch software utility, including how to find it and launch it, as well as how to use it to create 9-patch assets.

You took a hands-on approach and created the one-pixel black border line segments for a screw-down frame border for your Table of Contents on both the left and top, to see how the Draw 9-patch user interface controls worked and to see how the preview area on the right side responded.

You also learned about the option checkboxes on the bottom of the left side editing area, and how they allow you to better visualize what you are doing in the left editing side of the Draw 9-patch software utility.

Next, you defined your 9-patch padding area using the one-pixel black border line segments on the right and bottom sides of the editing area located on the left side of the Draw 9-patch software tool. You saw the preview result refined into professional-looking 9-patch image asset results in all of the sample preview orientations on the right side of the Draw 9-patch utility, including the square, portrait, and landscape sample preview orientations.

Finally, you saved out your **NinePatchFrame.9.png** 9-patch image asset and did the necessary file transfer into a **/workspace/GraphicsDesign/res/drawable** project folder. Then you renamed the file using only lowercase letters and numbers, as required by Android.

Next, you created the XML markup to implement this 9-patch image asset as a background image to provide graphics design detail around the perimeter of your Table of Contents LinearLayout container UI design.

After previewing your 9-patch results in the Graphical Layout Editor pane, you added an **android:textSize** parameter with a value of 13sp to prevent your TextView UI elements from wrapping to the next line, and then you used the Nexus One emulator to preview your results in both portrait and landscape modes. You did this in order to see exactly how the 9-patch image asset can scale, with seamless flexibly, to different screen shapes (aspect ratios).

In the next chapter, you will learn about digital image and animation asset **Blending** in Android, using the Android **PorterDuff** class and its many image compositing and blending modes and constants. This will allow you to ratchet your Android graphics design special effects work to an entirely new level, including building upon what you learned in this chapter regarding 9-patch design and implementation.

Chapter 11

Advanced Image Blending: Using Android PorterDuff Classes

In this eleventh chapter, we'll take a close look at the role that **blending modes** play in digital image compositing, as well as how to implement these digital image blending modes in Android, using the Android **PorterDuff** classes.

A blending mode allows advanced digital image compositing to be performed between two or more layers within a digital image composite. Each pixel in each layer is run through an algorithm to determine how it will be applied (or not applied) to the layer or layers underneath it.

Applying blending modes is usually done using a digital image editing and compositing software tool, such as Adobe Photoshop CS6 or the open source digital image software package GIMP, which we have been using throughout in this book, because it is quite advanced, and free for commercial use.

The fact that these PorterDuff blending modes (sometimes termed **transfer modes**) are in Android, along with the ability to work with layers via the Android LayerDrawable class, which we are covering in the next chapter, puts a lot of the power, which is normally only found in software packages such as Photoshop CS6 and GIMP 2.8, into the hands of Android developers.

This allows Android developers to take their graphics design creativity to an entirely new level by applying these types of algorithmic special effects, which are possible using layer blending mode in GIMP 2.8.6, to UI design, graphics design, digital imaging, digital video, and 2D animation in their Android applications.

Examples of use of image blending include photo software, games, e-books, iTV programs for GoogleTV, wallpapers, screensavers, and other graphics-related uses that your imagination can come up with. With clever coding, all of these areas can even be made to be interactive, so your graphics-design-related image blending possibilities are literally limited only by your digitalized imagination.

Pixel Blending: Take Image Compositing to the Next Level

Let's get an overview of what pixel blending is, and what blending modes, or transfer modes as they are sometimes called, are useful for in graphics design, before we get deeper into classes and constructors and nested enum classes and constants and all of those fun technical Java constructs that allow us to implement image asset blending inside of an Android application.

By and large, blending or transfer modes are most often utilized with image compositing objectives, which most digital imaging artisans perform using Adobe Photoshop CS6 or GIMP 2.8.6 or later professional imaging software.

Blending is used when there is more than one compositing layer holding image assets that need to be combined in some advanced way to achieve some end result, which could be anything from text overlays to special effects.

It is important to note that as long as you're great at implementing alpha channels, you don't have to necessarily implement blending modes to create an effective image composite, as we've already seen in previous chapters.

Thus, alpha channels are still important to the foundation of digital image compositing, and then on top of that blending allows us to generate better or more subtle effects. So always start with getting your composite clean by fine-tuning the alpha-channel-based compositing, and then add blending modes in as the next step in your work process to refine your compositing effect and end result.

Blending modes combine images, actually on a pixel-by-pixel basis, using algorithms that allow the resulting pixels (images) to be something more than a "normal mode" (zero blending modes invoked) image composite. So if you had an image where you wanted to add yellow pixels to the red pixels in another image layer to create orange pixels in your resulting image composite, you would utilize a blending mode to accomplish the desired end result, while still being able to keep the original yellow and red source digital image assets separate and individually unaffected.

We will cover the blending modes that are currently available in Android in a future section, which covers the class in Android that specifically holds **enum constants** that we can use to call or implement these blending algorithms for our own graphics design objectives inside our Android apps.

It is important to again note that blended pixels should "obey" your alpha channel, so that they know their place in the image compositing hierarchy. The alpha channel should take precedence over blending modes in that chain of calculation, which is implemented in an image compositing process, whether that is inside Android OS or in Adobe Photoshop CS6 or GIMP 2.8.6 or later.

A pixel will only be blended if it has some level of translucency defined. 100% transparent pixels, as defined by the alpha channel, are not factored into a blending algorithm. Let's get into how Android implements blending!

Android's PorterDuff Class: The Foundation for Blending

The Android **PorterDuff** class is a direct subclass of the **java.lang.Object** master class; it is an **algorithm** class that was essentially scratch-coded, and thus it was not based on any other types of superclass functionality currently found within the Android OS. The PorterDuff class is thus a completely unique class, and provides the foundational implementation in Android OS for **pixel blending algorithms**.

The PorterDuff class Java hierarchy is structured as follows:

```
java.lang.Object
  > android.graphics.PorterDuff
```

Android's PorterDuff class is part of the **android.graphics** package, and as such, its **import statement** references the **android.graphics.PorterDuff** package import path, as we will see later on in the chapter when we write Java code that implements PorterDuff blending for a variety of purposes.

In case you are wondering who Porter Duff is, it is actually two people who laid the mathematical foundation for blending modes and transfer modes. One was named **Thomas Porter** and the other was named **Tom Duff**, and in **1984**, they wrote a white paper detailing the mathematics behind pixel blending.

The Android PorterDuff class is deceptively simple, as it contains only a single **PorterDuff()** constructor method, as well as just one single nested class, which is called the **PorterDuff.Mode** Enum class.

We will go into these classes and other PorterDuff related classes in detail over the many sections of this chapter. These PorterDuff classes contain all of the available blending mode algorithms, functions, transfer constants and blending constants that allow developers to implement advanced image compositing in their Android application graphics design and UI design.

As I mentioned, blending modes are also sometimes called **transfer modes** because some of these modes don't really blend any pixel values together. Instead, some of them act much like a **Boolean set operator** (intersections, unions, differences, and so on) would function. Thus these modes could be considered transfer modes, as they are not really blending pixel values but simply transferring them from the source and destination image into the final image compositing result (the target or created composite image asset).

For this reason, some of these PorterDuff constants act more like transfer mode constants than they do blending mode constants. As a result, we'll go over each of these PorterDuff constants in fine detail in order to see what capabilities they afford to us as Pro Android graphics designers, and if they blend, or transfer, the pixels between our source and destination image assets. Once we have gone over the **PorterDuff.Mode** nested class, we can start to implement some of this cool digital image blending knowledge!

You may be wondering how CPU intensive these blending and transfer modes are, as well as which of them are more processor intensive. From what I have heard from other developers, the blending modes are about three times more processor intensive than the transfer modes because they are calculating a new pixel color value rather than simply calculating if a pixel needs to be displayed or not.

The PorterDuff.Mode Class: Android Blending Constants

Android's **PorterDuff.Mode** class is a direct subclass of the **java.lang.Enum** class, which is a subclass of the **java.lang.Object** master class, and it is therefore an **Enumerator** class designed to hold **Enum** constants, so it works hand-in-hand with the PorterDuff class it is nested underneath.

The PorterDuff.Mode class is also a completely unique class, and provides developers with the **blending mode constants** that are needed in Android OS to implement advanced **pixel blending** for their compositing operations.

The PorterDuff.Mode class Java hierarchy is structured as follows:

```
java.lang.Object
  > java.lang.Enum<E extends java.lang.Enum<E>>
    > android.graphics.PorterDuff
```

This PorterDuff.Mode class is also a part of the **android.graphics** package, and its **import statement** references an **android.graphics.PorterDuff.Mode** package import path, as you will see later on in the chapter when you write Java code that implements the PorterDuff.Mode blending mode constants.

There are currently **18** PorterDuff.Mode constants defined within this class. We will go over the pixel blending constants, which include **SCREEN**, **OVERLAY**, **LIGHTEN**, **DARKEN**, **MULTIPLY**, and **ADD** first, as these allow the most special imaging effects to be applied to the image compositing process.

After that, we will take a look at the **CLEAR**, **XOR**, and the **SRC** (source) and **DST** (destination) image transfer modes, which are also very useful for the application of advanced graphics design work processes or special effects.

If, while you're reading this section of the chapter, you can't visualize in your head what each of these algorithmic equations is doing with the pixel blending, don't worry, as we'll be taking a look visually at what these do later on in this chapter, so you will get plenty of "blending" experience!

It is important to note that the only way to really get familiar with what these blending modes are going to do in any given compositing application is to spend some time **experimenting** with or working with them. As you gain more time with and **experience** in using the blending modes, you will be more able to accurately speculate what any given blending mode is going to result in, given the combination of two totally different images.

The first blending constant we will look at is one of the most frequently used, the **ADD** constant, which adds the **saturation** of the source with the destination image asset, or in equation form, **Saturate(S+D)**. As you may have guessed, in these equations **S** means **Source** and **D** means **Destination**.

The second constant we're going to look at isn't a blending or a transfer, but rather a **utility constant**. A **CLEAR** constant clears the blending result area of all pixel data, and thus takes the equation form of **[0,0]**.

The third constant is popular with image compositors, the **DARKEN** constant, which **darkens** the destination image asset using the source image asset, or in equation form, **[Sa+Da - Sa*Da, Sc*(1-Da) + Dc*(1-Sa) + min(Sc, Dc)]**.

There is also a **LIGHTEN** constant, which is also used quite often by image compositors. As you might have guessed, this is the opposite of the **DARKEN** constant. This blending algorithm **lightens** the destination image asset by using the source image asset as a lightening guide, or in equation form, **[Sa+Da - Sa*Da, Sc*(1-Da) + Dc*(1-Sa) + max(Sc, Dc)],** which is the same as the DARKEN algorithm, except using the max function instead of the min.

There is also a **MULTIPLY** blending constant, which is one of my favorites; it **multiplies** the pixel values between the source and destination imaging assets by using the following equation: **[Sa*Da, Sc*Dc]**. This usually results in a darkening effect. The lowercase **a** and **c** stand for **alpha** (Channel) and **color** (RGB).

A slightly more complicated version of the MULTIPLY blending mode is the **SCREEN** blending mode constant, which allows you to essentially **ghost** the source image over the destination image, which allows us to obtain some really cool special effects. This SCREEN blending algorithm uses the following equation: **[Sa+Da - Sa*Da, Sc+Dc - Sc*Dc]**.

Another favorite of mine is the **OVERLAY** blending constant, which is one of the most-used blending constants for special effects. It combines a SCREEN blending mode with a MULTIPLY blending mode. As you may have guessed given its name, it **overlays** pixel values between a source and destination image, so that a source image looks like it's **ghosted** on top of the destination.

OVERLAY is a more advanced version of the SCREEN blending constant, where pixels are either multiplied or screened based on their luminosity values; lighter parts of the image become lighter (screen) and darker parts of the image become darker (multiply).

There are five **DST** related (destination-related) constants, which focus on the destination image asset. The first of these is the **DST** constant, which **isolates** only the destination image, meaning it shows only the destination image, hiding the source image, and thus its equation is **[Da, Dc]**.

The **DST_ATOP** constant takes that portion of the destination image that is over (intersecting with) the source image, and displays only this portion on TOP of (or, ATOP) the source image. The equation to produce this result is as follows: **[Sa, Sa*Dc + Sc*(1-Da)]**.

The **DST_IN** constant takes the portion of the destination image that lies **inside** (intersecting with) the source image, and displays only the portion of that destination image that is contained within (IN or INSIDE) the source image, but does not show any of the source image itself. This is an equivalent to the Boolean **intersection operation**. The equation to produce this digital image intersection result is **[Sa*Da, Sa*Dc]**.

The **DST_OUT** constant does the exact opposite of what the DST_IN constant does, and takes the portion of the destination image that lies **outside** of (not intersecting with) the source image, and displays only the portion of the destination image that is not intersecting with (OUT or OUTSIDE OF) the source image, but does not show any of the source itself. This is the equivalent of a **Boolean subtraction operation**, as the source image portion that overlays the destination image is essentially subtracted from the destination image. An algorithm or equation that produces this end result is written as follows: **[Da*(1-Sa), Dc*(1-Sa)]**.

The **DST_OVER** constant overlays the destination image on top of the source image. This is thus an equivalent of the **Boolean union operation**, which is sometimes called a Boolean add operation. The equation is as follows: **[Sa + (1-Sa)*Da, Rc = Dc+(1-Da)*Sc]**.

There are five **SRC** related (source-related) constants, which focus on source image assets. These are essentially the same as DST constants, only the opposite in the sense that they involve the source image, rather than the destination image. The first of them is a **SRC** constant, which **isolates** only the source image, meaning it shows only the source image, hiding the destination image, and thus, its very simple equation is **[Sa, Sc]**.

The **SRC_ATOP** constant takes the portion of the source image that is over (intersecting with) the destination image, and displays only this portion, on TOP of (or ATOP) the destination image. The algorithm or equation that produces this result is as follows: **[Da, Sc*Da + (1-Sa)*Dc]**.

The **SRC_IN** constant takes the portion of the source image that lies **inside** (intersecting with) the destination image and displays only the portion of the source image that is contained within (IN) the destination image, but does not show any of the destination image itself. A Boolean operation equivalent would be the same for both the SRC and DST mode type, if you're wondering. The equation to produce this result is **[Sa*Da, Sa*Dc]**.

The **SRC_OUT** constant does exactly the opposite of what the SRC_IN constant does, and will take the portion of the source image that lies **outside** of (not intersecting with) a destination image, and displays only the portion of the source image that is not intersecting with (OUT or OUTSIDE OF) the destination image, but does not show any of the destination image itself. The equation that produces this result is **[Sa*(1-Da), Sc*(1-Da)]**.

The **SRC_OVER** constant overlays the source image on top of the destination image. The algorithmic equation that produces this end result is **[Sa + (1-Sa)*Da, Rc = Dc + (1-Da)*Sc]**.

Finally, there is the **XOR** blending mode constant, which stands for either-or, and shows either the source image or the destination image, but never both. As a result, where both the source and destination images overlap, nothing is shown, but wherever there is no overlap either the source or destination image shows through (it's a **Boolean exclude operation**). An equation for this is **[Sa+Da - 2*Sa*Da, Sc*(1-Da) + (1-Sa)*Dc]**.

The PorterDuffColorFilter Class: Blending Your ColorFilter

Android has a specialized class for applying color values, in conjunction with PorterDuff blending mode constants, called the **PorterDuffColorFilter** class. The class is a direct subclass of the **android.graphics.ColorFilter** class. This class allows **color filters** to be applied to image assets using blending modes, which gives developers more flexibility in applying color changes to their image assets algorithmically, allowing objectives such as color correction, or even creating a hundred different color image assets, using one image source file, which can save megabytes in data footprint.

The PorterDuffColorFilter class Java hierarchy is structured as follows:

```
java.lang.Object
  > android.graphics.ColorFilter
    > android.graphics.PorterDuffColorFilter
```

The Android PorterDuffColorFilter class is a part of the **android.graphics** package. As such, its **import statement** is constructed to reference the **android.graphics.PorterDuffColorFilter** package import path.

It's interesting to note here that you do not absolutely have to construct a PorterDuffColorFilter object in order to apply your PorterDuff.Mode Enum constants to a color filtering operation. As you'll see in a future section of this chapter, there is a version of the **.setColorFilter()** method, which is part of the ImageView class and accommodates a PorterDuff.Mode blending constant in its parameter list. The method is utilized as follows:

```
myDigitalImageObjectName.setColorFilter( integer color, PorterDuff.Mode mode );
```

It is actually fairly easy to set this up, and thus apply the power of the PorterDuff class to any of your ImageView (and thus, ImageButton subclass) objects. Applying a ColorFilter algorithm in conjunction with a PorterDuff blending mode is actually a very powerful and useful capability as far as graphics design and image compositing is concerned, so we'll cover it now.

Let's do this in your **GraphicsDesign** application **BookmarkActivity** class to show you how to apply a PorterDuff blending mode with a ColorFilter method using only a couple lines of Java code.

Applying ColorFilter Effects to Image Assets Using PorterDuff

Fire up Eclipse ADT, if it isn't open on your desktop already, and open up your **GraphicsDesign** project. Right-click your **BookmarkActivity.java** file and use **Open** or **F3** to open it for editing in the central editing pane of Eclipse. The first thing you need to do is to instantiate your ImageView, which you defined in your **activity_bookmark.xml** UI definition XML file, so enter the following line of Java code to do this:

```
ImageView porterDuffImage = (ImageView)findViewById(R.id.currentBookmarkImage);
```

As you can see in Figure 11-1, you'll need to mouse-over the wavy red error highlighting, and select the **Import ImageView (android.widget)** option; Eclipse will then write this **Import android.widget. ImageView** statement for you, as you will see a bit later on in this chapter in Figure 11-2.

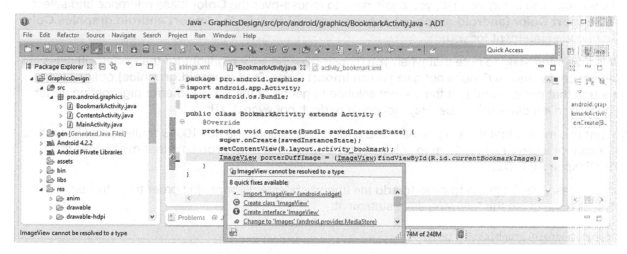

Figure 11-1. Instantiating currentBookmarkImage ImageView to create a Java Object in the BookmarkActivity class

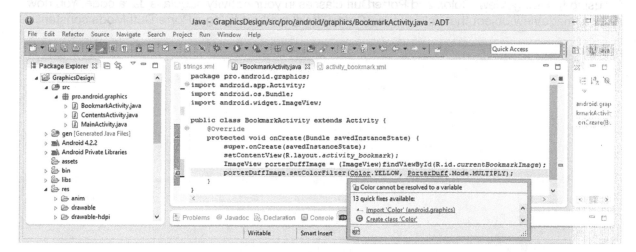

Figure 11-2. Fixing error highlighting by importing android.graphics.Color and android.graphics.PorterDuff classes

Now that your ImageView object instantiation is error-free, you can utilize this porterDuffImage ImageView object to call your **.setColorFilter()** method, which you learned about in the previous section of this chapter. This is done using the following single line of Java programming code:

```
porterDuffImage.setColorFilter(Color.YELLOW, PorterDuff.Mode.MULTIPLY);
```

What this line of Java code does is to call your .setColorFilter() method and pass into it two parameters. The first is the **color value** that you want to apply via your PorterDuff blending mode. In this case, it is the Android OS **Color.YELLOW** constant. A second parameter is one of the PorterDuff.Mode blending constant that you will use to specify your **blending mode algorithm**.

In this initial case, you will be using the **MULTIPLY** constant, as that is the most frequently used blending mode for applying a color change, or special coloration effect, on a digital image asset. This MULTIPLY mode will often increase image contrast as well, making the results look more realistic.

As you can see in Figure 11-2, you again have to mouse-over the **Color** class reference and select the **Import Color (android.graphics)** option to get ADT to write the **Import android.graphics.Color** Java code statement for you.

It is also interesting to note that when you mouse-over the error highlight for the PorterDuff class reference, Eclipse ADT does not give you an **Import PorterDuff (android.graphics)** option, even though that option would be the correct solution to get rid of the wavy red error highlighting under the PorterDuff class reference. Hey, nobody's perfect; not even ADT!

What this means that the Eclipse ADT IDE error helper dialogs are not 100% "bullet-proof," and that we cannot always rely on them to solve all of the Java code error problems that might arise inside our Eclipse ADT IDE.

In this case, you're going to need to add the Import statement yourself in order to fix this error. This is done using the following Java statement:

```
Import android.graphics.PorterDuff;
```

As you can see in Figure 11-3, your code is now error-free, and your Import statements are now in place for using the ImageView, Color, and PorterDuff classes in your Activity subclass Java code. You now have a ImageView object that calls the **.setColorFilter()** method using a PorterDuff.Mode constant.

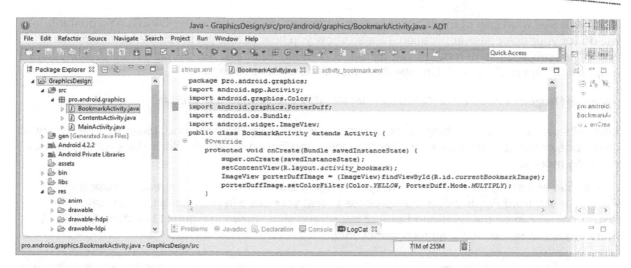

Figure 11-3. Using the .setColorFilter() method to apply a color value change using a PorterDuff MULTIPLY mode

Since the Graphical Layout Editor pane does not support applying imaging algorithms, you will need to use the Nexus One emulator to see the result of a PorterDuff blending mode color filtration digital image application.

As you can see on the left side of Figure 11-4, the yellow color value has been applied to the porterDuffImage ImageView object that references your currentBookmarkImage <ImageView> XML tag definition, which references your digital image asset.

Figure 11-4. Testing the PorterDuff MULTIPLY mode (left) and OVERLAY mode (right) in the Nexus One emulator

Next, let's see what one of the other popular blending mode constants, the **OVERLAY** constant, will do for your color filter application. I'll also show you how to apply a precise 24-bit color value within the .setColorFilter() method call, as that is normally what you are going to want to apply as a graphics design professional. Change the second line of Java code to read

```
porterDuffImage.setColorFilter(Color.rgb(216,192,96), PorterDuff.Mode.OVERLAY);
```

This calls your Color class **.rbg()** method inside your .setColorFilter() method, using a more advanced Java code construct that allows for a more precise application of 24-bit color values with PorterDuff blending modes.

As you can see in Figure 11-5, the Java code is again error-free and you are ready to use a **Run As ➤ Android Application** work process to test your code in the Nexus One emulator. The results are shown on the right-hand side of the screen shot shown in Figure 11-4. Alas, OVERLAY mode does not respect your alpha channel data!

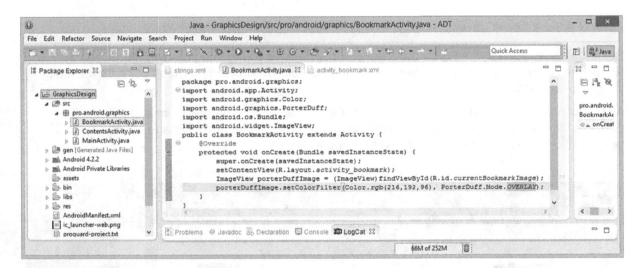

Figure 11-5. Replacing Color.YELLOW constant with an .rgb() method call to allow any color value to be specified

Sometimes there are bugs in the more advanced Android classes, and this OVERLAY algorithm referenced by the OVERLAY blending mode constant should "respect" the alpha channel that you've set up in your original image asset.

What I mean by **respect** is that the algorithm should only apply the OVERLAY blending mode to pixels that are not 100% transparent, so you should not see any of the goldenrod (RGB 216,192,96) color values where the alpha channel transparency is defined in your original digital image compositing asset.

This points out that this PorterDuff class and its modes are not yet fully perfected in Android, probably because this is an advanced feature that is not as often used by the majority of the Android developer community. That said, I am sure that eventually the Android development team will get around to adding a healthy dose of "respect" in the OVERLAY algorithm for the referenced source image alpha channel so that this blending mode works with digital image assets that include an alpha channel for compositing.

What seems to be happening currently is that the algorithm is applying the mode to a alpha channel using its grayscale representation of transparency, rather than first looking at the alpha channel as a guide and using it to determine if the color pixel value should be deemed to be present (or not) in the image composite end result. Just my guess, but there should not be an area of solid color in the resulting OVERLAY mode application shown in Figure 11-4; only the hoop and logo text should be lightened.

Next, let's change your PorterDuff.Mode constant reference back to MULTIPLY. Also, until the SCREEN and OVERLAY algorithms are updated to include alpha channel support, you'll use MULTIPLY to blend color changes using your alpha channel objects (see Figure 11-6). It is important to note that the blending modes will work fine for images (such as photographs) that do not use an alpha channel for image compositing or for other special effects purposes.

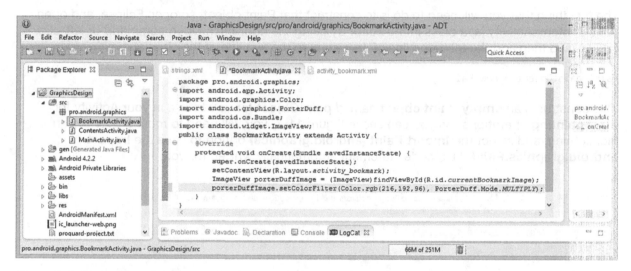

Figure 11-6. Final .setColorFilter() Java structure to use to color-shift digital image assets using alpha channels

In the next section, we will get a bit more advanced and utilize the **Paint**, **Bitmap**, **BitmapFactory**, and **Canvas** classes to apply a PorterDuff blending mode of choice between two different digital image assets.

The PorterDuffXfermode Class: Apply Blending Constants

Android has a specialized class for applying the PorterDuff image blending modes and transfer modes in conjunction with the PorterDuff.MODE constants and the PorterDuff class itself. The class is called the Android **PorterDuffXfermode** class and it's a direct subclass of the Android **Xfermode** class. This Xfermode subclass is modified to allow **PorterDuff algorithms** to be applied to your image assets by using the predefined blending mode constants that you learned about earlier.

The PorterDuffXfermode class Java hierarchy is structured as follows:

```
java.lang.Object
  > android.graphics.Xfermode
    > android.graphics.PorterDuffXfermode
```

The Android PorterDuffXfermode class is also part of the **android.graphics** package. As such, its **import statement** is constructed so that it will reference an **android.graphics.PorterDuffXfermode** package import path.

As you will see a bit later on in the chapter when you start writing Java code to implement PorterDuff transfer modes in your digital image assets, the Android **Paint** class **.setXfermode()** method is used in conjunction with your **PorterDuffXfermode** object and PorterDuff.Mode constant to "load" the Paint object with a blending algorithm, which it will utilize to "paint" one image asset onto another image asset using that blending algorithm.

The Paint Class: Apply a Blending Constant Onto an Image

The first thing that you will need to do is to construct that Paint object, so open Eclipse, and open your ContentsActivity.java class in the editor by using the right-click Open command or left-click F3 key, and then add the following line of Java code to the first line of the class above Override:

```
Paint paintObject = new Paint();
```

This constructs an **empty Paint object** named **paintObject** for you to use in your Activity for **pixel painting** operations. As you can see in Figure 11-7, you will need to mouse-over the error highlighting, and select the **Import Paint (android.graphics)** option to have the **Import android.graphics.Paint** Java code statement automatically written for you.

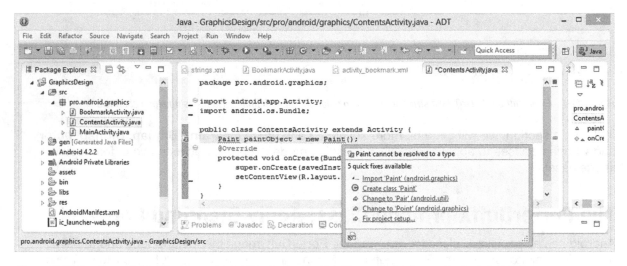

Figure 11-7. Creating a Paint object named paintObject using the Paint() constructor in your ContentsActivity.java

The Android **Paint** class is used to draw or "paint" pixels on the display screen, and as such it contains the style, alpha, modes, fonts, and color information necessary to be able to draw geometry, text, and bitmaps.

The Paint class is a direct subclass of the **java.lang.Object** class and is thus a unique capability not based on any other type of class in Android. It is one of the core classes used for graphics in Android, along with the Bitmap and Canvas classes, which you will be learning about in this chapter as well, since all three of these graphics classes must work together to allow an advanced operation such as PorterDuff blending to be performed.

The Android Paint class Java hierarchy is thus structured as follows:

```
java.lang.Object
  > android.graphics.Paint
```

You will see how this Paint class is used a bit later on in this chapter.

Using Bitmap Classes to Apply PorterDuff Between Images

Now that you have your Paint object set up, you can create the Bitmap objects. These will hold your backgroundImage and foregroundImage image assets, which you will load into your Bitmap objects using Android's **BitmapFactory** class.

You'll also need to use the **.copy()** method to make your Bitmap objects into what are termed **mutable** Bitmap objects in Android. Mutable means that your Bitmap object's pixels can be edited (changed). For this to happen it must be loaded into system memory, which is why you use a .copy() method to take your image asset from its drawable resource area and place it into system memory.

All the Bitmap work is done using these following four lines of Java code:

```
Bitmap backgroundImage = BitmapFactory.decodeResource(getResources(), R.drawable.cloudsky);
Bitmap mutableBackgroundImage = backgroundImage.copy(Bitmap.Config.ARGB_8888, true);
Bitmap foregroundImage = BitmapFactory.decodeResource(getResources(), R.drawable.cloudsky);
Bitmap mutableForegroundImage = foregroundImage.copy(Bitmap.Config.ARGB_8888, true);
```

The first statement uses your **BitmapFactory** class **.decodeResource()** method to load your Bitmap object named **backgroundImage** with your **cloudsky.jpg** image asset in your **drawable** folder using the **.getResources()** method call.

The second statement takes this Bitmap object, and uses the **.copy()** method to load it in system memory and specify that it needs **32-bit memory space** by using the **Bitmap.Config.ARGB_888** constant along with an **isMutable** flag which is set to true.

As you can see in Figure 11-8, you'll need to mouse-over your Bitmap class and BitmapFactory class references in Eclipse and invoke the Import option for both classes to get Eclipse to write those Import statements for you.

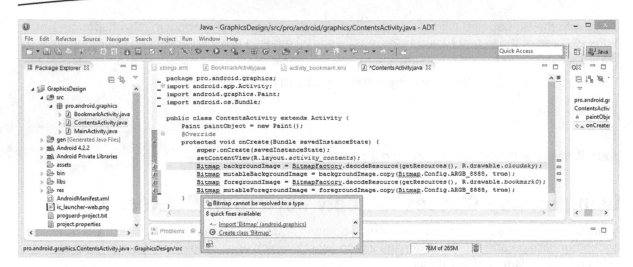

Figure 11-8. Creating Bitmap objects for backgroundImage and foregroundImage using the BitmapFactory class

Now that your Bitmap objects are loaded from your /res/drawable resources area, as well as loaded (copied) into memory as 32-bit data with alpha channels and the **isMutable** flag set to **true** so that you can edit (use) this data in your Android Paint and Xfermode operations, you are ready to use your Paint object and .setXfermode() method to load your PorterDuff mode of choice, so that your Paint object knows how you want it to function.

Using .setXfermode() Method to Apply PorterDuffXfermode

The next line of Java code will set up your Paint object, named paintObject, to be able to load a PorterDuff.Mode.XOR constant using the PorterDuffXfermode object you learned about earlier. This is done using the .setXfermode() method called off the Paint object, as follows:

```
paintObject.setXfermode(new PorterDuffXfermode(PorterDuff.Mode.XOR));
```

This calls the .setXfermode() method off of the paintObject Paint object using dot notation while at the same time, inside the .setXfermode() method call, creates a new PorterDuffXfermode object and sets it equal to the PorterDuff.Mode.XOR constant using its parameter list.

As you can see in Figure 11-9, after you type this line of Java code in, you will need to mouse-over the **PorterDuffXfermode** class reference, which after you **Import PorterDuffXfermode (android.graphics)** will also remove that **.setXfermode()** error highlighting. As you now know, you might need to write the Import android.graphics.PorterDuff statement by hand, as Eclipse does not seem to be seeing the PorterDuff class as needing to be imported.

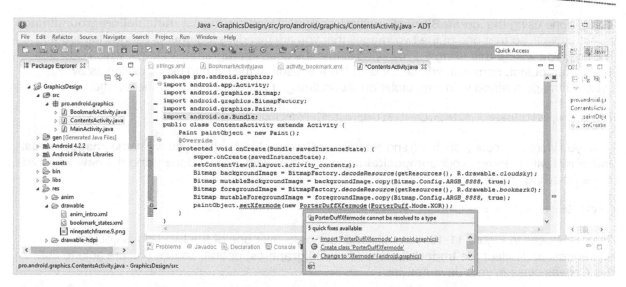

Figure 11-9. Using the .setXfermode() method of the paintObject to create a new PorterDuffXfermode XOR object

Now that your Paint object is configured, you can set up your **Canvas** object.

The Canvas Class: Creating a Canvas for Our Compositing

The Android **Canvas** class is used as an engine to draw on a display screen. If you are familiar with game design, you have heard of the Canvas before; it is a common term for graphics designers, and is available not only for Android but also other popular programming paradigms, such as HTML5 Apps.

In order to draw graphics to the screen, you will need to have four basic components. The first of these is a **Bitmap** object to hold your pixels in system memory; the second is the **Canvas** to execute the draw instructions (writing data onto the Bitmap object); the third is a drawing "**primitive**" object, for instance, a **Rect**, **Path**, **Text**, or **Bitmap** object; and finally, a **Paint** object, which is used to describe the colors, modes, and styles that will be applied by the Canvas rendering engine, through the primitive, to the Bitmap object. Graphics in Android is no walk in the park, to be sure.

The Android Canvas class is another one of those 100% original code direct subclasses of java.lang. Object. This is because it needs to be customized specifically for the Android OS. Thus, its Java hierarchy is as follows:

```
java.lang.Object
  > android.graphics.Canvas
```

You will utilize this Canvas class next, since you need its rendering engine capabilities to be able to perform this PorterDuff blending mode execution for the Java code that you are writing to demonstrate how to blend imagery.

The next step in setting up your image compositing stack in Android is the creation of a **Canvas** for you to paint on. This involves creating your target composite image, which is going to be another **Bitmap** object, one that you're going to aptly name **compositeImage** since it will hold your composite image.

This is done using the **.createBitmap()** method, and you'll load it with your **mutableForegroundImage** object as well, so that one of the two images that you are blending together is already loaded and in place. You will do this using the following single line of Java programming logic, which declares the Bitmap object, names it, and sets it equal to the result of the Bitmap class, calling its own .createBitmap() method with a mutableForegroundImage parameter inside of the function call:

```
Bitmap compositeImage = Bitmap.createBitmap(mutableForegroundImage);
```

Next, you want to create (construct) and set up your Canvas object, which you will name **imageCanvas,** and which will reference your **compositeImage** Bitmap object. This is done using the **new** keyword in the following line of code:

```
Canvas imageCanvas = new Canvas(compositeImage);
```

As you can see in Figure 11-10, you will need to mouse-over one of the two Canvas object references, and select the **Import Canvas (android.graphics)** option, so that you are able to use this Canvas class in your Java Activity.

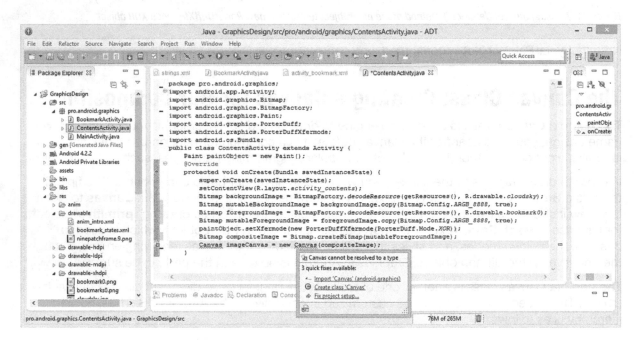

Figure 11-10. Creating a compositeImage Bitmap object using .createBitmap() and imageCanvas Canvas object

Now that you've set up your Bitmaps, Paint object, and Canvas object, you can write the line of code that brings them all together in one place and performs your compositing operation. This line of code uses the Canvas class **.drawBitmap()** method, which takes four parameters.

The first parameter is your Bitmap object, in this case the other Bitmap object you are blending; the second is a source rectangle (Rect object), in this case **null** since your image is the source; the third is the destination rectangle, in this case you create a **new Rect** object with the dimensions of the **cloudsky.jpg** image asset; and the fourth is that Paint object you named **paintObject,** which you created earlier and loaded with a PorterDuffXfermode object that references a **PorterDuff.Mode.XOR** blending algorithm constant.

```
imageCanvas.drawBitmap(mutableBackgroundImage, null, new Rect(0, 0, 1000, 1000), paintObject);
```

As you can see in Figure 11-11, there is only one class that you need to import, the **Rect** class, so mouse-over the Rect, and select your **Import Rect (android.graphics)** option to add that Import statement, and clear all of your image compositing Java code of those pesky red error highlights.

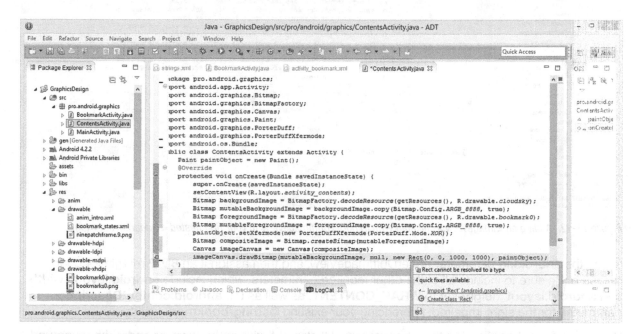

Figure 11-11. Using the .drawBitmap() method on the imageCanvas object to apply the paintObject to the image

Now you have set up all of this fantastic bitmap image compositing blending painting using the Canvas engine in system memory, but unless you send that data into an ImageView object so that you can see it on the screen, you will be sorely disappointed in all of this work that you've done. This means you get to do some easy XML markup, at least in comparison to the Java coding that you've just done to implement image blending in Android! So let's set up an ImageView child tag in your XML to use to display an image composite!

Open your activity_contents.xml XML definition file in your center editing pane of Eclipse, or if it is already open, click the tab to bring it up for editing, and you'll add your <ImageView> child tag next.

Creating an ImageView in XML and Java to Display Canvas

Add an <ImageView> child tag, right underneath the <ImageButton> child tag inside your first nested child <LinearLayout> container, as shown in Figure 11-12. This will place a blend compositing ImageView underneath your ImageButton, in the bottom left corner of your Table of Contents UI screen.

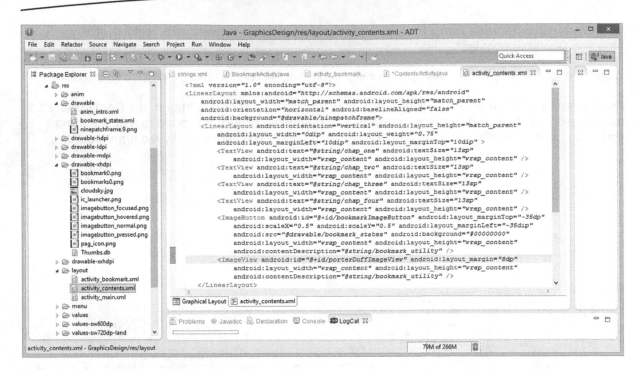

Figure 11-12. *Adding an <ImageView> child tag with ID porterDuffImageView to your first nested <LinearLayout> tag*

Name the **android:id** parameter porterDuffImageView, and then assign it an **8DIP** margin for good measure. Be sure to include all of the other required parameters, which include **android:layout_width** and **android:layout_height** set to **WRAP_CONTENT**, as well as the **android:contentDescription** parameter, for the sight impaired, referencing your existing **@string/bookmark_utility**.

Since you are not configuring this <ImageView> UI element with android:src or android:background parameters, because you are going to define this in your Java code, you won't be able to see it in the Graphical Layout Editor tab, unless you select (or have your cursor inside) the ImageView tag or one of its five parameters before you switch into the GLE editing mode.

If you have any of the ImageView selected, you will still be able to see a selection widget with handles around its perimeter, showing you that your ImageView UI widget is indeed included in your user interface definition.

Now you can instantiate your ImageView object, as shown in Figure 11-13.

Figure 11-13. Instantiating your ImageView Java object named porterDuffImageComposite and referencing XML

As you can see in Figure 11-13, you have not used any ImageView objects yet in this Activity subclass, so mouse-over the ImageView class reference and Import ImageView (android.widget). Also, notice that you gave the ImageView object a logical name (porterDuffImageComposite) using the following code:

```
ImageView porterDuffImageComposite=(ImageView)findViewById(R.id.porterDuffImageView);
```

Now all you have to do is wire your compositeImage Bitmap object to the porterDuffImageComposite ImageView object and you will be ready to test a bunch of the PorterDuff blending modes using less than a dozen lines of Java code, which is pretty concise for pulling off such an advanced image graphics operation like image compositing using PorterDuff blending modes!

Writing the Canvas to an ImageView Via .setBitmapImage()

Finally, click your **ContentsActivity.java** editing tab at the top of ADT and add the final line of code, which uses the **.setImageBitmap()** method called off of the porterDuffImageComposite ImageView object using dot notation, and pass it the compositeImage Bitmap object as its parameter, as shown in Figure 11-14 and in the following line of Java code:

```
porterDuffImageComposite.setImageBitmap(compositeImage);
```

Figure 11-14. Using a .setBitmapImage() method to write the Canvas object named imageCanvas to ImageView

This takes the compositeImage Bitmap object that is used as a canvas by the Canvas object and maps it (sets it, points it, references it, wires it) to the ImageView, so that whatever happens in the Canvas is displayed in the ImageView.

Now everything is wired up together (referencing each other correctly) and you can use the **Run As ➤ Android Application** work process to test your Java code in the Nexus One emulator. As you can see in Figure 11-15, the XOR PorterDuff mode shows nothing where your two images overlap.

Figure 11-15. Testing the XOR (left) and the MULTIPLY (right) PorterDuff.Mode constants in the Nexus One

This also demonstrates that the XOR PorterDuff.Mode constant correctly "respects" the alpha channel. If it didn't factor in the alpha channel transparency, the entire image would be white, not just the circular part of the image that is defined by the alpha channel as being opaque.

Next, go into your Java code and replace the **PorterDuff.Mode.XOR** constant with the **PorterDuff.Mode.MULTIPLY** constant, and again use your **Run As ➤ Android Application** work process to take a look at how the MULTIPLY blend mode multiplies these two images together, as shown in Figure 11-15 on the right-hand side of the screen shot. As you can clearly see, a PorterDuff.Mode.MULTIPLY constant also correctly respects (factors in) your alpha channel data for the digital image asset.

If you find that the other PorterDuff blending modes also respect your alpha channel when you use the PorterDuffXfermode class, then the problem you saw earlier in the PorterDuffColorFilter section of this chapter might just be confined to the PorterDuffColorFilter class.

This means that you will be able to blend images that have an alpha channel correctly by using the PorterDuffXfermode class. Let's find out, and use the other four blending modes in your ContentsActivity Java code, and you will see what happens first hand, by actually using these modes.

Go into the image compositing and blending that you just wrote, and change your PorterDuff.Mode. MULTIPLY constant to **PorterDuff.Mode.OVERLAY**, and again use the **Run As ➤ Android Application** to see the results, which are shown in Figure 11-16 on the left-hand side of the screen shot.

Figure 11-16. Testing the OVERLAY (left) and the SCREEN (right) PorterDuff.Mode constants in the Nexus One

As you can see, the alpha channel seems to be respected and the CloudSky image is blended into the bookmark image for a subtle effect in the text area and perimeter metal hoop.

Next, let's try the **SCREEN** blending mode, so again go into your Java code, and change your PorterDuff.Mode.OVERLAY constant to **PorterDuff.Mode.SCREEN**, and again use the **Run As ➤ Android Application** to see the results, which are shown in Figure 11-16 on the right-hand side of the screen shot.

As you can see, the bookmark image alpha channel seems to be respected and the CloudSky image is being blended into the bookmark image, this time for a not-so-subtle effect in the text area and in the perimeter metal hoop.

If you remember that the OVERLAY mode is like SCREEN and MULTIPLY, you can see that the BLACK area of your bookmark image is treated 100% differently (the exact opposite of) in the SCREEN mode than in the OVERLAY mode, which is something important for you to note here for any future compositing and blending endeavors.

Next, let's try a **LIGHTEN** blending mode, so again go into your Java code, and change your PorterDuff.Mode.SCREEN constant to **PorterDuff.Mode.LIGHTEN** constant, and again use a **Run As ➤ Android Application** to see the results, which are shown in Figure 11-17 on the left-hand side of the screen shot.

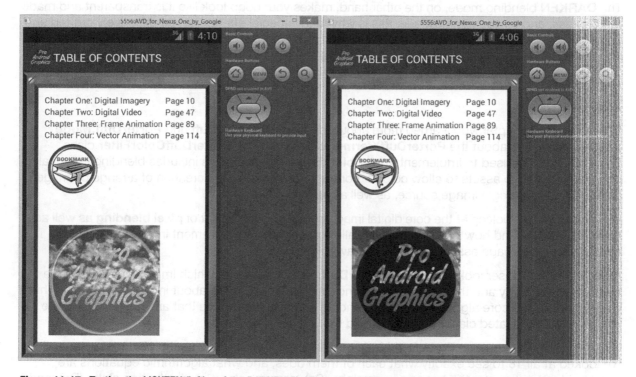

Figure 11-17. *Testing the LIGHTEN (left) and the DARKEN (right) PorterDuff.Mode constants in the Nexus One emulator*

As you can see, SCREEN and LIGHTEN blending modes are quite similar indeed, and at least with the SCREEN blending mode your text is readable, whereas with LIGHTEN blending mode it is difficult to discern. The blending mode does seem to be respecting the alpha channel data, however, so it's looking like PorterDuffXfermode, PorterDuff, and PorterDuff.Mode classes are error-free and the problem we saw earlier may just be with the ColorFilter class or with the PorterDuffColorFilter class code.

Finally, let's take a look at the last of Android's pixel blending modes, the **DARKEN** mode, and see how it works using these two source image assets.

Go into your Java code in Eclipse, and change your PorterDuff.Mode.LIGHTEN constant to be a **PorterDuff.Mode.DARKEN** constant, and again use a **Run As ➤ Android Application** to see the results, which are shown in Figure 11-17 on the right-hand side of the screen shot. The DARKEN constant has the effect of making your foregroundImage (bookmark0.png) look transparent like glass.

As you can see when comparing OVERLAY in Figure 11-16 and DARKEN in Figure 11-17, the **OVERLAY** renders your CloudSky onto your bookmark UI hoop as if it were a **texture map**, also called a **reflection map**, which is quite common in 3D. This blending mode seems to keep that metallic appearance of this hoop design element intact, and provides you with a nice 3D rendering effect.

The **DARKEN** blending mode, on the other hand, makes your hoop look like it is transparent and made out of glass, and as you can now see, this is why many special effects can be effectively crafted and implemented using the blending modes, whether it is in Adobe Photoshop, GIMP, or even right here inside the Android application code. Pixel blending is a powerful tool.

Summary

In this eleventh chapter, you learned more about the Android **PorterDuff** and **PorterDuff.Mode** classes, as well as about the **PorterDuffXfermode** class and the **PorterDuffColorFilter** class. These classes are used to implement **image blending** in Android. This includes blending color value changes into image assets to allow color or contrast correction or the creation of a range of image assets using one single image source, as well as special effects.

We started out by looking at the core digital image compositing concept of **pixel blending** as well as **transfer modes,** and how these capabilities allow developers to implement impressive special effects using the image assets in their /res/drawable folders.

Next, we took a closer look at the core **PorterDuff** class in Android, which implements the image blending technology and the pixel transfer concepts that you learned about in the first section. This class contains the core algorithms for the blending and transfer modes that are invoked using the other PorterDuff related classes in the Android OS.

You then learned about the PorterDuff.Mode nested class, which contains the **18 constants**, and we looked at all 18 to see exactly what each of them does, and what algorithmic equations are used to blend or transfer the image source alpha (Sa), source color (Sc), destination alpha (Da), and destination color (Dc) pixel data values into a resulting composite image.

We first looked at the five image blending algorithms and the one utility algorithm, and then we looked at the pixel transfer algorithms, and how they were similar to **Boolean set operations**. Once we had this overview of what was available to us via PorterDuff.Mode constants, it was time to take a look at the PorterDuffColorFilter class to implement pixel color blending.

Then we were ready to implement the first of two specialized PorterDuff classes in Android, the PorterDuffColorFilter class. We looked at how to implement this class using the **.setColorFilter()** method along with color values and a PorterDuff.Mode constant specification as parameter values.

Next, we took a look at the more advanced PorterDuffXfermode class, which allows us to apply PorterDuff transfer modes (Xfermode) and blending mode constants between other types of graphics assets. In this case, we utilized digital image assets, as bitmaps provide the latitude necessary to produce impressive image compositing special effects in the Android OS.

You took a hands-on approach, and created around a dozen lines of advanced Java code, as well as added the XML <ImageView> tag, implementing digital image blending in your GraphicsDesign application's ContentsActivity class.

While you were doing this, you learned about all of the major graphics-related classes in the Android OS, including the **Bitmap**, **BitmapFactory**, **Paint**, and **Canvas** classes. You learned what each of these classes does for graphics in Android, and you saw how they all worked together to allow you to implement image blending modes, so that you could composite two of your digital image assets together. This allowed you to visualize the blending modes, which you will be using on images in your applications to invoke image composites and special effects.

We looked at all six of the major blending modes that you will be using for digital image compositing and special effects, and you used them in your code to ascertain exactly what they will do with two existing images in your app.

These transfer (XOR) and blending modes included **OVERLAY**, **SCREEN**, **LIGHTEN**, **DARKEN**, **MULTIPLY**, and **XOR**. I encourage readers to try all of the PorterDuff modes in the code that they wrote in this chapter in order to experiment with what these modes offer as far as image processing power goes.

In the next chapter, you will learn about using digital image **layers** in the Android OS and how to use the **LayerDrawable** class in Android. This will allow you to ratchet your Android image compositing graphics design and special effects work to yet another level, which will include building upon what you have already learned in this chapter regarding the PorterDuff blending modes and their implementations, using the PorterDuffXfermode and the PorterDuffColorFilter classes, in conjunction with the PorterDuff.Mode nested class.

Chapter 12

Advanced Image Compositing: Using the LayerDrawable Class

In this twelfth chapter, we'll take a closer look at the role that **layers** play in Android and digital image compositing, as well as how to implement LayerDrawable objects in Android to enhance our digital image compositing capabilities.

Layers are created and managed in Android applications by using one of the subclasses of the **Drawable** superclass. This subclass specifically manages layer stacks and is called the **LayerDrawable** class.

A layer will allow more advanced digital image compositing to be performed because it allows more than just an image or two to be composited together, such as you did in the previous chapter on PorterDuff image blending modes.

A LayerDrawable object in Android is a good example of the concept of Java objects being made up of other Java objects, as the LayerDrawable contains other Drawable objects. This is often BitmapDrawable objects, in the case of graphics design, and the objective is usually the creation of composite graphics objects that are made up of component image parts.

This is usually done to either create a special effect or to allow for the optimization of the application image assets total data footprint by using layers to break images down into their component parts so that the indexed color space can be used to save each image asset, and thereby to save 100% or more on the total data footprint. The way this works is that if you can save image parts (as layers) into files that can effectively provide great image quality using 256 (indexed) colors instead of 16,777,216 (truecolor) colors, and later composite them into an image that looks like it is using truecolor but is really a LayerDrawable object using indexed color assets.

Layer Drawables: Take Image Compositing to a New Level

Let's get an overview of how digital imaging layers are implemented in Android. In Android, layers are called **Layer Drawables,** and use Android's **LayerDrawable** class. We will also take a look at where layers can be used to their best advantage in an Android application and in your Pro Android Graphics design work process.

By and large, layers are most often utilized with digital image compositing objectives, which many digital imaging artisans perform using professional digital imaging software packages such as Adobe Photoshop CS6, GIMP 2.8.6, or Corel's Painter, CorelDraw, or PaintShop Pro software packages.

The same compositing objectives that can be accomplished in these popular digital image compositing software packages can also be obtained inside the Android OS. However, you need to be advanced enough to code your very own image compositing rendering pipeline using XML and Java; you will be learning about some of the Android classes and the work processes that can be utilized to accomplish this later on in this chapter.

Be advised that this is significantly more difficult than just using one of these digital imaging software packages itself, and that alone can be very complicated in and of itself, as you've seen earlier on in this book.

Layers are used in Android when there is more than one Drawable asset that needs to be combined in your application in an advanced way to achieve any end result. This could be anything from text overlays to image blending to special effects applications. You can use any type of Android Drawable for use in a LayerDrawable layer stack, so it is a very flexible layer system.

It is important to note that as long as you're great at implementing alpha channels, you don't have to necessarily implement blending modes to create an effective image composite, as you've already seen in previous chapters.

Layers in Android can be made to be very similar to the layers found in popular digital imaging software packages such as GIMP 2.8.6. Android layers can have opacity values assigned; they can also access blending modes and utilize alpha channels as well as most of the other core things that a graphics artist would need to implement special digital imaging effects into their graphics rendering pipeline.

You'll add LayerDrawable capabilities into what Android PorterDuff blending modes do, since you already wrote the code in the previous chapter to blend images on a pixel-by-pixel basis.

So, by the end of this chapter, you will have combined the blending and transfer modes that you learned in the previous chapter with the layer capabilities of the LayerDrawable object into one comprehensive Java-based image compositing and blending rendering pipeline.

Android's LayerDrawable Class: A Foundation for Layers

The Android **LayerDrawable** class is a direct subclass of the Drawable class, which is itself a direct subclass of the **java.lang.Object** master class.

LayerDrawable is therefore a **Drawable subclass** that implements all of the features of the Drawable class as well as the additional features necessary for layer management that are specific to the LayerDrawable class.

The Android LayerDrawable class hierarchy is structured as follows:

```
java.lang.Object
  > android.graphics.drawable.Drawable
    > android.graphics.drawable.LayerDrawable
```

The Android LayerDrawable class is a part of its **android.graphics.drawable** package, and as such, its **import statement** logically references your **android.graphics.drawable.LayerDrawable** package import path, as you'll see later on in the chapter when you write the Java app code that implements LayerDrawable objects for your own layer management objectives.

The LayerDrawable class also has one direct subclass of its own called the TransitionDrawable class. We will be covering the TransitionDrawable class in the next chapter of this book, so stay tuned.

A LayerDrawable object is a type of Drawable object in Android that has the ability to create and manage an **array** of other Drawable objects. The Drawable objects within the array are always drawn to the screen using their **array order**, so the Drawable element that features the largest **index number** will always be drawn on the top of the **layer stack**. You'll see exactly how this works later, after you implement your LayerDrawable object.

A LayerDrawable object is usually defined by using an XML definition file, and by then using the **<layer-list>** parent tag. Each Drawable object inside your LayerDrawable container object defined by this <layer-list> parent tag will then be defined by using a nested **<item>** child tag, as you'll see in the next section of the chapter when you create your own LayerDrawable.

A LayerDrawable class has **six** XML attributes or parameters. Obviously, the most important are your **android:drawable** parameter, which allows you to specify your drawable image assets, and your **android:id** parameter, which allows you to specify an ID for a layer so that it can be referenced later inside your Java code.

The other four parameters specify each layer's coordinates or positioning, using pixels (PX), device-independent pixels (DIP or DP), millimeter (MM), inches (IN), or scaled pixels (SP) as the unit of measurement along with a floating point value. The parameters include **android:top**, **android:bottom**, **android:left**, and **android:right**, and are not necessary if your image assets each fill their Drawable (and thus their LayerDrawable) containers.

The <layer-list> Parent Tag: Setting Up Layers Using XML

Let's continue working in your ContentsActivity.java and activity_contents XML file tabs in Eclipse to implement a LayerDrawable object in your image composite. Fire up Eclipse ADT if it is not still open on your desktop, and right-click the /res/drawable folder as shown in Figure 12-1, and select the **New ➤ Android XML File** menu sequence. This will allow you to create your new LayerDrawable XML file and will automatically put it into your drawable folder. This root /res/drawable folder is where you've been storing assets, such as 9-patch image assets, ImageButton states, frame animation, and now this LayerDrawable object definition, each of which are related to Android Drawable objects and their configuration (frames, states, layers, patches, and other XML that defines how an image asset or assets will be implemented).

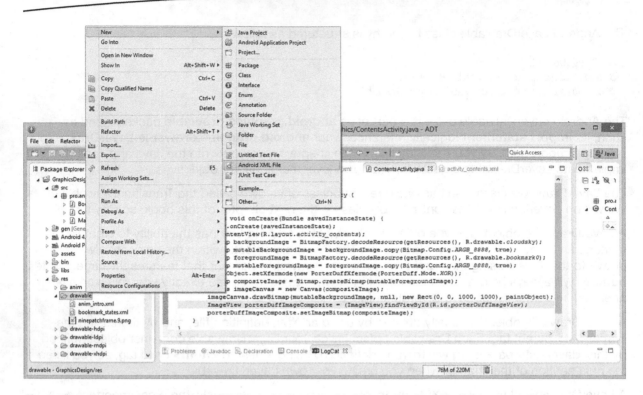

Figure 12-1. Creating a New ➤ Android XML File in the /res/drawable folder using the right-click context menu

Once you select this menu command sequence, you will get a **New Android XML File** dialog, which is shown in Figure 12-2. This is already configured for the **GraphicsDesign** project and **Drawable** resource type, due to your folder hierarchy and the fact that you clicked the correct folder (as shown in Figure 12-1) to invoke the dialog. Now, all you have to do is to select the **<layer-list>** Parent Tag **Root Element** and name the file contents_layers to show that you are defining the layers for your ContentsActivity class.

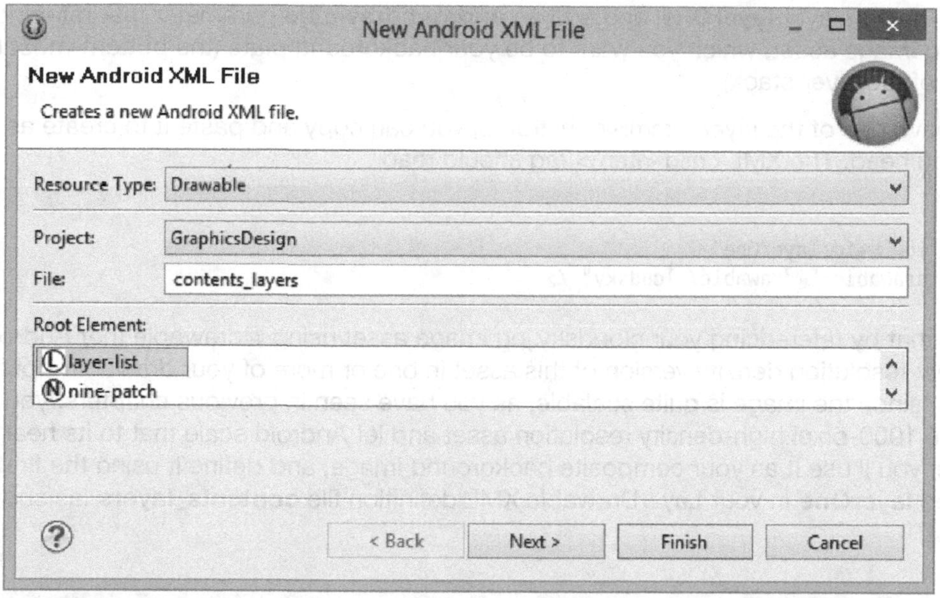

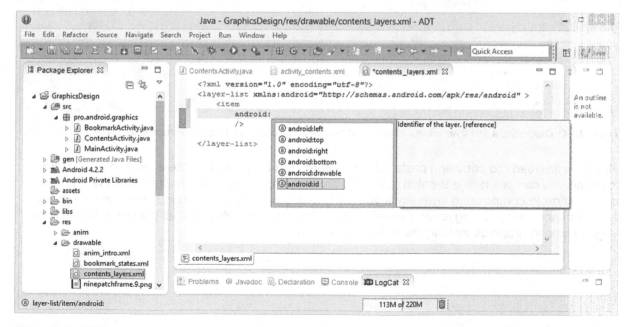

Figure 12-2. Selecting a <layer-list> Root Element for your New Android XML File

Once you are done setting your Drawable XML file parameters in the dialog, click the **Finish** button and you will see a new **contents_layers.xml** file in your Eclipse central editing pane, ready for use, as shown in Figure 12-3. Split your **<item> </item>** child tag container into one **<item />** container so that you can add parameters, and then use the **android:** work process to invoke the helper dialog with the six parameters you learned about earlier. You'll add the **android:id** parameter first, so your layer object has a name.

Figure 12-3. Adding <item> child tags inside of a <layer-list> parent tag, and accessing an android: helper dialog

Let's name the first layer **layerOne**, and add an **android:drawable** parameter that references your cloudsky.jpg image asset, which you want to be your background plate (the bottom-most layer at the bottom of the layer stack).

Once you have one of the layer <item> constructs, you can copy and paste it to create as many layers as you need. The XML child <item> tag should read

```
<item
    android:id="@+id/layerOne"
    android:drawable="@drawable/cloudsky" />
```

Remember that by referencing your cloudsky.jpg image asset using @drawable that Android will go find a correct resolution density version of this asset in one or more of your drawable-dpi subfolders. In this case, since the image is quite scalable, as you have seen in previous chapters, you will use only the one 1000-pixel high-density resolution asset and let Android scale that to its heart's content. In this case, you'll use it as your composite background image, and define it using the first (bottom) layer, named **layerOne** in your LayerDrawable XML definition file **contents_layers** (as shown in Figure 12-4).

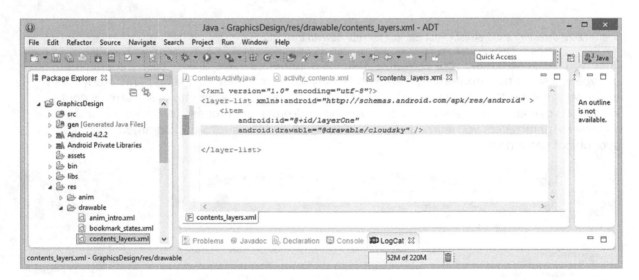

Figure 12-4. Completing a first layer <item> child tag, referencing a cloudsky.jpg background image in ID layerOne

Now you are ready to copy and paste this first <item> tag in order to create a second and a third layer, so you can see how a 9-patch asset and an image asset that has an alpha channel will work on the Android compositing layer stack you are creating here. Actually, your 9-patch asset has an alpha channel and padding areas defined as well; thus you are pulling out all the stops to use some very advanced graphics techniques in this first example.

Select and copy the first child <item> tag in your <layer-list> parent tag in its entirety, and paste it two more times underneath itself to create a layerTwo and layerThree image composite layer in your LayerDrawable object. The XML markup for a second and third layer will look like the following:

```
<item
    android:id="@+id/layerTwo"
    android:drawable="@drawable/bookmark0" />
<item
    android:id="@+id/layerThree"
    android:drawable="@drawable/ninepatchframe" />
```

All you have to do is edit the **ID** to change it to **layerTwo** and **layerThree**, and then edit the reference from **cloudsky** to **bookmark0** and **ninepatchframe**, respectively, as shown in Figure 12-5. You are now ready to see the results of your digital image compositing work process inside Android.

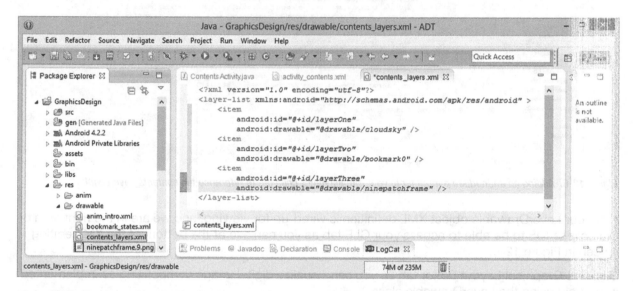

Figure 12-5. Copying and pasting the first layer <item> tag to create the second and the third layer <item> definitions

Notice in Figure 12-5 that there is no Graphical Layout Editor tab located at the bottom of the contents_layers.xml editing pane, only an XML editing tab. This should give you a clue as to the final step that you're going to need to perform in order to be able to visualize a LayerDrawable object inside Eclipse ADT and the Nexus One AVD emulator.

The contents_layers.xml file is an XML definition file which defines the image asset layers, but you'll still need to reference it from the inside of an ImageView object in order to visualize it inside ADT or in Android OS.

So, let's modify the **<ImageView>** child tag in your **contents_activity.xml** file to display this LayerDrawable object definition using an **android:src** parameter. You'll put your existing parameters on lines two through four of the tag and add a source image reference pointing to your **contents_layers** XML file using the following XML markup, as shown in Figure 12-6.

```
<ImageView android:src="@drawable/contents_layers"
    android:id="@+id/porterDuffImageView" android:layout_margin="8dp"
    android:layout_width="wrap_content" android:layout_height="wrap_content"
    android:contentDescription="@string/bookmark_utility" />
```

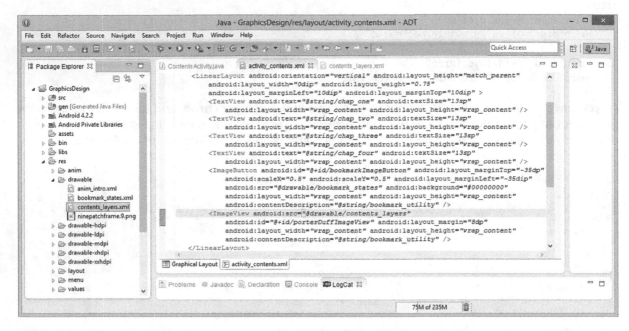

Figure 12-6. Adding an android:src parameter to your <ImageView> child tag to reference the contents_layers.xml

Now, our LayerDrawable object XML definition is wired-up for viewing, and we are in the right area of the Eclipse IDE to be able to access your GLE tab as you can see at the bottom of the XML editing screen in Figure 12-6.

Click the Graphical Layout Editor tab so you can visualize digital image compositing as implemented in Android using the LayerDrawable class.

As you can see in Figure 12-7, your ImageView UI element, shown selected as we still have our editing cursor in its boundaries in the XML editing pane, now shows a three-layer image compositing stack with a cloudsky.jpg image on the bottom, a bookmark0.png image on top of that, and a ninepatchframe 9-patch image asset on top of both of those, all seamlessly composited.

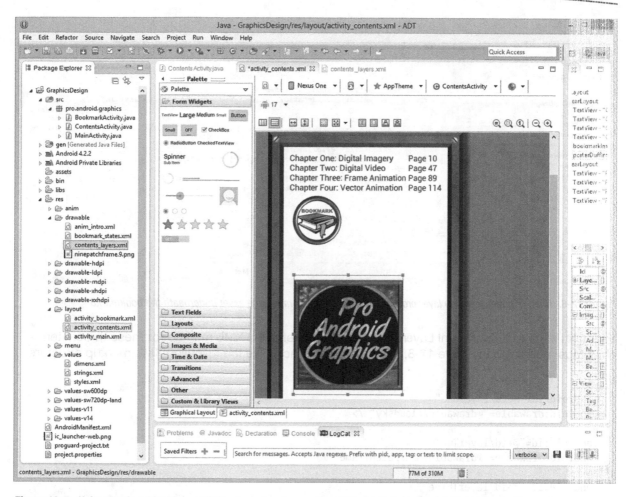

Figure 12-7. Using the Graphical Layout Editor to review the results of the contents_layers.xml LayerDrawable

Somehow this image composite does not look as professional as one would like it to, so next let's change the order of the digital image assets so that the hoop does not get cut off by the tiling of the 9-patch image asset frame around your composite's perimeter.

It's important to note that this is now easy to do because of the way that your image layer stack, or LayerDrawable object, is set up. By using an XML definition file, you have decentralized the graphics design for your digital image layering, and so all you have to do is switch up two android:drawable parameter references for the second and third child <item> tags, and this is done in the blink of an eye.

Let's do that next so that you can see the results of this different layer stack order, rendered by Android (and by Eclipse ADT via the GLE). They might not be exactly what you are expecting!

Next, click the **contents_layer.xml** tab at the top of Eclipse and switch back into LayerDrawable object XML definition editing mode to make these two parameter image asset reference changes, as shown in Figure 12-8.

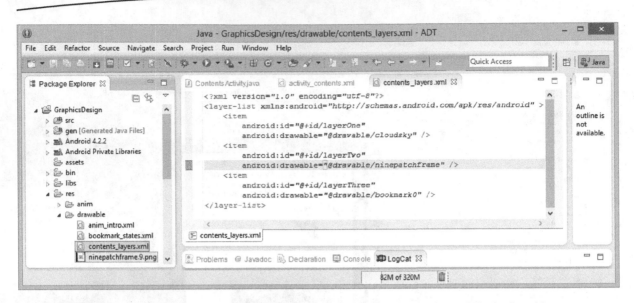

Figure 12-8. Changing the drawable layer order to place ninepatchframe image asset underneath the bookmark0

Your final contents_layers.xml LayerDrawable object definition XML markup for these three <item> child tags, as shown in Figure 12-8, should appear exactly like the following XML markup structure:

```
<item
    android:id="@+id/layerOne"
    android:drawable="@drawable/cloudsky" />
<item
    android:id="@+id/layerTwo"
    android:drawable="@drawable/ninepatchframe" />
<item
    android:id="@+id/layerThree"
    android:drawable="@drawable/bookmark0" />
```

Now you are ready to test your new layer compositing stack in the Graphical Layout Editor tab. Since that's not available to you in the contents_layers XML editing pane shown in Figure 12-8, you will need to click the **activity_contents.xml** tab at the top of Eclipse and then the **Graphical Layout Editor** tab at the bottom in order to view your revised image assets multi-layer composite (LayerDrawable object), as shown in Figure 12-9.

Figure 12-9. Using the Graphical Layout Editor to review new results of the contents_layers.xml LayerDrawable

The first thing that you will notice is that the hoop part of the bookmark image does not overlay on top of the ninepatchframe image layer, as you may have expected it to. Think for a moment about what attributes of a 9-patch image asset might be influencing the rendering pipeline calculation for this particular layer stack compositing order. Did you figure it out yet?

Think back to the chapter covering Android's **NinePatch** class (Chapter 10), when you defined your **padding values** for this 9-patch image asset using the right and bottom one-pixel black border line segments. If you recall, what this padding area does is to define (or force) anything placed inside this NinePatch asset inside the padding area you previously specified. Essentially the padding makes sure your NinePatch asset's "perimeter artwork" is not obscured.

This is what you are seeing here for the bookmark image asset layer on top of and thus rendered inside your ninepatchframe 9-patch image asset.

So how do I get the hoop to overlay the 9-patch image asset frame, you may be wondering. To accomplish this, go back into your **Draw 9-patch** utility, and extend the black lines on the bottom and right all the way to the edges of the image asset. This will tell Android that you want your contents in (or on top of, in this case) the 9-patch asset to be able to overlap the asset's image component, as well as its interior space. You can also define an alpha channel inside that interior 9-patch space so you can use this 9-patch for future compositing, such as you are doing here.

The next step that you should take is to now test this LayerDrawable in the Nexus One emulator and visualize the results, and make sure that your LayerDrawable object is working with your Java compositing code.

Use your **Run As ➤ Android Application** work process and launch your Android application in the Nexus One emulator; notice on the left hand side of Figure 12-10 that your LayerDrawable rendering pipeline (which you saw before in the Graphical Layout Editor shown in Figure 12-9) is not showing up in the Nexus One. This is not the fault of your XML markup, which you know due to the GLE is working fine, so it must be an issue with your Java code.

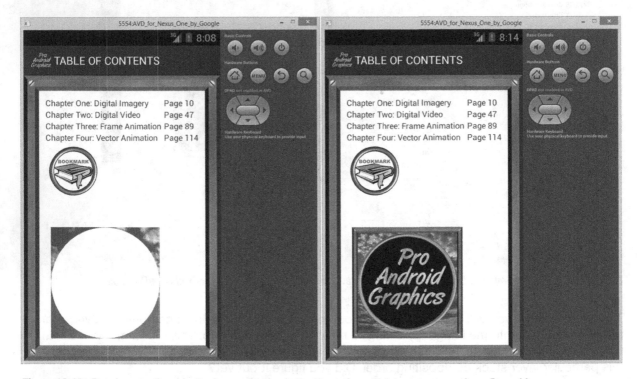

Figure 12-10. Running your GraphicsDesign application in the Nexus One emulator to see your LayerDrawable

Let's click the ContentsActivity.java tab and take a look at your Java code. As you can see in Figure 12-11 at the bottom of the code listing, I found the problem and commented it out so the XML definition will display.

Figure 12-11. Removing the .setImageBitmap() method call to allow the LayerDrawable XML definition to display

What was happening was that in the last two lines of your Java code you were instantiating the ImageView object—this line of code will still work great for displaying your LayerDrawable definition—but then you were writing your Canvas object into that ImageView using a .setImageView() method call. The last line of code was thus obscuring your LayerDrawable from view, so I commented it out and obtained the intended results, as shown on the right-hand side of the screen shot in Figure 12-10.

So, from a processing standpoint in Android, what was happening is that you were defining your LayerDrawable in XML and setting your ImageView object to display it correctly, which you confirmed by using the Graphical Layout tab in Eclipse earlier during your design and markup coding work process.

However, in your image compositing Java code, which you have been writing in your ContentsActivity, this LayerDrawable object was being overwritten via your programming call to place the image contents of your Canvas object into (over) this LayerDrawable composite, unbeknown to you, at least at the time that you coded it.

Ultimately, you are going to have to redo some of this code to incorporate using a LayerDrawable, and to see how to extract LayerDrawable object image layers and put them into a PorterDuff image blending pipeline. For now, I simply utilized the comment feature, and placed two forward slashes at the beginning of the line of code. This of course removed it from play, fixing the problem temporarily. I did this just to confirm that the LayerDrawable was indeed set up correctly in the XML markup, and was also visible using the current Java code (or at least the majority of the Java code).

The next challenge is to integrate LayerDrawable object layers into a PorterDuff blending pipeline, so you are going to have to modify your Java code in the next section to instantiate your LayerDrawable object, extract the layers that you wish to run through the PorterDuff blending infrastructure that you created, convert those Drawable objects to Bitmap objects and make them mutable (put them into system memory as 32-bit image data), and then make sure they are in the Paint ➤ Canvas rendering cycle.

Not simple, by any means; and, as you will see in the coming sections, not yet 100% perfected in the Android OS either! That is one of the caveats of working with a new OS and platform, such as Android; you have to work with (and around) what is currently available to you as a developer, and working well enough to be utilized, while waiting for new features to be added, as they invariably will at some point in time.

Now, you are set up to be able to bring this LayerDrawable object into your Java code, and incorporate it with the PorterDuff Java code that you wrote in the previous chapter. This will show you how to instantiate your Layer Drawable in Java and how to access the individual layers within your XML definition. You will also learn how to extract the image data that you have defined within these layers, and how to apply further processing in a more advanced image compositing and blending pipeline, such as using the layers in conjunction with Android's PorterDuff blending (or transfer) modes.

Instantiating a LayerDrawable for PorterDuff Compositing

The first thing that you need to do in your Java code is to instantiate this LayerDrawable object, inflating it with your contents_layers.xml definition to create the object's attributes, so fire up Eclipse ADT, and click the ContentsActivity.java tab to get back into your compositing code.

Add a newline (return) character after your setContentView() method call, at the top of the onCreate() method, and add this line of Java code, which will instantiate a **LayerDrawable** object named **layerComposite**, and then use the **getResources().getDrawable()** method chain to load your XML definition:

```
LayerDrawable layerComposite =
(LayerDrawable)getResources().getDrawable(R.drawable.contents_layers);
```

As you can see in Figure 12-12, you will then need to mouse-over your wavy red error highlighting underneath the LayerDrawable class reference, which will tell ADT to write your Import android.graphics.drawable.LayerDrawable Java statement for you. Once you do this, you will notice that your object name of **layerComposite** will also have a wavy yellow warning highlighting, as it is currently unused, at least until you write your next line of code.

Figure 12-12. Instantiating a LayerDrawable object in Java and naming it layerComposite and invoke .getDrawable()

Next, you will need to create a Drawable object to hold the contents of your LayerDrawable, which you will implement inside your current PorterDuff image blending rendering pipeline. You wrote this code in the previous chapter, and you will enhance it to work with LayerDrawable objects in this chapter.

Create a Drawable Object to Hold the LayerDrawable Asset

Now that you have your LayerDrawable object created and loaded into memory, the next step is to extract one of the layers that is a part of the object so that you can use it in your previously created PorterDuff image blending (or pixel transfer) pipeline, which you are going to expand to include support for LayerDrawable objects (layers).

The first step in this process is to create an Android Drawable object, which you will name **layerOne**, as shown in Figure 12-13. What you are going to do with this Drawable is use it to cast a LayerDrawable into a Drawable object, and then specify the layer within it that you wish to use using the .findDrawableByLayerId() method using a single line of code, as follows:

```
Drawable layerOne = ((LayerDrawable)layerComposite).findDrawableByLayerId(R.id.layerThree);
```

Figure 12-13. Creating a Drawable object named layerOne, cast to a LayerDrawable via findDrawableByLayerId()

What this does, all in a single line of code, is create a **Drawable** object, and name it **layerOne**, and then set the object equal to (load it with) the **LayerDrawable** object you instantiated earlier named **layerComposite**, and then use dot notation to call the **.findDrawableByLayerId()** method, passing the reference to the **layerThree** <item> that you defined earlier in the chapter.

Now that your layerOne Drawable object is loaded with a LayerDrawable layer that you want to use in your PorterDuff blending pipeline, you can proceed!

Cast a Drawable to a BitmapDrawable and Extract a Bitmap

The next step towards getting the Bitmap object data that you are going to need in order to utilize your existing PorterDuff image blending pipeline is to again cast this Drawable object into a BitmapDrawable object. You do this so that you can extract a Bitmap object from the BitmapDrawable object using the .getBitmap() method, and you will do all of this again using only one single line of Java code, written as follows:

```
Bitmap composite = ((BitmapDrawable)layerOne).getBitmap();
```

What this does, using very compact Java code, is to create a **Bitmap** object and name it **composite**, and then set the Bitmap object equal to (or load it with) the **Drawable** object you instantiated earlier named **layerOne,** and then use dot notation to call the **.getBitmap()** method, which gets the Bitmap in the Drawable object, which is actually now cast as a BitmapDrawable object and loads that digital image data into the Bitmap object named composite. As you can see in Figure 12-14, you will also need to mouse-over the error highlighting, so that Eclipse will write the **Import BitmapDrawable (android.graphics.drawable)** Java statement for you.

Figure 12-14. *Casting a Drawable to a BitmapDrawable, then using .getBitmap() method to convert to a Bitmap object*

Now that your **composite Bitmap** object is loaded with your **layerOne Drawable** object, which was previously loaded with your LayerDrawable layer, which you ultimately wish to use in your PorterDuff blending pipeline, you can now proceed to create a mutable Bitmap object (in memory) so you can process it!

You already know how to create a **mutable Bitmap** object by using the **.copy()** method, specifying a **Config.ARGB_8888** constant, called off a Bitmap class. Just in case you forgot how this is structured in Java, here is the code:

```
Bitmap mutableComposite = composite.copy(Bitmap.Config.ARGB_8888, true);
```

Now you have reached the final mutable Bitmap object "destination" that you reached in the PorterDuff image blending chapter, so all you really have to do next is to substitute the mutableComposite Bitmap object for either the mutableForegroundImage or the mutableBackgroundImage object references in your existing PorterDuff image blending (and pixel transfer) pipeline.

As you can see in Figure 12-15, I have not done this as yet, which is why you see wavy yellow underline warning highlighting on the mutableComposite Bitmap object, as it is currently unused, until I plug it into the render pipeline, which you will do next.

Figure 12-15. Creating a mutable Bitmap object named mutableComposite using .copy() method with ARGB_8888

Let's substitute your mutableComposite object (LayerDrawable to Drawable to BitmapDrawable to Bitmap cast object, actually) for the foregroundImage and mutableForegroundImage objects, which you really should comment out of your Java code so they do not take up any system memory while you put them on the shelf, so to speak. You can see the commenting operation you invoked in Figure 12-16 in green; all you had to do was put two forward slashes at the beginning of each line of code, and they vanished from Android's view!

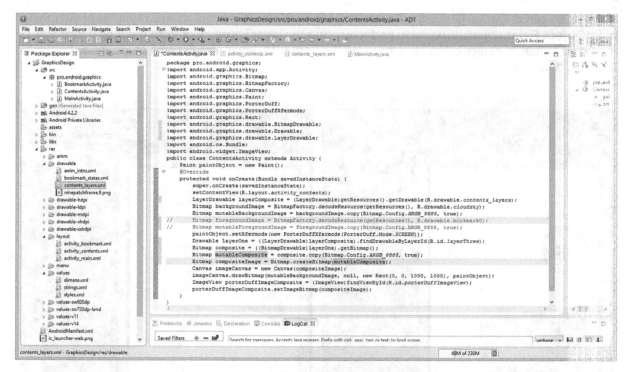

Figure 12-16. Modifying compositeImage Canvas target to reference your LayerDrawable mutableComposite Bitmap

Let's modify your PorterDuff pipeline to reference your cast LayerDrawable and incorporate layer compositing into your image-blending Java code next!

Modifying the PorterDuff Pipeline to Use a LayerDrawable

Let's replace the mutableForegroundImage object you created previously, and recently commented out of your Java code (for now), inside your existing **compositeImage** Bitmap object. This object is referenced by your **imageCanvas** Canvas object. You will do this by using the following line of Java code:

```
Bitmap compositeImage = Bitmap.createBitmap(mutableComposite);
```

What this does is to incorporate the drawable image asset that is defined in your LayerDrawable object in layerThree, which is the bookmark0.jpg image asset, into the image blending PorterDuff pipeline. As you can see in Figure 12-16, your code is error-free and ready to test out in the Nexus One emulator. If you count the commented-out lines of code, you have implemented layer support and image blending using only 15 lines of (dense) Java code.

Now, it is time to see if your digital image compositing pipeline Java code actually works! Utilize your **Run As ➤ Android Application** work process to launch your Nexus One emulator. Once your application loads, click your **MENU** button and select the **Table of Contents** menu selection. Let's take a look at your digital image layer blending and compositing results. You'll try using one pixel transfer mode and an image blending mode to test both!

As you can see in Figure 12-17, the **PorterDuff.Mode.SCREEN** constant, which you have set in your **paintObject Paint** object, is working perfectly using the **layerThree** layer from the LayerDrawable object you created earlier in the chapter using the **contents_layer.xml** file and its **<layer-list>** parent tag XML definition.

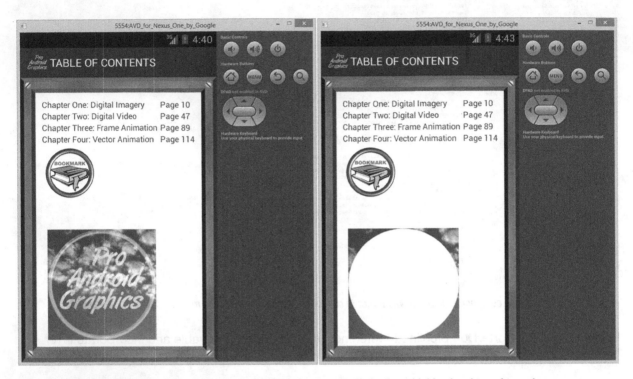

Figure 12-17. Testing the LayerDrawable asset in your existing PorterDuff pipeline with blend and transfer modes

Next, let's change this PorterDuff.Mode constant to the **XOR** constant, and make sure pixel blending is working as well. As you can see on the right-hand side of Figure 12-17, the XOR image transfer mode is also working as expected, so you have implemented both image blending and pixel transfers using your LayerDrawable object.

If you look very closely at the left-hand side of Figure 12-17, there is something wrong with the backgroundImage plate. Your cloudsky.jpg is no longer being scaled to fit the ImageView UI display container, as it is in the Graphical Layout Editor preview. It is using original **unscaled** image pixels, so all you see behind your bookmark foreground image, which is being extracted from the LayerDrawable, is the clouds from the upper-left (0,0) corner of the CloudSky image.

Let's change some things around and see if we can figure out why the scale has changed for one of your composite image assets inside your PorterDuff rendering pipeline. Offhand, I don't see any obvious reason why this would have occurred, but let's change some things around a bit and investigate!

Switch LayerDrawable Image Asset: Source to Destination

So let's try switching your source and destination image plates, so that the **mutableComposite** (a cast LayerDrawable) is called in the **.drawBitmap()** method along with the **paintObject**, and put the **mutableForegroundImage** into the **.createBitmap()** method, called off of the **compositeImage Bitmap** object that is used in the **Canvas** object as its canvas (surface) image data. This switch can be seen in Figure 12-18; also, notice that we have commented out the backgroundImage and mutableBackgroundImage Bitmap objects.

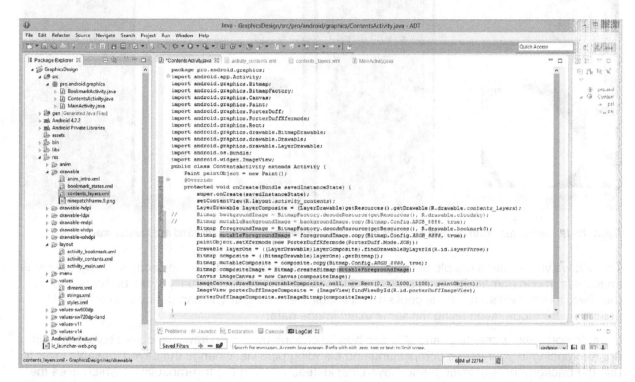

Figure 12-18. Switching the mutableComposite LayerDrawable cast Bitmap into the .drawBitmap() method

Now, uncomment your foregroundImage and mutableForegroundImage Bitmap objects so that you can temporarily use your bookmark PNG for both your source and destination digital image compositing plates. You are doing this so that you can visualize exactly what will happen when you use the same image in both source and destination image plates inside the digital image compositing pipeline that you have coded.

As you can see in Figure 12-19, one of the bookmark0 PNG image datasets is getting scaled to fit the ImageView UI container and the other one, which is exactly the same data, shows the raw, unscaled source pixels, displayed pixel-for-pixel using the image origin of 0,0 and with zero scaling.

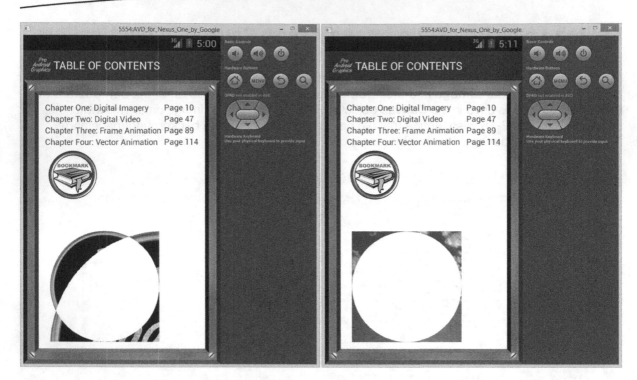

Figure 12-19. Testing the LayerDrawable asset in a different PorterDuff pipeline plate with blend and transfer modes

This allows you to see a couple of things here. One is the quality of the image scaling using the same image within one composite, both scaled and unscaled. The scaling actually looks pretty decent to me! Two, this shows some of the cool special imaging effects that you can get by using the XOR pixel transfer mode, even using the same exact image data.

Let's do some experimenting, and also see how to change the LayerDrawable object layer that you are referencing in your image compositing and blending pipeline. Change the LayerDrawable layer to use the background sky layer (named layerOne) instead of using the top-most layer, which uses the bookmark0.png as its image asset (named layerThree).

Changing the LayerDrawable Layer Used in Our Pipeline

Go back into your Java code; in the line of code that uses the method called **.findDrawableByLayerId()**, change its parameter from **layerThree** to **layerOne**, as shown in Figure 12-20.

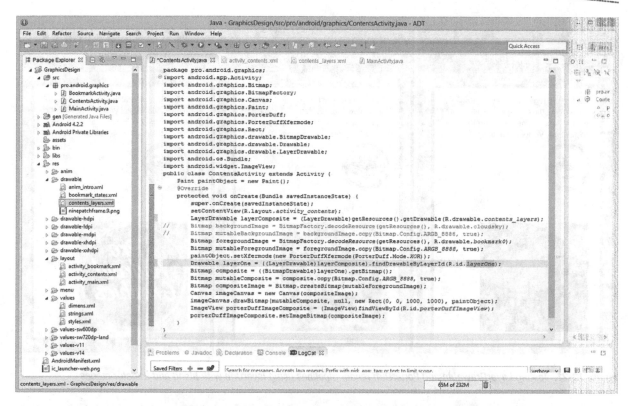

Figure 12-20. Changing the LayerDrawable cast Drawable to reference layerOne using .findDrawableByLayerId()

Notice that you have not changed the Bitmap objects that are referenced in the .drawBitmap() and .createBitmap() method calls because you want to only change one variable at a time and see the result; this time you are changing a LayerDrawable layer reference from layerThree to layerOne.

This change is happening much "higher up" in your "processing chain," and shows that you can change LayerDrawable object layer references without having to touch any of your image compositing, blending, painting, drawing, transfer, canvas, or other core Java image processing pipeline code.

This changes your background plate, which is coming from the LayerDrawable and being called in the imageCanvas object's **drawBitmap()** method call, and as you can see in Figure 12-21, in the middle rendered (OVERLAY Mode) view especially, an entire cloudsky.jpg sunset is now shown in the final render pipeline for your composite image. This proves that it is the LayerDrawable that is getting scaled, and the Bitmap composited plate image that is not.

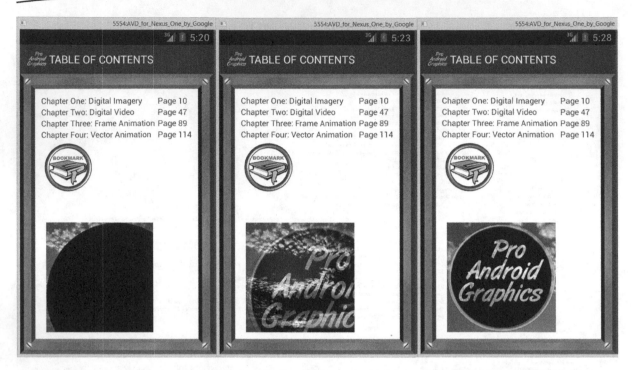

Figure 12-21. Testing LayerDrawable and PorterDuff render pipelines using layerOne with blend and transfer modes

I've found that the best way to figure out why this may be happening is to work backwards (from the bottom of the code up, in this instance) from the ImageView, which we know scales an image both in XML (GLE) and in Java (in the emulator and on the device). So let's trace things from the ImageView, and step our way backwards, up through the compositing rendering pipeline.

The last line of rendering code calls the **.setImageBitmap()** method, which references the **compositeImage Bitmap** object. This method is called off of your **porterDuffImageComposite ImageView** object. This compositeImage Bitmap is wired into (is utilized by) the **imageCanvas Canvas** object (the engine).

This imageCanvas object is then used to call a **.drawBitmap()** method, which references the **mutableComposite Bitmap** object. The mutableComposite Bitmap object references the **composite Bitmap** that was cast from a BitmapDrawable, which was cast from the **layerOne Drawable** object. The layerOne Drawable was cast from a layerComposite layerDrawable object, which was instantiated and loaded using a .findDrawableBylayerId() method.

So, you have traced your **ImageView** source data back up through your rendering pipeline to the **LayerDrawable** object layer source image, which makes sense as this is the image source that is scaling correctly, which means that it is the ImageView object at the end of this pipeline that is most likely scaling this object.

On the other hand, the other Bitmap object that you reference image data for directly, from the drawable resource folder, must be the image plate (source) that is not being scaled. Change the PorterDuff.Mode to OVERLAY and use the Run As ➤ Android Application work process to generate the view in the middle of Figure 12-21. The left side shows the XOR mode constant.

Next, let's switch the two Bitmap image references back the way that they were, with the mutableComposite inside the Canvas object compositeImage canvas image and the mutableForegroundImage inside the drawBitmap() method call, which invokes (applied) your paintObject Paint object to the imageCanvas Canvas object.

As you can see on the right-hand side of Figure 12-21, switching the image plate referencing makes this bookmark image fit, and the cloudsky imagery scales pixel for pixel. Thus, what you analyzed seems to be exactly what is happening.

By the way, we are using a PorterDuff.Mode.SCREEN constant to obtain the pixel-blending effect, which you see on the right-hand screen shot of the Nexus One emulator in Figure 12-21.

The final Java code for this final image compositing pipeline testing scenario can be seen in Figure 12-22.

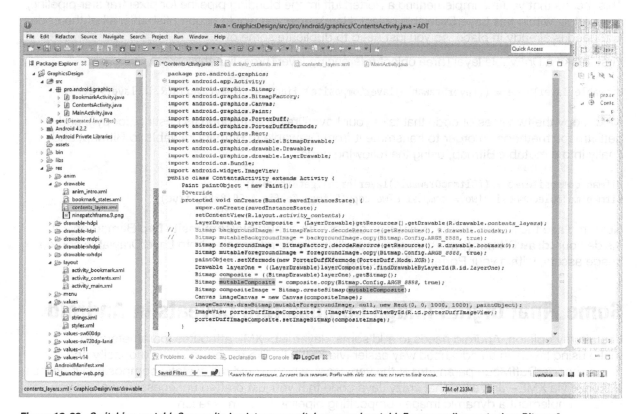

Figure 12-22. Switching mutableComposite back to compositeImage and mutableForegroundImage to drawBitmap()

The only thing left to do is to implement the entire rendering pipeline out of the LayerDrawable layers; however, I think I will make this into an exercise for the reader, just to make sure that everyone understands this entire pipeline and the casting and referencing processes within it.

Exercise for the Reader: Using Two LayerDrawable Assets

Here is a little test for you to do on your own, to get some practice working with Android graphics package classes like Canvas, Paint, Bitmap, Drawable, BitmapDrawable, LayerDrawable, and all of the PorterDuff classes.

I'll tell you how to do it; it only involves copying a few lines of code and changing some object names and references, so it should not be too difficult for you to implement.

What I want you to do first is to comment out both Bitmap (as well as the mutable Bitmap) objects that you used for the original PorterDuff blending pipelines in the previous chapter. You will do this because you are about to implement the PorterDuff blending pipeline using only the Drawable digital image data (assets), which are available via the LayerDrawable object.

This means that you are implementing a PorterDuff image blending pipeline (or pixel transfer pipeline) completely within this LayerDrawable object. Here's how you would accomplish this; all of the code you need is already in place, so you just need to duplicate some of it.

First, make a Drawable layerThree object referencing layerThree, like this:

```
Drawable layerThree = ((LayerDrawable)layerComposite).findDrawableByLayerId(R.id.layerThree);
```

Next, copy the two lines of code that take your LayerDrawable through its casting, .copy(), and getBitmap() methods, in order to transmute it from Drawable to BitmapDrawable to Bitmap, and finally into a mutable Bitmap, using the following code:

```
Bitmap compositeTwo = ((BitmapDrawable)layerThree).getBitmap();
Bitmap mutableCompositeTwo = compositeTwo.copy(Bitmap.Config.ARGB_8888, true);
```

Next, replace the `mutableForegroundImage` object with a **mutableCompositeTwo** Bitmap object inside your **.drawBitmap()** method, and you will finally be referencing both LayerDrawable source image assets, within your PorterDuff rendering pipeline.

Some Final Digital Image Compositing Caveats in Android

First, in my opinion, Android needs to add some <layer-list> XML attributes (parameters) to make using layers in an advanced way easier (via XML). I'd like to see an android:opacity and android:porterDuffMode parameter at the very least, which would make static compositing pipelines a breeze via XML—and all of that crazy Java code that you just crafted unnecessary, unless you need to implement a dynamic image compositing pipeline for some reason.

The other thing that you may have noticed is that I did not reference the 9-patch layerTwo in the LayerDrawable in the Java code. This is because it crashes the emulator. My guess is that Android has a difficult time casting a 9-patch through all of those Drawable types, and so for now, you will need to find a way to implement your 9-patches statically, as a background image using the android:background parameter, for instance.

Notice that 9-patch image assets do work in a static (XML) implementation of LayerDrawables and, as you saw, conformed to all of the 9-patch "rules."

Summary

In this twelfth chapter, you learned about using layers in Android for image compositing, and the Android **LayerDrawable** class. You also got the chance to use the **Drawable** and **BitmapDrawable** classes through casting.

We started out looking at some of the core concepts of how layers are used for digital image compositing pipelines, and then we looked at the Android LayerDrawable class and the features it provides to Android developers for implementing layer-based compositing pipelines in our code.

Next, we looked at the <layer-list> parent XML tag and its child <item> tags, and you learned how to define a LayerDrawable object by using an XML definition file. You defined your own LayerDrawable using a contents_layers XML file to define your image layers and name them and assign image assets to them, which you later used in your PorterDuff rendering pipeline.

Next, you dove into the Java side of things and modified the Image blending pipeline that you wrote in the previous chapter to implement LayerDrawable objects into the compositing and blending pipeline. You learned how to cast a LayerDrawable into a Drawable object and then into a BitmapDrawable and finally into a Bitmap object that you could then turn into a mutable Bitmap object, as you did in the previous chapter for the PorterDuff image blending pipeline.

You tested your code in a lot of different ways, and wired it up different ways in order to ascertain exactly what was happening in the compositing and rendering pipeline. Finally, you took part in an exercise to try implementing this code, and you learned some of the caveats about layers in Android.

In the next chapter, you will learn about using digital image **Transitions** in the Android OS, and how to use the **TransitionDrawable** class in Android. This will allow you to take your Android image compositing graphics design and special effects work to a higher level via image animation.

Chapter 13

Digital Image Transitions: Using the TransitionDrawable Class

In this thirteenth chapter, we will take a close look at the role that an image **Transition** plays in Android, and in digital image animation, as well as how to implement an image transition in Android. Transitions allow developers to enhance their core digital image animation capabilities.

Transitions are created and managed in Android applications using one of the indirect subclasses of the **Drawable** superclass. The **TransitionDrawable** subclass specifically manages image transitions and it's a direct subclass of the **LayerDrawable** class. Since you learned about LayerDrawables in the last chapter, this is a good follow-up chapter.

The TransitionDrawable object allows more advanced digital image animation to be performed in Android using the layering and blending features covered in the previous two chapters. Thus, a TransitionDrawable object allows developers to create image animation in the most simple of ways: by transitioning between two image layers using a blending or opacity change.

There are far more advanced forms of animation in Android, such as Bitmap or **frame animation** (sometimes called raster animation), and Vector or **procedural animation** (sometimes called tweening). You will be learning about these in detail over the next two chapters, as the unique forms of animation in Android each require their own chapter.

We will start with the basics of image transitions, and then get into the TransitionDrawable class specifically; after that you will implement your own TransitionDrawable object in your GraphicsDesign application using XML markup to define a transition and Java to run it.

Transitions: Image Blending to Create an Illusion of Motion

Let's get an overview of what digital imaging transitions are. In Android, these are technically called **Transition Drawables**, and these LayerDrawable objects are constructed and maintained using the **TransitionDrawable** class.

We'll also take a look at where image transitions can be utilized to best advantage in an Android application, and ways to use them that will provide some wow-factor and graphics design professionalism for your Android applications.

Image transitions can be implemented by using the types of digital imagery compositing pipelines that you have been implementing over the past couple of chapters, so this chapter should be fairly easy for you to assimilate into your professional Android graphics design work process.

A differentiating characteristic that makes digital image asset transition programming different is that the blending and opacity variables that are usually **static** in an image composite are run through a processing loop (in the Java code) where an image transition processing pipeline is concerned.

Making the image compositing pipeline dynamic in this way makes your image assets appear to be **animated**. This is probably a reason why Google Android developers created the TransitionDrawable class, so that we would not have to write this code ourselves, and to provide a popular new media feature.

Image transitions create this appearance of animation using only **two** image assets, so it is great both from an ease-of-use standpoint and a data-footprint-optimization standpoint.

Since image transitions can give your application an animated feature set, and a dynamic look and feel using a fairly easy setup, I'm going to cover this topic before we dive into frame animation and procedural animation in Android, which we will be doing over the next two chapters, so stay tuned.

Image transitions in Android use LayerDrawable objects because these types of Drawables in Android have characteristics that are needed to implement this animated compositing type of special effect. These include **opacity** or **alpha blending** as well as location parameters (top, bottom, left, or right) and the ability to assign an ID and reference the drawable asset resource.

Imaging transitions within Android can be used for many different purposes and in many different areas of the graphics design and the user interface design work process, so it is important you master them in this chapter.

TransitionDrawable objects are essentially Drawable assets, so they can be utilized in the **source** parameter for ImageView and ImageButton UI elements or in the **background** plate (parameter) for ImageView classes (or subclass) objects. These can also be used via an **android:background** parameter for adding special effects to your layout containers, which can add a wow-factor to your user interface screen design quickly, efficiently, and effectively.

Android's TransitionDrawable Class: A Transition Engine

Android's **TransitionDrawable** class is an indirect subclass of the **Drawable** class, which is a direct subclass of the **java.lang.Object** master class. The TransitionDrawable is a direct subclass of the Android LayerDrawable class, which is a direct subclass of the Android Drawable class.

As a **LayerDrawable subclass**, the TransitionDrawable class thus implements all of the features of the LayerDrawable class, which you learned about in the previous chapter. It also implements additional opacity animation features necessary to implement digital image transitions; these are specific to this TransitionDrawable class, as would be expected.

The Android TransitionDrawable class hierarchy is structured as follows:

```
java.lang.Object
  > android.graphics.drawable.Drawable
    > android.graphics.drawable.LayerDrawable
      > android.graphics.drawable.TransitionDrawable
```

The TransitionDrawable class is also part of the **android.graphics.drawable** package. So its import **statement** references an **android.graphics.drawable.TransitionDrawable** package import path. You will see an example of this later in this chapter, when you write your Java application code to implement a TransitionDrawable object for use with your digital image animation for your Pro Android Graphics programming objectives.

A TransitionDrawable object is a type of Drawable object in Android, which has the ability to create and manage an array of two Drawable objects for the purpose of creating an image transition between the Drawable objects.

The TransitionDrawable class was written to be an extension of the Android LayerDrawable class, which is intended to crossfade (or transition) between the first and second layer of an image drawable. This is the reason it is a LayerDrawable subclass: because it will use the LayerDrawable class's code infrastructure as its foundation and then add an animation aspect by running LayerDrawable attribute (parameter) values through additional Java processing (Java loop structures).

A TransitionDrawable object can be defined **statically** in your XML file using a **<transition>** parent tag XML element. Each Layer Drawable in a transition is defined using a nested **<item>** child tag. We will go over this in detail in the next section of this chapter, so that you can see how this is done.

To **start** the image transition in your Java code, you call the method **.startTransition()** using a reference to your TransitionDrawable object XML definition, which, as you may have guessed, will be in your **drawable** folder.

To **reset** an ImageView to show your source layer instead of the destination (final) layer, you call the method **.resetTransition()**, after you are sure your user is no longer viewing the screen, to prevent image flashing.

The <transition> Parent Tag: Setting Up Transitions in XML

Let's continue working in your ContentsActivity.java and activity_contents XML file tabs in Eclipse, and implement a TransitionDrawable object in your Table of Contents Activity screen so that you can see how this is achieved.

Fire up your Eclipse ADT IDE, if it is not still open on your desktop, and right-click the **/res/drawable** folder, as shown in Figure 13-1, and select the **New ➤ Android XML File** menu sequence to open the file creation dialog.

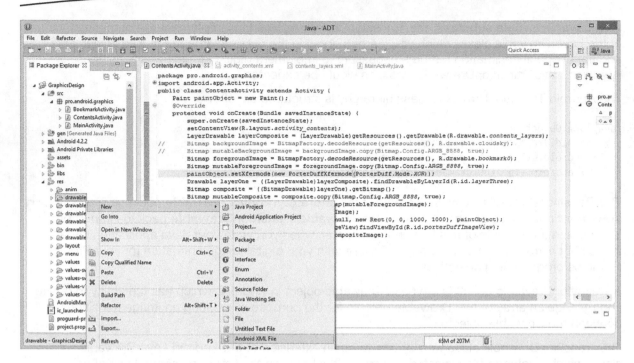

Figure 13-1. Right-clicking the /res/drawable folder, and then selecting the New ➤ Android XML File menu sequence

You are going to create your new TransitionDrawable XML definition file, and this work process will automatically put it into your **drawable** folder. This **/res/drawable** folder is where you have been storing all your drawable assets, such as LayerDrawable layer definitions, 9-patch image assets, ImageButton states, frame animation definitions, and now your TransitionDrawable object definition. Soon you'll be storing procedural animation definitions here!

It's important to note that each of the assets in the /res/drawable folder are related to Drawable objects, and to their definitions (frames, states, layers, patches, vectors, etc.), but not to actual image assets themselves, with the exception of the 9-patch asset, which is both a patch definition and an image asset in one file format. Actual image assets go into other drawable-dpi folders, which are located alongside the /res/drawable folder.

Thus, any XML definitions in your /res/drawable folder will **automatically** reference these image assets (using their different resolution densities), which are stored in Android's five standard /res/drawable-dpi imagery and animation asset folders. These were created for you when you created your **New Android Application** using the series of dialogs shown in Chapter 2.

Once you select this menu command sequence, you will get a **New Android XML File** dialog, which is shown in Figure 13-2. This is already configured for the **GraphicsDesign** project and **Drawable** resource type due to your folder hierarchy, and the fact that you clicked the correct folder, shown in Figure 13-1, to invoke the dialog. Now, all you have to do is to select the **<transition>** Parent Tag **root element** and name the file **trans_contents.xml** to show that you are defining a transition for your ContentsActivity class.

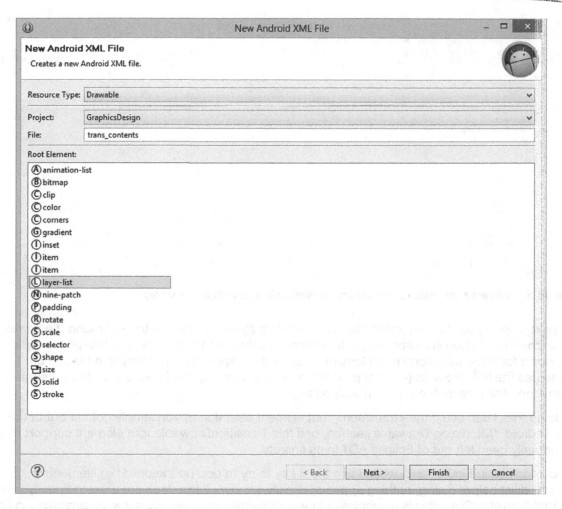

Figure 13-2. Looking for the <transition> root element in the New Android XML File dialog

As you can see in Figure 13-2, you've hit your first problem in implementing TransitionDrawable objects in this chapter. Notice that there is no parent (root element) tag available for a **<transition>**, although there should be.

I assume this is an oversight by the Eclipse ADT development team, and we can't worry about that now; we just need to conform to the next best work process that is available to us. Since the TransitionDrawable is a Layer Drawable, select the <layer-list> parent tag, or root element, and change this to be a <transition> parent tag once you're in the Eclipse editing pane. So, select the **<layer-list>** root element, and name the file **trans_contents.xml**, and then click the **Finish** button.

Once you are done setting your Drawable XML file parameters in the dialog, you will see the new **trans_contents.xml** file in your Eclipse editing pane, ready for use. Replace the <layer-list> with your <transition> text in the parent tag (root element) containers, as shown in Figure 13-3.

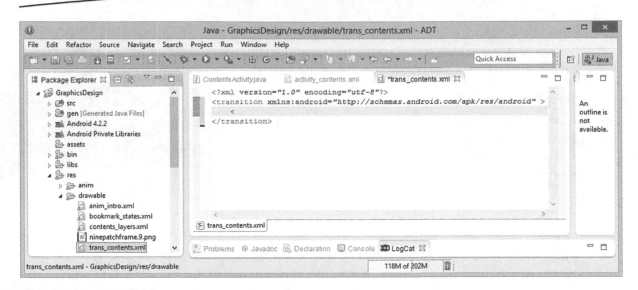

Figure 13-3. Modifying a <layer-list> parent tag (root element) to be a <transition> parent tag

The next step in your "work-around process," which is the work process to get around the barrier you encountered when implementing a TransitionDrawable, is to ascertain how "deep" this lack of support for the <transition> root element goes inside Eclipse ADT. The way that I found out was to use the **left chevron (<)** work process, and try to bring up the list of supported parent tag parameters while inside the parent Transition tag.

By doing this, I can see if the <transition> root element selection option simply got left out of the New Android XML dialog Drawable section, or if this TransitionDrawable root element support has accidentally been left out of Eclipse ADT in its entirety.

As you can see in Figure 13-3, when I use the < key to try to pop up the child tag elements supported list helper dialog, nothing appears. Luckily, I know <item> tags are used to specify layers, and that TransitionDrawable is a subclass of LayerDrawable and uses the same parameters, so I can get around this second barrier to implementation as well using manual actions.

Since Eclipse did not give us automatic **<item> </item>** child tag container tags, we don't need to split these into one **<item />** container like we did in the previous chapter; we can just type them in this way manually.

Name your first transition layer **imageSource**, since it is the source image for the TransitionDrawable object using the android:id parameter.

Next, you will add the **android:drawable** parameter, which will reference the **cloudsky.jpg** image asset that you want to be your background (bottom) plate (the bottom-most layer at the bottom of your transition image layer stack).

Once you have one of the transition <item> child tag constructs, you can copy and paste it to create the other transition layer that you need. Your XML child <item> tag should read

```
<item
    android:id="@+id/imageSource"
    android:drawable="@drawable/cloudsky" />
```

Remember that by referencing your **cloudsky.jpg** image asset using **@drawable** that Android will find a correct resolution density version of this asset in one or more of your drawable-dpi sub-folders. In this case, since the image is quite scalable, as you have seen in previous chapters, you will use only the one 1000-pixel high-density resolution asset, and let Android find and scale that one high-resolution image asset, as you know this image will scale well in any usage scenario.

In this case, you'll utilize the CloudSky digital image asset as your transition background image, and define it using the first (bottom) layer, named **imageSource**, for an XML definition for the TransitionDrawable object defined in the file **trans_contents.xml**.

Now you are ready to copy and paste this first <item> tag so you can create your second transition layer. Let's use a 9-patch asset so that you can see if one will work inside a TransitionDrawable object.

Your 9-patch image asset features an alpha channel; this transparency area will lend some additional capabilities (flexibility in implementation) to your TransitionDrawable object, as you will see later in this chapter.

Select and copy the first child <item> tag in your <transition> parent tag in its entirety, and then paste it again underneath itself, creating an **imageDestination** transition layer for your TransitionDrawable object's XML definition. The XML markup for the first and the second transition object layer definitions will ultimately look exactly like the following markup:

```
<item
    android:id="@+id/imageSource"
    android:drawable="@drawable/cloudsky" />
<item
    android:id="@+id/imageDestination"
    android:drawable="@drawable/ninepatchframe" />
```

As you can see in Figure 13-4, your XML is error-free, and you can now go into your UI layout container's XML definition and reference this new Drawable.

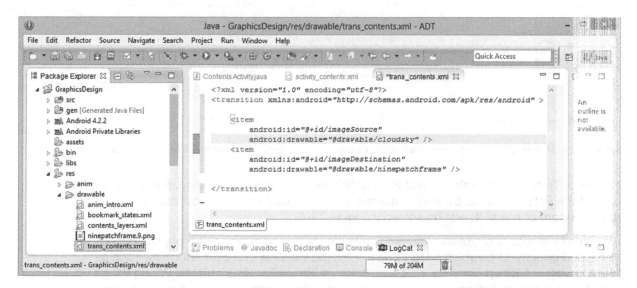

Figure 13-4. The completed TransitionDrawable object XML definition in the trans_contents.xml file in Eclipse

Notice in Figure 13-4 that there is no Graphical Layout Editor tab located at the bottom of your trans_contents.xml editing pane, only the XML editing tab. This is because Android Drawable objects (definition) aren't directly renderable, but a View object (or a ViewGroup layout container object) is.

This trans_contents.xml file is a definition file, which defines the image asset layers, but you'll still need to reference it from the inside an **ImageView** object in order to visualize it inside ADT or in Android OS.

So, let's modify your **<ImageView>** child tag in your **contents_activity.xml** file to display the TransitionDrawable object XML definition by modifying an **android:src** parameter. You have put your existing parameters on lines two through four of the tag, and edited the image asset source reference that is pointing to your trans_contents.xml file. You will accomplish this change by using the following XML markup (this is also shown in Figure 13-5):

```
<ImageView android:src="@drawable/trans_contents"
    android:id="@+id/porterDuffImageView" android:layout_margin="8dp"
    android:layout_width="wrap_content" android:layout_height="wrap_content"
    android:contentDescription="@string/bookmark_utility" />
```

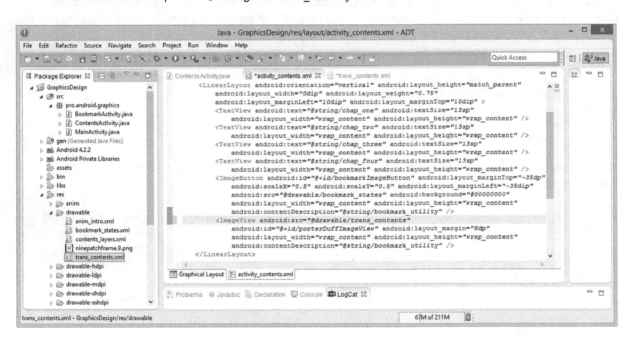

Figure 13-5. Modifying the <ImageView> android:src parameter to reference TransitionDrawable trans_contents.xml

Now your TransitionDrawable object XML definition is wired up for viewing, and you are in the right area of the Eclipse ADT to be able to access your Graphical Layout Editor tab, as you can now see at the bottom of the XML editing screen in Figure 13-5.

As you saw in recent chapters, Android Drawable class (and subclassed) objects cannot be visualized directly. Drawables need to be referenced via View class (or subclass, such as ViewGroup), or Bitmap class (or subclass, such as BitmapFactory) objects. Wiring things up, as I call it, in Android can sometimes take several layers of referencing as well as transmutation.

Take a look at your work so far, and click your Eclipse Graphical Layout Editor tab so that you can visualize this digital image transition plate that you have implemented inside Android using XML for the Transition Drawable object (class).

As you can see in Figure 13-6, your ImageView User Interface element, shown at the bottom of the Table of Contents UI design, now shows the background cloudsky.jpg image asset for a TransitionDrawable layer compositing stack.

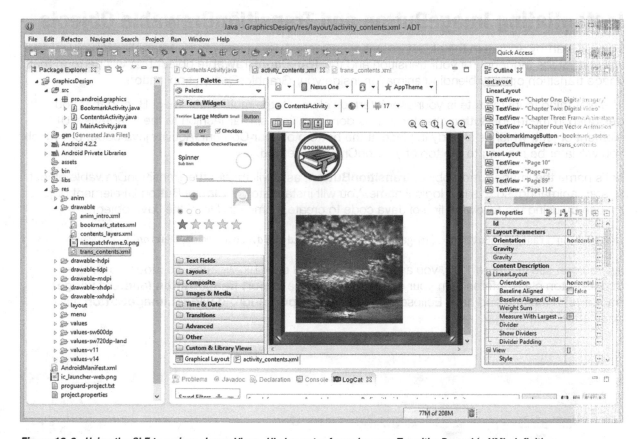

Figure 13-6. Using the GLE to review <ImageView> UI element referencing your TransitionDrawable XML definition

Now you can see that your TransitionDrawable object is defined using XML in your trans_content. xml file and is referenced through your <LinearLayout> UI container ViewGroup, which is using your <ImageView> UI widget container and its source image parameter to load your Drawable object into a View object.

Now that your TransitionDrawable object is installed and configured using only XML markup, it is important to notice (and be grateful for) the fact that you just defined a high-level digital image transition special effect entirely using low-level XML markup, and zero Java code. You can now get into Java programming and jump through the various image compositing hoops required for that more complicated side of things.

Once the Java instantiation and imports and referencing and event handling and all of that more complicated stuff is in place, you'll be able to test and enjoy your application's new digital image transition capabilities.

Now you are ready to tackle some Java coding, so go into Eclipse and click the ContentsActivity. java tab at the top of the central editing pane.

Instantiating ImageButton and TransitionDrawable Objects

You will start by adding in the object instantiation lines of Java code for the **ImageButton** object that will control the triggering of your transition and the **TransitionDrawable** object that will perform that image transition opacity blending animation inside your GraphicsDesign application.

The first thing to instantiate is your user interface element, the multi-state ImageButton that you designed in the ImageButton chapter. This is done in a very similar fashion to the ImageView UI element object, which is already in place at the bottom of your ContentsActivity.java code, but which you will later be moving to the top of your onCreate() method.

Let's name the ImageButton object **transitionButton**, as it will trigger the TransitionDrawable object to start animating, so this is a logical name. You will instantiate your ImageButton UI element object for use by using the following line of Java code to create, name, and load the Java object:

```
ImageButton transitionButton = (ImageButton)findViewById(R.id.bookmarkImageButton);
```

As you can see in Figure 13-7, you are getting wavy red error highlighting, so mouse-over the ImageButton class reference in your code and select the **Import ImageButton (android.widget package)** reference and have Eclipse ADT write the **Import android.widget.ImageButton** Java code statement for you.

Figure 13-7. Instantiating an ImageButton object named transitionButton and using findViewById to reference its ID

Next, let's instantiate your TransitionDrawable object. Initially, you'll do this in the most standard way, much like you did with your Paint object. So let's add this short line of Java code, instantiating (and naming) your TransitionDrawable. You will use the name **transition** for this object, using the following Java statement at the top of your ContentsActivity class:

```
TransitionDrawable transition;
```

As you can see in Figure 13-8, this instantiation statement is now in place and error-free. Notice that your Import statement for the ImageButton is now visible at the top of your Activity subclass as well.

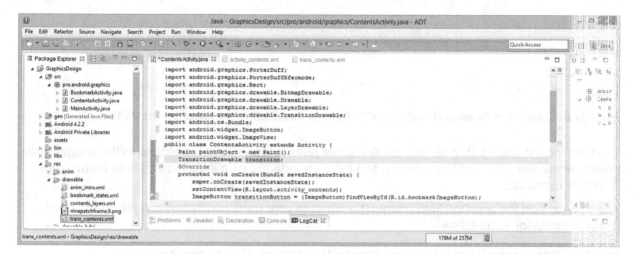

Figure 13-8. *Instantiating a TransitionDrawable object named transition at the top of the ContentsActivity.java class*

The next line of Java code that you will need to put into place is the line of code that will load the TransitionDrawable object with the Drawable XML XML definition, which you created in the previous section of the chapter.

This will load your TransitionDrawable object, which is currently declared or instantiated, but is empty (not loaded, or configured). To do this, you must get the Drawable (in this case TransitionDrawable) object definition.

This would normally be done with the **.getDrawable()** method, called off of the **transition TransitionDrawable** object, using the following Java code:

```
transition.getDrawable(R.drawable.trans_contents);
```

As you can see in Figure 13-9, this code also comes up as error-free, at least as far as Eclipse ADT is concerned. You can see that there is one warning in Eclipse, shown in both Figures 13-8 and 13-9, because you have not yet utilized your transitionButton ImageButton object instantiation.

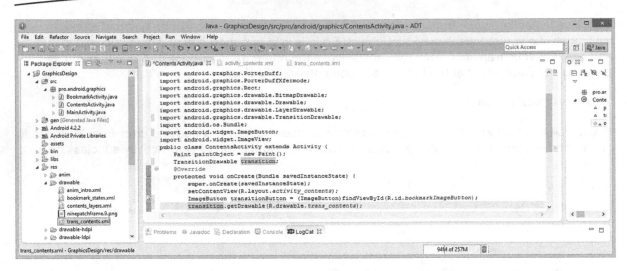

Figure 13-9. Calling the .getDrawable() method off of the transition TransitionDrawable object to reference XML

The next logical coding step for you to take at this point is adding event handling to the ImageButton object, which will get rid of that warning and more importantly, wire it up to be able to trigger your TransitionDrawable.

The code to add the **.setOnClickListener()** method to your transitionButton ImageButton object using dot notation is as follows:

```
transitionButton.setOnClickListener(new View.OnClickListener(){ code goes here });
```

This calls the .setOnClickListener and creates a new **.OnClickListener()** inside the method, using the **new** keyword and off of the **View** class.

As you can see in Figure 13-10, you will need to mouse-over this View class reference and **Import View (android.view)** in order to get rid of the wavy red line error highlighting.

Figure 13-10. *Adding Event Listening to the transitionButton ImageButton using the .setOnClickListener() method*

As you can see in Figure 13-11, this writes your Import android.view.View statement for you, but also brings up another wavy red error highlight. This time it is because there is nothing inside your curly braces, and Android expects to see your **.onClick()** event handling method implemented inside those curly braces, but there isn't one implemented in there yet.

Figure 13-11. *Adding an unimplemented onClick() method automatically using Eclipse's error pop-up solution dialog*

Again, mouse-over the wavy red error highlighting, and select the option to **Add unimplemented methods**, as shown in Figure 13-11. Eclipse ADT will write an .onClick() event handling method bootstrap for you automatically.

Now, all you need to do is add in your Java programming logic, which will live inside of this empty .onClick() event handling method.

The code that you add inside this event handling method will be called (triggered, or executed) when one of your users (initially, this will be yourself, during your software testing phase) clicks your multi-state transitionButton ImageButton UI element, which you created in Chapter 9.

What you want to happen when your user clicks your ImageButton is for the image transition that is controlled by the TransitionDrawable object that you are setting up here to start its playback, just like you would start your other animation assets (which we'll be getting into in much greater depth over the next couple of chapters).

After all, a TransitionDrawable object, that is, an image transition, will be considered an animation by most of your viewers. Technically, however, it is simply an image-opacity-blending compositing effect where an opacity value is slowly changed over time via a Java programming loop.

The method call used is thus very similar to other animation start method calls, and is termed the **.startTransition()** method call. This is what will be inside your .onClick() event handling method and is called off of the transition TransitionDrawable object that you have instantiated and loaded (or so it seems).

The parameter that you pass into this method call is an integer value that determines how many milliseconds your image transition animation will take. This is also another indication that the Android OS considers image transition to be a type of animation asset, as animation assets deal with milliseconds, so as to give developers extremely fine-tuned timing control over their motion graphics assets. The event handler code looks like this:

```
@Override
public void onClick(View arg0) {
    transition.startTransition(5000);
}
```

As you can see in Figure 13-12, your Java code is still error-free, and you are ready to move your ImageView-related Java programming logic, which is currently located at the bottom of the onCreate() method, to the top where your ImageButton and TransitionDrawable Java logic are located. You will do this so that you can see all the related code in one location, and so that your ImageView is instantiated and initialized alongside the other two Java objects that you're using for this digital image transition implementation.

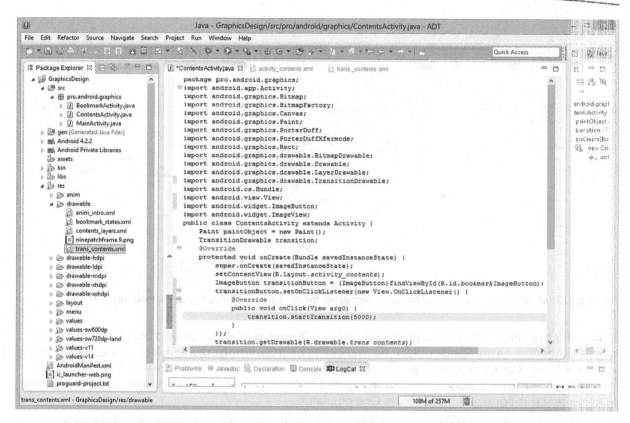

Figure 13-12. *Coding an onClick() event handling method to call a .startTransition() method off the transition object*

So go to the bottom of your onCreate() method, and cut and paste your two lines of code that create the ImageView, and name it porterDuffImageView, and call the **.setImageBitmap()** method off your porterDuffImageView object, and place these two lines of Java code right after the line of code that calls the **.getDrawable()** method off of the **transition** TransitionDrawable object, as shown in Figure 13-13.

Figure 13-13. Moving the ImageView and transition logic above the ImageButton and calling .setImageDrawable()

Since your transition TransitionDrawable object is a Drawable object type and not a Bitmap object type, change the **.setImageBitmap()** method call to be a **.setImageDrawable()** method call, and then reference your **transition** object as the Drawable object (type) that you are now wiring up into your ImageView object. As you can see in Figure 13-13, your code is still error-free, and you are now ready to test this code using the Nexus One emulator.

Right-click your GraphicsDesign project folder and use the **Run As ➤ Android Application** work process to launch the Nexus One emulator. When you click the MENU button and select the Table of Contents menu item, the GraphicsDesign application crashes! Now we need to go into investigate mode and find out what may be happening to cause this. I am going to take you through this process here, as this is a common occurrence in app development, so I want you to see the work (and thought) process.

The first thing I looked for in the online developer documentation was when the TransitionDrawable class support was added into the Android OS, as that will advise me of the API Level support the feature requires to be able to run (at all). My research uncovered that **API Level 16** support is required to use these image transition features in Android. Thus, the next step is to right-click the AndroidManifest.xml file at the bottom of the project hierarchy in Eclipse and open the AndroidManifest.xml file in the central editing pane in order to see what API Level support (Minimum and Target) is defined for this app.

When you do this, you will see that your app's Minimum SDK Level of support is set at **API Level 8**, so you need to change this to **API Level 16** by changing the parameter for your **<uses-sdk>** child tag from **android:minSdkVersion="8"** to **android:minSdkVersion="16"**, as shown in Figure 13-14.

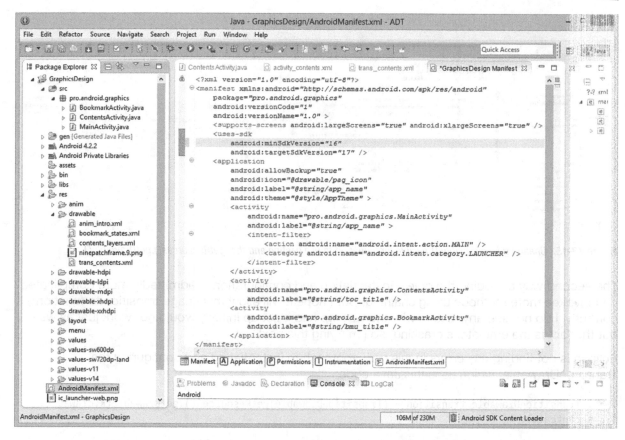

Figure 13-14. Editing the AndroidManifest.xml file to upgrade the application Minimum SDK Version to Level 16

Now you can again use your **Run As ➤ Android Application** work process, and test your GraphicsDesign application, and see if this AndroidManifest.xml application configuration parameter refinement has solved the problem.

Indeed this should solve the problem, since you had your SDK set incorrectly for what you are doing with these image transitions inside the Android OS.

When you click your emulator (hardware) MENU button, and select your Table of Contents menu item, you are still getting this runtime error, which is crashing Android. My next step in ferreting out this bug that Eclipse is not seeing in the code is to look in the LogCat tab at the bottom of ADT.

The LogCat is saying there's an error in the line of code that relates to the TransitionDrawable and how you are loading its Drawable asset, so I am going to try a different approach to the instantiation and loading of this TransitionDrawable object. This second approach is more aligned to what we are doing with our ImageView and ImageButton instantiation. This new **final** access control modifier line of Java code will create, name, cast, and call two chained methods, **.getResources()** and **.getDrawable()**, all using one very long line of Java code, which is shown near the top of Figure 13-15.

Figure 13-15. Changing the TransitionDrawable instantiation to use casting and the .getResources().getDrawable()

The second way of coding the object instantiation and configuration is admittedly more complicated and invokes more methods using chaining. But I hope it will allow this image transition to function correctly. I do not see any reason why the way we had it set up initially would not work just as well, but the fact is the emulator's crashing, so I'm trying this next.

Eclipse is not finding any errors in this new approach to instantiating and configuring the TransitionDrawable, which uses this Java code:

```
final TransitionDrawable transition = (TransitionDrawable)getResources().getDrawable(R.drawable.
trans_contents);
```

Use your **Run As ➤ Android Application** work process a third time, and launch the Nexus One emulator; as you can see in Figure 13-16, it works!

Figure 13-16. Using the Nexus One emulator to test your TransitionDrawable using different drawable image assets

From the new line of code, it looks like you need to call a **.getResources()** method off of the TransitionDrawable first to get the Drawable object that contains the TransitionDrawable object definition. Then, the getResources() method passes this Drawable resource object data into your .getDrawable() method call. Since the transition TransitionDrawable object is called from inside your event handling methods, which are coded even deeper within the onCreate() method, you use the **final** access control modifier to allow the Java code inside the onCreate() method call to see all the way up to the transition object declared at the top of the onCreate() method.

Using the .reverseTransition() Method for Pong Transitions

Now that you have your image transitions working, you can play around with the code or image assets a bit in order to see what TransitionDrawable objects can do. You may have noticed that I am using a **9-patch** image as one of the transition image assets, and yes, this was my first test to see if 9-patch assets would work with TransitionDrawable objects.

As you can see in the middle of Figure 13-16, a 9-patch image asset works just fine when installed as a sub-object (layer) in an TransitionDrawable object. Next, I want to play around with the alternate method calls that are available with the TransitionDrawable object, namely this **.reverseTransition()** method call that allows the equivalent of a PONG animation effect to be achieved within your digital image transition.

Inside your onClick() event handler method, change your **.startTransition()** method call to instead be a **.reverseTransition()** method call by using the following line of Java code:

```
transition.reverseTransition(5000);
```

The code is error-free and can be seen inside Eclipse in Figure 13-17.

Figure 13-17. *Changing the .startTransition() method call to .reverseTransition() method call to ping-pong transition*

Next, use your **Run As ➤ Android Application** work process, and test your new code in the Nexus One emulator. As you can see, now every time you click an ImageButton UI element, the 9-patch frame asset will fade in and then fade out, just like a Pong animation will do. Using the .StartTransition() method, the fade only goes in one direction (fade in), so this alternate method call actually gives you a great deal of latitude in how you implement the animation of your TransitionDrawable objects.

Next, let's edit your TransitionDrawable object's XML definition, and use a normal (non-9-patch) image asset in place of the ninepatchframe object. You will edit the second <item> tag to reference the bookmark0.png asset file, rather than the ninepatchframe.9.png file as it is currently. Click the trans_contents.xml tab at the top of Eclipse and make the necessary edits.

The final trans_contents.xml Transition Drawable object's XML definition markup for these two <item> child tags, shown in Figure 13-18, should appear exactly as follows:

```
<item
    android:id="@+id/imageSource"
    android:drawable="@drawable/cloudsky" />
<item
    android:id="@+id/imageDestination"
    android:drawable="@drawable/bookmark0" />
```

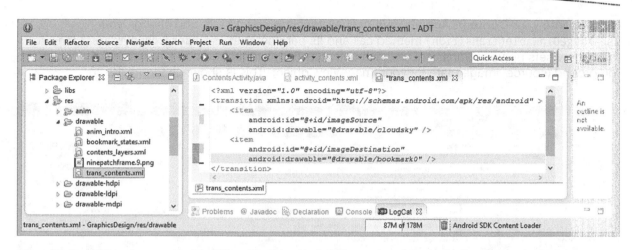

Figure 13-18. Editing a trans_contents.xml TransitionDrawable definition to change the destination image to bookmark

Now you can use the **Run As ➤ Android Application** sequence to review the new transition image crossfade using the bookmark image asset, which fades in over the cloudsky background plate nicely. It is important to note that using PNG32 images, which have an alpha channel installed inside them, can really enhance what you can achieve with Android image transition code; instead of one image replacing another, much more advanced effects can be achieved.

Now let's combine image transitions with **compositing** with your ImageView UI element by using both its **source** (foreground) and **background** image plates.

Advanced TransitionDrawable Compositing via ImageView

Let's go back into your **activity_contents.xml** UI layout definition file and edit your <ImageView> child tag to change your **android:src** parameter to use your **ninepatchframe** image asset as the foreground image plate, and then add an **android:background** parameter that references your **trans_contents.xml** XML TransitionDrawable object definition, as shown in Figure 13-19.

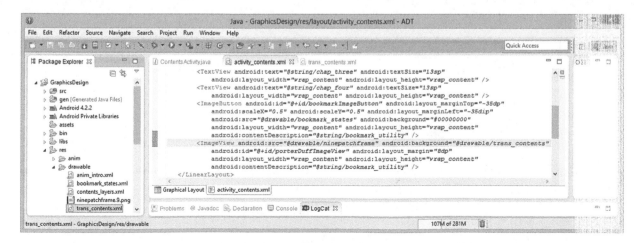

Figure 13-19. Changing the android:src parameter to a ninepatchframe and android:background to trans_contents

Next, go into your **ContentsActivity.java** Activity subclass editing tab, and change your
.setImageDrawable(transition) method call and its parameter to .setBackground(transition) so
that it now sets up your TransitionDrawable object as (in) your background plate, rather than your
foreground (source) image plate for your ImageView object. This is shown in Figure 13-20.

Figure 13-20.   Changing the ImageView object .setImageDrawable() method call to a .setbackground() method call

Now let's test this more advanced use of the TransitionDrawable object with three image assets, two
of which use alpha channels, and one of which is a 9-patch asset. We're throwing everything that
we can at TransitionDrawable to see if it can handle it: foreground and background image plates,
9-patch image assets, 32-bit PNG images with 8-bit alpha channel—all triggered using a multi-state
ImageButton.

As you can see in Figure 13-21, all of these new code and image assets are working well together
as expected, using the ninepatchframe.9.png image asset as the new foreground image plate
overlaying the TransitionDrawable, which is now installed in the background image plate of the
ImageView UI object, and fading in and out at each click of the ImageButton UI element.

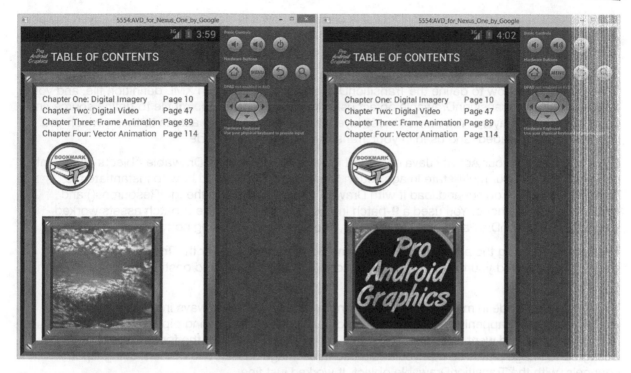

Figure 13-21. Testing your ImageView foreground and background image composite with your TransitionDrawable

As you can see, the TransitionDrawable object animated image asset can be used as a foreground (source image plate) graphics design element or as a background graphics design element for any Android ImageView class (this includes ImageButton), so make sure to use this amazing power creatively in your future Android applications graphics design.

As you get more advanced as you move through this book, keep in mind that everything that you have learned (and will be learning) can be utilized in conjunction with each other using the correct XML markup and Java coding constructs. This includes layers, PorterDuff blending and transfer modes, alpha channels (PNG32), 9-patches, animation, digital video, and much more!

Summary

In this thirteenth chapter, you learned about using digital image transitions in Android via the **TransitionDrawable** class.

We started out looking at some of the core concepts of how transitions are used to simulate animation for digital new media applications, and how the transition effect is closely related to layer-based compositing pipelines.

Since we covered image compositing, layers, and blending in the past couple of chapters, this TransitionDrawable chapter was a good way to segue into the frame animation and vector (procedural) animation chapters coming next, which cover more advanced types of 2D animation, such as using more than two image assets to create a 2D animation effect that goes beyond basic image crossfading.

Next, we took a look at the TransitionDrawable class and how it is closely related to the LayerDrawable class, which was covered in the previous chapter. We looked at the TransitionDrawable class **.startTransition()** Java method call as well as the **.resetTransition()** Java method call.

Next, we looked at the root element **<transition>** parent XML tag as well as its child **<item>** tag. Then you learned how to define the TransitionDrawable object using an XML definition file, and you defined your own TransitionDrawable object using the **trans_contents.xml** file to define source and destination image layers. You named these layers and assigned image assets to them, which you later referenced, loaded, and used in your TransitionDrawable Java code.

Next, you opened your Activity Java code and implemented TransitionDrawable objects and event handler code for your multi-state ImageButton UI element. You learned how to instantiate the TransitionDrawable object and load it with Drawable asset data using the .getResources() and .getDrawable() methods. You used a 9-patch image asset to make sure 9-patch assets worked inside the TransitionDrawable class framework, and you also tried using normal assets.

Then you tried using the alternate **.reverseTransition()** method call for the TransitionDrawable class, which allowed you to "pong" back and forth between source and destination image blending transitions.

You tested your code in many different ways and wired it up different ways in order to ascertain exactly what was happening in the image blend transitions and rendering pipeline. Then you got really advanced and went into your ImageView and implemented both the foreground and the background image plates so that you could use three image assets, two of them using alpha channels, with the TransitionDrawable object. It worked just fine.

In the next chapter, you will learn how to use **Frame Animation** in Android OS and how to use the **AnimationDrawable** class in Android. This will allow you to take your Android digital-image-based animation graphics design and special effects work to a higher level via digital image animation.

Frame-Based Animation: Using the AnimationDrawable Class

In this fourteenth chapter, we will take a closer look at the Java coding side of implementing frame animation in Android. We looked at the concepts behind frame-based animation and how to set up frame animation using the XML definition file work process back in Chapter 3, because I thought you should be able to at least get basic animation running in your application early on in the game (in this book).

The task we're going to focus on in this chapter is how to implement frame animation using only Java code, and zero XML, which is a bit more advanced than the way that we implemented frame animation for an application splash screen back in Chapter 3, as Java coding is generally far more complicated structurally than XML markup is ever going to be.

Doing everything with Java methods will allow you to see how the methods available in the **AnimationDrawable** class, which is the frame animation class for the Android OS, function via the Java side of your Android application code. In this way, if you want to add other Java code functionality inside or around this frame animation code, everything that you are doing using your frame animation processing pipeline will be implemented with the Java programming language.

One of the reasons I am doing this is because if you Google topics such as frame animation, procedural animation, transitions, and similar graphics-related Android topics, invariably one of the prominent developer requests always seems to be the "how can I implement this using only Java code and no XML" request. We are going to do that here.

The AnimationDrawable Class: A Frame Animation Engine

An Android **AnimationDrawable** class is an indirect subclass of the **Drawable** class, which is a direct subclass of the **java.lang.Object** master class. The AnimationDrawable is a direct subclass of a **DrawableContainer** class, which is a direct subclass of the Android Drawable class. The AnimationDrawable Android Java class hierarchy is thus structured as follows:

```
java.lang.Object
  > android.graphics.drawable.Drawable
    > android.graphics.drawable.DrawableContainer
      > android.graphics.drawable.AnimationDrawable
```

As a Drawable subclass, the AnimationDrawable class thus implements all of the features of the Drawable and DrawableContainer class, which you will be learning more about soon.

The AnimationDrawable class implements some additional frame animation features, such as the frame asset definition, a looping parameter, and frame display duration. These are needed to implement frame animation and are specific to this AnimationDrawable class, as would be expected.

An AnimationDrawable class is also a part of the **android.graphics.drawable** package. Since this is the case, its import statement thus references the **android.graphics.drawable.AnimationDrawable** package import path, as you will see later on in this chapter when you write your Java application to implement an AnimationDrawable object for use with your digital image animation for your splash screen animation programming objectives.

An AnimationDrawable object is instantiated in order to create individual frame-by-frame animation, commonly referred to as frame animation and also sometimes termed **bitmap animation** or **raster animation**.

An AnimationDrawable object will always be defined by a series of Drawable objects, which can then be used as the View object background image plate, or as a foreground (source) image plate in View or ViewGroup type objects.

Whichever View (ViewGroup) image container you leverage, remember that you can use alpha channels in your image assets. If you take advantage of this, you will be able to **composite** your animation, both within the View object that it is contained within and the parent View objects that your View is contained within. This goes for ViewGroup layout containers as well.

As you learned in Chapter 3, the simple way to create frame animation is to define the animation in an XML file using the <animation-list> parent tag, or root element. Once that is completed, you can then place that animation XML definition, which becomes a Drawable asset for your application, into your project **/res/drawable** folder and set it as the background, or even a source image asset, for one of your View objects. To trigger the animation, you call a **.start()** method to run the animation. Let's do all of this using Java!

The DrawableContainer Class: A Multi-Drawable Drawable

As the AnimationDrawable class is a direct subclass of the **DrawableContainer** class, and thus inherits all of its functionality, I'm going to spend some time covering this class as well, before you start writing code to implement frame animation using only the Java programming language.

The Android DrawableContainer class is a direct subclass of the **Drawable** class, which is a direct subclass of the **java.lang.Object** master class. Android's DrawableContainer class is part of the **android.graphics.drawable** package. Note that you would never use it in an Import statement, as it is a class that is designed to be used to create other subclasses that are imported. A DrawableContainer class hierarchy is structured as follows:

```
java.lang.Object
  > android.graphics.drawable.Drawable
    > android.graphics.drawable.DrawableContainer
```

As a Drawable subclass, this DrawableContainer class implements all of the features of the Drawable class, which you'll be learning about in detail in a future chapter, once you get done learning about all of its subclasses!

There are three direct subclasses of DrawableContainer in Android OS. They are the **AnimationDrawable** class, which we're covering in this chapter, as well as the **LevelListDrawable** class and the **StateListDrawable** class.

The LevelListDrawable class was created to allow developers to be able to manage a number of different Drawable objects. Each is assigned a maximum and a minimum numerical value in the XML definition file using parameters called **android:maxLevel** and **android:minLevel**. To then change your Drawable based on those levels you have set, use the **public boolean .onLevelChange()** method, which will return a **true** value if, when called, the Drawable is in fact changed. An example of a LevelListDrawable would be the battery level indicator used in the Android OS to visualize hardware power remaining.

The StateListDrawable class allows you to assign any number of images to a single Drawable, and later swap out the visible item by referencing string ID values. A StateListDrawable object is defined by using an XML file with a **<selector>** parent tag. A StateListDrawable child Drawable object is then defined using nested **<item>** elements. The StateListDrawable class features more XML parameters, most of which are **android:state_** parameters, such as **state_active**, **state_activated**, **state_checked**, **state_checkable**, **state_last**, **state_first**, **state_middle**, **state_focused**, **state_pressed**, and many others.

DrawableContainer is essentially what Android terms a **"helper"** class. This class was created to contain several Drawable objects and to then be able to easily select which one to use. The class was not meant to be used directly; however, you can subclass it in order to create your own classes, or you can use one its child classes, which are already coded for you, simply by using your handy Import statement at the top of your class.

Creating Your AnimationDrawable Splashscreen Using Java

Over the next two chapters you are going to completely replace the XML-generated animation currently used on your MainActivity.java Activity subclass splash screen with an identical Java-generated animation, so you can see exactly how to do the same frame and procedural animation programming, but using only Java code and zero XML definition files.

Fire up Eclipse and right-click your MainActivity.java file to open it, and then delete the Import statements for the ImageView (you'll add these back soon as part of the new workflow) as well as the AnimationDrawable and the Animation and AnimationUtils classes.

Next, delete all code statements in the class except for the core **onCreate()** statements that Eclipse created for you back in Chapter 2; you can leave your **onCreateOptionsMenu()** and **onOptionsItemSelected()** methods so you can continue to access (test) your other application's Activity subclasses.

Now you have a blank slate, at least as far as your splash screen is concerned, and you can re-create it all using Java code in the frame animation chapter and the next chapter on procedural animation (the **Animation** class).

The first thing that you want to do is declare your **AnimationDrawable** object for use at the top of the MainActivity class and name it something logical like **frameAnimation**, as shown in Figure 14-1.

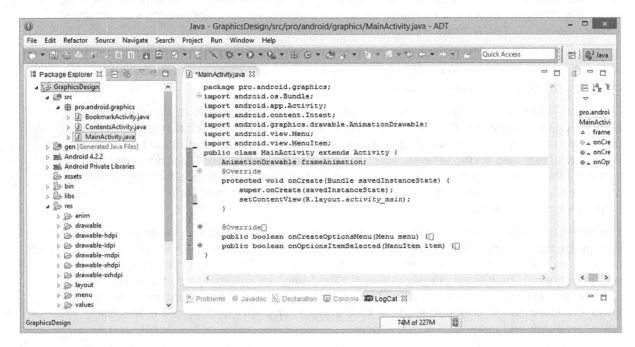

Figure 14-1. Instantiating an AnimationDrawable object and naming it frameAnimation at the top of the MainActivity.java class

You do this using the following basic object-declaring Java statement:

```
AnimationDrawable frameAnimation;
```

Next, you need to create a class called **animStarter** that implements **Runnable**; inside of that, you will code a **run()** method that will contain your **.start()** method, which you will need to call off your **frameAnimation** object in order to start your frameAnimation AnimationDrawable object.

Let's learn more about the Runnable class first, and then write this code.

Using the Android Runnable Class to Run Your Animation

You are going to utilize the Java **Runnable** public interface, and its **run()** method to run your AnimationDrawable in a separate thread, so that it can process the Drawable (BitmapDrawable frames in this case) asynchronously.

This Java **Runnable** interface is not a direct subclass (or even a class at all, for that matter, it is an **interface**) of your **java.lang.Object** master class; I guess there is a first time for everything!

Runnable is actually on the same java.lang level as Object, and thus would be referenced as the **java.lang.Runnable** interface; as a core member of the java.lang package it does not need to be inherently imported into your class in order for you to harness its power, as you'll see in Figure 14-2.

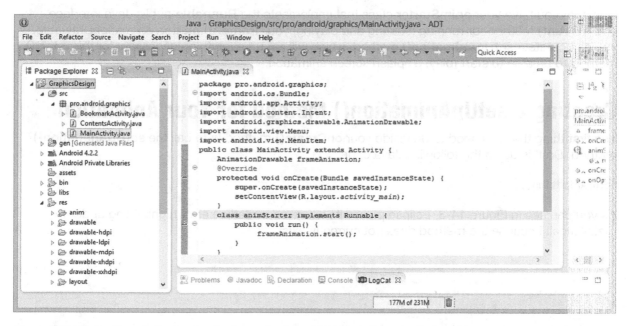

Figure 14-2. Coding the animStarter class implementing Runnable and a run() method inside with .start() method

The Java Runnable interface has ten indirect subclasses, other than the AnimationDrawable subclass, that implement its interface, and one of these just happens to be the Android **Thread** class.

This might give you some clue as to what the Runnable class, and the run() method, are supposed to be used for. That is right; they are used to spawn threads! Threads are operating system processes that are able to allocate their own separate memory space and sometimes their own CPU (especially on multi-core system hardware) upon which processing-intensive tasks, such as animation, downloading, or video playback (codecs), can run **asynchronously**.

While asynchronous simply means **out of sync**, it more accurately signifies a process that does not **interfere** (is not forced to synchronize) with the processing tasks currently underway inside your **User Interface Thread**. The UI Thread is the primary thread for your application and handles tasks such as writing your UI elements to the display screen and scaling them if needed (for instance, if your user rotates their device screen 90 degrees).

The Java code to implement **Runnable** and call your **.start()** method inside its **.run()** method is deceptively simple compared to how powerful it is.

```
class animStarter implements Runnable {
    public void run() {
        frameAnimation.start();
    }
}
```

As you can see in Figure 14-2, the code is error-free and the declaration of your **frameAnimation** AnimationDrawable at the top of your class code now is used via the **.start()** method inside your **run()** method inside your **animStarter** class, which is implementing the Java Runnable interface.

Now that you have your **animStarter** class that implements the **Runnable** public Java interface, and the **run()** method for running (starting and playing) your **frameAnimation** AnimationDrawable, you can create a **setUpAnimation()** method, which will set up everything necessary for this **.start()** method to be able to start (play) a splash screen animation.

Creating a setUpAnimation() Method for Your Animation

The first thing that you need to do inside your **onCreate()** method is to call the **setUpAnimation()** method. Do this using the following Java code:

```
setUpAnimation();
```

As you can see in Figure 14-3, Eclipse places its wavy red underline error highlighting under the method call because the method does not currently exist.

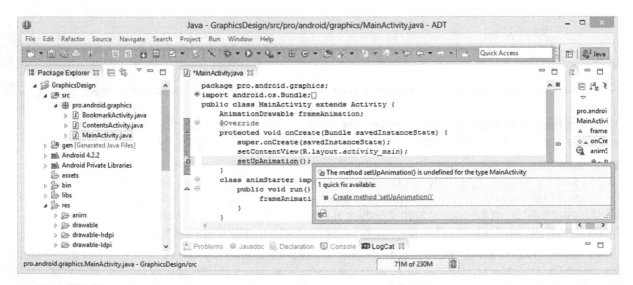

Figure 14-3. Adding a setUpAnimation() method call to your onCreate() method and having Eclipse create it for you

Mouse-over the error highlighting and see if you can get Eclipse ADT to write some code for you, as you often are able to invoke using these pop-up dialogs. Sure enough, there is a Create method setUpAnimation() option, so click that option's link and have this bootstrap method code written for you, saving you approximately three dozen keystrokes.

Once a **private void setUpAnimation()** method is in place, delete the comment and replace it with your ImageView object instantiation, which you deleted earlier. Remember, practice makes perfect! Here's the line of code in case you forgot how to instantiate, name, and load it with your XML definition:

```
ImageView pag = (ImageView) findViewById(R.id.pagImageView);
```

As you can see in Figure 14-4, you will need to mouse-over your ImageView class reference and select the **Import ImageView (android.widget)** option.

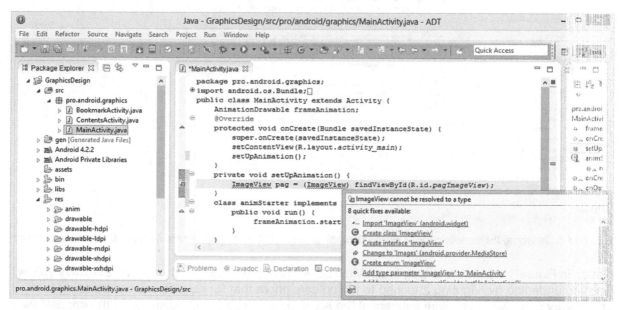

Figure 14-4. Adding the ImageView object instantiation and naming and loading it using a findViewById() method

Now that your ImageView object is set up to receive image output from your **frameAnimation** AnimationDrawable object, you can proceed with the Java code that sets up the AnimationDrawable object itself, which you had handled via XML markup previously, but which you are now going to do using Java code.

Creating a New AnimationDrawable Object and Referencing Its Frames

The first thing that you'll need to do is to initialize your **frameAnimation** object, which you declared at the top of the MainActivity class but did not initialize. You'll initialize this object by using the Java **new** keyword and creating an AnimationDrawable object via the **AnimationDrawable()** constructor method, and then assigning it to the **frameAnimation** object that you created in the first line of code for your Activity subclass. This can be accomplished by using the following line of Java code:

```
frameAnimation = new AnimationDrawable();
```

As you can see in Figure 14-5, the code is error-free, and your Java object is now instantiated, constructed, and even triggered via the **animStarter()** method. However, it is still basically an empty AnimationDrawable object, so let's write the Java code next that loads it with animation frame data.

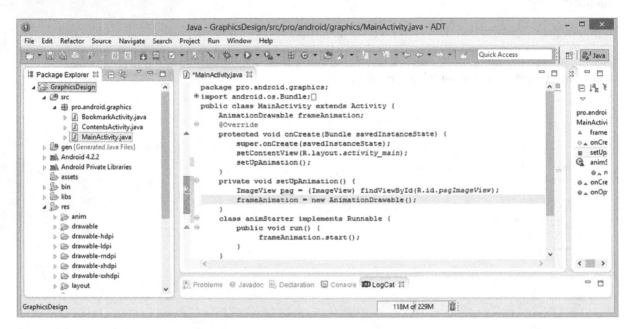

Figure 14-5. Initializing the frameAnimation AnimationDrawable object using the new keyword and AnimationDrawable() constructor

Notice in Figure 14-5 that your **pag** ImageView object is not used as yet, thus it has the wavy yellow warning underline highlighting attached to it. You can ignore that for now as you will be using that object very soon when you wire (reference) the AnimationDrawable up to display via the ImageView.

Using the AnimationDrawable Class's .addFrame() Method

Now that you have constructed an empty AnimationDrawable object, you can use the **.addFrame()** method to add frames and their durations to your object in much the same way that you did using your XML <animation-list> parent tag and <item> child tags.

You'll extract your Drawable references using the same method chaining that you used in the previous chapter, on the inside of the **.addFrame()** method call, using the following somewhat long Java code construct:

```
frameAnimation.addFrame(getResources().getDrawable(R.drawable.pag0), 112);
```

This calls an **.addFrame()** method off of a **frameAnimation** AnimationDrawable object. Inside the **.addFrame()** method, in order to reference a Drawable object parameter, you use the **getResources().getDrawable()** method chaining to obtain your pag0.png image asset that is in your /res/drawable-xhdpi folder.

The second parameter is the duration in milliseconds, and as you know, you are using the 112 millisecond value for the first frame and 111 for the remaining frames, which you'll cut and paste to put into place. As you can see in Figure 14-6, your code is error-free and you can continue on.

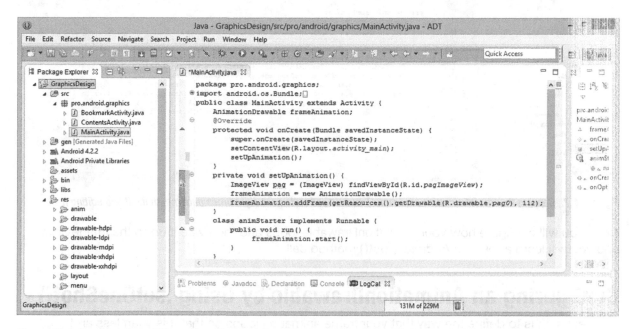

Figure 14-6. *Invoking the .addFrame() method and the getResources().getDrawable() method chain to load frames*

Now, select the entire line of code that you just wrote, and cut and paste it eight more times underneath itself, specifying the pag1.png through pag8.png image asset file names (without the .png extension, of course), and a 111 millisecond frame duration value for each, totaling one second. The completed frame loading lines of code can be seen in Figure 14-7.

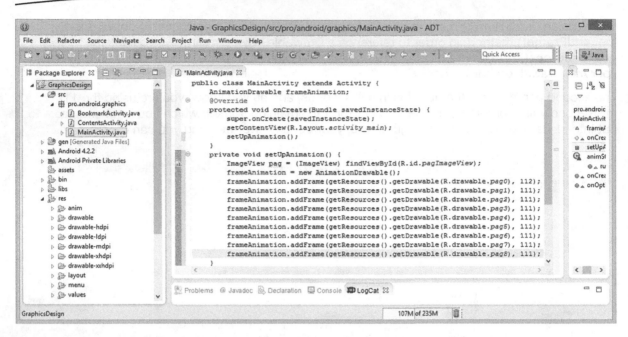

Figure 14-7. Copying the frameAnimation.addFrame() method call statement eight times underneath itself and editing it

Next, you will configure how your AnimationDrawable loops and then wire it up to the ImageView, and you will learn about the Android **.post()** method call.

Configuring an AnimationDrawable by Using .setOneShot()

The next step is to define the way that your frame animation loops so that it is seamless and continuous. In Java code, this is done by using a method called **.setOneShot()**, with a Boolean value of **true** (do not loop) or **false** (seamless looping animation). This is akin to what you would set up in your XML definition file using the **android:oneShot** parameter.

Let's go ahead and use this method to set your animation frames to continue to play forever by using a **false** parameter value via the following code:

```
frameAnimation.setOneShot(false);
```

Your next step is to wire up your **pag** ImageView animation display UI widget with the **frameAnimation** AnimationDrawable object that contains the data that will be sent to the ImageView to be displayed. You will do this using the now-familiar **.setImageDrawable()** method with the **frameAnimation** AnimationDrawable object passed as the parameter value. This is done using the following line of Java code, as shown in Figure 14-8:

```
pag.setImageDrawable(frameAnimation);
```

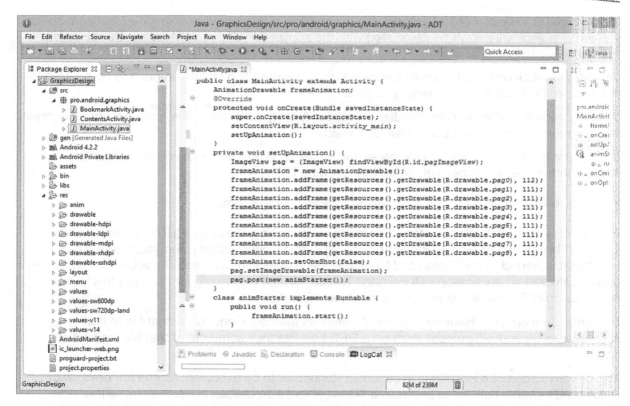

Figure 14-8. Configuring the AnimationDrawable using .setOneShot() and ImageView using .setImageDrawable()

Next, you need to start the AnimationDrawable object by using its **.start()** method, which means calling your **animStarter** Runnable class .run() method.

This is done using a method that is a part of the Android **Handler** class, called the **.post()** method, so let's take a moment and learn exactly what the **.post()** method and its Handler class do for us within Android.

Scheduling an AnimationDrawable Using the Handler Class

The Android **Handler** class is also a direct subclass of **java.lang.Object**, which is Java's master **Object** class, and this makes a Handler an Object.

Android's Handler class is part of the **android.os.Handler** package. It is imported when you have an **Import android.os** statement in your application, which imports all of the OS related functions necessary for your application development, such as Bundle, Handler, and similar OS utilities.

The Android OS Handler class hierarchy is structured as follows:

```
java.lang.Object
 > android.os.Handler
```

The Android OS Handler object enables you to send and process a Runnable (or a Message) object. A Handler object will always be associated with the application UI thread **MessageQueue** object that spawned the Handler object.

This MessageQueue object will hold any processing or messaging tasks that need to be processed in a First In, First Out (FIFO) scheduling algorithm.

You only need to implement one Handler object per Activity subclass, where your background thread will communicate with it to update your UI Thread.

If you want to research Android's MessageQueue class and how it works, you can find more information on the developer web site at the following URL:

http://developer.android.com/reference/android/os/MessageQueue.html

Each Android **Handler** object instantiation is associated using its spawning Thread, and with that parent's **Thread** and **MessageQueue** objects. What this means is that when you create a new Handler, it is **bound** to the Thread and MessageQueue objects of a parent Thread, which is usually (but not always) an application's UI (primary) Thread, which is spawning (or creating) this Handler object as child Thread and MessageQueue object instantiations.

From that time on, your **Handler** object will deliver its messages and (or) runnables to that MessageQueue and will process them on a FIFO basis as they come out of that MessageQueue object.

The primary usage of a Handler is to schedule Runnables to be executed, as you are doing with your AnimationDrawable here, or to schedule a Message to be processed at some point further down the processing line. You could also utilize Handler objects to queue up some action to be performed using a different Thread than the one Thread that you are currently using.

After your app UI Process is created when you launch your application, its main (or UI) thread begins running a MessageQueue object. The MessageQueue object takes care of managing all of your Android application Java classes (Activity, Service, BroadcastReceiver, ContentProvider, etc.) and objects, as well as any windows that your Activity may create on a display screen.

You can create your own Threads, and these will communicate with your main application (UI) thread using a Handler. This is accomplished via calls to the same **.post()** (or the custom **.sendMessage()** methods for Message objects) methods as before, but from your new thread.

Any given Runnable object, or Message object, will eventually be scheduled in that Handler's message queue and then processed later when appropriate.

Three methods have been created to handle Runnable object scheduling in Android: the one that you are using, **.post(Runnable)**, as well as **.postAtTime(Runnable, long)** and **.postDelayed(Runnable, long)**.

These three **.post(Runnable)** method versions allow you to queue up the **Runnable** object to be called by a **MessageQueue** object when it is received. In your application example, the **Runnable** is implemented in the **animStarter** class and contains the **.run()** method, which in turn contains the **.start()**.

There are also .sendMessage() methods, including a **.sendMessage(Message),** **.sendMessageAtTime(Message, long)**, **.sendMessageDelayed(Message, long)**, and

.sendEmptyMessage(int), which are Message object-specific, as you can see by the Message object that is passed inside the parameter list, rather than being **Runnable** object-specific, as the **.post()** methods are.

The .sendMessage() methods also permit developers to queue up Message objects containing a **Bundle** object containing data that will be processed by that Handler's **.handleMessage(Message)** method, which requires that you implement a subclass of the Android Handler class.

Now that I have covered a little bit of background on **Runnable** and how it will **.run()** this **frameAnimation.startAnimation()** processing statement, you can test your frame animation, now converted from XML to Java code, in the Nexus One emulator. Use the **Run As ➤ Android Application** work process to launch your application, and as you can see in Figure 14-9, the animation loops seamlessly forever when your app launches, just like it did before.

Figure 14-9. Testing your AnimationDrawable in the Nexus One emulator

Now that you have simulated the frame animation you had in place from before (you are going to add in the procedural animation part in the next chapter), let's get a bit more advanced. You're going to learn how to trigger animation using event handlers, so you can click your PAG logo to start it animating.

Designing an AnimationDrawable to Loop Back to Frame 1

You are going to first set up your AnimationDrawable to loop seamlessly one time, because as it is now, the last frame is not quite "vertical" as far as the logo is concerned. To accomplish this, you are going to copy the first **.addFrame()** method call in your code and paste it after the last **.addFrame()** method call, as shown in Figure 14-10. To keep the timing the same, use a duration value of 111 (like the others) in the first method call, and a value of 1 (the remainder to make a full second) in the last method call.

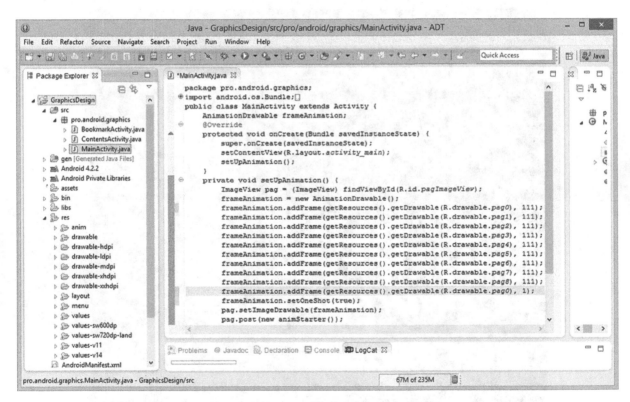

Figure 14-10. Setting your .setOneShot() method to true and adding an end frame so logo is flat to screen at end

This makes sure to draw the first frame of the animation to the screen right at the end of the animation, so your PAG logo looks like it did when you started the animation. This won't matter when you have the **.setOneShot()** method set to false, but as you can see in Figure 14-10, you are going to set it to **true**, which is why what you are doing is necessary!

Use your **Run As ➤ Android Animation** work process, and when your application launches (watch carefully), your animation will loop one time and return to its upright position. Attention passengers: Please return your animations to their upright positions! Thank you for flying Apress.

Next, you're going to change back to forever looping animation and implement event handling so that you can control your animation using click and long-click events. This is so that if you are implementing something cool, like an animated children's storybook app, for instance, your readers can click graphic elements in the page to start them animating (and stop them, using a long-click). We will go through the work process to implement all of this next, using only Java code, of course.

Adding Event Handling to Allow Frame Animation by Click

To allow your graphical element—in your case, it is your PAG logo, but it could also be a fish in your aquarium children's storybook (free idea for you)—to animate on command (onClick), you need to attach an event handler to the ImageView that displays your AnimationDrawable object contents. You will do this by calling a **.setOnClickListener()** method on your **pag** object, as shown in Figure 14-11. This is similar to the handlers you coded before.

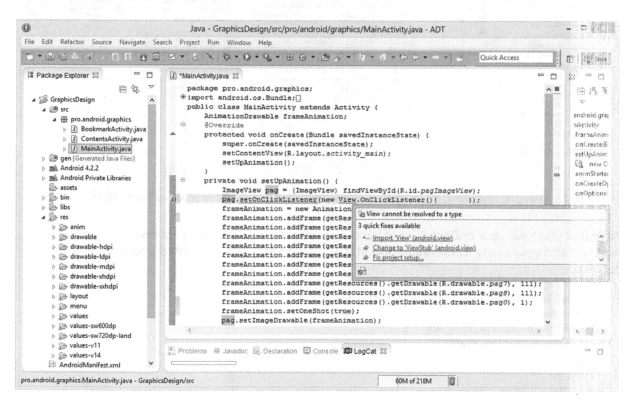

Figure 14-11. Adding a .setOnClickListener() method and View.OnClickListener() method to your pag ImageView

Next, mouse-over your View class reference, and have Eclipse **Import View (android.view)** for you, and then you will get the wavy red error highlight shown in Figure 14-12. You can mouse-over this and have Eclipse again write your method bootstrap code for you automatically. It is always a pleasure when your IDE sees what you are doing and offers to do some of it for you!

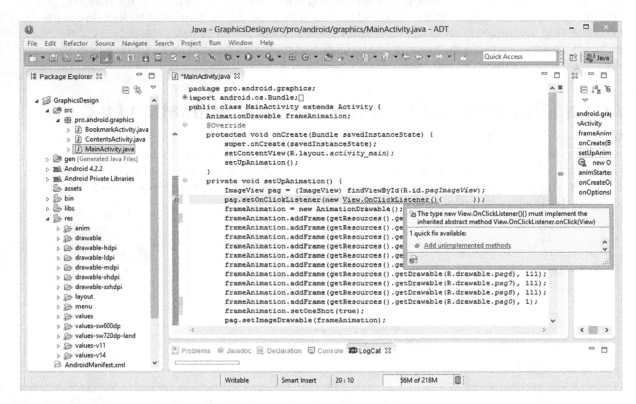

Figure 14-12. Adding an unimplemented onClick() event handling method by using the error pop-up helper dialog

Now that you have your **onClick()** event handling method written for you, as shown in Figure 14-13, you can add your trusty **frameAnimation.start()** method call. The completed code block is as follows:

```
pag.setOnClickListener(new View.OnClickListener() }
    @Override
    public void onClick(View arg0) {
        frameAnimation.start();
}});
```

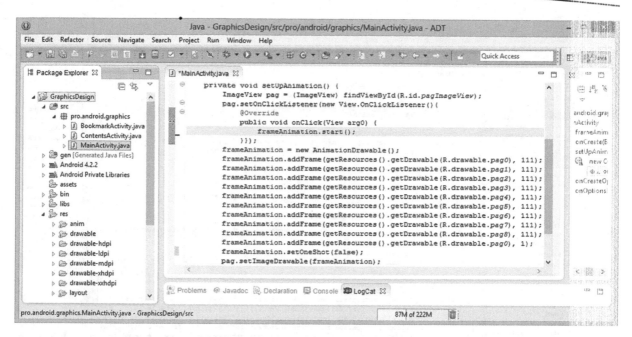

Figure 14-13. *Adding a .start() method call to your frameAnimation object inside your onClick() event handler*

Notice that I have combined both closing curly braces for both methods to exist on the same line of code to save a line of space in my code listing. It is good for you to get comfortable with different personal styles of coding in case you need to look at other programmers' Java code, which you should be doing as often as you can in order to learn more about how other developers implement Java code. There are many different ways of doing the exact same thing where computer programming is concerned!

Also, make sure to change your **.setOneShot()** method's parameter value back to **false**, so that you can have your AnimationDrawable object loop seamlessly forever. You'll need to use a **false** setting to be able to see if your event handling code is indeed starting (and eventually, stopping) it correctly.

Next, you can remove the **animStarter** class that implements **Runnable**, as you are now going to **.start()** (and soon **.stop()** as well) your AnimationDrawable object "manually." More accurately, your users are going to be controlling (start and stop) the AnimationDrawable objects now using clicks and long-clicks! Thus, you are essentially making your graphic element interactive as far as animation is concerned; your user now controls when it animates and when it is static.

As you might well imagine, I'm not going to show the code listing for this **animStarter** class now that it is deleted, as there would be nothing to see. Trust that it is now deleted; if you like, you can leave it in your code because you are not calling it, so it won't be utilized anyway.

It is important to note that it is always a good idea to remove any unused classes, methods, objects, and variables. You should always do this simply to make sure that your application's memory is not allocated for something that is not even being utilized! That would be inefficient.

Next, you're going to save yourself some keystrokes, and cut and paste the **onClick()** event handling code block, in order to create your **onLongClick()** event handling code block, as shown in Figure 14-14. Add the word **Long** before **Click** in all copied code (**onLongClickListener, onLongClick,** etc.).

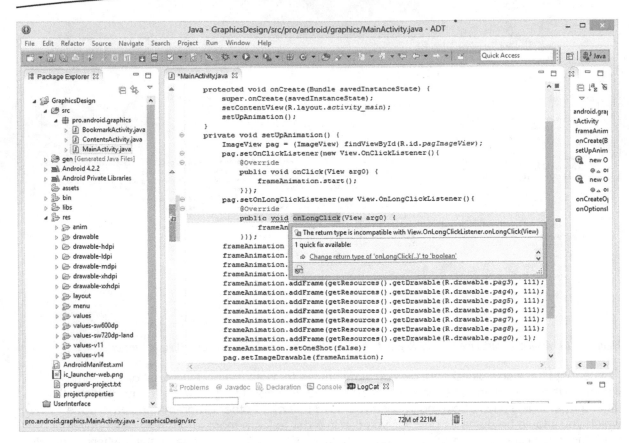

Figure 14-14. Changing the onLongClick() method return type from void to boolean using the error pop-up helper

As you can see, Eclipse has detected an inaccurate method modifier and is offering to fix it for you. Mouse-over your wavy red underlined **void** return type and have Eclipse ADT **change return type of onLongClick() to boolean**, as suggested in the pop-up error dialog shown in Figure 14-14.

As you can see in Figure 14-15, this fixes your return type, which is now **boolean** as required by the **onLongClick()** event handing method, but brings up a new error, which you'll mouse-over and have Eclipse again fix for you.

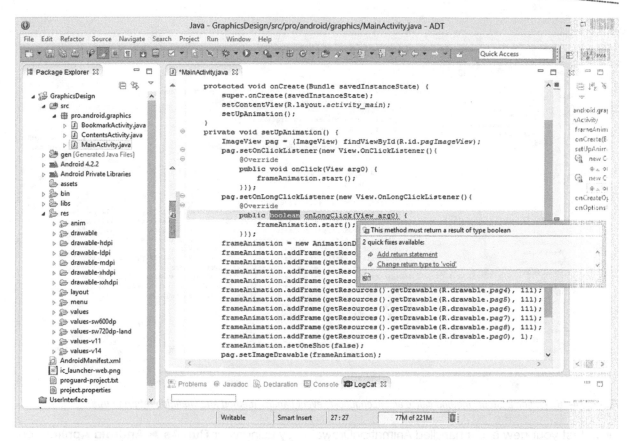

Figure 14-15. Adding a return statement to your onLongClick() event handling method using the error pop-up helper

The pop-up error dialog informs you that you need to add a **return** statement, which is required since your method is of the type **boolean** and the calling entity is expecting a **true** (handled successfully) or **false** (failed) return value. As you can seen in Figure 14-15, one of the error dialog's solution options is to **add a return statement**, and that is the option you should select.

Unfortunately, the Eclipse helper dialog adds an incorrect return value of **false**, when you want to return a value of **true** once your AnimationDrawable object has been started. Nobody is perfect, not even the Eclipse ADT IDE, which does seem to have a mind of its own sometimes!

Let's edit this **false** return value, and change it to **true**. You should also edit the copied **.start()** method call, and change it to the **.stop()** method call, since Long-Click events are going to stop your AnimationDrawable, and another Click event should start it right up again. The final Java code in your **onLongClick()** method is shown in Figure 14-16 and looks like the following programming logic **onLongClickListener** event handling construct:

```
pag.setOnLongClickListener(new View.OnLongClickListener() }
    @Override
    public boolean onLongClick(View arg0) {
        frameAnimation.stop();
        return true;
    }});
```

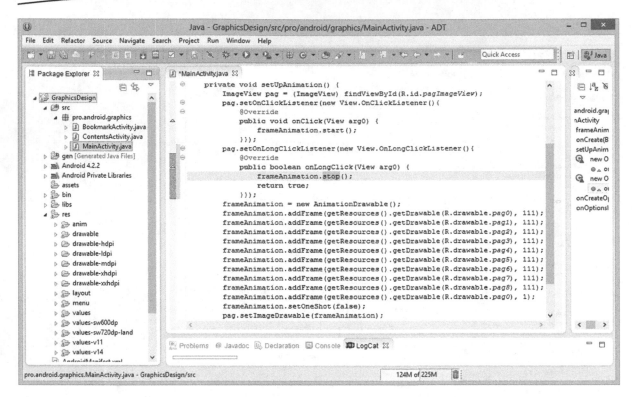

Figure 14-16. Adding a .stop() method call to an onLongClick() event handler method and changing return to true

Now, test your new event handled AnimationDrawable by using your **Run As ➤ Android Application** work process. When the application starts, click the PAG logo to start it animating. So far, so good. Next, long-click, or click and hold for a second (or longer), and you will see the animation stop. But there is a problem: the animation is not stopping on Frame 1, which looks unprofessional, so you're not done with your Java coding as yet!

What you need to do to fix this problem is to "reset" your AnimationDrawable to Frame 1, but wouldn't you know it, Android left the **.reset()** method out of the AnimationDrawable class! Quite a glaring oversight as far as frame animation is concerned, but I'm sure they will add it in there someday.

You will need to figure out a different way of getting your frame animation set back to the first frame when your users perform a Long-Click operation on the **pag** ImageView UI element that contains your frame animation assets.

The first thing I am going to try is to put the statement that initializes the frameAnimation object via the **.setImageDrawable()** method call inside the **onLongClick()** method and after the **frameAnimation.stop()** method call.

As you can see in Figure 14-17, once you place the method call inside an **onLongClick()** nested method, the nested **pag** object reference used to call the **.setImageDrawable()** method becomes unable to see this ImageView object instantiation at the top of your **setUpAnimation()** method. So Eclipse puts a wavy red error highlight under the **pag** ImageView reference to let you know.

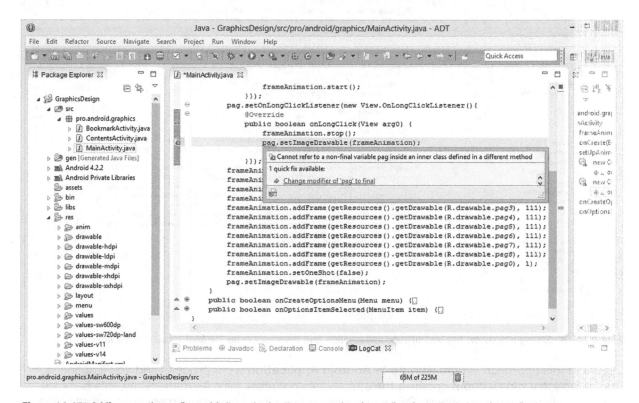

Figure 14-17. Adding a .setImageDrawable() method call to reset animation to first frame and changing to final

If you mouse-over the error highlighting and pop up the helper suggestion dialog, it will suggest making your **pag** ImageView object instantiation (and loading) line of Java code use a **final** access modifier. You will accept the suggestion and allow Eclipse to do this for you, as shown in Figure 14-18.

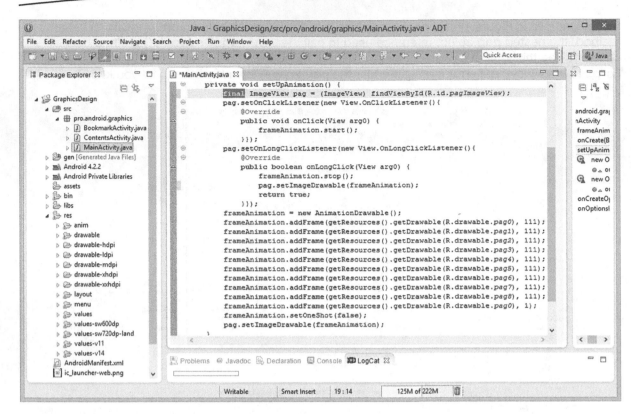

Figure 14-18. Setting ImageView pag instantiation and inflation Java statement to be the final access control modifier

Let's test this approach via the **Run As ➤ Android Application** work process and you'll notice that, although it runs without crashing the app, it does not reset your AnimationDrawable back to Frame 1, which is what you need. This is because an AnimationDrawable object contains all of the references regarding which frame of animation is playing (or is stopped) and when it is playing (or where it is stopped).

So you will need to figure something else out to achieve your desired end result of a perfect seamless Frame 1 to Frame 1 animation stop operation.

Thus, the next thing that you will try is to set this pag ImageView to your Frame 1 image asset directly, which you already have the Java code in place to do. This code is currently used inside the **.addFrame()** method call.

Copy the **getResources().getDrawable()** method chaining code from inside the first parameter (Drawable) portion of your **.addFrame()** method call and paste it inside the **.setImageDrawable()** method call. This is done using the following single line of Java code:

```java
pag.setImageDrawable(getResources.getDrawable(R.drawable.pag0));
```

As you can see in Figure 14-19, your code is error-free and ready to test!

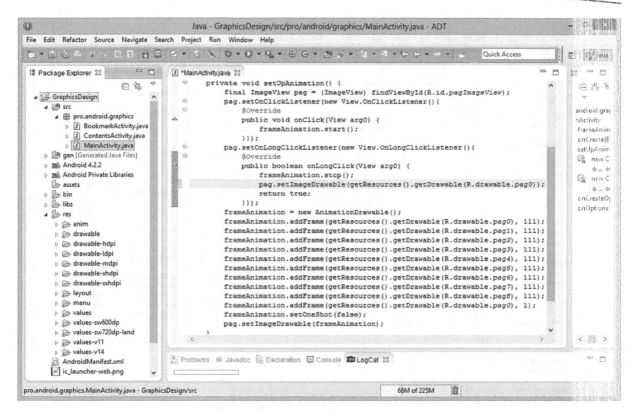

Figure 14-19. Changing the .setImageDrawable() method to directly reference the first frame of the animation

Now, let's use your **Run As ➤ Android Application** work process and see if you have achieved perfection yet. When your application launches, click the PAG logo and watch it animate. The next step in your testing cycle would be to long-click on the animating PAG logo and watch it stop and reset itself to Frame 1. So far, so good! The final step in your testing cycle is to click on the PAG logo and see if it starts animating again so you can "toggle" the animation on and off. Alas, a click does not restart the PAG animation, so again you need to go back to the drawing (coding) board!

Let's think for a moment why your AnimationDrawable object would not start animating again on your second click. The reason is because the ImageView is not set to display your AnimationDrawable object anymore; it is now set to directly reference the Frame 1 Drawable image asset, so you will need to move the **.setImageDrawable(frameAnimation)** method call inside, and to the top of, your **onClick()** event handling code structure.

This is acceptable from a logic standpoint, because you don't animate until you click the ImageView anyway. So, since the AnimationDrawable class has no **.reset()** method and you thus have to manually set Frame 1 in an **onLongClick .stop()** code structure, you can set this **pag** ImageView back to referencing the AnimationDrawable object using your **onClick .start()** code structure.

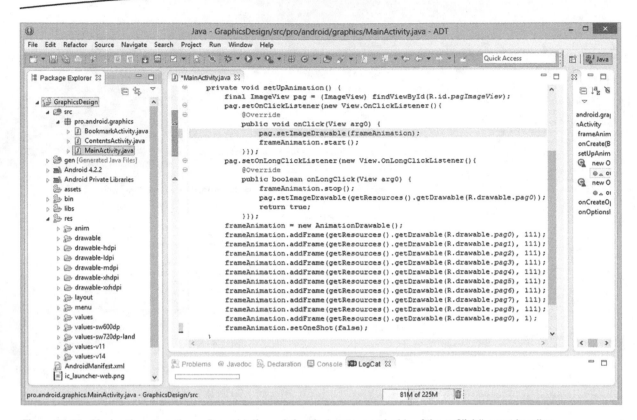

Figure 14-20. Moving the pag.setImageDrawable(frameAnimation) statement inside of the onClick() event handler

Again, let's use a **Run As ➤ Android Application** work process and see if you finally have achieved perfection. When your application launches, click the PAG logo and again watch it animate. Perform the next step in the test cycle and long-click on the animating PAG logo, watching it stop and reset itself to Frame 1.

The final step in your testing cycle is the important one here, so click the PAG logo and see if it starts animating again! It works now, so as a final testing process, click and long-click several times in order to make sure that it works over time and with numerous repetitions. This is called testing thoroughly or robustly. Great job, folks! Next, you'll add procedural animation elements to your frame animation treatment using only Java code.

Summary

In this fourteenth chapter, you learned how to use only Java code, and no XML markup, to implement your splash screen frame animation in Android OS via methods and constructors from the **AnimationDrawable** class.

We started out by looking at Android's **AnimationDrawable** class itself, and how it is a direct subclass of the **DrawableContainer** class. You have seen how it contains your animation frames, durations, and looping parameters, as well as methods to start and stop your frame animation playback cycle.

Next, we covered the **DrawableContainer** class, which you can use to create Drawable objects that are contained in DrawableContainer object structures with other closely-related Drawable objects.

Examples include frames in an animation, or AnimationDrawables, or states and levels of a graphic object, such as are found in the **StateListDrawable** class and in the **LevelListDrawable** class.

Then, you dove right into re-creating your application's splash screen frame animation using only Java code. You removed all of the code referencing your XML definition, and started over from scratch, creating an all-new method named **setUpAnimation()** to set up your **AnimationDrawable** object.

You also created an **animStart** class implementing the **Runnable** interface and **.run()** method, so that a frame animation will start running automatically when your application launches.

You learned about the Java **Runnable** and **.run()** method, and the Android **Handler** class and the **.post()** method. We went over **processes** and **Thread** objects and **MessageQueue** objects to see how all of that works in the Android OS.

Next, instead of using Runnable and .run() to auto-start your animation, you implemented event handling code, which allows you to trigger the animation playback using Click and eventually Long-Click events.

You saw how to use event handling with both **looping**, or **.setOneShot(false)**, as well as **play it once**, or **.setOneShot(true)**, animation configurations.

You learned how to configure your AnimationDrawable object in Java to get a seamless-loop, one-time, Frame-1-to-Frame-1 (resting place) result. You also saw how to modify your code to be able to Long-Click and top the animation cycle without it hanging the logo on any frame other than its front-facing first frame.

In the next chapter, you will learn how to use the **Animation** class for implementing procedural, or vector, animation inside the Android OS. This will allow you to take your Android digital-image-based frame animation that you re-created in this chapter and finish implementing the translate, rotate, scale, and alpha procedural animation special effects that you created via XML back in Chapter 4 to combine with your frame-based PAG logo animation.

This will take your current Android 2D animation knowledge base to an even more advanced level as you will be implementing a complex procedural frame-based animation combination implemented using only Java programming logic.

Chapter 15

Procedural Animation: Using the Animation Classes

In this fifteenth chapter, we will take a detailed look at the Java coding side of implementing procedural animation within Android. We examined the concepts behind procedural animation, and how to set up a procedural animation using an XML definition file work process, back in Chapter 4. I did this early in the book because I thought that you should at least be able to get basic procedural animation running inside your application early on in your professional Android graphics design work process.

The task we're going to focus on in this chapter is how to implement the procedural animation "moves" that we implemented in Chapter 4, but now using only Java code and zero XML. This is a bit more advanced than the way in which we implemented procedural animation for your application splash screen back in Chapter 4, as Java code is generally far more complicated due to its compact, chained code structures than XML markup will ever be, no matter how complex your XML nested structure may become.

Doing everything with Java methods will allow you to see how the methods available in the **Animation** class and its **five** subclasses work. The Animation class is the procedural animation superclass for the Android OS. You will be learning all about this class and Animation objects, as well as how to implement procedural animation functions using only the Java side of your Android application's graphics programming logic.

We are doing this so that if you wish to add other Java code functionality in with, or around, your procedural animation's Java programming pipeline, everything that you are doing using your procedural animation processing pipeline will be implemented 100% within the Java programming language.

The Animation Class: Your Procedural Animation Engine

An Android **Animation** class is a direct subclass of the **java.lang.Object** master class, which means that it was scratch-coded specifically for the purpose of providing a procedural animation foundation for the Android OS. By scratch-coded I mean coded from scratch, or not based on any other existing code (classes, methods, interfaces, constants, etc.).

The Android Animation Java class hierarchy is structured as follows:

```
java.lang.Object
  > android.view.animation.Animation
```

The Animation class is a part of the **android.view.animation** package. Since this is the case, an **import statement** for an Animation class thereby references the **android.view.animation.Animation** package import path.

An Animation object is instantiated in order to create interpolated **vector** or **procedural** animation. This type of animation does not use frames or bitmaps, but rather applies mathematical vectors or algorithms to existing Drawable objects to achieve effects such as scaling (resizing), rotation, alpha blending (alpha channel fading), and translations (X and Y movement).

The Animation class is a **public abstract** class, which means that it is not mean to be used directly other than declaring Animation objects initially; it was created to be used to create other subclasses, such as the classes that we will be using during this chapter to implement 2D procedural animation special effects.

So the Animation class has five direct subclasses that are of importance, all of which you will be learning about in detail during this chapter. Subclasses include **ScaleAnimation** for scaling View objects, **AlphaAnimation** for alpha blending (fading in and fading out) View (or ViewGroup) objects, **RotateAnimation** for rotating View objects, and finally, **TranslateAnimation** for moving View objects around on the screen.

There is also a fifth **AnimationSet** subclass, which is much more complicated as it allows **composite animations** to be created using the other four types of Animation subclasses. The AnimationSet class and object allows sets, or grouping, and even sub-grouping, of Animation objects to form more complex hierarchies of procedural animation to allow virtually any result that you can imagine to be achieved.

We'll get into all of these during this chapter as you code your animation pipeline application, which will combine the frame animation that you coded in the previous chapter with procedural animation that you will code around it and on top of it during this chapter.

You will implement many of these Animation class and subclass objects for your use within a digital image animation. You will add procedural animation "moves" to your splash screen animation using most of the Android Animation class subclasses, each of which you will learn about as you use them during your progression through this chapter on procedural animation in Android.

TranslateAnimation Class: Animation Subclass for Moving

Since this is the one procedural animation transform that we are not going to be implementing directly within this chapter, other than the "try this" suggested exercise section I'm going to put at the end of the chapter, we will cover this Animation subclass first, as it's fairly straightforward.

As mentioned, the Android **TranslateAnimation** class is a direct subclass of the **android.view. animation.Animation** abstract class. This class is used to animate movement in the X and Y coordinate directions around the screen of the user's Android device. As such, it is very simple and yet extremely useful for a variety of purposes, from animated elements to moving things on and off of the user's display screen.

The Android TranslateAnimation Java class hierarchy is structured as follows:

```
java.lang.Object
  > android.view.animation.Animation
    > android.view.animation.TranslateAnimation
```

The TranslateAnimation class is part of the **android.view.animation** package and, since this is the case, its **import statement** thus references the **android.view.animation.TranslateAnimation** package import path.

The constructor method that you want to use to create a TranslateAnimation object takes the following format, as you'll see later on in the chapter:

```
TranslateAnimation(float fromX, float toX, float fromY, float toY);
```

The ScaleAnimation Class: Animation Subclass for Scaling

As you know, the Android **ScaleAnimation** class is another direct subclass of the **android.view. animation.Animation** abstract class. This class is used to scale View objects, again by using the X and Y coordinates in 2D space.

The Android ScaleAnimation Java class hierarchy is structured as follows:

```
java.lang.Object
  > android.view.animation.Animation
    > android.view.animation.ScaleAnimation
```

A ScaleAnimation class is also part of the **android.view.animation** package. Its **import statement** references the **android.view.animation.ScaleAnimation** package import path, as you'll see in the next section when you use it to scale your PAG frame animation to make it look like it is coming out of the distance and landing in the center of your display screen.

The constructor method that you want to use to create your ScaleAnimation object takes the following format, as you will see in the next section:

```
ScaleAnimation(float fromX, float toX, float fromY, float toY, int pivotXType, float pivotXValue,
int pivotYType, float pivotYValue);
```

Scaling Up Your Logo: Using the ScaleAnimation Class

Now it is time to fire up Eclipse and add procedural scaling animation to your PAG logo frame animation, exactly like you did in Chapter 4 using XML.

Open your **MainActivity.java** code, in a tab in Eclipse's central editing pane, and declare an **Animation** object named **scaleZeroToFullAnimation** right after your AnimationDrawable object declaration, as shown in Figure 15-1.

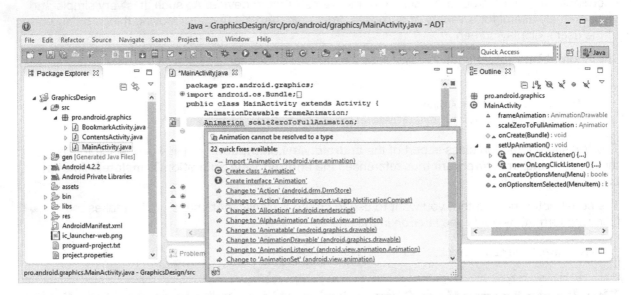

Figure 15-1. Declaring your scaleZeroToFullAnimation Animation object at the top of your MainActivity.java Activity

As you can see, you have not added the Import statement for the Animation class to your code, so mouse-over the wavy red error highlight and select the **Import Animation (android.view.animation package)** option so that ADT will write the **Import android.view.animation.Animation** Java statement for you. Now that you have declared and named your Animation object for use, you can initialize it inside your setUpAnimation() method.

Next, add in a line of space after your frameAnimation AnimationDrawable initialization statement, and add a similar statement to initialize your now-declared scaleZeroToFullAnimation object, using the following single line of Java code:

```
scaleZeroToFullAnimation = new ScaleAnimation();
```

As you can see in Figure 15-2, there is some wavy red error highlighting to investigate! Let's mouse-over the ScaleAnimation() constructor method, and select the **Import ScaleAnimation (android.view.animation package)** option.

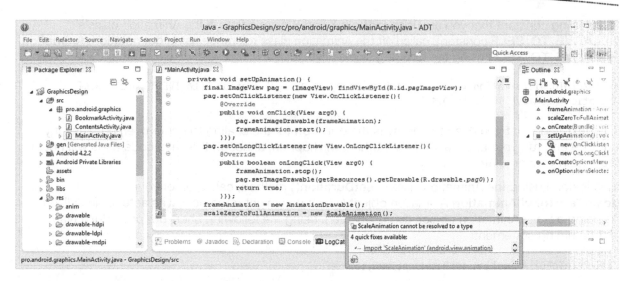

Figure 15-2. Instantiating a scaleZeroToFullAnimation Animation object using a new ScaleAnimation() constructor

As you can see once you select that option, this does not remove this wavy red error highlighting; however, it does write an Import statement for you!

The reason that the wavy red error highlighting does not go away (in fact, all that changes is the pop-up helper's suggestion) is because you need to pass parameters (variables) into this constructor method outlining how you want this object to be constructed (configured initially, if you will).

Let's add float values; I used **0** (0%), and **1** (100%), for the **fromX** and **toX** parameter values and the same values for **fromY** and **toY** parameters, as shown in Figure 15-3. You should also specify **constants** and **float** values of **0.5f**, or 50% for each of these **pivotX** and **pivotY** parameter value positions. Notice that float value positions will accept integer values and convert them for you.

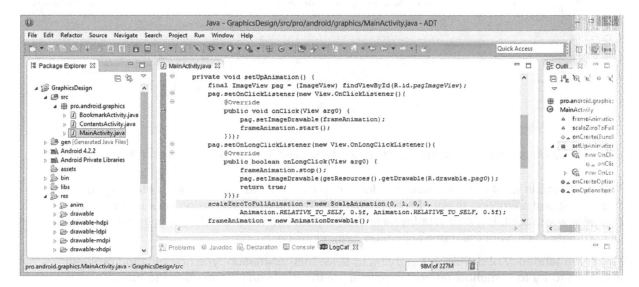

Figure 15-3. Configuring a ScaleAnimation() constructor method call with scale variables and pivot point constants

The scaling constant that you are using for both X and Y pivot points is the Animation class's **RELATIVE_TO_SELF** constant, called off the Animation class reference using dot notation (**Animation. RELATIVE_TO_SELF**) using the following single (if you use a widescreen display) line of code:

```
scaleZeroToFullAnimation = new ScaleAnimation(0, 1, 0, 1, Animation.RELATIVE_TO_SELF, 0.5f,
Animation.RELATIVE_TO_SELF, 0.5f);
```

The next thing that you need to specify is the **duration** for the scaling to occur over, because if you compile and run your application now, nothing will happen, although the Java code as-is will not in fact crash your emulator.

This is done using the Animation class's **.setDuration()** method, called off of your **scaleZeroToFullAnimation** Animation object (which you might remember was actually initialized as being a ScaleAnimation object; confused yet?), using the following short but powerful Java programming statement:

```
scaleZeroToFullAnimation.setDuration(5000);
```

I am using a data value of **5000 milliseconds**, or five seconds, as shown in Figure 15-4. I am using this time value so that you can see the logo scaling happen over a reasonably long duration of elapsed time.

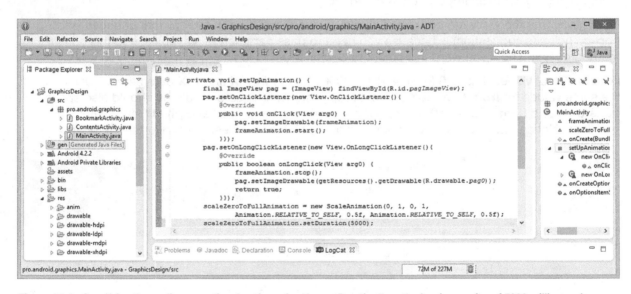

Figure 15-4. *Specifying the scaling operation duration using the .setDuration() method, using a value of 5000 milliseconds*

This next step is what throws developers for a loop (no pun intended): how exactly do you apply this procedural animation to your frame animation? The answer is by using your ImageView, as the ImageView will contain (hold) your frame animation, but you will procedurally animate that ImageView UI container itself, with the frame animation running inside it.

I think the tendency of developers in trying to solve this "animation type combination problem" would be to try to somehow reference (or wire up) the frame animation object to the procedural animation object, or vice versa.

As you can see in Figure 15-5, you've already installed your **frameAnimation AnimationDrawable** configured inside of the **pag** ImageView object using the `pag.setImageDrawable(frameAnimation)` Java code statement, so now you will utilize a **.startAnimation()** method called off the exact same pag ImageView object, wiring it up to the **scaleZeroToFullAnimation ScaleAnimation** object using the following short but critical (pivotal) Java code statement:

```
pag.startAnimation(scaleZeroToFullAnimation);
```

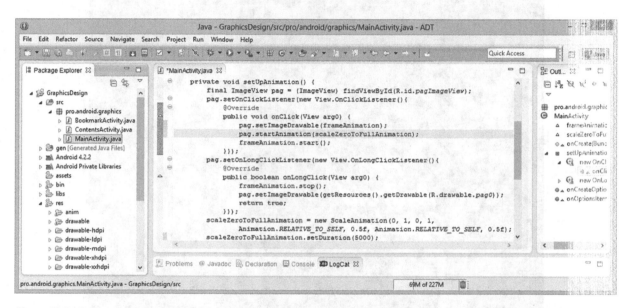

Figure 15-5. *Setting the ScaleAnimation scaleZeroToFullAnimation Animation object to scale using .startAnimation()*

As you can see in Figure 15-5, Eclipse has no problems with this code, so let's go ahead and test it, and see if you can get procedural animation to affect your frame animation using the ImageView UI element as a go-between.

Use the **Run As ➤ Android Application** work process to launch the Nexus One emulator, and run and test your application (see Figure 15-6). When you click the logo, it disappears into the distance immediately, as expected, and then animates in from your horizon, scaling up, and spinning in, exactly like it did in Chapter 4 when you implemented this cool special effect using XML markup for the most part. Here you did the entire special effect using only Java code, and you're not done yet, not by a long shot!

Figure 15-6. Testing the ScaleAnimation in the Nexus One emulator

In case you are wondering why you haven't added some of the parameters to the ScaleAnimation object that you did in Chapter 4, it is because you are going to add these to the AnimationSet later in the chapter as this is more efficient. Once you learn about those methods, you can add them to your ScaleAnimation (locally), simply by calling them off of your object's name; this can be done at the local level to fine-tune component parts of your aggregate special effect, or if all of the component parts use the same offsets and interpolators, it can all be done using the AnimationSet.

The next thing you did in Chapter 4 was to add an alpha blending effect to make this coming-in-from-the-distance special effect even more realistic. You accomplished this by additionally fading the scaling, spinning logo by using alpha blending in Android, which is also supported in the Animation classes and package, as you will see in the next two sections of the chapter.

You will bring your spinning, scaling frame and vector combination animation in from the distance more realistically by taking it from 100% transparent to being 100% opaque once it reaches a final resting place on the screen.

Let's learn about the Android AlphaAnimation class, so that you have a good technical foundation regarding the class before you implement the Java code that will fade your PAG logo into view as it emerges out of the distance.

After that you can get back into some Java coding and have some more fun with your Java-only frame animation and procedural animation combination pipeline, which you are creating using dozens of lines of dense Java code.

AlphaAnimation Class: Animation Subclass for Blending

As you know, the Android **AlphaAnimation** class is another direct subclass of the **android.view.animation.Animation** public abstract class. This animation class is used to implement alpha blending for View objects. It does this by using the alpha (transparency) values for any View object. Essentially, this makes this procedural animation class useful for fading, either in or out, and it can be used in conjunction with the other three transform types to create some pretty spectacular effects, regardless of how simple it is in and of itself.

The Android AlphaAnimation class hierarchy is structured as follows:

```
java.lang.Object
  > android.view.animation.Animation
    > android.view.animation.AlphaAnimation
```

An AlphaAnimation class is also part of the **android.view.animation** package.

Its **import statement** references your **android.view.animation.AlphaAnimation** package import path, as you'll soon see in the next section when you use it to fade in your PAG frame animation.

You are going to use an AlphaAnimation object to enhance your scale special effect even further, to make it look like the logo is coming from an even greater distance than that of the scale animation you just implemented.

The constructor method that you want to use to create your AlphaAnimation object is significantly more basic than the eight-parameter ScaleAnimation constructor method. The AlphaAnimation constructor method will take the following format, so pay attention as you will be implementing this in the next section of this chapter:

```
AlphaAnimation(float fromAlpha, float toAlpha);
```

Technically, an Alpha Channel blending operation is not usually classified as a transform type of animation, like a movement (translation), rotation, or scaling operation would be. This is especially true where 3D software packages are concerned, where object blending is handled by the application of materials and opacity texture mapping, and similar operations.

However, for some reason the Android OS groups alpha blending, which is really more of an image compositing function than a 2D transform, with the three foundational transform operations.

That said, it is very useful in conjunction with these transformational operations, and so we will cover all four in this chapter, as well as the AnimationSet grouping operation, to provide a complete overview.

Fading In Your PAG Logo: Using the AlphaAnimation Class

Let's go back into Eclipse and into your MainActivity.java editing tab and add an **Animation** object at the top of your Activity subclass, as shown in Figure 15-7. Name the object **alphaZeroToFullAnimation** and then go into the **setUpAnimation()** method you are coding and add an object instantiation for the object close to (above or below) the scaleZeroToFullAnimation object.

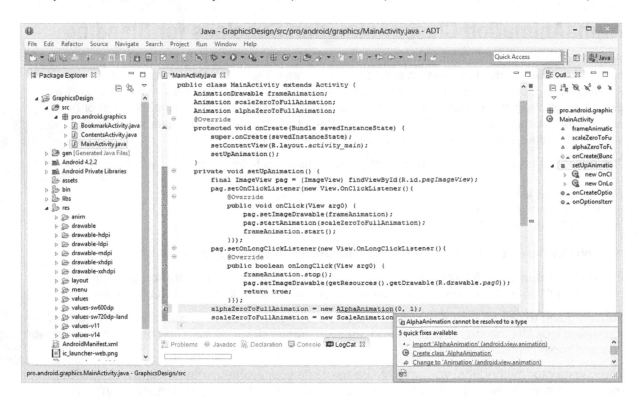

Figure 15-7. Adding an alphaZeroToFullAnimation Animation object instantiation using an AlphaAnimation() constructor

This would be identical to what you did with your scaleZeroToFullAnimation object instantiation, except using the **AlphaAnimation()** constructor method instead of the ScaleAnimation() class constructor method. The results are shown in Figure 15-7, using the following Java programming statement:

```
alphaZeroToFullAnimation = new AlphaAnimation(0, 1);
```

Note that you will have to mouse-over the new AlphaAnimation() constructor (and class) that you have invoked in your code and select the **Import Alpha Animation (android.view.animation package)** option to generate your Import statement for the class at the top of your Activity subclass code listing. That will clean all of the error flags out of your code, and you can then add a **.setDuration()** method call to set a 5 second alpha blended fade-in time.

This is done in a similar fashion to what you did with your scale animation, only using your alphaZeroToFullAnimation object, through the following code:

```
alphaZeroToFullAnimation.setDuration(5000);
```

As you can see in Figure 15-8, your Java code seems to be error-free (thus far, at least), and you are ready to attach this AlphaAnimation constructed alphaZeroToFullAnimation Animation object to your pag ImageView object.

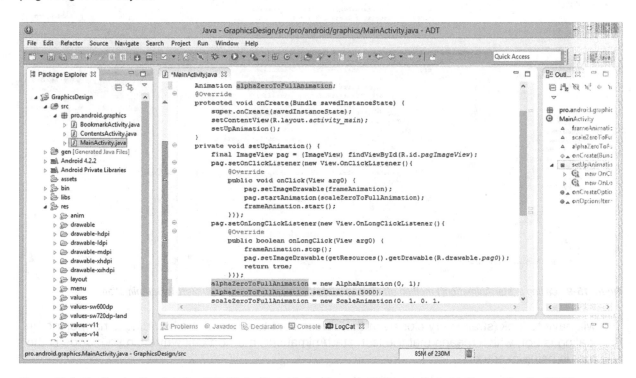

Figure 15-8. Configuring the alphaZeroToFullAnimation object with zero to 100% opacity and calling .setDuration(5000)

Now you need to go up into your onClick() event handling code construct, and add a call similar to the one that you did for the scaleZeroToFullAnimation object, using the **.startAnimation()** method called off of the pag ImageView object via the following single line of Java code:

```
pag.startAnimation(alphaZeroToFullAnimation);
```

As you can see in Figure 15-6, your code is error-free (still), and so the time has come to test your code in the Nexus One AVD emulator. It should be interesting to see if having more than one .startAnimation() method call will actually work, and if it doesn't, how it prioritizes the method calls to process (start) more than one procedural Animation object.

Use the **Run As ➤ Android Application** work process, and launch your app in the Nexus One emulator. When the logo appears, click it to start both the frame animation and the procedural animation object constructs, which you have put into place simultaneously inside your Java processing pipeline.

As you can see in Figure 15-9, I pulled this screen shot very early in the alpha blending operation so that you could observe the size (scale) of your PAG logo to ascertain if it is blending or scaling or doing both!

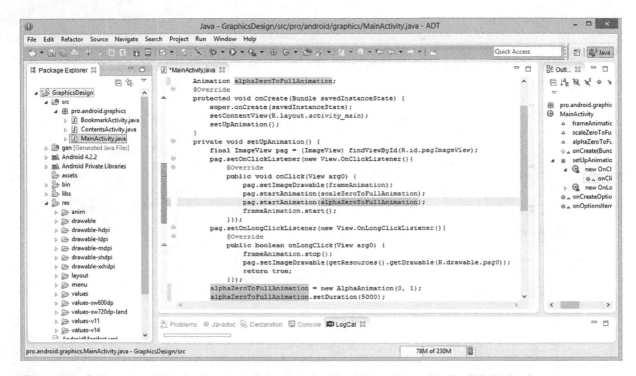

Figure 15-9. *Calling a .startAnimation() method off the pag ImageView object with an alphaZeroToFullAnimation*

You will have to look (strain) very closely at this screen shot to see that the blending is happening but the scaling is not, which means that the last .startAnimation() method call written in your code is the one that is being executed.

This either means that the ScaleAnimation object processing was skipped over or that it was started and then immediately replaced by the alpha blending operation contained in the AlphaAnimation object. Either way you slice it, you are only going to be able to make one procedural animation .startAnimation() method call, which means that you will have to implement an AnimationSet object to be able to combine procedural animation types.

This is really no surprise, but I had to try it anyway, both for my own curiosity as well as a part of the overall learning and discovery process regarding procedural and frame animation pipelines in the Android OS, and seeing exactly how far we can push these classes and methods into achieving our desired end result. Besides, this is as good a time as any to get into an AnimationSet discussion, and after we do we can get back into covering the RotateAnimation class, implementing that procedural animation object into the AnimationSet object that it looks like we're going to be implementing!

Figure 15-10. Testing the Scale and Alpha Animations in Nexus One

Since you need to implement the AnimationSet class and construct an AnimationSet object next, let's take some time to go over this class and get some technical background on what it does and why we need to use it.

The AnimationSet Class: Creating Complex Animation Sets

As you're already aware, the Android **AnimationSet** class is another direct subclass of the **android.view.animation.Animation** public abstract class.

This animation class is used to "group" your other four types of Animation subclasses into "sets" in order to create far more complex multi-transform animations for application to Android View objects.

An AnimationSet object would thus represent logical groupings of Animation subclass (ScaleAnimation, AlphaAnimation, RotateAnimation, etc.) objects, which are intended to be played together, in parallel, at the same time.

Essentially this makes this procedural animation class useful for creating complex animations which cannot be achieved using any of the other Animation subclasses individually. These four transforms are each fairly basic conceptually, but in structured combination with each other they can do almost anything that you can imagine!

The Android AnimationSet class hierarchy is structured as follows:

```
java.lang.Object
  > android.view.animation.Animation
   > android.view.animation.AnimationSet
```

The AnimationSet class is also part of the **android.view.animation** package. So its **import statement** references the **android.view.animation.AnimationSet** package import path, as you'll see in the next section when you use it to create a complex scaling and blending procedural animation set.

The procedural transformations that are specified using each individual (child) Animation object are composed together into one single unified transform by using the (parent) AnimationSet object (class).

If the AnimationSet object sets properties that its children also set (for example, duration or startOffset), values that are set for an AnimationSet parent object will always override its child Animation object values.

The way AnimationSet inherits parameters from an Animation transform, and vice versa, is important to understand. Some parameters or attributes set in an AnimationSet object will affect the entire AnimationSet object. Some parameters will be pushed down and thus applied to the child's transforms, and some are ignored. For this reason, you'll need to learn **where to apply certain parameters** when utilizing these AnimationSet objects.

The **duration**, **repeatMode**, **fillBefore**, and **fillAfter** parameters, also called **properties**, will be **pushed down** to all child transforms when they are set on an AnimationSet object. The solution to this behavior is to always set these parameters **locally**, within your Animation objects, and to **never** set these in the parent AnimationSet object. If you do this, then Android has nothing to push down, and there is no confusion as to where the parameter is going to be applied in the procedural animation processing pipeline.

The **repeatCount** and **fillEnabled** parameters, or properties, are **ignored** for an AnimationSet altogether, and thus you will always apply these parameters locally to each Animation object if you wish to access them properly.

On the other hand, the **startOffset** and **shareInterpolator** parameters can be applied to the AnimationSet object. Note that the startOffset can also be applied locally to transforms to fine-tune the timing of the animation by introducing a delay into the looping cycle or to when it starts animating.

So a good **rule of thumb** would be to apply your transformational parameters locally, rather than at the AnimationSet object level, unless it is the **shareInterpolator** parameter, which is obviously intended for usage in a group level operation, as that is the only way that we can "share" things in a procedural animation. So, **always set transform parameters locally**.

Creating an AnimationSet for Your PAG Logo Animation

Let's get back into Eclipse ADT and into your MainActivity.java editing tab and add in an AnimationSet object instantiation at the top of your Activity subclass, as shown in Figure 15-11, using the following line of Java code:

```java
AnimationSet pagAnimationSet = new AnimationSet(true);
```

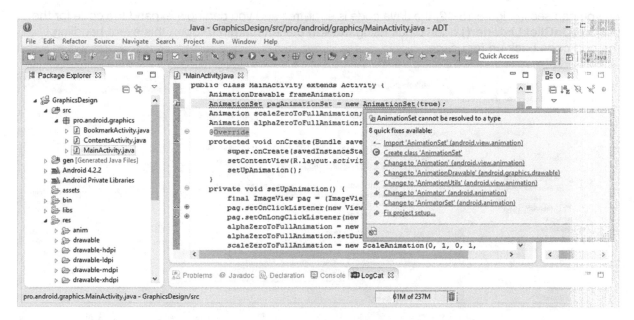

Figure 15-11.   Creating your new AnimationSet object named pagAnimationSet at the top of the MainActivity class

As you can see, you will need to mouse-over the **AnimationSet()** constructor and select the option to **Import AnimationSet (android.view.animation)**, and have the Import statement put into place for you at the top of your class.

You are going to name your AnimationSet object **pagAnimationSet** and set it to **true**, which specifies in this constructor method's parameter list that the **shareInterpolator** flag for the AnimationSet object should be set to **true**.

This shareInterpolator parameter is used to specify whether or not you wish your child Animation objects for its parent AnimationSet object to share Interpolator constants that you set for the AnimationSet object.

In your case, you do desire this since you want your scale, blend, and rotate procedural animations to act in the exact same fashion. So, you pass a true value in your constructor parameter list (item), since all the Animation child objects in this parent AnimationSet object should "share" the same Interpolator constant that you associate with this AnimationSet.

If you've used a **.setInterpolator()** method within your Animation objects, pass a **false** value instead so each Animation uses its own Interpolator.

Your next step is going to be adding your ScaleAnimation and AlphaAnimation child objects to your new parent AnimationSet object using the, you guessed it, **.addAnimation()** method call. Add two Java code statements to your Java method that call this method off of the **pagAnimationSet** object and pass in object names for each of your Animation objects, using the following code:

```
pagAnimationSet.addAnimation(scaleZeroToFullAnimation);
pagAnimationSet.addAnimation(alphaZeroToFullAnimation);
```

As you can see in Figure 15-12, the Java code is error-free and you can now expand the code for the **pag.setOnClickListener()** code block using the **+** in the left margin to open this event handling method code back up for usage.

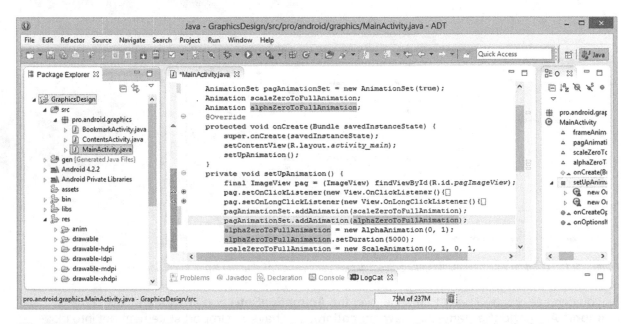

Figure 15-12.   Using .addAnimation() method to add ScaleAnimation and AlphaAnimation objects to AnimationSet

Let's remove the second **.startAnimation()** method call and change the first one to reference your new parent pagAnimationSet object instead. This will allow you to "wire up" your two ScaleAnimation and AlphaAnimation objects into one AnimationSet object construct that can then be called using a single **.startAnimation()** method call, as shown in Figure 15-13.

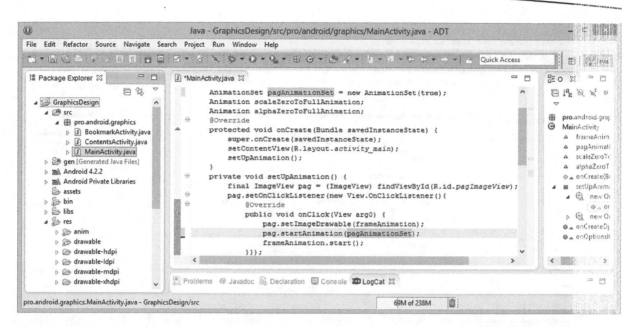

Figure 15-13. Changing the .startAnimation() method called off the pag ImageView object to reference pagAnimationSet

Now you are again ready to test your application using the **Run As ➤ Android Application** work process to launch the Nexus One emulator; let's see what happens! This application, as coded currently, crashes the emulator!

Eclipse is not finding any syntax errors in the code, but let's see if we can ascertain what might be going on by looking closely at the Animation processing pipeline. The only possible issue I can see is that you're adding your child Animation objects to your parent AnimationSet object **before** they have been initialized using the **new** keyword and their constructor methods.

So let's first try to cut and paste the two lines of code that call the **.addAnimation()** method off of your **pagAnimationSet** AnimationSet object, and relocate them right underneath (after) your four lines of Java code which instantiate and configure your ScaleAnimation and AlphaAnimation objects.

If this turns out to be the problem, then this reinforces the factor of **code order** being as important as having correct Java code statements in the first place. In order to produce a correct object and event processing pipeline, you must have both the correct Java code and the correct Java code processing order.

As you can see in Figure 15-14, Eclipse is still deeming your Java code to be error-free, so let's again test your Java code in the Nexus One emulator and try to get your GraphicsDesign application working again!

Figure 15-14. Moving the .addAnimation() method calls after AlphaAnimation and ScaleAnimation instantiations

Use the **Run As ➤ Android Application** work process to launch the Nexus One emulator, and click the PAG logo once it appears to set it into motion.

This application, as coded currently, now works, and your scale and blend animations implemented via an AnimationSet object work quite well together!

Now that you have implemented the basic scaling and blending animations, it is time to add in your other options, which will allow you to control the **type of motion** and the **initial timing** for the AnimationSet that you have now successfully created (and debugged).

You will begin with the method call that allows you to fine-tune the **start timing** of your Animation object, or AnimationSet object, depending on what object you call it from by using dot notation.

This method call is called the **.setStartOffset()** method call, and it takes an **integer milliseconds** value. Since we really don't require a StartOffset for the AnimationSet object, I'll include it here by using an insignificant quarter-second (or 250 milliseconds) parameter value, just to show you how to implement this in your Java code.

Let's attach a **.setStartOffset(250)** method call off of your **pagAnimationSet** object by using the following basic Java programming statement:

```
pagAnimationSet.setStartOffset(250);
```

As you can see in Figure 15-15, the code is error-free, and you are ready to add other AnimationSet parameters to this AnimationSet object, such as the **Acceleration** Motion Interpolator constant, which you are going to add next.

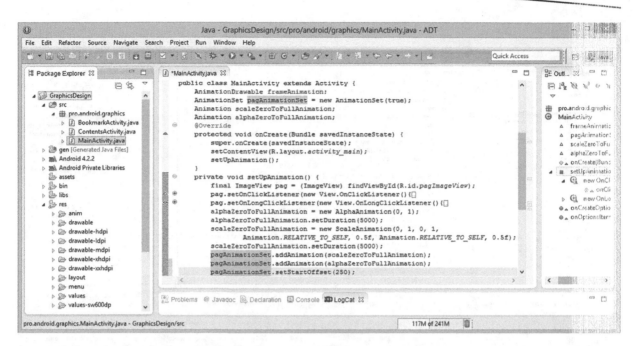

Figure 15-15. Adding an animation StartOffset to the pagAnimationSet object, using the .setStartOffset() method

If you like, you can use the **Run As ➤ Android Application** work process to make sure the code runs at this juncture and does not crash the Nexus One emulator. However, it is doubtful that you will be able to visualize this quarter-second startOffset delay as scale and blend settings are initially set at zero, so a startOffset value would only be useful for fine-tuning.

Now it's time to add an **ACCELERATE** Interpolator constant, which in Java is done via the **AccelerateInterpolator** class and its **AccelerateInterpolator()** constructor method call.

You will call the AccelerateInterpolator object, and construct it using the same line of code, by first calling the **.setInterpolator()** method off of your **pagAnimationSet** AnimationSet object and then utilizing the **new** keyword inside of this method call with your **AccelerateInterpolator()** constructor method call, which will all be accomplished using the following Java code:

```
pagAnimationSet.setInterpolator( new AccelerateInterpolator() );
```

I spaced the Java code statement inside the method call parameter area out a bit using a couple of space characters on each end to make it more readable. This will not affect the compilation of the Java statement, but I have left the more compact version in the screen shot.

You can see the Java code in Figure 15-16, and you will notice that your method call to the AccelerateInterpolator class constructor method will require that you add an Import statement at the top of your MainActivity class.

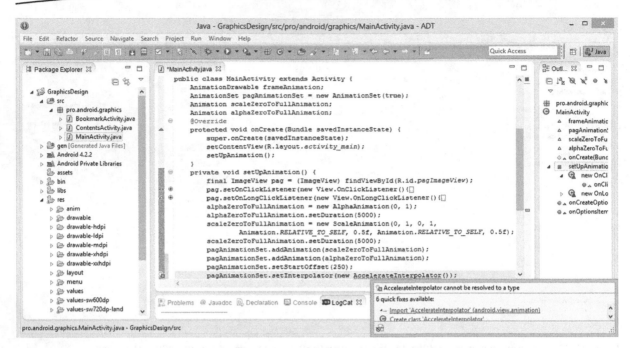

Figure 15-16. Adding an animation AccelerateInterpolator to the pagAnimationSet object using the .setInterpolator() method

This is indicated to you, as usual, by Eclipse ADT using a wavy red error underlining indicator. If you mouse-over the **AccelerateInterpolator** class and constructor method, and select the first option, Eclipse will install this **Import android.view.animation.AccelerateInterpolator** Java statement for you automatically.

When you use the **Run As ➤ Android Application** work process and test your code using the Nexus One emulator, it works perfectly, as shown in Figure 15-17.

Figure 15-17. Testing your AnimationSet in the Nexus One AVD

RotateAnimation Class: Animation Subclass for Rotation

As mentioned in the chapter introduction, an Android **RotateAnimation** class is yet another direct subclass of the **android.view.animation.Animation** public abstract class. The Android RotateAnimation Java class hierarchy is structured as follows:

```
java.lang.Object
  > android.view.animation.Animation
    > android.view.animation.RotateAnimation
```

The RotateAnimation class is a part of the **android.view.animation** package.

Its **import statement** references the **android.view.animation.RotateAnimation** package import path, as you'll see in the next section when you use it to rotate your PAG frame animation, as it also scales and fades into view. This animation class is utilized to implement 2D rotation of View objects.

This rotation will take place in an X-Y plane. This technically means that the rotation is taking place around the **Z axis**. In 3D, there are three axes including the normal X (left to right) axis and Y (top to bottom) axis you find in 2D, as well as a Z axis that is represented by a line coming out of the intersection of the X and Y axes, towards (and away from) your screen (or towards and away from your viewer).

So technically the RotateAnimation object is implementing Z-axis rotation, around (using) a pivot point **origin**, which is set by the developer using X and Y coordinates, as you will see firsthand in the next section.

Besides the **pivot point origin** around which your View object will rotate, you must also specify your amount of rotation using a **range**, which starts with the degrees to **rotate from**, usually zero or "normal" View positioning, and ends with the degrees to **rotate to**, such as 90 degrees (clockwise), or -90 degrees (counter-clockwise), or 180 degrees (upside down), or, in your case, 360 degrees, or a full seamless View object (ImageView) rotation.

The RotateAnimation procedural animation class is thus useful for rotating Views as well as flipping them on their sides or upside down, which can be done quickly if that effect is desired by using a short duration value.

This RotateAnimation procedural animation class can be used in conjunction with the other three procedural animation object types to create extremely impressive special effects, regardless of how simple this class may seem to be when it is standing (used) alone.

The constructor method that you want to use to create the RotateAnimation object is similar to the eight-parameter ScaleAnimation constructor method that you have already implemented. RotateAnimation constructor methods will leverage the following advanced rotation specification format in your app:

```
RotateAnimation(float fromDegrees, float toDegrees, int pivotXType, float pivotXValue, int
pivotYType, float pivotYValue);
```

Rotating Your PAG Logo: Using the RotateAnimation Class

Finally, it is time to add your RotateAnimation object, and finish off the Java version of the animation you implemented via XML markup in Chapter 4.

Open up Eclipse and the MainActivity.java editing tab and add an Animation object declaration at the top, right after your scale and alpha Animation objects, and name it **rotateZeroToFullAnimation**, as shown in Figure 15-18.

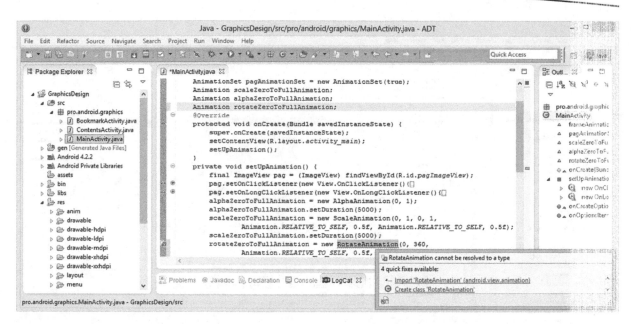

Figure 15-18. Adding rotateZeroToFullAnimation Animation object declaration and new RotateAnimation() constructor

Next, close up your event listener code blocks so that you can see all your instantiation code, which is shown at the bottom of Figure 15-18, and add in the RotateAnimation object instantiation using the following Java code:

```
rotateZeroToFullAnimation = new RotateAnimation(0, 360, Animation.RELATIVE_TO_SELF, 0.5f,
Animation.RELATIVE_TO_SELF, 0.5f);
```

The next thing that you need to do is to call the **.setDuration()** method off of the **rotateZeroToFullAnimation** object, now that it is initialized, and pass it a value of **5000** milliseconds (5 seconds) using the following code:

```
rotateZeroToFullAnimation.setDuration(5000);
```

Finally, you need to add this **rotateZeroToFullAnimation** Animation object to the **pagAnimationSet** AnimationSet object, using the **.addAnimation()** method, by using the following single line of Java code, as shown in Figure 15-19:

```
pagAnimationSet.addAnimation(rotateZeroToFullAnimation);
```

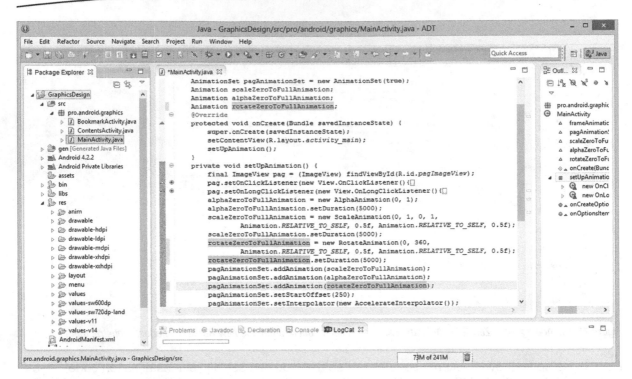

Figure 15-19. Configuring RotationAnimation with duration, degrees and pivot and adding to AnimationSet with .addAnimation()

Since all of your offset timing and motion interpolation parameters are set at the parent AnimationSet object level, you do not need to worry about any of those global parameters, which is one of the advantages to creating an advanced AnimationSet procedural animation pipeline, as you can see here.

Now it is time to test your AnimationSet object procedural animation and see if it works and if you have replicated everything that you did in Chapter 3 and Chapter 4—but now using only Java code.

Use the **Run As ➤ Android Application** work process to run the Nexus One AVD emulator, and click your PAG logo, and watch it spin, fade, rotate, and scale in from the distance, as shown in Figure 15-20.

Figure 15-20. Testing your pagAnimationSet in a Nexus One emulator

You have implemented the same XML tags and parameters that you did using markup in the earlier chapters in the book, which showed you the easier way to implement frame and procedural animation (together), by using only Java code constructs to create your View Animation object pipeline.

Now you have a pretty good introduction to many of the Drawable object types in Android, so in the next chapter I want to go back to the drawing board (Drawable board, no pun intended) and take another closer look at the foundational Drawable class, so that some more light bulbs go off in your head, because that is really what this book is all about, isn't it?

I sure hope so! Great job implementing frame and procedural animation!

Next, I'm going to give you a couple of things to try on your own, things we have done already, so it will just be repetition for the sake of experience to get you familiar with all of the classes and methods that you have been learning about in this book.

Using an Android Runnable Class to Run the AnimationSet

In the previous chapter, you utilized the Java **Runnable** public interface and its **run()** method to run your AnimationDrawable in a separate thread. You coded the method so that your app could process frame animation Drawable objects (BitmapDrawable frames, in that case) asynchronously.

For practice, what I want you to do now is comment out your event handling methods, and re-implement your **animStarter** class implementing the **Runnable** public Java interface and the **run()** method, and install the code that's in your onClick() event handler to automatically start both the frame and the procedural animations when your application launches. Don't forget to put your **.setImageDrawable()** method call back where you had it in Chapter 14!

Creating a TranslateAnimation Object for Your AnimationSet

The one other thing that I want you to play around with is adding a move component to the current AnimationSet object that starts your animation higher up on the screen and moves it down the Y axis as the scale and fade occur to make the animation look like it is coming down out of the sky.

To do this, you would declare an Animation object named **translateSkyToZero** at the top of your class, as you did with the other transformation objects, and then initialize the object using the **new** keyword and configure a list of parameters using the constructor method, just as you did with the other three Animation subclass objects and in the same location in your code.

Make sure to add the new TranslateAnimation object into your AnimationSet object using the **.addAnimation()** method call and **translateSkyToZero** value to pass that new Animation object into the method as a parameter, which will add it into the AnimationSet (group) object complex animation definition.

Finally, experiment with calling some of the other parameter method calls off of your AnimationSet object once your TranslateAnimation object has been added (wired up) to it! Some of the parameter methods that we did not specifically declare (use) because we were relying on their default values include the **.setRepeatMode()** or **.setRepeatCount()** methods that you learned about and implemented back in Chapter 4.

Summary

In this fifteenth chapter, you learned how to use only Java code, and no XML markup, to implement a splash screen procedural animation in Android OS by using methods and constructors from the **Animation** class and its five subclasses: **ScaleAnimation**, **AlphaAnimation**, **AnimationSet**, **RotateAnimation**, and **TranslateAnimation**.

We started out by looking at Android's **Animation** class itself, and how it is a direct subclass of the **java.lang.Object** master class, which means it was essentially written from scratch to provide view animation, or vector animation, also known as procedural animation, to the Android OS.

Next, we looked at the TranslateAnimation subclass and how it allows us to move View objects in an animated fashion around the X-Y screen space. We then looked at the ScaleAnimation subclass and how it allows us to scale a View objects within this X-Y 2D screen dimension, and we looked at how the constructor methods for both of these procedural animation classes work.

Next, you jumped right into your Java coding by implementing a ScaleAnimation object in your GraphicDesign application to see how Animation objects and their transform subclasses work together in your Java coding environment.

You then learned about the AlphaAnimation class and how it allows us to add alpha blending to our procedural animation bag of tricks. You also learned how to use a relatively simple constructor method to implement fade-in or fade-out effects to a View object (in your case an ImageView), thereby animating it.

Then, you again dove back into your Java coding and added another Animation object to define your AlphaAnimation objectives, and attempted to implement two serial calls to the **.startAnimation()** method, which failed, forcing you to then learn about the Android AnimationSet class, which turned out to be a really positive experience. Peace, Love, and AnimationSet, man (or woman)!

After we reviewed the AnimationSet class particulars, we got right back in Eclipse ADT, and you started implementing even more advanced Java procedural animation programming. You created an AnimationSet animation group pipeline to implement complex procedural animation, and you did this using only Java programming logic.

Once you had your AnimationSet working, it was much easier to add a rotation to your animation set by using the RotateAnimation class and constructor method, and then adding it into your AnimationSet using the **.addAnimation()** method call. By this time, you were getting pretty good at using Animation class and its functional subclasses inside your Android application.

Finally, you implemented that exact same frame and procedural animation combination sequence using Java, which you had implemented using XML back in Chapters 3 and 4. At this point I suggested (for practice) trying to add a TranslationAnimation object to your AnimationSet and trying to make an app auto-start logo animation by re-implementing your animStarter class.

In the next chapter, we'll focus on gaining a more advanced understanding of the Android **Drawable** class, now that you have learned about and utilized many of its subclasses to implement animation and blending and other very advanced graphics-related Android programming gymnastics. This will allow you to "finish off" your comprehension of Drawable classes and objects in Android, which are the cornerstone of graphics design and implementation within the Android operating system, and thus very important.

Chapter 16

Advanced Graphics: Mastering the Drawable Class

In this sixteenth chapter, we will take a lower-level look at the **Drawable** class within the Android OS, as it provides a foundation for all graphics-related objects in the operating system.

Now that you've had some deep experience with, and exposure to, a variety of advanced Drawable object types in Android, it's time for us to examine the base class that these came from, and to take a look at some of the other types of Drawable objects that are available to you in Android OS.

Many of these different types of Drawables, such as the Shape Drawable, we simply have not had a compelling reason to cover as of yet. This is mainly due to the fact that digital images, digital video, 2D animation, blending, and transitions are more in-demand topics for you, the reader, than topics such as vector illustration (shapes), fonts (text objects), or gradients. Still, vector illustration is a popular topic, so we'll cover it in this chapter.

So, never fear, we'll get around to it all, and that is one of the reasons that I was sure to include a chapter on Android's Drawable class, so that I could be sure to cover all of the different types of Drawable subclasses and objects, as they all can affect graphics design in one way or another.

You will also be learning about several other important Android classes in this chapter that directly relate to professional Android graphics design, classes that are used with the Drawable class and its many subclasses. These include Android's **Shader** and **BitmapShader** classes, **Rect** and **RectF** classes, the **InputStream** class, and the **ShapeDrawable** class. You will also reinforce your usage and knowledge of the **Bitmap**, **Paint**, and **Canvas** classes as well.

Android Drawable Resources: Types of Drawable Objects

Android has over one dozen different types of Drawable Resources that you can apply to the Android application graphics design pipeline. You already have leveraged a significant number of these more advanced Drawable object types at this juncture of the book, so we will just make sure you're aware of everything that is available in Android, where Drawables are concerned.

Android Drawable Resources are a foundational concept for a graphic that can be drawn to your user's display screen and that you can retrieve with method calls such as **.getDrawable()** or apply using an XML definition along with parameters like , **android:iconandroid:background**, or **android:src**.

There are a number of different Drawable object types in Android including **Bitmap**, **9-Patch**, **Layer**, **State**, **Level**, **Animation**, **Transition**, **Shape**, **Scale**, **Rotate**, **Inset**, **Clip**, **Picture**, **Paint**, and **Color**, just to name a few.

We will go over each of these primary types of Drawable objects in Android and see exactly what they are and what they do, during this first overview section for this chapter. We're doing this so that you will have a broader perspective regarding what is available for you in Android as a professional graphics designer. We'll cover the Drawable types you've already utilized first, and then introduce you to some new and exciting Drawables after that.

A **BitmapDrawable** uses a digital image asset, either a **PNG**, **JPG**, or **GIF**, to populate a Drawable object with an array of pixels, called a Bitmap. You've already seen how to cast Drawables to BitmapDrawables and more during your construction of an image compositing and blending pipeline in Chapter 11.

As you saw in Chapter 10, **NinePatchDrawable** objects leverage a **PNG32** image file format, and customize it using one-pixel black border areas to create scalable X and/or Y regions to allow dynamic image resizing in either an X or Y dimension based on the image asset content design. A NinePatch object image asset uses a special file name designation of **thefilename.9.png**, and can also use **PNG24** (truecolor, no alpha channel) and **PNG8** (indexed color).

As you saw in Chapter 12, **LayerDrawable** objects allow collections of other types of Drawable objects, which can be used for layered compositing. These Drawable objects are drawn using the LayerDrawable object's array order so that the child layer element with the largest index will be drawn on top.

As you saw in Chapter 13, **TransitionDrawable** objects are typically defined using an XML file that allows a cross-fade to take place between two Drawable asset resources.

As you saw in Chapter 14 and Chapter 3, **AnimationDrawable** objects can be used either via XML markup or Java code to define a series of frames that play back as specified by the developer using parameters to form 2D frame animation assets. AnimationDrawable objects can be further processed using Animation objects, which will apply vector (algorithmic) transformations.

A **StateListDrawable** is also usually defined using an XML definition file that references a series of bitmap graphic image assets that highlight different functional states. You utilized states back in Chapter 9 when you created a multi-state ImageButton UI element that implements a different image for each button state, such as when a button is hovered over, or is pressed, or has the focus.

A **LevelListDrawable** is usually defined using an XML file that inflates a Drawable object that manages a number of alternate Drawable objects, each assigned a minimum and a maximum numerical value utilized at runtime to ascertain what level the LevelListDrawable currently references.

The **InsetDrawable** object is defined using an XML definition file that defines a Drawable XML asset that creates an inset within another Drawable object at a specified DIP distance. This is useful when your View object needs a background Drawable that is smaller than your View object's actual boundaries.

A **ClipDrawable** object is defined using an XML file that defines a Drawable object that implements a clipping plane or region on another Drawable that is based on your ClipDrawable object's current level values. This is often utilized to create special effects, or utilities, such as a progress bar.

A **ScaleDrawable** object is also defined using an XML definition file that specifies a Drawable object that changes the scaling of another Drawable object based on the current level value of the ScaleDrawable object.

A **ShapeDrawable** object is defined via an XML file that defines a geometric shape. The shape definition can also include other nested shapes, borders, colors, or color gradients. The ShapeDrawable object essentially gives the Android OS many of the vector capabilities found in software packages such as Freehand, Illustrator, or InkScape.

We are going to cover Shape and ShapeDrawable objects in the next sections of this chapter, as digital illustration is a popular topic in new media.

It's important to note, before we get into ShapeDrawable objects, that any of your Color Resources, usually defined in your Colors.xml file, can also be used as a Drawable object by using referencing inside XML definitions.

To give an example, when creating your StateListDrawable object, you could reference a color resource for the android:drawable attribute, which makes it a Color Drawable asset of sorts. This would be done using the following parameter in your View object tag inside your XML markup:

```
android:drawable="@color/green"
```

Next, let's take a look at how to create vector illustration in Android by using XML markup and the **<shape>** root element to create the ShapeDrawable object. Once you've created your own vector illustrations in Android, we'll take a look at the Shape and ShapeDrawable classes in Android in greater detail. Since we covered vector animation in the previous chapter, it is only logical that we cover **static vector imagery** as well in this chapter.

Creating a ShapeDrawable Object: XML <shape> Parent Tag

Let's fire up Eclipse again, or if it is open on your desktop already, you can simply right-click your GraphicsDesign **/res/drawable** folder. Select the **New ➤ Android XML File** menu command sequence, as shown in Figure 16-1.

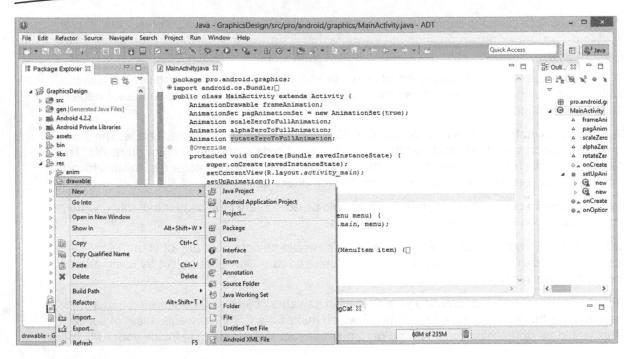

Figure 16-1. *Creating a New* ➤ *Android XML File so that you can create a ShapeDrawable object XML definition*

In the New Android XML File dialog, shown in Figure 16-2, name the file **contents_shape**, and then select the **<shape>** root element, which makes this a **ShapeDrawable XML** definition file. Notice that since you clicked on the /res/drawable folder in your GraphicsDesign project, Eclipse was able to infer these first two **Resource Type** and **Project** setting fields for you. When you are finished, select the **Finish** button in order to create your ShapeDrawable XML definition file.

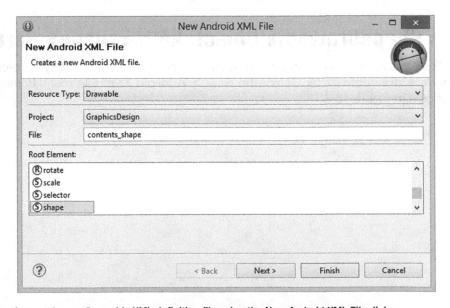

Figure 16-2. *Creating a <shape> Drawable XML definition file using the New Android XML File dialog*

Once the ShapeDrawable XML definition file opens up in the central editing pane of Eclipse, put your cursor at the end of the **xmlns:android** parameter, and press the **return** key, and type **android**, and then press the **colon** key to pop up the helper dialog that contains all of the parameters that can be used with this tag, as shown in Figure 16-3. Select the **android:shape** option, which allows you to define the shape, and double-click it, which will add it as a parameter for your **<shape>** parent tag.

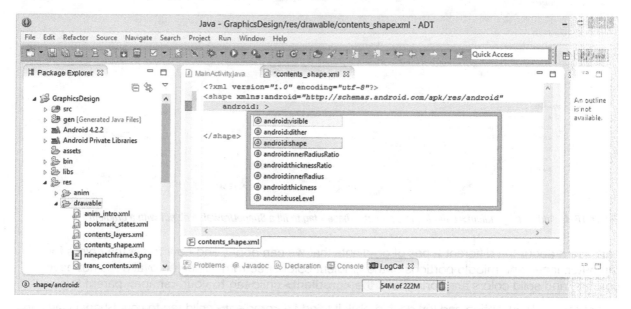

Figure 16-3. Adding an android:shape parameter to define what shape you want your ShapeDrawable to utilize

When the parameter appears, add a shape type of oval inside the quotation marks. Next, put your cursor inside your <shape> parent tag container, or on the line of space that's underneath the "end" chevron of the opening <shape> tag, where you can start working on adding nested, or child, tags.

Add a left facing < chevron character to call up the Eclipse helper dialog that contains all of the child tags available for use with a <shape> root element, as shown in Figure 16-4.

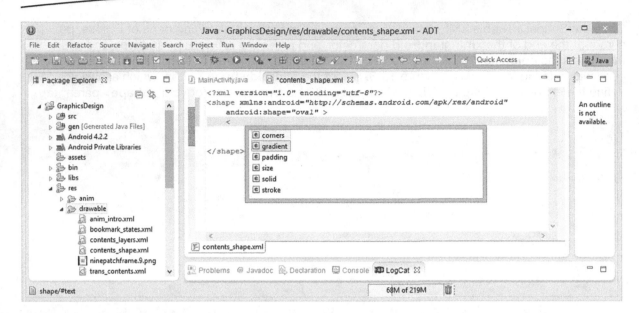

Figure 16-4. Adding a <gradient> child tag to a parent <shape> tag to fill a ShapeDrawable object with a gradient

Let's learn about the different types of gradients that we can apply, and how to set the colors for the outer, inner, and middle portions of the gradient color spectrum. Since an oval does not have corners, and solid colors are boring, add the **<gradient>** child tag to your <shape> parent tag.

Select the gradient option and (or) double-click it to add a <gradient> child tag to your ShapeDrawable XML definition. You will notice that only the **<gradient** portion of the child tag is added, so you must complete the container for Eclipse by adding a space and then a **/>** closing tag portion.

Once this is done, you can place your cursor after your **<gradient** opening tag and press the return key to access the **auto-indent** feature of Eclipse.

Type in the word **android** and hit the **colon** key to bring up the list of the parameters that we can use with the <gradient> tag. As you can see, there are nine of them, seven of which you will use before you are done with this section. Double-click the **android:startColor** parameter, which will add it into your <gradient> tag, as shown in Figure 16-5, and you will start the process of configuring the gradient for your oval ShapeDrawable object.

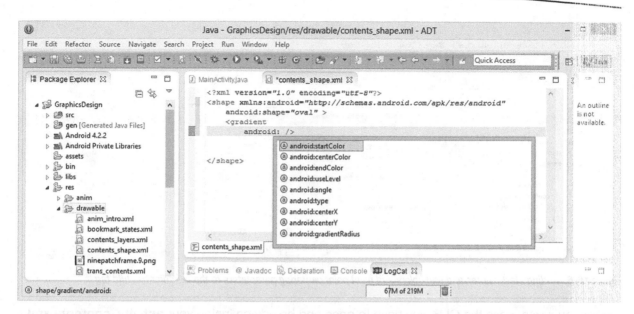

Figure 16-5. Using the android: work process to bring up all of the parameter options for the <gradient> tag

Set a hexadecimal color value of **100% red** channel using **#FF0000** in the **android:startColor** parameter, and use **100% yellow** (red plus green) for the **android:centerColor** parameter using the hexadecimal value **#FFFF00**. For the **android:endColor**, use a **100% green** hexadecimal color value, or **#00FF00**, so that you're using colors that will blend well in your gradient.

Next, let's specify the pivot point, or a center point as it is called with a gradient, using the **android:centerX** and **android:centerY** parameter both set to the **exact middle (50%)** of the shape, by using float values of **0.5**.

When you are done adding these five parameters, the XML definition for the **oval Shape** with a **linear (default)** gradient of red, yellow, and green color values will look exactly like this following block of XML markup:

```
<? xml version="1.0" encoding="utf-8" ?>
<shape xmlns:android=http://schemas.android.com/apk/res/android
    android:shape="oval" >
    <gradient
        android:startColor="#FF0000"
        android:centerColor="#FFFF00"
        android:endColor="#00FF00"
        android:centerX="0.5"
        android:centerY="0.5" />
</shape>
```

As you can see in Figure 16-6, the markup is error- and warning-free, and you are ready to test your ShapeDrawable definition using the Graphical Layout Editor pane inside the Eclipse ADT.

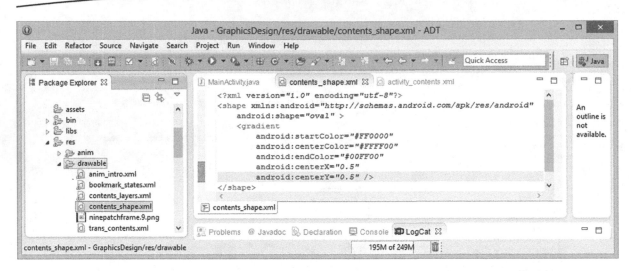

Figure 16-6. Adding start, center, and end colors and pivot point centering parameters to the <gradient> child tag

Before you can access the GLE, you have to open and be editing inside your **activity_contents.xml** definition tab, so right-click that file in your **/res/layout** folder and select the **Open** option, or click that tab at the top of the Eclipse central editing area if it is already open in your IDE.

Since your ShapeDrawable is not currently being referenced by the ImageView UI element in your layout container definition, you will need to change your NinePatchDrawable reference to instead point to your new ShapeDrawable XML definition file. This is done by changing your **android:src** parameter to a value of **@drawable/contents_shape** by using the following XML markup:

```
android:src="@drawable/contents_shape"
```

You can leave your android:background parameter configured the way that it is currently, so that you can see how Android **anti-aliases** (pixel smoothes) its vector artwork when bitmap assets are in use in the background plate.

As you can see in Figure 16-7, your ImageView user interface object is now referencing two different types of Drawable Resources, a ShapeDrawable and a TransitionDrawable. Both of your Drawable Resources are using XML markup to define their image assets, and thus you are not referencing any of your image assets (directly) in your ImageView UI element anymore, although you are referencing them inside your TransitionDrawable object XML definition.

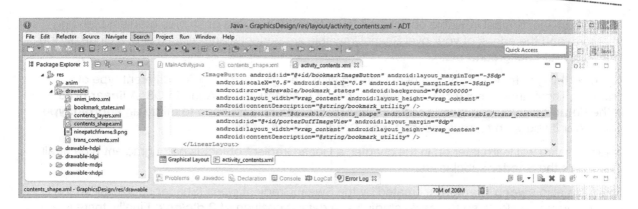

Figure 16-7. Editing activity_contents.xml UI definition to change your <ImageView> tag to reference contents_shape

In fact, if you wanted to see the TransitionDrawable that you created back in Chapter 13 provide an image transition behind your ShapeDrawable vector illustration, you could use the **Run As ➤ Android Application** work process at any time during this process and check the results out for yourself. I am not going to waste any time doing that now, as we have a lot to cover in this chapter, but it might be fun for you to do, both to get some more practice with using the AVD emulator and to see what a great job Android does in compositing Bitmap (Transition Drawable) and Vector (Shape Drawable) graphics design elements. You will be pleased with the results!

Once you have reconfigured your ImageView source image parameter, click your **Graphical Layout Editor** tab, as shown in Figure 16-8, so you can review the results of your ShapeDrawable object's XML definition thus far.

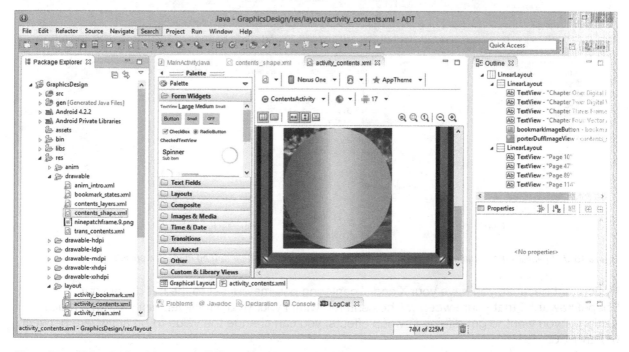

Figure 16-8. Using the Graphical Layout Editor to preview your oval ShapeDrawable and linear gradient settings

As you can see, ShapeDrawable objects render in the GLE and you get a nice gradient blending of colors, and the edges of your oval ShapeDrawable are perfectly anti-aliased with a cloudsky.jpg image in your background plate.

The next thing to try while you are here working with the <gradient> tag is a different type of gradient. There are currently three different types of gradients in the Android OS. A **linear gradient** is the **default**, as you can clearly see in Figure 16-8, so there is no need to utilize an **android:type** parameter if you wish to implement a **LinearGradient** gradient type.

In fact, as you will learn later on in the chapter, a LinearGradient object is not a gradient type at all; it is one of the **Shader** subclasses.

There are also **sweep gradients**, created by the SweepGradient class (Shader subclass), which sweeps around a clock, so to speak, starting at a default position of **3 o'clock**. Finally, there is a **RadialGradient class**, and this gradient starts at the center of the ShapeDrawable and radiates outwards.

It is important to note that if the center of your ShapeDrawable, as specified by the **android:centerX** and **android:centerY** parameters, is not set using the value of **0.5** (or 50%), the radial gradient will emanate from wherever you have set your centering X and Y coordinates and radiate outward from that point. This gives you a lot of control over placing your radial gradient and thus over the types of special effects you can create.

Let's add an **android:type** parameter and set it to a value of **sweep**, as shown in Figure 16-9, in order to see what different gradient effects this setting, and its various constants, will have on your ShapeDrawable object.

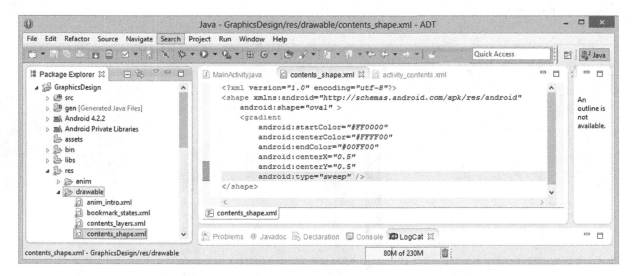

Figure 16-9. Changing the <gradient> type via android:type from the default linear setting to the sweep setting

Notice that because you have your X and Y centering parameters set to the middle of your ShapeDrawable, that your sweep will be centered within your oval. However, just as with a radial setting, if you want to get different sweep effects, you can change the value to be anywhere between 0.0 and 1.0.

After you've made your android:type="sweep" parameter addition, click back over to activate your activity_contents.xml editing tab, and then click the Graphical Layout Editor tab at the bottom in order to preview your new ShapeDrawable object with the sweep gradient type displayed inside it, as shown in Figure 16-10.

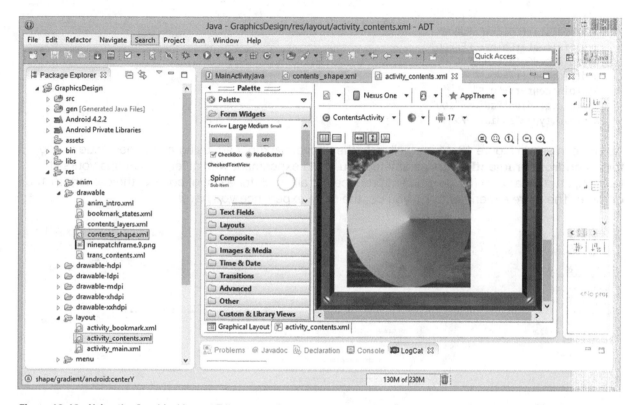

Figure 16-10. Using the Graphical Layout Editor to preview your oval ShapeDrawable and sweep gradient settings

Finally, you will try to implement the **radial constant** for the android:type parameter and generate a radial gradient, so that you can visualize exactly what this type of gradient effect looks like, and provides, for your vector illustration pipeline in Android. Remember, a radial android:type constant is actually referencing an Android **RadialGradient** class, which is a Shader subclass. You'll be learning about the Shader class and subclasses later.

There is one related parameter that you will need to add in when using the android:type="radial" parameter. The parameter is an **android:gradientRadius** parameter, which specifies a **radius** for the radial gradient. It's just not that surprising that your radial gradient needs its radius to be specified!

As I found out the hard way, Eclipse will throw an error (and not a pretty highlighted one, either) if you attempt to use the radial type of gradient without first installing this **android:gradientRadius** parameter.

Later, if you like, you can remove this parameter, if you are the curious type, and use the **CRTL-S** keystroke combination to save your XML markup so that Eclipse will evaluate it. This will provide you with these error messages, inside an **Error Log** tab located at the bottom of your IDE.

So let's add in the two parameters now that you will need to implement a radial gradient inside your ShapeDrawable object, a gradient radius by using the **android:gradientRadius** parameter, and the radial gradient by using the `android:type="radial"` parameter, using the following gradient XML markup:

```
<gradient
    android:startColor="FF0000"
    android:centerColor="FFFF00"
    android:endColor="00FF00"
    android:centerX="0.5"
    android:centerY="0.5"
    android:gradientRadius="100"
    android:type="radial" />
```

As you can see in Figure 16-11, as well as in the above markup, I am using an integer value of 100 for my **android:gradientRadius** parameter. You could experiment with different settings yourself later on, starting at zero (for no gradient produced at all), to 5 (for a dot of color at the center), to 100 or more. The more experimentation you do, the more experience you have!

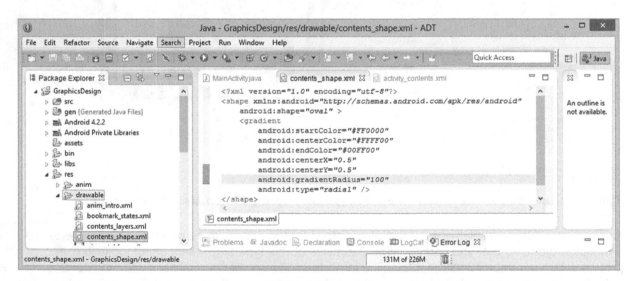

Figure 16-11. Adding an android:gradientRadius parameter so that you can implement an android:type="radial"

An android:gradientRadius parameter setting of 100 will produce the radial gradient three color stratification shown in Figure 16-12, where approximately 35% of your radial gradient is red, 15% is yellow, and 50% of the radial gradient is green. Higher numbers will yield more red color.

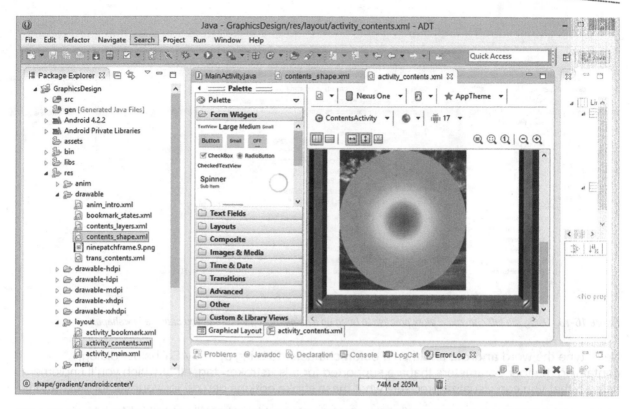

Figure 16-12. Using the Graphical Layout Editor to preview your oval ShapeDrawable and radial gradient settings

Click your activity_contents.xml tab at the top of Eclipse and then click a Graphical Layout tab at the bottom to see a result, shown in Figure 16-12.

Next, you are going to add another child tag attribute, a stroke tag, to your ShapeDrawable to add some detail to the **perimeter** of this ShapeDrawable.

To do this, use the left chevron < work process, as shown in Figure 16-13, to bring up the helper dialog with all of the child tag options in it, and select the **stroke** tag option at the bottom, and (or) double-click it to insert the **<stroke>** child tag.

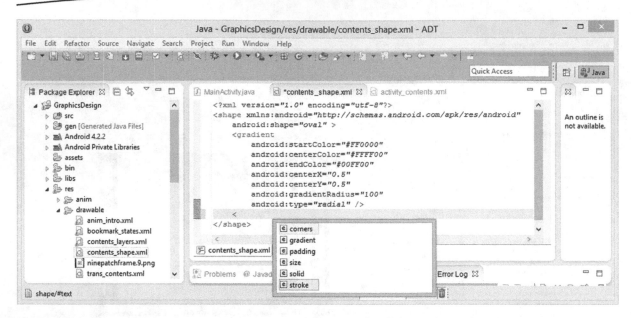

Figure 16-13. Using the left chevron < work process to bring up a helper dialog with tags you can use in <shape>

Next, type the word **android** and then a **colon** character to bring up the ADT helper dialog, containing the four parameters that are supported for this <stroke> tag, all of which you'll implement here so that you can visualize precisely what these stroke options can do for your vector illustrations.

The **android:color** parameter specifies the **stroke color**, which you will set to be black to give you a nice dark border; the **android:width** parameter specifies the **thickness of the stroke** around the perimeter. I will utilize a setting of **5 DIP** so that the stroke around the oval is highly visible.

The last two parameters allow you to add **dashed line effects**, which you'll use to make the perimeter of your radial gradient oval look like it is a gear. The **android:dashWidth** defines the **width** of the dashes, which I set to a value of **4 DIP**, and the **android:dashGap** defines how much **gap** (space) is between each dash. I used a value of **3 DIP** for my dashGap parameter.

```
<stroke
    android:color="#000000"
    android:width="5dip"
    android:dashWidth="4dip"
    android:dashGap="3dip"  />
```

As you can see in Figure 16-14, you have utilized all four of the <stroke> parameters, and your XML markup is evaluating as error- and warning-free.

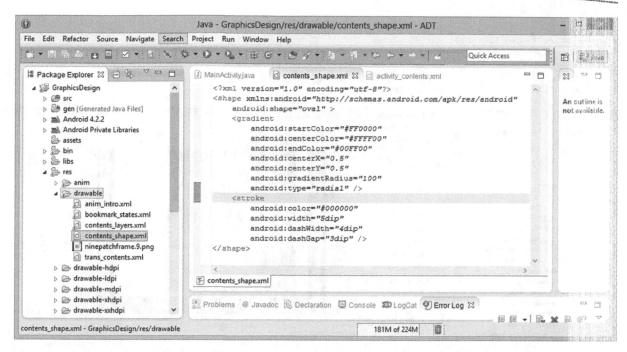

Figure 16-14. Adding <stroke> tag parameters for android:color, android:width, android:dashWidth, and dashGap

Click the activity_contents and GLE tabs; Figure 16-15 shows your results.

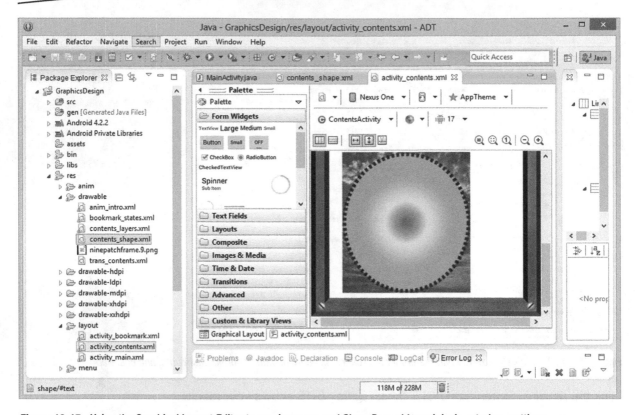

Figure 16-15. Using the Graphical Layout Editor to preview your oval ShapeDrawable and dash <stroke> settings

The Android Drawable Class: The Blueprint for Graphics

The Android **Drawable** class is yet another one of the direct subclasses of the **java.lang.Object** master class. This indicates that this Drawable class was designed specifically for the purpose of **defining graphics objects** for the Android OS, and as such, it is important for us to cover in detail.

The Android Drawable class hierarchy is structured as follows:

```
java.lang.Object
   > android.graphics.drawable.Drawable
```

Android's Drawable class belongs to the **android.graphics.drawable** package. Thus the **import statement** for a Drawable class references the **android.graphics.drawable.Drawable** package as its class import path.

A Drawable class is a **public abstract** class. This type of access modifier pair signifies that this class is not meant to be used directly other than to declare Drawable objects initially, or to be used to create subclasses, such as classes that you will be using (and creating) during this chapter.

A Drawable (class or object) is the term that the Android OS has chosen to represent a graphic object of some sort or another. It was probably coined as a term derivative from a supposition that "something that can be drawn should be called a Drawable." Android likes to create its own terms for OS components and functions, such as Activities and Receivers and Drawables.

As you have seen throughout this book, you will deal with Drawable objects when you require some type of graphic-related object (in memory) resource. You'll instantiate a Drawable (or one of its subclass Drawable types, such as the BitmapDrawable) when you wish to draw something onto your display.

The Drawable class represents a foundation for graphics design in Android, and was designed to provide the generic API for dealing with an underlying graphics resource. This graphic resource could take a variety of forms, as we saw in the first section of the chapter when we looked at many of the different types of Drawable objects that can be utilized within Android.

The Drawable object in Android does not have any capabilities of receiving events, nor does it allow any interaction with your users. This is instead handled by your **View** object, oftentimes an ImageView, which will "contain" (or reference) your Drawable objects inside it, either in a foreground parameter, which holds your source image plate (holder), or background parameter, which holds your background image plate (or alternately, just a simple ARGB color value)

There are five functional areas of support provided by the Drawable master class for all of the other types of Drawable subclasses. These include the Drawable object's **padding**, **boundaries**, **animation**, **state control**, and **level**.

We've already taken a look at some of these concepts during this book, for instance, with padding values the Drawable class **.getPadding()** method will return from a Drawable object, if applicable, information regarding how to place the content contained inside that Drawable object.

For example, a Drawable object such as the NinePatchDrawable object, which is intended to be utilized as a graphic frame for a Button UI widget, will need to return a padding Rect value that accurately places the text label inside the NinePatchDrawable asset, within your Button UI element. This **.getPadding()** method call uses the Rect object, which you will learn about later on in the chapter, as its parameter via the following method call code:

```
yourDrawableObjectNameHere.getPadding(Rect);
```

We have also looked at AnimationDrawable (frame animation) objects quite a bit in this book. Any Drawable subclass can support animation by "calling back" to its parent using one of two nested classes in the Drawable class.

This **Drawable.Callback** interface should be implemented for any subclass in which you wish to create an animated Drawable object that will extend the Drawable class.

A subclass can support the interface via a .setCallback(Drawable.Callback) method call, so that animation will function properly within your Drawable subclass. The simplest way to do this is by using your method call (off of the custom Drawable object) to Drawable's **.setBackgroundDrawable()** method.

We've also looked at **multi-state** ImageButton objects and similar Drawables that take the state of the UI element or graphic into account in order to set the Drawable asset to reference and display the correct image asset.

The Drawable class contains a **.setState()** method that allows the Drawable subclass to tell the Drawable object that it creates precisely which state each of your Drawable assets needs to be drawn for: for instance, when the mouse is hovered, or when the UI element is focused, or when the object is selected, or even when a custom-defined state is being used by your users.

The Drawable objects that support setting states will modify their source images based upon this state or state-change information. You have created a multi-state Drawable already in this book, in Chapter 9 when you created an ImageButton Drawable that featured four different button UI states.

Drawable objects can also respond to different **levels** using a **.setLevel()** method. This method allows a Drawable object to respond to any controller, which can send level information to trigger exactly which Drawable asset is displayed. Levels would be especially useful for use with Android hardware, for instance, to display a battery level in real time, or set an altimeter level, if the hardware supported that feature, such as will most likely be the case with the new Android watches coming out this year.

Finally, the Drawable class supports boundaries by using the **.setBounds()** method, which needs to be utilized to tell your Drawable where it needs to be drawn and how large it should be on your screen. You will be leveraging the **.getBounds()** method in the next section of this chapter when you create your own custom Drawable subclass, the **ImageRoundingDrawable** class.

Android developers can find out the preferred size for any given Drawable object by using the **.getIntrinsicHeight()** or **.getIntrinsicWidth()** methods.

Creating Your Custom Drawable: ImageRoundingDrawable

Let's go back into Eclipse and create your own custom Drawable subclass so that you can see exactly how this is done. Right-click your project **/src/** folder, and select the **New ➤ Class** menu command sequence, as shown in Figure 16-16 on the left-hand side of the screen shot.

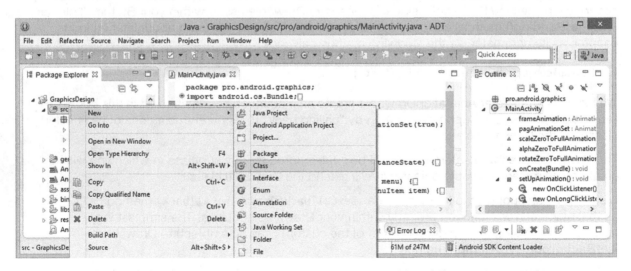

Figure 16-16. Right-clicking the /src folder and selecting the New ➤ Class menu sequence to create your new class

This will bring up a **New Java Class** dialog, shown in Figure 16-17, and will auto-populate the **Source folder** field since you right-clicked the GraphicsDesign/src/ folder earlier in order to invoke this dialog.

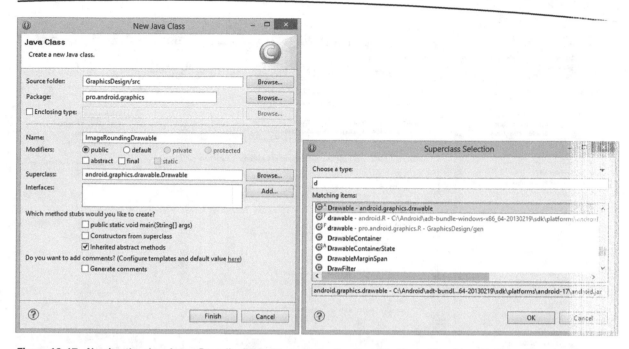

Figure 16-17. Naming the class ImageRoundingDrawable and selecting the android.graphics.drawable.Drawable superclass

Click the **Browse** button on the right of the **Package** field and select your **pro.android.graphics** Java Package from the bottom of the provided list.

In the Name field, type the Drawable subclass name of **ImageRoundingDrawable** and leave the **public** modifier set (checked) as shown below the Name field.

Next, click the **Browse** button on the right side of the **Superclass** field. This will open up the **Superclass Selection** dialog, shown on the right-hand side of Figure 16-17, where you can search for the Drawable Superclass.

At the top of the Superclass Selection dialog you will see a **Choose a Type** field, which acts as a search function to narrow down your search through the hundreds of classes that are a part of the Android OS.

Type the letter "**d**," as shown in Figure 16-17, and then find the **Drawable** class reference, which will specify its **android.graphics.drawable** package origin. When you click the Drawable class reference, the package origin information will appear to the right of the class, confirming that this is the primary Drawable superclass that you wish to subclass. This is similar to the way package origins are detailed in Eclipse pop-up helper dialogs.

After you have located and selected the Drawable superclass, as shown in Figure 16-17 on the right, click the **OK** button, which will return you to your New Java Class dialog where you can finally click the **Finish** button to create the public class ImageRoundingDrawable extends Drawable bootstrap, as well as the four methods within it that Android wishes to see implemented, or at least in place, for your Drawable subclass.

As you can see in the empty bootstrap Drawable subclass framework shown in Figure 16-18, Eclipse has written almost two dozen lines of Java code for you, providing an initial framework for you to build the Drawable subclass on top of, which you will be doing next.

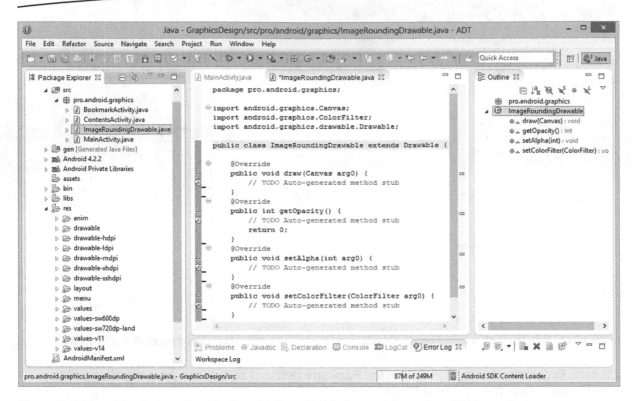

Figure 16-18. Examining the ImageRoundingDrawable Drawable subclass bootstrap code and its four methods

Besides the **package** statement, there are three **import** statements provided, which support the class (extends) and method (parameter objects) usage in your Drawable subclass. These include the **Canvas**, **ColorFilter**, and **Drawable** classes, all of which we have covered in detail at some point during this book. Next, you see the ImageRoundingDrawable class declaration, and inside that are four @Override methods that, if implemented, will override the same methods that live in the Drawable superclass.

Two of these, the **.draw()** and **.getOpacity()** methods, you will be upgrading to implement your own Java code to control the opacity of your Drawable and to specify exactly how it will be drawn to the Canvas.

The other two methods, **.setAlpha()** and **.setColorFilter()**, will not be implemented for this exercise because your ImageRoundingDrawable won't use them.

Next, you will start to add in object declarations and build the constructor class for your custom Drawable subclass. You'll start with declaring a Paint object, which you will later utilize to paint Bitmaps on your Canvas object.

Creating a Paint Object to Use to Paint the Drawable Canvas

The first thing you'll add, on the first line of your ImageRoundingDrawable class definition, is a Paint object variable declaration. This is done by using the following simple Java code statement:

```
private Paint paintObject;
```

You will use private access control so that only your ImageRoundingDrawable class can access and utilize this soon-to-be-customized Paint object.

As you can see in Figure 16-19, you will need to mouse-over and select the option to import the Paint class, which is a part of the android.graphics package. Once this has been done, you will be able to start to implement your **ImageRoundingDrawable()** constructor method, which will utilize this Paint object, in conjunction with the Canvas and Bitmap classes, as you saw in Chapter 11 when you worked with PorterDuff image blending modes.

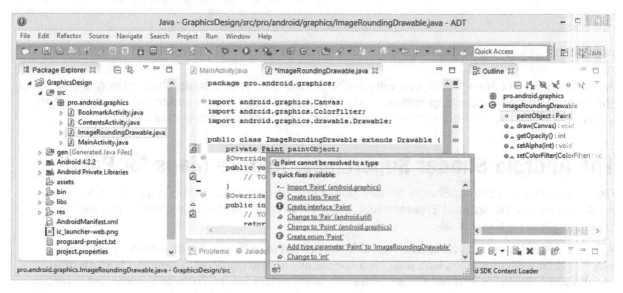

Figure 16-19. *Declaring a private Paint object named paintObject for use in ImageRoundingDrawable() constructor*

Next, let's declare your constructor method, as shown in Figure 16-20, using the same exact name as your **ImageRoundingDrawable** class name, and using the **public** access control modifier designation, so that it can be accessed by the other classes in your GraphicsDesign project and package. You will use a **sourceImage Bitmap** object as the parameter that is passed into the method, which allows you to specify the image that you want to be rounded. The code to create this empty constructor method is as follows:

```
public ImageRoundingDrawable(Bitmap sourceImage) { constructor code goes in here }
```

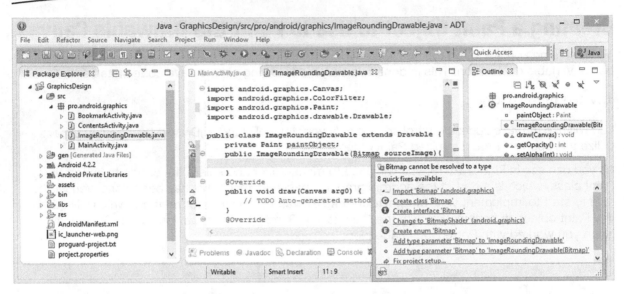

Figure 16-20. Creating a public ImageRoundingDrawable constructor method with sourceImage Bitmap object parameter

As you can see in Figure 16-20, you will need to mouse-over your Bitmap class reference and select the **Import Bitmap (android.graphics)** option. Notice the Paint import statement at the top of your class, which is a result of doing this same exact work process in the previous step.

The Android Shader Superclass: Texture Maps for Painting

Before you create a BitmapShader Shader object in a future section of this chapter, I wanted to introduce you to the Android **Shader** class, since the **BitmapShader** class, which you will be using soon, is one of its subclasses.

Android's **Shader** class is another direct subclass of the **java.lang.Object** master class. This signifies that a Shader class was designed specifically for the purpose of defining **texture map** (or shader) objects for Android OS and, as such, is important for us to cover in some detail before we use it.

The Android Shader class hierarchy is structured as follows:

```
java.lang.Object
  > android.graphics.Shader
```

Android's Shader class belongs to the **android.graphics** package. Therefore, an **import statement** for using the Shader class in your app references the **android.graphics.Shader** package as the correct class import path.

This Shader class is a **public** class and has several indirect subclasses including the **BitmapShader**, which you will use next, and the three gradient classes you utilized earlier in the chapter: **LinearGradient**, **SweepGradient**, and **RadialGradient**.

The Shader class is used to create objects that generate horizontal color rendering during draw (Paint) operations. Any Shader subclass (object) can be installed inside a Paint object by calling the **.setShader()** method.

After this .setShader() method call configures a Shader object for a Paint object, any Canvas object that is drawn using that Paint object will draw on your canvas using color information retrieved from that Shader object.

The Shader class has one `nested class` called **Shader.TileMode** that provides **tiling mode constants** which developers can use when declaring their Shader objects. Since this is an important class, we will cover it in detail next.

The Shader.TileMode Nested Class: Shader Tiling Modes

Android's **Shader.TileMode** class is a **public static final enum** class and is another of those **java.lang.Enum** direct subclasses of the **java.lang.Object** master class that provides **Enumerated Constants** for use with related Java classes. In this case, the related Java classes are the Shader class and its subclasses, many of which you will be implementing in this chapter.

This means that the Shader.TileMode nested class was designed specifically for the purpose of defining texture (or shader) tiling mode constants. The Shader.TileMode Enum class hierarchy is structured as follows:

```
java.lang.Object
  > java.lang.Enum<E extends java.lang.Enum<E>>
    > android.graphics.Shader.TileMode
```

This Shader.TileMode nested class belongs to the **android.graphics** package. Because of this, the **import statement** for the Shader class is sufficient to access the TileMode constants, and references the **android.graphics.Shader** package and class name as its class import path, as you will see in a bit when you implement a BitmapShader with Shader.TileMode constants.

There are three TileMode constants that define the texture map, or shader, tiling modes that are currently available within the Android OS: **CLAMP**, **MIRROR**, and **REPEAT**.

The **TileMode.CLAMP** will replicate the image edge color if the shader draws outside its original bounds. This might look a bit strange when using a Bitmap object, so if you plan to exceed boundaries, you may want to have a one-pixel solid color border (much like what is used in a NinePatch). What the **CLAMP** mode essentially means is **zero tiling** or **do not tile** this image!

The **TileMode.MIRROR** will repeat your shader image horizontally as well as vertically. This mode will **flip,** or mirror, image tiles in an alternating fashion. This is done so that adjacent image tiles never exhibit a "seam." Thus, your image tiling results with the MIRROR constant will be seamless, even if you utilize images that were not originally designed (or meant) to be tiled. This mode can also create some cool kaleidoscope effects if you implement the right digital image assets.

The **TileMode.REPEAT** will repeat your shader image horizontally as well as vertically. This is known as "straight tiling" and can be used for images that you have designed (using GIMP 2.8) to be seamlessly tiled in the first place. Note that MIRROR also works well for image tiles that you have designed to be seamless, so always preview both constants!

The BitmapShader Class: Texture Mapping Using Bitmaps

Before you create your BitmapShader Shader object in the next section I want to introduce you to Android's **BitmapShader** class in greater detail first.

The Android BitmapShader class is a direct subclass from the Shader class. As such, the BitmapShader class inherits all of the capabilities, methods, constants, and so on from its Shader superclass.

The Android BitmapShader class hierarchy is structured as follows:

```
java.lang.Object
  > android.graphics.Shader
    > android.graphics.BitmapShader
```

Android's BitmapShader class also belongs to the **android.graphics** package. Therefore, the **import statement** for the BitmapShader class references the **android.graphics.BitmapShader** package as its class import path.

The BitmapShader class is a **public** class, and creates a Shader object that can be utilized to draw a Bitmap object as a texture map in a Paint object to be applied to a Canvas object. This Bitmap object can be CLAMP, REPEAT, or MIRROR tiled by setting the appropriate (desired) TileMode constants.

It is important to point out that you can use a different constant for the X axis than for the Y axis, so you can MIRROR in one dimension and REPEAT in another, giving you fine-tuned control over your image tiling.

The BitmapShader constructor method specifies a source image Bitmap object as well as X and Y Shader.TileMode constants using the following format:

```
BitmapShader(Bitmap bmpName, Shader.TileMode Xconstant, Shader.TileMode Yconstant)
```

Now you can implement Shader objects in your ImageRoundingDrawable subclass.

Creating and Configuring a BitmapShader for the Drawable

Declare your **BitmapShader** object at the top of your ImageRoundingDrawable constructor method and name it **imageShader,** as shown in Figure 16-21.

```
BitmapShader imageShader;
```

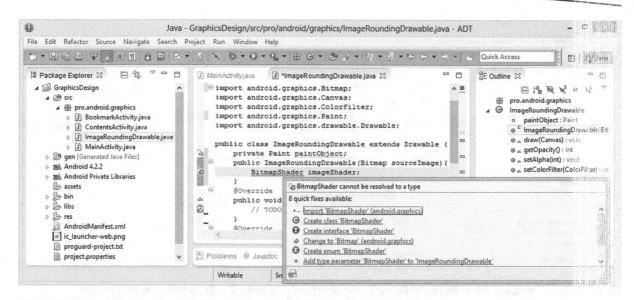

Figure 16-21. Declaring the BitmapShader object and naming it imageShader for use in your constructor method

As you now know, the **BitmapShader** object is used to hold the **Bitmap** object and will tell Android how to apply, or **render**, a Bitmap object image asset within the Paint object. As you know, your Paint object is used to control how graphics are drawn, or applied (painted), onto your Drawable's Canvas.

As you may know, the concept of a **shader** is most prevalent in the world of 3D rendering, where a shader is a component of the **texture mapping** process of placing a **skin** or **surface** on top of the 3D mesh or wireframe object so that it has a **solid appearance instead of a mesh or wireframe appearance**.

A BitmapShader object performs this same surface mapping process, only in 2D instead of in 3D, and is used to apply your 2D image asset to the Paint surface. You can think of a Paint object as a **virtual paintbrush**, and this shader information as designating how the Bitmap object will be painted or, more accurately, **mapped** to the resulting Canvas object's 2D surface.

Next, let's instantiate your imageShader BitmapShader object and configure it with a source image asset, as well as constants that tell it how to **map** (or tile) the image along the X and Y 2D coordinates of your shader object.

You will use a **TileMode** constant values of **CLAMP** for your X and Y dimension, and call these off of the Shader class on the inside of your BitmapShader constructor method call, which you will invoke by using a Java **new** keyword.

You will pass your **sourceImage** Bitmap object, which has been passed into your ImageRoundingDrawable constructor method as a primary parameter, into this BitmapShader constructor method as its first parameter. You will then need to specify the X and Y **TileMode constants** called off of the **Shader** class by using the following single line of Java code, as shown in Figure 16-22:

```
imageShader = new BitmapShader(sourceImage, Shader.TileMode.CLAMP, Shader.TileMode.CLAMP);
```

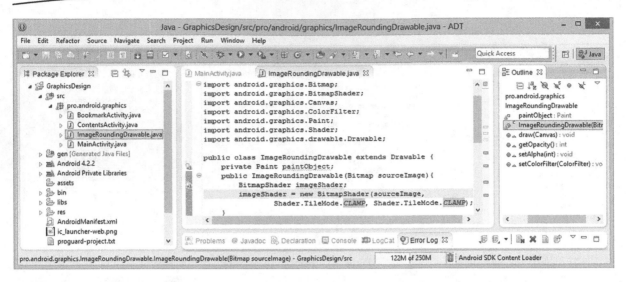

Figure 16-22. Instantiating the imageShader BitmapShader object and configuring it with sourceImage and constant

It is interesting to note in Figure 16-22 that even though you instantiated and configured your imageShader BitmapShader object, the Eclipse IDE does not considering the object as having been used (utilized) as of yet. Objects can be declared, and even instantiated (loaded) and configured, and not be used!

This is the reason that your wavy yellow warning highlighting will remain under the original imageShader declaration until you actually do something with this object. I just wanted to point this out and to clarify what was going on here, in case you were wondering why we "used" the imageShader we declared in the previous line of code, but the warning that the object was still not used remained. So technically an object instantiation does not constitute usage! This is quite logical, if you think about it.

Now that your imageShader BitmapShader object has been instantiated and is configured, you can focus on setting up your paintObject Paint object. First, you must instantiate the Paint object using the new keyword; since you have already declared it for use and named it at the top of your subclass, you can accomplish this using one simple, short-but-sweet Java statement:

```
paintObject = new Paint();
```

Now that you have a properly declared and instantiated a Paint object named paintObject, you can invoke method calls off of it to configure it for your usage. The first thing that you want to set is the AntiAliasing flag, which you will set to a value of true (on) using the **.setAntiAlias()** method call. This is a fairly straightforward but important step, as it gives us a high-quality visual result, and is accomplished using the following statement:

```
paintObject.setAntiAlias(true);
```

As you can see in Figure 16-23, you have now created your Paint object and your BitmapShader object constructs, and configured them to work the way you want them to, as far as image tiling and anti-aliasing are concerned.

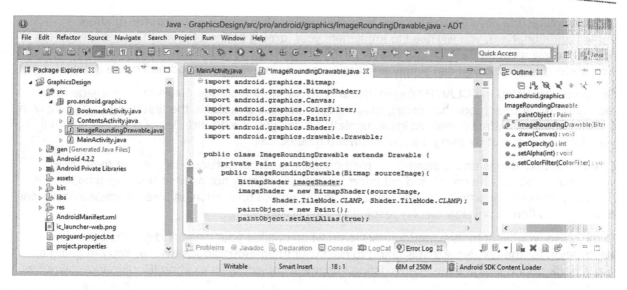

Figure 16-23. Instantiating the paintObject and setting the .setAntiAlias() method to true to turn on AntiAliasing feature

Now, all you have left to do is "wire up" your BitmapShader object construct to your Paint construct via a **.setShader()** method you learned about earlier.

This is accomplished by calling the .setShader() method off of the Paint object, and passing the BitmapShader object as the configuring parameter, as shown in Figure 16-24. The Java code to perform this configuration of the **paintObject** with the **imageShader** is as follows:

```
paintObject.setShader(imageShader);
```

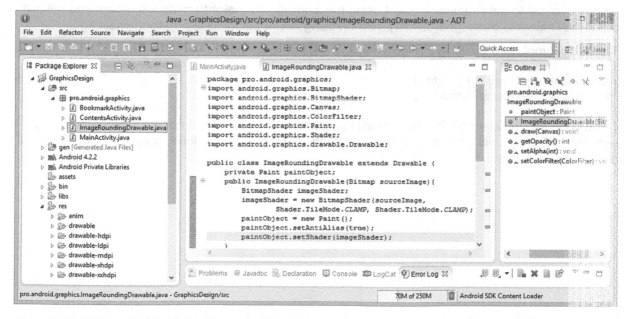

Figure 16-24. Wiring paintObject Paint object to the imageShader BitmapShader object using .setShader() method

This completes the Java coding for your **ImageRoundingDrawable() constructor** method implementation. Next, you will need to implement your **.draw()** method for your Drawable subclass so it can draw an ImageRoundingDrawable to the screen. As you recall, the .draw() method bootstrap was coded for you, so you can simply add the Java code inside the method and make it draw!

Since you are using the CLAMP tiling mode, and do not want the edge pixels of your image to be replicated (to appear more than once), which would look like a mistake, the first thing that you'll want to accomplish in a .draw() method implementation is to "get" the boundaries of the container holding your Drawable object by using the **.getBounds()** method call.

One of the cool things about these "get" method calls, such as .getBounds(), is that they allow your code to go "up the chain" and get information that you may not have at develop-time (versus runtime), or more importantly, do not want to specify in fixed units such as pixels because each user device has different physical display resolution specifications.

In this case, you want to use .getBounds() to crawl up outside your class and get the boundary information for the container that is going to hold your ImageRoundingDrawable. You are going to use a background image plate in an existing ImageView object in an existing (BookmarkActivity.java) class.

Since that ImageView is designed using XML parameters to conform itself to the user's device screen, you will need to find out width and height values for that ImageView. The ImageView uses the **MATCH_PARENT** parameter so that it will display its contents using the entire screen. For this reason, your .getBounds() method call also equates, in this particular UI design setup at least, to "getting" your BookmarkActivity.java Activity subclass display screen area's total (full screen) width and height data values.

Since you don't have variables declared to hold these width and height data values, you will do all of this work using one single line of Java code for each of the width and height dimensions. You declare the **integer** data type, name your variables **canvasW** and **canvasH**, and then set these variables equal to data values obtained using the **.width()** and **.height()** methods, which you will call off of the Drawable class .getBounds() method using dot-notation-based method chaining.

This is accomplished by using the following two lines of Java code:

```
int canvasH = getBounds().height();
int canvasW = getBounds().width();
```

As you can see in Figure 16-25, the canvasH and canvasW variables are not yet implemented and exhibit the wavy yellow warning underline highlights. The next step of defining your drawing area will alleviate this problem.

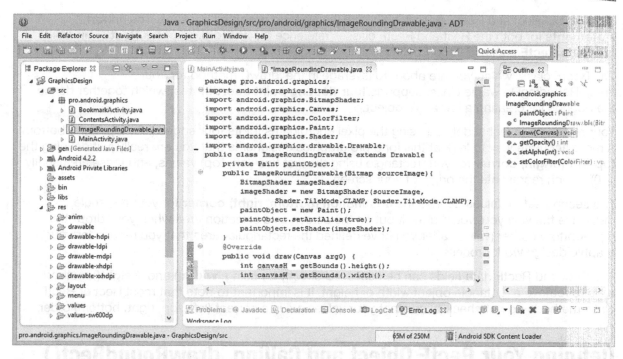

Figure 16-25. Implementing a public void draw() method and Canvas object named arg0 for your Drawable subclass

Next, you'll use the **RectF** class to define your drawable area for the method.

Android Rect and RectF Classes: Defining the Draw Area

Before you code your rectangular drawing area object, I need to familiarize you with Android's Rect and **RectF** classes first. The primary difference in these two classes, at least at a fundamental level, is that the **Rect** class uses **integer** values to define a Rect (rectangle) object and a **RectF** class uses **float** (real number) values to define a RectF object.

That said, due to the differences stemming from using integers versus real numbers, the methods for each class are different from each other. This is mainly due to the different code mathematics involved in the calculations performed within these different types of (numeric) methods.

The Android Rect and RectF classes are direct subclasses of Java's master class **java.lang.Object**. For this reason, you know they were created just for implementing rectangular areas in Android. These areas are most often utilized for graphics, and are often used in drawing operations with the Paint and Canvas classes.

The Android Rect and RectF class hierarchy is structured as follows:

```
java.lang.Object
  > android.graphics.Rect
```

```
java.lang.Object
  > android.graphics.RectF
```

The Android Rect and RectF classes belong to the **android.graphics** package. The **import statements** for both the Rect and RectF classes reference the **android.graphics.Rect** or **android. graphics.RectF** package import paths.

The RectF class, which you are about to leverage in the .draw() method for your ImageRoundingDrawable class, supports **four floating point coordinates**, which together define the bounds for creating a rectangle object.

Your rectangle object is defined using the pixel coordinates for its four edges (left, top, right, bottom). A more accurate way to look at this for a pro graphics designer is that you are really just defining the **top-left (origin) corner** for your rectangle using the first two (left, top) values, and these are usually (0,0), which represents the origin of your screen.

The second set of values defines the **destination (bottom, right) corner** for your rectangle, much like the way you would draw it out on the screen as a selection area when you "drop" the right-bottom corner (value), after you have defined the rectangular area that you require for your graphic design work process.

The Rect and RectF data fields can be accessed directly by using **.width()** and **.height()** method calls to retrieve a rectangle object width or height. It is important to note that most Rect or RectF class methods do not check to see that your values are in a correct (left, top, right, bottom) order.

Defining Your RectF Object and Calling .drawRoundRect( )

Next, let's finish off your .draw() method by defining and instantiating your RectF object, and then calling the actual drawing method, which you require for your class. You'll do this by harnessing all of the RectF, Paint, Canvas, and Shader objects that you have set up thus far. This is getting exciting in its complexity, and yet it's really all so very logical once you get it in the right sequence in your mind's eye (understanding, or Ah-Ha moment).

This is done by declaring the **RectF** object, naming it **drawRect**, and then using the **new** keyword and **RectF()** constructor method, with the 0,0 screen origin that you learned about earlier, and destination bottom-right corner.

The destination corner location data values will logically be set by using the **.getBounds().width()** and the **.getBounds().height()** method calls, which you already coded, and stored in your canvasW and canvasH integer variables.

This can be done via a single line of Java code, as shown in Figure 16-26:

```
RectF drawRect = new RectF(0.0f, 0.0f, canvasW, canvasH);
```

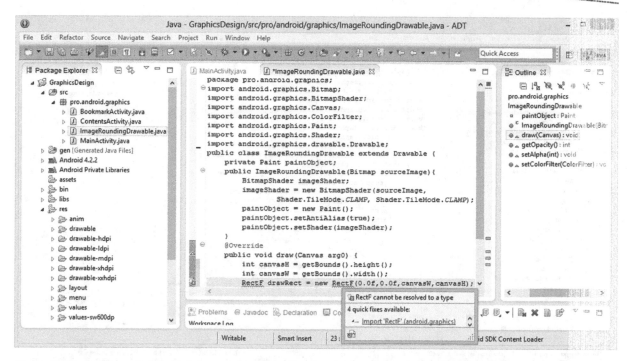

Figure 16-26. Creating a RectF object named drawRect and configuring it with Drawable width and height boundary

Next, you will use the Canvas object named **arg0** (the first argument for the method is the naming convention Eclipse ADT followed) to invoke your Canvas class drawing method that will perform an image rounding operation for you. Once you deal with your opacity, you'll be done creating your custom Drawable.

To call the Canvas class's **.drawRoundRect()** method off your arg0 Canvas object, you need to have your **drawRect** RectF object, X and Y **corner rounding values** (higher values yield rounder corners), and finally, your **paintObject** Paint object. Since you have all of those in place, let's write this method call by using the following line of Java code, as shown in Figure 16-27:

```
arg0.drawRoundRect(drawRect, 50, 50, paintObject);
```

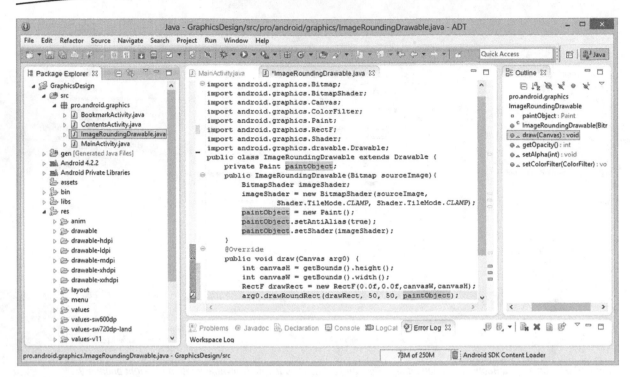

Figure 16-27. Calling a .drawRoundRect() method off of a Canvas object named arg0 using RectF and Paint objects

As you can also see in Figure 16-27, I clicked the paintObject variable inside the method call to highlight the chain of paintObject declaration, instantiation, configuration, and the Shader object connection. I did this so that you could visualize this important progression much more clearly.

You will need to implement any of these empty methods which were bootstrapped for you which your class needs to utilize to add features to your custom Drawable subclass. In this case, you need to change the .getOpacity() method return value for your Drawable (object) subclass to be opaque (a 255 data value), instead of being transparent (a 0 data value).

I really cannot give you an answer as to why Eclipse ADT would default the .getOpacity() method's return data value to zero (transparent), as I would suspect most developers would want to return a fully opaque data value for their Drawable subclass objects.

As you can see in Figure 16-28, you are going to change the zero to a **255** data value for the .getOpacity() method's return value. You will do this by using the following Java statement inside the .getOpacity() method:

```
return 255;
```

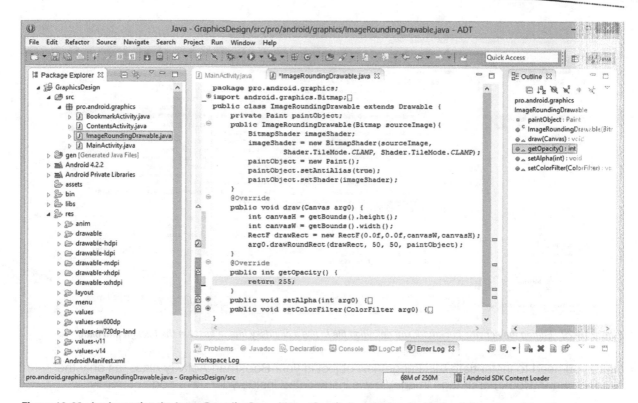

Figure 16-28. *Implementing the ImageRoundingDrawable .getOpacity() method and returning fully opaque data value*

As you can see in Figure 16-28, your Java code is error-free and your new ImageRoundingDrawable class is now complete.

Now that you have finished creating an ImageRoundingDrawable class Drawable subclass, you need to make some minor tweaks in your **activity_bookmark.xml**, which is the XML definition for your **BookmarkActivity.java** class (Activity subclass). You will edit the first ImageView UI element, which holds the cloudsky image asset, and change the foreground plate **android:src** image reference to a background plate **android:background** image reference.

Find the **activity_bookmark.xml** file in your **/res/layout** folder, and right-click it, and select the **Open** option (or select it and press the **F3** key).

In the first <ImageView> tag, shown in Figure 16-29, change the source image reference to be a background image reference by changing android:src to android:background in your XML. Both of these will reference your cloudsky.jpg image asset, so what you are doing is switching the image asset from the front plate of the ImageView container to the back plate.

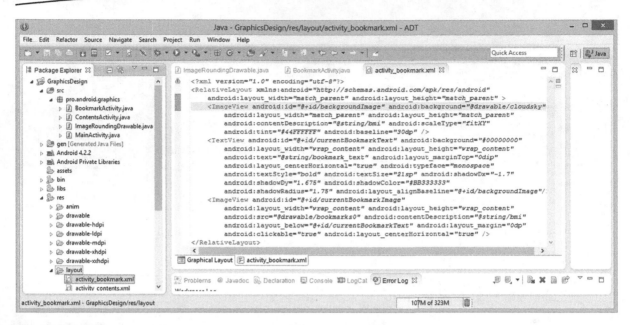

Figure 16-29. Editing the activity_bookmark.xml definition file to use a cloudsky image asset in the background plate

Next, you need to instantiate this ImageView object in your BookmarkActivity class, as only the second currentBookmarkImage ImageView is instantiated inside your Java code currently.

Add a line of code after the .setColorFilter() method call, and instantiate the ImageView, and name it backgroundImage, using the following Java code:

```
ImageView backgroundImage = (ImageView)findViewById(R.id.backgroundImage);
```

As you can see in Figure 16-30, Eclipse warns us that the backgroundImage object you have just instantiated is not yet utilized. Ignore this, as soon you will be calling a key method using this ImageView object in order to be able to implement your newborn ImageRoundingDrawable class and object.

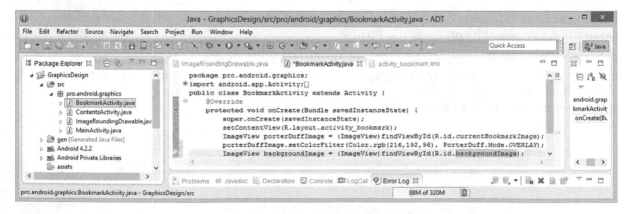

Figure 16-30. Instantiating another ImageView object named backgroundImage in your BookmarkActivity.java file

Next, you will be using the **InputStream** Java.IO class to read the raw data (pixels) from your cloudsky.jpg image asset, so let's get an overview of this class in the next section before you actually utilize it in your code.

The Java InputStream Class: Reading Raw Data Streams

The Java **InputStream** class is a direct subclass of the Java master class **java.lang.Object**. InputStream is part of the **java.io** package, which, as its name indicates, deals with input and output. There is an output counterpart to the InputStream class that is called **OutputStream**.

The Java InputStream class hierarchy is structured as follows:

```
java.lang.Object
  > java.io.InputStream
```

The Java InputStream class belongs to the **java.io** input and output utility package. The **import statement** for the Java IO InputStream class references the **java.io.InputStream** package import path, as you'll see next.

The InputStream class (and thus object) was created to provide developers with a source of raw data bytes that are readable by their applications.

Most applications will leverage input streams that read data using a file system, such as you will be doing next. InputStream can also handle reading raw data over a network using a **.getInputStream()** method call, as well as access data from a byte array, which will be located in system memory.

You will load your **InputStream** object, which you will name **rawImage**, by using the **.openRawResource()** method called off of the invaluable .getResources() method, which you have used quite often at this point to process your data.

You will do this all using one line of Java code, as shown in Figure 16-31:

```
InputStream rawImage = getResources().openRawResource(R.drawable.cloudsky);
```

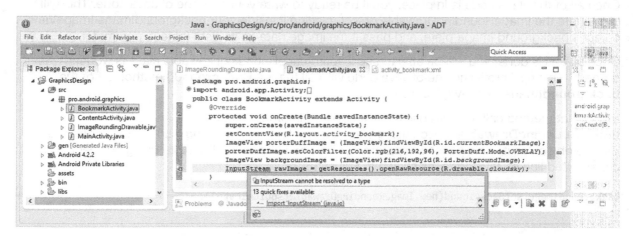

Figure 16-31. Instantiating a InputStream object named rawImage and loading it with cloudsky image via .getResources()

The next thing that you'll need to do is to turn this **rawImage** data stream of pixel information into a more processable Bitmap object. You'll do this by using the **BitmapFactory** class, along with its **.decodeStream()** method.

First, you will declare a **Bitmap** object and name it **sourceImage**. Then you'll set it equal to the result of your **.decodeStream()** method call, which you'll call off of Android's **BitmapFactory** class. You will use your **rawImage** object as the method call parameter, and you will accomplish all of this using one single line of Java code, as shown in Figure 16-32:

```
Bitmap sourceImage = BitmapFactory.decodeStream(rawImage);
```

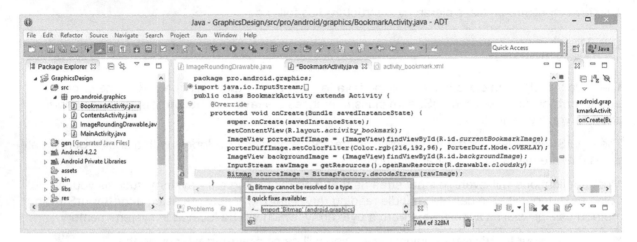

Figure 16-32. *Creating a Bitmap object named sourceImage and using BitmapFactory class to load it with rawImage*

As you can see in Figure 16-32, you'll now need to mouse-over the reference to the Bitmap class and select the **Import Bitmap (android.graphics)** option in order to have the necessary import statement written for you at the top of your BookmarkActivity.java class Activity subclass.

Once all of this Java code is in place, you'll be ready to write your final line of Java code. This will instantiate the ImageRoundingDrawable object, placing it inside your backgroundImage ImageView object's background image plate, and pass it the image data as its data (object) parameter.

Once all this is done, you will be able to see if your ImageRoundingDrawable class is working properly. This final crowning line of Java code will call the **.setBackground()** method off of the **backgroundImage** ImageView object.

Inside that method call, you will use the new keyword in order to instantiate an **ImageRoundingDrawable** object, using your constructor method, along with the **sourceImage** Bitmap object, as its sole passed-in parameter. This can all accomplished by using one very well constructed line of Java code, as shown in Figure 16-33.

```
backgroundImage.setBackground(new ImageRoundingDrawable(sourceImage));
```

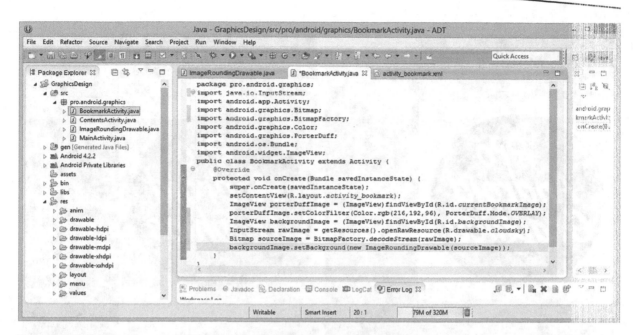

Figure 16-33. Constructing a new ImageRoundingDrawable object using sourceImage object via .setbackground()

Now use your **Run As ➤ Android Application** to view the result in Nexus One!

What you are seeing on the left side of the screen shot in Figure 16-34 is my first attempt at running the ImageRoundingDrawable class, when I still was using the android:src parameter for my cloudsky, instead of using the background plate, so my ImageRoundingDrawable was obscured from view. Also shown is a PorterDuff.Mode.SCREEN constant, which was in the original code and which does not respect the Alpha for the currentBookmarkImage. As this looks less than professional, I changed over to a **PorterDuff.Mode.MULTIPLY** constant, as shown in Figure 16-35, which provided a more professional end result, as can be seen on the right side of Figure 16-34.

Figure 16-34. Testing the ImageRoundingDrawable class in the Nexus One emulator using different image plates

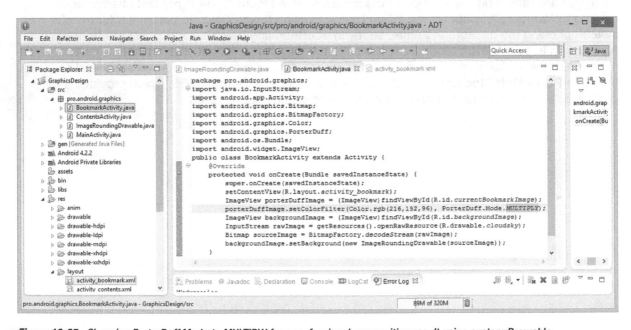

Figure 16-35. Changing PorterDuff.Mode to MULTIPLY for a professional compositing result using custom Drawable

Summary

In this sixteenth chapter, you learned how to use the **Drawable** class to create your own custom Drawable objects in Android. We covered all of the different types of Drawable objects available in Android, as well as how to create custom ShapeDrawables by using the <shape> parent tag in an XML ShapeDrawable object definition file.

We took a look at some of the child tags that can be utilized inside a parent <shape> tag, including the <gradient> tag to define different types of gradients, which you learned were actually Shader object types, as well as the <stroke> tag, which allows us to create a border around the ShapeDrawable object.

Along the way you learned about some other important classes for graphics, including the **Shader** class for creating texture maps (Shaders) for use with the Paint class, the **Rect** and **RectF** classes for creating rectangle objects, and the **InputStream** class for importing raw data streams.

You learned about the all-important Android Drawable class, and then you learned how to create your very own custom ImageRoundingDrawable class Drawable subclass, starting by using a New ➤ Class function in Eclipse.

You created an **ImageRoundingDrawable()** constructor method, and leveraged the Paint, Bitmap, Shader, and Canvas classes to craft and add your own custom type of Drawable object to the Android OS (your version, at least).

You learned about the Android Shader class and the **Shader.TileMode** nested class and its tiling mode constants, and you implemented these in your code. You also learned about the **BitmapShader** subclass of Shader and how to use it to apply Bitmap image assets as shaders. You will be using this knowledge to do something really cool in the next chapter.

You also learned about the Rect and RectF classes, used for defining rectangular areas often used for drawing and other graphics-related operations, and you learned about the InputStream class, which allows you to open up raw data input streams and to bring graphics data into your application in new and more powerful ways.

In the next chapter, we'll focus on gaining more advanced understanding of Android's **Paint and Canvas** classes and how to allow our users to use the onDraw() method to draw graphics to their screens in real time.

17

Interactive Drawing: Using Paint and Canvas Classes Interactively

In this seventeenth chapter, you will learn how to use the Android **Paint** and **Canvas** classes interactively, in real time, using your Android device's touchscreen. You will implement touchscreen event handling using the **OnTouchListener()** method and class, and learn how to enable your user to **draw** on their Android device's screen interactively and in real time.

You will learn about the Android **MotionEvent**, **List**, **ArrayList**, and **Context** classes, as well as much more detail regarding Android's Paint and Canvas classes. We will also look specifically at the **.onDraw()** method in Android as well as how drawing to the user's display functions within Android OS.

You will be creating your own custom **View** subclass called **SketchPadView**, and you will use this View subclass to create your own **SketchPad Activity** that will allow your users to create their own graphic designs on their screen.

You will start off learning how the Canvas and Paint classes function with the Android .onDraw() method. This foundational information, which we will cover in the first portion of this chapter, will show you how Android allows developers to create their own custom graphics applications.

After we've looked at these core classes and methods that allow developers to create graphics applications, you will create your own **SketchPad Utility**. During that portion of the chapter we will cover some of the ancillary classes and methods that will need to be leveraged in order to make Canvas drawing functions interactive for your application's user base. By the end of this chapter, you will have created your own custom View, and painted on it using the Canvas, Paint, Context, List, ArrayList, and Context classes!

The Android onDraw() Method: Drawing onto Your Screen

The function that is the most central or critical to drawing on your custom SketchPadView subclass, which you will be creating later in the chapter, is to **override** the View subclass's **onDraw()** method, implementing your own version of it within your SketchPadView.java class.

This onDraw() method contains one single parameter, which is, as you might imagine, a **Canvas** object, usually named canvas. Your View subclass can use this Canvas object to allow your users to draw on the View surface.

As you will see in the next section, the Canvas class defines a great many .draw() methods, which can be used to draw **colors**, **text**, **shapes**, **vertices**, **bitmaps**, **paths**, **points**, or any other type of **Drawable** graphic object.

You can use any and all of these methods in your onDraw() implementation to create your own custom drawing applications, as well as anything else that you can imagine, such as interactive coloring books, for that matter.

As you have already learned in this book, prior to calling your onDraw() method, you must first declare and instantiate your **Paint** object.

As you've seen in the second half of this book, Android's **android.graphics** package and graphics design framework separates the drawing and display function into two discrete functional areas: where to draw the graphics to, as defined by your Canvas object, and what to draw upon the Canvas object, which is defined by your Paint object. Near the end of the chapter you'll see why this is a smart thing for Android to do, as you add **image cloning** to your SketchPad Utility using only a few lines of **Paint** and **Shader** code.

Before you start coding your **SketchPad** Activity subclass and **SketchPadView** View subclass to implement custom drawing on the display for your user, I need to give you the overview of both the Canvas and the Paint classes so that you have this foundational information under your belt. If you intend on mastering graphics in Android OS, you will want to familiarize yourself with both of these core classes; go to the developer.android.com web site for more information.

The Android Canvas Class: The Digital Artisan's Canvas

Android's **Canvas** class is a direct subclass of the **java.lang.Object** class. As you now know, this indicates that the Canvas class was designed specifically for the purpose of providing **canvas** objects used in graphics applications in the Android OS (named after the canvas that artists paint upon using brush strokes, or in the case of Android application development, graphics operations).

The Android Canvas class hierarchy is therefore structured as follows:

```
java.lang.Object
  > android.graphics.Canvas
```

Android's Canvas class belongs to the **android.graphics** package. Therefore, an **import statement** for using the Canvas class in your app references the **android.graphics.Canvas** package, as you've already seen in this book.

This Canvas class is a **public** class and has two nested subclasses that handle special advanced canvas characteristics. These are **Canvas.EdgeType**, which allows a special type of edge to be specified for the Canvas object, and **Canvas.VertexMode**, which allows a Canvas to use Vertex Mode. **Vertices** are commonly utilized in **3D** operations using **OpenGL ES 3.0**.

The Canvas class holds all of the Android OS **.draw()** related method calls. In order to draw graphics onto a Canvas object, you will need to implement at least **four** essential components for the draw operation. These include a **Bitmap** object used to contain your image's pixels; the **Canvas** object that will implement your **.draw()** method calls to modify the Bitmap object as you direct it to for your graphics design objective; an object to be used as a **drawing primitive**, for instance the **RectF** object or **Bitmap** object (as you have utilized in the book already) or a **Path** object or **Text** object; and finally, a **Paint** object to specify colors, images, and styles for the draw operation you are implementing.

Some of the more mainstream .draw() related method calls include the **.drawCircle()** method, which you will be using to allow your user to draw on their screen using a **brush stroke thickness** of five **pixels** (initially), as well as the **.drawRoundRect()** method, which you used in Chapter 16, and the **.drawBitmap()** method, which you used back in Chapter 11, as well as useful methods such as **.drawPoints()**, **.drawColor()**, **.drawLines()**, **.drawPath()**, **.drawTextOnPath()**, **.drawPaint()**, **.drawText()**, **.drawVertices()**, **.drawArc()**, **.drawRGB()**, and many others.

There are more than two dozen .draw() related method calls in this Canvas class, which you can implement within your .onDraw() method instance, for instance, in your SketchPadView View subclass, later on in the chapter, if you wish to experiment with them. This is a great way to see what they do!

Experimentation will allow you to observe what each method call does and how it is implemented. In this way, you can learn more about graphics in Android and gain experience with your Java coding at the very same time.

The Android Paint Class: The Digital Artisan's Paintbrush

The Android **Paint** class is a direct subclass of the **java.lang.Object** class, just like the Canvas class is. This means the Paint class was specifically designed for use with Android OS for the purpose of defining **paint** objects for use in your Canvas objects for your Pro Android graphics applications.

The Android Paint class hierarchy is structured as follows:

```
java.lang.Object
  > android.graphics.Paint
```

Android's Paint class belongs to the **android.graphics** package. Therefore, an **import statement** for using the Paint class in your app references the **android.graphics.Paint** package, as you have already seen in this book.

The Paint class is a **public** class that holds **style** and **color** information that describes to the Canvas object how to draw geometry, text, or bitmaps.

The Paint class features **six nested subclasses**. The nested subclasses are utilized when developers need to specify (further) special Paint object characteristics for their primary Paint object configuration definitions.

Paint.Align is an **Enum class**, and as such it uses constants to specify how the **.drawText()** method call will align a Text object relative to X and Y coordinates within your Canvas (and ultimately your View) objects that you are drawing on. The default setting for Paint.Align is the **LEFT** constant, and the other two constants are **RIGHT** or **CENTER**.

The **Paint.Cap** nested class is also an Enum class type and the **Cap constant** allows developers to specify the visual treatment (look) for the beginning and the ending of your lines (strokes) and paths (2D curves). Your default is the **BUTT** constant, and the other two constants are **ROUND** and **SQUARE**. In case you are wondering what BUTT means, it **butts up against** the connecting line or curve, providing as close to a **seamless connection** as you're going to get. "Hanging starts and ends" use the ROUND and SQUARE constants.

The **Paint.FontMetrics** class describes assorted "font metrics," for all you fontographers out there. These are used to describe **font attributes**. There is **no default**, and the **five** constants are **ascent**, **bottom**, **descent**, **leading**, and **top**. According to the developer documentation, these constants are not capitalized, although they probably can all be used that way, if you wish.

The closely related **Paint.FontMetricsInt** class provides the "convenience" method to **Paint.FontMetrics** for those elite method calls needing to have their FontMetrics data values provided via the in-vogue **Integer** data type.

The **Paint.Join** is an Enum class that allows developers to specify exactly how their line segments and curve segments will **join** when stroked along a path. The default constant is **MITER**, which joins outer edges of a curve or a line (or both) using a **sharp angle** where they meet or intersect. A **BEVEL** constant will provide a **straight line** intersection at the outer edges of a join, whereas a **ROUND** constant will use a **circular arc** to join your edges.

The **Paint.Style** is an Enum class that allows developers to specify if the **Shape** primitive being drawn to a Canvas is to be **filled**, **stroked**, or **both** by using predefined constants **FILL**, **STROKE**, or **FILL_AND_STROKE**. The default Paint.Style constant setting is FILL.

The Paint class also defines **eleven constants** that allow you to configure the Paint object itself. These are all in the form of **switches** or **flags**, which you can turn **on (true)** or **off (false)** depending on how much graphics processing power (overhead) you wish your application's graphics rendering pipeline to consume! Most of these are related to font support or quality.

These features are turned on (they are **off by default**) by utilizing the constants to **enable**, by using a **true** Boolean value, or **disable**, by using a **false** Boolean value, each of these following graphics processing features.

The **ANTI_ALIAS_FLAG** constant provides the flag that can be used to enable **anti-aliasing**, which is off (disabled) as a default, as it is an algorithm that utilizes significant system resources (memory and processor cycles).

The **DEV_KERN_TEXT_FLAG** constant provides a flag that can be used to enable device-side **kerning** for fonts (Text objects). Kerning is the spacing found between individual characters within a given font definition.

The **DITHER_FLAG** constant provides a flag that is used to enable **dithering**. Dithering is also turned off as a default because it also involves processing and memory resources to implement; it is an algorithm that provides an ability to **simulate more colors** when a device is running in a less than 24-bit (**truecolor**) display color environment, such as the **indexed color** (8-bit) 256 colorspace, or the **highcolor** (15-bit or 16-bit) colorspace.

The **FAKE_BOLD_TEXT_FLAG** provides a flag that allows developers to enable the **fake-bold text algorithm**, which is also turned off as a default because it uses system resources, as the great algorithms usually do. This algorithm can provide Text object (font) bolding when the font that the Text object is referencing does not feature a bold component or font definition within its font definition files currently installed in the Android OS.

The **FILTER_BITMAP_FLAG** will allow developers to set a flag enabling **bitmap filtering,** which is off by default. The constant allows developers to turn on **bilinear interpolation**, also known as **bilinear filtering**, which is only one algorithmic step down from the pristine **bicubic interpolation** found in Photoshop or the **cubic interpolation** found in GIMP. This is turned off as a default because it is processor intensive, but it will provide your application with better **scaling** results if quality is your objective. I would have included this flag in the SketchPad app, but the app doesn't scale images!

The **LINEAR_TEXT_FLAG** allows the developer to set the flag that will enable "**linear-text.**" This constant sets a flag that will **disable system caching** of Text objects, specifically their font definitions. This allows fonts to bypass the system font cache and display directly to your display screen.

The **STRIKE_THRU_TEXT_FLAG** allows developers to set the flag that enables a feature called strike-thru text. A strike-through will put horizontal lines through the content contained within a Text object. This is another one of those "afterthought algorithms" that provides missing font feature definition enhancements algorithmically, but can slow an app down.

The **SUBPIXEL_TEXT_FLAG** allows developers to set the flag that enables the rendering of **subpixel-text**, which essentially amounts to **text anti-aliasing** and makes text look crisper on **low-DPI** hardware devices. It is also off by default because it's quite processor intensive. With all the high DPI displays in the market these days, with their super-fine dot pitches, it is usually unnecessary to use this feature, especially with sans-serif font families.

The **UNDERLINE_TEXT_FLAG** allows developers to set the flag that enables a Text object to be **underlined**. This is similar to the BOLD and STRIKE_THRU constants, as it provides support for fonts that don't feature underline font components. Again, don't ask me why there is no ITALIC_TEXT_FLAG, but my speculation is that an algorithm for italicized text would be too resource intensive, or possibly not yet perfected across different fonts.

The last two constants are the **HINTING_OFF** and **HINTING_ON** constants, which provide **subpixel text hinting** option constants for use when you are using the **.setHinting()** method call. **Font hinting** is an advanced feature that is usually used in conjunction with subpixel text rendering and anti-aliasing. Font hinting is also called **font instructing** and is designed to provide a higher quality visual result at lower screen resolutions. This constant is somewhat unnecessary on most Android devices, which have high resolution and high density (a fine dot pitch) at the same time. Don't ask me why this hinting flag was set up using _OFF and _ON extensions, whereas the others were not, as I don't have the answer to that one for you!

Now that we have spent a few pages covering .onDraw() as well as the Paint and Canvas classes, it is time to get your hands dirty with some Java coding. Since you are going to create a SketchPad utility for your GraphicsDesign application, you'll need to first modify several of your application XML and Java files and create a couple of new Java classes.

You will need to add a new **Menu Item** on your **MainActivity.java** home screen; create a new **SketchPad** Activity subclass and **SketchPadView** View subclass; add the new SketchPad Activity class to your **AndroidManifest.xml** file using an **<activity>** tag; add a **String constant** XML definition to your **strings.xml** and a MenuItem **<item>** tag to your **main.xml** Menu XML definition file; add a **case statement** and new **Intent** object to your onOptionsItemSelected() method; and finally code your SketchPad and SketchPadView classes from scratch, or at least from the bootstrap code that the **New ➤ Class** dialog provides for you. So, you have a ton of work to do over these next couple dozen pages!

Setting Up Your GraphicsDesign Project for Your SketchPad

The first addition you're going to make to your GraphicsDesign application's MainActivity.java Activity subclass is to add a **MenuItem** object called **The PAG SketchPad**. Open your project's **/res/menu** folder and right-click the **main.xml** file, and select the **Open** menu option or left-click it and press the **F3** key. Copy and paste the second **bookmark_utility** <item> tag and edit it to create a third MenuItem object definition with an **ID** of **sketchPad**.

Your XML markup, shown in Figure 17-1, should look like the following:

```
<item android:id="@+id/sketchPad"
      android:orderInCategory="300"
      android:showAsAction="never"
      android:title="@string/sketchPad_utility" />
```

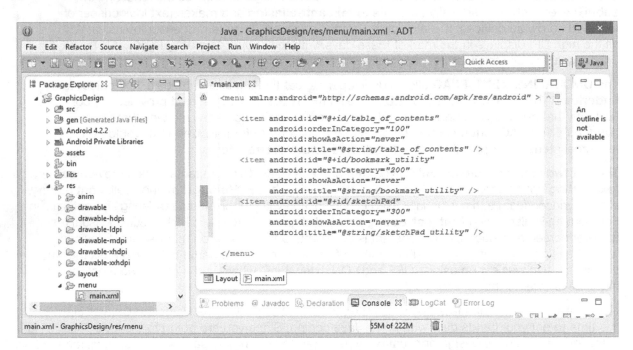

Figure 17-1. Adding the PAG SketchPad Utility to the application menu using the /res/menu folder's main.xml file

Since you referenced this String constant named **sketchPad_utility**, your next step will be to get into your **strings.xml** file, which is in your **/res/values** folder, and add that <string> tag to define this constant for use inside your menu title, or label, as I like to call it. Let's code this next.

As you can see in Figure 17-2, I added the **< string >** tag to the **strings.xml** file, naming it **sketchPad_utility** with a text value of **The PAG SketchPad**.

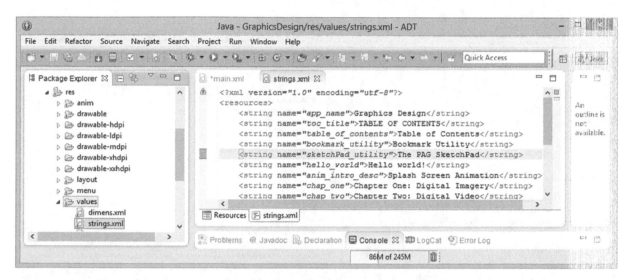

Figure 17-2. Adding a < string > constant for The PAG SketchPad menu item to the /res/values folder's strings.xml file

Right-click the **/src** folder, and use a **New ➤ Class** menu sequence to create the framework for a **SketchPad Activity** subclass, as shown in Figure 17-3.

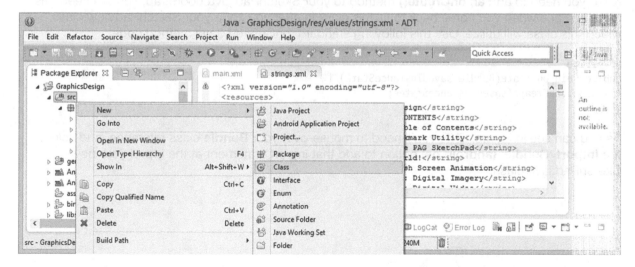

Figure 17-3. Right-clicking the /src folder and creating a New ➤ Class for a custom Activity subclass SketchPad.java

Name the class **SketchPad** and select an **android.app.Activity** superclass, as shown in Figure 17-4. Be sure to specify the **pro.android.graphics** package.

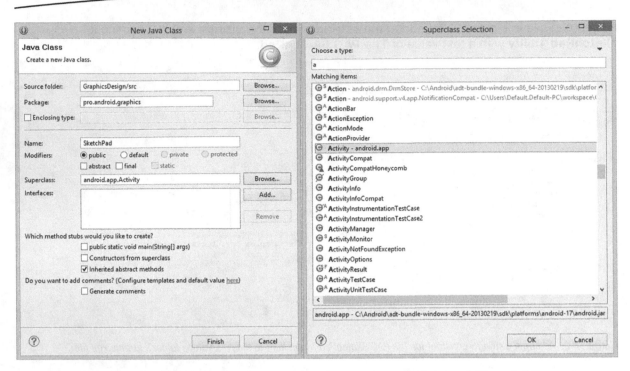

Figure 17-4. Naming this new Java class SketchPad, and defining its superclass selection as android.app.Activity

Next, you need to add an **onCreate()** method to your SketchPad.java bootstrap; you will need this to be in place when you come back to fill this class in after you code your SketchPadView class, which this class will utilize. Use this following standard .onCreate() Java method code:

```
@Override
public void onCreate(Bundle savedInstanceState) {
    super.onCreate(savedInstanceState);
}
```

As you can see in Figure 17-5, you'll need to mouse-over your **Bundle** class reference, and select the **Import 'Bundle' (android.os)** option to add that import statement at the top of your new SketchPad.java class.

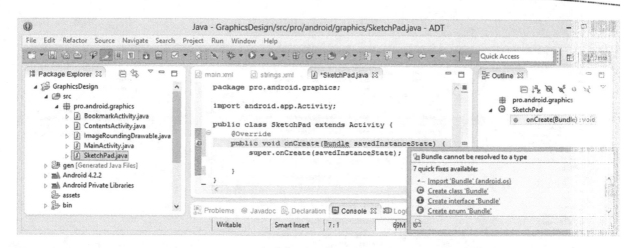

Figure 17-5. Adding the .onCreate() method to the new SketchPad Activity subclass and importing the Bundle class

Now that you have an empty SketchPad.java Activity subclass, which will not throw any errors or exceptions and admittedly does absolutely nothing at this point in time, you can move on and add the class to your application AndroidManifest and Menu object XML definition files. Let's do this next.

Right-click your **AndroidManifest.xml** file, located near the bottom of your project folder hierarchy, and select the **Open** option, or left-click it and use the **F3** function key, located at the top (left) of your keyboard.

As you may remember, you need to **declare an Activity** for use in your Manifest by using the **< activity >** tag and **android:name** and **android:label** parameters.

The fastest and easiest way to implement this is to copy the last tag for the Activity declaration that's in your AndroidManifest file currently, so select the BookmarkActivity < activity > tag in its entirety, use the **CRTL-C** combination to copy it, and then insert a line right underneath it, and use **CTRL-V** to paste it again, underneath itself, and then edit it to point to the new class by using the following XML markup, which is shown in Figure 17-6:

```
<activity android:name="pro.android.graphics.SketchPad"
          android:label="@string/sketchPad_utility" />
```

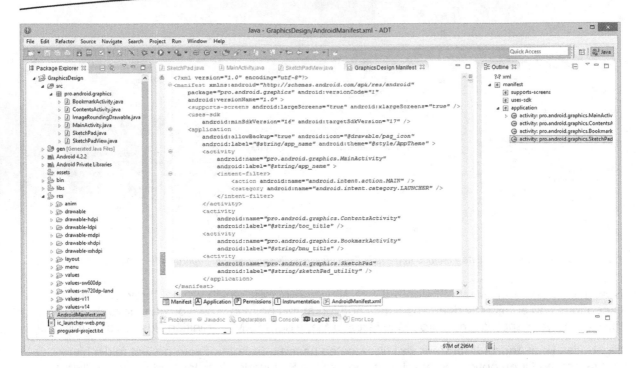

Figure 17-6. Adding a SketchPad < activity > definition to the AndroidManifest.xml file for the GraphicsDesign project

Notice that you are using that same Menu labeling < string > constant for the Activity subclass label, displayed at the top of the Activity. Speaking of MenuItem objects, you need to go back into your MainActivity.java class, and add a switch statement **case** entry and **Intent** declaration and instantiation for the third MenuItem object that you created earlier in your main.xml file so that this MenuItem becomes functional and calls your new SketchPad.java Activity, which currently (and proudly, I might add) does absolutely nothing for your application at the moment. They (women) say good things take time.

Right-click the **MainActivity.java** file in your **/src** folder, and **Open** it for editing, and copy the last case statement in the **onOptionsItemSelected** method and paste it again underneath itself so you can edit it, and create a new SketchPad Intent to be able to call your SketchPad.java Activity.

The case statement should reference your **sketchPad** MenuItem XML < item > tag defined in your main.xml file and create a new Intent named **intent-spu** for SketchPadUtility, passing it your current Activity **Context** (this), as well as the **SketchPad.class** reference parameter. Then call the **.startActivity()** method off of the current Activity Context object (we will delve into the Context class a bit later on in this chapter) via the following Java code:

```
case R.id.sketchPad:
    Intent intent_spu = new Intent(this, SketchPad.class);
    this.startActivity(intent_spu);
    break;
```

As you can see in Figure 17-7, your code is error-free, and you are ready to create your pivotal SketchPadView.java View subclass, which will do all of the heavy lifting for the interactive graphics pipeline that you are about to code, using a number of new (to you, that is) Android and Java classes.

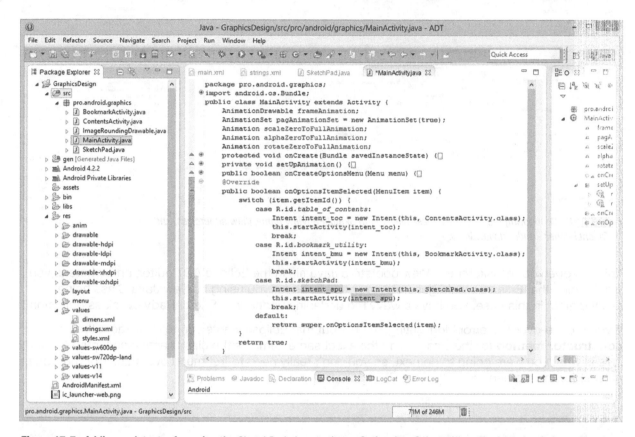

Figure 17-7. Adding an Intent referencing the SketchPad.class to the .onOptionsItemSelected() method case switch

Next, you are going to create a **SketchPadView** class that **extends** the **View** class and **implements** the OnTouchListener class, so that you have the View subclass framework in place that will hold your **.onDraw()** method calls to your **Canvas** and **Paint** objects, which you are about to create from scratch.

Creating a Custom View Class: Your SketchPadView Class

Right-click the /src folder for your project and select the **New ➤ Class** menu sequence just like you did for the SketchPad.java class (for a visual, see Figure 17-3), and you will get a New Java Class dialog and several subdialogs, as shown in Figure 17-8. Name your new class **SketchPadView**, and select the **superclass android.view.View** as well as the **Interface OnTouchListener** from the **android.view.View** package path, and finally, click the **Finish** button.

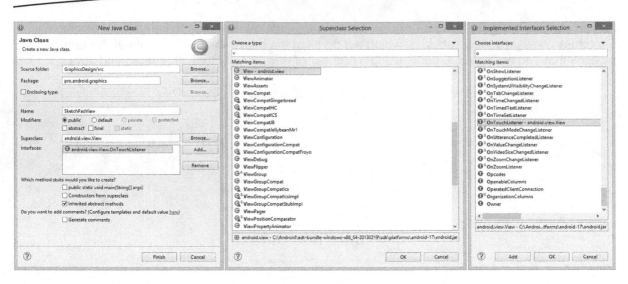

Figure 17-8. *Configuring the New Java Class dialog with SketchPadView name, View superclass, and OnTouchListener - android.view.View*

This will open up the SketchPadView bootstrap Java file in the Eclipse ADT editor, and whereas you would think that Eclipse would generate error-free code for you using its New Java Class helper utility dialog, in this case, you have a wavy red underline under your SketchPadView class definition!

If you mouse-over this error highlighting, it turns out that Eclipse wants you to implement the **constructor method** for the class, using the exact same name as the class name (see Figure 17-9). This is what you were going to do next, so you don't really need to fret much over this error message, at least for the moment.

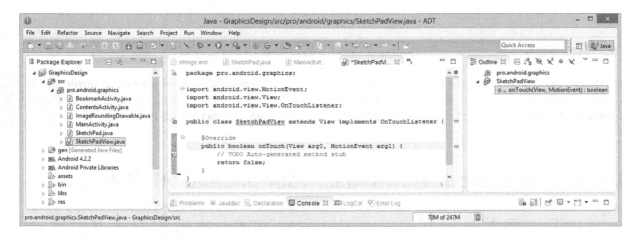

Figure 17-9. *Examining the SketchPadView public class bootstrap code in Eclipse*

As you see in Figure 17-10, Eclipse offers to code a bootstrap constructor method for you, complete with its **Context** object parameter, and most likely **Import** statements as well. Click this first **Add constructor** option now.

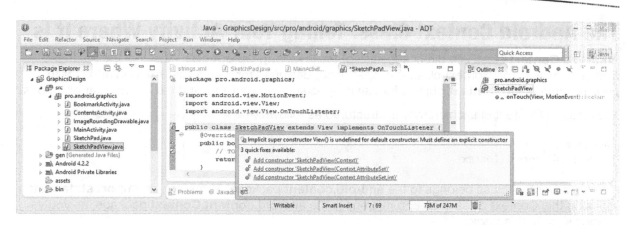

Figure 17-10. *Adding the SketchPadView(Context) constructor method bootstrap code to eliminate class's error highlighting*

As you can see in Figure 17-11, you have now coded your second Java class in this chapter that does absolutely nothing. The primary goal is error-free code, the secondary goal is code that actually does something, the tertiary goal is code that works across all devices, and the final goal is sales.

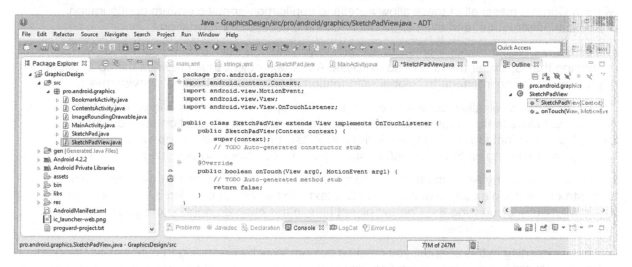

Figure 17-11. *Examining a SketchPadView() constructor method, super(context) call, and Context Import statement*

Let's take a look at your error-free SketchPadView class and its **OnTouch()** method, which takes the **View** object (which it is) and a **MotionEvent** object as parameters, and returns a **false** value, which Eclipse coded in this way probably because the method currently does nothing, so false (says nothing was accomplished during this method call) is technically correct in this particular use-case. Later, you will be changing this return value to **true**.

The **SketchPadView()** method is a bit more interesting as it will create and set up your SketchPadView custom View object that you are creating with this class. The method has only one parameter passed into it by the Android OS, a **Context** object named **context**. Let's learn a bit more about Context now!

The Android Context Class: Telling Your Activity Where It Is

Android's **Context** class is a direct subclass of the **java.lang.Object** class, just like the Paint and Canvas classes. The Context class was specifically designed for use in your Android apps for the purpose of defining **Context** objects for use in apps such as your Pro Android graphics applications.

The Android Context class hierarchy is structured as follows:

```
java.lang.Object
  > android.content.Context
```

Android's Context class belongs to the **android.content** package. Therefore, an **import statement** for using this Context class in an app references the **android.content.Context** package, as you've already seen in this book.

The Context class is a **public abstract** class, which holds an application's **contextual information**. This information contained within a Context object serves to describe **all information regarding your app** that is relevant to the Android OS and its ability to wire the application together properly.

Essentially, a Context object allows the application component referencing it to look "above" itself into the construction of your application. More than two dozen **.get()** related methods are included within a Context class; all of these allow access to application-specific system configuration, or application structure, and even application resource access or information.

In a sense, a Context object represents everything you cannot "see" before your very eyes; everything that is "under the hood," so to speak. A Context object thus provides the component that references it with an interface to "global" information about your application's environment.

The Context class will allow access to your application-specific resources and your custom classes. The Context class features methods that implement "up-calls" to application-level operations. Examples of this include launching an Activity subclass, broadcasting an app-wide message, sending and receiving an Intent object, or starting a Service object's processing.

Now you can see why Android chose the name Context for this class and for the object that it constructs. A good example of the use of Context can be seen in creating a View subclass; this is why we're discussing the Context object here in this chapter, right before you create a SketchPadView View subclass.

As you are learning in this chapter, you create a custom View by extending the View class using an **extends** keyword in the class declaration. You also saw that you must provide a constructor method that takes a Context object as its parameter. This is so that once you instantiate the custom View, you also are forced to pass in your Context object containing the context for your application. This is due to the fact that your View subclass needs to be able to have access to your application resources, classes, themes, and other similar application configuration details that a View needs to use.

Creating a View subclass is actually the perfect example to use for why a Context object needs to be passed into a constructor method. Each Context object features various data fields that are set up by the Android OS to describe your application parameters, such as display dimension or screen density, or what visual OS theme (if defined) to use with the View object.

Next, we will take a look at some of the key methods exposed by the Context class. This will provide an overview for you regarding what data a Context object might contain. For your **application**, there's a **.getApplicationInfo()** method call, as well as a **.getApplicationContext()** method call.

To grab onto your **application resources**, there is a **.getAssets()** as well as a **.getResources()** and **.getSharedResources()** method call, a **.getText()** and a **.getString()** method call, and even a **.getContentResolver()** method call.

To access your **package**, there's a **.getPackageName()**, **.getPackageManager()**, **.getPackageCodePath()**, and **.getPackageResourcePath()** method call.

To access **application settings**, there is a **.getTheme()** and **.getWallpaper()** method call, and to access **data path settings**, there is a **.getDatabasePath()** and **.getExternalFilesDir()** method call along with a **.getFileStreamPath()**, **.getDir()**, **.getFilesDir()**, and finally, a **.getCacheDir()** method call.

What do all these method calls have in common? They all enable whoever has access to a Context object the ability to reference application resources.

Context, in other words, hooks the component that has a reference to it in with all of your other application environment's components and resources. Think of it as kind of like an AndroidManifest definition for a component.

The Context class is one of the more advanced classes in Android, and for this reason, you really shouldn't worry too much if you do not understand Context objects very well at this early stage of your development.

As Pro Android programmers, as long as you understand context conceptually (I was tempted to say contextually) as well as why it is needed to provide "context" to the Android OS, regarding what your application is trying to accomplish in its entirety, you should be able to leverage it successfully and productively in your professional graphics design work for Android OS.

Configuring Your SketchPadView() Constructor Method

Now that you know more about what the Context object is doing, let's create your Paint object named **paintScreen** at the top of your class that you can use in the constructor method, which you are going to code next.

As you can see in Figure 17-12, you'll need to mouse-over and **Import 'Paint' (android.graphics)**, since you are using it in your class, and then you will be ready to start coding the constructor method, which will create and set up the SketchPadView object, after it is declared and instantiated by your SketchPad class a bit later on during this chapter.

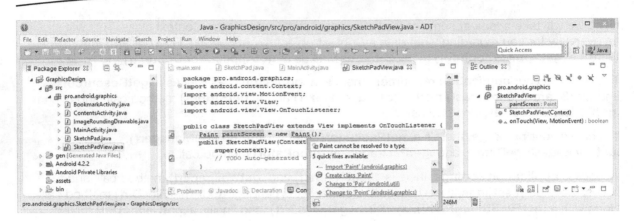

Figure 17-12.   Declaring and instantiating the paintScreen Paint object to be used to use to paint on the Canvas

Since Eclipse already coded the super(context); statement that passes the current context up to the View superclass for you, the next statement that you need to add is one that calls the **.setOnTouchListener()** method off of the current context and passes the current context as its parameter.

This is done via one short line of Java code, which will use the Java **this** keyword. In its first use-case, it refers to "this" object, the one that will be created when the SketchPadView class is declared and instantiated.

The **this** object (keyword) calls the **.setOnTouchListener()** method, passing in the **this** object (keyword) yet again, by using the following Java code:

```
this.setOnTouchListener(this);
```

As you can see in Figure 17-13, the statement generates no error warnings.

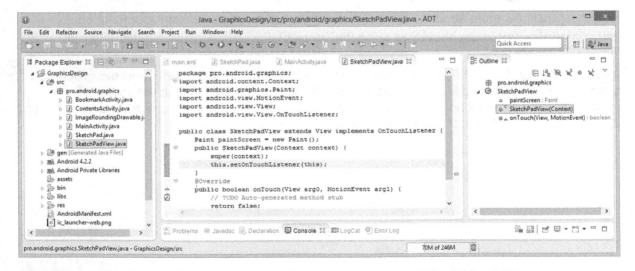

Figure 17-13.   Setting the OnTouchListener to the current Context by using the this.setOnTouchListener(this) method

The second **this** is representing a (soon to be instantiated) SketchPadView object (class), plus its Context within the overall scheme of things. You could simply imagine that the (this) Context here contains both your object (class) definition itself and the context of how your object fits into your overall application infrastructure.

Remember, Context is provided so that Android can keep everything properly connected (I like to say **wired**) together. Do not worry too much regarding what **this** (Context) is doing; instead, worry about how to implement (pass, or reference) Context (this; the object reference and Context) correctly.

Next, you will want to configure your paintScreen Paint object to anti-alias everything that you do, as well as to set its color to a system Color class constant of **CYAN**. Be careful when you use CYAN in an IDE (CYANIDE). Configure Paint by calling **.setColor()** and **.setAntiAlias()** methods off of a Paint object, using the following two lines of Java code:

```
paintScreen.setAntiAlias(true);
paintScreen.setColor(Color.CYAN);
```

Notice in Figure 17-14, that after you type in the Android **Color** class and then the **period** character, that Eclipse will bring up a **ColorPicker Helper Dialog** that contains all of the possible values available to you as color constant values within the Android OS. This can be quite helpful.

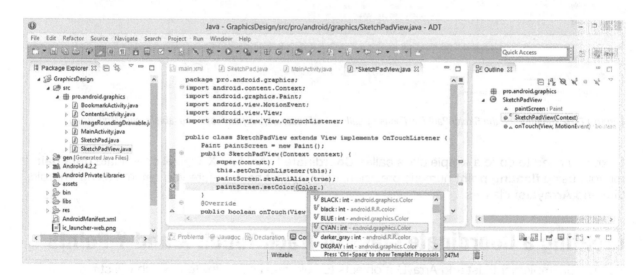

Figure 17-14. Configuring the paintScreen Paint object anti-aliasing and CYAN color constant using method calls

The next thing that you will need to do in the constructor method is to make sure that your SketchPadView object can be used by the user when the View (Activity) screen appears. You do this by making the View focusable. This is done by calling a **.setFocusable()** method. Because you are using Android Touch Mode and OnTouchListener() event handling, you must also call a

.setFocusableInTouchMode() method call as well just to make sure you have everything covered. This is done using these following lines of Java code:

```
setFocusableInTouchMode(true);
setFocusable(true);
```

As you can see in Figure 17-15, your code is error-free and your constructor method is now implemented and sets up your SketchPadView custom View object to pass its Context upwards to handle Touch events, anti-alias all pixels drawn, use a CYAN Color constant, and finally to set the View as Focusable as well as FocusableInTouchMode.

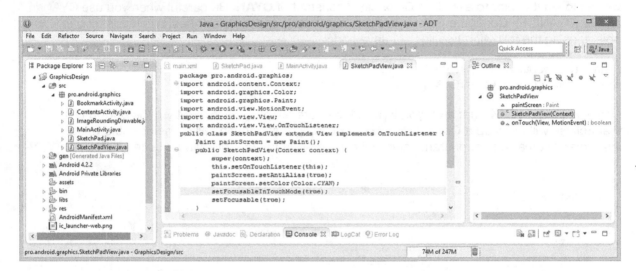

Figure 17-15. Configuring the SketchPadView Focus by calling .setFocusable(true) and .setFocusableInTouchMode(true)

Next, you need to code a simple class called **Coordinate** to hold an **X,Y** pixel coordinate **data pair** for you, using **floating point** numeric precision. Let's do that next, before you get into using Android **List** and **ArrayList** classes.

Creating a Coordinate Class to Track Touch X and Y Points

Before you implement List and ArrayList objects to hold **pixel coordinates**, which will stream out of your OnTouchListener() method as the user draws on the screen using their finger, let's write the shortest Java class that you will ever write in your lifetime, using one single line of code! In fact, you'll utilize only 32 text characters to code the entire Coordinate class!

```
class Coordinate { float x, y; }
```

This class provides a **Coordinate** object for a single pixel or point on the touchscreen, using **float** or floating point numeric precision to store the X and the Y position data values for the point's (pixel's) screen location or **coordinate**. As you can see in Figure 17-16, your class is error-free. Now you're ready to learn more about List and ArrayList classes in Android next since you are going to harness these classes in your SketchPadView class.

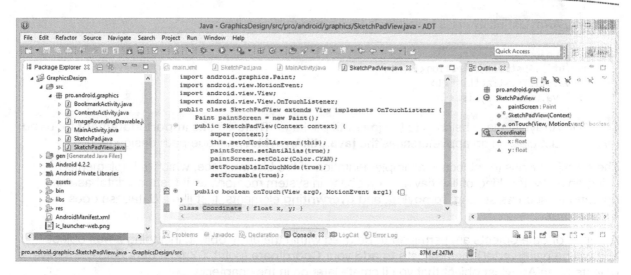

Figure 17-16. Creating a Coordinate class to provide a floating point X and Y data pair to track mouse/touch points

Before you implement your ArrayList object Coordinate List construct, which you will be naming **coordinates**, let's go over what the Android List and ArrayList classes do and exactly how they are related to each other.

The Java List Utility Class: Get Your Collections in Order

The Java **List** construct is not a class but rather a **public interface** that implements **Collection<E>** and is part of the **java.util** package.

The Java List public interface hierarchy is structured as follows:

```
java.util.List<E>
```

This Java List interface belongs to the **java.util** package. Therefore, the **import statement** for using this List interface in your app references the **java.util.List** package.

The List public interface is a **collection**, which maintains an ordering for its individual data elements. Each element in this List includes an **index**.

Each List element can later be accessed by using its index, with the first index numbered **zero**. Normally, a List will allow you to insert **duplicate** elements. This is different than using the data Set class, where each of the data elements needs to be 100 % completely unique.

Java's ArrayList Utility Class: An Array of Collection List

The Java **ArrayList** class is a **public class**, which extends **AbstractList<E>** and implements the **Serializable Cloneable RandomAccess**.

The Java ArrayList utility class hierarchy is thus structured as follows:

```
java.lang.Object
   > java.util.AbstractCollection<E>
      > java.util.AbstractList<E>
         > java.util.ArrayList<E>
```

The Java ArrayList class belongs to the **java.util** package. Therefore, its **import statement** for using this ArrayList class in an app references the **java.util.ArrayList** package path designation.

The ArrayList class (or object) is an implementation of the List interface, which is implemented using an array. It is kind of like having a database in system memory, as it features database-like operations, such as **adding**, **removing**, and **overwriting** elements, just like a database does with records.

All types of data objects are permitted to be used within the array object, including a **null** object. You will be using **.add()** method calls to **add** your **Coordinate** (point X,Y float data pair) class Java objects to an ArrayList object that you'll create later on in the chapter.

ArrayList would be a good choice to use for a default List implementation.

Creating an ArrayList Object to Hold Your Touch Point Data

Add a line of code at the top of your SketchPadView class, right under the **paintScreen** object instantiation, to set up a **coordinates** ArrayList object by using a **new** keyword to create the ArrayList, as shown in Figure 17-17.

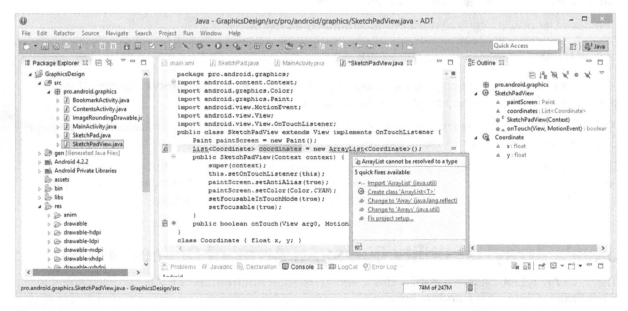

Figure 17-17. Using the new keyword to create an ArrayList List<Coordinate> object named coordinates to hold points

The Java code that you are going to write to accomplish this is as follows:

```
List<Coordinate> coordinates = new ArrayList<Coordinate>();
```

What this does is to instantiate a new **ArrayList** object based upon your **Coordinate** class and name it **coordinates**, as it is going to contain the coordinates of where your user touches the screen (over time) in the form of a List of Coordinate objects, designated in code as **List<Coordinate>**.

As you will see in Figure 17-17 and in Figure 17-18, you will also need to mouse-over this ArrayList class in your code, and **import ArrayList** (from a **java.util** package), as well as your List class, to **import List (java.util)** before you can utilize either the List<Coordinate>List collection object or the ArrayList<Coordinate>array object for your SketchViewView class.

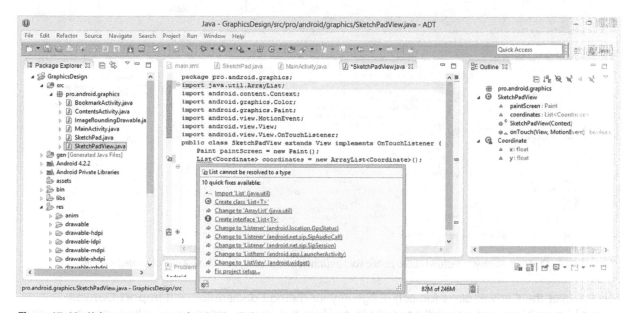

Figure 17-18. Using mouse-over to invoke the Eclipse pop-up helper dialog to import the List class from java.util package

Now you have the code infrastructure in place to create your **onDraw()** method, which will contain the **processing core** of your SketchPadView View subclass.

Implementing Your .onDraw() Method: Painting Your Canvas

The first thing that you need to do to implement your onDraw() method is to put the framework in place to hold your Java processing logic.

This is done by coding the following method declaration and parameter list right underneath your SketchPadView constructor method, as shown in Figure 17-19. The method bootstrap Java code will look just like the following:

```
public void onDraw(Canvas canvas) { draw processing pipeline code will go in here }
```

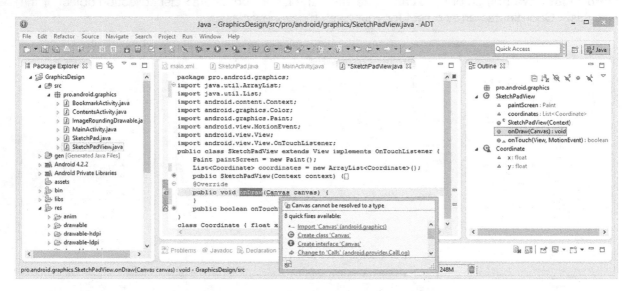

Figure 17-19. Creating an empty method called public void onDraw() and passing in a Canvas object named canvas

Mouse-over the Canvas class (object) usage in your method declaration and **import Canvas (android.graphics)**, and you will be ready to code your drawing processing pipeline engine by using a **for loop** to process X,Y coordinates.

Next, code the for loop controlled by data in the **coordinates** ArrayList you just created. Inside the for loop code is a construct calling a **.drawCircle()** method off of the Canvas object named **canvas**, as shown in Figure 17-20.

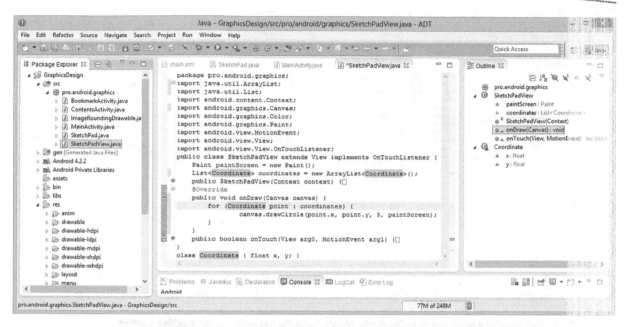

Figure 17-20. Creating a for loop that reads a coordinates ArrayList object and calls a .drawCircle() using point data

This is done using the following for loop Java code processing construct:

```
for ( Coordinate point : coordinates ) {
   canvas.drawCircle(point.x, point.y, 5, paintScreen); }
```

You will be instantiating a **point** object using your **Coordinate** class in the next section when you code an **OnTouchListener()** Touch event handler method. This will finish your Java coding for your SketchPadView View subclass. For now, what this does is use the contents of your **coordinates** ArrayList array inside this for loop structure as your "counter" for this for loop.

Inside the for loop curly brackets is one powerful Java statement that calls the .drawCircle() method off of the Canvas object named canvas, which was passed into the .onDraw() method as a parameter or attribute.

The **.drawCircle()** method is configured to draw a circle (your paintbrush) **5** pixels in diameter and at a **point.x** and **point.y** coordinate location, using the settings collection that you created for your **paintScreen** Paint object.

Creating Your OnTouchListener() Method: Event Handling

Next, you will collapse (using the minus icon on the left) the methods that you aren't working on and expand (using the plus icon also on the left) your onTouch() method call, as shown in Figure 17-21. As you can see, the first thing that you want to do each time you process a Touch(screen) event is to instantiate a **Coordinate** object named **point** using a **new** keyword like this:

```
Coordinate point = new Coordinate();
```

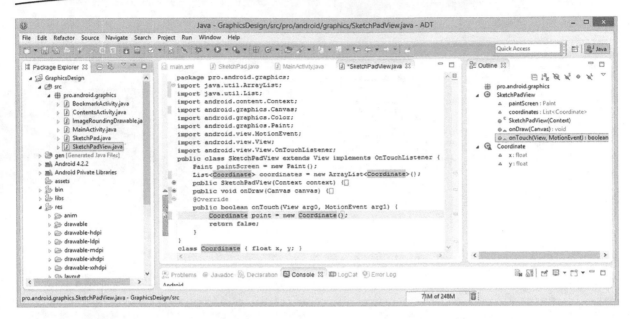

Figure 17-21. Constructing a point to a new Coordinate object inside the onTouch() event handling method

Android's MotionEvent Class: Movement Data in Android

The Android **MotionEvent** class is a **public class**, which extends **InputEvent** and **implements Parcelable**.

Android's MotionEvent class hierarchy is structured as follows:

```
java.lang.Object
  > android.view.InputEvent
    > android.view.MotionEvent
```

The Android MotionEvent belongs to the **android.view** package, which is why you are using it in your SketchPadView View subclass. Therefore, the **import statement** for using this MotionEvent class in your app references the **android.view.MotionEvent** package path structure.

A MotionEvent is an object that can be utilized to report **movement** in the Android OS. This movement could come from a user's **finger** in TouchMode, or from a **Mouse**, **Trackball**, **NavKeys**, **LightPen**, **Game Controller**, **3D Trackball**, or similar Android hardware feature that can (will) generate MotionEvents.

MotionEvent objects can hold either **absolute** or **relative** movement data, as well as other types of related data. The data that will be loaded into the MotionEvent object data structure will ultimately depend upon what type of hardware device is generating this movement datastream in the first place.

MotionEvent objects encode movement data using an **action code** along with a set of **axis values**. Unless your user is using a 3D controller, axis values will usually be X and Y, as they are in your application in this chapter.

The action code will specify the **state change** that has occurred since the last MotionEvent, for instance, if the mouse pointer has gone down or up.

The axis values describe the **coordinate position** as well as other movement properties, and these are the values that you will be extracting from your **arg1 MotionEvent** object during the next section of this chapter.

Modern Android devices can track **multiple movement data** at the same time. Some Android hardware supports **MultiTouch** displays that can broadcast one movement data stream for each user's finger. Individual fingers and other objects that generate movement data streams are referred to as **pointers**.

We are not using MultiTouch movement data in the SketchPad app because the AVD emulator does not currently support it. We need to be able to run the software we are creating in this book using a platform (method) that every reader can access and utilize, so we're using the AVD in the Eclipse IDE.

MotionEvent objects contain information about all of the pointers that are currently in use, even if some of these pointers have not been moved since the last MotionEvent object was delivered by the Android operating system.

The Android MotionEvent class defines several different methods that can be used to access the coordinate position, as well as other properties of pointers. These include **.getX()** and **.getY()** method calls, which we'll use.

Other method calls for the MotionEvent class offer more fine-tuned or detailed data to be extracted from the MotionEvent object, such as **.getAction()**, **.getFlags()**, **.getOrientation()**, **.getSize()**, **.getAxisValue()**, **.getDeviceId()**, **.getSource()**, **.getMetaState()**, and a plethora of others.

MotionEvent method calls take a **pointer index** as the parameter rather than using the pointer ID value. The pointer index of each pointer contained in the MotionEvent object ranges from zero to one less than a value returned by a **.getPointerCount()** method call. As you have seen, it is necessary to use an **array** when dealing with MotionEvent objects due to the sheer volume of data that's flowing through your draw processing pipeline in real time.

The order in which individual pointer data might appear in the MotionEvent object is undefined. For this reason, the pointer index of the pointer may change from one MotionEvent object to another. However, a pointer id for a pointer will always remain constant as long as the pointer remains active.

Processing Your Movement Data: Using .getX() and .getY()

Once you have created a **point Coordinate** object to hold the floating point X and Y values that will be coming into your **onTouch()** method via the **arg1** MotionEvent object, you call **.getX()** or **.getY()** methods, as shown in Figure 17-22, to **extract** the X and Y coordinate data from this MotionEvent object structure, which has been passed into your onTouch() event handling method.

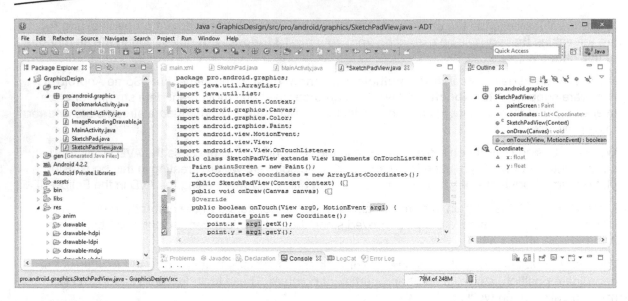

Figure 17-22. Calling a .getX() and .getY() method on the MotionEvent object named arg1 to set point object data

Now that you have created your **point Coordinate** object and loaded it with X and Y coordinate values, you can use the ArrayList class's **.add()** method to add this point (X,Y) object to your **coordinates** ArrayList object, which you created at the top of your SketchPadView class, as shown in Figure 17-23.

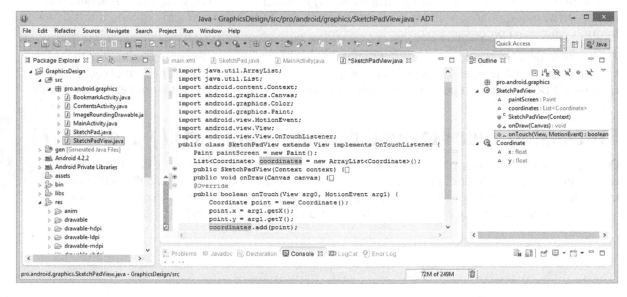

Figure 17-23. Using an ArrayList class .add() method to add a Coordinate object named point to coordinates array

You will accomplish this by using the following compact line of Java code:

```
coordinates.add(point);
```

Now that you have added this MotionEvent coordinate data to your coordinates ArrayList object, you can call the View class methods that will update your screen and return the **true** value to the calling entity, letting it know that your MotionEvent object data processing has been completed.

The next line of code that you will need to write in your onTouch() method is an **invalidate()** method call, which is shown in Figure 17-24. Calling an invalidate() method will trigger a **refresh** for your custom View object.

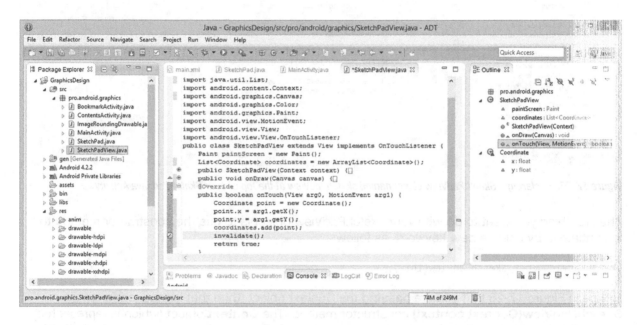

Figure 17-24. Calling View class's invalidate() method to update SketchPadView object once the XY data processed

Essentially what this means is that an invalidate() method call will serve to **redraw** the display screen using the latest graphics data available.

I'm not sure why this method call is named invalidate, other than possibly instructing the Android OS to invalidate what is currently displayed in a View object. This would signal that you wanted Android to perform a display screen **refresh operation** using the new information that you have drawn into the **framebuffer**. It's not the most intuitive method call in the OS, that's for sure, but as long as you know what it's doing, you're all set to draw.

A framebuffer is a 2D area held in system memory (such as a Canvas object) that has the same dimensions as the display screen and is used to compose graphics that will eventually be drawn to a screen (invalidated).

Finally, if you haven't done so already, change your return statement at the end of the onTouch() method from a false value over to a **true** value.

Coding Your SketchPad Activity: Using the SketchPadView

Now that you can create a new type of View object, called SketchPadView, you can click the SketchPad.java tab, as shown in Figure 17-25, and declare the SketchPadView object, named **sketchPadView**. You can now use a SketchPadView.

Figure 17-25.   Declaring a SketchPadView object named sketchPadView at the top of your SketchPad.java Activity

The first thing you want to do with your sketchPadView object is to use the constructor method to instantiate it, by using a **new** keyword, as follows:

```
sketchPadView = new SketchPadView(this);
```

Notice in Figure 17-26 that you are **passing** the Context object (**this**) that is required for your **SketchPadView(Context context)** constructor method. The **Context** object (which is represented via the **this** keyword, on this side of things, no pun intended), as you know, contains information describing how your SketchPad.java Activity class fits into your GraphicsDesign app.

Figure 17-26. Instantiating the sketchPadView object using the SketchPadView() constructor inside the onCreate()

Your next step will be to tell the **ContentView** object for your Activity what you want it to display. This is often set to an XML UI layout definition, as you've seen throughout this book. In this case, you'll set this to display your **sketchPadView** SketchPadView object instead, as shown in Figure 17-27.

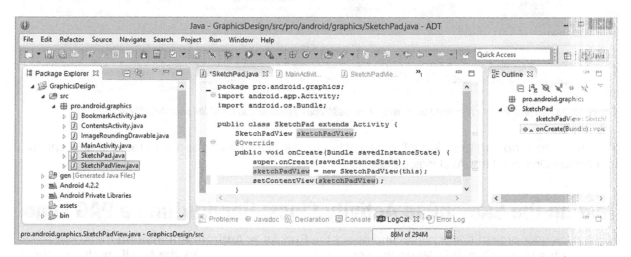

Figure 17-27. Setting ContentView for the SketchPad Activity subclass to the sketchPadView SketchPadView object

This is done by passing the **sketchPadView** object to the **ContentView** object by using a **.setContentView()** method, as shown in the following line of Java code:

```
setContentView(sketchPadView);
```

The next thing that you will need to do is to **activate** your SketchPad Activity screen surface for the user so it will send MotionEvent objects to your onTouch() event handing method. You do this by **requesting the focus** for the View from the Android OS, by calling the **.requestFocus()** method off of the **sketchPadView** object. This is done using the following line of Java code:

```
sketchPadView.requestFocus();
```

As you can see, in Figure 17-28, I clicked one of the sketchPadView object references in the Java code in the Eclipse IDE so that it would highlight an **object trail** for me (or in this case, for you). I did this so that you could see the object declaration and instantiation (tan highlighting), as well as its usage (grey highlighting, that is, the second two highlights).

Figure 17-28. *Calling the TouchScreen Focus using a .requestFocus() method call off of the sketchPadView object*

The final step in adding this SketchPad Utility to your GraphicsDesign app is to test the application in a Nexus One emulator AVD inside Eclipse.

Testing the SketchPad Activity Class: Handwriting a PAG Logo

Right-click your project folder name, and select the **Run As ➤ Android Application** menu sequence to launch the Nexus One AVD. When the app home screen appears, click the MENU button on the top-right of the emulator (second button in the bottom row), open your Options menu, click **The PAG SketchPad** menu item, and launch your SketchPad Activity subclass.

Click and hold your left mouse button, simulating your finger touch on the surface of your screen, and using your best handwriting, write **PAG** for me!

As you can see in Figure 17-29, the new addition to your GraphicsDesign app suite works great, and as you can see on the right side of the screenshot, the faster you move your finger, the more space appears between the 5-pixel circles that are drawn to the screen. I moved rapidly in my stroke at the end of this PAG handwriting exercise to show this visually on the screen.

Figure 17-29. Testing the PAG SketchPad Activity in the Nexus One AVD emulator and handwriting a PAG logo

This is all fairly cool, but let's take this SketchPad Utility to the next level by implementing something that we would find in a professional image editing software package, such as Photoshop or GIMP. One of the features I use in those packages is the **clone tool**, which allows me to select imagery that I want to turn into a **paintbrush source**, and paint using that image's pixel data. If we could implement something like this in the SketchPadView, it would be much more impressive (and useful) than basic cyan ink drawing.

Paint Using a Bitmap Source: Implementing Your InkShader

To accomplish this, you must essentially create an **InkShader** for your pen (or finger), which will require a number of classes that you have already used inside the fairly aggressive graphics pipeline constructions during this book.

The first thing that you need to do is to create a **paintImage** Bitmap object by using the **BitmapFactory** class and its **.decodeResource()** method call.

Inside this **BitmapFactory.decodeResource()** method call, you will want to nest yet another **getResources()** method call, as well as a reference to the **R.drawable.cloudsky** image asset. You will do this using the following code:

```
Bitmap paintImage = BitmapFactory.decodeResources(getResources(),R.drawable.cloudsky);
```

As you can see in Figure 17-30, you are placing this code right after your paintScreen object instantiation to keep your paintScreen and paintImage objects together. Sometimes you just have to take the initiative to make your Java coding romantic. Now that you have a paintImage Bitmap object to clone colored pixel data from, you can go ahead and create your Shader code.

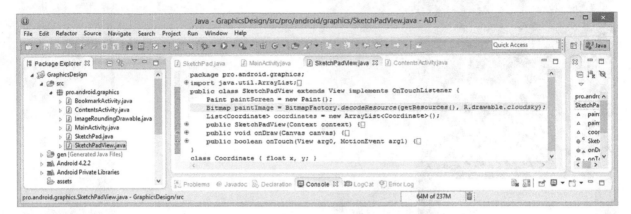

Figure 17-30. Creating the paintImage Bitmap object by using a BitmapFactory.decodeResource() method call

Now you can use your trusty **BitmapShader** class to create an **inkShader** object by instantiating a new (keyword) BitmapShader object using your **paintImage** as the Bitmap object parameter along with a **Shader.TileMode.CLAMP** constant for the X and the Y axis or dimension, as shown in Figure 17-31.

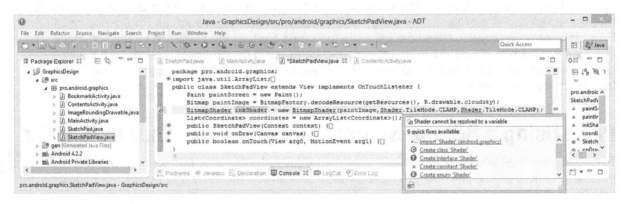

Figure 17-31. Creating an inkShader BitmapShader object using the new keyword and BitmapShader constructor

The Java code to accomplish this inkShader configuration looks like this:

```
BitmapShader inkShader = new BitmapShader( paintImage, Shader.TileMode.CLAMP, Shader.TileMode.CLAMP );
```

As you can see in Figure 17-31 and Figure 17-32, you need to mouse-over the Shader and BitmapShader class references, and have Eclipse import the Shader and BitmapShader classes from the android.graphics package.

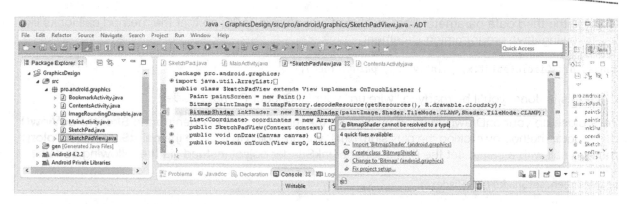

Figure 17-32. Mouse-over Shader and BitmapShader class references and have Eclipse code import statements for you

Next, so you can visualize painting with a Bitmap image asset source, change your thin 5 pixel paintbrush stroke width to a much wider **25 pixel paintbrush stroke** width, just like you would do if you were working in GIMP 2.8.6 or Photoshop CS6, only via Java code.

Click the plus icon next to the onDraw() method block of code in Eclipse, as shown in Figure 17-33, and open up the method so that you can edit the for loop and the canvas.drawCircle() method call that live inside it.

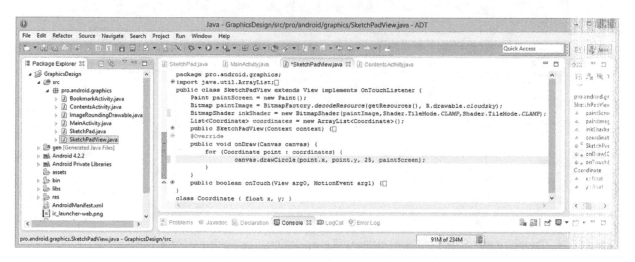

Figure 17-33. Changing brush stroke width from 5 pixels to 25 pixels in the .onDraw() method's .drawCircle() call

Change the third data parameter from a value of 5 to a value of **25**, so that the method call looks like the following Java programming statement:

```
canvas.drawCircle(point.x, point.y, 25, paintScreen);
```

Once this is done, you'll be ready to "wire up" your inkShader BitmapShader!

Let's close up your onDraw() method by clicking the minus sign, and open up the **SketchPadView()** constructor method by clicking the plus sign. Next, you are going to replace the **paintScreen.setColor()** method call with a call to set the BitmapShader inkShader object instead via the following code:

```
paintScreen.setShader(inkShader);
```

This wires up an **inkShader** BitmapShader object that contains a **paintImage** Bitmap object into your **paintScreen** Paint object, which is in turn used in the onDraw() method to create your paintbrush, and turns it into a **cloning tool**. As you can see in Figure 17-34, your code is error-free; thus, you are ready to have some fun cloning your cloudsky.jpg image asset via your Canvas object surface using fat 25 pixel brushstrokes, just like you'd do in GIMP.

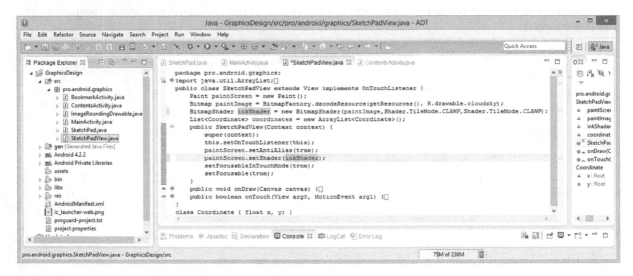

Figure 17-34. Changing a paintScreen.setColor() method call to a paintScreen.setShader(inkShader) method call

This will essentially look like you are erasing the white (default) system screen background color and exposing the cloudsky image behind it. However, this is not in fact what is happening; actually you are painting using your Bitmap image source onto this white canvas surface.

Let's use the **Run As ➤ Android Application** menu sequence and launch the Nexus One emulator so you can see your **shader drawing pipeline** in action.

Click the **MENU** button on the emulator, and select **The PAG SketchPad** menu item, and launch the SketchPad.java Activity subclass so that you can test your new code using the Nexus One AVD emulator one final time (we hope).

When the white screen appears, draw a huge PAG to expose some of the pixel color data that is being **culled** from your Bitmap object using the Shader and BitmapShader classes. As you can see in Figure 17-35, I also played around with the appearance of exposing the image behind the white overlay, which, although this is not really what is happening, you could always use this perceived effect to your advantage if you wanted to in your own apps!

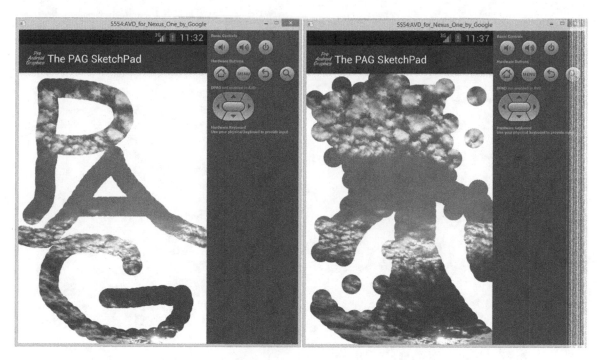

Figure 17-35. Testing your InkShader and image cloning drawing feature using the Nexus One AVD emulator

Summary

In this seventeenth chapter, you learned how to leverage an **.onDraw()** method in conjunction with the **Paint** and **Canvas** classes to create your own custom **SketchPad** graphics program in Android. We took a more detailed look at both the Canvas and the Paint classes. Then you coded your own drawing on a canvas pipeline to learn how to create interactive graphics applications using Paint, Canvas, onDraw(), and onTouch() with some other key classes.

Along the way you learned about some other important classes for graphics, including the **Context** class for providing the context for what you are doing to the Android OS, plus the **List** and **ArrayList** classes for creating **collections** (lists) and **arrays** of those collections.

You also learned more about the **MotionEvent** class, which you later utilized for **movement tracking** and touch event data processing in the Android OS and in interactive applications (in this case, your **SketchPadView** View subclass). You learned how to create your own **custom View** subclass, just like you learned how to create a custom Drawable subclass back in Chapter 16.

In the next chapter, we'll switch back into digital video editing and optimization mode, which you were learning about back in Chapter 2 before we got sidetracked by all of this other really cool graphics pipeline coding.

Chapter 18

Playing Captive Video Using the VideoView and MediaPlayer Classes

In this eighteenth chapter, you'll gain more experience using the Android **VideoView**, **Uri**, and **MediaPlayer** classes, as well as optimizing multiple "target" digital video asset resolutions for use with popular Android devices featuring different physical display screen resolutions and pixel pitch specifications.

We will also optimize for a range of digital video playback **data rates**, or bit rates, to accommodate processor power ranging from a single-core up to a quad-core and beyond (there are already octa-core devices available out there, such as the Galaxy S4 from Samsung Electronics).

We will first take a look at the various stages of a digital video asset's life cycle, which will give you that basic overview you'll need in order to understand the various method calls available for use with the Android MediaPlayer digital video playback engine.

You will learn about the Android **MediaPlayer** class and its **nested classes**, which allow you to implement **Listeners** that will run your custom Java code if needed during different stages of the digital video playback lifecycle.

You'll also implement one of the Listener nested classes in your application code. This will allow a digital video asset to loop seamlessly by setting up the video looping parameter in the video preparation stage of the video playback lifecycle. You'll learn how to make a digital video asset scale to fit different aspect ratios, as promised in Chapter 2. Finally, you will optimize digital video assets across 10 different industry standard device screen resolutions, including WVGA, WSVGA, Pseudo HD (1280 x 720), or True HD (1920 x 1080) resolution.

A Life of a Video: The Stages of a Video Playback Lifecycle

Before we look at the VideoView and MediaPlayer classes in depth, you need to first understand the different "stages" that a digital video asset goes through inside the Android operating system. Playing a digital video may seem quite simple on the surface: press Play, Pause, Rewind, and so on. Certainly these steps are part of the overall process. However, there are some "behind the scenes" steps that allow the Android OS to load the video asset in memory, set parameters for it, and other more system-level considerations which ultimately make for an optimal user experience.

When you implement a VideoView, which you have already done in this book by using around a dozen lines of XML markup and Java code, you also implement a MediaPlayer object that will play a digital video asset associated with this asset via the URI object reference.

When a MediaPlayer object is first instantiated, but is doing nothing, the MediaPlayer object is in what's called an **idle state**. Once you use the **URI** object via the **Uri.parse()** method call, or a **.setDataSource()** method call, your MediaPlayer object goes into what is termed an **initialized state**. You will learn about the Android URI class a bit later on in this chapter.

There is an intermediary state between the **initialized** MediaPlayer object state and a **started** MediaPlayer object state called a **prepared** MediaPlayer object state. This state is accessed using **MediaPlayer.OnPreparedListener**, a **nested class** that you will be learning about in the next section of this chapter and actually using inside your application's Java code.

Once your MediaPlayer object has been initialized (loaded with data), and prepared (configured), it can then be started. Once **started** (playing), it can be **stopped** using the **.stop()** method call, or **paused** using the **.pause()** method call. These three video states should be the most familiar to you.

The final type of MediaPlayer object state is a **playback completed** state, which means that the video asset will stop playing, unless a **.setLooping()** method call off of (to) the MediaPlayer object has been set to the **true** Boolean value, in which case your video will continue to loop seamlessly.

There are also **.start()** and **.reset()** method calls for a MediaPlayer object that can **start** and **reset** the MediaPlayer object again, at any time, based on the needs in your Java programming logic. Finally, there's a **.release()** method call, which invokes the **end state** for the MediaPlayer object, which will end the MediaPlayer object lifecycle and **remove it from memory**.

There are other **nested classes** that will also allow you to "listen" for **errors** (**MediaPlayer.OnErrorListener**), as well other states of the MediaPlayer, such as when it reaches a **playback completed** state (**MediaPlayer.OnCompletionListener**). You'll be looking at these in a future section when you look at the MediaPlayer class in detail to understand exactly how it works before you use it in your code!

Where Video Lives: The Data URI and Android's Uri Class

Before you look at the MediaPlayer class you must understand what a URI is, and what URI objects and Android's Uri class provide to us as developers.

URI stands for **Uniform Resource Identifier**, and is "uniform" because it is a **standard**, a "resource" because it **references** a data path to the data that your application will operate on (or utilize), and "identifier" because it **identifies** where you can get the data, also known as its **data path**.

A URI has four parts. First is the URI **schema**, such as **HTTP://**; next comes the **authority**, such as **apress.com**; next comes a **path**, such as **/data/files**; and finally the **data object**, usually some sort of file, such as **video.mp4**.

The Android **Uri** class is a direct subclass of the **java.lang.Object** master class. There is also a Uri class in the Java programming language, but as we are using Android here, we will take a look at the Android Uri class. A **java.net.Uri** class also exists; however I suggest that you use the Android-specific version of the class, as it is conformed for use with Android OS.

The Android Uri class hierarchy is structured as follows:

```
java.lang.Object
  > android.net.Uri
```

The Android Uri class belongs to the **android.net** package, making it a tool for accessing data across a network. For this reason, the **import statement** for using the Uri class inside your Android application references a package path of **android.net.Uri**, as you'll see later on in this chapter.

The Uri class is a **public abstract** class and has over three dozen methods that allow developers to work with URI objects (and data path references).

The Android Uri class allows developers to create **URI objects** that provide an **immutable** URI reference. You've had experience making your Bitmap objects immutable by placing them in system memory for use, and you need to do the same thing for your URI data path references by using Android's Uri class.

Your URI object reference includes a **URI specifier** as well as a **data path** reference, which is the component of your URI following the ://. The Uri class will take care of **building** and **parsing** a URI object that references data in a manner that conforms to the **RFC 2396** technical specification.

To optimize Android operating system and application performance, this Uri class performs very little data path validation. What this means is that a behavior is not defined for handling an invalid data input. This means the Uri class is very forgiving in the face of an invalid input specification.

Thus, as a developer you have to be very careful in what you are doing, as URI objects will return garbage rather than throw an exception, unless you specify otherwise using your Java code. **Error trapping** and **data path validation** are left up to the developer to do inside their code.

Android's MediaPlayer Class: Controlling Video Playback

We looked (briefly) at the MediaPlayer and MediaController classes back in Chapter 2, and now it's time to get into the MediaPlayer core media player class at an advanced level so that you can leverage it directly within your GraphicsDesign app's MainActivity.java class.

Later on in the chapter you will put your 3D virtual world fly-through video back in behind your logo to create an animated backdrop for your application splash screen. To do this you'll need to make it loop seamlessly, and you'll need to remove the MediaController UI component, making the digital video asset simply a part of your overall animated splash screen compositing operation.

The Android **MediaPlayer** class is a direct subclass of the **java.lang.Object** master class. This indicates that Android's MediaPlayer class was designed specifically for the purpose of providing **MediaPlayer** objects. These are a part of the VideoView widget, as you will see in the next section.

Android's MediaPlayer class hierarchy is therefore structured as follows:

```
java.lang.Object
  > android.media.MediaPlayer
```

The MediaPlayer class belongs to the **android.media** package. Therefore, the **import statement** for using a MediaPlayer class in your app references the **android.media.MediaPlayer** package, as you will soon see in this book.

The MediaPlayer class is a **public** class and features **nine** nested classes. Eight of these nested classes offer callbacks for determining information regarding the operation of the MediaPlayer video playback engine. The ninth nested class, a **MediaPlayer.TrackInfo** nested class, is utilized to return video, audio, or subtitle track metadata information.

The callback that you will be implementing later on in the chapter is the MediaPlayer. OnPreparedListener, which allows you to configure a MediaPlayer object before playback starts the first time. Other often-called callbacks include **MediaPlayer.OnErrorListener,** which can respond to (handle) error messages, and **MediaPlayer.OnCompletionListener**, which can run other Java statements once your video asset playback is completed.

There is also **MediaPlayer.OnSeekCompletedListener**, which is called when a **seek operation** is completed, and **MediaPlayer.OnBufferingUpdateListener**, which is called in order to obtain **data buffering status** for a video asset that is being streamed over a network.

There are also a couple of less often utilized nested classes, such as the **MediaPlayer. OnTimedTextListener** (used when **timed text** becomes available for display) and **MediaPlayer. OnInfoListener** (used to display **information** or **warnings** about certain video media). These are not used often, at least not to my knowledge, but are available if necessary.

The Android VideoView Class: The Video Asset Container

Behind the scenes (no pun intended), the Android MediaPlayer and VideoView classes are married together, wedded in a digital matrimonial bliss, which may not be apparent on the surface, as is the case with most marriages. In this section we'll investigate how these two classes are inexorably linked together so that you understand the best way to access the MediaPlayer in the VideoView object, which you'll be doing a bit later on in this chapter.

The Android **VideoView** class is a direct subclass of an Android **SurfaceView** layout container class, which is in turn the direct subclass of an Android **View** class, which is, finally, the direct subclass of the **java.lang.Object** master class.

The Android VideoView class hierarchy is therefore structured as follows:

```
java.lang.Object
  > android.view.View
    > android.view.SurfaceView
      > android.widget.VideoView
```

The Android VideoView class belongs to the **android.widget** package, making it a User Interface element, or widget. Therefore, the **import statement** for using the VideoView class in your Android application references **android.widget.VideoView** as its package, as you saw earlier in this book.

The VideoView class is a **public** class and has over two dozen method calls or callbacks, which one would think would be part of the MediaPlayer class, and in a way, as you know now, they're married together, deep in Java code.

We will take a look at some of the more important and useful method calls since we already covered the callbacks (in the previous section), just so that you're familiar with them in case you need to implement any of these extended digital video features in your own video playback applications.

The simplest method calls were discussed in the first section on MediaPlayer states; these include **.pause()**, **.resume()**, **.start()**, **.stop()**, **.suspend()**, and **.stopPlayback()**. We've already used the **.setMediaController()** and the **.setVideoURI()** method calls, and there is a **.setVideoPath()** method call as well, which accomplishes much the same end result.

There are four .get() method calls: **.getDuration()**, **.getCurrentPosition()**, **.getBufferPercentage()**, and **.getAudioSessionId()** as well as an **.isPlaying()** method call to see if the video is playing back currently. There are also three .can() method calls to ascertain what the MediaPlayer is able to do: **.canPause()**, **.canSeekBackward()**, and **.canSeekForward()**.

There are standard event handling method calls that are inherited from the View class, such as **.onTouchEvent()**, **onKeyDown()**, and **onTrackballEvent()**. Finally, there are specialized method calls such as **.resolveAdjustedSize()** or **.onInitializeAccessibilityEvent()** to implement accessibility standards.

Using the MediaPlayer Class: Looping a Video Seamlessly

The only real way to learn how to implement the MediaPlayer by using a VideoView widget is to get your hands dirty with Java code and XML markup! Let's shift into production mode, write code and optimize video, and add multi-resolution support for your video asset next.

Let's reinstall the digital video that you created in Chapter 2 (and disabled in the chapters that followed so that you could explore animation, compositing, blending, and the like without the visual distraction of background video and its processing overhead) and put those seven lines of code back in the **onCreate()** method of your primary Activity class so that it plays behind the PAG logo on your splash screen. As you can see in Figure 18-1, I've placed these seven lines of code right after the **.setUpAnimation()** method call, and you'll see later in the left-hand side of Figure 18-5 that everything is working together seamlessly.

Figure 18-1. Adding your Video Playback Java logic from Chapter 2 into your current animated splash screen code

The next thing that you want to have happen is that instead of a transport UI control for your digital video, you want it to loop seamlessly behind the logo. To accomplish this, you'll remove three lines of code, which are shown in Figure 18-2, by commenting them out. These are the lines of code to create and wire-in your MediaController object to your VideoView object.

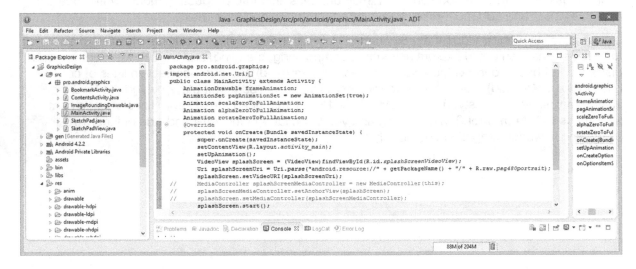

Figure 18-2. Removing the MediaController UI controls from your digital video playback to prepare to loop it forever

Next, use the **Run As ➤ Android Application** work process and notice that the digital video asset **still plays**, albeit once, using only the **four lines of code** that are left. This represents the least amount of code that you'll need to implement in order to get digital video assets to play back (once) in an application.

The fastest (and the simplest) way to get digital video to loop within the Android OS is to use the **.setLooping()** method with a **true** parameter. Since this is not available with the MediaController functionality (and for good reason, as if a video is looping forever, controlling it is not an option), you will need to use the MediaPlayer class, which does support this method.

You may think that declaring, instantiating, and constructing a MediaPlayer object and calling this function on it would be the best way to accomplish this, but there is a slicker way to obtain a reference to the MediaPlayer object that the VideoView object is utilizing (internally) to play video.

This is done by using one of those nested classes that you learned about earlier in this chapter. Since you only want to set this looping parameter one time, the logical nested class for you to utilize to achieve this is the **MediaPlayer.OnPreparedListener()** nested class.

Using this nested class, you can set your looping parameter just as Android is preparing the video, when Android is ascertaining how (or when) to play it optimally. This is a perfect time to set up parameters, such as looping parameters, in what I prefer to think of as a MediaPlayer "configuration" (also known as preparation) stage of your MediaPlayer's imminent lifecycle.

This can be done by calling this **.setOnPreparedLister()** method off of your **splashScreen** VideoView object and instantiating a **new** nested class inside that method call using the MediaPlayer.OnPreparedListener() reference.

The Java statement to do this is shown in Figure 18-3 and looks like this:

```
splashScreen.setOnPreparedListener(new MediaPlayer.OnPreparedListener(){Override});
```

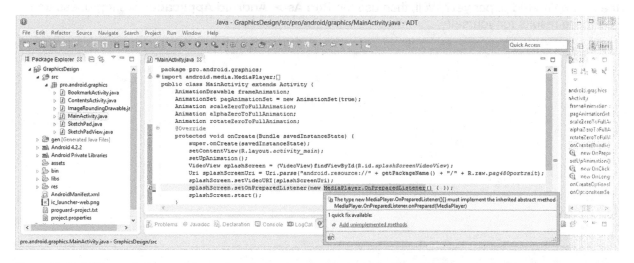

Figure 18-3. Adding .setOnPreparedListener() method to the splashScreen VideoView object to set loop parameter

As you can see in Figure 18-3, Eclipse is offering to write unimplemented method bootstrap code for you, so click the "**Add unimplemented method**" option and take a brief moment to thank goodness for small miracles.

Inside this **public void onPrepared(MediaPlayer arg0)** method structure, add your `.setLooping(true);` method call, and also notice that I took the liberty of naming the **MediaPlayer** object that is passed into this method **splashScreenMediaPlayer,** as that is what it is, not a pirate hurling some insult (Aarrrgh Zero). Weak joke, but strong code. So, as you can see in Figure 18-4, your method call is

```
splashScreenMediaPlayer.setLooping(true);
```

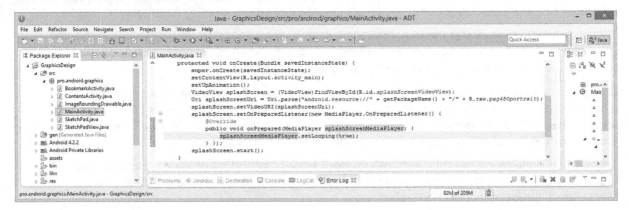

Figure 18-4. Coding an onPrepared() method to expose the MediaPlayer object and call the .setLooping() method off of it

As you can see in Figure 18-5, the digital video now will loop seamlessly. What? You are not using the new animated paper yet? Well, then use the **Run As ➤ Android Application** work process and see these results for yourself.

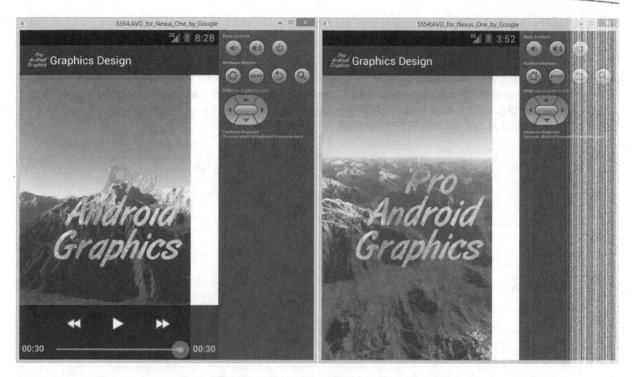

Figure 18-5. Before and after splash screen in Nexus One emulator, showing MediaController and looping video

If you look online for solutions to looping video, you will see a ton of recommendations to call the **.start()** method every time the video ends using the **MediaPlayer.OnCompletionListener()** nested class, which will also work. However, I think you will agree that this method is less complicated, less work for the OS, less memory-intensive, and less likely to incur a memory leak; and it's the proper way to set up your video to loop once so you can forget about it!

Next, you will modify your XML UI layout container code and UI widgets so your digital video asset will **non-uniformly scale** to fit slight variances in a user's display screen aspect ratio. This 3D virtual world video, much like your cloudsky.jpg asset that you used earlier in the book, is a good asset to scale in this fashion because it is difficult to fathom what the exact original motion imagery (video data) looked like in the first place.

Setting Up Scaling Video Assets to Fit any Screen Aspect Ratio

You are now going to see how to change your XML user interface definition to allow your digital video assets to "scale to fit" slightly different screen aspect ratios.

I'm not talking about drastic asymmetric scaling here, as you'll see later on in the chapter. You're going to develop a number of 16:9 or 16:10 aspect ratio video assets to hit the most popular Android device physical resolution specifications. You'll do this using Terragen 3, VirtualDub 1.9, and Sorenson Squeeze Pro 9, like we did in Chapter 2.

So you may be scaling 10% or so along one axis, but this should not be that noticeable, unless the content is a "talking head," of course. The virtual world video content we are using here isn't prone to noticeable distortion.

Right-click your **activity_main.xml** layout definition in your **/res/layout** folder and select the **Open** menu command, or left-click it and press the **F3** key. Edit the opening and closing **<FrameLayout>** container parent tag, and turn it into a **<RelativeLayout>** container by replacing the word Frame with the word Relative, as shown in Figure 18-6.

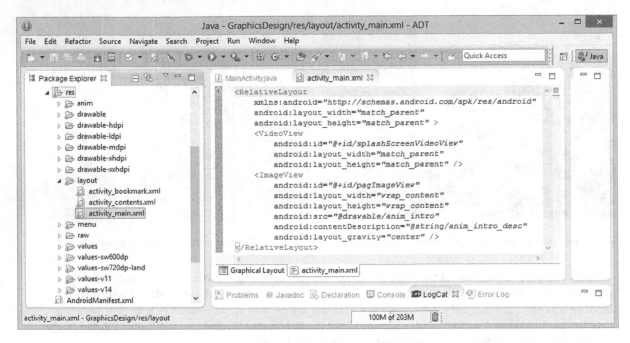

Figure 18-6. *Changing your <FrameLayout> parent container tag to be a <RelativeLayout> parent container tag*

Next, use a **Run As ➤ Android Application** work process (or use the **Graphical Layout Editor** tab, if you wish), and see if your UI layout results are the same when using a different type of user interface layout container (ViewGroup).

As you can see on the far left side of Figure 18-7, the parameters in your <ImageView> child tag UI widget are not compatible with a <RelativeLayout> parent tag container type. Thus, you will have to make some changes to that child tag and its parameters first to get it to center correctly again.

Figure 18-7. Testing your new <RelativeLayout> in the Nexus One as you adjust your child tag parameters to refine

Let's look at the parameters in the <ImageView> child tag in Figure 18-6 by one at a time and see if we can find the problem. We know the **ID**, the **SRC**, and the **LAYOUT_WIDTH** and **LAYOUT_HEIGHT** are standard for layout containers, and the **contentDescription** is required for image-based UI elements, so it must be the **layout_gravity="center"** parameter that is not compatible with a RelativeLayout. A concept of **gravity** is not supported in RelativeLayout, which stands to reason, as UI widgets are laid out relative to each other!

Let's delete the **:layout_gravity="center"** part of this last parameter, and then type the colon key again. This will again invoke Eclipse ADT's helper dialog, as shown in Figure 18-8.

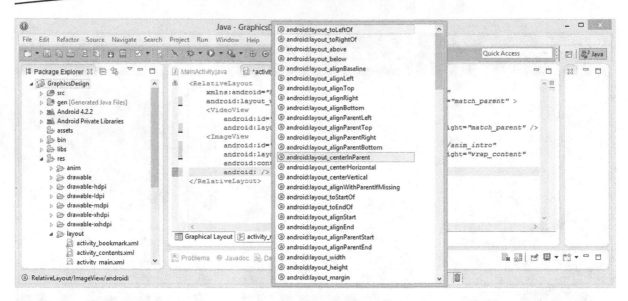

Figure 18-8. *Changing the <ImageView> layout_gravity="center" parameter to the android:layout_centerInParent parameter*

As you can see in this long parameter list for the <RelativeLayout> layout container, there is indeed a different tag that can be used for centering the <ImageView> UI widget child tag within its <RelativeLayout> UI layout parent tag. The correct parameter to implement within a RelativeLayout container is an **android:layout_centerInParent** parameter with a Boolean value of **"true."** If you now use your **Run As ➤ Android Application** work process, you can see you have fixed that problem, and your PAG logo is centered again, as shown in the middle of Figure 18-7. Your video still loops seamlessly behind it.

The next thing you need to figure out is how to implement the "fill the View" scaling effect that is shown on the right-hand side of Figure 18-7.

Let's get back into the Eclipse RelativeLayout parameter helper dialog, and figure out which of these parameters (there are dozens) can achieve this end result and provide something that can be used in any resolution and in any orientation. Then you will be able to move on to create your video asset targets and learn how to tell Android which to use with different devices (physical resolution and orientation asset auto-switching).

To get your video to scale to fit the entire screen, you will need to add a parameter to your <VideoView> child tag. What you want to do is to **align** the <VideoView> container with the <RelativeLayout> container, which has been configured using the **MATCH_PARENT** constant in both the X and Y dimensions. This makes the <RelativeLayout> parent tag fill the entire display screen.

It is important to notice that even though you also have these MATCH_PARENT constants set in your VideoView child tag as well, Android is "respecting" the aspect ratio of the digital video asset, so you must find a different parameter to "override" this behavior and scale the video (in the X dimension, in this case) to cover that white stripe of default background color that is showing behind the video.

Use your Eclipse helper dialog, by adding a line of space after your <VideoView> closing tag /> symbol, and typing **android** and then a **colon** and then the letter "a," as shown in Figure 18-9. As you can see, this will bring up the available parameters that begin with the letter "a," such as all of the **align**, **above**, and **alpha** parameters.

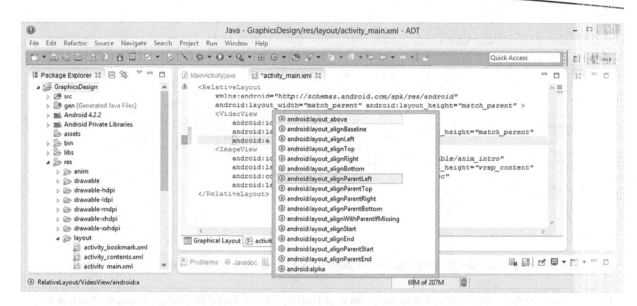

Figure 18-9. Using the Eclipse parameter helper dialog to find the four android:layout_alignParent parameters

You will see four **alignParent** parameters; they can be used to "pull" the VideoView over to match each edge of the parent RelativeLayout. I do wish there was an alignParentAll or just an alignParent parameter, so that we do not have to code four parameters to achieve our end result, but not everything in Android is going to be logical, optimal, or implemented the way that we want it to be 100% of the time. That's life for an Android, I guess! Being a programmer and a graphics designer in a single person will demand flexibility and creativity in working with the available tools and paradigms in order to figure out creative ways to interleave these disparate worlds together to create never-before-seen works of digital art.

As you can see in Figure 18-9, the first **alignParentLeft** parameter has been selected. Double-click this parameter to insert it into your child tag and set its value equal to **"true."** Next, do the same work process, and go back into the helper dialog and add the **alignParentTop**, **alignParentRight**, and **alignParentBottom** parameters to make sure the VideoView is scaled evenly.

As you can see in Figure 18-10, the four parameters are in place, and your markup is error-free, so now you can use the **Run As ➤ Android Application** work process to watch your video scale and play behind your PAG logo. In my emulator, the video actually played back even more smoothly as it filled the container, probably because it didn't have that white strip to render.

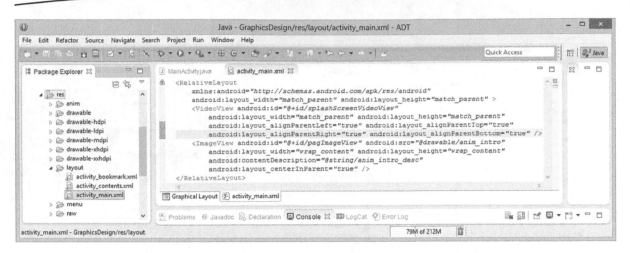

Figure 18-10. Adding all four sides for the android:layout_alignParent parameters to scale <VideoView> to fit screen

It is important to note that even if you have an eight-core, 64-bit 3.4GHz workstation, as I do, with 16GB of DDR3 1333 RAM, and a SSD (**Solid State Drive**) HDD (Hard Disk Drive), you still may not get the Eclipse AVD emulator performance you desire.

This is because your AVD is **virtualizing** your entire Android hardware and software environment. It is doing this using only software emulation, and that takes an inordinately massive amount of memory space, as well as huge amounts of processing cycles. That said, there may well be some "room" for improvement in optimizing the code that runs the AVD emulator part of this development software package, so let's hope that the Android team has some key team members deployed regarding that objective at Google headquarters.

If you can set up your Android development workstation to use a 3.8GHZ (or faster) 16-core AMD 64-bit CPU with 32GB or even 64GB of DDR3 1600 or 1800 (now very affordable) memory, then you may well want to do this, at least for the time being, until the emulator environment becomes more efficient! If you want the emulator to launch quickly, be sure to include an SSD HDD! The SSD HDD will ultimately make all your software (and OS) start rapidly.

Next, let's look at one more <VideoView> parameter you will want to know about. This **android:keepScreenOn** parameter will keep a user's display from that "power saving time out" feature that most Android devices implement aggressively to increase the battery life for any given charging cycle. You can see this parameter in Figure 18-11 in an Eclipse tag helper dialog, along with the pale yellow explanation screen fly-out, which will appear when each parameter that you are investigating is clicked.

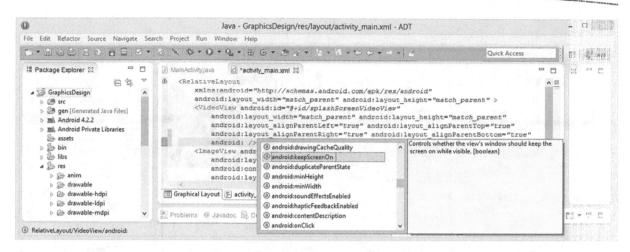

Figure 18-11. *Using the Eclipse parameter helper dialog to find the android:keepScreenOn VideoView parameter*

As you can see in the pale yellow explanation screen, this parameter will keep the user's screen on (back-lit) while the VideoView is visible. This also shows that the parameter is **Boolean**, so be sure to use the "**true**" value to indicate that you want to "keep the screen on" to the Android OS. Next, you need to optimize some more **target device resolution** video assets.

Optimizing Your Range of Video Asset Resolution Targets

Next, you will finish optimizing your **Wide VGA** 800x480 video assets. Since VGA uses a 640x480 resolution, add another 160 pixels of width and you have the **WVGA** resolution, which is extremely popular in Android smartphones and tablets because it an affordable screen size and has (barely) enough pixels to provide decent graphics quality to the end user. For this reason, it is a good resolution for you to consider using for your graphics applications digital video assets. Let's optimize your 800x480 landscape video asset.

Launch the Sorenson Squeeze Pro video application, and click the 480x800p Android preset you created back in Chapter 2. Once it is selected in light-blue, as shown on the far left side of Figure 18-12, click the center (create a copy or third icon of the five icons) on the bottom-left of the panel, and create a copy of the codec preset so that you can use it to create another preset for the WVGA landscape version for this widely-used resolution. It will be easier to create a new preset, especially one that uses similar data rate settings, by using this method.

Figure 18-12. Creating an 800x480p landscape digital video codec preset (also showing all completed presets)

The first thing that you want to do is to provide a correct **Name** and **Desc** field data entry, so name this new preset **Android800x480p** (this p stands for **progressive scan**, not pixels) and add a description of **Android 800x480 Landscape**, as shown in Figure 18-13. All of the other settings are the same, as the data is the same between the two presets, just flipped 90 degrees (or rotated from portrait display mode to landscape display mode).

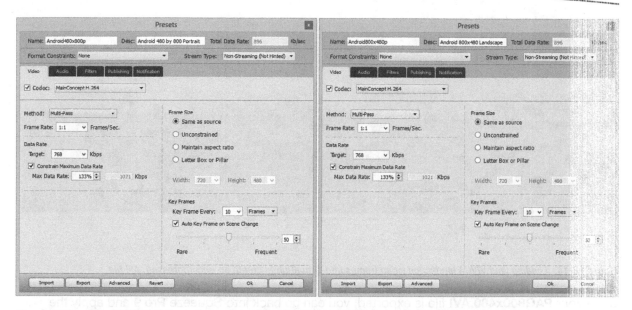

Figure 18-13. Android WVGA video codec presets using 768KPBS to 1MPBS data rate with high-quality codec

A progressive scan video is one where every line in the image (or video, in this case) is written to the display screen sequentially, all at once. The opposite of a progressive scan is an **interlaced scan**, like the old TV sets that wrote the even lines on one pass (scan) and the odd numbered lines on a second pass (scan), thus interlacing them (which is why they flickered).

Make sure your data rate ranges from 768 KBPS (3/4 MBPS) to 1 MBPS and that you have set 10 key frames every second of video (which is at 10 FPS) and that your frame size is set at **Same as source**.

Once your new WVGA preset is set up, click the **OK** button to create that preset, and you will be ready to go into VirtualDub and create your AVI source file. Let's do that now.

Start VirtualDub 1.9 using the shortcut icon and use the **File ➤ Open Video File** option. When the dialog opens, navigate to your system HDD, and find the first frame of your PAG800 rendered BMP file sequence, and select it. Once the 400-frame 3D rendering has loaded, use a **File ➤ Save AVI As** option to save an AVI to your **/AVIs** directory, just like you did in Chapter 2. If you need to revisit this work process, you can review the text or screen shots in Chapter 2. I show the VirtualDub software with the 800x480 Wide XGA landscape video loaded into its user interface in Figure 18-14.

Figure 18-14. Loading your WVGA landscape video frames into VirtualDub to create an uncompressed .AVI file

Once your **PAG800x480.AVI** file is exported, you can go back into Squeeze Pro 9 and apply the new preset, after you import the PAG800x480 video file and use the **Apply** button to attach the next preset you have created to it. Once all of this has been set up in Squeeze, you can click the Squeeze It! button and start the compression process. This will apply your WVGA preset setting to the AVI raw frame data via the MainConcept codec and MPEG-4 H.264 video encoding algorithm.

Once an AVI file is generated, you can use some math to see if you're getting the excellent compression you obtained in Chapter 2 on your 480x800 Portrait version of the file, which, as you can now see, actually compresses to be 35K smaller than a landscape version with the same number of pixels.

You are still getting a 99.2% compression, or the MP4 data file is 0.8% of the size of the original full frames uncompressed AVI source file, which is exactly the same size as the PAG480x800.AVI file (450MB), which stands to reason, as it has the same number of pixels and frames inside it.

Now you have digital video assets that will fit medium resolution, medium DPI, or **MDPI**, devices with WVGA resolution and 4-inch through 7-inch LED or LCD display screens.

Next, let's get the LDPI, or low DPI, screens out of the way so you can focus on your assets for the more mainstream HD Android devices and NetBook (1024 pixel) resolution devices after that.

One last note before we move on: a 800x480 resolution is not a "true" 16:9 widescreen aspect ratio. To calculate this, 800/16=50, and 50x9=450, so a true 16:9 aspect ratio is an 800x450 resolution, which is not a common physical screen (pixels) resolution for many Android devices. Since 480/50=9.6, the 800x480 resolution actually represents a **16:9.6** aspect ratio, or 60% of the way between a 16:9 and a 16:10 aspect ratio.

Using 16:9 Low Resolution 640x360 Digital Video Assets

This next resolution will also use the VGA 640x480 resolution to create its wide-screen resolution version, except that you're not going to add 160 pixels to the width, but instead, you are going to subtract 120 pixels from the height! This will give you 640 pixels of width and 360 pixels of height and will result in a 16:9 aspect ratio. To calculate this **640/16=40x9=360**, so 640x360 is a low-resolution version of a popular 16:9 HD aspect ratio.

Let's go back into Squeeze and use the work process that you learned in the previous section to copy the Android480x800p preset so that you can create an **Android360x640p** preset for use with lower resolution Android devices.

Such devices would include HDPI watches (2-inch screens with 640 pixels is 320 DPI and thus HDPI), entry-level Android phones with smaller 4-inch screens (4-inch screens with 640 pixels is 160 DPI and thus MDPI) and mini-tablets with 5-inch screens (5-inch screens with 640 pixels is 128 DPI and thus LDPI).

Create a copy of the WVGA preset, right-click it, and select the **Edit** menu option, as was shown in Figure 18-12. Once the Presets dialog opens up, as shown on the left side of Figure 18-15, name the preset **Android360x640p** and enter the description of **Android 360x640 Portrait**, and then you will be ready to set your data rates and related parameters. Set a **target data rate** of **512 KBPS,** and a **maximum data rate** of **150%** more than that, or **768 KBPS**. You can leave your settings on the right hand side of this Presets dialog the same, as you want to match resolution and use one keyframe per second. Once you finish the **portrait preset**, go back and create a **landscape preset**.

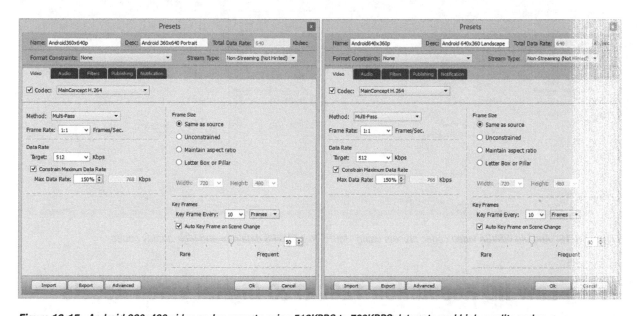

Figure 18-15. Android 360x480 video codec presets using 512KPBS to 768KBPS data rate and high-quality codec

Using NetBook Resolution 1024x600 Digital Video Asset

The 1024x600 resolution was made popular by the ultra-portable **netbook** products that appeared almost a decade ago, featuring a Wide SVGA resolution. SVGA, or "Super VGA," was 800x600, so if you add another 224 pixels of width, you will have a Wide Super VGA (or WSVGA) display screen.

Netbooks have 10.1-inch screens, making them **LDPI** (1024/10=102 pixels per inch), and now that Dell has an Android PC out, you will probably see the Android Netbooks market start to materialize as well. There are also some smartphones and tablets with this resolution that have 4- to 5-inch screens, and this puts them in the **HDPI** 240-pixels-per-inch screen density range.

The aspect ratio for this resolution is not quite 16:9, as 1024/16=64 and 64x9=576, so **1024x576** would represent a "true" 16:9 aspect ratio. Since 64 goes into 600 9.375 times, this would represent a **16:9.375** aspect ratio, or 3/8ths of the way from a widescreen 16:9 to a 16:10 aspect ratio.

Create a copy of the WVGA preset, right-click it, and select the **Edit** menu option, as was shown in Figure 18-12. Once the Presets dialog opens up, as shown on the left side of Figure 18-16, name the preset **Android600x1024p** and enter the description of **Android 600x1024 Portrait**. Set a **target data rate** of **1024KBPS**, and a **maximum data rate** of **150%** more than that, or **1536KBPS**. You can leave your settings on the right hand side of this Presets dialog the same, as you want to match resolution and use one keyframe per second. Once you finish the **portrait preset**, go back and create a **landscape preset**.

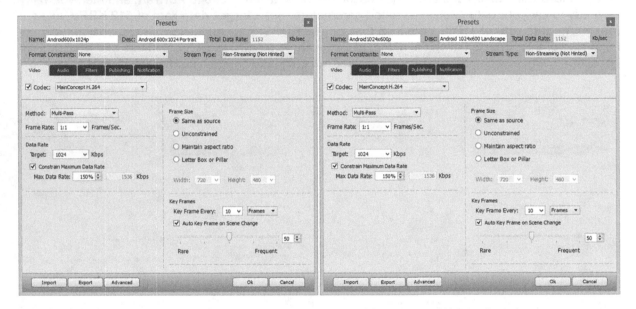

Figure 18-16. *Android WSVGA video codec presets using 1MBPS to 1.5MBPS data rate and high-quality codec*

Using Low HD Resolution 1280x720 Digital Video Assets

The first HD resolution to hit the digital scene, around a decade or more ago, was what I like to call "Pseudo HD," or 1280x720. This resolution has enough pixels (almost one million) to provide clear video content, but not so many so as to bog down the processor or data transfer bandwidth. It is also a true 16:9 aspect ratio, as **1280/16=80x9=720**.

Devices that use this resolution include **Phablets** (Phone-Tablets) such as the Samsung Galaxy Note II, which has a 5.5-inch screen, making it a 240 DPI HDPI device, as well as larger 8-inch tablets, which feature a 160 DPI MDPI screen density. Larger 10-inch tablets featuring this resolution fall into the LDPI or 120 DPI screen density category.

Create a copy of the WVGA preset, right-click it, and select the **Edit** menu option, as shown in Figure 18-12. Once the Presets dialog opens up, as shown on the left side of Figure 18-17, name the preset **Android720x1280p** and enter the description of **Android 720x1280 Portrait**. Set a **target data rate** of **1536KBPS**, and a **maximum data rate** of **133%** more than that, or **2048KBPS**.

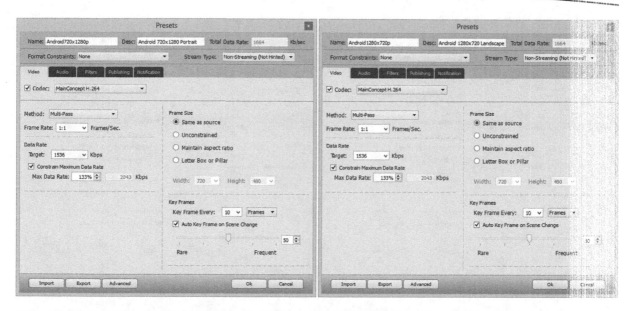

Figure 18-17. Android Pseudo HD video codec presets using 1.5MBPS to 2MBPS data rate and high-quality codec

You can leave your settings on the right hand side of this Presets dialog the same, as you want to match resolution, and use one keyframe per second.

Once you finish the Pseudo HD **portrait preset,** you can go back and perform the same work process in order to create your Pseudo HD **landscape preset**.

Finally, you'll create a True HD set of presets for iTV or high-end tablets.

Using a True HD 1920x1080 Digital Video Asset for iTVs

The second HD resolution to hit the digital scene, around a decade or more ago, was what the industry calls **True HD**, or **1920x1080**. This resolution is also an exact 16:9 aspect ratio and has more than enough pixels, at over 2 million, to provide crystal clear video playback. True HD resolution also has so many pixels that it could potentially bog down a weak (single core) processor and could also "crowd out" any smaller data transfer bandwidth.

Devices that use this HD resolution include **iTVs** (interactive television) as well as the Kindle Fire HD, which actually sports **True HD 16:10 1920x1200** resolution on an 8.9-inch screen, making it closer to a 240 DPI **HDPI** device. For an iTV set, screen size determines your DPI, so let's go in the other direction this time. 1920/240=8, so an 8-inch wide iTV (11-inch diagonal) is HDPI, and 1920/160=12, so a 12-inch wide iTV (16-inch diagonal) is MDPI, and 1920/120=16, so a 16-inch wide iTV (20-inch diagonal) is LDPI. This means most iTVs out there are **LDPI**.

Create a copy of the WVGA preset, right-click it, and select the **Edit** menu option, as shown in Figure 18-12. Once the Presets dialog opens up, as shown on the left side of Figure 18-18, name your preset **Android1080x1920p** and enter a description of **Android 1080x1920 Portrait**. Set a **target data rate** of **2048KBPS,** and a **maximum data rate** of **150%** more than that, or **3072KBPS**.

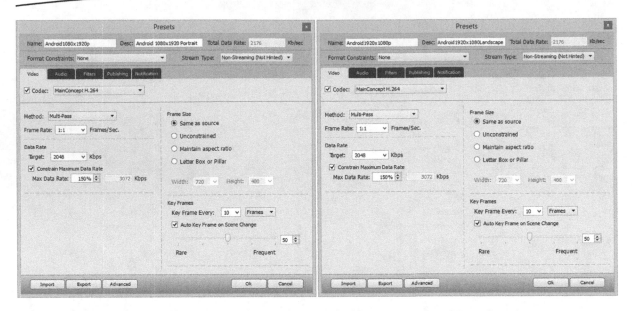

Figure 18-18. Android True HD video codec presets using 2MBPS to 3MBPS data rate and a high-quality codec

You can leave your settings on the right hand side of this Presets dialog the same, as you want to match resolution and use one keyframe per second.

Once you finish the True HD **portrait preset,** you can go through the same work process in order to create your True HD **landscape preset**. Now that you have generated all of your MPEG-4 digital video assets, you can see what kind of compression ratios you are getting and decide which ones would be the best to use for your application.

Analyzing Target Resolution Compression Ratio Results

Now that you have created compressed .MP4 files using your uncompressed .AVI files, you can calculate the compression ratios and percentage compressed to see which resolution yields the superior compression results. As you will see, higher resolutions give slightly better results. You also need to look at the digital video asset file size as well when making a decision. Table 18-1 collects the results of the calculations; you could do something similar in your studio using a spreadsheet, such as the open source OpenOffice Calc 4.0, available at www.openoffice.org.

Table 18-1. Industry Standard Hardware Screen Resolutions, Original Data Size, Compressed Size, and Ratios

Resolution	Original Data	Compressed	Compression Ratio	Percentage	Screen Orientation
640x360	270MB	2.5MB	108:1	0.93%	Landscape
800x480	450MB	3.8MB	119:1	0.84%	Landscape
1024x600	720MB	5.0MB	143:1	0.70%	Landscape
1280x720	1080MB	7.5MB	143:1	0.70%	Landscape

(continued)

Table 18-1. (*continued*)

Resolution	Original Data	Compressed	Compression Ratio	Percentage	Screen Orientation
1920x1080	2430MB	9.9MB	243:1	0.41%	Landscape
360x640	270MB	2.5MB	108:1	0.93%	Portrait
480x800	450MB	3.8MB	119:1	0.84%	Portrait
600x1024	720MB	5.0MB	143:1	0.70%	Portrait
720x1280	1080MB	7.5MB	143:1	0.70%	Portrait
1080x1920	2430MB	10 MB	243:1	0.41%	Portrait

What you want to look for is the best compression ratio, plus the smallest file size, with a resolution that has enough pixels to scale either up or down with good quality. Besides the **243:1** compression that the True HD is obtaining, I am leaning towards the **5MB WSVGA** compression result. A 243:1 result for this 1920 resolution makes me suspect that this codec has some additional optimizations for HD resolution, the resolution 99% of users of this product will be using the codec with for their mainstream video work!

I'd choose WSVGA as **1024** scales up to 1920 (or 2048) resolution screens by an even factor of **2X**, is close to 1280 resolution, and will scale down to any other resolution with great quality. Add to this the fine dot pitch of most Android devices, which tend to be HDPI and hide any scaling artifacts, and you have 400 frames of 3D animation using only 5MB, or **13KB** per frame.

A video file of 5MB represents **10%** of the total file size for your maximum **50MB** Android APK file size limitation, so that is fairly reasonable for a splash screen background video plate.

It is important to note that you can also have your applications access up to **two** additional **external data files** of up to **2GB** each, so if the app has a ton of captive video, it is not really an issue (problem) as long as you optimize your video well.

Let's try one more thing regarding this 1024x600 target resolution. Create an HQ (High Quality) preset using the work process you learned during this chapter (and Chapter 2) by selecting the 1024x600 preset and using the copy icon at the bottom to make a copy of the preset.

Right-click the copy, and select **Edit**, and use a higher quality data rate setting of **1200 KBPS** for the target data rate, and give it **170%** headroom to the maximum data rate of **2048 KBPS**, and let's see how much data overhead you add to your current 5MB file size by using these higher quality settings.

Import the **PAG1024x600.avi** AVI uncompressed source data and apply this new codec preset to it, and then press the SqueezeIt! button to compress the MP4 file. If you can get even more quality out of the file in **under 6MB**, Android will have an excellent quality video data source to scale up or down from.

As you can see in Figure 8-23, the MP4 comes in at **5.878** megabytes, so you could probably give it a little more quality at the lower (target) end; maybe use a **1250** or **1280** KBPS target data rate to make sure you have no visible artifacts even when you are viewing the data on large (LDPI) screens where pixels are large and artifacts are apparent.

This 1024x600 target resolution should scale up to 1280 or 1920 reasonably well, especially on HDPI screens (which are the norm), where pixels are so small that artifacts aren't even visible. Think of it like you are looking at one of the massive LED billboards in Las Vegas, while you're at the CES trade show doing your Android-related business. When you are up close, the pixels look terrible, but when you are farther away, this same multimedia content looks absolutely pristine. These smaller dot pitch displays so commonplace today serve to take your eye farther away from the content.

As you have seen, with 243:1 compression ratios, Sorenson Squeeze has shown that it can provide amazing video quality with a small data footprint, and that is with an older MPEG-4 codec. Using the newer WebM video codec could provide even better results, depending on the video content, of course. It could also provide the same or worse results; there is no real way to find out other than going into Squeeze and running your uncompressed AVI source file through a codec and seeing the results. Let's do that next.

Using the WebM VP8 Codec to Compress Pseudo HD Video

Let's go back into Sorenson and try one of the **WebM** presets for **HD 1280x720** resolution and **2000 KBPS,** which is included with Sorenson Squeeze Pro. Right-click this preset, and use the **Edit** command to modify the codec preset to use your **target 1536 KBPS** data rate, and, later on, to use your **maximum 2048 KBPS** data rate. The WebM codec does not support the data rate range like the MPEG-4 codec does, so you need to test both data rates.

What you are trying to accomplish here is to see if you can get any smaller of a data footprint than you did by using Squeeze's MainConcept MPEG4 H.264 codec. If you can, you might consider using the WebM format, if it gives you a significantly lower data footprint. If not, you should use the MPEG4 format as it is supported across more versions of Android OS (Pre-2.3 versions). Launch Sorenson Squeeze, and use the **Import File** icon on the upper-left to open the **PAG1280x720.avi** uncompressed AVI file, as shown in Figure 18-19.

Figure 18-19. Loading an uncompressed source PAG1280x720.avi file and selecting a WebM 1280x720p codec

Once the uncompressed .AVI data has loaded, apply the WebM preset that you have created, which uses the low-end (target) data rate of 1536 KBPS, as shown on the left side of Figure 18-20. Press the **SqueezeIt!** button and code the WebM file, and then either create a new preset or edit your existing one (you can right-click the applied codec in the bottom area of Squeeze's main editing view as well, if you like) and create a second 2048KBPS high-end (maximum) data rate preset. Apply that to your uncompressed source and then use the SqueezeIt! button to create a 2048KBPS data rate version of a WebM file so that you can see what kind of data footprint optimization you are getting. It is interesting to note that WebM supports only a "static," or unary (single) data rate, and not a range, like the MPEG-4 codec does.

Figure 18-20. Creating a 1536 target data rate WebM preset as well as a 2048 target data rate WebM preset

Since you got such a huge compression ratio boost (143:1 to 243:1), between Pseudo HD and True HD using the MPEG-4 codec, let's finally try using True HD video source on the WebM codec and see if it gives you the same results.

Using the WebM VP8 Codec to Compress True HD Video

Find the Squeeze WebM codec preset for 1080p, as shown on the right side of Figure 18-21, and edit the target data rate to be **3072 KBPS**, or **3 MBPS**, and use the optimal **2-Pass Variable Bit-Rate (VBR)** setting, and a **Maintain Aspect Ratio** setting, which you can see does the exact same thing, in this situation, as using the **Same as source** setting, which you used before. Use the same work process to copy this preset, creating a 2048 TDR preset.

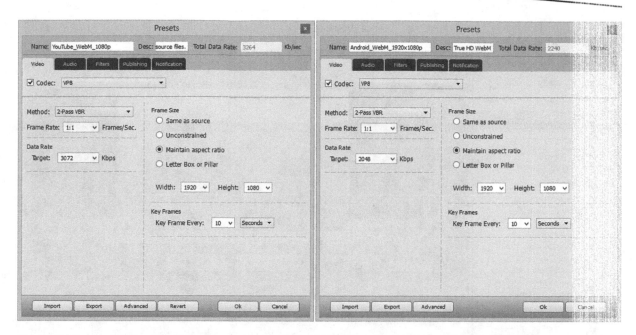

Figure 18-21. Creating True HD video compression presets for the WebM codec at 3072 and 2048 Kbps data rate

Next, use the Import File button on the upper-left of Squeeze and find the PAG1920x1080.avi uncompressed source file and load it so you can compress a WebM True HD video asset.

Apply your 3072 KBPS WebM preset to the True HD source data, and click the SqueezeIt! button and generate the WebM version of the digital video data.

As you will see later in the chapter, this gives you a **14MB** data footprint, so next let's compress the uncompressed source AVI using a 2048 KBPS codec preset and see if you can get a much smaller data footprint result.

Apply your 2048 KBPS WebM preset to the True HD source data, and click the SqueezeIt! button and generate the WebM version of the digital video data.

The result of this data rate setting is an 8MB file, which is a remarkable result if you consider that 400 frames of 3D imagery, at 6.22MB per frame, is essentially two and a half billion bytes of data being compressed down to only eight million bytes (see Figure 18-22).

Figure 18-22. Importing the uncompressed PAG1920x1080.avi True HD AVI file and applying the WebM preset to it

I played the WebM video in the Opera browser, which specializes in support for WebM videos, and it played back smooth as a banana milkshake! So, for a True HD video asset, especially one that will stream, I would choose this WebM codec and preset over the MPEG-4, or possibly find a way to provide both formats if I was hosting the data externally on a media server.

We will be taking a look at streaming video data using a remote web server in the next chapter, so this chapter and Chapter 2, will serve as a great foundational knowledge for that far more advanced video streaming chapter.

Finally, as a summary, let's take a look at all 38 of the source, data, and project files that you have generated, which are shown in Figure 18-23. At the top of this list are the .sqz Squeeze project files, and under those, in numeric X-axis order are ten different video asset file resolutions, and their uncompressed AVIs, and compressed MPEG-4s, and where you got curious, even compressed WebM files as well.

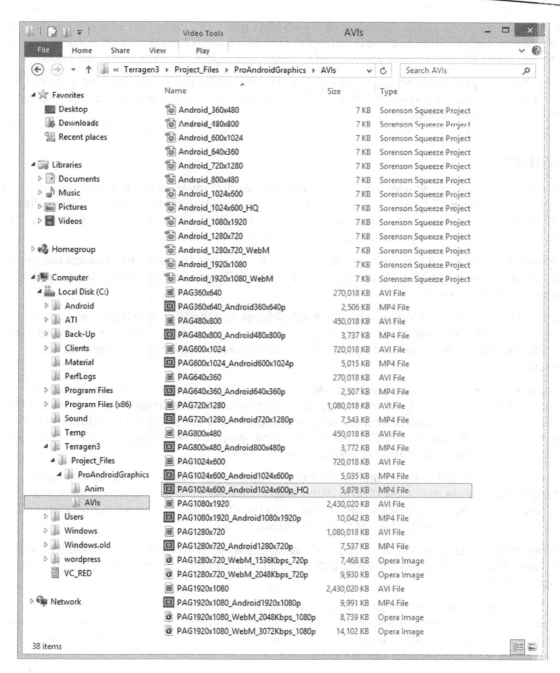

Figure 18-23. Windows Explorer file manager showing AVIs folder with compression result file sizes and formats

If you want to practice doing the math, switch numerator and denominator, or divisor and dividend, to change back and forth from compression ratios into compression percentages. To get the amount compressed, subtract your compression percentage from 100%, or in this case, from the number one.

Most of the calculations I have already done for you and placed in Table 18-1 to show you how to create a similar data table to keep your data footprint optimization results at hand in case your client asks to see them. Or, just in case you wanted to follow a "surgical" work process, like I do.

Now you have enough knowledge to proceed to the next chapter where you will take a look at video remote streaming coding and optimization, so that you can store your digital video assets on your server instead of in your app!

Summary

In this eighteenth chapter, you learned how to use your **MediaPlayer**, which is inherently contained inside your **VideoView** UI object. You took a close look at the **MediaPlayer**, **Uri**, and **VideoView** classes in Android, and saw what each of them do, and how they all work together to allow us to **locate**, **load** into memory, **access**, **play**, and **loop** a digital video asset.

You learned how to grab a MediaPlayer object reference by using the **OnPreparedListener** nested class, accessed using the MediaPlayer nested class **MediaPlayer.OnPreparedListener**, which **exposes** the MediaPlayer object.

We took a far more detailed look at both the **MediaPlayer** and the **VideoView** classes in this chapter than we did way back in Chapter 2, when you were just a simple graphics neophyte, before re-introducing your video asset into your splash screen code so that you could use it as your animated backplate.

You composited your video asset with the PAG logo animation treatment, which you created eons ago in Chapters 3 and 4. As expected, the video you created in Chapter 2 works behind the animated elements you created, because of your compositing work process and intelligent use of alpha channel data inside your PNG32 assets. You have learned well, Young Lukes and Lukessas. May the GeForce (nVidia graphics processor) be with you all.

Next, we got back into the digital video data footprint optimization work process and ascertained **five target resolutions** that "cover" 95% of the mainstream Android device screen resolutions (using physical pixels). Each of these also happens to be a "named" screen resolution standard, with the exception of the smallest, which is the 640x360 resolution.

We targeted **Wide VGA**, or WVGA, at **800x480; Wide Super VGA**, or WSVGA, at **1024x600; Pseudo HD** at **1280x720;** and **True HD** at **1920x1080**. The last two also happen to be video (television) broadcasting standards.

You set up codec presets for the portrait and landscape versions of these resolutions, and set standard data rates to match the size of the video with the intended playback device. You looked at the resulting file sizes and determined which result would best fit across the target Android devices that you intended to deliver your application across.

In the next chapter, you'll take a look at streaming a digital video asset over the Internet using the HTTP protocol, in case you have too much digital video to use "captive" assets in your application, and so that you can see how network bandwidth comes into play, using video compression and data streaming.

19

Streaming Digital Video from an External Media Server

In this nineteenth chapter, you will gain even deeper experience using the Android **VideoView**, **Uri**, and **MediaPlayer** classes. However, this time you'll be using digital video that is hosted external to your Android application.

If a video is played back on your user's Android device as the video asset data comes over the Internet for the first time (during its first playback loop, in the case of your code configuration), this is popularly known as a **streaming** digital video. The other way of using videos from remote digital video media servers is to **download** the digital video asset first, before a playback cycle (seamless looping, in your particular use-case) is started.

Either way, this approach differs from using captive video (as you did in the previous chapter) because you are using the **network connection** as the source of your digital video data stream and using an Android application as the playback engine (recipient) of this streaming (or downloaded) video data.

To give the user feedback while they are waiting for a video asset to **download** will require that you implement a **progress dialog**, and thus you will be learning in this chapter about Android's **ProgressDialog** class. This class allows you to implement the dialog that will alert users to the fact that they are downloading a video, and give them information regarding that download, such as what is being downloaded, using a progress animation.

Later on in this chapter, using Squeeze, you will also optimize your 480x800 digital video asset to utilize the **WebM** codec and file format. You'll also be learning about Android's **Display** and **WindowManager** classes, as you need to use them to detect what **screen orientation** a user is using.

Can I Stream Video? Setting a Manifest Internet Permission

Before you will be able to use the Internet with your application at all, you will first be required by the Android OS to declare an **INTERNET** permission constant in your **AndroidManifest.xml** file. This can be accomplished by using the Android **<uses-permission>** child tag, along with the INTERNET constant, using the following line of XML markup:

```
<uses-permission android:name="android.permission.INTERNET" />
```

This **permission flag**, located at the top of the Android Manifest XML file after your **<uses-sdk>** specifications (see Figure 19-1), will inform Android OS that you intend to go outside your user's device to access streaming data or other content for your application.

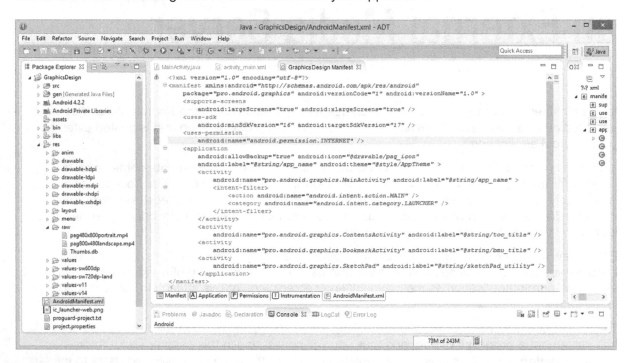

Figure 19-1. Adding the <uses-permission> child tag to the AndroidManifest file with android.permission.INTERNET

The reason that this is necessary is essentially because you need to inform the Android OS that it needs to watch out for potential security breaches. Once you put a hardware device onto a **public network**, such as the Internet, it can be **compromised** by third parties, such as **hackers**. This is why I keep most of my 3D content development workstations on their own private network, one that is not connected (visible or accessible) to the outside world. The same concept can be applied to a user's Android device.

When Video Lives Far Away: The HTTP URL and Your URI

Content internal to the Android OS (for video, this will be in the **/res/raw** folder) will usually use the **android.resource://** URI path reference since this content will always live in the **R** or **resource** area of the Android OS.

Database content, which uses what is termed a **content provider** in Android, uses the **content://** URI path reference. You will not be looking at that URI path reference location in this book (that is an entirely different book on database design for Android), although it's good to know about it!

We are going to be using a **web server** to host your digital video assets, so you are going to change this android.resource:// to the familiar **HTTP://** used to denote the **HyperText Transfer Protocol** schema.

This means that upgrading your current application code to utilize digital video streaming is as simple as changing the parameter that is passed to your **Uri.parse()** method call in the **splashScreenUri** object declaration and configuration line of code, as shown in Figure 19-2. Your new Java code should look something like the following Java code statement:

```
Uri splashScreenUri = Uri.parse(HTTP://www.e-bookclub.com/pag480x800portrait.mp4);
```

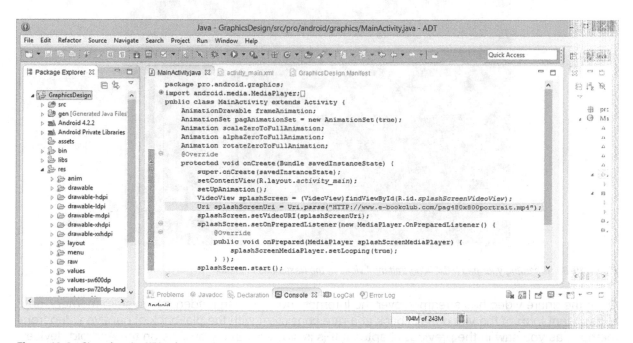

Figure 19-2. *Changing the URI reference for your internal video asset to an external HTTP video asset reference*

This is the only change you will need to make to the code you crafted in Chapter 18 in order to stream digital video assets from a new media web server to your Nexus One emulator (or Android hardware testing devices).

As you can see in Figure 19-3, the MPEG-4 digital video asset is streaming from the web server to the Nexus One emulator AVD frame by frame, as each frame comes over the Internet. I utilized a slower Internet connection to confirm this, and the video displayed frame by frame as each frame came over the Internet into my emulator.

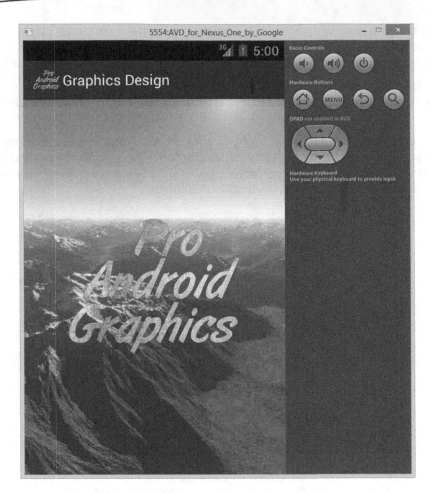

Figure 19-3. Streaming your pag480x800portrait.mp4 video in the Nexus One emulator

Once the entire video has streamed over the Internet and has been loaded into system memory, any subsequent loop of the video plays back at a rate consistent with the playback of captive video from memory, as you saw in the previous chapter. If this is slower than it would be on the Android device hardware, remember that the Android device does not need to both emulate itself and run your app, as the AVD has to do (thus its weak performance).

Next, you'll look at how to **preload** digital video assets over the Internet, just in case you want to make sure your users have smooth video playback.

The ProgressDialog Class: Show Your Download Progress

Android has a class called the **ProgressDialog** class, which makes it easy for you to show your users that a download is progressing so that they do not think that the application has "hung" but instead are assured that it is performing some sort of task in the background (downloading data) while they are waiting.

The Android **ProgressDialog** class is a direct subclass of the AlertDialog class, so it is a specialized type of AlertDialog object for Android OS. The AlertDialog class is itself a subclass of the Dialog class, which is used to create Dialog classes, and the Dialog class is a subclass of the **java.lang. Object** master class.

The Android ProgressDialog class hierarchy is thus structured as follows:

```
java.lang.Object
  > android.app.Dialog
    > android.app.AlertDialog
      > android.app.ProgressDialog
```

The ProgressDialog class, along with all the other types of Dialog classes in Android, belongs to the **android.app** package because it's something that is a part of every application, in one way or another. The **import statement** for using the ProgressDialog class (or object) in your app references the **android.app.ProgressDialog** package, as you will see in this chapter.

The ProgressDialog class is a **public** class and allows your application to implement a **progress dialog**, which displays an animated progress indicator and an optional text message. The animated progress indicator should use a spinning wheel for video downloading, since that's the industry "norm" for a video download.

A **spinning wheel indicator**, which you'll be using later on in this chapter, is the default indicator type for a ProgressBar object. The other progress indicator type is a **horizontal bar indicator**, which will show a percentage of the download that has been completed at any given time.

A ProgressDialog object can also implement a **View** object in place of your text message. This means that if you wanted to get fancy and use your own graphics or animation assets that you designed using what you learned over the past eighteen chapters in the book, you can make really awesome visual progress dialogs, if you so choose.

Only text messages or a View object can be used in ProgressDialog objects; currently both cannot be used at the same time. Of course, you will simply implement your text (drawable) in your View object, so that's not a problem for a Pro Android Graphics designer such as yourself! The ProgressDialog object can be made **cancelable** via a "back" key press or via a click "off" (outside) your ProgressDialog object (screen area) itself. The horizontal progress bar's numeric range is from 0 to 10000, in case you're wondering.

Implementing a ProgressDialog in the GraphicsDesign App

Let's implement a ProgressDialog object in your current streaming digital video codebase so that you can turn it from a streaming video into a video preload operation. The first thing that you will need to do is to declare a ProgressDialog object and name it **downloadProgress** via the following code:

```
ProgressDialog downloadProgress;
```

As you can see in Figure 19-4, you will need to mouse-over a reference to the ProgressDialog class and select the option to **Import 'ProgressDialog' (android.app)** so that Eclipse will write your Import statement for you. You can then proceed to utilize this class in the rest of your code.

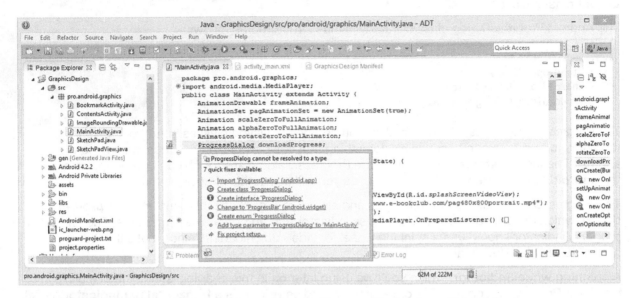

Figure 19-4. *Declaring a ProgressDialog object named downloadProgress at the top of your MainActivity class*

Next, you need to make sure that your video does not start to play until the download is completed. This might seem on first thought to involve a lot of complicated code to watch the download and start the video when it is finished, but it actually simply involves moving the **.start()** function call to the inside of the **onPrepared()** method from where it sits currently.

What this will do is start the digital video once it is "prepared." In this case, prepared means loaded into system memory, which, in this case, also means downloaded completely! So, let's accomplish this next; copy the splashScreen.start(); line of code from the outside of your .onPrepared() method that you wrote in the previous chapter, and paste it inside the onPrepared() method, right after your **.setLooping()** method call, as shown in Figure 19-5. As you can see, you have some error highlighting to address!

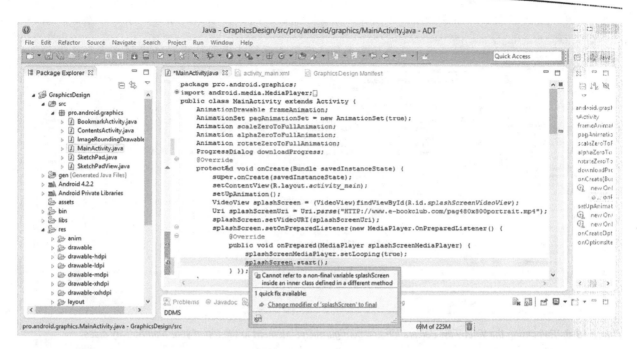

Figure 19-5. Relocating .start() method call to the inside of the onPrepared() method so video starts after download

By putting a splashScreen object reference call to the .start() method inside your onPrepared() method, it becomes difficult for the Activity subclass to "locate" it because your VideoView object is hidden further down inside your code (nesting) hierarchy.

If you mouse-over the error highlighting, you will see the suggestion that you use a **final access modifier** so that your splashScreen VideoView object can be seen (found or referenced) anywhere within your MainActivity class.

This is one solution that might also take a little bit of extra memory to implement, so let's try something different first: move your VideoView object declaration, naming, and configuration statement from inside your onCreate() method up to the top of the class along with the ProgressDialog and Animation related declarations.

As you can see in Figure 19-6, this takes care of your error messages, just like clicking that "**Change modifier of splashScreen to final**" option in Figure 19-5 would have, except in this way your VideoView object is visible to each method in your MainActivity Activity subclass as well as accessible to all of your methods in this class, if access is needed.

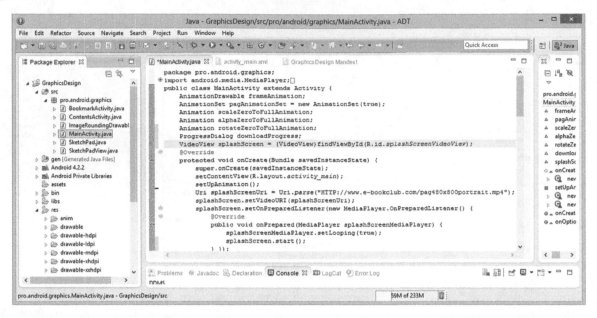

Figure 19-6. *Relocating the VideoView declaration and configuration statement to the top of your MainActivity class*

Now you can get into the work process of instantiating and configuring your ProgressDialog object so that you can use it to inform your users that you are downloading a video file for their viewing pleasure. Let's accomplish this next to prevent your users from fidgeting in their seats, which is never a good user experience indicator.

Add a line of space after the **setUpAnimation()** method call and instantiate a **ProgressDialog** object using the **new** keyword, using the following line of Java code, as shown in Figure 19-7:

```java
downloadProgress = new ProgressDialog(this);
```

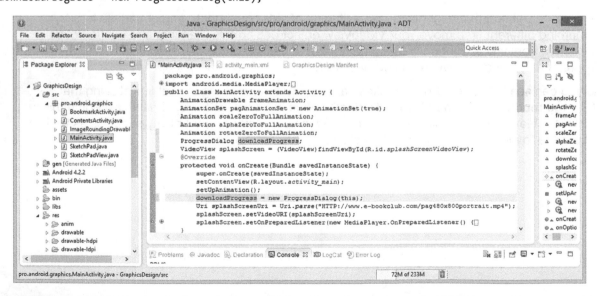

Figure 19-7. *Instantiating the downloadProgress ProgressDialog object using new keyword and this Context object*

You are passing your current Activity subclass's **Context object** into this **ProgressDialog constructor method** using the **this** keyword as a parameter. This gives your ProgressDialog object the proper context that it needs to know when (and where) to pop up and to display its messages, as you learned earlier in the book when I covered the Context class and "this" keyword.

Once your downloadProgress ProgressDialog object is instantiated, you can begin to customize it to do what you want it to do for your application. You will first create a **title** (caption) for your ProgressDialog object using the **.setTitle()** method call, by using the following line of Java code:

```
downloadProgress.setTitle("Terragen 3 Virtual World Fly-Through Video");
```

Next, you'll define a **message** shown next to an animated progress indicator using the **.setMessage()** method call, using the following Java statement:

```
downloadProgress.setMessage("Downloading Video from Media Server...");
```

As you can see in Figure 19-8, your Java code remains error-free and you can move on to set some flags that will define how the ProgressDialog object functions. The first function you want to control is your user's ability to **cancel** this dialog, as you want this dialog to **cancel itself** once the video has finished downloading from the remote media web server.

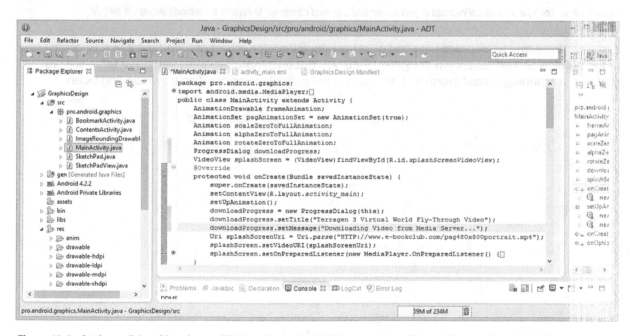

Figure 19-8. Setting a dialog title using .setTitle() method call and dialog message using .setMessage() method call

This is done by using the **.setCancelable()** method, with a Boolean value of **false**, as shown in Figure 19-9. As you can see in this screen shot, if you type in the ProgressDialog object name (**downloadProgress**), and then type a **period** character, you can pop up the **available methods helper dialog**.

Figure 19-9. Using a downloadProgress object name and a period character to invoke a methods available helper

Let's use the same work process to find a **.setIndeterminate()** method call, and set it to a Boolean value of **false** as well, as shown in Figure 19-10. An **indeterminate** progress setting of **false** will provide you with a **spinning wheel** progress bar, which is the normal indicator when downloading video.

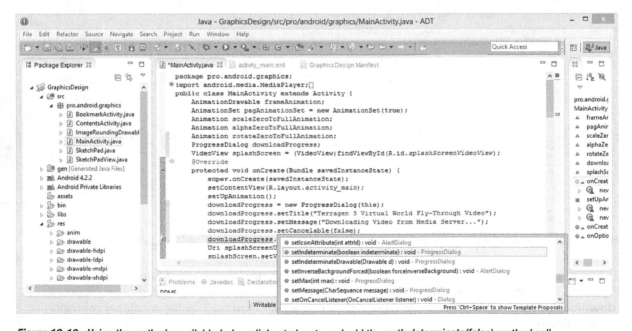

Figure 19-10. Using the methods available helper dialog to locate and add the .setIndeterminate(false) method call

Once you have configured your ProgressDialog object's title, message, cancel behavior, and animating progress icon type, you can finally show the user a progress dialog by calling the **.show()** method call off the ProgressDialog object by using the following line of Java code, as shown in Figure 19-11:

```
downloadProgress.show();
```

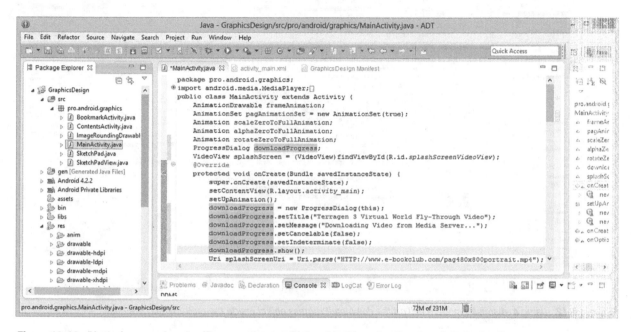

Figure 19-11. *Displaying your downloadProgress ProgressDialog object by using the .show() method call*

As you can see in Figure 19-11, I have clicked the downloadProgress object in the code to show the logical progression of its declaration, instantiation, and configuration using tan (declare and instantiate) and grey (configuration) object highlighting.

The next thing that you need to deal with is removing the ProgressDialog object from the screen once the video has finished downloading. This is done in the onPrepared() method, just like the .start() method call, for much the same reason. Once you know the video is prepared in system memory and is ready for playback, you also know that it is time to remove this ProgressDialog object from the user's screen.

Removing the ProgressDialog from the screen is accomplished by using the **.dismiss()** method call off of the downloadProgress ProgressDialog object. You should do this inside the **onPrepare()** method, after you set the video looping value to true, but before you actually start the video playback cycle. Add a line of space after the .setLooping() method call, and type in the following line of Java code, as shown in Figure 19-12:

```
downloadProgress.dismiss();
```

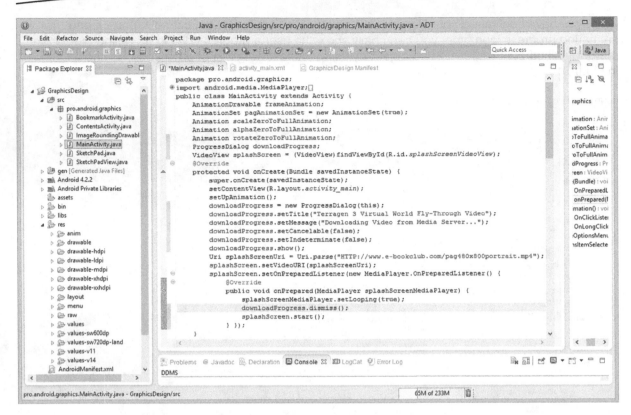

Figure 19-12. Using a .dismiss() method call off the downloadProgress object inside the onPrepared() method

Now it's time to test your new ProgressDialog object and the Java code that declares, names, instantiates, and configures it, inside the Nexus One emulator.

Testing the Progress Dialog: Dealing with Compiler Errors

Right-click your GraphicsDesign project folder and select the **Run As ➤ Android Application** menu sequence to launch the Nexus One emulator. After it loads, it should automatically launch your application, unless you are starting it for the first time, in which case you may need to swipe the screen to unlock it, just like you would do with a real Android device!

As you can see in Figure 19-13, something is amiss in the Java code you have added (or reconfigured), and you are getting a fatal crash on your screen, as indicated by this message: "**Unfortunately, Graphics Design has stopped.**" Click the **OK** button underneath the message, and return to the Eclipse ADT IDE, and look in your **LogCat** error log tab to see if you can ascertain what exactly needs to be changed for your application to work again! I also show some of the other application errors you will be getting (next) in this screenshot, so make sure not to peek (or get depressed)!

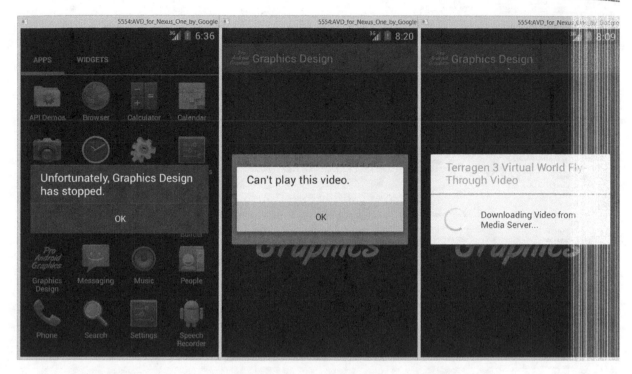

Figure 19-13. *Testing in the Nexus One emulator and some of the errors you can look forward to solving*

To give you some room in the IDE to look at your LogCat tab contents, place your cursor on the dividing line shown at the bottom of the IDE in Figure 19-14, and click and drag it up so that the half-dozen "problem" tabs at the bottom of the IDE have enough room to function in (about 60% open).

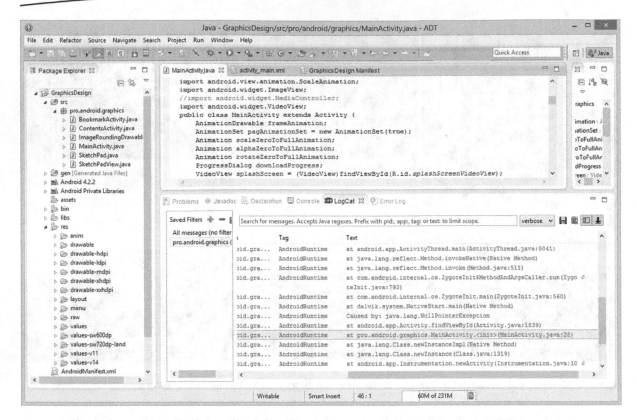

Figure 19-14. Pulling up the LogCat tab section of the IDE and looking for a reasonable line number (28) for your code

You will see a ton of red ink (code); scroll up through this "Red Sea" and part it, if you will (if you're a fan of the Bible), and look for code line numbers that are lines of code that you know that you wrote. What I mean by this is that clearly you haven't written 5,041, or even 511, lines of code in this app, so look for a number that you know is a line of code that you wrote, as the error is most likely in your code and not in Android's!

I found MainActivity.java code line 28 and highlighted it in this screen shot; it says that there is a problem in the initialization or <init> of one of the objects and that the problem occurs on line 28 of the code. This is that VideoView object declaration and configuration that we placed at the top of our class. Maybe we should have listened to Eclipse and used that **final** access modifier! Then again, maybe we don't need to. I'm pretty stubborn, so no worries; we'll figure it all out soon.

The way I did this was to count down 28 lines from the top of the class's code by expanding the import statements section and being sure to count each of those as well. I ended up at a VideoView object instantiation line of code, so I know that is the line of code I have to modify next.

The first thing that I am going to try is, of course, Eclipse's suggestion of using the final access modifier before this line of code and putting it back down in the onCreate() method after the setContentView() method call.

My thinking here is that the initialization problem we are encountering is coming from trying to access this **splashScreenVideoView** (ID) UI element, a part of the **activity_main.xml** UI definition, before that UI definition was referenced in our code, by using a setContentView(R.layout.activity_main); Java programming statement.

So to see if I can get the code working, I'm going to put this line of code right under the setContentView() method call, as shown in Figure 19-15, to test the application a second time to see if my hasty cut-and-paste of the VideoView to the top of the class was ultimately a fatal (error) mistake, at least as far as programming judgment is concerned.

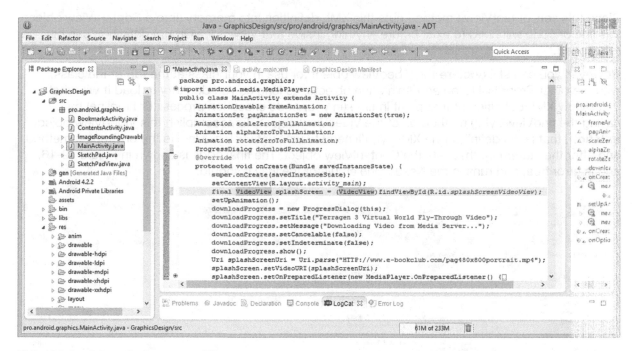

Figure 19-15. Using a final access modifier and placing a VideoView declaration and configuration inside onCreate()

Use the **Run As ➤ Android Application** work process after making this change and you will see that this was indeed the problem. But as I said, stubborn is as stubborn does, and I still want to find a way to code this without a **final** access modifier for the VideoView object. So let's figure out a way to accomplish this next, and then you can move along and part other oceans.

If you look at the line of code in question, you can see that it is fairly dense and could also be written using two lines of code, in this fashion:

```
VideoView splashScreen;
splashScreen = (VideoView) findViewById(R.id.splashScreenVideoView);
```

The fact that you can make this dense code more **verbose**, in this situation, at least, is exactly what's going to allow you to code your VideoView object without having to use the final access modifier keyword (and extra memory) at all. As you can see, sometimes stubbornness (relentlessness) can lead to clever solutions that use less memory and (or) advanced features, which are not really needed to elegantly implement the programming solution at hand. Like life, programming is never easy, and your decisions must be reviewed thoroughly after you have had time to take a break and revisit with a fresh viewpoint later.

If you remember, the reason the compiler was throwing an error was because you were trying to initialize a VideoView object before your definition of that object was established (put into place) using the .setContentView() method.

The VideoView UI object's structure was defined using XML in your activity_main.xml definition file, and you must bring this UI definition "into play" by utilizing the .setContentView() method call before you actually reference this data.

Since this setContentView() method puts this XML definition into memory (into a ContentView object) this line of code will need to exist before anything inside that View (ViewGroup) definition can be referenced.

However, you can still **declare** the VideoView object for use in your class at the top of the class, with the other ProgressDialog and Animation objects, as long as you don't try to load it with that VideoView XML definition at that point in time (in your code execution process or timeline) by calling the findViewById() method off of the VideoView object. To accomplish this VideoView object **inflation**, that is, its definition via XML, you'll need to wait until you are inside the onCreate() method and after the statement that sets the ContentView object. The final code is shown in Figure 19-16, and is error free, and runs in the Nexus One emulator the way it should.

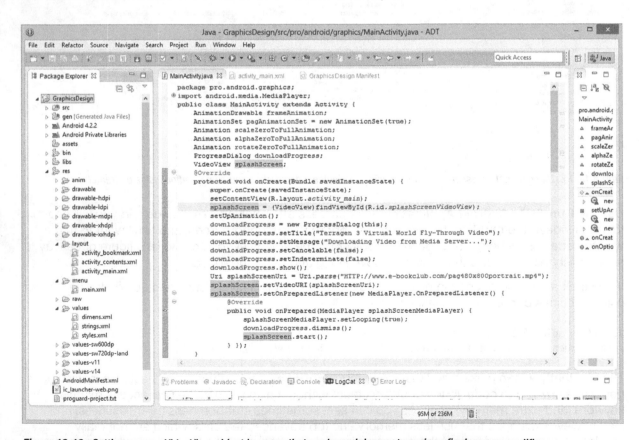

Figure 19-16. Setting up your VideoView object in a way that works and does not require a final access modifier

In the center of Figure 19-13, I showed an error screen informing us that the video file could not be played. The screen on the right of Figure 19-13 shows a view of what the screen will look like when your app is working correctly.

There are two reasons for the error message in the middle screen. The one that you need to check out thoroughly is that a file format is incompatible (MPEG-4), which you know is not the case, as you used this file in the last chapter on captive video playback and it worked.

The second reason for the "can't play this video" type of error message is that the Internet connection that you are using is either too slow or has some problem with data transfer currently. Mine was slow for some reason, possibly due to high traffic during peak usage hours, or a router issue (being serviced or upgraded) causing the Internet to have to re-route its traffic. Networking is a chaotic scenario and seldom provides a smooth, even stream of data.

Just to make sure that the file formats you're using are all correct, and so that I can provide you with a range of assets for these video chapters, using both MPEG-4 H.264 AVC and WebM VP8 video codecs (and file formats), in the next section I'm going to go through the process of creating a WebM digital video asset for this **pag480x800portrait** file that you're using with the Nexus One emulator AVD currently.

Streaming Digital Video Using the WebM VP8 Video Codec

Let's go back into Squeeze and create a WebM version of your 480x800 video asset, since you already have the uncompressed AVI ready to utilize. On the left side of Squeeze you will see a WebM (.webm) with a right-facing arrow next to it. Click this arrow, and open up the WebM presets, and find the WebM_480p preset, and either **copy** it or right-click and **edit** it to create your own custom **Android_WebM_480x800p** codec, as shown in Figure 19-17.

Figure 19-17. Creating a WebM 480x800p codec preset at 768 KBPS and compressing a 480x800 .webm asset

Let's use that same three-quarters of a megabyte per second that you used for the MPEG4 target data rate, so set the **Data Rate** parameter to **768 KBPS** and set the **Frame Size** selector to **Same as source**, and finally, leave your **Key Frames** default parameter to **Key Frame Every 10 Seconds**.

Name the preset **Android_WebM_480x800p** and use an **Android WebM** description, and then click the **OK** button to create the new preset, shown in Figure 19-17 on both the left and in the right side of the screen shot.

Once you are back in Squeeze, use the **Import File** icon at the upper left, and navigate to your uncompressed **PAG480x800.avi** AVI file and load it for compression. Click the new preset you just created to select it in light blue and then click the **Apply** button at the bottom right of your presets panel in order to apply it to the source AVI file that you just imported.

Now you are ready to click the SqueezeIt! button and apply the codec to the AVI file to create the WebM file. You will notice that the resulting file size is quite close to the MPEG4 file size, at around 3.8 megabytes.

Now all you really have left to do is to modify the code in your application to reference a new file by using a modified URL, as shown in Figure 19-18 as well as in the following line of Java code that sets up your Uri object:

```
Uri splashScreenUri = Uri.parse(HTTP://www.e-bookclub.com/pag480x800portrait.webm);
```

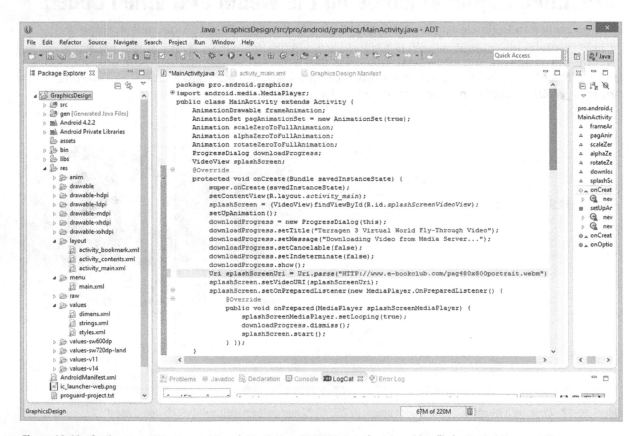

Figure 19-18. Setting your URI reference to point to the pag480x800portrait.webm video file instead of the .mp4 file

This time when I tested the app in the emulator the video downloaded and then played perfectly! You can see what it looked like before the download finished in Figure 19-13, and after the download finished in Figure 19-3.

It may well be that the WebM codec is designed to work more efficiently in low-bandwidth situations, such as the one I was encountering the week that I was working on this chapter. Although the file size is nearly identical between the MPEG-4 and WebM versions of this video asset data, the WebM seemed to play more smoothly and have a little bit better quality.

This could be what the development team for this WebM codec are trying to achieve; the codec and technology behind it, originally developed by ON2, are owned by Google. That is why it's part of Android and Chrome. It's easy to surmise, due to a **static data rate** (versus a target-to-max range allowed in MPEG4), that a strict setting parameter targets low-bandwidth networks.

Making Your Video Playback App Aware of Its Orientation

Next, I want to show you how to utilize the different portrait and landscape versions of the video assets that you have been creating during this book.

This will involve changing how you implement your Uri object a little bit because you will now be setting a Uri location definition inside a for loop or a switch (case) loop statement, so the first thing that you need to do is to move your Uri object declaration up to the top of your MainActivity class and outside any particular method.

This will involve deleting the Uri line of code that you just dealt with in Figure 19-18, starting over from scratch, and simplifying the line of code to just declare an object (for now), as shown in Figure 19-19, like this:

```
Uri SplashScreenUri;
```

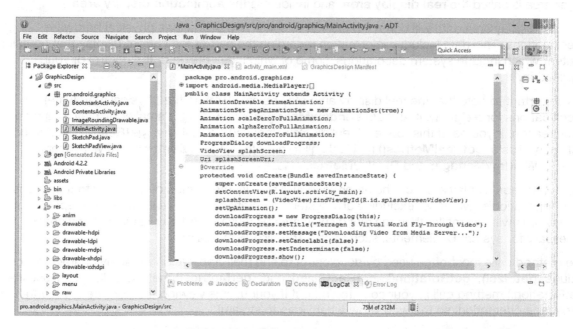

Figure 19-19. Placing the Uri object named splashScreenUri declaration at the top of the MainActivity class code

Now, when you put your Uri object definitions deep inside your switch loop full of case statements inside an OnCreate() method, references to the Uri object will be able to see the Uri object wherever they are. You'll set the Uri object path depending upon each case statement's **comparison constants**, which, once ascertained by the switch statement, will call the **Uri.parse()** method on the **splashScreenUri** Uri object that is now accessible globally.

Android's Display Class: Physical Display Characteristics

Android has a class called the **Display** class, which allows you to access a display's characteristics in real time from within your application code. There are several related classes that we will cover in this part of the chapter as well, including the **DisplayManager** class, the **DisplayMetrics** class, the **Surface** class, and the **WindowManager** class and nested classes.

This Android **Display** class is a direct subclass of the **java.lang.Object** master class, so it was created specifically to give display information. The Android Display class hierarchy is structured as follows:

```
java.lang.Object
  > android.view.Display
```

The Display class belongs in the **android.view** package because any View in Android could essentially be considered a "child" of the hardware display. The **import statement** for using the Display class (or object) in your apps should reference the **android.view.Display** package, as you'll soon see.

This Display class is a **public final** class and is used to provide various information regarding the pixel **size**, pixel **density**, **rotation** (portrait or landscape orientation), and **refresh rate** of the display being used by your app. There are two types of **display area terms** for an Android application. The larger area is called the **real display area**, and inside it is the **application display area**.

The real display area data will come the closest to specifying your user's physical hardware specifications. This data includes information regarding the part of the current display that contains content which include system decorations, some of which are outside of the control of your application.

It is important to note that the real display area may be smaller than the physical (hardware) specifications for a display, if Android **WindowManager** is emulating a smaller display area for any given reason. If you need this top-level real display area, you can utilize a **.getRealSize()** method call, as well as a **.getRealMetrics()** method call to get other **DisplayMetrics**. We will cover the Android **WindowManager** and **DisplayMetrics** classes very soon.

The application display area, on the other hand, will specify the portion of a display that contains your application's "window," excluding any system decoration screen real estate. The application display area will be smaller than the real display area because Android will subtract any space necessary for system UI elements, such as the Android OS status bar.

The method calls most often used by developers to find their application's display characteristics include **.getSize()**, **.getRotation()**, **.getRectSize()**, and **.getMetrics()** method calls. You'll use the .getRotation() method call in your code to find out if your user is viewing their device in a portrait or landscape orientation, so that you know what video to stream!

The Android DisplayManager Class: Managing the Display

Android also has a class called the **DisplayManager** class, which allows you to manage all of the displays, including any second (external) or presentation displays that may be attached to your user's Android devices.

Android's **DisplayManager** is another direct subclass of **java.lang.Object,** the master class, so it was also created specifically to provide display hardware management features to developers for the Android OS. The Android Display class hierarchy is structured as follows:

```
java.lang.Object
  > android.hardware.display.DisplayManager
```

The Display class belongs in the **android.hardware.display** package because it provides access to management of the Android device display hardware. A bridge between the display hardware and the operating system software is necessary due to the vast differences between screen sizes, pixel density, screen orientations, refresh rates, and similar display hardware specifics that need to be quantified and incorporated into your interactive graphics design programming logic pipelines.

The **import statement** for using the DisplayManager class (or object) in the app should reference the **android.hardware.display.DisplayManager** package.

The DisplayManager class is a **public final** class and is used to manage the properties of the primary Android device display as well as any externally attached displays that might also be in use with the Android device.

If you are familiar with the term "second screen" or technologies such as MiraCast or similar "shoot your content up onto the local big screen" iTV type of technologies, this Android class was created to allow these technologies to work with your applications.

The DisplayManager has one nested class, a **DisplayManager.DisplayListener** public interface, that allows your application to "listen" for changes in the display hardware configuration, such as when an external presentation display is attached to an Android device or is accessed wirelessly.

The DisplayManager also has one constant, a **DISPLAY_CATEGORY_PRESENTATION** constant, that is meant to be used to identify a secondary display that is deemed suitable for use as a presentation display. To implement this class, you need to get an instance of this object by calling the **.getSystemService()** method, using a parameter that references a **DISPLAY_SERVICE** constant called off of a **Context** object using the **WindowManager** class, which we will be covering next.

The Java code that you will be implementing in your app a bit later on will use **WindowManager**, a **Display** object, **Context** object, and the **DisplayManager** class's **.getSystemService()** method to obtain your user's display rotation.

Android's WindowManager Interface: Managing a Window

Android OS has a **windowing management** interface called the **WindowManager** interface. The WindowManager interface is a **public interface** implementing the **ViewManager** interface. The ViewManager interface allows you to add and delete child Views for your Activity subclass. A Window is a type of View.

A WindowManager interface will allow your applications to communicate with the Android OS **window manager**, which is part of Android's low-level (Linux) OS window or display layer. This lower-level layer interfaces the Linux OS Kernel at the fundamental (low) level with your Android device's hardware, upon which the Linux Kernel is running. I'm assuming here that you know that the Android OS runs on top of the pen source Linux kernel.

If you are familiar with Linux, you will be used to windowing managers, which can be swapped in and out of a Linux OS to give an entirely new look and feel (in other words, a new UI design for the Linux OS).

Each instance of a WindowManager object references one instance of a given Display object. If you wish to obtain a WindowManager object for different displays, you will want to utilize a **.createDisplayContext(Display)** method call to obtain the Context object for that Display object. You should then leverage the **.getSystemService(Context.WINDOW_SERVICE)** method call to get the WindowManager, which you will be doing in your code in the next section of this chapter.

If you want to show a window using an external display, the easiest way to accomplish this is to create a **Presentation** object. The Presentation class automatically obtains the WindowManager and the Context for that Display. A Presentation class is a subclass of the Android Dialog class.

The Android WindowManager interface is a part of the following package:

```
java.lang.Object
  > android.view.WindowManager
```

The Display class belongs in the **android.view** package because it provides access to View management by implementing a ViewManager public interface. The **import statement** for using the WindowManager class (or object) in the app should reference the **android.view.WindowManager** package.

The WindowManager interface has **three** nested classes, including the Layout Parameter nested class **WindowManager.LayoutParams**, which contains all the constants that are used as flags to tell your application how the Window object is currently configured. The **WindowManager. BadTokenException** nested class throws an exception when your application tries to add a View object whose WindowManager.LayoutParams token is not valid, and the **WindowManager. InvalidDisplayException** nested class throws an exception when your app calls an **.addView(View, ViewGroup.LayoutParams)** method on secondary Display objects that can't be found (do not exist).

Setting Up a Display Object to Ascertain the Device Rotation

Now let's use all of this newfound knowledge to accomplish something critical for your current streaming video application. What you are going to do is to finally implement the landscape version(s) of the video assets you have been creating by "polling" the Display object by using the WindowManager and .getSystemService() method call in order to ascertain a rotation vector (zero, 90, 180, or 270) so that your app can "see" the declination of the Android device in your user's hands. You will use this information to stream your digital video assets in the correct orientation.

The first thing you'll want to do, right after your **downloadProgress.show()** method call, is to declare your **Display** object and name it **rotationDegrees**. You will name the object rotationDegrees because you'll be using this object to find out the **device rotational declination** that your user is utilizing.

You will set this object equal to the current application's **Context** object, and call the **WINDOW_SERVICE** constant off this Context object inside the **.getSystemService()** method call, cast off the **WindowManager**, and then call the **.getDefaultDisplay()** method off of that programming construct using the following line of exceptionally dense Java code shown in Figure 19-20:

```
Display rotationDegrees =
((WindowManager)getSystemService(Context.WINDOW_SERVICE)).getDefaultDisplay();
```

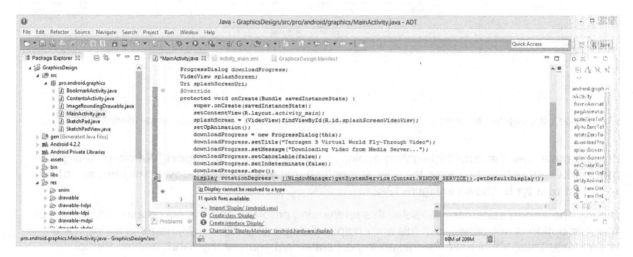

Figure 19-20. Writing your Display object named rotationDegrees code and importing the android.view.Display class

This loads the rotationDegrees Display object with the default (primary) display screen's characteristics, one of which is its current rotation, which will also give you its current (portrait or landscape) orientation.

As you can see in Figure 19-20, you will need to mouse-over your Display class reference and select the **Import 'Display' (android.view)** option first.

As you will see in Figure 19-21, this fixes part of the error highlighting, as you expected, but there is still a reference to the WindowManager class.

Figure 19-21. Mousing-over to ascertain remaining error; note that Eclipse is not offering to import the WindowManager class

If you mouse-over the error highlighting again, you expect to see the **Import 'WindowManager' (android.view)** option, however, the only admonition that you get is **WindowManager cannot be resolved to a type**, shown in Figure 19-21.

Clearly, the Import statement will solve this referencing problem, and the only reason I can think of that this option is not provided in this error helper dialog is that WindowManager is an interface and not a class. Thus, you'll have to write an Import statement yourself, by hand, heaven forbid!

Scroll up to the very top of your MainActivity.java code listing and click the plus icon next to the Import statements section to expand it, as shown in Figure 19-22. At the end, add an Import statement for the WindowManager class, using the following Java programming statement:

```
Import android.view.WindowManager;
```

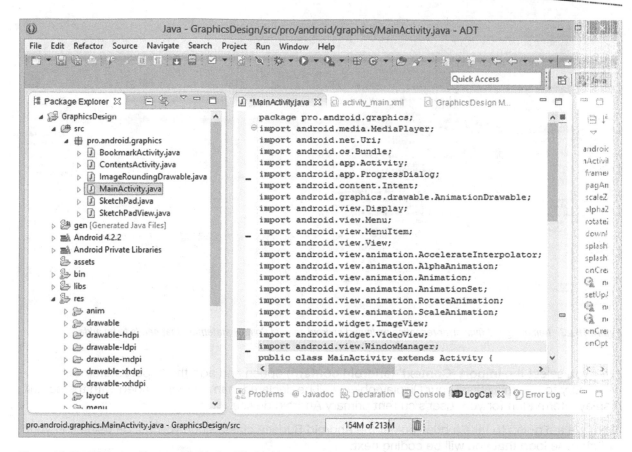

Figure 19-22. Writing an Import android.view.WindowManager statement to remove errors from the Display object

While you are here, looking at all of the Import statements for your Activity subclass, take a gander at the 20 different classes that you are using to implement animation and video streaming and progress dialogs and other complex graphics design pipelines and implementations, just in this one class. You've come a long way, baby! (Note that I am not advocating smoking; very few programmers smoke, in case you haven't noticed!)

Now that you have added the WindowManager import statement, you can use the Control-S (Save) keystroke combination, and Eclipse will re-evaluate the error messages, and you can see if you have completely eliminated all of the errors related to this complex line of Java code.

As you can see in Figure 19-22, you're almost finished with this dense line of code; you just have to import one last class and then you should be ready to move on and implement your switch programming construct.

As you can see in Figure 19-23, you still need to import the Context class.

Figure 19-23. Removing the final error regarding an Import android.content.Context statement that needs to be added

After you select the **Import 'Context' (android.content)** option and add the Import statement necessary to use this class, your Display object will be declared, named, and loaded with the default display information for your user's current primary Android device.

Next, we are going to take a brief look at the Android Surface class, since you will be using it in your switch case loop that you will be coding next.

Android's Surface Class: Grab Your Display's Raw Buffer

Android also has a class called the **Surface** class, which allows developers to directly access the "raw" or source memory "buffer" that draws what is on the Android device screen to the physical hardware itself. You are going to need to access this in order to determine how Android users have turned their devices (to the left, to the right, even upside down).

The Android **Surface** class is another direct subclass of **java.lang.Object**, the master class, so it was created specifically to provide this "handle" to a display screen surface for developers if they really need to use it. The Surface class also extends the android.os.Parcelable interface.

The Android Surface class hierarchy is structured as follows:

```
java.lang.Object
  > android.view.Surface
```

The Display class belongs in the **android.view** package because it directly accesses and (depending on your code) affects what is in your View object. The **import statement** for using the Surface class (or object) in your apps should reference the **android.view.Surface** package.

The Surface class is a **public** class and contains one nested class, called the **Surface. OutOfResourcesException** class. This class will throw an exception when the Surface object that you are trying to reference cannot be created, resized, rotated, or otherwise manipulated in the fashion that you are trying to achieve within your graphics processing code pipeline.

The Surface class also has one public constructor method that allows you to create a Surface object using a SurfaceTexture object. This is done via the following form: **Surface(SurfaceTexture surfaceTextureName)**.

The Surface class has four key constants, which you'll be leveraging in your code in the next section of this chapter, that are used to determine how the user is holding the Android device. These ROTATION constants not only determine if the Android device is being used in the portrait or landscape mode, but which direction that the device has been rotated into.

The four constants, like so many other things in Android, are positioned at 3, 6, 9, and 12 o'clock. They are named, as you might expect, **ROTATION_0**, **ROTATION_90**, **ROTATION_180** and **ROTATION_270**. Let's get to work and utilize the **Surface.ROTATION** constants in your code so you can see how they're used.

Using a .getRotation() Method Call to Drive a Switch Loop

Right after your Display object creation and configuration, you are going to add a switch loop (case statements) that will detect the **current rotation** or **orientation** (portrait or landscape) of the user's Android device.

The switch statement will evaluate a call to the **.getRotation()** method off of your **rotationDegrees** Display object that you created in the previous line of code. This method call returns one of four Surface.ROTATION constants, which you will then evaluate using case constructs, and then use to set your splashScreenUri Uri object's reference value to the correct video asset. This is done by using the following Java code, as shown in Figure 19-24:

```
switch(rotationDegrees.getRotation()){
case(Surface.ROTATION_0):
    splashScreenUri = Uri.parse(HTTP://www.e-bookclub.com/pag480x800portrait.webm);
    break;
case(Surface.ROTATION_90):
    splashScreenUri = Uri.parse(HTTP://www.e-bookclub.com/pag800x480landscape.webm);
    break;
}
```

Figure 19-24. Coding a switch statement to evaluate the results of a .getRotation() method call off a Display object

As you can see in Figure 19-24, you will need to mouse-over the reference to the Surface class and select the **Import Surface (android.view)** option.

Although using the ROTATION_0 and ROTATION_90 will tell you if the Android device has been rotated to the left (ROTATION_90) or has not been rotated, you also need to add support for those constants that tell you if the device has been rotated to the right (ROTATION_270) or been turned "upside down" (ROTATION_180), just to make 100% sure that your case statement will handle every single result that the **.getRotation()** method call is able to return.

If you handle each of the four Surface class constants, you will not need to add any default return statement to your switch programming statement, as you will be handling 100% of the values that can come into your statement's evaluation mechanism. So let's add the final two case statements to your switch construct using the following Java code, as shown in Figure 19-25:

```
case(Surface.ROTATION_180):
    splashScreenUri = Uri.parse(HTTP://www.e-bookclub.com/pag480x800portrait.webm);
    break;
case(Surface.ROTATION_270):
    splashScreenUri = Uri.parse(HTTP://www.e-bookclub.com/pag800x480landscape.webm);
    break;
```

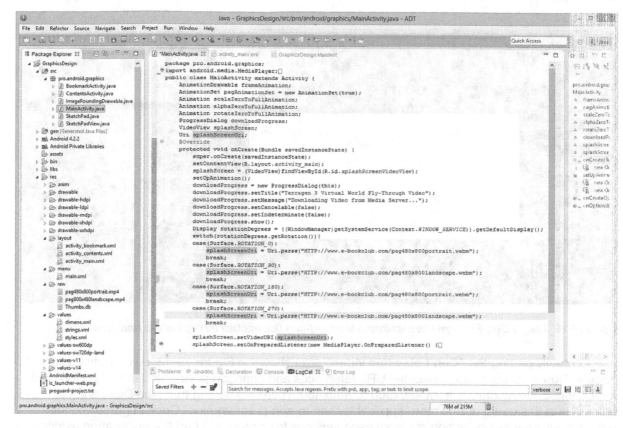

Figure 19-25. Adding all four screen rotation orientations to the switch statement to cover 0, 90, 180, and 270 degrees

Now you need to test the code to see if it's working the way you want it to!

Testing Streaming Video in Portrait and Landscape Orientations

Right-click your project folder, then use **Run As ➤ Android Application** so that you can see if your code works in the Nexus One emulator. Once the portrait version of the digital video streams successfully into your app, you can switch the emulator into a Landscape mode and see if the code gets the correct (landscape) version of your WSVGA digital video asset.

To switch the emulator into Landscape mode, use the **CTRL-F11** keystroke combination; as you can see in Figure 19-26, your application will fetch the correct video data from the media server.

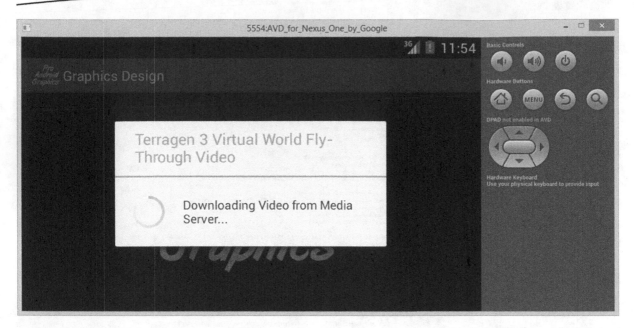

Figure 19-26. Using a CRTL-F11 keystroke combination to rotate Nexus One emulator 90 degrees into landscape

I was actually getting the "**Can't play this video**" error shown in Figure 19-13; if you notice in my code in Figure 19-25, I had copied the URL references and changed portrait to landscape, but had not changed the resolution from **480x800** to **800x480!** There is a saying that "the Devil is in the details" and this could not be more applicable than to app programming! Once I figured out this problem, which was preventing my landscape versions from playing, I had the application working perfectly in both orientations.

Before I figured out this simple (dumb) mistake, I changed the file name extension to .mp4 from .webm to see if that was the problem, as you can see in Figure 19-27. It is always a good idea to test both supported formats anyway, so I included this screen shot just so there was at least one screen shot in this chapter that had Java code in it that actually 100% works!

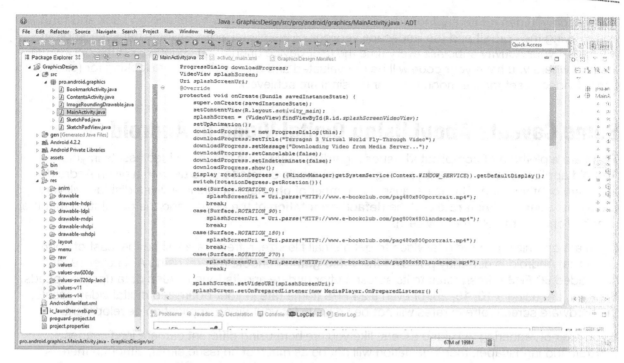

Figure 19-27. *Final code showing MPEG4 asset names and the corrected landscape resolution in asset names*

As you can see in Figure 19-28, all the hard work was worth the effort, as the Terragen virtual world fly-through is very impressive in landscape mode!

Figure 19-28. *The Terragen 3 planet fly-through playing in Nexus One in Landscape mode*

The reason you can rotate an Android device (or the emulator, in this case) and go back and forth from playing the portrait and the landscape versions of the digital video asset is because Android will restart your Activity subclass every time the user device orientation changes. So the onCreate() method where you have your code will be re-evaluated and the results you are looking for (playing a correct video asset for the mode the user is using) are achieved.

Some Caveats About Using Digital Video in Android

There are a plethora of complicated issues regarding playing the range of video assets in your Android applications if you want your digital video media assets to sync up with a given Android hardware configuration. This is because the number of **physical pixels** in a given display will vary widely, as will the **refresh rate** and the **default orientation** of the device and the orientation that the user has chosen to hold the device in.

If you are optimizing your digital video to get a small file size, refresh rate will be the least of your concerns. Android is currently pursuing the **video game console** market using API Level 19, and has added **60 FPS** refresh rates to its screen buffer update and its touchscreen data update speeds. So if you are using a 10, 15, 20, or even a 24 FPS frame rate in your optimized digital video assets, the hardware screen refresh rates will not be an issue for your video application development.

If you are not rendering 3D video assets, like you are here using different camera lens shapes (portrait and landscape), then orientation will not be as much of an issue either, although there is no "default" device rotation anymore because some tablets default to landscape operation mode default, while smartphones usually use a portrait operation mode default. Thus, this will remain an issue and challenge for developers, which is why I covered this subject in this chapter as well as in the previous chapters on video.

The most difficult (and costly, in data footprint) thing to do is provide a resolution-specific video asset for each physical display resolution out there. What I have suggested in the previous chapter is to ascertain a data "sweet spot" and select one asset that has both the **compression ratio** and the **resolution** (quality) to be able to scale up or down with great results. This will most likely be the 1024 or 1280 pixel resolution, as you have seen in the previous chapter; if you are targeting iTV, a 1920 pixel video asset will be used, but down-sampling it to low resolutions may be costly.

In case you are heck-bent (how politically correct of me) on providing a wide range of digital video assets within your application (or via a media server) and then polling the user device hardware to find out the physical pixel characteristics, I am going to cover the **DisplayMetrics** class before we finish up with this chapter so that you have the tools to do this via a switch loop or if-then loop structure, just like you did in this chapter.

Android's DisplayMetrics Class: A Display's Specifications

The Android OS has a class that allows developers to get all of the display-related information from their user's Android device. This class is called the **DisplayMetrics** utility class, and it is yet another direct subclass of the **java.lang.Object** master class.

The Android DisplayMetrics class hierarchy is thus structured as follows:

```
java.lang.Object
  > android.util.DisplayMetrics
```

The DisplayMetrics class belongs in the **android.util** package because it is an Android operating system utility for determining hardware environments. The **import statement** for using the DisplayMetrics class in your app should reference the **android.util.DisplayMetrics** package path.

The Android DisplayMetrics class is a **public** class, and it contains **eight** screen density constants: **DENSITY_DEFAULT**, **DENSITY_LOW**, **DENSITY_MEDIUM**, **DENSITY_TV**, **DENSITY_HIGH**, **DENSITY_XHIGH**, **DENSITY_XXHIGH**, and recently, **DENSITY_XXXHIGH**.

This DENSITY_XXXHIGH constant was recently added in Android 4.3 (API Level 18) in order to accommodate all the new "4K" UHD iTV products that are coming out and that feature "Ultra-High" 4096x2160 physical resolutions.

This DisplayMetrics object will provide developers with a data structure that contains fields that describe general information about the display hardware and how the Android OS is scaling its fonts to fit the hardware. This information includes the **physical display size** in pixels, the **pixel density**, and the **font scaling factor** Android is currently using for the display.

To access the DisplayMetrics object data, initialize the object like this:

```
DisplayMetrics displayMetricsObject = new DisplayMetrics();
getWindowManager().getDefaultDisplay().getMetrics(displayMetricsObject);
```

The data fields in the DisplayMetrics object that is returned by the above Java code construct will contain **seven** key information values, including a **density** floating point value for the logical screen density of the display as well as a **densityDPI** integer value providing the **dots per inch** for the display. There are also **heightPixels** and **widthPixels** integers, which give you the physical resolution for the current (primary) display screen. There are also **xdpi** and **ydpi** integers, which provide developers with the physical pixels per inch values for each of the X and Y dimensions, and finally, the **scaledDensity** floating point value that tells what font scaling is currently being applied to fonts by the Android OS. All of these values will be needed at some point or another by Android graphics designers inside their graphics processing pipeline Java code.

Summary

In this nineteenth chapter, you learned how to stream video using a media server. You learned how to implement a **ProgressDialog** object to give your users an animated downloading progress indicator, in case you did not want to stream your digital video but instead download it first and then play it back more smoothly directly out of the system memory.

You took a closer look at how to determine orientation using the **Display**, **DisplayManager**, **WindowManager**, and **Surface** classes in Android. You looked at what each of these classes do and how they all work together to allow your code to ascertain the various display characteristics for an end user's current (primary) Android device screen.

You learned how to define the **INTERNET** permission in your AndroidManifest XML file so that you could stream video from a remote video media server. You then implemented video streaming using an **HTTP://** URL in your URI, and then implemented downloaded video assets using the ProgressDialog class. I showed you all the bloody red ink I generated until I set up my VideoView object correctly, and how I ascertain which line(s) of code might contain the error(s). You also saw how to set up the VideoView object without the use of the final access modifier, and how stubborn programmers can become.

Next, you created WebM versions of your WSVGA digital video asset so that you had a landscape version in that resolution. Then you looked at screen orientation, and started learning about all of the Display-related classes, and how they all work together to allow you to bridge the hardware being used in your user's device with your graphics design code pipelines.

You learned about the Android **Display** class, the **DisplayManager** class, the **WindowManager** class, and even the **DisplayMetrics** class, albeit at the very end of the chapter. You then implemented these classes in your code to ascertain the rotation of your user's Android device so that you could set the correct URI value in your splashScreenUri Uri object and stream the correct version of your digital video asset to the user.

I hope that you had a challenging and rewarding experience while reading this book, as you implemented all of these cool graphics-related features that are available to us developers inside the Android APIs!

Index

▆ V

W

X, Y, Z